高等学校经济管理英文版教材

国际财务管理

（英文版·原书第4版）

International Financial Management

(4th Edition)

（美）

切奥尔 S. 尤恩（Cheol S. Eun）
乔治亚理工学院
布鲁斯 G. 雷斯尼克（Bruce G. Resnick）
威克林业大学

著

赵银德 张华 译注

机械工业出版社
China Machine Press

本书共21章。第一部分（第1~4章）主要介绍了国际财务管理方面的基础知识；第二部分（第5~7章）主要介绍了外汇市场、汇率的决定和货币衍生工具；第三部分（第8~10章）主要介绍了外汇风险暴露及其管理；第四部分（第11~15章）主要介绍了国际金融市场和国际金融机构；第五部分（第16~21章）主要介绍了跨国企业的财务管理。

本书作者从强调基础知识和强调管理视角这两个角度出发，在大多数章节的正文中提供了"国际财务实践"专栏，并在各章的末尾提供了"关键术语"、"问答题"、"思考题"、"网上练习"、"小型案例"等丰富多彩的练习材料。此外，各章末尾的"参考文献和推荐阅读"将有助于读者拓宽视野，涉猎更多的国际财务管理方面的知识。

本书版权登记号：图字：01-2006-3186

图书在版编目（CIP）数据

国际财务管理（英文版·原书第4版）/（美）尤恩（Eun, C. S.），（美）雷斯尼克（Resnick, B. G.）著；赵银德，张华译注. －北京：机械工业出版社，2007.1
（高等学校经济管理英文版教材）
书名原文：International Financial Management.
ISBN 7-111-20600-2

Ⅰ.国… Ⅱ.① 尤… ② 雷… ③ 赵… ④ 张… Ⅲ.国际财务管理－高等学校－教材－英文　Ⅳ.F811.2

中国版本图书馆CIP数据核字（2006）第155747号

机械工业出版社（北京市西城区百万庄大街22号　邮政编码 100037）
责任编辑：石美华　　版式设计：刘永青
北京瑞德印刷有限公司印刷·新华书店北京发行所发行
2008 年 6 月第 1 版第 4 次印刷
214mm×275mm·33.75 印张
定价：58.00 元

凡购本书，如有缺页、倒页、脱页，由本社发行部调换
本社购书热线：（010）68326294
投稿热线：（010）88379007

出版说明

教育部在2001年颁布了《关于加强高等学校本科教学工作提高教学质量的若干意见》，明确要求高校要积极开展双语教学。为适应经济全球化的挑战，培养符合现代社会需求的高级管理人才，推进高校"教育面向现代化、面向世界、面向未来"的发展，双语教学逐渐在我国大学教育中推广开来。

机械工业出版社华章分社为了满足国内广大师生了解、学习和借鉴国外先进经济管理理论、经验，开展双语教学的迫切需求，与国外著名出版公司合作影印出版了"高等学校经济管理英文版教材"系列。我社出版的该系列教材都是在国际上深受欢迎并被广泛采用的优秀教材，其中大部分教材是在国外多次再版并在该领域极具权威性的经典之作。为了让该系列教材更好地服务于读者，适应我国教育教学的客观需求，我社还专门邀请国内在该学术领域有一定研究的专家学者，结合国内教学的实际对这些图书中的重点内容精心加入中文注释，以方便读者快捷地把握学习重点，提高阅读研究的兴趣。

在此我们需要提请广大读者特别注意的是，由于我社所选择出版的该系列图书其原书作者均来自先进管理思想比较集中的欧美国家，他们所处国家的政治环境、经济发展状况、文化背景和历史发展过程等与我国社会发展状况之间存在着显著差异，同时作者个人人生观、价值观以及对各种问题的认识也仅仅只代表作者本人的观点和态度，并不意味着我们完全同意或者肯定其说法。敬请广大读者在阅读过程中，立足我国国情，以科学分析为依据，仔细斟辨，批判接受、客观学习和借鉴。

最后，这套中文注释版英文教材的出版，得到了清华大学、北京大学、南开大学、南京大学等高校很多专家学者的大力支持和帮助，对他们的辛勤劳动和精益求精的工作态度在此深表谢意！能为我国经济管理学科的理论教育与实践发展以及推动国家高校双语教学计划略尽绵薄之力是我们出版本套教材的初衷，也实为我们出版者之荣幸。

欢迎广大读者对我社出版的这套教材和各类经济管理类读物多提宝贵意见和建议，您可以通过hzjg@hzbook.com与我们联系。

机械工业出版社华章分社经管出版中心

作者简介

切奥尔 S. 尤恩（Cheol S. Eun）

切奥尔 S. 尤恩于1981年获纽约大学博士学位，现任乔治亚理工学院管理学院国际金融系托马斯 A. 威廉姆斯教授。在加盟乔治亚理工学院之前，他先后任教于明尼苏达大学和马里兰大学，还担任过宾夕法尼亚大学沃顿商学院、韩国高等科学技术院（KAIST）、新加坡管理大学（SMU）和德国埃斯林根（Esslingen）科技大学的客座教授。他发表了众多国际金融方面的学术论文，这些论文多刊登在著名的国际金融类学术期刊上，如《金融学》（*Journal of Finance*）、《金融数量分析》（*JFQA*）、《银行和金融》（*Journal of Banking and Finance*）、《国际货币金融》（*Journal of International Money and Finance*）、《管理科学》（*Management Science*）和《牛津经济论文集》（*Oxford Economic Papers*）等。目前，他还担任《银行和金融》、《金融研究》（*Journal of Financial Research*）、《世界金融》（*Global Finance Journal*）、《欧洲财务管理》（*European Financial Management*）等学术期刊的编委。他的研究成果被美国及其他很多国家的众多学术文章及教科书所广泛引用。

尤恩博士还是Fortis/Georgia Tech国际金融会议的首任主席。自1995年以来，该会议每年都举办，会议的首要目标是促进国际金融方面的研究，并为那些关注国际金融问题的学者、从业者和监管者提供一个交流的平台。

尤恩博士曾为本科生、研究生和管理人员教授过很多课程，而且在马里兰大学荣获克鲁（Krowe）杰出教师奖。他还担任世界银行、鼎洋投资（Apex Capital）、韩国发展协会（Korea Development Institute）等许多国内和国际机构的顾问，就资本市场自由化、全球资本筹集、国际投资和汇率风险控制等问题提出了建议。此外，他还经常在全球各地的各种学术会议或专家论坛上发表演讲。

布鲁斯 G. 雷斯尼克（Bruce G. Resnick）

雷斯尼克博士是位于美国北卡罗来纳州温斯顿－塞伦的威克林业大学（Wake Forest University）Babcock管理学院银行和财务系的Joseph M. Bryan Jr.教授。他于1979年在印第安纳大学获得金融领域的工商管理博士学位，还拥有科罗拉多大学的工商管理硕士和威斯康星大学的工商管理学士学位。在来Babcock管理学院任教之前，他已在印第安纳大学从教10年，在明尼苏达大学从教5年，在加利福尼亚州立大学从教2年。他还是位于澳大利亚昆士兰州金色海岸的Bond大学和芬兰赫尔辛基经济管理学院的客座教授。此外，他还担任印第安纳大学常驻荷兰马斯特里赫特的欧洲研究中心的主任，以及新加坡理工大学工商管理系的外聘主考官。

雷斯尼克博士在威克林业大学教授MBA课程。他的研究领域为投资学、证券投资管理和国际财务管理。雷斯尼克博士的研究兴趣包括期权和金融期货市场的有效性问题、资产定价模型的实证检验等。他一直以来所关注的是如何设计出最优的国际分散的证券投资组合，以解决参数的不确定性和汇率风险问题。近年来，他一直关注的是如何根据收益曲线所包含的信息来确定进行国际股票投资的最佳时机。他的研究论文发表在权威的金融学术期刊上，并为其他研究人员和教科书作者所广泛引用。他还担任了《金融研究》、《跨国财务管理》（*Journal of Multinational Financial Management*）和《经济学与商业》（*Journal of Economics and Business*）等学术期刊的副主编。

导　读

　　大凡国际财务管理类书籍都有一个老套抑或成熟的内容架构，这也使得许多此类书籍难受读者欢迎。然而，切奥尔 S. 尤恩和布鲁斯 G. 雷斯尼克两位教授超越了这一切，他们合力并倾心写出了具有独特风格、堪称国际财务管理类书籍中杰作的《国际财务管理》。概括而言，本书有着以下方面的特点：

　　首先，本书反映了作者在国际财务领域长期研究和教学的心得。一直以来，本书作者致力于国际财务的教学研究，积累了大量的教学与研究心得和课堂教学素材，而本书中的许多观点正是这一切的自然流露。

　　其次，本书呈现了作者对读者需求的响应。在整个图书市场供大于求的现实环境里，弄懂读者心自然成了赢得竞争的重要策略。显然，本书所秉承的两个写作原则——强调基础知识与注重经营需要——既便利了读者学习基础知识和掌握分析方法，也为读者提供了进行决策实践的标杆和案例。

　　第三，本书旨在启发而非说教读者。流畅而自然的章节配置，引人注意的财务实践专栏、案例应用和小型案例，众多最新的数据资料，让读者仿佛浑然置身在真实的职业世界里，正在进行着国际财务决策。

　　本书的特色来源于作者不断求变、不断求发展的理念。面对国际财务管理领域所出现的新进展，如技术的飞速发展、金融管制的日益放松、新产品的不断推出和世界市场的日渐一体化，本书都在尽最大努力来加以显现。

　　我非常高兴将本书推荐给大家。

赵银德

2006年10月于江苏大学

前言⊖

写作本书的原因

二十多年来，我们两人一直在乔治亚理工学院、威克林业大学以及其他几所我们到访过的大学为本科生和MBA学生讲授国际财务管理。在这一时期里，围绕国际金融市场的运作，我们开展了大量的调查研究并将研究结果发表在金融与统计类权威期刊上。当然，在此过程中，我们积累了在课堂上得到成功运用的大量教学资料。随着时光流逝，我们各自越来越依赖自己的教学资料和笔记，而对国际财务方面的教科书则依赖得越来越少，尽管过去我们曾一度使用了其中的不少教科书。

如你所知，伴随着金融市场管制的解除、产品的创新和技术的进步，国际财务所涉及的范围和内容一直在迅速演变。由于世界资本市场变得日益一体化，公司及时而正确的决策更加离不开对国际财务的深刻理解和把握。国际财务作为一门学科已变得日趋重要。这一点反映在企业界与学术界对国际财务领域专家的需求正在迅速增加这一事实上。

在写作《国际财务管理》（第4版）时，我们抱着这样一个目的——充分利用我们多年来在该领域所积累的教学和研究成果，对国际财务方面的最新观点和话题进行清晰而全面的阐述。我们希望本书能给学生提供一定的挑战，不过，这并不意味着本书缺乏可读性。本书在阐述各个主题时采用了方便读者的方式，独立描述每一主题。本书适合作为高年级本科生和MBA学生的教材或参考书。

写作本书所遵循的原则

与前三版一致，《国际财务管理》（第4版）仍然秉承两个原则：强调基础知识与注重经营需要。

强调基础知识。 我们确信只有掌握了扎实的基础知识，才能更好地学好各门功课。因此，本书的最初几章对国际财务的基本概念进行了介绍。掌握了这些基础内容，后续各章的学习就会变得容易了。对于层次较深的话题，本书常常会让读者回忆相关的基础知识。如此这般，我们相信读者就能掌握一种分析方法，以便他们在今后的职业生涯中加以应用。

注重经营需要。 本书强调如何教导学生进行经营决策。我们坚信财务管理者的基本职责是实现股东财富的最大化，并将这一观点贯穿于决策的整个过程。为了满足经营需要，本书提供了许多适当而真实的案例。

本书的结构

《国际财务管理》（第4版）对之前的版本进行了较大的调整。新的章节安排使得主题讨论变得更加流畅。与此同时，《国际财务管理》（第4版）在内容上也进行了全面的更新。在本书付梓时，书中所有的数据和统计资料都是最新的。此外，本书各章还编写了许多新的国际财务实践专栏，用真实案例来说明各章的主题和概念。下表给出了《国际财务管理》（第4版）中各章所涉及的主要变化。

⊖ 本书仅翻译了前言中的部分内容。——译者注

切奥尔 S. 尤恩（Cheol S. Eun）
cheol.eun@mgt.gatech.edu
布鲁斯 G. 雷斯尼克（Bruce G. Resnick）
bruce.resnick@mba.wfu.edu

目　录

第9章 经济风险暴露的管理 ··········222

第10章 换算风险暴露的管理 ·········244

第四篇 国际金融市场和 国际金融机构

第11章 国际银行与货币市场 ·········266

Contents

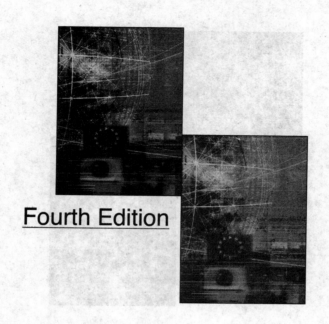

Fourth Edition

International
Financial
Management

PART ONE

Foundations of International Financial Management

PART ONE lays the macroeconomic and institutional foundation for all the topics to follow. A thorough understanding of this material is essential for understanding the advanced topics covered in the remaining sections.

CHAPTER 1 provides an introduction to International Financial Management. The chapter discusses why it is important to study international finance and distinguishes international finance from domestic finance.

CHAPTER 2 introduces the various types of international monetary systems under which the world economy can function and has functioned at various times. The chapter traces the historical development of the world's international monetary systems from the early 1800s to the present. Additionally, a detailed discussion of the European Monetary Union is presented.

CHAPTER 3 presents balance-of-payment concepts and accounting. The chapter shows that even a country must keep its "economic house in order" or else it will experience current account deficits that will undermine the value of its currency.

CHAPTER 4 provides an overview of corporate governance around the world. Corporate governance structure varies greatly across countries, reflecting diverse cultural, economic, political, and legal environments.

1 Globalization and the Multinational Firm

财务管理关注的是如何以最优方式做出关于投资、融资、股利分配和营运资本管理的各类公司财务决策，以期实现一系列既定的公司目标。

AS THE TITLE *International Financial Management* indicates, in this book we are concerned with financial management in an international setting. Financial management is mainly concerned with how to *optimally* make various corporate financial decisions, such as those pertaining to investment, financing, dividend policy, and working capital management, with a view to achieving a set of given corporate objectives. In Anglo-American countries as well as in many advanced countries with well-developed capital markets, maximizing shareholder wealth is generally considered the most important corporate objective.

世界经济的全球化与一体化

Why do we need to study "international" financial management? The answer to this question is straightforward: We are now living in a highly **globalized and integrated world economy.** American consumers, for example, routinely purchase oil imported from Saudi Arabia and Nigeria, TV sets and camcorders from Japan, automobiles from Germany, garments from China, shoes from Indonesia, pasta from Italy, and wine from France. Foreigners, in turn, purchase American-made aircraft, software, movies, jeans, wheat, and other products. Continued liberalization of international trade is certain to further internationalize consumption patterns around the world.

Like consumption, production of goods and services has become highly globalized. To a large extent, this has happened as a result of multinational corporations' (MNCs) relentless efforts to source inputs and locate production anywhere in the world where costs are lower and profits are higher. For example, personal computers sold in the world market might have been assembled in Malaysia with Chinese-made monitors, Korean-made keyboards, U.S.-made chips, and preinstalled software packages that were jointly developed by U.S. and Indian engineers. It has often become difficult to clearly associate a product with a single country of origin.

近来，金融市场已变得高度一体化，使得投资者可在国际范围内对其投资组合进行分散化运作。

Recently, financial markets have also become highly integrated. This development allows investors to diversify their investment portfolios internationally. In the words of a *Wall Street Journal* article, "Over the past decade, U.S. investors have poured buckets of money into overseas markets, in the form of international mutual funds.

In April 1996, the total assets in these funds reached a whopping $148.14 billion, far beyond the measly $2.49 billion reported in 1985."[1] At the same time, Japanese investors are investing heavily in U.S. and other foreign financial markets in efforts to recycle their enormous trade surpluses. In addition, many major corporations of the world, such as IBM, Daimler-Benz (now, DaimlerChrysler), and Sony, have their shares cross-listed on foreign stock exchanges, thereby rendering their shares internationally tradable and gaining access to foreign capital as well. Consequently, Daimler-Benz's venture, say, in China can be financed partly by American investors who purchase Daimler-Benz shares traded on the New York Stock Exchange.

Undoubtedly, we are now living in a world where all the major economic functions—consumption, production, and investment—are highly globalized. It is thus essential for financial managers to fully understand vital international dimensions of financial management. This *global shift* is in marked contrast to a few decades ago, when the authors of this book were learning finance. At that time, most professors customarily (and safely, to some extent) ignored international aspects of finance. This attitude has become untenable since then.

对于财务经理来
说，全面了解财务管理
中国际性因素就显得十
分必要。

What's Special about International Finance?

Although we may be convinced of the importance of studying international finance, we still have to ask ourselves, what's special about international finance? Put another way, how is international finance different from purely domestic finance (if such a thing exists)? Three major dimensions set international finance apart from domestic finance. They are:

1. 外汇风险与政治
风险。
2. 市场的不完全性。
3. 扩大的市场机遇。

正如我们看到的，
这些国际财务的主要特
征大部分来源于这样一
个事实，那些主权国家
有权力和能力发行货币，
制定它们的经济政策、
课税和控制劳动力及资
本的国际流动。

1. Foreign exchange and political risks.
2. Market imperfections.
3. Expanded opportunity set.

As we will see, these major dimensions of international finance largely stem from the fact that sovereign nations have the right and power to issue currencies, formulate their own economic policies, impose taxes, and regulate movements of people, goods, and capital across their borders. Before we move on, let us briefly describe each of the key dimensions of international financial management.

Foreign Exchange and Political Risks

Suppose Mexico is a major export market for your company and the Mexican peso depreciates drastically against the U.S. dollar, as it did in December 1994. This means that your company's products can be priced out of the Mexican market, as the peso price of American imports will rise following the peso's fall. If such countries as Indonesia, Thailand, and Korea are major export markets, your company would have faced the same difficult situation in the wake of the Asian currency crisis of 1997. The preceding examples suggest that when firms and individuals are engaged in cross-border transactions, they are potentially exposed to **foreign exchange risk** that they would not normally encounter in purely domestic transactions.

外汇风险

汇率变化的不确定
性对消费、生产和投资
等全部主要经济活动有
着普遍而深入的影响。

Currently, the exchange rates among such major currencies as the U.S. dollar, Japanese yen, British pound, and euro fluctuate continuously in an unpredictable manner. This has been the case since the early 1970s, when fixed exchange rates were abandoned. As can be seen from Exhibit 1.1, exchange rate volatility has exploded since 1973. Exchange rate uncertainty will have a pervasive influence on all the major economic functions, that is, consumption, production, and investment.

---

[1]Sara Calian, "Decision, Decision," *The Wall Street Journal*, June 27, 1996, p. R6.

5

EXHIBIT 1.1

Monthly Percentage Change in Japanese Yen–U.S. Dollar Exchange Rate

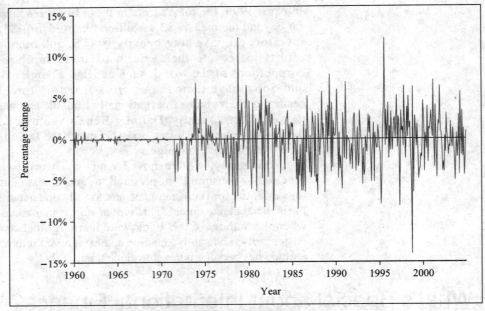

Source: International Monetary Fund, International Financial Statistics, various issues.

公司或个人参与国际经营时所面临的另一类风险就是**政治风险**。

在缺乏传统法律保护意识的国家进行投资时，跨国企业和投资者应特别关注政治风险。

Another risk that firms and individuals may encounter in an international setting is political risk. **Political risk** ranges from unexpected changes in tax rules to outright expropriation of assets held by foreigners. Political risk arises from the fact that a sovereign country can change the "rules of the game" and the affected parties may not have effective recourse. In 1992, for example, the Enron Development Corporation, a subsidiary of a Houston-based energy company, signed a contract to build India's largest power plant. After Enron had spent nearly $300 million, the project was canceled in 1995 by nationalist politicians in the Maharashtra state who argued India didn't need the power plant. The Enron episode illustrates the difficulty of enforcing contracts in foreign countries.[2]

Multinational firms and investors should be particularly aware of political risk when they invest in those countries without a tradition of the rule of law. The meltdown of Yukos, the largest Russian oil company, provides a compelling example. Following the arrest of Mikhail Khodorkovsky, the majority owner and a critic of the government, on fraud and tax evasion charges, the Russian authorities have been steadily hammering Yukos into bankruptcy. The authorities sued the company for more than $20 billion back taxes and auctioned off its assets to cover the alleged tax arrears. This government action against Yukos, widely viewed as politically motivated, inflicted a serious collateral damage on international shareholders of Yukos whose investment values were wiped out. It is important to understand that the property rights of shareholders and investors are not universally respected.

Market Imperfections

市场不完全性是指那些阻碍市场功能完全发挥的各种阻力和障碍，市场不完全在激励跨国公司到海外从事生产方面起着重要作用。

Although the world economy is much more integrated today than was the case 10 or 20 years ago, a variety of barriers still hamper free movements of people, goods, services, and capital across national boundaries. These barriers include legal restrictions, excessive transaction and transportation costs, information asymmetry, and discriminatory taxation. The world markets are thus highly imperfect. As we will discuss later in this book, **market imperfections,** which represent various frictions and

---

[2]Since then, Enron has renegotiated the deal with the Maharashtra state.

EXHIBIT 1.2

Daily Prices of Nestlé's Bearer and Registered Shares

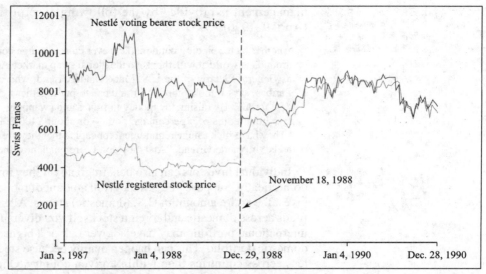

Source: Reprinted from Journal of Financial Economics, Volume 37, Issue 3, Claudio Loderer and Andreas Jacobs, "The Nestlè Crash," pp. 315–339, 1995, with kind permission from Elsevier Science S.A., P.O. Box 564, 1001 Lausanne, Switzerland.

世界金融市场的不完全性会限制投资者将投资组合分散化的程度。

在1988年11月18日，雀巢取消了对外国人的限制，允许他们除了持有不记名股外，还可持有记名股。声明过后，这两种雀巢股票的差价突然变小。如图1-2所示，不记名股的价格大幅下滑，而记名股的价格大幅上升。这意味着财富从外国人手中转到本国股东手中。在一个被普通人认为是风险避难所的国家中，持有不记名股的外国人遭受了政治风险。雀巢案例表明认识国际金融市场不完全性的重要性和政治风险的危险性。

Expanded Opportunity Set

当公司在国际市场投资时，它可以通过**市场机会增加**获益。前面曾经提过，企业可以在世界上任何国家和地区组织生产，以使它们的业绩最大化，也可以在资本成本最低的资本市场

impediments preventing markets from functioning perfectly, play an important role in motivating MNCs to locate production overseas. Honda, a Japanese automobile company, for instance, decided to establish production facilities in Ohio, mainly to circumvent trade barriers. One might even say that MNCs are a gift of market imperfections.

Imperfections in the world financial markets tend to restrict the extent to which investors can diversify their portfolios. An interesting example is provided by the Nestlé Corporation, a well-known Swiss MNC. Nestlé used to issue two different classes of common stock, bearer shares and registered shares, and foreigners were allowed to hold only bearer shares. As Exhibit 1.2 shows, bearer shares used to trade for about twice the price of registered shares, which were exclusively reserved for Swiss residents.[3] This kind of price disparity is a uniquely international phenomenon that is attributable to market imperfections.

On November 18, 1988, however, Nestlé lifted restrictions imposed on foreigners, allowing them to hold registered as well as bearer shares. After this announcement, the price spread between the two types of Nestlé shares narrowed drastically. As Exhibit 1.2 shows, the price of bearer shares declined sharply, whereas that of registered shares rose sharply. This implies that there was a major transfer of wealth from foreign shareholders to domestic shareholders. Foreigners holding Nestlé bearer shares were exposed to political risk in a country that is widely viewed as a haven from such risk. The Nestlé episode illustrates both the importance of considering market imperfections in international finance and the peril of political risk.

When firms venture into the arena of global markets, they can benefit from an **expanded opportunity set.** As previously mentioned, firms can locate production in any country or region of the world to maximize their performance and raise funds in any capital market where the cost of capital is the lowest. In addition, firms can gain from greater economies of scale when their tangible and intangible assets are deployed on a global basis. A real-world example showing the gains from a global approach to financial

---

[3] It is noted that bearer and registered shares of Nestlé had the same claims on dividends but differential voting rights. Chapter 17 provides a detailed discusiion of the Nestlé case.

[3] 雀巢的不记名股票和记名股票具有相同的股息，但投票权不一样，这将在17章详细论述。

上获得资金。另外，当
企业的有形和无形资产
处于国际环境中，它可
以获得最大的经济规模。

management is provided by the following excerpt from *The Wall Street Journal* (April 9, 1996):

> Another factor binding bond markets ever closer is large companies' flexibility to issue bonds around the world at will, thanks to the global swap market. At the vanguard are companies such as General Electric of the U.S. Mark VanderGriend, who runs the financing desk at Banque Paribas, says it took "about 15 minutes" to put together a four billion franc ($791.6 million) deal for GE. By raising the money in francs and swapping into dollars instantly, GE will save five hundredths of a percentage point—or about $400,000 annually on the nine-year deal. "They have such a huge requirement for capital that they are constantly looking for arbitrages," adds Mr. VanderGriend. "And they don't care much how they get there."

与只进行国内投资
相比，个体投资者也可
通过国际化投资获得巨
大的利益。

Individual investors can also benefit greatly if they invest internationally rather than domestically. Suppose you have a given amount of money to invest in stocks. You may invest the entire amount in U.S. (domestic) stocks. Alternatively, you may allocate the funds across domestic and foreign stocks. If you diversify internationally, the resulting international portfolio may have a lower risk or a higher return (or both) than a purely domestic portfolio. This can happen mainly because stock returns tend to covary much less across countries than within a given country. Once you are aware of overseas investment opportunities and are willing to diversify internationally, you face a much expanded opportunity set and you can benefit from it. It just doesn't make sense to play in only one corner of the sandbox.

Goals for International Financial Management

本书的重点自始至
终都放在如何用各种金
融工具来处理外汇风险
和适应不完善的市场，
并且在更广阔的国际机
遇中获得最大化利益。

The foregoing discussion implies that understanding and managing foreign exchange and political risks and coping with market imperfections have become important parts of the financial manager's job. *International Financial Management* is designed to provide today's financial managers with an understanding of the fundamental concepts and the tools necessary to be effective global managers. Throughout, the text emphasizes how to deal with exchange risk and market imperfections, using the various instruments and tools that are available, while at the same time maximizing the benefits from an expanded global opportunity set.

股东财富最大化 是
指公司所做的全部经营决
策和投资应着眼于使公司
的所有者——股东——较
过去财务状况更好或更
富有。

Effective financial management, however, is more than the application of the newest business techniques or operating more efficiently. There must be an underlying goal. *International Financial Management* is written from the perspective that the fundamental goal of sound financial management is shareholder wealth maximization. **Shareholder wealth maximization** means that the firm makes all business decisions and investments with an eye toward making the owners of the firm—the shareholders— better off financially, or more wealthy, than they were before.

尽管股东权益最大
化在澳大利亚、加拿大、
英国、尤其是美国这些
"Anglo-Saxon" 国家中
被视为财务管理中最重
要的目标，但这种观点
在世界的其他地方并不
适用。

Whereas shareholder wealth maximization is generally accepted as the ultimate goal of financial management in "Anglo-Saxon" countries, such as Australia, Canada, the United Kingdom, and especially the United States, it is not as widely embraced a goal in other parts of the world. In countries like France and Germany, for example, shareholders are generally viewed as one of the "stakeholders" of the firm, others being employees, customers, suppliers, banks, and so forth. European managers tend to consider the promotion of the firm's stakeholders' overall welfare as the most important corporate goal. In Japan, on the other hand, many companies form a small number of interlocking business groups called *keiretsu,* such as Mitsubishi, Mitsui, and Sumitomo, which arose from consolidation of family-owned business empires. Japanese managers tend to regard the prosperity and growth of their *keiretsu* as the critical goal; for instance, they tend to strive to maximize market share, rather than shareholder wealth.

It is pointed out, however, that as capital markets are becoming more liberalized and internationally integrated in recent years, even managers in France, Germany, Japan and other non-Anglo-Saxon countries are beginning to pay serious attention to shareholder wealth maximization. In Germany, for example, companies are now allowed to repurchase stocks, if necessary, for the benefit of shareholders. In accepting an unprecedented $183 billion takeover offer by Vodafone AirTouch, a leading British wireless phone company, Klaus Esser, CEO of Mannesmann of Germany, cited shareholder interests: "The shareholders clearly think that this company, Mannesmann, a great company, would be better together with Vodafone AirTouch. . . . The final decision belongs to shareholders."[4]

Obviously, the firm could pursue other goals. This does not mean, however, that the goal of shareholder wealth maximization is merely an alternative, or that the firm should enter into a debate as to its appropriate fundamental goal. Quite the contrary. If the firm seeks to maximize shareholder wealth, it will most likely simultaneously be accomplishing other legitimate goals that are perceived as worthwhile. Shareholder wealth maximization is a long-run goal. A firm cannot stay in business to maximize shareholder wealth if it treats employees poorly, produces shoddy merchandise, wastes raw materials and natural resources, operates inefficiently, or fails to satisfy customers. Only a well-managed business firm that profitably produces what is demanded in an efficient manner can expect to stay in business in the long run and thereby provide employment opportunities.

尽管受聘的经理人员必须使公司的经营符合股东利益，但无法保证经理人员一定会这么做。

While managers are hired to run the company for the interests of shareholders, there is no guarantee that they will actually do so. As shown by a series of recent corporate scandals at companies like Enron, WorldCom, and Global Crossing, managers may pursue their own private interests at the expense of shareholders when they are not closely monitored. Extensive corporate malfeasance and accounting manipulations at these companies eventually drove them into financial distress and bankruptcy, devastating shareholders and employees alike. Lamentably, some senior managers enriched themselves enormously in the process. Clearly, the boards of directors, the ultimate guardians of the interests of shareholders, failed to perform their duties at these companies. In the wake of these corporate calamities that have undermined the credibility of the free market system, the society has painfully learned the importance of **corporate governance,** that is, the financial and legal framework for regulating the relationship between a company's management and its shareholders. Needless to say, the corporate governance problem is not confined to the United States. In fact, it can be a much more serious problem in many other parts of the world, especially emerging and transition economies, such as Indonesia, Korea, and Russia, where legal protection of shareholders is weak or virtually nonexistent.

很明显，在这些公司里，作为股东权益守护人的董事会没有履行其职责。在这场灾难中，社会信用被彻底摧毁了。社会在沉痛的教训中认识到公司治理的重要性，也就是说要在公司管理层和股东之间建立起一种起到监控调节作用的财务及法律框架。

我们在第4章中将看到，各国的公司治理结构差异很大，这反映了不同国家不同的文化环境、法律环境、经济环境和政治环境。

As we will discuss in Chapter 4 in detail, corporate governance structure varies greatly across countries, reflecting different cultural, legal, economic, and political environments in different countries. In many countries where shareholders do not have strong legal rights, corporate ownership tends to be concentrated. The concentrated ownership of the firm, in turn, may give rise to the conflicts of interest between dominant shareholders (often the founding family) and small outside shareholders. The collapse of Parmalat, a family-controlled Italian company, after decades of accounting frauds, provides an example of corporate governance risk. The company allegedly hid debts, "invented" assets, and diverted funds to bail out failing ventures of the family members. Because only the Tanzi (founding) family and close associates knew how the company was run, it was possible to hide the questionable practices for decades. Outside shareholders who collectively control a 49 percent stake did not know how Parmalat was operating. Franco Ferrarotti, professor of sociology at the University of Rome, was quoted as saying, "The government is weak, there is no sense of state, public services are bad and social services are weak. The family is so strong because it is the only institution that doesn't let you down."[5]

[4]The source for this information is *The New York Times,* February 4, 2000, p. C9.
[5]*USA Today,* February 4, 2004, p. 2B.

Shareholders are the owners of the business; it is their capital that is at risk. It is only equitable that they receive a fair return on their investment. Private capital may not have been forthcoming for the business firm if it had intended to accomplish any other objective. As we will discuss shortly, the massive privatization that is currently taking place in developing and formerly socialist countries, which will eventually enhance the standard of living of these countries' citizens, depends on private investment. It is thus vitally important to strengthen corporate governance so that shareholders receive fair returns on their investments. In what follows, we are going to discuss in detail: (1) the globalization of the world economy, and (2) the growing role of MNCs in the world economy.

Globalization of the World Economy: Major Trends

四大世界经济发展新趋势：(i) 全球化金融市场的出现，(ii) 作为全球货币的欧元的诞生，(iii) 贸易自由化与经济一体化的持续发展，(iv) 国有企业的大规模私有化。

The term "globalization" became a popular buzzword for describing business practices in the last few decades, and it appears as if it will continue to be a key word for describing business management throughout the new century. In this section, we review a few key trends of the world economy: (i) the emergence of globalized financial markets, (ii) emergence of the euro as a global currency, (iii) continued trade liberalization and economic integration, and (iv) large-scale privatization of state-owned enterprises.

Emergence of Globalized Financial Markets

然而，可能最值得庆祝的解禁发生在1986年10月27日的伦敦，它被称为"大爆炸"。在那一天，伦敦股票交易所取消了交易数额的限制。1975年的五一节，美国也发生了同样的一幕。另外，那项做市商按顺序交易的规定也被取消了。在欧洲，金融机构可以有投资银行和商业银行的双重职能。因此，在伦敦的外国商业银行的分支机构是伦敦股票交易所的理想成员。

www.imf.org

Offers an overview of globalization and financial development.

金融市场管制的解除与金融服务业竞争水平的提高为金融工具创新提供了一个良好的环境。

The 1980s and 90s saw a rapid integration of international capital and financial markets. The impetus for globalized financial markets initially came from the governments of major countries that had begun to deregulate their foreign exchange and capital markets. For example, in 1980 Japan deregulated its foreign exchange market, and in 1985 the Tokyo Stock Exchange admitted as members a limited number of foreign brokerage firms. Additionally, the London Stock Exchange (LSE) began admitting foreign firms as full members in February 1986.

Perhaps the most celebrated deregulation, however, occurred in London on October 27, 1986, and is known as the "Big Bang." On that date, as on "May Day" in 1975 in the United States, the London Stock Exchange eliminated fixed brokerage commissions. Additionally, the regulation separating the order-taking function from the market-making function was eliminated. In Europe, financial institutions are allowed to perform both investment-banking and commercial-banking functions. Hence, the London affiliates of foreign commercial banks were eligible for membership on the LSE. These changes were designed to give London the most open and competitive capital markets in the world. It has worked, and today the competition in London is especially fierce among the world's major financial centers. The United States repealed the Glass-Steagall Act, which restricted commercial banks from investment banking activities (such as underwriting corporate securities), further promoting competition among financial institutions. Even developing countries such as Chile, Mexico, and Korea began to liberalize by allowing foreigners to directly invest in their financial markets.

Deregulated financial markets and heightened competition in financial services provided a natural environment for financial innovations that resulted in the introduction of various instruments. Examples of these innovative instruments include currency futures and options, multicurrency bonds, international mutual funds, country funds, and foreign stock index futures and options. Corporations also played an active role in integrating the world financial markets by listing their shares across borders. Such well-known non-U.S. companies as Seagram, Sony, Toyota Motor, Fiat, Telefonos de Mexico, KLM, British Petroleum, Glaxo, and Daimler are directly listed and traded on the New York Stock Exchange. At the same time, U.S. firms such as IBM and GM are listed on the Brussels, Frankfurt, London, and Paris stock exchanges. Such cross-

计算机和通信技术的发展为世界金融市场的形成做出了巨大贡献。以网络信息技术为代表的新技术给全世界的投资者提供了一种快速获得最新信息的手段，这些信息会对他们的投资产生影响，并大大缩减信息获取的费用。同样，用计算机交易也缩减了国际交易的费用。由于这些技术发展和金融市场自由化的结果，在最近几年跨国金融交易迅速发展起来。美国商务部的资料表明，使用计算机的费用在减少。以1960年的计算机使用费用作为基数100，到1970年已近减少到15.6，1980年为2.9，到1999年只达0.5。

Emergence of the Euro as a Global Currency

交易领域

欧洲中央银行 (ECB)

自1999年诞生以来，欧元已给欧洲金融业带来了革命性的变化。

border listings of stocks allow investors to buy and sell foreign shares as if they were domestic shares, facilitating international investments.[6]

Last but not least, advances in computer and telecommunications technology contributed in no small measure to the emergence of global financial markets. These technological advancements, especially Internet-based information technologies, gave investors around the world immediate access to the most recent news and information affecting their investments, sharply reducing information costs. Also, computerized order-processing and settlement procedures have reduced the costs of international transactions. Based on the U.S. Department of Commerce computer price deflator, the relative cost index of computing power declined from a level of 100 in 1960 to 15.6 in 1970, 2.9 in 1980, and only 0.5 in 1999. As a result of these technological developments and the liberalization of financial markets, cross-border financial transactions have exploded in recent years.

The advent of the euro at the start of 1999 represents a momentous event in the history of the world financial system that has profound ramifications for the world economy. Currently, more than 300 million Europeans in 12 countries (Austria, Belgium, Finland, France, Germany, Greece, Ireland, Italy, Luxembourg, the Netherlands, Portugal, and Spain) are using the common currency on a daily basis. No single currency has circulated so widely in Europe since the days of the Roman Empire. Considering that 10 countries, including the Czech Republic, Hungary, and Poland, newly joined the European Union (EU) in 2004, and that many of them would like to adopt the euro eventually, the **transactions domain** of the euro may become larger than that of the U.S. dollar in the near future.

Once a country adopts the common currency, it obviously cannot have its own monetary policy. The common monetary policy for the euro zone is now formulated by the **European Central Bank** (ECB) that is located in Frankfurt and partly modeled after the Bundesbank, the German central bank. ECB is legally mandated to achieve price stability for the euro zone. Considering the sheer size of the euro zone in terms of population, economic output, and world trade share and the prospect of monetary stability in Europe, the euro has a strong potential for becoming another global currency rivaling the U.S. dollar for dominance in international trade and finance. Reflecting the significance of the euro's introduction, Professor Robert Mundell, who is often referred to as the intellectual father of the euro, recently stated: "The creation of the euro area will eventually, but inevitably, lead to competition with the dollar area, both from the standpoint of excellence in monetary policy, and in the enlistment of other currencies."[7] The world thus faces a prospect of bipolar international monetary system.

Since its inception in 1999, the euro has already brought about revolutionary changes in European finance. For instance, by redenominating corporate and government bonds and stocks from 12 different currencies into the common currency, the euro has precipitated the emergence of continentwide capital markets in Europe that are comparable to U.S. markets in its depth and liquidity. Companies all over the world can benefit from this development as they can raise capital more easily on favorable terms in Europe. In addition, the recent surge in European M&A activities, cross-border alliances among financial exchanges, and lessening dependence on the banking sectors for capital raising are all manifestations of the profound effects of the euro. The International Finance in Practice box, "Why We Believe in the Euro," presents an upbeat view of the euro expressed by Jürgen Schrempp, former CEO of DaimlerChrysler.

[6]Various studies indicate that the liberalization of capital markets tends to lower the cost of capital. See, for example, Peter Henry, "Stock Market Liberalization, Economic Reform, and Emerging Market Equity Prices," *Journal Finance* (2000), pp. 529–64.

[7]Source: Robert Mundell, 2000, "Currency Area, Volatility and Intervention," *Journal of Policy Modeling 22* (3), 281–99.

Why We Believe in the Euro

By Jürgen Schrempp, CEO of DaimlerChrysler

In our company, we don't mean to waste even a day in putting the euro to work. On Jan. 1, 1999—day one for the new currency—our company will switch over completely to the euro as the internal and external unit of account. We expect to be one of the first German-based companies—perhaps the first—to make such a complete change. We'll also encourage our suppliers within Euroland to invoice us in euros from the very beginning. Our Euroland customers, of course, will have the option of paying in either euros or their domestic currency until 2001.

Nearly all major European companies are in favor of the single currency. But having recently agreed on a historic, transatlantic merger with Chrysler Corp. of the United States, we feel especially attuned to the forces of global competition that make the euro so essential. For our new company, DaimlerChrysler AG, and for Germany and Europe as a whole, economic and monetary union will bring substantial and lasting benefits as we take our place in the interdependent world of the 21st century.

Those benefits will take shape—indeed, are already occurring—in several realms at once. First and most fundamental is the political. The single currency will push the countries of Europe into cooperating more and more in seeking solutions to common economic problems. As they do so, they'll grow increasingly intertwined politically.

At the same time, the euro will unleash powerful market forces certain to transform the way Europeans live and work. The years ahead will bring increased efficiency, greater productivity, higher overall living standards and lower unemployment. For businesses, a common currency will reduce transaction costs—eliminating, among other things, the unnecessary waste of resources involved in dealing with several European currencies. At present, doing business across borders means having to buy and sell foreign currencies—and taking the risk that sudden changes in their relative value could upend an otherwise sound business strategy. The risks can be hedged, of course, but only at a cost that must ultimately be borne by customers.

The market forces unleashed by the euro will be felt not just by corporate managers but also by political leaders. Business executives are already working to rationalize their companies, enhancing productivity and improving labor flexibility. Elected officials, facing competition as they try to attract the investments that create jobs, will eventually lower corporate tax rates and streamline regulation. In so doing, governments will give corporations a boost, like the reduction in the cost of capital that came about as countries tightened their fiscal and monetary policies in preparation for EMU.

These changes are mutually reinforcing. And as they take hold, Euroland companies will grow more confident about committing resources to long-term projects. A look at the level of corporate mergers in recent years shows that

美元的优越地位反映了美国经济的主导地位、美国资本市场的成熟和开放程度、美国市场价格的稳定性和美国的政治与军事实力。

Since the end of World War I, the U.S. dollar has played the role of the dominant global currency, displacing the British pound. As a result, foreign exchange rates of currencies are quoted against the dollar and the lion's share of currency trading involves the dollar on either the buy or sell side. Similarly, international trade in primary commodities, such as petroleum, coffee, wheat, and gold, is conducted using the U.S. dollar as the invoice currency. Reflecting the dominant position of the dollar in the world economy, central banks of the world hold a major portion of their external reserves in dollars. The ascendance of the dollar reflects several key factors such as the dominant size of the U.S. economy, mature and open capital markets, price stability, and the political and military power of the United States. It is noted that the dominant global currency status of the dollar confers upon the United States many special privileges such as the ability to run trade deficits without having to hold much foreign exchange reserves, that is, "deficits without tears," and conduct a large portion of international transactions in dollars, without bearing exchange risks. However, once economic agents start to use the euro in earnest as an invoice, vehicle, and reserve currency, the dollar may have to share the aforementioned privileges with the euro.[8]

---

[8]A recent study by Eun and Lai, 2002, "The Power Contest in FX Markets: The Euro vs. the Dollar," indicates that within three years since its inception, the euro has succeeded in establishing its own currency bloc in Europe, comprising the currencies of Croatia, Czech Republic, Hungary, Norway, Slovakia, Slovenia, Sweden, and Switzerland. The study, however, shows that the U.S. dollar remains as the dominant global currency. In contrast, the Japanese yen does not have its own currency bloc in Asia.

managers have already stepped up their strategic decision making. Europe saw 237 such deals last year, worth $250 billion, of which 25 percent were European cross-border transactions. In 1995, by contrast, there were just 100 deals, worth $168 billion—and only 17 percent were European cross-border transactions.

Euroland will be a strong base for companies striving to compete globally. In 1997 its combined population numbered 290 million, compared with 268 million for the United States and 126 million for Japan. Its combined GDP was $6.3 trillion, versus $7.8 trillion for the United States and $4.2 trillion for Japan. Euroland already trades with the rest of the world as much as the United States does, and the picture will change in favor of Europe as soon as the United Kingdom, and others who have stayed out of the first wave, join the currency union. Such a development—the sooner the better—is something we would very much welcome.

Launching the new euro is one thing; successfully managing the EMU process in the years ahead is quite another. Implementation poses major challenges. Some will be technical; others will have to do with maintaining a unity of purpose among a diverse group of nations, regions, peoples and cultures. I believe, however, that Europe possesses the unshakable political will and financial expertise needed to keep this endeavor on track.

It will help that—as we at DaimlerChrysler well know—some of the payoffs are immediate and obvious.

Currently, one third of our group's revenues are earned in Deutsche marks, but nearly three quarters of our costs are incurred in that currency. That makes planning harder and running the company more complex. But with the coming of the euro, the disparity between our DM costs and DM revenues will diminish. As of January, 50 percent of our revenues will be in euros, with 80 percent of our costs incurred in the same currency.

How will the euro affect our ability to compete in the United States, our main export market outside the EU? In a word, positively. Higher productivity and a stable "home" currency will allow us to maintain a competitive pricing structure. Such long-term consistency in our business practices is something our U.S. customers have come to appreciate.

One final point. Thanks to the single market and the pending introduction of a single currency, Europe has matured both politically and economically. As a major transatlantic player, DaimlerChrysler is now in a position to communicate an important message to its business partners in that other great single-currency market, the United States. Working through the World Trade Organization and other groups, the globe has made great progress toward free and fair trade over the years. Now let us together examine opportunities for removing some of the remaining obstacles to trade between Europe and the United States. The beneficiaries will be consumers on both sides of the Atlantic.

Source: Newsweek, Special Issue. Winter 1998, p. 38. Reprinted with permission.

Trade Liberalization and Economic Integration

作为各国经济间的传统纽带，国际贸易正在不断扩大。

International trade, which has been the traditional link between national economies, continued to expand. As Exhibit 1.3 shows, the ratio of merchandise exports to GDP for the world has increased from 7.0 percent in 1950 to 20.0 percent in 2003. This implies that, over the same time period, international trade increased nearly three times as fast as world GDP. For some countries, international trade grew much faster; for Germany, the ratio rose from 6.2 percent to 31.1 percent, while for Korea it grew from 1.0 percent to 32.6 percent over the same time period. Latin American countries such as Argentina, Brazil, and Mexico used to have relatively low export-to-GDP ratios. In 1973, for example, the export-to-GDP ratio was 2.1 percent for Argentina, 2.6 percent for Brazil, and 2.2 percent for Mexico. This reflects the inward-looking, protectionist economic policies these countries pursued in the past. Even these once-protectionist countries are now increasingly pursuing free-market and open-economy policies because of the gains from international trade. In 2003, the export-to-GDP ratio was 22.8 percent for Argentina, 14.8 percent for Brazil, and 26.3 percent for Mexico.

比较优势理论

在李嘉图看来，如果每个国家专业化生产各自效率最高的商品，然后相互进行交换，那么参与各方都能获益。

The principal argument for international trade is based on the **theory of comparative advantage,** which was advanced by David Ricardo in his seminal book, *Principles of Political Economy* (1817). According to Ricardo, it is mutually beneficial for countries if they specialize in the production of those goods they can produce most efficiently and trade those goods among them. Suppose England produces textiles most efficiently, whereas France produces wine most efficiently. It then makes sense if England specializes in the production of textiles and France in the production of wine,

EXHIBIT 1.3

Long-Term Openness in Perspective (Merchandise Exports/GDP at 1990 Prices, in Percent)

Country	1870	1913	1929	1950	1973	2003
United States	2.5	3.7	3.6	3.0	5.0	6.5
Canada	12.0	12.2	15.8	13.0	19.9	33.4
Australia	7.4	12.8	11.2	9.1	11.2	13.5
United Kingdom	12.0	17.7	13.3	11.4	14.0	17.2
Germany	9.5	15.6	12.8	6.2	23.8	31.3
France	4.9	8.2	8.6	7.7	15.4	20.3
Spain	3.8	8.1	5.0	1.6	5.0	19.0
Japan	0.2	2.4	3.5	2.3	7.9	10.4
Korea	0.0	1.0	4.5	1.0	8.2	32.6
Thailand	2.1	6.7	6.6	7.0	4.5	54.6
Argentina	9.4	6.8	6.1	2.4	2.1	22.8
Brazil	11.8	9.5	7.1	4.0	2.6	14.8
Mexico	3.7	10.8	14.8	3.5	2.2	26.3
World	5.0	8.7	9.0	7.0	11.2	20.0

Source: Various issues of World Financial Markets, JP Morgan, and International Financial Statistics, IMF.

and the two countries then trade their products. By doing so, the two countries can increase their combined production of textiles and wine, which, in turn, allows both countries to consume more of both goods. This argument remains valid even if one country can produce both goods more efficiently than the other country.[9] Ricardo's theory has a clear policy implication: *Liberalization of international trade will enhance the welfare of the world's citizens.* In other words, international trade is not a "zero-sum" game in which one country benefits at the expense of another country—the view held by the "mercantilists." Rather, international trade could be an "increasing-sum" game at which all players become winners.

Although the theory of comparative advantage is not completely immune to valid criticism, it nevertheless provides a powerful intellectual rationale for promoting free trade among nations. Currently, international trade is becoming further liberalized at both the global and regional levels. At the global level, the **General Agreement on Tariffs and Trade (GATT),** which is a multilateral agreement among member countries, has played a key role in dismantling barriers to international trade. Since it was founded in 1947, GATT has been successful in gradually eliminating and reducing tariffs, subsidies, quotas, and other barriers to trade. The latest round of talks, the Uruguay Round launched in 1986, aims to (1) reduce the import tariffs worldwide by an average of 38 percent, (2) increase the proportion of duty-free products from 20 percent to 44 percent for industrialized countries, and (3) extend the rules of world trade to cover agriculture, services such as banking and insurance, and intellectual property rights. It also created a permanent **World Trade Organization (WTO)** to replace GATT. The WTO has more power to enforce the rules of international trade. China recently joined WTO. China's WTO membership will further legitimize the idea of free trade.

Inspired by Deng Xiaoping's pragmatic policies, that is, "to get rich is glorious," China began to implement market-oriented economic reforms in the late 1970s. Since then, the China economy has grown rapidly, often at an astounding rate of 10 percent per annum, and in the process has lifted tens of millions of local citizens from poverty. China's impressive economic growth has been driven by burgeoning international trade and foreign direct investment. China's demand for natural resources, capital goods, and technologies, in turn, has boosted exports to China from the rest of the world. India has also joined China in recent years in opening its

尽管比较优势理论并非无懈可击，但它仍为促进各国间的自由贸易提供了强大的理论基础。

关贸总协定（GATT）

www.wto.org/

The World Trade Organization website covers news and data about international trade development.

世界贸易组织（WTO）

---

[9]Readers are referred to Appendix 1A for a detailed discussion of the theory of comparative advantage.

www.lib.berkeley.edu/GSSI/ eu.html

The University of California at Berkeley library provides a web guide to resources related to the European Union.

欧盟（EU）

从区域范围来看，各国间所签署的正式协议也促进了经济的一体化。

北美自由贸易协定（NAFTA）

economy and attracting foreign investment. India has implemented its own market-oriented reforms since the early 1990s, gradually dismantling "license-raj" or quota system in all economic spheres and encouraging private entrepreneurship. As is well known, India has emerged as the most important center for outsourcing information technology (IT) services, back-office support, and R&D functions. The huge supplies of labor, highly skilled and disciplined, in China and India are bound to alter the structure of the world economy in a major way. In terms of purchasing power, China already is the second largest economy in the world, second only to the U.S. India, on the other hand, is the fourth largest economy after Japan. The importance of China and India is likely to grow further, profoundly altering the pattern of international production, trade, and investment.

On the regional level, formal arrangements among countries have been instituted to promote economic integration. The **European Union (EU)** is a prime example. The European Union is the direct descendent of the European Community (formerly the European Economic Community), which was established to foster economic integration among the countries of Western Europe. Today the EU includes 25 member states that have eliminated barriers to the free flow of goods, capital, and people. The member states of the EU hope this move will strengthen its economic position relative to the United States and Japan. In January 1999, 11 member countries of EU successfully adopted a single common currency, the euro, which may rival the U.S. dollar as a dominant currency for international trade and investment. Greece joined the euro club in January 2001. The launch of the euro has spurred a rush by European companies into seeking pan-European and global alliances. Merger and acquisition (M&A) deals in Europe totaled $1.2 trillion in 1999, exceeding the figure for U.S. deals for the first time.

Whereas the economic and monetary union planned by the EU is one of the most advanced forms of economic integration, a free trade area is the most basic. In 1994, Canada, the United States, and Mexico entered into the **North American Free Trade Agreement (NAFTA).** Canada is the United States' largest trading partner and Mexico is the third-largest. In a free trade area, all impediments to trade, such as tariffs and import quotas, are eliminated among members. The terms of NAFTA call for phasing out tariffs over a 15-year period. Many observers believe that NAFTA will foster increased trade among its members, resulting in an increase in the number of jobs and the standard of living in all member countries. It is interesting to note from Exhibit 1.3 that for Mexico, the ratio of export to GDP has increased dramatically from 2.2 percent in 1973 to 26.3 percent in 2003. This dramatic increase in Mexico's propensity to trade should be attributable to NAFTA.

Multinational Corporations

除了国际贸易之外，跨国公司的国外直接投资也是促进世界经济一体化的主要动力。

In addition to international trade, foreign direct investment by MNCs is a major force driving globalization of the world economy. According to a UN report, there are about 60,000 MNCs in the world with over 500,000 foreign affiliates.[11] Throughout the 1990s, foreign direct investment by MNCs grew at the annual rate of about 10 percent. In comparison, international trade grew at the rate of 3.5 percent during the same period. MNCs' worldwide sales reached $11 trillion in 1998, compared to about $7 trillion of world exports in the same year.[12] As indicated in the International Finance in Practice box, "Multinationals More Efficient," MNCs are reshaping the structure of the world economy.

---

[11]The source for this information is the United Nations' *World Investment Report 1999*.
[12]The source of this information is *World Investment Report 1999*, the United Nations.

www.unctad.org/wir/
This UNCTAD website provides a broad coverage of cross-border investment activities by multinational corporations.

跨国公司可以通过手段繁多的全球经营方式来获得利益。

A **multinational corporation (MNC)** is a business firm incorporated in one country that has production and sales operations in several other countries. The term suggests a firm obtaining raw materials from one national market and financial capital from another, producing goods with labor and capital equipment in a third country, and selling the finished product in yet other national markets. Indeed, some MNCs have operations in dozens of different countries. MNCs obtain financing from major money centers around the world in many different currencies to finance their operations. Global operations force the treasurer's office to establish international banking relationships, place short-term funds in several currency denominations, and effectively manage foreign exchange risk.

Exhibit 1.4 lists the top 40 of the largest 100 MNCs ranked by the size of foreign assets. The list was compiled by the United Nations Conference on Trade and Development (UNCTAD). Many of the firms on the list are well-known MNCs with household names because of their presence in consumer product markets. For example, General Electric (GE), General Motors, British Petroleum (BP), Toyota, BMW, IBM, Wal-Mart Stores, Unilever, Nestlé, Sony, and Siemens are names recognized by most people. By country of origin, U.S. MNCs, with 26 out of the total of 100, constitute the largest group. France ranks second with 14 MNCs in the top 100, followed by Germany with 13, U.K. with 12, and Japan with 7. It is interesting to note that some Swiss firms are extremely multinational. Novartis, for instance, derived about 98.6 percent of its sales from overseas markets.

MNCs may gain from their global presence in a variety of ways. First of all, MNCs can benefit from the economy of scale by (1) spreading R&D expenditures and advertising costs over their global sales, (2) pooling global purchasing power over suppliers, (3) utilizing their technological and managerial know-how globally with minimum additional costs, and so forth. Furthermore, MNCs can use their global presence to take advantage of underpriced labor services available in certain developing countries, and gain access to special R&D capabilities residing in advanced foreign countries. MNCs can indeed leverage their global presence to boost their profit margins and create shareholder value.

SUMMARY

本章对国际财务管理做了总体介绍。

1. 如今，人们生活在一个高度国际化和一体化的世界经济中，因此，了解财务管理的"国际性"一面就变得十分必要。鉴于国际贸易和投资的持续自由化，以及通信和运输技术的迅速发展，世界经济将变得更加一体化。

2. 国际财务管理与国内财务管理的区别主要体现在以下三个方面：外汇风险和政治风险，市场不完全性，市场机会增加。

3. 跨国公司的财务经理必须懂得如何使用合适的工具来管理外汇风险和政治风险，以处理（或利用）市场的不完全性并从增加的市场机会中获益。这样，财务经理就能为股东财富最大化做出贡献，而这正是国际财务管理的最终目标。

4. 比较优势理论表明如果每个国家生产具有比较优势的产品并进行交易，那么经济福利就会增加。比较优势理论为自由贸易提供了有力的理论依据。目前，无论是在全球

This chapter provided an introduction to *International Financial Management*.

1. It is essential to study "international" financial management because we are now living in a highly globalized and integrated world economy. Owing to the (a) continuous liberalization of international trade and investment, and (b) rapid advances in telecommunications and transportation technologies, the world economy will become even more integrated.

2. Three major dimensions distinguish international finance from domestic finance. They are (a) foreign exchange and political risks, (b) market imperfections, and (c) an expanded opportunity set.

3. Financial managers of MNCs should learn how to manage foreign exchange and political risks using proper tools and instruments, deal with (and take advantage of) market imperfections, and benefit from the expanded investment and financing opportunities. By doing so, financial managers can contribute to shareholder wealth maximization, which is the ultimate goal of international financial management.

4. The theory of comparative advantage states that economic well-being is enhanced if countries produce those goods for which they have comparative advantages and then trade those goods. The theory of comparative advantage provides a powerful

Multinationals More Efficient

Foreign-owned manufacturing companies in the world's most highly developed countries are generally more productive and pay their workers more than comparable locally-owned businesses, according to the Organisation for Economic Co-operation and Development.

The Paris-based organisation also says that the proportion of manufacturing under foreign ownership in European Union countries rose substantially during the 1990s, a sign of increasing economic integration.

In a report on the global role of multinationals, the OECD points out that for some countries, the level of production abroad by foreign subsidiaries of national businesses was comparable to total exports from these countries.

The finding underlines the increasing importance in the world economy of large companies with bases scattered across the globe.

Gross output per employee, a measure of productivity, in most OECD nations tends to be greater in multinationals than in locally-owned companies, the report says.

This is partly a factor of the multinationals being bigger and more geared to operating according to worldclass levels of efficiency. But it also reflects their ability to transfer new thinking in production technologies through an international factory network.

Reflecting the greater efficiencies, workers in foreignowned plants tend to earn more money than those in locally-owned ones.

In Turkey, employees of multinationals earn double the wages of their counterparts. The equivalent figure in the UK is 23 per cent and in the US it is 9 per cent.

In the EU in 1998, a quarter of total manufacturing production was controlled by a foreign subsidiary of a bigger company compared to 17 per cent in 1990. The

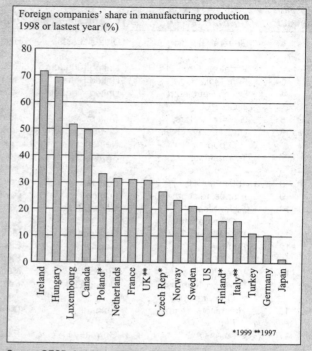

Foreign companies' share in manufacturing production 1998 or lastest year (%)

*1999 **1997

Source: OECD, Activities of Foreign Affiliates database.

figure has probably increased since then, and is expected to climb further as the impact of the euro tightens the link between member countries' economies.

Measuring Globalisation: The Role of Multinationals in OECD Economies. For details see www.oecd.org

Source: Peter Marsh, Financial Times, March 20, 2002, p. 6. Reprinted with permission.

层面上还是在地区层面上，国际贸易正在变得更加自由化。在全球层面上，世界贸易组织在促进自由贸易方面起着重要的作用。在地区层面上，欧盟和北美自由贸易协定在消除区域内贸易壁垒方面起着至关重要的作用。

5. 在当今时代，决定一个国家相对于其他国家拥有比较优势的因素，从本质上讲并不是一个国家所处的地理位置，而是资本和技术的控制者或管理者——跨国公司。一家跨国公司会用某一国家的资本设备来生产产品，其资本设备的融资则通过向投资者发行各种货币的证券来完成，而后跨国公司再将产品销售给其他国家的消费者。今天，这种情形已变得司空见惯了。

rationale for free trade. Currently, international trade is becoming liberalized at both the global and the regional levels. At the global level, WTO plays a key role in promoting free trade. At the regional level, the European Union and NAFTA play a vital role in dismantling trade barriers within regions.

5. In modern times, it is not a country per se but rather a controller of capital and know-how that gives the country in which it is domiciled a comparative advantage over another country. These controllers of capital and technology are multinational corporations (MNCs). Today, it is not uncommon for a MNC to produce merchandise in one country on capital equipment financed by funds raised in a number of different currencies through issuing securities to investors in many countries and then selling the finished product to customers in yet other countries.

EXHIBIT 1.4	The World's Top 40 MNCs Ranked by Foreign Assets, 2002 (Billions of Dollars)						
Ranking by Foreign Assets	**Corporation**	**Country**	**Industry**	**Assets**		**Sales**	
				Foreign	**Total**	**Foreign**	**Total**
1	General Electric	United States	Electrical & Electronic equipment	229.0	575.2	45.4	131.7
2	Vodafone Group PLC	United Kingdom	Telecommunications	207.6	232.8	33.6	42.3
3	Ford Motor Co.	United States	Motor vehicles	165.0	295.2	54.5	163.4
4	British Petroleum Co. PLC	United Kingdom	Petroleum expl./ref./distr.	121.1	159.1	146.0	180.2
5	General Motors	United States	Motor vehicles	107.9	370.8	48.1	186.8
6	Royal Dutch/ Shell Group	United Kingdom/ Netherlands	Petroleum expl./ref./distr.	94.4	145.4	114.3	179.4
7	Toyota Motor Corporation	Japan	Motor vehicles	79.4	167.3	72.8	127.1
8	Total Fina Elf	France	Petroleum expl./ref./distr.	79.0	89.4	77.5	97.0
9	France Telecom	France	Telecommunications	73.5	111.7	18.2	44.1
10	ExxonMobile Corporation	United States	Petroleum expl./ref./distr.	60.8	94.9	141.3	200.9
11	Volkswagen Group	Germany	Motor vehicles	57.1	114.1	59.7	82.2
12	E.On	Germany	Electricity, gas and water	52.3	118.5	13.1	35.1
13	RWE Group	Germany	Electricity, gas and water	50.7	105.1	17.6	44.1
14	Vivendi Universal	France	Media	49.6	72.7	30.0	55.0
15	Chevron Texaco Corporation	United States	Petroleum expl./ref./distr.	48.5	77.3	55.1	98.7
16	Hutchison Whampoa Limited	China	Diversified	48.0	63.3	8.1	14.2
17	Siemens AG	Germany	Electrical & Electronic equipment	47.5	76.5	50.7	77.2
18	Electricité de France	France	Electricity, gas and water	47.4	151.8	12.6	45.7
19	Fiat Spa	Italy	Motor vehicles	46.2	97.0	24.6	52.6
20	Honda Motor Co Ltd	Japan	Motor vehicles	43.6	63.8	49.2	65.4
21	News Corporation	Australia	Media	40.3	45.2	16.0	17.4
22	Roche Group	Switzerland	Pharmaceuticals	40.2	46.2	18.8	19.2
23	Suez	France	Electricity, gas and water	38.7	44.8	34.2	43.6
24	BMW AG	Germany	Motor vehicles	37.6	58.2	30.2	40.0
25	Eni Group	Italy	Petroleum expl./ref./distr.	37.0	69.0	22.8	45.3
26	Nestlé SA	Switzerland	Food & beverages	36.1	63.0	34.9	57.5
27	DaimlerChrysler AG	Germany/ United States	Motor vehicles	35.8	196.4	46.1	141.5
28	Telefonica SA	Spain	Telecommunications	35.7	71.3	11.3	26.9
29	IBM	United States	Electrical & Electronic equipment	35.0	96.5	48.4	81.2
30	ConocoPhillips	United States	Petroleum expl./ref./distr.	32.1	76.8	10.1	56.7
31	Wal-Mart Stores	United States	Retail	30.7	94.7	40.8	244.5
32	Sony Corporation	Japan	Electrical & Electronic equipment	29.8	69.5	42.9	61.3
33	Carrefour SA	France	Retail	28.6	40.8	31.8	65.0
34	Hewlett-Packard	United States	Electrical & Electronic equipment	28.2	70.7	33.3	56.6
35	ABB	Switzerland	Machinery and equipment	28.2	29.5	17.1	18.3
36	Unilever	United Kingdom/ Netherlands	Diversified	27.9	46.8	27.6	46.1
37	Philips Electronics	Netherlands	Electrical & Electronic equipment	27.9	33.8	28.7	30.1
38	Novartis	Switzerland	Pharmaceuticals	25.9	45.6	20.6	20.9
39	Aventis SA	France	Pharmaceuticals	23.8	32.6	14.8	19.5
40	AOL Time Warner Inc	United States	Media	23.5	115.5	8.3	41.0

Source: World Investment Report 2004, United Nations.

KEY WORDS

corporate governance, *9*
European Central Bank, *11*
European Union (EU), *15*
expanded opportunity
   set, *7*
foreign exchange risk, *5*
General Agreement on
   Tariffs and Trade
   (GATT), *14*

globalized and integrated
   world economy, *4*
market imperfections, *6*
multinational corporation
   (MNC), *16*
North American Free
   Trade Agreement
   (NAFTA), *15*
political risk, *6*

shareholder wealth
   maximization, *8*
theory of comparative
   advantage, *13*
transactions domain, *11*
World Trade
   Organization
   (WTO), *14*

QUESTIONS

1. Why is it important to study international financial management?

2. How is international financial management different from domestic financial management?

3. Discuss the three major trends that have prevailed in international business during the last two decades.

4. How is a country's economic well-being enhanced through free international trade in goods and services?

5. What considerations might limit the extent to which the theory of comparative advantage is realistic?

6. What are multinational corporations (MNCs) and what economic roles do they play?

7. Ross Perot, a former presidential candidate of the Reform Party, which is a third political party in the United States, had strongly objected to the creation of the North American Trade Agreement (NAFTA), which nonetheless was inaugurated in 1994. Perot feared the loss of American jobs to Mexico where it is much cheaper to hire workers. What are the merits and demerits of Perot's position on NAFTA? Considering the recent economic developments in North America, how would you assess Perot's position on NAFTA?

8. In 1995, a working group of French chief executive officers was set up by the Confederation of French Industry (CNPF) and the French Association of Private Companies (AFEP) to study the French corporate governance structure. The group reported the following, among other things: "The board of directors should not simply aim at maximizing share values as in the U.K. and the U.S. Rather, its goal should be to serve the company, whose interests should be clearly distinguished from those of its shareholders, employees, creditors, suppliers and clients but still equated with their general common interest, which is to safeguard the prosperity and continuity of the company." Evaluate the above recommendation of the working group.[13]

9. Emphasizing the importance of voluntary compliance, as opposed to enforcement, in the aftermath of such corporate scandals as those involving Enron and WorldCom, U.S. President George W. Bush stated that while tougher laws might help, "ultimately, the ethics of American business depends on the conscience of America's business leaders." Describe your view on this statement.

10. Suppose you are interested in investing in shares of Nokia Corporation of Finland, which is a world leader in wireless communication. But before you make an investment decision, you would like to learn about the company. Visit the website of CNN Financial Network (money.cnn.com) and collect information about Nokia,

---

[13]This question draws on the article by François Degeorge, "French Boardrooms Wake Up Slowly to the Need for Reform," in the Complete MBA Companion in Global Business, *Financial Times,* 1999, pp. 156–60.

including the recent stock price history and analysts' views of the company. Discuss what you learn about the company. Also discuss how the instantaneous access to information via Internet would affect the nature and workings of financial markets.

INTERNET EXERCISES

1. Visit the corporate websites of Nestlé, one of the most multinational companies in the world, and study the scope of geographical diversification of its sales and revenues. Also, gather and evaluate the company's financial information from the related websites. You may use such Internet search engines as Netscape, Microsoft Internet Explorer, and Yahoo.

MINI CASE

Nike and Sweatshop Labor

Nike, a company headquartered in Beaverton, Oregon, is a major force in the sports footwear and fashion industry, with annual sales exceeding $12 billion, more than half of which now come from outside the United States. The company was co-founded in 1964 by Phil Knight, a CPA at Price Waterhouse, and Bill Bowerman, college track coach, each investing $500 to start. The company, initially called Blue Ribbon Sports, changed its name to Nike in 1971 and adopted the "Swoosh" logo—recognizable around the world—originally designed by a college student for $35. Nike became highly successful in designing and marketing mass-appealing products such as the Air Jordan, the best selling athletic shoe of all time.

Nike has no production facilities in the United States. Rather, the company manufactures athletic shoes and garments in such Asian countries as China, Indonesia, and Vietnam using subcontractors, and sells the products in the U.S. and international markets. In each of those Asian countries where Nike has production facilities, the rates of unemployment and under-employment are quite high. The wage rate is very low in those countries by U.S. standards—the hourly wage rate in the manufacturing sector is less than $1 in each of those countries, compared with about $20 in the United States. In addition, workers in those countries often operate in poor and unhealthy environments and their rights are not particularly well protected. Understandably, host countries are eager to attract foreign investments like Nike's to develop their economies and raise the living standards of their citizens. Recently, however, Nike came under worldwide criticism for its practice of hiring workers for such a low rate of pay—"next to nothing" in the words of critics—and condoning poor working conditions in host countries.

Initially, Nike denied the sweatshop charges and lashed out at critics. But later, the company began monitoring the labor practices at its overseas factories and grading the factories in order to improve labor standards. Nike also agreed to random factory inspections by disinterested parties.

Discussion points:

1. Do you think the criticism of Nike is fair, considering that the host countries are in dire needs of creating jobs?

2. What do you think Nike's executives might have done differently to prevent the sensitive charges of sweatshop labor in overseas factories?

3. Do firms need to consider the so-called corporate social responsibilities in making investment decisions?

REFERENCES & SUGGESTED READINGS

Basic Finance References

Bodie, Zvi, Alex Kane, and Alan J. Marcus. *Investments,* 5th ed. New York: Irwin/McGraw-Hill, 2001.

Ross, Stephen A., Randolph W. Westerfield, and Jeffrey F. Jaffee. *Corporate Finance,* 6th ed. New York: Irwin/ McGraw-Hill, 2002.

International Accounting References

Al Hashim, Dhia D., and Jeffrey S. Arpan. *International Dimensions of Accounting,* 3rd ed. Boston: PWS-Kent, 1992.

Meuller, Gerhard G., Helen Gernon, and Gary Meek. *Accounting: An International Perspective,* 5th ed. Burr Ridge, Ill.: Richard D. Irwin, 2000.

International Economics References

Baker, Stephen A. *An Introduction to International Economics.* San Diego: Harcourt Brace Jovanovich, 1990.

Husted, Steven, and Michael Melvin. *International Economics,* 5th ed. Reading, Mass.: Addison-Wesley, 2000.

Krugman, Paul R., and Maurice Obstfeld. *International Economics: Theory and Policy,* 6th ed. Reading, Mass.: Addison-Wesley, 2002.

Rivera-Batiz, Francisco L., and Luis Rivera-Batiz. *International Finance and Open Economy Macroeconomics,* 2nd ed. Upper Saddle River, N.J.: Prentice Hall, 1994.

1A Gain from Trade: The Theory of Comparative Advantage

比较优势理论由19世纪经济学家大卫·李嘉图提出，解释了为什么国家间要进行贸易。这个理论说明如果一个国家生产有比较优势的产品并进行交易，那么经济利益就会扩大。这个理论的前提是国家间存在自由贸易并且生产要素（土地、厂房、劳动力、技术、资本）相对静止，看看表A.1所举的例子，它说明了这个理论。

The theory of comparative advantage was originally advanced by the 19th-century economist David Ricardo as an explanation for why nations trade with one another. The theory claims that economic well-being is enhanced if each country's citizens produce that which they have a comparative advantage in producing relative to the citizens of other countries, and then trade products. Underlying the theory are the assumptions of free trade between nations and that the factors of production (land, labor, technology, and capital) are relatively immobile. Consider the example described in Exhibit A.1 as a vehicle for explaining the theory.

Exhibit A.1 assumes two countries, A and B, which each produce only food and textiles, but they do not trade with one another. Country A and B each have 60,000,000 units of input. Each country presently allocates 40,000,000 units to the production of food and 20,000,000 units to the production of textiles. Examination of the exhibit shows that Country A can produce five pounds of food with one unit of production or three yards of textiles. Country B has an absolute advantage over Country A in the production of both food and textiles. Country B can produce 15 pounds of food or four yards of textiles with one unit of production. When all units of production are employed, Country A can produce 200,000,000 pounds of food and 60,000,000 yards of textiles. Country B can produce 600,000,000 pounds of food and 80,000,000 yards of textiles. Total output is 800,000,000 pounds of food and 140,000,000 yards of textiles. Without trade, each nation's citizens can consume only what they produce.

While it is clear from the examination of Exhibit A.1 that Country B has an absolute advantage in the production of food and textiles, it is not so clear that Country A (B) has a relative advantage over Country B (A) in producing textiles (food). Note that in using units of production, Country A can "trade off" one unit of production needed to produce five pounds of food for three yards of textiles. Thus, a yard of textiles has an

---

EXHIBIT A.1

Input/Output without Trade

		Country A	Country B	Total
I.	Units of input (000,000)			
	Food	40	40	
	Textiles	20	20	
II.	Output per unit of input (lbs. or yards)			
	Food	5	15	
	Textiles	3	4	
III.	Total output (lbs. or yards) (000,000)			
	Food	200	600	800
	Textiles	60	80	140
IV.	Consumption (lbs. or yards) (000,000)			
	Food	200	600	800
	Textiles	60	80	140

EXHIBIT A.2

Input/Output with free Trade

		Country		
		A	B	Total
I.	Units of input (000,000)			
	Food	20	50	
	Textiles	40	10	
II.	Output per unit of input (lbs. or yards)			
	Food	5	15	
	Textiles	3	4	
III.	Total output (lbs. or yards) (000,000)			
	Food	100	750	850
	Textiles	120	40	160
IV.	Consumption (lbs. or yards) (000,000)			
	Food	225	625	850
	Textiles	70	90	160

opportunity cost of 5/3 = 1.67 pounds of food, or a pound of food has an opportunity cost of 3/5 = .60 yards of textiles. Analogously, Country B has an opportunity cost of 15/4 = 3.75 pounds of food per yard of textiles, or 4/15 = .27 yards of textiles per pound of food. When viewed in terms of opportunity costs it is clear that Country A is relatively more efficient in producing textiles and Country B is relatively more efficient in producing food. That is, Country A's (B's) opportunity cost for producing textiles (food) is less than Country B's (A's). A *relative efficiency* that shows up via a lower opportunity cost is referred to as a comparative advantage.

Exhibit A.2 shows that when there are no restrictions or impediments to free trade, such as import quotas, import tariffs, or costly transportation, the economic well-being of the citizens of both countries is enhanced through trade. Exhibit A.2 shows that Country A has shifted 20,000,000 units from the production of food to the production of textiles where it has a comparative advantage and that Country B has shifted 10,000,000 units from the production of textiles to the production of food where it has a comparative advantage. Total output is now 850,000,000 pounds of food and 160,000,000 yards of textiles. Suppose that Country A and Country B agree on a price of 2.50 pounds of food for one yard of textiles, and that Country A sells Country B 50,000,000 yards of textiles for 125,000,000 pounds of food. With free trade, Exhibit A.2 makes it clear that the citizens of each country have increased their consumption of food by 25,000,000 pounds and textiles by 10,000,000 yards.

PROBLEMS

1. Country C can produce seven pounds of food or four yards of textiles per unit of input. Compute the opportunity cost of producing food instead of textiles. Similarly, compute the opportunity cost of producing textiles instead of food.

2. Consider the no-trade input/output situation presented in the following table for countries X and Y. Assuming that free trade is allowed, develop a scenario that will benefit the citizens of both countries.

Input/Output without Trade

		Country		Total
		X	Y	
I.	Units of input (000,000)			
	Food	70	60	
	Textiles	40	30	
II.	Output per unit of input (lbs. or yards)			
	Food	17	5	
	Textiles	5	2	
III.	Total output (lbs. or yards) (000,000)			
	Food	1,190	500	1,490
	Textiles	200	60	260
IV.	Consumption (lbs. or yards) (000,000)			
	Food	1,190	500	1,490
	Textiles	200	60	260

2 International Monetary System

国际货币体系是指跨国公司和国际投资者从中开展经营活动的整体金融环境。

欧元

国际货币体系是关于进行国际支付、调节资金流动和确定各种货币间汇率的组织框架。

THIS CHAPTER EXAMINES the **international monetary system,** which defines the overall financial environment in which multinational corporations and international investors operate. As mentioned in Chapter 1, the exchange rates among major currencies, such as the U.S. dollar, British pound, Swiss franc, and Japanese yen, have been fluctuating since the fixed exchange rate regime was abandoned in 1973. Consequently, corporations nowadays are operating in an environment in which exchange rate changes may adversely affect their competitive positions in the marketplace. This situation, in turn, makes it necessary for many firms to carefully measure and manage their exchange risk exposure. Similarly, international investors face the problem of fluctuating exchange rates affecting their portfolio returns. As we will discuss shortly, however, many European countries have adopted a common currency called the **euro,** rendering intra-European trade and investment much less susceptible to exchange risk. The complex international monetary arrangements imply that for adroit financial decision making, it is essential for managers to understand, in detail, the arrangements and workings of the international monetary system.

The international monetary system can be defined as the *institutional framework within which international payments are made, movements of capital are accommodated,* and *exchange rates among currencies are determined.* It is a complex whole of agreements, rules, institutions, mechanisms, and policies regarding exchange rates, international payments, and the flow of capital. The international monetary system has evolved over time and will continue to do so in the future as the fundamental business and political conditions underlying the world economy continue to shift. In this chapter, we will review the history of the international monetary system and contemplate its future prospects. In addition, we will compare and contrast the alternative exchange rate systems, that is, fixed versus flexible exchange rates. For astute financial management, it is important to understand the dynamic nature of international monetary environments.

Evolution of the International Monetary System

1. 1875年前的金银复本位制时期。
2. 1875～1914年的古典金本位制时期。
3. 1915～1944年的战争时期。
4. 1945～1972年的布雷顿森林体系时期。
5. 1973年后的浮动汇率制。

The international monetary system went through several distinct stages of evolution. These stages are summarized as follows:

1. Bimetallism: Before 1875.
2. Classical gold standard: 1875–1914.
3. Interwar period: 1915–1944.
4. Bretton Woods system: 1945–1972.
5. Flexible exchange rate regime: Since 1973.

We now examine each of the five stages in some detail.

Bimetallism: Before 1875

复本位制

Prior to the 1870s, many countries had **bimetallism,** that is, a double standard in that free coinage was maintained for both gold and silver. In Great Britain, for example, bimetallism was maintained until 1816 (after the conclusion of the Napoleonic Wars) when Parliament passed a law maintaining free coinage of gold only, abolishing the free coinage of silver. In the United States, bimetallism was adopted by the Coinage Act of 1792 and remained a legal standard until 1873, when Congress dropped the silver dollar from the list of coins to be minted. France, on the other hand, introduced and maintained its bimetallism from the French Revolution to 1878. Some other countries such as China, India, Germany, and Holland were on the silver standard.

从某种意义上说，19世纪70年代以前的国际货币体系是以金银复本位制为标志的，金和银不仅可以作为国际支付手段，而且可根据金或银的成色来确定各国货币之间的汇率。

The international monetary system before the 1870s can be characterized as "bimetallism" in the sense that both gold and silver were used as international means of payment and that the exchange rates among currencies were determined by either their gold or silver contents.[1] Around 1870, for example, the exchange rate between the British pound, which was fully on a gold standard, and the French franc, which was officially on a bimetallic standard, was determined by the gold content of the two currencies. On the other hand, the exchange rate between the franc and the German mark, which was on a silver standard, was determined by the silver content of the currencies. The exchange rate between the pound and the mark was determined by their exchange rates against the franc. It is also worth noting that, due to various wars and political upheavals, some major countries such as the United States, Russia, and Austria-Hungary had irredeemable currencies at one time or another during the period 1848–79. One might say that the international monetary system was less than fully *systematic* up until the 1870s.

按照"格雷欣法则"，"良"币（数量不足）会被"劣"币（数量充足）逐出流通市场。

Countries that were on the bimetallic standard often experienced the well-known phenomenon referred to as **Gresham's law.** Since the exchange ratio between the two metals was fixed officially, only the abundant metal was used as money, driving more scarce metal out of circulation. This is Gresham's law, according to which "bad" (abundant) money drives out "good" (scarce) money. For example, when gold from newly discovered mines in California and Australia poured into the market in the 1850s, the value of gold became depressed, causing overvaluation of gold under the French official ratio, which equated a gold franc to a silver franc 15½ times as heavy. As a result, the franc effectively became a gold currency.

---

[1]This does not imply that each individual country was on a bimetallic standard. In fact, many countries were on either a gold standard or a silver standard by 1870.

Classical Gold Standard: 1875–1914

金本位制

Mankind's fondness for gold as a storage of wealth and means of exchange dates back to antiquity and was shared widely by diverse civilizations. Christopher Columbus once said, "Gold constitutes treasure, and he who possesses it has all he needs in this world." The first full-fledged **gold standard,** however, was not established until 1821 in Great Britain, when notes from the Bank of England were made fully redeemable for gold. As previously mentioned, France was effectively on the gold standard beginning in the 1850s and formally adopted the standard in 1878. The newly emergent German empire, which was to receive a sizable war indemnity from France, converted to the gold standard in 1875, discontinuing free coinage of silver. The United States adopted the gold standard in 1879, Russia and Japan in 1897.

One can say roughly that the *international* gold standard existed as a historical reality during the period 1875–1914. The majority of countries got off gold in 1914 when World War I broke out. The classical gold standard as an international monetary system thus lasted for about 40 years. During this period, London became the center of the international financial system, reflecting Britain's advanced economy and its preeminent position in international trade.

An *international* gold standard can be said to exist when, in most major countries, (1) gold alone is assured of unrestricted coinage, (2) there is two-way convertibility between gold and national currencies at a stable ratio, and (3) gold may be freely exported or imported. In order to support unrestricted convertibility into gold, banknotes need to be backed by a gold reserve of a minimum stated ratio. In addition, the domestic money stock should rise and fall as gold flows in and out of the country. The above conditions were roughly met between 1875 and 1914.

在金本位制下，任何两种货币间的汇率应根据它们的含金量来确定。

Under the gold standard, the exchange rate between any two currencies will be determined by their gold content. For example, suppose that the pound is pegged to gold at six pounds per ounce, whereas one ounce of gold is worth 12 francs. The exchange rate between the pound and the franc should then be two francs per pound. To the extent that the pound and the franc remain pegged to gold at given prices, the exchange rate between the two currencies will remain stable. There were indeed no significant changes in exchange rates among the currencies of such major countries as Great Britain, France, Germany, and the United States during the entire period. For example, the dollar–sterling exchange rate remained within a narrow range of $4.84 and $4.90 per pound. Highly stable exchange rates under the classical gold standard provided an environment that was conducive to international trade and investment.

在金本位制下，汇率偏差能够通过黄金的跨国自由流动而实现自动矫正。

Under the gold standard, misalignment of the exchange rate will be automatically corrected by cross-border flows of gold. In the above example, suppose that one pound is trading for 1.80 francs at the moment. Since the pound is undervalued in the exchange market, people will buy pounds with francs, but not francs with pounds. For people who need francs, it would be cheaper first to buy gold from the Bank of England and ship it to France and sell it for francs. For example, suppose that you need to buy 1,000 francs using pounds. If you buy 1,000 francs in the exchange market, it will cost you £555.56 at the exchange rate of Fr1.80/£. Alternatively, you can buy 83.33 = 1,000/12 ounces of gold from the Bank of England for £500:

$$£500 = (1,000/12) \times 6$$

Then you could ship it to France and sell it to the Bank of France for 1,000 francs. This way, you can save about £55.56.[2] Since people only want to buy, not sell, pounds

---

[2]In this example, we ignored shipping costs. But as long as the shipping costs do not exceed £55.56, it is still advantageous to buy francs via "gold export" than via the foreign exchange market.

at the exchange rate of Fr1.80/£, the pound will eventually appreciate to its fair value, namely, Fr2.0/£.

在金本位制下，国际收支不平衡也可以实现自动矫正。

Under the gold standard, international imbalances of payment will also be corrected automatically. Consider a situation where Great Britain exported more to France than the former imported from the latter. This kind of trade imbalance will not persist under the gold standard. Net export from Great Britain to France will be accompanied by a net flow of gold in the opposite direction. This flow of gold will lead to a lower price level in France and, at the same time, a higher price level in Great Britain. (Recall that under the gold standard, the domestic money stock is supposed to rise or fall as the country experiences an inflow or outflow of gold.) The resultant change in the relative price level, in turn, will slow exports from Great Britain and encourage exports from France. As a result, the initial net export from Great Britain will eventually disappear. This adjustment mechanism is referred to as the **price-specie-flow mechanism,** which is attributed to David Hume, a Scottish philosopher.[3]

价格-铸币-流动机制

Despite its demise a long time ago, the gold standard still has ardent supporters in academic, business, and political circles, which view it as an ultimate hedge against price inflation. Gold has a natural scarcity and no one can increase its quantity at will. Therefore, if gold serves as the sole base for domestic money creation, the money supply cannot get out of control and cause inflation. In addition, if gold is used as the sole international means of payment, then countries' balance of payments will be regulated automatically via the movements of gold.[4]

国际金本位制在本质上缺乏一种迫使各主要国家遵守游戏规则的机制。

The gold standard, however, has a few key shortcomings. First of all, the supply of newly minted gold is so restricted that the growth of world trade and investment can be seriously hampered for the lack of sufficient monetary reserves. The world economy can face deflationary pressures. Second, whenever the government finds it politically necessary to pursue national objectives that are inconsistent with maintaining the gold standard, it can abandon the gold standard. In other words, the international gold standard per se has no mechanism to compel each major country to abide by the rules of the game.[5] For such reasons, it is not very likely that the classical gold standard will be restored in the foreseeable future.

Interwar Period: 1915–1944

World War I ended the classical gold standard in August 1914, as major countries such as Great Britain, France, Germany, and Russia suspended redemption of banknotes in gold and imposed embargoes on gold exports. After the war, many countries, especially Germany, Austria, Hungary, Poland, and Russia, suffered hyperinflation. The German experience provides a classic example of hyperinflation: By the end of 1923, the wholesale price index in Germany was more than 1 trillion times as high as the prewar level. Freed from wartime pegging, exchange rates among currencies were fluctuating in the early 1920s. During this period, countries widely used "predatory" depreciations of their currencies as a means of gaining advantages in the world export market.

As major countries began to recover from the war and stabilize their economies, they attempted to restore the gold standard. The United States, which replaced Great Britain as the dominant financial power, spearheaded efforts to restore the gold standard.

---

[3]The price-specie-flow mechanism will work only if governments are willing to abide by the rules of the game by letting the money stock rise and fall as gold flows in and out. Once the government demonetizes (neutralizes) gold, the mechanism will break down. In addition, the effectiveness of the mechanism depends on the price elasticity of the demand for imports.

[4]The balance of payments will be discussed in detail in Chapter 3.

[5]This point need not be viewed as a weakness of the gold standard per se, but it casts doubt on the long-term feasibility of the gold standard.

With only mild inflation, the United States was able to lift restrictions on gold exports and return to a gold standard in 1919. In Great Britain, Winston Churchill, the chancellor of the Exchequer, played a key role in restoring the gold standard in 1925. Besides Great Britain, such countries as Switzerland, France, and the Scandinavian countries restored the gold standard by 1928.

The international gold standard of the late 1920s, however, was not much more than a façade. Most major countries gave priority to the stabilization of domestic economies and systematically followed a policy of **sterilization of gold** by matching inflows and outflows of gold respectively with reductions and increases in domestic money and credit. The Federal Reserve of the United States, for example, kept some gold outside the credit base by circulating it as gold certificates. The Bank of England also followed the policy of keeping the amount of available domestic credit stable by neutralizing the effects of gold flows. In a word, countries lacked the political will to abide by the "rules of the game," and so the automatic adjustment mechanism of the gold standard was unable to work.

Even the façade of the restored gold standard was destroyed in the wake of the Great Depression and the accompanying financial crises. Following the stock market crash and the onset of the Great Depression in 1929, many banks, especially in Austria, Germany, and the United States, suffered sharp declines in their portfolio values, touching off runs on the banks. Against this backdrop, Britain experienced a massive outflow of gold, which resulted from chronic balance-of-payment deficits and lack of confidence in the pound sterling. Despite coordinated international efforts to rescue the pound, British gold reserves continued to fall to the point where it was impossible to maintain the gold standard. In September 1931, the British government suspended gold payments and let the pound float. As Great Britain got off gold, countries such as Canada, Sweden, Austria, and Japan followed suit by the end of 1931. The United States got off gold in April 1933 after experiencing a spate of bank failures and outflows of gold. Lastly, France abandoned the gold standard in 1936 because of the flight from the franc, which, in turn, reflected the economic and political instability following the inception of the socialist Popular Front government led by Leon Blum. Paper standards came into being when the gold standard was abandoned.

In sum, the interwar period was characterized by economic nationalism, halfhearted attempts and failure to restore the gold standard, economic and political instabilities, bank failures, and panicky flights of capital across borders. No coherent international monetary system prevailed during this period, with profoundly detrimental effects on international trade and investment. It is during this period that the U.S. dollar emerged as the dominant world currency, gradually replacing the British pound for the role.

Bretton Woods System: 1945–1972

In July 1944, representatives of 44 nations gathered at Bretton Woods, New Hampshire, to discuss and design the postwar international monetary system. After lengthy discussions and bargains, representatives succeeded in drafting and signing the Articles of Agreement of the International Monetary Fund (IMF), which constitutes the core of the **Bretton Woods system.** The agreement was subsequently ratified by the majority of countries to launch the IMF in 1945. The IMF embodied an explicit set of rules about the conduct of international monetary policies and was responsible for enforcing these rules. Delegates also created a sister institution, the International Bank for Reconstruction and Development (IBRD), better known as the World Bank, that was chiefly responsible for financing individual development projects.

In designing the Bretton Woods system, representatives were concerned with how to prevent the recurrence of economic nationalism with destructive "beggar-thy-neighbor" policies and how to address the lack of clear rules of the game plaguing the interwar

EXHIBIT 2.1

The Design of the Gold-Exchange System

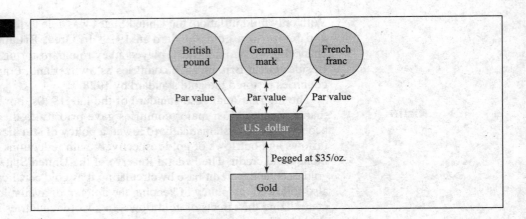

years. The British delegates led by John Maynard Keynes proposed an international clearing union that would create an international reserve asset called "bancor." Countries would accept payments in bancor to settle international transactions, without limit. They would also be allowed to acquire bancor by using overdraft facilities with the clearing union. On the other hand, the American delegates, headed by Harry Dexter White, proposed a currency pool to which member countries would make contributions and from which they might borrow to tide themselves over during short-term balance-of-payments deficits. Both delegates desired exchange rate stability without restoring an international gold standard. The American proposal was largely incorporated into the Articles of Agreement of the IMF.

Under the Bretton Woods system, each country established a **par value** in relation to the U.S. dollar, which was pegged to gold at $35 per ounce. This point is illustrated in Exhibit 2.1. Each country was responsible for maintaining its exchange rate within ±1 percent of the adopted par value by buying or selling foreign exchanges as necessary. However, a member country with a "fundamental disequilibrium" may be allowed to make a change in the par value of its currency. Under the Bretton Woods system, the U.S. dollar was the only currency that was fully convertible to gold; other currencies were not directly convertible to gold. Countries held U.S. dollars, as well as gold, for use as an international means of payment. Because of these arrangements, the Bretton Woods system can be described as a dollar-based **gold-exchange standard.** A country on the gold-exchange standard holds most of its reserves in the form of currency of a country that is *really* on the gold standard.

Advocates of the gold-exchange system argue that the system economizes on gold because countries can use not only gold but also foreign exchanges as an international means of payment. Foreign exchange reserves offset the deflationary effects of limited addition to the world's monetary gold stock. Another advantage of the gold-exchange system is that individual countries can earn interest on their foreign exchange holdings, whereas gold holdings yield no returns. In addition, countries can save transaction costs associated with transporting gold across countries under the gold-exchange system. An ample supply of international monetary reserves coupled with stable exchange rates provided an environment highly conducive to the growth of international trade and investment throughout the 1950s and 1960s.

Professor Robert Triffin warned, however, that the gold-exchange system was programmed to collapse in the long run. To satisfy the growing need for reserves, the United States had to run balance-of-payments deficits continuously. Yet if the United States ran perennial balance-of-payments deficits, it would eventually impair the public confidence in the dollar, triggering a run on the dollar. Under the gold-exchange system, the reserve-currency country should run balance-of-payments deficits to supply reserves, but if such deficits are large and persistent, they can lead to

按照布雷顿森林体系，每个国家都建立其货币与美元挂钩的**平价**制度，而美元与黄金挂钩，即每盎司黄金价值35美元。

金汇兑本位制

充裕的国际货币储备以及稳定的货币汇率为20世纪50年代和60年代间国际贸易和投资的发展提供了一个良好的环境。

特里芬难题

a crisis of confidence in the reserve currency itself, causing the downfall of the system. This dilemma, known as the **Triffin paradox,** was indeed responsible for the eventual collapse of the dollar-based gold-exchange system in the early 1970s.

The United States began to experience trade deficits with the rest of the world in the late 1950s, and the problem persisted into the 1960s. By the early 1960s the total value of the U.S. gold stock, when valued at $35 per ounce, fell short of foreign dollar holdings. This naturally created concern about the viability of the dollar-based system. Against this backdrop, President Charles de Gaulle prodded the Bank of France to buy gold from the U.S. Treasury, unloading its dollar holdings. Efforts to remedy the problem centered on (1) a series of dollar defense measures taken by the U.S. government and (2) the creation of a new reserve asset, **special drawing rights (SDRs),** by the IMF.

对这次美元危机采取了两种补救措施：一是美国政府采取了一系列保护美元价值的措施；二是国际货币基金组织创建了**特别提款权（SDR）**这种新的储备资产。

In 1963, President John Kennedy imposed the Interest Equalization Tax (IET) on U.S. purchases of foreign securities in order to stem the outflow of dollars. The IET was designed to increase the cost of foreign borrowing in the U.S. bond market. In 1965, the Federal Reserve introduced the U.S. voluntary Foreign Credit Restraint Program (FCRP), which regulated the amount of dollars U.S. banks could lend to U.S. multinational companies engaged in foreign direct investments. In 1968, these regulations became legally binding. Such measures as IET and FCRP lent a strong impetus to the rapid growth of the Eurodollar market, which is a transnational, unregulated fund market.

www.imf.org/external/fin.htm/
Provides detailed information about the SDR, such as SDR exchange rates, interests, allocations, etc.

To partially alleviate the pressure on the dollar as the central reserve currency, the IMF created an artificial international reserve called the SDR in 1970. The SDR, which is a basket currency comprising major individual currencies, was allotted to the members of the IMF, who could then use it for transactions among themselves or with the IMF. In addition to gold and foreign exchanges, countries could use the SDR to make international payments.

Initially, the SDR was designed to be the weighted average of 16 currencies of those countries whose shares in world exports were more than 1 percent. The percentage share of each currency in the SDR was about the same as the country's share in world exports. In 1981, however, the SDR was greatly simplified to comprise only five major currencies: U.S. dollar, German mark, Japanese yen, British pound, and French franc. As Exhibit 2.2 shows, the weight for each currency is updated periodically, reflecting the relative importance of each country in the world trade of goods and services and the amount of the currencies held as reserves by the members of the IMF. Currently, the SDR is comprised of four major currencies-the U.S. dollar (45 percent weight), euro (29 percent), Japanese yen (15 percent), and British pound (11 percent).

特别提款权不仅可以充当储备资产，而且可以充当国际贸易的计价货币。

The SDR is used not only as a reserve asset but also as a denomination currency for international transactions. Since the SDR is a "portfolio" of currencies, its value tends to be more stable than the value of any individual currency included in the SDR. The portfolio nature of the SDR makes it an attractive denomination currency for international commercial and financial contracts under exchange rate uncertainty.

EXHIBIT 2.2

The Composition of the Special Drawing Right (SDR)[a]

Currencies	1981–85	1986–90	1991–95	1996–2000	2001–2005
U.S. dollar	42%	42%	40%	39%	45%
Euro	—	—	—	—	29
German mark	19	19	21	21	—
Japanese yen	13	15	17	18	15
British pound	13	12	11	11	11
French franc	13	12	11	11	—

[a]The composition of the SDR changes every five years.
Source: The International Monetary Fund.

The efforts to support the dollar-based gold-exchange standard, however, turned out to be ineffective in the face of expansionary monetary policy and rising inflation in the United States, which were related to the financing of the Vietnam War and the Great Society program. In the early 1970s, it became clear that the dollar was overvalued, especially relative to the mark and the yen. As a result, the German and Japanese central banks had to make massive interventions in the foreign exchange market to maintain their par values. Given the unwillingness of the United States to control its monetary expansion, the repeated central bank interventions could not solve the underlying disparities. In August 1971, President Richard Nixon suspended the convertibility of the dollar into gold and imposed a 10 percent import surcharge. The foundation of the Bretton Woods system cracked under the strain.

《史密森协议》

In an attempt to save the Bretton Woods system, 10 major countries, known as the Group of Ten, met at the Smithsonian Institution in Washington, D.C., in December 1971. They reached the **Smithsonian Agreement,** according to which (1) the price of gold was raised to $38 per ounce, (2) each of the other countries revalued its currency against the U.S. dollar by up to 10 percent, and (3) the band within which the exchange rates were allowed to move was expanded from 1 percent to 2.25 percent in either direction.

The Smithsonian Agreement lasted for little more than a year before it came under attack again. Clearly, the devaluation of the dollar was not sufficient to stabilize the situation. In February 1973, the dollar came under heavy selling pressure, again prompting central banks around the world to buy dollars. The price of gold was further raised from $38 to $42 per ounce. By March 1973, European and Japanese currencies were allowed to float, completing the decline and fall of the Bretton Woods system. Since then, the exchange rates among such major currencies as the dollar, the mark (later succeeded by the euro), the pound, and the yen have been fluctuating against each other.

自那以来，美元、马克（后被欧元取代）、英镑、日元等主要货币间的汇率一直在变动。

The Flexible Exchange Rate Regime: 1973–Present

The flexible exchange rate regime that followed the demise of the Bretton Woods system was ratified after the fact in January 1976 when the IMF members met in Jamaica and agreed to a new set of rules for the international monetary system. The key elements of the **Jamaica Agreement** include:

《牙买加协议》

1. Flexible exchange rates were declared acceptable to the IMF members, and central banks were allowed to intervene in the exchange markets to iron out unwarranted volatilities.

2. Gold was officially abandoned (i.e., demonetized) as an international reserve asset. Half of the IMF's gold holdings were returned to the members and the other half were sold, with the proceeds to be used to help poor nations.

3. Non-oil-exporting countries and less-developed countries were given greater access to IMF funds.

The IMF continued to provide assistance to countries facing balance-of-payments and exchange rate difficulties. The IMF, however, extended assistance and loans to the member countries on the condition that those countries follow the IMF's macroeconomic policy prescriptions. This "conditionality," which often involves deflationary macroeconomic policies and elimination of various subsidy programs, provoked resentment among the people of developing countries receiving the IMF's balance-of-payments loans.

IMF的"援助条款"常常要求受援国实行通货紧缩政策和取消各种补助项目，结果引起了接受IMF国际收支贷款的发展中国家的愤恨。

As can be expected, exchange rates have become substantially more volatile since March 1973 than they were under the Bretton Woods system. Exhibit 2.3 summarizes

EXHIBIT 2.3	The Value of the U.S. Dollar since 1965[a]

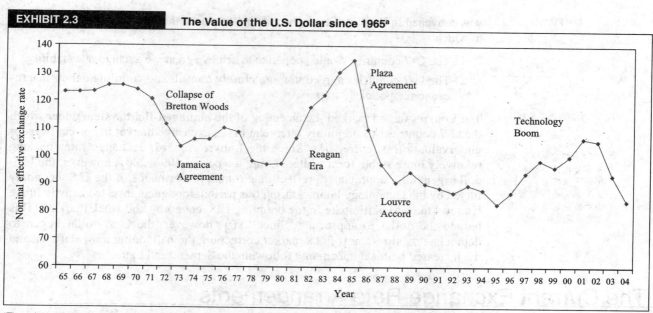

[a]The value of the U.S. dollar represents the nominal effective exchange rate index (2000 = 100) with weights derived from trade among 22 industrialized countries.
Source: The International Monetary Fund.

http://cibs.sauder.ubc.ca

Provides a list of all the currencies of the world with information on each country's exchange rate regime. Also provides current and historical exchange rates.

国外投资者对美元的大量需求推动了外汇市场上美元的升值。

《广场协议》

the behavior of the dollar exchange rate since 1965. The exhibit shows the exchange rate between the U.S. dollar and a weighted basket of 21 other major currencies. The decline of the dollar between 1970 and 1973 represents the transition from the Bretton Woods to the flexible exchange rate system. The most conspicuous phenomena shown in Exhibit 2.3 are the dollar's spectacular rise between 1980 and 1984 and its equally spectacular decline between 1985 and 1988. These unusual episodes merit some discussion.

Following the U.S. presidential election of 1980, the Reagan administration ushered in a period of growing U.S. budget deficits and balance-of-payments deficits. The U.S. dollar, however, experienced a major appreciation throughout the first half of the 1980s because of the large-scale inflows of foreign capital caused by unusually high real interest rates available in the United States. To attract foreign investment to help finance the budget deficit, the United States had to offer high real interest rates. The heavy demand for dollars by foreign investors pushed up the value of the dollar in the exchange market.

The value of the dollar reached its peak in February 1985 and then began a persistent downward drift until it stabilized in 1988. The reversal in the exchange rate trend partially reflected the effect of the record-high U.S. trade deficit, about $160 billion in 1985, brought about by the soaring dollar. The downward trend was also reinforced by concerted government interventions. In September 1985, the so-called G-5 countries (France, Japan, Germany, the U.K., and the United States) met at the Plaza Hotel in New York and reached what became known as the **Plaza Accord.** They agreed that it would be desirable for the dollar to depreciate against most major currencies to solve the U.S. trade deficit problem and expressed their willingness to intervene in the exchange market to realize this objective. The slide of the dollar that had begun in February was further precipitated by the Plaza Accord.

As the dollar continued its decline, the governments of the major industrial countries began to worry that the dollar may fall too far. To address the problem of exchange rate volatility and other related issues, the G-7 economic summit meeting

《卢浮宫协议》

was convened in Paris in 1987.[6] The meeting produced the **Louvre Accord,** according to which:

1. The G-7 countries would cooperate to achieve greater exchange rate stability.
2. The G-7 countries agreed to more closely consult and coordinate their macroeconomic policies.

管理浮动汇率制

《卢浮宫协议》标志
着有管理的浮动汇率制
度的开始实行。在这种
制度下，七国集团会联
合干预外汇市场以调整
货币价值的过度波动。

The Louvre Accord marked the inception of the **managed-float system** under which the G-7 countries would jointly intervene in the exchange market to correct over- or undervaluation of currencies. Since the Louvre Accord, exchange rates became relatively more stable for a while. During the period 1996–2001, however, the U.S. dollar generally appreciated, reflecting a robust performance of the U.S. economy fueled by the technology boom. During this period, foreigners invested heavily in the United States to participate in the booming U.S. economy and stock markets. This helped the dollar to appreciate. Since 2001, however, the U.S. dollar began to depreciate due to a sharp stock market correction, the ballooning trade deficits, and the increased political uncertainty following the September 11 attack.

The Current Exchange Rate Arrangements

尽管美元、日元、
英镑和欧元等全球交易
最活跃的货币相互间可
以自由浮动，但世界上
仍有相当数量的货币仍
然只是与某一种货币挂
钩，特别是与美元、欧
元或SDR之类的一篮子
货币挂钩。

Although the most actively traded currencies of the world, such as the dollar, the yen, the pound, and the euro, may be fluctuating against each other, a significant number of the world's currencies are pegged to single currencies, particularly the U.S. dollar and the euro, or baskets of currencies such as the SDR. The current exchange rate arrangements as classified by the IMF are provided in Exhibit 2.4.

As can be seen from the exhibit, the IMF currently classifies exchange rate arrangements into eight separate regimes:[7]

钉住组合货币的汇
率制度

Exchange arrangements with no separate legal tender: The currency of another country circulates as the sole legal tender or the country belongs to a monetary or currency union in which the same legal tender is shared by the members of the union. Examples include Ecuador, El Salvador, and Panama using the U.S. dollar and the 12 euro zone member countries (like France, Germany, and Italy) sharing the common currency, the euro.

货币局制度

Currency board arrangements: A monetary regime based on an explicit legislative commitment to exchange domestic currency for a specified foreign currency at a fixed exchange rate, combined with restrictions on the issuing authority to ensure the fulfillment of its legal obligation. Examples include China-Hong Kong SAR fixed to the U.S. dollar and Estonia fixed to the euro.

其他传统的固定汇
率制

Other conventional fixed peg arrangement: The country pegs its currency (formally or de facto) at a fixed rate to a major currency or a basket of currencies where the exchange rate fluctuates within a narrow margin of less than 1 percent, plus or minus, around a central rate. Examples include Morocco, Saudi Arabia, and Ukraine.

钉住幅度汇率制

Pegged exchange rates within horizontal bands: The value of the currency is maintained within margins of fluctuation around a formal or de facto fixed peg that are wider than at least 1 percent, plus or minus, around a central rate. Examples include Denmark, Slovenia, and Hungary.

有管理的钉住汇率制

Crawling pegs: The currency is adjusted periodically in small amounts at a fixed, preannounced rate or in response to changes in selective quantitative indicators. Examples are Bolivia, Costa Rica, and Tunisia.

---

[6]The G-7 is composed of Canada, France, Japan, Germany, Italy, the U.K., and the United States.
[7]We draw on IMF classifications provided in *International Financial Statistics*.

爬行钉住汇率制

Exchange rates within crawling bands: The currency is maintained within certain fluctuation margins around a central rate that is adjusted periodically at a fixed preannounced rate or in response to changes in selective quantitative indicators. Examples are Belarus and Romania.

有管理的浮动汇率制

Managed floating with no preannounced path for the exchange rate: The monetary authority influences the movements of the exchange rate through active intervention in the foreign exchange market without specifying, or precommitting to, a preannounced path for the exchange rate. Examples include Algeria, China, P.R., Czech Republic, India, Russia, Singapore, and Thailand.

自由浮动汇率制

Independent floating: The exchange rate is market determined, with any foreign exchange intervention aimed at moderating the rate of change and preventing undue fluctuations in the exchange rate rather than at establishing a level for it. Examples include Australia, Brazil, Canada, Korea, Mexico, the U.K., Japan, Switzerland, and the United States.

截至2005年7月，澳大利亚、加拿大、日本、英国和美国等很多国家都容许其货币对其他货币可自由浮动，即这些国家的汇率基本上由市场来决定。

As of July 2005, a large number of countries (36), including Australia, Canada, Japan, the United Kingdom, and the United States, allow their currencies to float independently against other currencies; the exchange rates of these countries are essentially determined by market forces. Fifty countries, including China, India, Russia, and Singapore, adopt some forms of "managed floating" system that combines market forces and government intervention in setting the exchange rates. In contrast, 41 countries do not have their own national currencies. For example, 14 central and western African countries jointly use the CFA-franc, which is fixed to the euro through the historical ties with the French franc. Seven countries including Bulgaria, and Estonia, on the other hand, maintain national currencies but they are permanently fixed to such hard currencies as the U.S. dollar or euro. The remaining countries adopt a mixture of fixed and floating exchange rate regimes. As is well known, the European Union has pursued Europe-wide monetary integration by first establishing the European Monetary System and then the European Monetary Union. These topics deserve a detailed discussion.

European Monetary System

According to the Smithsonian Agreement, which was signed in December 1971, the band of exchange rate movements was expanded from the original plus or minus 1 percent to plus or minus 2.25 percent. Members of the European Economic Community (EEC), however, decided on a narrower band of ±1.125 percent for their currencies. This scaled-down, European version of the fixed exchange rate system that arose concurrently with the decline of the Bretton Woods system was called the **snake.** The name "snake" was derived from the way the EEC currencies moved closely together within the wider band allowed for other currencies like the dollar.

蛇形浮动

欧共体之所以采用"蛇形浮动"制，是因为它们认为稳定的汇率制度是促进欧共体内部贸易和深化经济一体化的必要条件。

欧洲货币体系（EMS）

The EEC countries adopted the snake because they felt that stable exchange rates among the EEC countries were essential for promoting intra-EEC trade and deepening economic integration. The snake arrangement was replaced by the **European Monetary System (EMS)** in 1979. The EMS, which was originally proposed by German Chancellor Helmut Schmidt, was formally launched in March 1979. Among its chief objectives are:

1. To establish a "zone of monetary stability" in Europe.

2. To coordinate exchange rate policies vis-à-vis the non-EMS currencies.

3. To pave the way for the eventual European monetary union.

At the political level, the EMS represented a Franco-German initiative to speed up the movement toward European economic and political unification. All EEC member

EXHIBIT 2.4 Exchange Rate Regimes and Anchors of Monetary Policy (As of July 31, 2005)[1]

Exchange Rate Regime (Number of Regions or Countries)	Monetary Policy Framework				
	Exchange Rate Anchor	Monetary Aggregate Target	Inflation Targeting Framework	Fund-Supported or Other Monetary Program	Other
Exchange Arrangements with No Separate Legal Tender (41)	**Another currency as legal tender** Ecuador[†] El Salvador[4] Kiribati Marshall Islands, Rep. of Micronesia, Fed. States of Palau Panama San Marino Timor-Leste **ECCU**[3] Antigua & Barbuda Dominica Grenada St. Kitts & Nevis St. Lucia St. Vincent & the Grenadines **CFA Franc Zone** **WAEMU** Benin[†] Burkina Faso[†] Côte d'Ivoire[†] Guinea-Bissau[†] Mali[†] Niger[†] Senegal[†] Togo **CAEMC** Cameroon[†] C. African Rep.[†] Chad[†] Congo, Rep. of[†] Equatorial Guinea[†] Gabon[†]				Euro Area[4,5] Austria Belgium Finland France Germany Greece Ireland Italy Luxembourg Netherlands Portugal Spain
Currency Board Arrangements (7)	Bosnia and Herzegovina[†] Brunei Darussalam Bulgaria[†] China-Hong Kong SAR Djibouti[†] Estonia[†] Lithuania[†]				
Other Conventional Fixed Peg Arrangements (Including De Facto Peg Arrangements under Managed Floating) (40)	**Against a single currency (32)** Aruba Bahamas, The[6] Bahrain, Kingdom of Barbados Belize Bhutan Cape Verde Comoros[9] Eritrea Guinea Iraq Jordan[17] Kuwait Lebanon[7] Lesotho[†] Macedonia, FYR[17] Maldives[7] Namibia Nepal Netherlands Antilles Oman Qatar[7,8] Saudi Arabia[7,8] Seychelles Suriname[6,7] Swaziland Syrian Arab Republic[6] Turkmenistan[7] Ukraine United Arab Emirates[7,8] Venezuela Zimbabwe[7] **Against a composite (8)** Botswana[6] Fiji Latvia[†] Libyan A.J. Malta Morocco Samoa Vanuatu	China, P.R.: Mainland[*7]			
Pegged Exchange Rates within Horizontal Bands (5)[10]	**Within a cooperative arrangement** **ERM II (2)** Denmark Slovenia **Other band arrangements (3)** Cyprus Hungary[*] Tonga		Hungary[*]		
Crawling Pegs (6)	Bolivia[†] Costa Rica[7] Honduras Nicaragua[†] Solomon Islands[7] Tunisia	Tunisia		Honduras	

Exchange rate regime						
Exchange Rates within Crawling Bands (2)[11]	Belarus	Romania[17]		Israel*		
Managed Floating with No Predetermined Path for Exchange Rate (50)			Bangladesh, Cambodia, Egypt, Ghana†, Guyana†, Indonesia†, Iran, Jamaica[17], Mauritius, Moldova, Sudan, Zambia	Czech Rep., Peru, Thailand†	Argentina, Azerbaijan, Croatia, Ethiopia, Georgia, Haiti, Kenya, Kyrgyz Republic, Lao PDR[6], Mongolia, Mozambique, Pakistan, Rwanda, Serbia and Montenegro, Tajikistan, Vietnam	Afghanistan, Algeria[4], Angola[4], Burundi[4], China, P.R., Gambia, India[4], Kazakhstan, Malaysia, Mauritania, Myanmar[4,6,7], Nigeria, Paraguay[4], Russian Federation, São Tomé and Príncipe, Singapore[4], Slovak Rep.[4], Trinidad and Tobago, Uzbekistan[4,6]
Independently Floating (36)			Malawi†, Sierra Leone†, Sri Lanka, Uruguay†, Yemen†	Australia, Brazil[†3], Canada, Chile[6], Colombia†, Guatemala, Iceland, Israel, Korea, Mexico, New Zealand, Norway, Philippines, Poland, South Africa, Sweden, Turkey, United Kingdom	Albania, Armenia, Congo, Dem. Rep., Madagascar, Tanzania, Uganda	Dominican Rep., Japan[4], Liberia[4], Papua New Guinea[4], Somalia[6,12], Switzerland[4], United States[4]

Source: www.imf.org/external/np/mfd/er/2005.

Note: "Country" in this publication does not always refer to a territorial entity that is a state as understood by international law and practice; the term also covers the euro area and some nonsovereign territorial entities for which statistical data are provided internationally on a separate basis.

[1] A country with * indicates that the country adopts more than one nominal anchor in conducting monetary policy. It should be noted, however, that it would not be possible, for practical reasons, to infer from this table which nominal anchor plays the principal role in conducting monetary policy.

[2] A country with † indicates that the country has a Fund supported or other monetary program.

[3] These countries have a currency board arrangement.

[4] The country has no explicitly stated nominal anchor, but rather monitors various indicators in conducting monetary policy.

[5] Until they are withdrawn in February 2002, national currencies will retain their status as legal tender within their home territories.

[6] Member maintained exchange regimes involving more than one market. The regime shown is that maintained in the major market.

[7] The indicated country has a de facto regime which differs from its de jure regime.

[8] Exchange rates are determined on the basis of a fixed relationship to the SDR, within margins of up to ±7.25%. However, because of the maintenance of a relatively stable relationship with the U.S. dollar, these margins are not always observed.

[9] Comoros has the same arrangement with the French Treasury as do the CFA Franc Zone countries.

[10] The band width for these countries is: Cyprus (±2.25%), Denmark (±2.25%), Hungary (±15%), Slovenia (±15%), and Tonga (±5%).

[11] The band for these countries is: Belarus (±5%) and Romania (unannounced).

[12] There is no relevant information available for the country.

[13] Brazil maintains a Fund-supported program.

[14] For El Salvador, the printing of new colones, the domestic currency, is prohibited, but the existing stock of colones will continue to circulate, along with the U.S. dollar, as legal tender until all notes physically wear out.

[15] Peru's exchange rate regime has been reclassified, retroactively, as Peru has been maintaining an independently floating exchange rate.

countries, except the United Kingdom and Greece, joined the EMS. The two main instruments of the EMS are the European Currency Unit and the Exchange Rate Mechanism.

欧洲货币单位(ECU)

The **European Currency Unit (ECU)** is a "basket" currency constructed as a weighted average of the currencies of member countries of the European Union (EU). The weights are based on each currency's relative GNP and share in intra-EU trade. The ECU serves as the accounting unit of the EMS and plays an important role in the workings of the exchange rate mechanism.

汇率机制（ERM）

The **Exchange Rate Mechanism (ERM)** refers to the procedure by which EMS member countries collectively manage their exchange rates. The ERM is based on a "parity grid" system, which is a system of par values among ERM currencies. The par values in the parity grid are computed by first defining the par values of EMS currencies in terms of the ECU.

在1979年欧洲货币体系成立之初，各成员国货币按规定对其他货币可偏离平价一定的幅度，除意大利里拉的最大偏离幅度为±6%之外，其他各国货币的最大偏离幅度为±2.25%。

When the EMS was launched in 1979, a currency was allowed to deviate from the parities with other currencies by a maximum of plus or minus 2.25 percent, with the exception of the Italian lira, for which a maximum deviation of plus or minus 6 percent was allowed. In September 1993, however, the band was widened to a maximum of plus or minus 15 percent. When a currency is at the lower or upper bound, the central banks of both countries are required to intervene in the foreign exchange markets to keep the market exchange rate within the band. To intervene in the exchange markets, the central banks can borrow from a credit fund to which member countries contribute gold and foreign reserves.

Since the EMS members were less than fully committed to coordinating their economic policies, the EMS went through a series of realignments. The Italian lira, for instance, was devalued by 6 percent in July 1985 and again by 3.7 percent in January 1990. In September 1992, Italy and the U.K. pulled out of the ERM as high German interest rates were inducing massive capital flows into Germany. Following German reunification in October 1990, the German government experienced substantial budget deficits, which were not accommodated by the monetary policy. Germany would not lower its interest rates for fear of inflation, and the U.K. and Italy were not willing to raise their interest rates (which was necessary to maintain their exchange rates) for fear of higher unemployment. Italy, however, rejoined the ERM in December 1996 in an effort to participate in the European monetary union. However, the U.K. still remains outside the European monetary union.

《马斯特里赫特条约》

Despite the recurrent turbulence in the EMS, European Union members met at Maastricht (Netherlands) in December 1991 and signed the **Maastricht Treaty.** According to the treaty, the EMS will irrevocably fix exchange rates among the member currencies by January 1, 1999, and subsequently introduce a common European currency, replacing individual national currencies. The European Central Bank, to be located in Frankfurt, Germany, will be solely responsible for the issuance of common currency and conducting monetary policy in the euro zone. National central banks of individual countries then will function pretty much like regional member banks of the U.S. Federal Reserve System. Exhibit 2.5 provides a chronology of the European Union.

为了给欧洲货币联盟的启动铺平道路，欧盟货币体系的成员国同意紧密协调各自的财政政策、货币政策及汇率政策以实现经济趋同。

To pave the way for the European Monetary Union (EMU), the member countries of the European Monetary System agreed to closely coordinate their fiscal, monetary, and exchange rate policies and achieve a *convergence* of their economies. Specifically, each member country shall strive to: (1) keep the ratio of government budget deficits to gross domestic product (GDP) below 3 percent, (2) keep gross public debts below 60 percent of GDP, (3) achieve a high degree of price stability, and (4) maintain its currency within the prescribed exchange rate ranges of the ERM. Currently, "convergence" is the buzz word in such countries as the Czech Republic, Hungary, and Poland that would like to join the EMU in the near future.

EXHIBIT 2.5		
Chronology of the European Union	1951	The treaty establishing the European Coal and Steel Community (ECSC), which was inspired by French Foreign Minister Robert Schuman, was signed in Paris by six countries: France, Germany, Italy, Netherlands, Belgium, and Luxembourg.
	1957	The treaty establishing the European Economic Community (EEC) was signed in Rome.
	1968	The Custom Union became fully operational; trade restrictions among the EEC member countries were abolished and a common external tariff system was established.
	1973	The U.K., Ireland, and Denmark became EEC members.
	1978	The EEC became the European Community (EC).
	1979	The European Monetary System (EMS) was established for the purpose of promoting exchange rate stability among the EC member countries.
	1980	Greece became an EC member.
	1986	Portugal and Spain became EC members.
	1987	The Single European Act was adopted to provide a framework within which the common internal market can be achieved by the end of 1992.
	1991	The Maastricht Treaty was signed and subsequently ratified by 12 member states. The treaty establishes a timetable for fulfilling the European Monetary Union (EMU). The treaty also commits the EC to political union.
	1994	The European Community was renamed the European Union (EU).
	1995	Austria, Finland, and Sweden became EU members.
	1999	A common European currency, the euro, was adopted by 11 EU member countries.
	2001	Greece adopted the euro on January 1.
	2002	Euro notes and coins were introduced; national currencies were withdrawn from circulation.
	2004	EU expanded by admitting 10 new member countries: Cyprus, Czech Republic, Estonia, Hungary, Latvia, Lithuania, Malta, Poland, Slovak Republic, and Slovenia.

The Euro and the European Monetary Union

1999年1月1日，国际金融领域发生了一件历史性事件：欧盟15个成员国中的11个国家自愿放弃本国的货币主权，开始统一使用欧元。

On January 1, 1999, an epochal event took place in the arena of international finance: Eleven of 15 EU countries adopted a common currency called the euro, voluntarily giving up their monetary sovereignty. The original euro-11 includes Austria, Belgium, Finland, France, Germany, Ireland, Italy, Luxembourg, the Netherlands, Portugal, and Spain. Four member countries of the European Union-Denmark, Greece, Sweden, and the United Kingdom-did not join the first wave. Greece, however, joined the euro club in 2001 when it could satisfy the convergence criteria.

The advent of a European single currency, which may potentially rival the U.S. dollar as a global currency, has profound implications for various aspects of international finance. In this section, we are going to (1) describe briefly the historical background for the euro and its implementation process, (2) discuss the potential benefits and costs of the euro from the perspective of the member countries, and (3) investigate the broad impacts of the euro on international finance in general.

A Brief History of the Euro

Considering that no European currency has been in circulation since the fall of the Roman Empire, the advent of the euro in January 1999 indeed qualifies as an epochal event. The Roman emperor Gaius Diocletianus, A.D. 286–301, reformed the coinage and established a single currency throughout the realm. The advent of the euro also marks the first time that sovereign countries voluntarily have given up their monetary independence to foster economic integration. The euro thus represents a historically unprecedented experiment, the outcome of which will have far-reaching implications.

EXHIBIT 2.6

Euro Conversion Rates

1 Euro Is Equal to	
Austrian schilling	13.7603
Belgian franc	40.3399
Dutch guilder	2.20371
Finnish markka	5.94573
French franc	6.55957
German mark	1.95583
Irish punt	0.78756
Italian lira	1936.27
Luxembourg franc	40.3399
Portuguese escudo	200.482
Spanish peseta	166.386
U.S. dollar*	1.2976
Japanese yen*	139.93
British pound*	0.6860

*Represents the market exchange rates of April 11, 2005.
Source: The Wall Street Journal.

www.ecb.int/

Website of the European Central Bank offers a comprehensive coverage of the euro and links to EU central banks.

欧洲货币联盟（EMU）

欧元启动后，11个欧元成员国的货币必须按1999年1月1日的兑换率与欧元挂钩。

欧洲中央银行（ECB）

欧元区各成员国的中央银行与欧洲中央银行组成了类似于美国联邦储备体系的**欧洲中央银行体系**（ESCB）。

If the experiment succeeds, for example, both the euro and the dollar will dominate the world of international finance. In addition, a successful euro may give a powerful impetus to the political unionization of Europe.

The euro should be viewed as a product of historical evolution toward an ever deepening integration of Europe, which began in earnest with the formation of the European Economic Community in 1958. As discussed previously, the European Monetary System (EMS) was created in 1979 to establish a European zone of monetary stability; members were required to restrict fluctuations of their currencies. In 1991, the Maastricht European Council reached agreement on a draft Treaty on the European Union, which called for the introduction of a single European currency by 1999. With the launching of the euro on January 1, 1999, the **European Monetary Union (EMU)** was created. The EMU is a logical extension of the EMS, and the European Currency Unit (ECU) was the precursor of the euro. Indeed, ECU contracts were required by EU law to be converted to euro contracts on a one-to-one basis.

As the euro was introduced, each national currency of the euro-11 countries was *irrevocably* fixed to the euro at a conversion rate as of January 1, 1999. The conversion rates are provided in Exhibit 2.6. On January 1, 2002, euro notes and coins were introduced to circulation while national bills and coins were being gradually withdrawn. Once the changeover was completed by July 1, 2002, the legal-tender status of national currencies was canceled, leaving the euro as the sole legal tender in the euro-12 countries.

Monetary policy for the euro-12 countries is now conducted by the **European Central Bank (ECB)** headquartered in Frankfurt, Germany, whose primary objective is to maintain price stability. The independence of the ECB is legally guaranteed so that in conducting its monetary policy, it will not be unduly subjected to political pressure from any member countries or institutions. By and large, the ECB is modeled after the German Bundesbank, which was highly successful in achieving price stability in Germany. Willem (Wim) Duisenberg, the first president of the ECB, who previously served as the president of the Dutch National Bank, recently defined "price stability" as an annual inflation rate of "less than but close to 2 percent."

The national central banks of the euro-12 countries will not disappear. Together with the European Central Bank, they form the **European System of Central Banks (ESCB),** which is in a way similar to the Federal Reserve System of the United States. The tasks of the ESCB are threefold: (1) to define and implement the common monetary policy of the Union; (2) to conduct foreign exchange operations; and (3) to

EXHIBIT 2.7

The Daily Dollar–Euro Exchange Rate since the Euro's Inception

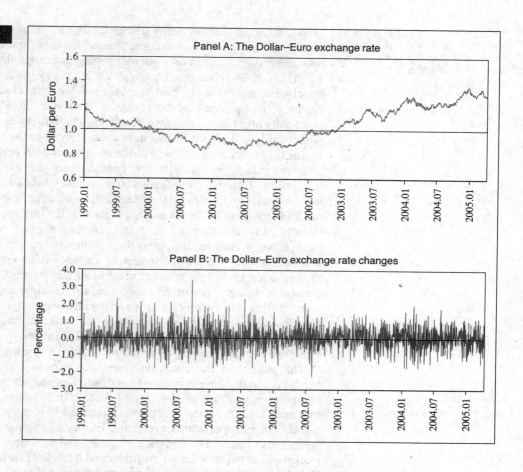

虽然各国中央银行
要执行ECB所制定的政
策，但在信贷分配、资
源筹集、收支系统管理
等权限方面仍然担当重
要职能。

hold and manage the official foreign reserves of the euro member states. In addition, governors of national central banks will sit on the Governing Council of the ECB. Although national central banks will have to follow the policies of the ECB, they will continue to perform important functions in their jurisdiction such as distributing credit, collecting resources, and managing payment systems.

Before we proceed, let us briefly examine the behavior of exchange rate between the dollar and euro. Panel A of Exhibit 2.7 plots the daily dollar–euro exchange rate since the inception of the euro, whereas Panel B plots the rate of change of the exchange rate. As can be seen from Panel A, since its introduction at $1.18 per euro in January 1999, the euro has been steadily depreciating against the dollar, reaching a low point of $0.83 per euro in October 2000. The depreciation of the euro during this period reflects a robust performance of the U.S. economy and massive European investments in the United States. From the start of 2002, however, the euro began to appreciate against the dollar, reaching a rough parity by July 2002. This, in turn, reflects a slowdown of the U.S. economy and lessening European investments in the United States. The euro continued to strengthen against the dollar, reaching $1.36 per euro at the end of 2004 before it started to ease a bit. Panel B confirms that the dollar–euro exchange rate is highly volatile.

What Are the Benefits of Monetary Union?

The euro-12 countries obviously decided to form a monetary union with a common currency because they believed the benefits from such a union would outweigh the associated costs-in contrast to those eligible countries that chose not to adopt the single currency. It is thus important to understand the potential benefits and costs of monetary union.

采用统一货币的直
接和即时利益就是可以
降低交易成本、消除汇
率变动的不确定性。

What are the main benefits from adopting a common currency? The most direct and immediate benefits are reduced transaction costs and the elimination of exchange rate uncertainty. There was a popular saying in Europe that if one travels through all 15 EU countries, changing money in each country but not actually spending it, one returns home with only half the original amount. Once countries use the same currency, transactions costs will be reduced substantially. These savings will accrue to practically all economic agents, benefiting individuals, companies, and governments. Although it is difficult to estimate accurately the magnitude of foreign exchange transaction costs, a consensus estimation is around 0.4 percent of Europe's GDP.

Economic agents should also benefit from the elimination of exchange rate uncertainty. Companies will not suffer currency loss anymore from intra–euro zone transactions. Companies that used to hedge exchange risk will save hedging costs. As price comparison becomes easier because of the common currency, consumers can benefit from comparison shopping. Increased price transparency will promote Europe-wide competition, exerting a downward pressure on prices. Reduced transaction costs and the elimination of currency risk together will have the net effect of promoting cross-border investment and trade within the euro zone. By furthering economic integration of Europe, the single currency will promote corporate restructuring via mergers and acquisitions, encourage optimal business location decisions, and ultimately strengthen the international competitive position of European companies. Thus, the enhanced efficiency and competitiveness of the European economy can be regarded as the third major benefit of the monetary union.

The advent of the common European currency also helps create conditions conducive to the development of continental capital markets with depth and liquidity comparable to those of the United States. In the past, national currencies and a localized legal/regulatory framework resulted in largely illiquid, fragmented capital markets in Europe, which prevented European companies from raising capital on competitive terms. The common currency and the integration of European financial markets pave the way for a European capital market in which both European and non-European companies can raise money at favorable rates. A study by Bris, Koskinen, and Nilsson (2004) indeed documents that the adoption of the euro as the common European currency has lowered firms' cost of capital in the euro zone and enhanced the firm value by about 17 percent on average. The increases in firm valuation are larger for firms that were exposed to intra-European currency risks, that is, those firms that were expected to benefit more from the common currency.

最后，统一货币将
促进欧洲地区的政治合
作与和平。

Last but not least, sharing a common currency should promote political cooperation and peace in Europe. The founding fathers of the European Union, including Jean Monnet, Paul-Henri Spaak, Robert Schuman, and their successors, took a series of economic measures designed to link European countries together. They envisioned a new Europe in which economic interdependence and cooperation among regions and countries replace nationalistic rivalries which so often led to calamitous wars in the past. In this context Helmut Kohl, a former German chancellor, said that the European Monetary Union was a "matter of war and peace." If the euro proves to be successful, it will advance the political integration of Europe in a major way, eventually making a "United States of Europe" feasible.

Costs of Monetary Union

The main cost of monetary union is the loss of national monetary and exchange rate policy independence. Suppose Finland, a country heavily dependent on the paper and pulp industries, faces a sudden drop in world paper and pulp prices. This price drop could severely hurt the Finnish economy, causing unemployment and income decline while scarcely affecting other euro zone countries. Finland thus faces an "asymmetric shock." Generally speaking, a country would be more prone to asymmetric shocks the less diversified and more trade-dependent its economy is.

If Finland maintained monetary independence, the country could consider lowering domestic interest rates to stimulate the weak economy as well as letting its currency depreciate to boost foreigners' demand for Finnish products. But because Finland has joined the EMU, the country no longer has these policy options at its disposal. Further, with the rest of the euro zone unaffected by Finland's particular problem, the ECB is not likely to tune its monetary policy to address a local Finnish shock. In other words, a common monetary policy dictated in Frankfurt cannot address asymmetric economic shocks that affect only a particular country or subregion; it can only deal with euro zone–wide shocks.

If, however, wage and price levels in Finland are flexible, then the country may still be able to deal with an asymmetric shock; lower wage and price levels in Finland would have economic effects similar to those of a depreciation of the Finnish currency. Furthermore, if capital flows freely across the euro zone and workers are willing to relocate to where jobs are, then again much of the asymmetric shock can be absorbed without monetary adjustments. If these conditions are not met, however, the asymmetric shock can cause a severe and prolonged economic dislocation in the affected country. In this case, monetary union will become a costly venture. According to the theory of **optimum currency areas,** originally conceived by Professor Robert Mundell of Columbia University in 1961, the relevant criterion for identifying and designing a common currency zone is the degree of factor (i.e., capital and labor) mobility within the zone; a high degree of factor mobility would provide an adjustment mechanism, providing an alternative to country-specific monetary/currency adjustments.

Considering the high degree of capital and labor mobility in the United States, one might argue that the United States approximates an optimum currency area; it would be suboptimal for each of the 50 states to issue its own currency. In contrast, unemployed workers in Helsinki, for example, are not very likely to move to Milan or Stuttgart for job opportunities because of cultural, religious, linguistic, and other barriers. The stability pact of EMU, designed to discourage irresponsible fiscal behavior in the post-EMU era, also constrains the Finnish government to restrict its budget deficit to 3 percent of GDP at most. At the same time, Finland cannot expect to receive a major transfer payment from Brussels, because of a rather low degree of fiscal integration among EU countries. These considerations taken together suggest that the European Monetary Union will involve significant economic costs. Due to the sluggish economic conditions, France and Germany often let the budget deficit exceed the 3 percent limit. This violation of the stability pact compromises the fiscal discipline necessary for supporting the euro.

An empirical study by von Hagen and Neumann (1994) identified Austria, Belgium, France, Luxembourg, the Netherlands, and Germany as nations that satisfy the conditions for an optimum currency area. However, Denmark, Italy, and the United Kingdom do not. It is interesting to note that Denmark and the United Kingdom actually chose to stay out of the EMU. Von Hagen and Neumann's study suggests that Italy joined the EMU prematurely. The International Finance in Practice box, "Mundell Wins Nobel Prize in Economics," explains Professor Mundell's view on the monetary union.

换言之，在法兰克福所确定的共同货币政策并不能应对影响特定国家或地区的不对称经济冲击，它只能应对影响整个欧元区的经济冲击。

www.columbia.edu/~ram15

This homepage of Professor Robert Mundell provides a synopsis of his academic works, Nobel lecture, etc.

最优货币区

综合考虑以上各方面的因素，欧洲货币联盟的运行需要付出巨额的经济成本。

Prospects of the Euro: Some Critical Questions

Will the euro succeed? The first real test of the euro will come when the euro zone experiences major asymmetric shocks. A successful response to these shocks will require wage, price, and fiscal flexibility. A cautionary note is in order: Asymmetric shocks can occur even within a country. In the United States, for example, when oil prices jumped in the 1970s, oil-consuming regions such as New England suffered a severe recession, whereas Texas, a major oil-producing state, experienced a major boom. Likewise, in Italy, the highly industrialized Genoa–Milan region and the

Mundell Wins Nobel Prize in Economics

Robert A. Mundell, one of the intellectual fathers of both the new European common currency and Reagan-era supply-side economics, won the Nobel Memorial Prize in Economic Science.

Mr. Mundell conducted innovative research into common currencies when the idea of the euro, Europe's new currency, was still a fantasy. The 66-year-old Columbia University professor, a native of Canada, also examined the implications of cross-border capital flows and flexible foreign-exchange rates when capital flows were still restricted and currencies still fixed to each other.

"Mundell chose his problems with uncommon—almost prophetic—accuracy in terms of predicting the future development of international monetary arrangements and capital markets," the selection committee said in announcing the prize.

An eccentric, white-haired figure who once bought an abandoned Italian castle as a hedge against inflation, Mr. Mundell later became a hero of the economic Right with his dogged defense of the gold standard and early advocacy of the controversial tax-cutting, supply-side economics that became the hallmark of the Reagan administration.

While the Nobel committee sidestepped his political impact in awarding Mr. Mundell the $975,000 prize for his work in the 1960s, his conservative fans celebrated the award as an endorsement of supply-side thinking.

"I know it will take a little longer, but history eventually will note that it was Mundell who made it possible for Ronald Reagan to be elected president," by providing the intellectual backing for the Reagan tax cuts, wrote conservative economist Jude Wanniski on his Web site.

Mr. Mundell's advocacy of supply-side economics sprang from his work in the 1960s examining what fiscal and monetary policies are appropriate if exchange rates

Mundell's View

Great currencies and great powers according to Robert Mundell:

Country	Period
Greece	7th–3rd C. B.C.
Persia	6th–4th C. B.C.
Macedonia	4th–2nd C. B.C.
Rome	2nd C. B.C.–4th C.
Byzantium	5th–13th C.
Franks	8th–11th C.
Italian city states	13th–6th C.
France	13th–18th C.
Holland	17th–18th C.
Germany (thaler)	14th–19th C.
France (franc)	1803–1870
Britain (pound)	1820–1914
U.S. (dollar)	1915–present
E.U. (euro)	1999

Source: The Euro and the Stability of the International Monetary System, Robert Mundell, Columbia University.

are either fixed—as they were prior to the collapse of the gold-based Bretton Woods system in the early 1970s—or floating, as they are in the U.S. and many other countries today.

One major finding has since become conventional wisdom: When money can move freely across borders, policy makers must choose between exchange-rate stability and an independent monetary policy. They can't have both.

Mr. Mundell's work has long had an impact on policy makers. In 1962, he wrote a paper addressing the Kennedy administration's predicament of how to spur the

southern Mezzogiorno, an underdeveloped region, can be in very different phases of the business cycle. But these countries have managed their economies with a common national monetary policy. Although asymmetric shocks are no doubt more serious internationally, one should be careful not to exaggerate their significance as an impediment to monetary union. In addition, since the advent of the EMS in 1979, the EMU member countries have restricted their monetary policies in order to maintain exchange rate stability in Europe. Considering that intra–euro zone trade accounts for about 60 percent of foreign trade of the euro-12 countries, benefits from the EMU are likely to exceed substantially the associated costs. Furthermore, leaders in political and business circles in Europe have invested substantial political capital in the success of the euro. It seems safe to predict that the euro will be a success.

我们可以预见，欧元必将有一个辉煌的未来。

Will the euro become a global currency rivaling the U.S. dollar? The U.S. dollar has been the dominant global currency since the end of the First World War, replacing the British pound as the currency of choice in international commercial and financial transactions. Even after the dollar got off the gold standard in 1971, it retained its economy while facing a balance-of-payments deficit. "The only correct way to do it was to have a tax cut and then protect the balance of payments by tight money," he recalled in a 1996 interview. The Kennedy administration eventually came around to the same way of thinking.

Mr. Mundell traces the supply-side movement to a 1971 meeting of distinguished economists, including Paul Volcker and Paul Samuelson, at the Treasury Department. At the time, most economists were stumped by the onset of stagflation—a combination of inflationary pressures, a troubled dollar, a worsening balance of payments and persistent unemployment. They thought any tightening of monetary or fiscal policy would bolster the dollar and improve the balance of payments, but worsen unemployment. An easing of monetary or fiscal policy might generate jobs, but weaken the dollar, lift prices and expand the balance-of-payments deficit.

Mr. Mundell suggested a heretical solution: Raise interest rates to protect the dollar, but cut taxes to spur the economy. Most others in the room were aghast at the idea, fearing tax cuts would lead to a swelling budget deficit—something many nonsupply-siders believe was exactly what happened during the Reagan years.

"I knew I was in the minority," he said in an 1988 interview. "But I thought my vote should count much more than the others because I understood the subject."

At the University of Chicago early in his career, Mr. Mundell befriended a student named Arthur Laffer, and together they were at the core of the supply-side movement. Even today, Mr. Mundell predicts similar policies will be necessary to keep the U.S. economic expansion going. "Monetary policy isn't going to be enough to stay up there and avoid a recession," he said in an interview yesterday. "We'll have to have tax reduction, too."

While in Chicago, he found himself constantly at odds with Milton Friedman, who advocated monetary rules and floating exchange rates. Mr. Mundell joined Columbia in 1974, two years before Mr. Friedman won the economics Nobel.

Ever the maverick, Mr. Mundell remains a fan of the gold standard and fixed exchange rates at a time when they're out of favor with most other economists. "You have fixed rates between New York and California, and it works perfectly," he said.

The Nobel committee also praised Mr. Mundell's research into common currency zones, which laid the intellectual foundation for the 11-country euro. In 1961, when European countries still clung to their national currencies, he described the circumstances in which nations could share a common currency.

"At the time, it just seemed like such a wacko thing to work on, and that's why it's so visionary," said Kenneth Rogoff, a Harvard economist.

In particular, Mr. Mundell argued that in any successful currency zone, workers must be able to move freely from areas that are slowing to areas that are booming. Some critics suggest the euro nations don't fit his description.

But Mr. Mundell believes the new currency will eventually challenge the dollar for global dominance. "The benefits will derive from transparency of pricing, stability of expectations and lower transactions costs, as well as a common monetary policy run by the best minds that Europe can muster," Mr. Mundell wrote last year. He began working on the euro project as a consultant to European monetary authorities in 1969.

Outside academia, Mr. Mundell has led a colorful life. Worried about the onset of inflation in the late 1960s, he bought and renovated a 16th century Italian castle originally built for Pandolfo Petrucci, the "Strong Man of Siena." Mr. Mundell has four children, who range in age from one to 40.

Source: Michael M. Phillips, The Wall Street Journal, October 14, 1999. p. A2. © 1999 Dow Jones & Company, Inc. All Rights Reserved Worldwide.

dominant position in the world economy. This dominance was possible because the dollar was backed by the sheer size of the U.S. economy and the relatively sound monetary policy of the Federal Reserve. Now, as can be seen from Exhibit 2.8, the euro zone is remarkably comparable to the United States in terms of population size, GDP, and international trade share. Exhibit 2.8 also shows that the euro is as important a denomination currency as the dollar in international bond markets. In contrast, the Japanese yen plays an insignificant role in international bond markets. As previously discussed, there is little doubt that the ECB will pursue a sound monetary policy. Considering both the size of the euro zone economy and the mandate of the ECB, the euro is likely to emerge as the second global currency in the near future, ending the dollar's sole dominance. A significant depreciation of the U.S. dollar in recent years seems to be precipitating the emergence of the euro as another global currency. The Japanese yen is likely to be a junior partner in the dollar–euro condominium. However, the emergence of the euro as another global currency may prompt Japan and other Asian countries to explore cooperative monetary arrangements for the region.

然而，作为另一种全球货币，欧元的诞生必将刺激日本和亚洲其他国家就本地区的货币合作做出安排。

The New World Order of Finance

Global financial panics erupt every decade or so. But even by historical standards, Mexico's currency collapse ranks among the scariest. With the crisis stretching into its seventh week, investors were stampeding. Worse yet, the panic was spreading from Buenos Aires to Budapest. Even the dollar was taking an unexpected shellacking. Some were bracing for another 1987 crash—not just in Mexico City, but in New York, London, and Tokyo.

It took forceful action to stop the runaway markets before they dragged the world economy down with them: $49.8 billion in loans and guarantees for Mexico from the U.S. and its allies. Some bankers say the total could reach $53 billion or more. Certainly, this will go down as the largest socialization of market risk in international history.

Ambitious Labor

With the U.S. spreading the gospel of democracy and free-market economics throughout the developing world, Clinton and his cohorts had little choice but to assemble the megaplan. As the club of emerging-market nations expands, the rich nations' obligation to provide a safety net for poorer trading partners is growing exponentially. America and its allies must mount a collective drive to ensure global monetary and economic stability—much like their efforts to maintain geopolitical order in the post-cold-war era.

Such ambitious labor is needed because the nature of financial markets has changed since Latin America's last financial crisis in 1982. Back then, it was gunslinger bankers who lent to Latin America. Because banks could lend for the long haul and absorb losses, they were a valuable shock absorber for the financial system. When enough Latin loans eventually went bad, it still took years to craft and conclude their restructuring.

Since then, bankers have wised up. Now, others with a shorter time horizon make the emerging-market deals. This time, it was mutual-, hedge-, and pension-fund gunslingers who provided the capital. Mexico attracted $45 billion in mutual-fund cash in the past three years. And when the peso dived, fund managers bolted. In this global market, all it takes is a phone call to Fidelity to send money hurtling toward Monterey—or zooming back. And world leaders should be able to act with similar speed.

Clinton's $40 billion in loan guarantees for Mexico got nowhere because Congress objected to bailing out Wall Street. Legislators also did not like the U.S. shouldering most of the cost. They were right. Emerging markets will stay volatile, and countries and investors shouldn't expect a handout every time an economy hits a rough patch. And when a rescue is necessary, it should be global.

Bridge the Gap

Europe and Japan, after all, will benefit from a healthy Mexican economy and thus should bear the burden of supporting it in times of crisis. Likewise, Washington should be obliged to lend a hand to European or Asian allies if Poland or Indonesia come unglued. One way to keep the next crisis at bay: bridge the gap between short-term money and long-term investment needs.

In addition, emerging economies need to take steps to immunize themselves from the vagaries of a fund-dominated world. It would help a lot if more of them developed mandatory pension schemes to build up domestic savings. Along with that should come privatization. With capital so flighty, it may take hard decisions to make money stay put. But if the first world wants to encourage capitalism, it will have to underwrite it—even if the cost is huge.

Source: Reprinted from February 13, 1995 issue of BusinessWeek by special permission, © 1995 by The McGraw-Hill Companies, Inc.

EXHIBIT 2.8

Macroeconomic Data for Major Economies[a]

Economy	Population (Million)	GDP ($ Billion)	Annual Inflation	World Trade Share	International Bonds Outstanding ($ Billion)
United States	294.0	10,951.3	2.2%	17.9%	3,073.4
Euro-12	306.3	7,744.5	2.3%	15.7	5,002.6
Japan	127.7	3,624.6	−0.6	6.6	269.6
United Kingdom	59.3	1,774.1	2.1	5.6	1,134.0

[a]The inflation rate is the annual average from 2001 to 2003. GDP is estimated based on purchasing power parity as of the end of 2003. The remaining data are the 2003 figures.
Source: Datastream; International Financial Statistics; and BIS Quarterly Review, June 2004.

The Mexican Peso Crisis

墨西哥比索危机具有深远的意义，因为它是首次因证券投资资本的跨国逃逸而导致的严重的国际金融危机。

On December 20, 1994, the Mexican government under new president Ernesto Zedillo announced its decision to devalue the peso against the dollar by 14 percent. This decision, however, touched off a stampede to sell pesos as well as Mexican stocks and bonds. As Exhibit 2.9 shows, by early January 1995 the peso fell against the U.S. dollar by as much as 40 percent, forcing the Mexican government to float the peso. As concerned international investors reduced their holdings of emerging market securities, the peso crisis rapidly spilled over to other Latin American and Asian financial markets.

Faced with an impending default by the Mexican government and the possibility of a global financial meltdown, the Clinton administration, together with the International Monetary Fund (IMF) and the Bank for International Settlement (BIS), put together a $53 billion package to bail out Mexico.[8] As the bailout plan was put together and announced on January 31, the world's, as well as Mexico's, financial markets began to stabilize.

The Mexican peso crisis is significant in that it is perhaps the first serious international financial crisis touched off by cross-border flight of portfolio capital. International mutual funds are known to have invested more than $45 billion in Mexican securities during a three-year period prior to the peso crisis. As the peso fell, fund managers quickly liquidated their holdings of Mexican securities as well as other emerging market securities. This had a highly destabilizing, contagious effect on the world financial system. The same point is discussed in the International Finance in Practice box, "The New World Order of Finance" on page 46.

必须建立恰当的多国安全网络来保障世界金融体系免受比索危机之类事件的冲击。

As the world's financial markets are becoming more integrated, this type of contagious financial crisis is likely to occur more often. Two lessons emerge from the peso crisis. First, it is essential to have a multinational safety net in place to safeguard the world financial system from the peso-type crisis. No single country or institution can handle a potentially global crisis alone. In addition, in the face of rapidly changing market conditions, usually slow and parochial political processes cannot cope with rapidly changing market conditions. In fact, the Clinton administration faced

---

EXHIBIT 2.9

U.S. Dollar versus Mexican Peso Exchange Rate
(November 1, 1994– January 31, 1995)

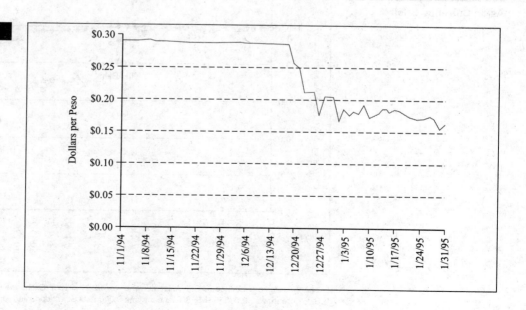

---

[8]The United States contributed $20 billion out of its Exchange Stabilization Fund, whereas IMF and BIS contributed, respectively, $17.8 billion and $10 billion. Canada, Latin American countries, and commercial banks collectively contributed $5 billion.

stiff opposition in Congress and from foreign allies when it was working out a bailout package for Mexico. As a result, early containment of the crisis was not possible. Fortunately, the G-7 countries endorsed a $50 billion bailout fund for countries in financial distress, which would be administered by the IMF, and a series of increased disclosure requirements to be followed by all countries. The reluctance of the outgoing Salinas administration to disclose the true state of the Mexican economy, that is, the rapid depletion of foreign exchange reserves and serious trade deficits, contributed to the sudden collapse of the peso. Transparency always helps prevent financial crises.

外资的大量流入也会引起较高的国内通货膨胀和比索的高估，从而损害了墨西哥的贸易平衡。

Second, Mexico excessively depended on foreign portfolio capital to finance its economic development. In hindsight, the country should have saved more domestically and depended more on long-term rather than short-term foreign capital investments. As Professor Robert MacKinnon of Stanford University pointed out, a flood of foreign money had two undesirable effects. It led to an easy credit policy on domestic borrowings, which caused Mexicans to consume more and save less.[9] Foreign capital influx also caused a higher domestic inflation and an overvalued peso, which hurt Mexico's trade balances.

The Asian Currency Crisis

1997年7月2日，长期钉住美元的泰国货币泰铢突然贬值，金融危机迅速蔓延成全球金融危机。

On July 2, 1997, the Thai baht, which had been largely fixed to the U.S. dollar, was suddenly devalued. What at first appeared to be a local financial crisis in Thailand quickly escalated into a global financial crisis, first spreading to other Asian countries-Indonesia, Korea, Malaysia, and the Philippines-then far afield to Russia and Latin America, especially Brazil. As can be seen from Exhibit 2.10, at the height of the crisis the Korean won fell by about 50 percent in its dollar value from its precrisis level, whereas the Indonesian rupiah fell an incredible 80 percent.

EXHIBIT 2.10

Asian Currency Crisis

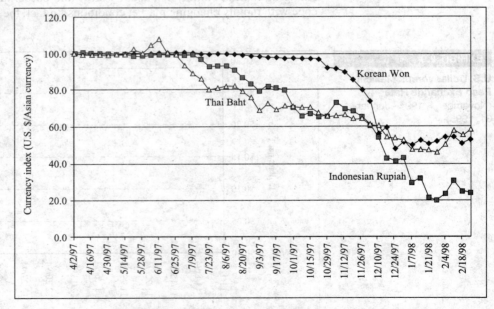

Exchange rates are indexed (U.S. $/Asian currency on 4/2/97 = 100). Exchange rates on 4/2/97: 0.00112 U.S. $/Korean won, 0.03856 U.S. $/Thai baht, and 0.00041 U.S. $/Indonesian rupiah.

---

[9]See "Flood of Dollars, Sunken Pesos," *New York Times,* January 20, 1995. p. A2g.

The 1997 Asian crisis is the third major currency crisis of the 1990s, preceded by the crises of the European Monetary System (EMS) of 1992 and the Mexican peso in 1994–95. The Asian crisis, however, turned out to be far more serious than its two predecessors in terms of the extent of contagion and the severity of resultant economic and social costs. Following the massive depreciations of local currencies, financial institutions and corporations with foreign-currency debts in the afflicted countries were driven to extreme financial distress and many were forced to default. What's worse, the currency crisis led to an unprecedentedly deep, widespread, and long-lasting recession in East Asia, a region that, for the last few decades, has enjoyed the most rapidly growing economy in the world. At the same time, many lenders and investors from the developed countries also suffered large capital losses from their investments in emerging-market securities. For example, Long Term Capital Management (LTCM), one of the largest and, until then, profitable hedge funds, experienced a near bankruptcy due to its exposure to Russian bonds. In mid-August 1998, the Russian ruble fell sharply from 6.3 rubles per dollar to about 20 rubbles per dollar. The prices of Russian stocks and bonds also fell sharply. The Federal Reserve System, which feared a domino-like systematic financial failure in the United States, orchestrated a $3.5 billion bailout of LTCM in September 1998.

Given the global effects of the Asian currency crisis and the challenges it poses for the world financial system, it would be useful to understand its origins and causes and discuss how similar crises might be prevented in the future.

考虑到亚洲货币危机的全球影响以及对世界金融体制所提出的挑战，有必要清楚其成因，也有必要讨论如何避免类似的危机再次发生。

Origins of the Asian Currency Crisis

Several factors are responsible for the onset of the Asian currency crisis: a weak domestic financial system, free international capital flows, the contagion effects of changing market sentiment, and inconsistent economic policies. In recent years, both developing and developed countries were encouraged to liberalize their financial markets and allow free flows of capital across countries. As capital markets were liberalized, both firms and financial institutions in the Asian developing countries eagerly borrowed foreign currencies from U.S., Japanese, and European investors, who were attracted to these fast-growing emerging markets for extra returns for their portfolios. In 1996 alone, for example, five Asian countries-Indonesia, Korea, Malaysia, the Philippines, and Thailand-experienced a new inflow of private capital worth $93 billion. In contrast, there was a net outflow of $12 billion from the five countries in 1997.

20世纪90年代早中期，私人资本的大量流入导致亚洲国家的信贷急剧膨胀。

Large inflows of private capital resulted in a credit boom in the Asian countries in the early and mid-1990s. The credit boom was often directed to speculations in real estate and stock markets as well as to investments in marginal industrial projects. Fixed or stable exchange rates also encouraged unhedged financial transactions and excessive risk-taking by both lenders and borrowers, who were not much concerned with exchange risk. As asset prices declined (as happened in Thailand prior to the currency crisis) in part due to the government's effort to control the overheated economy, the quality of banks' loan portfolios also declined as the same assets were held as collateral for the loans. Clearly, banks and other financial institutions in the afflicted countries practiced poor risk management and were poorly supervised. In addition, their lending decisions were often influenced by political considerations, likely leading to suboptimal allocation of resources. However, the so-called crony capitalism was not a new condition, and the East Asian economies achieved an economic miracle under the same system.

Meanwhile, the booming economy with a fixed or stable nominal exchange rate inevitably brought about an appreciation of the real exchange rate. This, in turn, resulted in a marked slowdown in export growth in such Asian countries as Thailand and Korea. In addition, a long-lasting recession in Japan and the yen's depreciation against the dollar hurt Japan's neighbors, further worsening the trade balances of the Asian developing countries. If the Asian currencies had been allowed to depreciate in

EXHIBIT 2.11

Financial Vulnerability Indicators

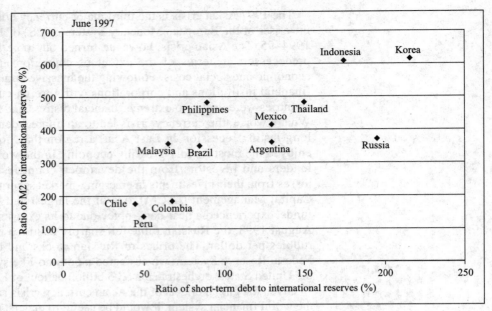

Source: The World Bank, International Monetary Fund.

real terms, which was not possible because of the fixed nominal exchange rates, such catastrophic, sudden changes of the exchange rates as observed in 1997 might have been avoided.

In Thailand, as the run on the baht started, the Thai central bank initially injected liquidity to the domestic financial system and tried to defend the exchange rate by drawing on its foreign exchange reserves. With its foreign reserves declining rapidly, the central bank eventually decided to devalue the baht. The sudden collapse of the baht touched off a panicky flight of capital from other Asian countries with a high degree of financial vulnerability. It is interesting to note from Exhibit 2.11 that the three Asian countries hardest hit by the crisis are among the most financially vulnerable as measured by (1) the ratio of short-term foreign debts to international reserve and (2) the ratio of broad money, M2 (which represents the banking sector's liabilities) to international reserve. Contagion of the currency crisis was caused at least in part by the panicky, indiscriminate flight of capital from the Asian countries for fear of a spreading crisis. Fear thus became self-fulfilling. As lenders withdrew their capital and refused to renew short-term loans, the former credit boom turned into a credit crunch, hurting creditworthy as well as marginal borrowers.

As the crisis unfolded, the International Monetary Fund (IMF) came to rescue the three hardest-hit Asian countries-Indonesia, Korea, and Thailand-with bailout plans. As a condition for the bailing out, however, the IMF imposed a set of austerity measures, such as raising domestic interest rates and curtailing government expenditures, that were designed to support the exchange rate. Since these austerity measures, contractionary in nature, were implemented when the economies had already been contracting because of a severe credit crunch, the Asian economies consequently suffered a deep, long-lasting recession. According to a World Bank report (1999), one-year declines in industrial production of 20 percent or more in Thailand and Indonesia are comparable to those in the United States and Germany during the Great Depression. One can thus argue that the IMF initially prescribed the wrong medicine for the afflicted Asian economies. The IMF bailout plans were also criticized on another ground: moral hazard. IMF bailouts may breed dependency in

IMF 的援助不仅有可能滋长发展中国家的依赖性，也可能刺激国际信贷贷者的冒险投资。

developing countries and encourage risk-taking on the part of international lenders. There is a sentiment that taxpayers' money should not be used to bail out "fat-cat" investors. Former U.S. senator Lauch Faircloth was quoted as saying: "Through the IMF we have privatized profits and socialized losses." No bailout, however, can be compared with the proposal to get rid of the only fire department in town so that people will be more careful about fire.

Lessons from the Asian Currency Crisis

总之，一个国家应先完善国内金融体系，而后再寻求金融市场的自由化。

www.adb.org/

Provides a broad coverage of Asian financial developments.

托宾税

就像往车轮上撒点沙子一样，"托宾税"对于预防金融动荡，稳定世界金融市场很有作用。

矛盾的三位一体

Generally speaking, liberalization of financial markets when combined with a weak, underdeveloped domestic financial system tends to create an environment susceptible to currency and financial crises. Interestingly, both Mexico and Korea experienced a major currency crisis within a few years after joining the OECD, which required a significant liberalization of financial markets. It seems safe to recommend that countries first strengthen their domestic financial system and then liberalize their financial markets.

A number of measures can and should be undertaken to strengthen a nation's domestic financial system. Among other things, the government should strengthen its system of financial-sector regulation and supervision. One way of doing so is to sign on to the "Core Principle of Effective Banking Supervision" drafted by the Basle Committee on Banking Supervision and to monitor its compliance with the principle. In addition, banks should be encouraged to base their lending decisions solely on economic merits rather than political considerations. Furthermore, firms, financial institutions, and the government should be required to provide the public with reliable financial data in a timely fashion. A higher level of disclosure of financial information and the resultant transparency about the state of the economy will make it easier for all the concerned parties to monitor the situation better and mitigate the destabilizing cycles of investor euphoria and panic accentuated by the lack of reliable information.

Even if a country decides to liberalize its financial markets by allowing cross-border capital flows, it should encourage foreign direct investments and equity and long-term bond investments; it should not encourage short-term investments that can be reversed overnight, causing financial turmoil. As Chile has successfully implemented, some form of **"Tobin tax"** on the international flow of hot money can be useful. Throwing some sand in the wheels of international finance can have a stabilizing effect on the world's financial markets.

A fixed but adjustable exchange rate is problematic in the face of integrated international financial markets. Such a rate arrangement often invites speculative attack at the time of financial vulnerability. Countries should not try to restore the same fixed exchange rate system unless they are willing to impose capital controls. According to the so-called "trilemma" that economists are fond of talking about, a country can attain only two of the following three conditions: (1) a fixed exchange rate, (2) free international flows of capital, and (3) an independent monetary policy. It is very difficult, if not impossible, to have all three conditions. This difficulty is also known as the **incompatible trinity.** If a country would like to maintain monetary policy independence to pursue its own domestic economic goals and still would like to keep a fixed exchange rate between its currency and other currencies, then the country should restrict free flows of capital. China and India were not noticeably affected by the Asian currency crisis because both countries maintain capital controls, segmenting their capital markets from the rest of the world. China-Hong Kong SAR was less affected by the crisis for a different reason. China-Hong Kong SAR has fixed its exchange rate permanently to the U.S. dollar via a currency board and allowed free flows of capital; in consequence, China-Hong Kong SAR gave up its monetary independence. A currency board is an extreme form of the fixed exchange rate regime under which local currency is "fully" backed by the

随着国际资本市场
的不断一体化，为了避
免货币危机，一国可以
实行固定汇率制或浮动
汇率制，但绝不能实行
可调整的固定汇率制。

dollar (or another chosen standard currency). China-Hong Kong SAR has essentially dollarized its economy. To avoid currency crises, a country can have a really fixed exchange rate or flexible exchange rate, but not a fixed yet adjustable exchange rate, when international capital markets are integrated.

The Argentine Peso Crisis

2002年的阿根廷比
索危机表明，货币局制度
也并不能完全避免崩溃的
风险。

The 2002 crisis of the Argentine peso, however, shows that even a currency board arrangement cannot be completely safe from a possible collapse. Exhibit 2.12 shows how the peso–dollar exchange rate, fixed at parity throughout much of the 1990s, collapsed in January 2002. Short of a complete dollarization (as is the case with Panama, for example), a currency board arrangement can collapse unless the arrangement is backed by the political will and economic discipline to defend it.

When the peso was first linked to the U.S. dollar at parity in February 1991 under the Convertibility Law, initial economic effects were quite positive: Argentina's chronic inflation was curtailed dramatically and foreign investment began to pour in, leading to an economic boom. Over time, however, the peso has appreciated against the majority of currencies as the U.S. dollar became increasingly stronger in the second half of the 1990s. A strong peso hurt exports from Argentina and caused a protracted economic downturn that eventually led to the abandonment of the peso–dollar parity in January 2002. This change, in turn, caused severe economic and political distress in the country. The unemployment rate rose above 20 percent and inflation reached a monthly rate of about 20 percent in April 2002. In contrast, China-Hong Kong SAR was able to successfully defend its currency board arrangement during the Asian financial crisis, a major stress test for the arrangement.

Although there is no clear consensus on the causes of the Argentine crisis, there are at least three factors that are related to the collapse of the currency board system and ensuing economic crisis: (1) the lack of fiscal discipline, (2) labor market inflexibility, and (3) contagion from the financial crises in Russia and Brazil. Reflecting the traditional sociopolitical divisions in the Argentine society, competing claims on economic resources by different groups were accommodated by increasing public sector indebtedness. Argentina is said to have a "European-style welfare system in a Third World economy." The federal government of Argentina borrowed heavily in dollars throughout the 1990s. As the economy entered a recession in the late 1990s,

EXHIBIT 2.12

Collapse of the Currency Board Arrangement in Argentina

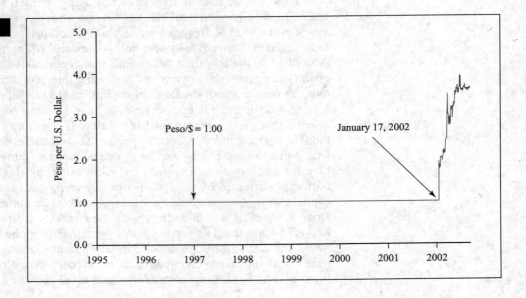

the government encountered an increasing difficulty in raising debts, eventually defaulting on its internal and external debts. The hard fixed exchange rate that Argentina adopted under the currency board system made it impossible to restore competitiveness by a traditional currency depreciation. Further, a powerful labor union also made it difficult to lower wages and thus cut production costs that could have effectively achieved the same real currency depreciation with the fixed nominal exchange rate. The situation was exacerbated by a slowdown of international capital inflows following the financial crises in Russia and Brazil. Also, a sharp depreciation of the Brazil real in 1999 hampered exports from Argentina.

虽然货币危机过去了，但债务问题尚未得到全部解决。

While the currency crisis is over, the debt problem has not been completely resolved. The government of Argentina ceased all debt payments in December 2001 in the wake of persistent recession and rising social and political unrest. It represents the largest sovereign default in history. Argentina faces a complex task of restructuring over $100 billion borrowed in seven different currencies and governed by the laws of eight legal jurisdictions. In June 2004, the Argentine government made a 'final' offer amounting to a 75 percent reduction in the net present value of the debt. Foreign bondholders have rejected this offer and asked for an improved offer.

Fixed versus Flexible Exchange Rate Regimes

Since some countries, including the United States and possibly Japan, prefer flexible exchange rates, while others, notably the members of the EMU and many developing countries, would like to maintain fixed exchange rates, it is worthwhile to examine some of the arguments advanced in favor of fixed versus flexible exchange rates.

The key arguments for flexible exchange rates rest on (1) easier external adjustments and (2) national policy autonomy. Suppose a country is experiencing a balance-of-payments deficit at the moment. This means that there is an excess supply of the country's currency at the prevailing exchange rate in the foreign exchange market. Under a flexible exchange rate regime, the external value of the country's currency will simply depreciate to the level at which there is no excess supply of the country's currency. At the new exchange rate level, the balance-of-payments disequilibrium will disappear.

只要汇率由市场供求来决定，那么外部平衡就能自动实现。

As long as the exchange rate is allowed to be determined according to market forces, external balance will be achieved automatically. Consequently, the government does not have to take policy actions to correct the balance-of-payments disequilibrium. With flexible exchange rates, therefore, the government can use its monetary and fiscal policies to pursue whatever economic goals it chooses. Under a fixed rate regime, however, the government may have to take contractionary (expansionary) monetary and fiscal policies to correct the balance-of-payments deficit (surplus) at the existing exchange rate. Since policy tools need to be committed to maintaining the exchange rate, the government cannot use the same policy tools to pursue other economic objectives. As a result, the government loses its policy autonomy under a fixed exchange rate regime.

Using the British pound as the representative foreign exchange, Exhibit 2.13 illustrates the preceding discussion on how the balance-of-payment disequilibrium is corrected under alternative exchange rate regimes. As is the case with most other commodities, the demand for British pounds would be downward sloping, whereas the supply of British pounds would be upward sloping. Suppose that the exchange rate is $1.40/£ at the moment. As can be seen from the exhibit, the demand for British pounds far exceeds the supply (i.e., the supply of U.S. dollars far exceeds the demand) at this exchange rate. The United States experiences trade (or balance of payment) deficits. Under the flexible exchange rate regime, the dollar will simply depreciate to a new level of exchange rate, $1.60/£, at which the excess demand for British pounds (and

EXHIBIT 2.13

External Adjustment Mechanism: Fixed versus Flexible Exchange Rates

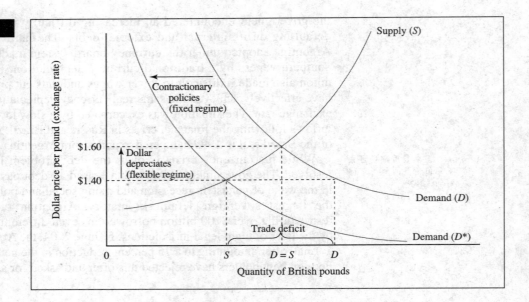

thus the trade deficit) will disappear. Now, suppose that the exchange rate is "fixed" at $1.40/£, and thus the excess demand for British pounds cannot be eliminated by the exchange rate adjustment. Facing this situation, the U.S. Federal Reserve Bank may initially draw on its foreign exchange reserve holdings to satisfy the excess demand for British pounds. If the excess demand persists, however, the U.S. government may have to resort to contractionary monetary and fiscal policies so that the demand curve can shift to the left (from D to D^* in the exhibit) until the excess demand for British pounds can be eliminated at the fixed exchange rate, $1.40/£. In other words, it is necessary for the government to take policy actions to maintain the fixed exchange rate.

A possible drawback of the flexible exchange rate regime is that exchange rate uncertainty may hamper international trade and investment. Proponents of the fixed exchange rate regime argue that when future exchange rates are uncertain, businesses tend to shun foreign trade. Since countries cannot fully benefit from international trade under exchange rate uncertainty, resources will be allocated suboptimally on a global basis. Proponents of the fixed exchange rate regime argue that fixed exchange rates eliminate such uncertainty and thus promote international trade. However, to the extent that firms can hedge exchange risk by means of currency forward or options contracts, uncertain exchange rates do not necessarily hamper international trade.

As the above discussion suggests, the choice between the alternative exchange rate regimes is likely to involve a trade-off between national policy independence and international economic integration. If countries would like to pursue their respective domestic economic goals, they are likely to pursue divergent macroeconomic policies, rendering fixed exchange rates infeasible. On the other hand, if countries are committed to promoting international economic integration (as is the case with the core members of the European Union like France and Germany), the benefits of fixed exchange rates are likely to outweigh the associated costs.

A "good" (or ideal) international monetary system should provide (1) liquidity, (2) adjustment, and (3) confidence. In other words, a good IMS should be able to provide the world economy with sufficient monetary reserves to support the growth of international trade and investment. It should also provide an effective mechanism that restores the balance-of-payments equilibrium whenever it is disturbed. Lastly, it should offer a safeguard to prevent crises of confidence in the system that result in panicked flights from one reserve asset to another. Politicians and economists should keep these three criteria in mind when they design and evaluate the international monetary system.

上述分析表明，汇率制度的选择涉及到对一国货币政策的自主性和国际经济的一体化进行权衡。

"好"的（或理想的）国际货币体系应具有：流动性、可调性和信任性。

SUMMARY

本章从总体上介绍了作为跨国公司经营运作环境的国际货币体系。

1. 国际货币体系是关于进行国际支付、调节资金流动和确定各种货币间汇率的组织框架。

2. 国际货币体系经历了5个演变阶段：（1）金银复本位制时期，（2）古典金本位制时期，（3）战争时期，（4）布雷顿森林体系时期，（5）浮动汇率制时期。

3. 古典金本位制存在于1875~1914年。在该制度下，两种货币间的汇率是由它们的含金量决定的。国际收支失衡可通过价格-铸币-流动机制而得到自动调整。今天，金本位制的忠实追随者仍坚信，金本位制可有效解决通货膨胀问题。然而，在金本位制下，世界经济会因货币黄金供应量的不足而面临紧缩的压力。

4. 为了避免战争时期因没有明确的"游戏规则"而产生的经济民族主义卷土重来，44个国家的代表汇聚在新罕布什尔州的布雷顿森林城，组建了新的国际货币体系。在布雷顿森林体系下，各国货币与可以全部兑换成黄金的美元建立了平价关系。各国以外汇，特别是美元和黄金作为国际支付手段。建立布雷顿森林体系的初衷是要维持汇率稳定并节约黄金。由于美国国内发生通货膨胀并出现持续的国际收支赤字，布雷顿森林体系最终于1973年崩溃。

5. 《牙买加协议》确立了替代布雷顿森林体系的浮动汇率制。随着20世纪80年代美元价值的大起大落，主要工业化国家决定相互合作以维持汇率的稳定性。1987年"卢浮宫协议"的签署标志着有管理的浮动汇率制的启动。在该制度下，七国集团（G7）将联合干预外汇市场以纠正货币价值的高估或低估。

6. 1979年，欧洲经济共同体国家建立了欧洲货币体系，试图在欧洲建立一个"货币稳定区"。欧洲货币体系的两个主要工具是欧洲货币单位和汇率机制。欧洲货币单位是由欧洲货币体系的成员国货币所组成的一篮子货币，并作为欧洲货币体系的核算单位。而汇率机制是指欧洲货币体系成员国集体管理其汇率的过程。汇率机制建立在各成员国维持平价网的基础之上。

7. 1999年1月1日，包括法国和德国在内的11个欧洲国家开始采用统一货币——欧元。希腊于2001年加入欧元区。鉴于欧元最终可能成为与美元相抗衡的全球流通货币，因此，单一欧洲货币的启动对欧洲乃至世界经济有着深远的影响。欧元区的12个国家可以交易成本的减低和汇率不确定的消除中受益。此外，欧元的启动也有助于欧洲大陆资本市场的发展，使得公司能以有利的条件筹集到资金。

8. 在欧洲货币联盟内，位于法兰克福的欧洲中央银行负责制定12个欧元区国家的共同货币政策。欧洲中央银行具有维持欧洲物价稳定的法定

This chapter provides an overview of the international monetary system, which defines an environment in which multinational corporations operate.

1. The international monetary system can be defined as the institutional framework within which international payments are made, the movements of capital are accommodated, and exchange rates among currencies are determined.

2. The international monetary system went through five stages of evolution: (a) bimetallism, (b) classical gold standard, (c) interwar period, (d) Bretton Woods system, and (e) flexible exchange rate regime.

3. The classical gold standard spanned 1875 to 1914. Under the gold standard, the exchange rate between two currencies is determined by the gold contents of the currencies. Balance-of-payments disequilibrium is automatically corrected through the price-specie-flow mechanism. The gold standard still has ardent supporters who believe that it provides an effective hedge against price inflation. Under the gold standard, however, the world economy can be subject to deflationary pressure due to the limited supply of monetary gold.

4. To prevent the recurrence of economic nationalism with no clear "rules of the game" witnessed during the interwar period, representatives of 44 nations met at Bretton Woods, New Hampshire, in 1944 and adopted a new international monetary system. Under the Bretton Woods system, each country established a par value in relation to the U.S. dollar, which was fully convertible to gold. Countries used foreign exchanges, especially the U.S. dollar, as well as gold as international means of payments. The Bretton Woods system was designed to maintain stable exchange rates and economize on gold. The Bretton Woods system eventually collapsed in 1973 mainly because of U.S. domestic inflation and the persistent balance-of-payments deficits.

5. The flexible exchange rate regime that replaced the Bretton Woods system was ratified by the Jamaica Agreement. Following a spectacular rise and fall of the U.S. dollar in the 1980s, major industrial countries agreed to cooperate to achieve greater exchange rate stability. The Louvre Accord of 1987 marked the inception of the managed-float system under which the G-7 countries would jointly intervene in the foreign exchange market to correct over- or undervaluation of currencies.

6. In 1979, the EEC countries launched the European Monetary System (EMS) to establish a "zone of monetary stability" in Europe. The two main instruments of the EMS are the European Currency Unit (ECU) and the Exchange Rate Mechanism (ERM). The ECU is a basket currency comprising the currencies of the EMS members and serves as the accounting unit of the EMS. The ERM refers to the procedure by which EMS members collectively manage their exchange rates. The ERM is based on a parity grid that the member countries are required to maintain.

7. On January 1, 1999, eleven European countries including France and Germany adopted a common currency called the euro. Greece adopted the euro in 2001. The advent of a single European currency, which may eventually rival the U.S. dollar as a global vehicle currency, will have major implications for the European as well as world economy. Euro-12 countries will benefit from reduced transaction costs and the elimination of exchange rate uncertainty. The advent of the euro will also help develop continentwide capital markets where companies can raise capital at favorable rates.

8. Under the European Monetary Union (EMU), the common monetary policy for the euro-12 countries is formulated by the European Central Bank (ECB) located in Frankfurt. The ECB is legally mandated to maintain price stability in Europe. Together with the ECB, the national central banks of the euro-12 countries form the European System of Central Banks (ESBC), which is responsible for defining and implementing the common monetary policy for the EMU.

权力。欧洲中央银行与12个欧元区
成员国的中央银行共同组成了欧洲
中央银行体系，负责制定并实施欧
洲货币联盟的共同货币政策。

9. 包括法国和德国在内的欧洲
货币联盟的核心成员国显然主张实
行固定汇率制，而美国和日本之类
的其他主要国家则更倾向于采用浮
动汇率制。在浮动汇率制下，因为
外部平衡可通过汇率的自行调整而
非政策干预来实现，因而政府能够
维持政策的独立性。然而，汇率的
不确定性可能会妨碍国际贸易和投
资，因此，选择何种汇率制度也需
要对维持本国政策独立性和寻求国
际经济一体化进行权衡。

9. While the core EMU members, including France and Germany, apparently prefer the fixed exchange rate regime, other major countries such as the United States and Japan are willing to live with flexible exchange rates. Under the flexible exchange rate regime, governments can retain policy independence because the external balance will be achieved by the exchange rate adjustments rather than by policy intervention. Exchange rate uncertainty, however, can potentially hamper international trade and investment. The choice between the alternative exchange rate regimes is likely to involve a trade-off between national policy autonomy and international economic integration.

KEY WORDS

bimetallism, 26
Bretton Woods
    system, 29
currency board, 34
euro, 25
European Central Bank
    (ECB), 40
European Currency Unit
    (ECU), 38
European Monetary
    System (EMS), 35
European Monetary
    Union (EMU), 40
Exchange Rate
    Mechanism (ERM), 38

European System of
    Central Banks
    (ESCB), 40
gold-exchange
    standard, 30
gold standard, 27
Gresham's law, 26
incompatible trinity, 51
international monetary
    system, 25
Jamaica Agreement, 32
Louvre Accord, 34
Maastricht Treaty, 38
managed-float
    system, 34

optimum currency
    area, 43
par value, 30
Plaza Accord, 33
price-specie-flow
    mechanism, 28
Smithsonian
    Agreement, 32
snake, 35
special drawing rights
    (SDRs), 31
sterilization of
    gold, 29
"Tobin tax," 51
Triffin paradox, 31

QUESTIONS

1. Explain Gresham's law.

2. Explain the mechanism that restores the balance-of-payments equilibrium when it is disturbed under the gold standard.

3. Suppose that the pound is pegged to gold at 6 pounds per ounce, whereas the franc is pegged to gold at 12 francs per ounce. This, of course, implies that the equilibrium exchange rate should be two francs per pound. If the current market exchange rate is 2.2 francs per pound, how would you take advantage of this situation? What would be the effect of shipping costs?

4. Discuss the advantages and disadvantages of the gold standard.

5. What were the main objectives of the Bretton Woods system?

6. Comment on the proposition that the Bretton Woods system was programmed to an eventual demise.

7. Explain how special drawing rights (SDR) are constructed. Also, discuss the circumstances under which the SDR was created.

8. Explain the arrangements and workings of the European Monetary System (EMS).

9. There are arguments for and against the alternative exchange rate regimes.

   a. List the advantages of the flexible exchange rate regime.

   b. Criticize the flexible exchange rate regime from the viewpoint of the proponents of the fixed exchange rate regime.

   c. Rebut the above criticism from the viewpoint of the proponents of the flexible exchange rate regime.

10. In an integrated world financial market, a financial crisis in a country can be quickly transmitted to other countries, causing a global crisis. What kind of measures would you propose to prevent the recurrence of an Asia-type crisis?

11. Discuss the criteria for a "good" international monetary system.

12. Once capital markets are integrated, it is difficult for a country to maintain a fixed exchange rate. Explain why this may be so.

13. Assess the possibility for the euro to become another global currency rivaling the U.S. dollar. If the euro really becomes a global currency, what impact will it have on the U.S. dollar and the world economy?

INTERNET EXERCISES

1. Using the data from http://cibs.sauder.ubc.ca, first plot the monthly exchange rate between the euro and the U.S. dollar since January 1999, and try to explain why the exchange rate behaved the way it did.

MINI CASE

Will the United Kingdom Join the Euro Club?

When the euro was introduced in January 1999, the United Kingdom was conspicuously absent from the list of European countries adopting the common currency. Although the current Labour government led by Prime Minister Tony Blair appears to be in favor of joining the euro club, it is not clear at the moment if that will actually happen. The opposition Tory party is not in favor of adopting the euro and thus giving up monetary sovereignty of the country. Public opinion is also divided on the issue.

Whether the United Kingdom will eventually join the euro club is a matter of considerable importance for the future of the European Union as well as that of the United Kingdom. If the United Kingdom, with its sophisticated finance industry, joins, it will most certainly propel the euro into a global currency status rivaling the U.S. dollar. The United Kingdom for its part will firmly join the process of economic and political unionization of Europe, abandoning its traditional balancing role.

Investigate the political, economic, and historical situations surrounding British participation in the European economic and monetary integration and write your own assessment of the prospect of Britain joining the euro club. In doing so, assess from the British perspective, among other things, (1) potential benefits and costs of adopting the euro, (2) economic and political constraints facing the country, and (3) the potential impact of British adoption of the euro on the international financial system, including the role of the U.S. dollar.

REFERENCES & SUGGESTED READINGS

Bris, Arturo, Yrjö Koskinen, and Mattias Nilsson. The Euro and Corporate Valuation. Working Paper (2004).

Cooper, Richard N. *The International Monetary System: Essays in World Economics*. Cambridge, Mass.: MIT Press, 1987.

Eichengreen, Barry. *The Gold Standard in Theory and History*. Mathuen: London, 1985, pp. 39–48.

Friedman, Milton. *Essays in Positive Economics*. Chicago: University of Chicago Press, 1953.

Jorion, Philippe. "Properties of the ECU as a Currency Basket," *Journal of Multinational Financial Management* 1 (1991), pp. 1–24.

Machlup, Fritz. *Remaking the International Monetary System: The Rio Agreement and Beyond*. Baltimore: Johns Hopkins Press, 1968.

Mundell, Robert. "A Theory of Optimum Currency Areas." *American Economic Review* 51 (1961), pp. 657–65.

———. "Currency Areas, Volatility and Intervention," *Journal of Policy Modeling* 22 (2000), pp. 281–99.

Nurkse, Ragnar. *International Currency Experience: Lessons of the Interwar Period*. Geneva: League of Nations, 1944.

Solomon, Robert. *The International Monetary System, 1945–1981*. New York: Harper & Row, 1982.

Stiglitz, Joseph. "Reforming the Global Economic Architecture: Lessons from Recent Crisis." *Journal of Finance* 54 (1999), pp. 1508–21.

Tobin, James. "Financial Globalization," unpublished manuscript presented at American Philosophical Society, 1998.

Triffin, Robert. *Gold and the Dollar Crisis*. New Haven, Conn.: Yale University Press, 1960.

3 Balance of Payments

THE TERM **balance of payments** is often mentioned in the news media and continues to be a popular subject of economic and political discourse around the world. It is not always clear, however, exactly what is meant by the term when it is mentioned in various contexts. This ambiguity is often attributable to misunderstanding and misuse of the term. The balance of payments, which is a statistical record of a country's transactions with the rest of the world, is worth studying for a few reasons.

国际收支是一个国家与其他国家经济交易的统计记录。

First, the balance of payments provides detailed information concerning the demand and supply of a country's currency. For example, if the United States imports more than it exports, then this means that the supply of dollars is likely to exceed the demand in the foreign exchange market, *ceteris paribus*. One can thus infer that the U.S. dollar would be under pressure to depreciate against other currencies. On the other hand, if the United States exports more than it imports, then the dollar would be likely to appreciate.

拥有巨大国际收支顺差的国家更有可能扩大进口，能为外国企业提供营销机会，同时也不太可能实行外汇限制。

Second, a country's balance-of-payment data may signal its potential as a business partner for the rest of the world. If a country is grappling with a major balance-of-payment difficulty, it may not be able to expand imports from the outside world. Instead, the country may be tempted to impose measures to restrict imports and discourage capital outflows in order to improve the balance-of-payment situation. On the other hand, a country experiencing a significant balance-of-payment surplus would be more likely to expand imports, offering marketing opportunities for foreign enterprises, and less likely to impose foreign exchange restrictions.

Third, balance-of-payments data can be used to evaluate the performance of the country in international economic competition. Suppose a country is experiencing trade deficits year after year. This trade data may then signal that the country's domestic industries lack international competitiveness. To interpret balance-of-payments data properly, it is necessary to understand how the balance-of-payments account is constructed.

Balance-of-Payments Accounting

国际收支的正式定义为：以复式记账的形式对一个国家在某一时期内的国际经济交易所做的统计记录。

The balance of payments can be formally defined as *the statistical record of a country's international transactions over a certain period of time presented in the form of double-entry bookkeeping*. Examples of international transactions include import and export of goods and services and cross-border investments in businesses, bank accounts, bonds, stocks, and real estate. Since the balance of payments is recorded over a certain period of time (i.e., a quarter or a year), it has the same time dimension as national income accounting.[1]

Generally speaking, any transaction that results in a receipt from foreigners will be recorded as a credit, with a positive sign, in the U.S. balance of payments, whereas any transaction that gives rise to a payment to foreigners will be recorded as a debit, with a negative sign. Credit entries in the U.S. balance of payments result from foreign sales of U.S. goods and services, goodwill, financial claims, and real assets. Debit entries, on the other hand, arise from U.S. purchases of foreign goods and services, goodwill, financial claims, and real assets. Further, credit entries give rise to the demand for dollars, whereas debit entries give rise to the supply of dollars. Note that the demand (supply) for dollars is associated with the supply (demand) of foreign exchange.

国际收支采用复式记账法，每一个贷方账户都必然有一个与之平衡的借方账户，反之亦然。

Since the balance of payments is presented as a system of double-entry bookkeeping, every credit in the account is balanced by a matching debit and vice versa.

EXAMPLE 3.1

For example, suppose that Boeing Corporation exported a Boeing 747 aircraft to Japan Airlines for $50 million, and that Japan Airlines pays from its dollar bank account kept with Chase Manhattan Bank in New York City. Then, the receipt of $50 million by Boeing will be recorded as a credit (+), which will be matched by a debit (−) of the same amount representing a reduction of the U.S. bank's liabilities.

EXAMPLE 3.2

Suppose, for another example, that Boeing imports jet engines produced by Rolls-Royce for $30 million, and that Boeing makes payment by transferring the funds to a New York bank account kept by Rolls-Royce. In this case, payment by Boeing will be recorded as a debit (−), whereas the deposit of the funds by Rolls-Royce will be recorded as a credit (+).

As shown by the preceding examples, every credit in the balance of payments is matched by a debit somewhere to conform to the principle of double-entry bookkeeping.

---

[1]In fact, the current account balance, which is the difference between a country's exports and imports, is a component of the country's GNP. Other components of GNP include consumption and investment and government expenditure.

Not only international trade, that is, exports and imports, but also cross-border investments are recorded in the balance of payments.

EXAMPLE 3.3

Suppose that Ford acquires Jaguar, a British car manufacturer, for $750 million, and that Jaguar deposits the money in Barclays Bank in London, which, in turn, uses the sum to purchase U.S. treasury notes. In this case, the payment of $750 million by Ford will be recorded as a debit (−), whereas Barclays' purchase of the U.S. Treasury notes will be recorded as a credit (+).

The above examples can be summarized as follows:

Transactions	Credit	Debit
Boeing's export	+$50 million	
Withdrawal from U.S. bank		−$50 million
Boeing's import		−$30 million
Deposit at U.S. bank	+$30 million	
Ford's acquisition of Jaguar		−$750 million
Barclays' purchase of U.S. securities	+$750 million	

Balance-of-Payments Accounts

一国的国际交易账户可分为三大类：经常账户、资本账户和官方储备账户。

Since the balance of payments records all types of international transactions a country consummates over a certain period of time, it contains a wide variety of accounts. However, a country's international transactions can be grouped into the following three main types:

1. The current account.
2. The capital account.
3. The official reserve account.

经常账户
资本账户
官方储备账户

The **current account** includes the export and import of goods and services, whereas the **capital account** includes all purchases and sales of assets such as stocks, bonds, bank accounts, real estate, and businesses. The **official reserve account,** on the other hand, covers all purchases and sales of international reserve assets such as dollars, foreign exchanges, gold, and special drawing rights (SDRs).

Let us now examine a detailed description of the balance-of-payments accounts. Exhibit 3.1 summarizes the U.S. balance-of-payments accounts for the year 2004 that we are going to use as an example.

The Current Account

Exhibit 3.1 shows that U.S. exports were $1,516.2 billion in 2004 while U.S. imports were $2,109.1 billion. The current account balance, which is defined as exports minus imports plus unilateral transfers, that is, (1) + (2) + (3) in Exhibit 3.1, was negative, −$665.9 billion. The United States thus had a balance-of-payments deficit on the current account in 2004. The current account deficit implies that the United States

EXHIBIT 3.1

A Summary of the U.S. Balance of Payments for 2004 (in $ billion)

	Credits	Debits
Current Account		
(1) Exports	1,516.2	
(1.1) Merchandise	811.1	
(1.2) Services	336.1	
(1.3) Factor income	369.0	
(2) Imports		−2,109.1
(2.1) Merchandise		−1,473.1
(2.2) Services		−291.1
(2.3) Factor income		−344.9
(3) Unilateral transfer	16.4	−89.4
Balance on current account		−665.9
[(1) + (2) + (3)]		
Capital Account		
(4) Direct investment	115.5	−248.5
(5) Portfolio investment	794.4	−90.8
(5.1) Equity securities	57.6	−93.0
(5.2) Debt securities	736.8	2.2
(6) Other investment	524.3	−483.7
Balance on capital account	611.2	
[(4) + (5) + (6)]		
(7) Statistical discrepancies	51.9	
Overall balance		−2.8
Official Reserve Account	2.8	

Source: IMF, International Financial Statistics Yearbook, 2005.

经常账户可分为四个细目：**商品贸易**（merchandise trade）、服务、要素收入以及单方面转移。

交易余额（**trade balance**）

服务是经常账户的第二个细目，包括法律服务、咨询服务、工程维护、专利和知识产权、保险、运输、旅行等方面的收入与支出。

无形交易（**invisible trade**）

used up more output than it produced.[2] Since a country must finance its current account deficit either by borrowing from foreigners or by drawing down on its previously accumulated foreign wealth, a current account deficit represents a reduction in the country's net foreign wealth. On the other hand, a country with a current account surplus acquires IOUs from foreigners, thereby increasing its net foreign wealth.

The current account is divided into four finer categories: merchandise trade, services, factor income, and unilateral transfers. **Merchandise trade** represents exports and imports of tangible goods, such as oil, wheat, clothes, automobiles, computers, and so on. As Exhibit 3.1 shows, U.S. merchandise exports were $811.1 billion in 2004 while imports were $1,473.1 billion. The United States thus had a deficit on the **trade balance** or a trade deficit. The trade balance represents the net merchandise export. As is well known, the United States has experienced persistent trade deficits since the early 1980s, whereas such key trading partners as China, Japan, and Germany have generally realized trade surpluses. This continuous trade imbalance between the United States and her key trading partners set the stage for the relative decline of the dollar observed since 2001.

Services, the second category of the current account, include payments and receipts for legal, consulting, and engineering services, royalties for patents and intellectual properties, insurance premiums, shipping fees, and tourist expenditures. These trades in services are sometimes called **invisible trade.** In 2004, U.S. service exports were $336.1 billion and imports were $291.1 billion, realizing a surplus of $45.0 billion. Clearly, the U.S. performed better in services than in merchandise trade.

---

[2]The current account balance (BCA) can be written as the difference between national output (Y) and domestic absorption, which comprises consumption (C), investment (I), and government expenditures (G):

$$BCA = Y - (C + I + G)$$

If a country's domestic absorption falls short of its national output, the country's current account must be in surplus. for more detailed discussion, refer to appendix 3A.

要素收入

Factor income, the third category of the current account, consists largely of payments and receipts of interest, dividends, and other income on foreign investments that were previously made. If U.S. investors receive interest on their holdings of foreign bonds, for instance, it will be recorded as a credit in the balance of payments. On the other hand, interest payments by U.S. borrowers to foreign creditors will be recorded as debits. In 2004, U.S. residents paid out $344.9 billion to foreigners as factor income and received $369.0 billion, realizing a $24.1 billion surplus. Considering, however, that the United States has heavily borrowed from foreigners in recent years, U.S. payments of interest and dividends to foreigners are likely to rise sharply. This can increase the U.S. current account deficit in the future, *ceteris paribus*.

单方面转移

Unilateral transfers, the fourth category of the current account, involve "unrequited" payments. Examples include foreign aid, reparations, official and private grants, and gifts. Unlike other accounts in the balance of payments, unilateral transfers have only one-directional flows, without offsetting flows. In the case of merchandise trade, for example, goods flow in one direction and payments flow in the opposite direction. For the purpose of preserving the double-entry bookkeeping rule, unilateral transfers are regarded as an act of buying *goodwill* from the recipients. So a country that gives foreign aid to another country can be viewed as importing goodwill from the latter. As can be expected, the United States made a net unilateral transfer of $73.0 billion, which is the receipt of transfer payments ($16.4 billion) minus transfer payments to foreign entities ($89.4 billion).

经常账户余额，尤其是贸易余额，对汇率变化十分敏感。

The current account balance, especially the trade balance, tends to be sensitive to exchange rate changes. When a country's currency depreciates against the currencies of major trading partners, the country's exports tend to rise and imports fall, improving the trade balance. For example, Mexico experienced continuous deficits in its trade balance of about $4.5 billion per quarter throughout 1994. Following the depreciation of the peso in December 1994, however, Mexico's trade balance began to improve immediately, realizing a surplus of about $7 billion for the year 1995.

J—曲线效应表明，在货币贬值后，一国的贸易收支会发生先恶化、后改善的情形。

The effect of currency depreciation on a country's trade balance can be more complicated than the case described above. Indeed, following a depreciation, the trade balance may at first deteriorate for a while. Eventually, however, the trade balance will tend to improve over time. This particular reaction pattern of the trade balance to a depreciation is referred to as the **J-curve effect,** which is illustrated in Exhibit 3.2. The curve shows the initial deterioration and the eventual improvement of the trade balance following a depreciation. The J-curve effect received wide attention when the British trade balance worsened after a devaluation of the pound in 1967. Sebastian Edwards (1989) examined various cases of devaluations carried out by developing countries in the 1960s through 1980s, and confirmed the existence of the J-curve effect in about 40 percent of the cases. (See the References and Suggested Readings at the end of this chapter for more information about this study.)

EXHIBIT 3.2

A Currency Depreciation and the Time-Path of the Trade Balance: The J-Curve Effect

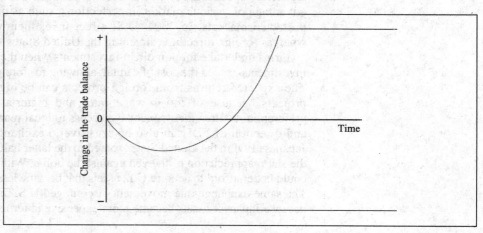

如果进口和出口对汇率变化敏感，那么贬值后，贸易收支会很快得到改善。

A depreciation will begin to improve the trade balance immediately if imports and exports are *responsive* to the exchange rate changes. On the other hand, if imports and exports are inelastic, the trade balance will worsen following a depreciation. Following a depreciation of the domestic currency and the resultant rise in import prices, domestic residents may still continue to purchase imports because it is difficult to change their consumption habits in a short period of time. With higher import prices, the domestic country comes to spend more on imports. Even if domestic residents are willing to switch to less expensive domestic substitutes for foreign imports, it may take time for domestic producers to supply import substitutes. Likewise, foreigners' demand for domestic products, which become less expensive with a depreciation of the domestic currency, can be inelastic essentially for the same reasons. In the long run, however, both imports and exports tend to be responsive to exchange rate changes, exerting positive influences on the trade balance.

The Capital Account

The capital account balance measures the difference between U.S. sales of assets to foreigners and U.S. purchases of foreign assets. U.S. sales (or exports) of assets are recorded as credits, as they result in *capital inflow*. On the other hand, U.S. purchases (imports) of foreign assets are recorded as debits, as they lead to *capital outflow*. Unlike trades in goods and services, trades in financial assets affect future payments and receipts of factor income.

Exhibit 3.1 shows that the United States had a capital account surplus of $611.2 billion in 2004, implying that capital inflow to the United States far exceeded capital outflow. Clearly, the current account deficit was largely offset by the capital account surplus. As previously mentioned, a country's current account deficit must be paid for either by borrowing from foreigners or by selling off past foreign investments. In the absence of the government's reserve transactions, the current account balance must be equal to the capital account balance but with the opposite sign. When nothing is excluded, a country's balance of payments must necessarily balance.

资本账户可以分为三个细目：直接投资、证券投资以及其他投资。

The capital account can be divided into three categories: direct investment, portfolio investment, and other investment. Direct investment occurs when the investor acquires a measure of control of the foreign business. In the U.S. balance of payments, acquisition of 10 percent or more of the voting shares of a business is considered giving a measure of control to the investor.

对外直接投资（FDI）

When Honda, a Japanese automobile manufacturer, built an assembly factory in Ohio, it was engaged in **foreign direct investment (FDI).** Another example of direct investment was provided by Nestlé Corporation, a Swiss multinational firm, when it *acquired* Carnation, a U.S. firm. Of course, U.S. firms also are engaged in direct investments in foreign countries. For instance, Coca-Cola built bottling facilities all over the world. In recent years, many U.S. corporations moved their production facilities to Mexico and China to take advantage of lower costs of production. Generally speaking, foreign direct investments take place as firms attempt to take advantage of various market imperfections, such as underpriced labor services and protected markets. In 2004, U.S. direct investment overseas was $248.5 billion, whereas foreign direct investment in the United States was $115.5 billion.

Firms undertake foreign direct investments when the expected returns from foreign investments exceed the cost of capital, allowing for foreign exchange and political risks. The expected returns from foreign projects can be higher than those from domestic projects because of lower wage rates and material costs, subsidized financing, preferential tax treatment, exclusive access to local markets, and the like. The volume and direction of FDI can also be sensitive to exchange rate changes. For instance, Japanese FDI in the United States soared in the latter half of the 1980s, partly because of the sharp appreciation of the yen against the dollar. With a stronger yen, Japanese firms could better afford to acquire U.S. assets that became less expensive in terms of the yen. The same exchange rate movement discouraged U.S. firms from making FDI in Japan because Japanese assets became more expensive in terms of the dollar.

证券投资是资本账户下的第二个细目，主要反映的是不涉及控制权转让的股票和债券等国外金融资产的买卖。

Portfolio investment, the second category of the capital account, mostly represents sales and purchases of foreign financial assets such as stocks and bonds that do not involve a transfer of control. International portfolio investments have boomed in recent years, partly due to the general relaxation of capital controls and regulations in many countries, and partly due to investors' desire to diversify risk globally. Portfolio investment comprises equity securities and debt securities. Equity securities include corporate shares, whereas debt securities include (1) bonds and notes, (2) money market instruments, and (3) financial derivatives like options. Exhibit 3.1 shows that in 2004, foreigners invested $794.4 billion in U.S. financial securities whereas Americans invested $90.8 billion in foreign securities, realizing a major surplus, $703.6 billion, for the United States. Much of the surplus represents foreigners' investment in U.S. debt securities. Exhibit 3.1 shows that foreigners invested $736.8 billion in U.S. debt securities in 2004. The exhibit also shows that U.S. investors liquidated some of their foreign debt holdings, repatriating $2.2 billion in 2004. It is unusual to have a positive entry ($2.2 billion) under debits but it represents net U.S. sales of foreign bonds.

Investors typically diversify their investment portfolios to reduce risk. Since security returns tend to have low correlations among countries, investors can reduce risk more effectively if they diversify their portfolio holdings internationally rather than purely domestically. In addition, investors may be able to benefit from higher expected returns from some foreign markets.[3]

The third category of the capital account is **other investment,** which includes transactions in currency, bank deposits, trade credits, and so forth. These investments are quite sensitive to both changes in relative interest rates between countries and the anticipated change in the exchange rate. If the interest rate rises in the United States while other variables remain constant, the United States will experience capital inflows, as investors would like to deposit or invest in the United States to take advantage of the higher interest rate. On the other hand, if a higher U.S. interest rate is more or less offset by an expected depreciation of the U.S. dollar, capital inflows to the United States will not materialize.[4] Since both interest rates and exchange rate expectations are volatile, these capital flows are highly reversible. In 2004, the United States experienced a net inflow of $40.6 billion in this category.

Statistical Discrepancy

国际交易引起的支付与收入记录是在不同时间和地点完成的，且可能采用了不同的方法。

Exhibit 3.1 shows that there was a statistical discrepancy of $51.9 billion in 2004, representing omitted and misrecorded transactions. Recordings of payments and receipts arising from international transactions are done at different times and places, possibly using different methods. As a result, these recordings, upon which the balance-of-payments statistics are constructed, are bound to be imperfect. While merchandise trade can be recorded with a certain degree of accuracy at the customs houses, provisions of invisible services like consulting can escape detection. Cross-border financial transactions, a bulk of which might have been conducted electronically, are far more difficult to keep track of. For this reason, the balance of payments always presents a "balancing" debit or credit as a statistical discrepancy.[5] It is interesting to note that the sum of the balance on capital account and the statistical discrepancy is very close to the balance of current account in magnitude, −$665.9 billion. This suggests that financial transactions may be mainly responsible for the discrepancy.

When we compute the *cumulative* balance of payments including the current account, capital account, and the statistical discrepancies, we obtain the so-called

---

[3]Refer to Chapter 15 for a detailed discussion of international portfolio investment.

[4]We will discuss the relationship between the relative interest rates and the expected exchange rate change in Chapter 6.

[5]Readers might wonder how to compute the statistical discrepancies in the balance of payments. Statistical discrepancies, which represent errors and omissions, by definition, cannot be known. Since, however, the balance of payments must balance to zero when every item is included, one can determine the statistical discrepancies in the "residual" manner.

总余额
官方结算差额

总余额也是一个国
家货币面临贬值或升值
压力的指标。

overall balance or **official settlement balance.** All the transactions comprising the overall balance take place *autonomously* for their own sake.[6] The overall balance is significant because it indicates a country's international payment gap that must be *accommodated* with the government's official reserve transactions.

It is also indicative of the pressure that a country's currency faces for depreciation or appreciation. If, for example, a country continuously realizes deficits on the overall balance, the country will eventually run out of reserve holdings and its currency may have to depreciate against foreign currencies. In 2004, the United States had a $2.8 billion deficit on the overall balance. This means that the U.S. had to make a net payment equal to that amount to the rest of the world. If the United States had realized a surplus on the overall balance, the U.S. would have received a net payment from the rest of the world.

Official Reserve Account
官方储备资产

官方储备账户包括
政府为平衡总余额及干
预外汇市场而进行的交
易。

When a country must make a net payment to foreigners because of a balance-of-payments deficit, the central bank of the country (the Federal Reserve System in the United States) should either run down its **official reserve assets,** such as gold, foreign exchanges, and SDRs, or borrow anew from foreign central banks. On the other hand, if a country has a balance-of-payments surplus, its central bank will either retire some of its foreign debts or acquire additional reserve assets from foreigners. Exhibit 3.1 shows that to take care of a $2.8 billion balance-of-payment deficit, the U.S. decreased its external reserve holdings by the same amount. When the U.S. decreases its reserve holdings by either liquidating its reserve holdings or borrowing anew, it will receive funds, which will be recorded under credits.

The official reserve account includes transactions undertaken by the authorities to finance the overall balance and intervene in foreign exchange markets. When the United States and foreign governments wish to support the value of the dollar in the foreign exchange markets, they sell foreign exchanges, SDRs, or gold to "buy" dollars. These transactions, which give rise to the demand for dollars, will be recorded as a positive entry under official reserves. On the other hand, if governments would like to see a weaker dollar, they "sell" dollars and buy gold, foreign exchanges, and so forth. These transactions, which give rise to the supply of dollars, will be recorded as a negative entry under official reserves. The more actively governments intervene in the foreign exchange markets, the greater the official reserve entry.

Until the advent of the Bretton Woods System in 1945, gold was the predominant international reserve asset. After 1945, however, international reserve assets comprise:

1. Gold.
2. Foreign exchanges.
3. Special drawing rights (SDRs).
4. Reserve positions in the International Monetary Fund (IMF).

As can be seen from Exhibit 3.3, the relative importance of gold as an international means of payment has steadily declined, whereas the importance of foreign exchanges has grown substantially. As of 2004, foreign exchanges account for about 95 percent of the total reserve assets held by IMF member countries, with gold accounting for less than 2 percent of the total reserves.

As can be seen from Exhibit 3.4, the U.S. dollar's share in the world's foreign exchange reserves was 50.9 percent in 1991, followed by the German mark (15.7 percent), ECU (10.0 percent), Japanese yen (8.7 percent), British pound (3.4 percent), French franc (2.8 percent), Swiss franc (1.2 percent), and Dutch guilder (1.1 percent). The "predecessor" currencies of the euro, including the German mark, French franc, Dutch guilder, and ECU, collectively received a substantial weight, about 30 percent,

---

[6]Autonomous transactions refer to those transactions that occur without regard to the goal of achieving the balance-of-payments equilibrium.

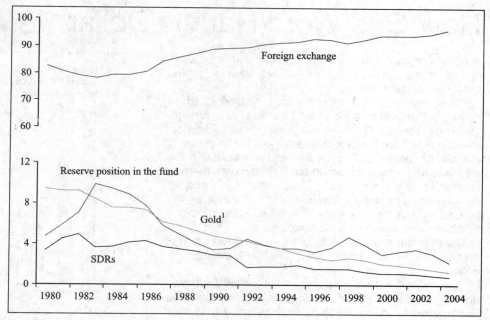

EXHIBIT 3.3

Composition of Total Official Reserves
(in Percent)

[1]Values at SDR 35 per ounce.
Source: IMF, International Financial Statistics Yearbook, 2004.

in the world's foreign exchange reserves. For comparison, in 1997, the world's reserves comprised the U.S. dollar (59.1 percent), German mark (13.7 percent), Japanese yen (5.1 percent), British pound (3.3 percent), French franc (1.5 percent), ECU (5.0 percent), Swiss franc (0.5 percent), Dutch guilder (0.5 percent), and miscellaneous currencies (11.3 percent). In other words, the U.S. dollar's share has increased substantially throughout the 1990s at the expense of other currencies. This change can be attributed to a strong performance of the dollar in the 1990s and the uncertainty associated with the introduction of the new currency, that is, the euro. In 2003, the world reserves comprised the U.S. dollar (63.8 percent), euro (19.7 percent), Japanese yen (4.8 percent), British pound (4.4 percent), Swiss franc (0.4 percent), and miscellaneous currencies (6.8 percent). The dollar's dominant position in the world's reserve holdings may decline to a certain extent as the euro becomes a "known quantity" and its external value becomes more stable. In fact, the euro's share has increased from 13.5 percent in 1999 to 19.7 percent in 2003.

EXHIBIT 3.4	**Currency Composition of the World's Foreign Exchange Reserves** (Percent of Total)								
Currency	**1987**	**1989**	**1991**	**1993**	**1995**	**1997**	**1999**	**2001**	**2003**
U.S. dollar	56.0	51.9	50.9	56.2	53.4	59.1	64.9	66.9	63.8
Japanese yen	7.0	7.3	8.7	8.0	6.7	5.1	5.4	5.5	4.8
Pound sterling	2.2	2.6	3.4	3.1	2.8	3.3	3.6	4.0	4.4
Swiss franc	1.8	1.4	1.2	1.2	0.5	0.5	0.4	0.5	0.4
Euro	—	—	—	—	—	—	13.5	16.7	19.7
Deutsche mark	13.4	18.0	15.7	14.1	14.7	13.7	—	—	—
French franc	0.8	1.4	2.8	2.2	2.4	1.5	—	—	—
Netherlands guilder	1.2	1.1	1.1	0.6	0.5	0.5	—	—	—
ECU	14.2	10.5	10.0	8.3	6.8	5.0	—	—	—
Other currencies	3.4	5.7	6.2	6.2	12.1	11.3	12.1	6.4	6.8

Source: IMF, Annual Report of the Executive Board, 1996, 2004.

How One Word Haunts Dollar

A new bogeyman is haunting the dollar and U.S. fixed-income markets. It goes by the innocuous name of "central bank reserve diversification."

Three weeks ago, the South Korean central bank told the country's Parliament it intended to diversify its foreign-exchange reserves. Before Korea, it was Russia. Early last week, it was China, which said it always had a policy to diversify reserves. Last Thursday, it was the Japanese prime minister's turn, with Junichiro Koizumi telling a parliamentary committee that, in general, Japan needs to consider diversifying its foreign-exchange reserves. A day later, the governor of the Reserve Bank of India said diversification was being discussed within his central bank.

Given that the vast majority of these foreign-exchange reserves are held in dollars, that in effect is a slight on the dollar.

"Diversification is not a word you want to hear if you hold dollars," says Bob Prince, co-chief investment officer at Bridgewater Associates. "Since most central banks hold almost all of their reserves in U.S. dollars, diversification always means 'sell dollars and buy euros and yen.'"

Most central banks that talked of diversification also have said officially that they aren't selling dollars. Still, it is the possibility that the central banks might in the future that has spooked investors almost as much as if there were irrefutable evidence that they actually had. In the past month, the dollar has fallen nearly 3 percent against the euro and retreated 1.4 percent against the yen. In New York yesterday afternoon, the euro stood at $1.3420, while the dollar was at 104.16 yen.

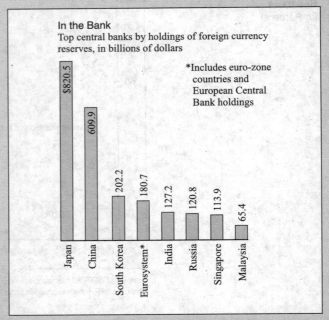

In the Bank
Top central banks by holdings of foreign currency reserves, in billions of dollars

*Includes euro-zone countries and European Central Bank holdings

Japan $820.5
China 609.9
South Korea 202.2
Eurosystem* 180.7
India 127.2
Russia 120.8
Singapore 113.9
Malaysia 65.4

Note: Figures for China, Eurosystem, Russia and Malaysia are as of Dec. 31, 2004; other countries are as of Feb. 28, 2005.
Sources: The Bank of Tokyo–Mitsubishi, Bloomberg.

Measured by reserves, the six biggest Asian central banks—Japan, China, South Korea, India, Singapore and Malaysia—combined hold roughly $2.3 trillion in foreign currency, the overwhelming amount in dollars. These

如果国际收支账户得到正确记录，那么经常账户余额、资本账户余额与储备账户余额的和为零。

In addition to the emergence of the euro as a credible reserve currency, continued U.S. trade deficits and foreigners' desire to diversify their currency holdings away from U.S. dollars could further diminish the position of the U.S. dollar as the dominant reserve currency. As pointed out by the International Finance in Practice box, "How One Word Haunts Dollar," the value of the U.S. dollar would also be very much affected by the currency diversification decisions of Asian central banks. These banks collectively hold an enormous amount of foreign currency reserves, mostly in dollars, arising from trade surpluses. Asian central banks also purchase U.S. dollars in foreign exchange markets in order to keep their local currencies from appreciating against the dollar.

The Balance-of-Payments Identity

When the balance-of-payments accounts are recorded correctly, the combined balance of the current account, the capital account, and the reserves account must be zero, that is,

$$BCA + BKA + BRA = 0 \tag{3.1}$$

where:

BCA = balance on the current account

BKA = balance on the capital account

BRA = balance on the reserves account

reserves for the most part are the product of accumulated trade surpluses, foreign direct investment, funds held for emergency purposes and central-bank dollar purchases through market intervention.

Rather than just hoarding piles of cash, the central banks typically use their dollars to buy dollar-denominated short-term U.S. government debt, which has been a big factor in keeping Treasurys prices high and yields low.

Mr. Prince figures that if central banks stopped purchasing dollars "cold turkey," U.S. bond yields would have to rise about 1.5 percentage points from about 4.5 percent now and the dollar would have to decline roughly 30 percent to attract sufficient private-investor capital to offset lost central-bank purchases.

Despite the rhetoric from central bankers, there is much debate over whether and to what degree central banks really are diversifying away from the dollar. Most don't reveal the composition of their reserves, and data collected by the U.S. Treasury and most international organizations tend to be incomplete.

For instance, Japan's Treasury holdings declined in four out of five months through January, according to U.S. Treasury International Capital (TIC) data—a sign to some that Japan's central bank is starting to diversify its currency exposure. Yet some note that TIC data fail to capture money held by central banks in bank accounts and some purchases of U.S. securities, such as those bought from a foreign entity outside the U.S.

In fact, many currency strategists believe that, so far, diversification talk is more bark than bite. "There is little reliable evidence of any notable diversification out of the dollar by Asian central banks," says Derek Halpenny, a senior currency economist at Bank of Tokyo-Mitsubishi.

Even so, they acknowledge that the motives to diversify are growing. Even after Korean officials last month insisted they had no plans to sell dollars, they confirmed that the central bank intends to invest in "higher yielding" securities, including nongovernment debt.

There also are signs that central banks are looking at other investments, even dollar-denominated, other than Treasurys. Chinese official institutions were net buyers of $12 billion of corporate bonds last year, accounting for 26 percent of China's net purchases of U.S. securities, according to Treasury data. By contrast, corporate bonds in each of the previous three years amounted to only 7 percent to 13 percent of the country's new investments in the U.S. These purchases appear to have come at the expense of safer, but lower-yielding, U.S. Treasurys and federal-agency debt.

Others note, however, that big Asian central banks are unlikely to aggressively begin dumping their dollar holdings, if only because they would be shooting themselves in the foot. The value of their U.S. investments would plummet along with the dollar; they would risk damaging demand in their main export market, the U.S.; and they might prompt a political backlash, says Mark Cliffe, chief economist at ING Financial Markets.

Source: The Wall Street Journal, March 17, 2005, p. C16. Reprinted with permission.

国际收支恒等式
(BOPI)

The balance on the reserves account, BRA, represents the change in the official reserves.

Equation 3.1 is the **balance-of-payments identity (BOPI)** that must necessarily hold. The BOPI equation indicates that a country can run a balance-of-payments surplus or deficit by increasing or decreasing its official reserves. Under the fixed exchange rate regime, countries maintain official reserves that allow them to have balance-of-payments disequilibrium, that is, BCA + BKA is nonzero, without adjusting the exchange rate. Under the fixed exchange rate regime, the combined balance on the current and capital accounts will be equal in size, but opposite in sign, to the change in the official reserves:

$$BCA + BKA = -BRA \qquad (3.2)$$

For example, if a country runs a deficit on the overall balance, that is, BCA + BKA is negative, the central bank of the country can supply foreign exchanges out of its reserve holdings. But if the deficit persists, the central bank will eventually run out of its reserves, and the country may be forced to devalue its currency. This is roughly what happened to the Mexican peso in December 1994.

在完全浮动汇率制
下，央行不会干涉外汇
市场。

Under the *pure* flexible exchange rate regime, central banks will not intervene in the foreign exchange markets. In fact, central banks do not need to maintain official reserves. Under this regime, the overall balance thus must necessarily balance, that is,

$$BCA = -BKA \qquad (3.3)$$

In other words, a current account surplus or deficit must be matched by a capital account deficit or surplus, and vice versa. In a *dirty* floating exchange rate system under which the central banks discreetly buy and sell foreign exchanges, Equation 3.3 will not hold tightly.

经常账户赤字（盈余）可能会导致资本账户发生盈余（赤字），反过来也成立。

Being an identity, Equation 3.3 does not imply a causality by itself. A current account deficit (surplus) may cause a capital account surplus (deficit), or the opposite may hold. It has often been suggested that the persistent U.S. current account deficits made it necessary for the United States to run matching capital account surpluses, implying that the former *causes* the latter. One can argue, with equal justification, that the persistent U.S. capital account surpluses, which may have been caused by high U.S. interest rates, have caused the persistent current account deficits by strengthening the value of the dollar. The issue can be settled only by careful empirical studies.

Balance-of-Payments Trends in Major Countries

Considering the significant attention that balance-of-payments data receive in the news media, it is useful to closely examine balance-of-payments trends in some of the major countries. Exhibit 3.5 provides the balance on the current account (BCA) as well as the balance on the capital account (BKA) for each of the five key countries, China, Japan, Germany, the United Kingdom, and the United States, during the period 1982–2003.

自1992年始，美国出现了持续的经常账户赤字及资本账户盈余。

Exhibit 3.5 shows first that the United States has experienced continuous deficits on the current account since 1982 and continuous surpluses on the capital account. Clearly, the magnitude of U.S. current account deficits is far greater than

EXHIBIT 3.5	Balances on the Current (BCA) and Capital (BKA) Accounts of Five Major Countries: 1982–2003 ($ billion)[a]									
	China		Japan		Germany		United Kingdom		United States	
Year	BCA	BKA	BCA	BKA	BCA	BKA	BCA	BKA	BCA	BKA
1982	5.7	0.6	6.9	−11.6	4.9	−2.0	8.0	−10.6	−11.6	16.6
1983	4.2	−0.1	20.8	−19.3	4.6	−6.6	5.3	−7.1	−44.2	45.4
1984	2.0	−1.9	35.0	−32.9	9.6	−9.9	1.8	−2.8	−99.0	102.1
1985	−11.4	9.0	51.1	−51.6	17.6	−15.4	3.3	−0.7	−124.5	128.3
1986	−7.0	5.0	85.9	−70.7	40.9	−35.5	−1.3	5.0	−150.5	150.2
1987	0.3	4.5	84.4	−46.3	46.4	−24.9	−8.1	28.2	−166.5	157.3
1988	−3.8	6.2	79.2	−61.7	50.4	−66.0	−29.3	33.9	−127.7	131.6
1989	−4.3	3.8	63.2	−76.3	57.0	−54.1	−36.7	28.6	−104.3	129.5
1990	12.0	0.1	44.1	−53.2	48.3	−41.1	−32.5	32.5	−94.3	96.5
1991	13.3	1.3	68.2	−76.6	−17.7	11.5	−14.3	19.0	−9.3	3.5
1992	6.4	−8.5	112.6	−112.0	−19.1	56.3	−18.4	11.7	−61.4	57.4
1993	−11.6	13.4	131.6	−104.2	−13.9	−0.3	−15.5	21.0	−90.6	91.9
1994	6.9	23.5	130.3	−105.0	−20.9	18.9	−2.3	3.8	−132.9	127.6
1995	1.6	20.9	111.0	−52.4	−22.6	29.8	−5.9	5.0	−129.2	138.9
1996	7.2	24.5	65.9	−30.7	−13.8	12.6	−3.7	3.2	−148.7	142.1
1997	29.7	6.1	94.4	−87.8	−1.2	2.6	6.8	−11.0	−166.8	167.8
1998	31.5	−6.3	120.7	−116.8	−6.4	17.63	−8.0	0.2	−217.4	151.6
1999	21.1	5.2	106.9	−31.1	−18.0	−40.5	−31.9	31.0	−324.4	367.9
2000	20.5	2.0	116.9	−75.5	−18.7	13.2	−28.8	26.2	−444.7	443.6
2001	17.4	34.8	87.8	−51.0	1.7	−24.1	−32.1	31.5	−385.7	419.9
2002	35.4	32.3	112.4	−66.7	43.4	−70.4	−26.2	17.3	−473.9	572.7
2003	45.9	52.7	136.2	67.9	54.9	−79.3	−30.5	24.8	−530.7	541.2

[a]The balance on the capital account (BKA) includes statistical discrepancies.
Source: IMF, International Financial Statistics Yearbook, various issues.

EXHIBIT 3.6

**The U.S.'s
Balance-of-Payments Trend:
1982–2004**

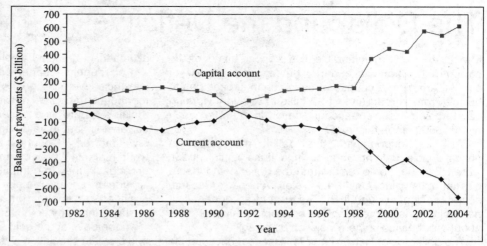

Source: IMF, International Financial Statistics Yearbook, various issues.

any that other countries ever experienced during the 22-year sample period. In 2003, the U.S. current account deficit reached $531 billion. The U.S. balance-of-payments trend is illustrated in Exhibit 3.6. The exhibit shows that the U.S. current account deficit has increased sharply since 1998. This situation has led some politicians and commentators to lament that Americans are living far beyond their means. As a matter of fact, the net international investment position of the United States turned negative in 1987 for the first time in decades and continued to deteriorate. The overseas debt burden of the United States-the difference between the value of foreign-owned assets in the United States and the value of U.S.-owned assets abroad-reached about $2,430 billion at the end of 2003, when valued by the replacement cost of the investments made abroad and at home. As recently as 1986, the United States was considered a net creditor nation, with about $35 billion more in assets overseas than foreigners owned in the United States. The International Finance in Practice box "The Dollar and the Deficit" addresses the issues associated with the U.S. trade deficit.

从1982年到20世纪90年代中期，尽管日元一直保持稳定升值，但日本的经常账户持续保持盈余。

Second, Exhibit 3.5 reveals that Japan has had an unbroken string of current account surpluses since 1982 despite the fact that the value of the yen rose steadily until the mid-1990s. As can be expected, during this period Japan realized continuous capital account deficits; Japan invested heavily in foreign stocks and bonds, businesses, real estates, art objects, and the like to recycle its huge, persistent current account surpluses. Consequently, Japan emerged as the world's largest creditor nation, whereas the United States became the largest debtor nation. It is noted that Japan has a capital account surplus in 2003, reflecting increased foreign investments in Japanese securities and businesses. The persistent current account disequilibrium has been a major source of friction between Japan and its key trading partners, especially the United States. In fact, Japan has often been criticized for pursuing **mercantilism** to ensure continuous trade surpluses.[7]

重商主义

与美国一样，英国近来也一直存在经常账户与资本账户盈余并存的情形。

Third, like the United States, the United Kingdom recently experienced continuous current account deficits, coupled with capital account surpluses. The

[7]Mercantilism, which originated in Europe during the period of absolute monarchies, holds that precious metals like gold and silver are the key components of national wealth, and that a continuing trade surplus should be a major policy goal as it ensures a continuing inflow of precious metals and thus continuous increases in national wealth. Mercantilists, therefore, abhor trade deficits and argue for imposing various restrictions on imports. Mercantilist ideas were criticized by such British thinkers as David Hume and Adam Smith. Both argued that the main source of wealth of a country is its productive capacity, not precious metals.

The Dollar and the Deficit

The dollar is looking vulnerable. It is propped up not by the strength of America's exports, but by vast imports of capital. America, a country already rich in capital, has to borrow from abroad almost $2 billion net every working day to cover a current-account deficit forecast to reach almost $500 billion this year.

To most economists, this deficit represents an unsustainable drain on world savings. If the capital inflows were to dry up, some reckon that the dollar could lose a quarter of its value. Only Paul O'Neill, America's treasury secretary, appears unruffled. The current-account deficit, he declares, is a "meaningless concept," which he talks about only because others insist on doing so.

The dollar is not just a matter for America, because the dollar is not just America's currency. Over half of all dollar bills in circulation are held outside American's borders, and almost half of America's Treasury bonds are held as reserves by foreign central banks. The euro cannot yet rival this global reach. International financiers borrow and lend in dollars, and international traders use dollars, even if Americans are at neither end of the deal. No asset since gold has enjoyed such widespread acceptance as a medium of exchange and store of value. In fact, some economists, such as Paul Davidson of the University of Tennessee and Ronald McKinnon of Stanford University, take the argument a step further (see references at end). They argue that the world is on a de facto dollar standard,

akin to the 19th-century gold standard.

For roughly a century up to 1914, the world's main currencies were pegged to gold. You could buy an ounce for about four pounds or twenty dollars. The contemporary "dollar standard" is a looser affair. In principle, the world's currencies float in value against each other, but in reality few float freely. Countries fear losing competitiveness on world markets if their currency rises too much against the greenback; they fear inflation if it falls too far. As long as American prices remain stable, the dollar therefore provides an anchor for world currencies and prices, ensuring that they do not become completely unmoored.

In the days of the gold standard, the volume of money and credit in circulation was tied to the amount of gold in a country's vaults. Economies laboured under the "tyranny" of the gold regime, booming when gold was abundant, deflating when it was scarce. The dollar standard is a more liberal system. Central banks retain the right to expand the volume of domestic credit to keep pace with the growth of the home economy.

Eventually, however, growth in the world's economies translates into a growing demand for dollar assets. The more money central banks print, the more dollars they like to hold in reserve to underpin their currency. The more business is done across borders, the more dollars

---

www.ecb.int/stats

This website provides balance-of-payment data on the euro-12 countries.

与日本相同，中国在经常账户下也出现了国际收支盈余。不过，不同的是中国的资本账户也发生了盈余。

magnitude, however, is far less than that of the United States. Germany, on the other hand, traditionally had current account surpluses. Since 1991, however, Germany has been experiencing current account deficits. This is largely due to German reunification and the resultant need to absorb more output domestically to rebuild the East German region. This has left less output available for exports. Since 2001, however, Germany starts to realize current account surpluses and capital account deficits, returning to the earlier pattern.

Fourth, like Japan, China tends to have a balance-of-payment surplus on the current account. Unlike Japan, however, China tends to realize a surplus on the capital account as well. In 2003, for instance, China had a $45.9 billion surplus on the current account and, at the same time, a $52.7 billion surplus on the capital account. This implies that China's official reserve holdings must have gone up for the year. In fact, China's official reserves have increased sharply in recent years, reaching about $610 billion in 2004.

While perennial balance-of-payments deficits or surpluses can be a problem, each country need not achieve balance-of-payments equilibrium every year. Suppose a country is currently experiencing a trade deficit because of the import demand for capital goods that are necessary for economic development projects. In this case, the trade deficit can be self-correcting in the long run because once the projects are completed, the country may be able to export more or import less by substituting domestic products for foreign imports. In contrast, if the trade deficit is the result of importing consumption goods, the situation will not correct by itself. Thus, what matters is the nature and causes of the disequilibrium.

因此，真正重要的是不平衡性的性质和原因。

traders need to cover their transactions. If the greenback is the new gold, Alan Greenspan, the Federal Reserve chairman, is the world's alchemist, responsible for concocting enough liquidity to keep world trade bubbling along nicely.

But America can play this role only if it is happy to allow foreigners to build up a huge mass of claims on its assets—and if foreigners are happy to go along. Some economists watch with consternation as the rest of the world's claims on America outstrip America's claims on the rest of the world. As they point out, even a dollar bill is an American liability, a promise of ultimate payment by the US Treasury. Can America keep making these promises to foreigners, without eventually emptying them of value?

According to Mr. Davidson, the world cannot risk America stopping. America's external deficit means an extra $500 billion is going into circulation in the world economy each year. If America reined in its current account, international commerce would suffer a liquidity crunch, as it did periodically under the gold standard. Hence America's deficit is neither a "meaningless concept" nor a lamentable drain on world savings. It is an indispensable fount of liquidity for world trade.

Spigot by Nature

But is the deficit sustainable? Many of America's creditors, Mr. McKinnon argues, have a stake in preserving the dollar standard, whatever the euro's potential charms. In particular, a large share of America's more liquid assets are held by foreign central banks, particularly in Asia,

which dare not offload them for fear of undermining the competitiveness of their own currencies. "Willy nilly," Mr. McKinnon says, "foreign governments cannot avoid being important creditors of the United States." China, for one, added $60 billion to its reserves in the year to June by ploughing most of its trade surplus with America back into American assets.

This is not the first time America's external deficits have raised alarm. In 1966, as America's post-war trade surpluses began to dwindle, The Economist ran an article entitled "The dollar and world liquidity: a minority view." According to this view, the build-up of dollar claims by foreigners was not a "deficit" in need of "correction." Rather, the American capital market was acting like a global financial intermediary, providing essential liquidity to foreign governments and enterprises. In their own ways, Mr. Davidson and Mr. McKinnon echo this minority view today. A "correction" of America's current deficit, they say, would create more problems than it would solve. Whether the world's holders of dollars will always agree remains to be seen.

"Financial Markets, Money and the Real World" by Paul Davidson. Edward Elgar 2002.

"The International Dollar Standard and Sustainability of the U.S. Current Account Deficit" by Ronald McKinnon 2001. Available on www.stanford.edu/~mckinnon/papers.htm

Source: The Economist, September 14, 2002, p. 74. Reprinted with permission.

SUMMARY

1. 国际收支的定义为：以复式记账的形式对一个国家在某一时期内的国际经济交易所做的统计记录。

2. 在国际收支中，任何导致从国外获得收入的交易记在贷方，用正号表示；而任何导致对国外进行支付的交易记在借方，用负号表示。

3. 一国的国际交易账户可分为三大类：经常账户、资本账户和官方储备账户。经常账户包括商品与服务的进出口，资本账户包括股票、债券、银行往来账款、不动产等资产的买卖。官方储备账户则包括美元、外汇、黄金以及特别提款权等国际储备资产的买卖。

4. 经常账户可分为四个细目：商品贸易、服务、生产要素收入以及单方面转移。商品贸易代表有形商品的进出口，服务贸易包括法律服务、咨询服务、工程维护、专利和知识产权、保险、运输、旅行等方面的收入与支出；生产要素收入账户包括利息、股利以及国外投资利得方面的收入

1. The balance of payments can be defined as the statistical record of a country's international transactions over a certain period of time presented in the form of double-entry bookkeeping.

2. In the balance of payments, any transaction resulting in a receipt from foreigners is recorded as a credit, with a positive sign, whereas any transaction resulting in a payment to foreigners is recorded as a debit, with a minus sign.

3. A country's international transactions can be grouped into three main categories: the current account, the capital account, and the official reserve account. The current account includes exports and imports of goods and services, whereas the capital account includes all purchases and sales of assets such as stocks, bonds, bank accounts, real estate, and businesses. The official reserve account covers all purchases and sales of international reserve assets, such as dollars, foreign exchanges, gold, and SDRs.

4. The current account is divided into four subcategories: merchandise trade, services, factor income, and unilateral transfers. Merchandise trade represents exports and imports of tangible goods, whereas trade in services includes payments and receipts for legal, engineering, consulting, and other performed services and tourist expenditures. Factor income consists of payments and receipts of interest, dividends, and other income on previously made foreign investments. Lastly, unilateral transfer involves unrequited payments such as gifts, foreign aid, and reparations.

与支出；单方面转移指无偿支付，如礼物、国外援助、赔款等。

5. 资本账户可以分为三个细目：直接投资、证券投资以及其他投资。直接投资是指投资者为获得国外公司的一部分控制权而进行的投资；证券投资是指不涉及控制权转让的股票和债券等国外金融资产的买卖；其他投资包括货币、银行存款、贸易信贷等方面的交易。

6. 国际收支账户中经常账户、资本账户及统计误差的累计值称为总余额或官方结算余额。总余额反映了一国的国际收支缺口。该缺口必须通过政府的官方储备交易来进行调节。当一国由于国际收支赤字而必须向外国进行净支付时，该国的中央银行就得减少黄金、外汇、特别提款权等官方储备资产或者向外国进行再借款。

7. 一国可以通过增加或减少它的官方储备来调整国际收支盈余或赤字。在固定汇率制下，经常账户余额与资本账户余额的和在数量上等于官方储备的变化，但符号相反。在完全浮动汇率制下，中央银行不需要维持任何官方储备，经常账户盈余或赤字必须与资本账户的赤字或盈余相匹配。

5. The capital account is divided into three subcategories: direct investment, portfolio investment, and other investment. Direct investment involves acquisitions of controlling interests in foreign businesses. Portfolio investment represents investments in foreign stocks and bonds that do not involve acquisitions of control. Other investment includes bank deposits, currency investment, trade credit, and the like.

6. When we compute the cumulative balance of payments including the current account, capital account, and the statistical discrepancies, we obtain the overall balance or official settlement balance. The overall balance is indicative of a country's balance-of-payments gap that must be accommodated by official reserve transactions. If a country must make a net payment to foreigners because of a balance-of-payments deficit, the country should either run down its official reserve assets, such as gold, foreign exchanges, and SDRs, or borrow anew from foreigners.

7. A country can run a balance-of-payments surplus or deficit by increasing or decreasing its official reserves. Under the fixed exchange rate regime, the combined balance on the current and capital accounts will be equal in size, but opposite in sign, to the change in the official reserves. Under the pure flexible exchange rate regime where the central bank does not maintain any official reserves, a current account surplus or deficit must be matched by a capital account deficit or surplus.

KEY WORDS

balance of payments, 59
balance-of-payments
    identity (BOPI), 69
capital account, 61
current account, 61
factor income, 63
foreign direct investment
    (FDI), 64

invisible trade, 62
J-curve effect, 63
mercantilism, 71
merchandise trade, 62
official reserve
    account, 61
official reserve
    assets, 66

official settlement
    balance, 66
other investment, 65
overall balance, 66
portfolio investment, 65
services, 62
trade balance, 62
unilateral transfer, 63

QUESTIONS

1. Define *balance of payments*.

2. Why would it be useful to examine a country's balance-of-payments data?

3. The United States has experienced continuous current account deficits since the early 1980s. What do you think are the main causes for the deficits? What would be the consequences of continuous U.S. current account deficits?

4. In contrast to the United States, Japan has realized continuous current account surpluses. What could be the main causes for these surpluses? Is it desirable to have continuous current account surpluses?

5. Comment on the following statement: "Since the United States imports more than it exports, it is necessary for the United States to import capital from foreign countries to finance its current account deficits."

6. Explain how a country can run an overall balance-of-payments deficit or surplus.

7. Explain *official reserve assets* and its major components.

8. Explain how to compute the overall balance and discuss its significance.

9. Since the early 1980s, foreign portfolio investors have purchased a significant portion of U.S. Treasury bond issues. Discuss the short-term and long-term effects of foreigners' portfolio investment on the U.S. balance of payments.

10. Describe the *balance-of-payments identity* and discuss its implications under the fixed and flexible exchange rate regimes.

11. Exhibit 3.5 indicates that in 1999, Germany had a current account deficit and at the same time a capital account deficit. Explain how this can happen.

12. Explain how each of the following transactions will be classified and recorded in the debit and credit of the U.S. balance of payments:

    a. A Japanese insurance company purchases U.S. Treasury bonds and pays out of its bank account kept in New York City.

    b. A U.S. citizen consumes a meal at a restaurant in Paris and pays with her American Express card.

    c. An Indian immigrant living in Los Angeles sends a check drawn on his LA bank account as a gift to his parents living in Bombay.

    d. A U.S. computer programmer is hired by a British company for consulting and gets paid from the U.S. bank account maintained by the British company.

13. Construct the balance-of-payment table for Japan for the year of 1998 which is comparable in format to Exhibit 3.1, and interpret the numerical data. You may consult *International Financial Statistics* published by IMF or search for useful websites for the data yourself.

PROBLEMS

1. Examine the following summary of the U.S. balance of payments for 2000 (in $ billion) and fill in the blank entries.

	Credits	Debits
Current Account		
(1) Exports	1,418.64	
(1.1) Merchandise	774.86	
(1.2) Services	290.88	
(1.3) Factor income	352.90	
(2) Imports		−1,809.18
(2.1) Merchandise		☐
(2.2) Services		−217.07
(2.3) Factor income		−367.68
(3) Unilateral transfer	10.24	−64.39
Balance on current account		☐
Capital Account		
(4) Direct investment	287.68	−152.44
(5) Portfolio investment	474.59	−124.94
(5.1) Equity securities	193.85	−99.74
(5.2) Debt securities	280.74	−25.20
(6) Other investment	262.64	−303.27
Balance on capital account	☐	
(7) Statistical discrepancies	☐	
Overall balance	0.30	
Official Reserve Account		−0.30

Source: IMF, International Financial Statistics Yearbook, 2001.

INTERNET EXERCISES

1. Study the website of the International Monetary Fund (IMF), www.imf.org/external, and discuss the role of IMF in dealing with balance-of-payment and currency crises.

MINI CASE

Mexico's Balance-of-Payments Problem

Recently, Mexico experienced large-scale trade deficits, depletion of foreign reserve holdings, and a major currency devaluation in December 1994, followed by the decision to freely float the peso. These events also brought about a severe recession and higher unemployment in Mexico. Since the devaluation, however, the trade balance has improved.

Investigate the Mexican experiences in detail and write a report on the subject. In the report, you may:

1. Document the trend in Mexico's key economic indicators, such as the balance of payments, the exchange rate, and foreign reserve holdings, during the period 1994.1 through 1995.12.

2. Investigate the causes of Mexico's balance-of-payments difficulties prior to the peso devaluation.

3. Discuss what policy actions might have prevented or mitigated the balance-of-payments problem and the subsequent collapse of the peso.

4. Derive lessons from the Mexican experience that may be useful for other developing countries.

In your report, you may identify and address any other relevant issues concerning Mexico's balance-of-payments problem. Internatonal Financial Statistics published by IMF provides basic macroeconomic data on Mexico.

REFERENCES & SUGGESTED READINGS

Edwards, Sebastian. *Real Exchange Rates, Devaluation and Adjustment: Exchange Rate Policy in Developing Countries.* Cambridge, Mass.: MIT Press, 1989.

Grabbe, Orlin. *International Financial Markets.* New York: Elsevier, 1991.

Kemp, Donald. "Balance of Payments Concepts—What Do They Really Mean?" *Federal Reserve Bank of St. Louis Review,* July 1975, pp. 14–23.

Ohmae, Kenichi. "Lies, Damned Lies and Statistics: Why the Trade Deficit Doesn't Matter in a Borderless World."

Journal of Applied Corporate World, Winter, 1991, pp. 98–106.

Salop, Joan, and Erich Spitaller. "Why Does the Current Account Matter?" International Monetary Fund, *Staff Papers,* March 1980, pp. 101–34.

U.S. Department of Commerce. "Report of the Advisory Committee on the Presentation of the Balance of Payments Statistics." *Survey of Current Business,* June, 1991, pp. 18–25.

Yeager, Leland. *International Monetary Relations.* New York: Harper & Row, 1965.

3A The Relationship between Balance of Payments and National Income Accounting

This section is designed to explore the mathematical relationship between balance-of-payments accounting and national income accounting and to discuss the implications of this relationship. National income (Y), or gross domestic product (GDP), is identically equal to the sum of nominal consumption (C) of goods and services, private investment expenditures (I), government expenditures (G), and the difference between exports (X) and imports (M) of goods and services:

$$GDP \equiv Y \equiv C + I + G + X - M. \tag{3A.1}$$

Private savings (S) is defined as the amount left from national income after consumption and taxes (T) are paid:

$$S \equiv Y - C - T, \quad or \tag{3A.2}$$

$$S \equiv C + I + G + X - M - C - T. \tag{3A.3}$$

Noting that the BCA $\equiv X - M$, equation (3A.3) can be rearranged as:

$$(S - I) + (T - G) \equiv X - M \equiv BCA. \tag{3A.4}$$

Equation (3A.4) shows that there is an intimate relationship between a country's BCA and how the country finances its domestic investment and pays for government expenditures. In equation (3A.4), $(S - I)$ is the difference between a country's savings and investment. If $(S - I)$ is negative, it implies that a country's domestic savings is insufficient to finance domestic investment. Similarly, $(T - G)$ is the difference between tax revenue and government expenditures. If $(T - G)$ is negative, it implies that tax revenue is insufficient to cover government spending and a government budget deficit exists. This deficit must be financed by the government issuing debt securities.

Equation (3A.4) also shows that when a country imports more than it exports, its BCA will be negative because through trade foreigners obtain a larger claim to domestic assets than the claim the country's citizens obtain to foreign assets. Consequently, when BCA is negative, it implies that government budget deficits and/or part of domestic investment are being financed with foreign-controlled capital. In order for a country to reduce a BCA deficit, one of the following must occur:

1. For a given level of S and I, the government budget deficit $(T - G)$ must be reduced.

2. For a given level of I and $(T - G)$, S must be increased.

3. For a given level S and $(T - G)$, I must fall.

4 Corporate Governance around the World

IN CHAPTER 1, we argue that the key goal of financial management should be shareholder wealth maximization. In reality, however, there is no guarantee that managers would run the company to maximize the welfare of shareholders. In fact, the recent spate of corporate scandals and failures, including Enron, WorldCom, and Global Crossing in the United States, Daewoo Group (a major *chaebol*) in Korea, Parmalat in Italy, and HIH (a major insurance group) in Australia, has raised serious questions about the way public corporations are governed around the world. When "self-interested" managers take control of the company, they sometimes engage in actions that are profoundly detrimental to the interests of shareholders and other stakeholders. For example, such managers may give themselves excessive salaries and indulgent perquisites, squander resources for corporate empire building, divert the company's cash and assets for private benefits, engage in cronyism, and steal business opportunities from the company. A recent report in the *Harvard Business Review* (January 2003) describes how American executives "treat their companies like ATMs, awarding themselves millions of dollars in corporate perks." In many less developed and transitional countries, corporate governance mechanisms are either very weak or virtually nonexistent. In Russia, for example, a weak corporate governance system allows managers to divert assets from newly privatized companies on a large scale.

    When managerial self-dealings are excessive and left unchecked, they can have serious negative effects on corporate values and the proper functions of capital markets. In fact, there is a growing consensus around the world that it is vitally important to strengthen **corporate governance** to protect **shareholder rights,** curb managerial excesses, and restore confidence in capital markets. *Corporate governance* can be defined as *the economic, legal, and institutional framework in which corporate control and cash flow rights are distributed among shareholders, managers, and other stakeholders of the company.* Other stakeholders may include workers, creditors, banks, institutional investors, and even the government. As we will

股东权利（**share-
holder rights**）

公司治理（**corporate
governance**）是公司的
控制权和现金流在公司
股东、经理人员和公司
的其他利益相关者之间进

行分配所依赖的经济、
法律和制度方面的框架。

see later, corporate governance structure varies a great deal across countries, reflecting divergent cultural, economic, political, and legal environments. It is thus essential for international investors and multinational corporations to have a solid understanding of the corporate governance environments around the world. An example of governance risk is provided by Citigroup's dealings with Parmalat. According to BBC News (March 18, 2005), William Mills of Citigroup said, "Citigroup is a victim of Parmalat's fraud and lost more than 500 million euros as a result. . . . If Citigroup had known the truth, it would not have done business with Parmalat."

Governance of the Public Corporation: Key Issues

公众公司是经济发
展所带来的一种主要的
组织创新，这种公司为
众多股东共同拥有并受
有限责任所保护。

The **public corporation,** which is jointly owned by a multitude of shareholders protected with limited liability, is a major organizational innovation of vast economic consequences. The majority of global corporations that drive economic growth and innovations worldwide, including Microsoft, General Electric (GE), IBM, Toyota, Sony, British Petroleum (BP), Nokia, and DaimlerChrysler, are chartered as public corporations rather than as private companies. The genius of public corporations stems from their capacity to allow efficient sharing or spreading of risk among many investors, who can buy and sell their ownership shares on liquid stock exchanges and let professional managers run the company on behalf of shareholders. This efficient risk-sharing mechanism enables public corporations to raise large amounts of capital at relatively low costs and undertake many investment projects that individual entrepreneurs or private investors might eschew because of the costs and/or risks. Public corporations have played a pivotal role in spreading economic growth and capitalism worldwide for the last few centuries.

公众公司的一个致
命的弱点就是公司经理
人与股东之间存在着利
益冲突。

However, the public corporation has a key weakness-namely, the conflicts of interest between managers and shareholders. The separation of the company's ownership and control, which is especially prevalent in such countries as the United States and the United Kingdom, where corporate ownership is highly diffused, gives rise to possible conflicts between shareholders and managers. In principle, shareholders elect the board of directors of the company, which in turn hires managers to run the company for the interests of shareholders. In the United States, managers are legally bound by the "duty of loyalty" to shareholders. Managers are thus supposed to be agents working for their principals, that is, shareholders, who are the real owners of the company. In a public company with diffused ownership, the board of directors is entrusted with the vital tasks of monitoring the management and safeguarding the interests of shareholders.

In reality, however, management-friendly insiders often dominate the board of directors, with relatively few outside directors who can independently monitor the management. In the case of Enron and similarly dysfunctional companies, the boards of directors grossly failed to safeguard shareholder interests. Furthermore, with diffused ownership, few shareholders have strong enough incentive to incur the costs of monitoring management themselves when the benefits from such monitoring accrue to all shareholders alike. The benefits are shared, but not the costs. When company ownership is highly diffused, this "free-rider" problem discourages shareholder activism. As a result, the interests of managers and shareholders are often allowed to diverge. With an ineffective and unmotivated board of directors, shareholders are basically left without effective recourse to control managerial self-dealings. Recognition of this key weakness of the public corporation can be traced at least as far back as to Adam Smith's *Wealth of Nations* (1776), which stated:

> The directors of such joint-stocks companies, however, being the managers rather of other people's money than of their own, it cannot well be expected that they should watch over it with the same anxious vigilance with which the partners of a private copartnery frequently

watch over their own. . . . Negligence and profusion, therefore, must always prevail, more or less, in the management of the affairs of such a company.

Two hundred years later, Jensen and Meckling (1976) provided a formal analysis of the "agency problem" of the public corporation in their celebrated paper "Theory of the Firm: Managerial Behavior, Agency Costs, and Ownership Structure." The Jensen-Meckling agency theory drew attention to this vitally important corporate finance problem.

It is suggested, however, that outside the United States and the United Kingdom, diffused ownership of the company is more the exception than the rule. In Italy, for instance, the three largest shareholders control, on average, about 60 percent of the shares of a public company. The average comparable ownership by the three largest shareholders is 54 percent in China-Hong Kong SAR, 64 percent in Mexico, 48 percent in Germany, 40 percent in India, and 51 percent in Israel.[1] These large shareholders (often including founding families of the company) effectively control managers and may run the company for their own interests, expropriating outside shareholders in one way or another. In many countries with concentrated corporate ownership, conflicts of interest are greater between large controlling shareholders and small outside shareholders than between managers and shareholders.

In a series of influential studies, La Porta, Lopez-de-Silanes, Shleifer, and Vishny (LLSV, hereafter) document sharp differences among countries with regard to (1) corporate ownership structure, (2) depth and breadth of capital markets, (3) access of firms to external financing, and (4) dividend policies. LLSV argue that these differences among countries can be explained largely by how well investors are protected by law from expropriation by the managers and controlling shareholders of firms. LLSV also argue that the degree of legal protection of investors significantly depends on the "legal origin" of countries. Specifically, English common law countries, such as Canada, the United States, and the U.K., provide the strongest protection for investors, whereas French civil law countries, such as Belgium, Italy, and Mexico, provide the weakest. We will revisit the issue of law and corporate governance later in the chapter.

Shareholders in different countries may indeed face divergent corporate governance systems. However, the central problem in corporate governance remains the same everywhere: *how to best protect outside investors from expropriation by the controlling insiders so that the former can receive fair returns on their investments.* How to deal with this problem has enormous practical implications for shareholder welfare, corporate allocation of resources, corporate financing and valuation, development of capital markets, and economic growth. In the rest of this chapter, we will discuss the following issues in detail:[2]

- Agency problem
- Remedies for the agency problem
- Law and corporate governance
- Consequences of law
- Corporate governance reform

在公司所有权集中的许多国家里，控股大股东与外部小股东之间的利益冲突会大于经理人员和股东之间的利益冲突。

www.oecd.org/maintopic/corporategovernance

This site provides an overview of corporate governance in OECD countries.

不同国家的股东的确面临着不同的公司治理制度。

The Agency Problem

完备合同

Suppose that the manager (or entrepreneur) and the investors sign a contract that specifies how the manager will use the funds and also how the investment returns will be divided between the manager and the investors. If the two sides can write a **complete contract**

---

[1]Source: R. La Porta, F. Lopez-de-Silanes, A. Shleifer, and R. Vishny, "Law and Finance," *Journal of Political Economy* 106 (1998), pp. 1113–55.

[2]Our discussion here draws on the contributions of Jensen and Meckling (1976), Jensen (1989), La Porta, Lopez-de-Silanes, Shleifer, and Vishny (1997–2002), and Denis and McConnell (2002).

代理问题

剩余控制权

按照以上所阐述的公司契约理论，代理问题事实上就产生于外部投资者难以确保获得公平投资收益。

管理防御效应

自由现金流是指满足了所有营利性投资项目所需资金后的企业的内生资金。

that specifies exactly what the manager will do under each of all possible future contingencies, there will be no room for any conflicts of interest or managerial discretion. Thus, under a complete contract, there will be no **agency problem.** However, it is practically impossible to foresee all future contingencies and write a complete contract. This means that the manager and the investors will have to allocate the rights (control) to make decisions under those contingencies that are not specifically covered by the contract. Because the outside investors may be neither qualified nor interested in making business decisions, the manager often ends up acquiring most of this **residual control right.** The investors supply funds to the company but are not involved in the company's daily decision making. As a result, many public companies come to have "strong managers and weak shareholders."

Having captured residual control rights, the manager can exercise substantial discretion over the disposition and allocation of investors' capital. Under this situation, the investors are no longer assured of receiving fair returns on their funds. In the contractual view of the firm described above, the agency problem arises from the difficulty that outside investors face in assuring that they actually receive fair returns on their capital.[3]

With the control rights, the manager may allow himself or herself to consume exorbitant perquisites. For example, Steve Jobs, the CEO of Apple Computer, reportedly has a $90 million company jet at his disposal.[4] Sometimes, the manager simply steals investors' funds. Alternatively, the manager may use a more sophisticated scheme, setting up an independent company that he owns and diverting to it the main company's cash and assets through *transfer pricing*. For example, the manager can sell the main company's output to the company he owns at below market prices, or buy the output of the company he owns at above market prices. Some Russian oil companies are known to sell oil to manager-owned trading companies at below market prices and not always bother to collect the bills.[5]

Self-interested managers may also waste funds by undertaking unprofitable projects that benefit themselves but not investors. For example, managers may misallocate funds to take over other companies and overpay for the targets if it serves their private interests. Needless to say, this type of investment will destroy shareholder value. What is more, the same managers may adopt antitakeover measures for their own company in order to ensure their personal job security and perpetuate private benefits. In the same vein, managers may resist any attempts to be replaced even if shareholders' interests will be better served by their dismissal. These **managerial entrenchment** efforts are clear signs of the agency problem.

As pointed out by Jensen (1989), the agency problem tends to be more serious in companies with "free cash flows." **Free cash flows** represent a firm's internally generated funds in excess of the amount needed to undertake all profitable investment projects, that is, those with positive net present values (NPVs). Free cash flows tend to be high in mature industries with low future growth prospects, such as the steel, chemical, tobacco, paper, and textile industries. It is the *fiduciary duty* of managers to return free cash flows to shareholders as dividends. However, managers in these cash-rich and mature industries will be most tempted to waste cash flows to undertake unprofitable projects, destroying shareholders' wealth but possibly benefiting themselves.

There are a few important incentives for managers to retain cash flows. First, cash reserves provide corporate managers with a measure of independence from the capital markets, insulating them from external scrutiny and discipline. This will make life easier for managers. Second, growing the size of the company via retention of cash tends to have the effect of raising managerial compensation. As is well known,

---

[3]The contractual view of the firm was developed by Coarse (1937) and Jensen and Meckling (1976).
[4]Source: *Financial Times,* November 27, 2002, p. 15.
[5]Source: A. Shleifer and R. Vishny, "A Survey of Corporate Governance," *Journal of Finance* (1997).

executive compensation depends as much on the size of the company as on its profitability, if not more. Third, senior executives can boost their social and political power and prestige by increasing the size of their company. Executives presiding over large companies are likely to enjoy greater social prominence and visibility than those running small companies. Also, the company's size itself can be a way of satisfying the executive ego.

In the face of strong managerial incentives for retaining cash, few effective mechanisms exist that can compel the managers to disgorge cash flows to shareholders. Jensen cites a revealing example of this widespread problem (1989, p. 66):

> A vivid example is the senior management of Ford Motor Company, which sits on nearly $15 billion in cash and marketable securities in an industry with excess capacity. Ford's management has been deliberating about acquiring financial service companies, aerospace companies, or making some other multibillion-dollar diversification move-rather than deliberating about effectively distributing Ford's excess cash to its owners so they can decide how to reinvest it.

He also points out that in the 1980s, many Japanese public companies retained enormous amounts of free cash flow, far exceeding what they needed to finance profitable internal projects. For example, Toyota Motor Company, with a cash hoard of more than $10 billion, was known as the "Toyota Bank." Lacking effective internal control and external monitoring mechanisms, these companies went on an overinvestment binge in the 1980s, engaging in unprofitable acquisitions and diversification moves. This wasteful corporate spending is, at least in part, responsible for the economic slump that Japan has experienced since the early 1990s.

代理问题的核心是经理人和外部投资者就如何处理自由现金流所存在的利益冲突。

The preceding examples show that the heart of the agency problem is the conflicts of interest between managers and the outside investors over the disposition of free cash flows. However, in high-growth industries, such as biotechnology, financial services, and pharmaceuticals, where companies' internally generated funds fall short of profitable investment opportunities, managers are less likely to waste funds in unprofitable projects. After all, managers in these industries need to have a "good reputation," as they must repeatedly come back to capital markets for funding. Once the managers of a company are known for wasting funds for private benefits, external funding for the company may dry up quickly. The managers in these industries thus have an incentive to serve the interests of outside investors and build a reputation so that they can raise the funds needed for undertaking their "good" investment projects.

Remedies for the Agency Problem

显然，对于股东而言，控制代理问题至关重要，否则，他们就会无法得到本该属于他们的钱。

Obviously, it is a matter of vital importance for shareholders to control the agency problem; otherwise, they may not be able to get their money back. It is also important for society as a whole to solve the agency problem, since the agency problem leads to waste of scarce resources, hampers capital market functions, and retards economic growth. Several governance mechanisms exist to alleviate or remedy the agency problem:

1. Board of directors
2. Incentive contracts
3. Concentrated ownership
4. Accounting transparency
5. Debt
6. Overseas stock listings
7. Market for corporate control

In the following sections, we discuss the corporate governance role of each of these mechanisms.

Board of Directors

In the United States, shareholders have the right to elect the board of directors, which is legally charged with representing the interests of shareholders. If the board of directors remains independent of management, it can serve as an effective mechanism for curbing the agency problem. For example, studies show that the appointment of outside directors is associated with a higher turnover rate of CEOs following poor firm performances, thus curbing managerial entrenchment. In the same vein, in a study of corporate governance in the United Kingdom, Dahya, McConnell, and Travlos (2002) report that the board of directors is more likely to appoint an outside CEO after an increase in outsiders' representation on the board. But due to the diffused ownership structure of the public company, management often gets to choose board members who are likely to be friendly to management. As can be seen from the International Finance in Practice box "When Boards Are All in the Family," the insider-dominated board becomes a poor governance mechanism.

不同国家在公司董事会的结构和法律责任方面存有很大的差异。

The structure and legal charge of corporate boards vary greatly across countries. In Germany, for instance, the corporate board is not legally charged with representing the interests of shareholders. Rather, it is charged with looking after the interests of stakeholders (e.g., workers, creditors, etc.) in general, not just shareholders. In Germany, there are two-tier boards consisting of supervisory and management boards. Based on the German *codetermination* system, the law requires that workers be represented on the supervisory board. Likewise, some U.S. companies have labor union representatives on their boards, although it is not legally mandated. In the United Kingdom, the majority of public companies voluntarily abide by the *Code of Best Practice* on corporate governance recommended by the *Cadbury Committee*. The code recommends that there should be at least three outside directors and that the board chairman and the CEO should be different individuals. Apart from outside directors, separation of the chairman and CEO positions can further enhance the independence of the board of directors. In Japan, most corporate boards are insider-dominated and are primarily concerned with the welfare of the *keiretsu* to which the company belongs.

Incentive Contracts

如前所述，因为经理人取得了公司的剩余控制权，所以也就掌握了公司的经营大权。

As previously discussed, managers capture residual control rights and thus have enormous discretion over how to run the company. But they own relatively little of the equity of the company they manage. To the extent that managers do not own equity shares, they do not have cash flow rights. Although managers run the company at their own discretion, they may not significantly benefit from the profit generated from their efforts and expertise. Jensen and Murphy (1990) show that the pay of American executives changes only by about $3 per every $1,000 change of shareholder wealth; executive pay is nearly insensitive to changes in shareholder wealth. This situation implies that managers may not be very interested in the maximization of shareholder wealth. This "wedge" between managerial control rights and cash flow rights may exacerbate the agency problem. *When professional managers have small equity positions of their own in a company with diffused ownership, they have both power and a motive to engage in self-dealings.*

为了使经理人与投资者的利益更好地一致起来，许多公司对经理人提供**激励合约**，如股票和股票期权。

Aware of this situation, many companies provide managers with **incentive contracts,** such as stocks and stock options, in order to reduce this wedge and better align the interests of managers with those of investors. With the grant of stocks or stock options, managers can be given an incentive to run the company in such a way that enhances shareholder wealth as well as their own. Against this backdrop, incentive contracts for senior executives have become common among public companies in the United States. As we have seen lately, however, senior executives can abuse

When Boards Are All in the Family

There is much talk these days about the need to increase the independence of directors on company boards. That has been obvious for a long time. Indeed, it is fairly easy to spot those boards for which chief executives have handpicked friends or business associates who are not truly independent.

This characteristic is a reliable indicator of whether a chief executive acts as a baronial owner of the company, or as one chosen by—and responsible to—the stakeholders. In fact, one can argue that making boards more independent is the single most important thing we can do in the current reform climate to restore public confidence.

By now it is well documented that boards dominated by their chief executives are prone to trouble. W.R. Grace is a good example. Peter Grace, the company's chief executive, was too powerful. He controlled his board as if the enterprise were his personal fief.

Even though the business was foundering in the late 1990s, the board allowed Mr. Grace to negotiate a retirement package that included generous perks—including use of a corporate jet and a company-owned apartment. The directors also sold a subsidiary to Mr. Grace's son and bestowed other benefits that they neglected to disclose to shareholders. This non-disclosure was against the law and resulted in an SEC-type enforcement action.

Another example is Apple, whose board I was once asked, briefly, to consider joining. Apart from Steve Jobs, the CEO, the board currently has only four members while Mr. Jobs searches for a replacement for his friend Larry Ellison of Oracle, who resigned from Apple's board in September.

That is all to the good, as Mr. Ellison attended fewer than half of Apple's board meetings anyway. Bill Campbell, another director, is nominally independent but may not be truly so. Mr. Campbell, who chairs the company's audit committee, qualifies as an independent director, because he is not currently connected with Apple. But he formerly worked at Apple and sold his software company, Claris, to Apple.

Another member of Apple's audit committee, Jerome York, is the chief executive of MicroWarehouse, whose Mac Warehouse catalogue was responsible for nearly $150m of Apple's $5.4bn sales in 2001. As a former chief financial officer for International Business Machines and

Chrysler Mr. York is well qualified but his presence on the all-important audit committee had to be treated as an exceptional circumstance by the Nasdaq market.

Such choices, to my mind, can yield bad judgment. In January 2000, for example, Apple's board awarded Mr. Jobs 20m shares, worth $550m if the share price increased 5 percent over 10 years. They also authorised the company to buy a $90m Gulfstream jet for him. The share price sank, putting Mr. Jobs's options under water. So the board granted him 7.5m more shares. At the time of the grant, Apple shares were underperforming other stocks in their industry sub-class by 28 percent.

There is plenty of evidence that public scrutiny and a spotlight can help improve corporate governance. The California Public Employees' Retirement System began pressing underperforming companies to change the composition of their boards in 1993. Calpers drew up a list of corporate governance standards: make independent directors a majority on boards; let these directors meet the chief executive separately three times a year; make boards perform an annual assessment of their own performance, and so on.

A study by Wilshire Associates looked at the performance of 62 companies named by Calpers as poor performers. These companies' stocks underperformed the Standard & Poor's 500 index by an average of 89 percent in the five years before they were singled out. After the spotlight was shone on them, they outperformed the index by an average of 23 percent over five years.

This does not, of course, mean all companies will fail without a model board of directors. At Warren Buffett's Berkshire Hathaway, the seven directors include Mr. Buffet's wife, his son, his business partner Charlie Munger, a partner at his company's law firm and a co-investor with Berkshire Hathaway in other companies.

Mr. Buffett makes a persuasive argument that the best directors may well be those who have the greatest personal economic stake in the company. But the correlation of seduced boards with underperforming or ethically flawed enterprises suggests that independent overseers are much less likely to give into temptation or corruption.

Source: Arthur Levitt, Financial Times, November 27, 2002. p. 15. Reprinted with permission.

董事会有必要成立一个独立的薪酬委员会来仔细设计与经理人的激励合同，并努力控制经理人的行为。

incentive contracts by artificially manipulating accounting numbers, sometimes with the connivance of auditors (for example, Arthur Andersen's involvements with the Enron debacle), or by altering investment policies so that they can reap enormous personal benefits. It is thus important for the board of directors to set up an independent compensation committee that can carefully design incentive contracts for executives and diligently monitor their actions.

Concentrated Ownership

减轻代理问题影响的一种有效办法就是所有权集中。

An effective way to alleviate the agency problem is to concentrate shareholdings. If one or a few large investors own significant portions of the company, they will have a strong incentive to monitor management. For example, if an investor owns 51 percent of the company, he or she can definitely control the management (he can easily hire or fire managers) and will make sure that shareholders' rights are respected in the conduct of the company's affairs. With **concentrated ownership** and high stakes, the free-rider problem afflicting small, atomistic shareholders dissipates.

In the United States and the United Kingdom, concentrated ownership of a public company is relatively rare. Elsewhere in the world, however, concentrated ownership is the norm. In Germany, for example, commercial banks, insurance companies, other companies, and families often own significant blocks of company stock. Similarly, extensive cross-holdings of equities among *keiretsu* member companies and main banks are commonplace in Japan. Also in France, cross-holdings and "core" investors are common. In Asia and Latin America, many companies are controlled by founders or their family members. In China, the government is often the controlling shareholder for public companies. Previous studies indicate that concentrated ownership has a positive effect on a company's performance and value. For example, Kang and Shivdasani (1995) report such positive effects for Japan, and Gorton and Schmid (2000) for Germany. This suggests that large shareholders indeed play a significant governance role.

过去的研究表明，管理层所拥有的股权量与公司价值和绩效之间存在一种非线性的关系。

Of particular interest here is the effect of managerial equity holdings. Previous studies suggest that there can be a nonlinear relationship between managerial ownership share and firm value and performance. Specifically, as the managerial ownership share increases, firm value may initially increase, since the interests of managers and outside investors become better aligned (thus reducing agency costs). But if the managerial ownership share exceeds a certain point, firm value may actually start to decline as managers become more entrenched. With larger shareholdings, for example, managers may be able to more effectively resist takeover bids and extract larger private benefits at the expense of outside investors. If the managerial ownership share continues to rise, however, the alignment effect may become dominant again. When managers are large shareholders, they do not want to rob themselves. To summarize, there can be an "interim range" of managerial ownership share over which the entrenchment effect is dominant.

This situation is illustrated in Exhibit 4.1, depicting a possible relationship between managerial ownership share and firm value. According to Morck, Shleifer, and Vishny

EXHIBIT 4.1

The Alignment versus Entrenchment Effects of Managerial Ownership

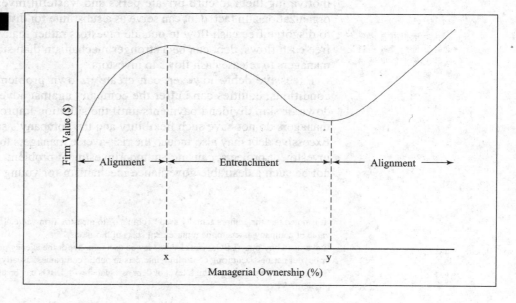

(1988), who studied the relationship for *Fortune* 500 U.S. companies, the first turning point (*x*) is reached at about 5 percent and the second (*y*) at about 25 percent. This means that the "entrenchment effect" is roughly dominant over the range of managerial ownership between 5 percent and 25 percent, whereas the "alignment effect" is dominant for the ownership shares less than 5 percent and exceeding 25 percent.[6] The relationship between managerial ownership and firm value is likely to vary across countries. For instance, Short and Keasey (1999) indicate that the inflection point (*x*) is reached at 12 percent in the United Kingdom, a much higher level of managerial ownership than in the United States. They attribute this difference to more effective monitoring by U.K. institutional investors and the lesser ability of U.K. managers to resist takeover.

Accounting Transparency

一般地，更为透明的会计信息披露能减少公司内部人与公众间的信息不对称，有助于减少内部交易。

Considering that major corporate scandals, such as Enron and Parmalat, are associated with massive accounting frauds, strengthening accounting standards can be an effective way of alleviating the agency problem. Self-interested managers or corporate insiders can have an incentive to "cook the books" (for example, inflating earnings and hiding debts) to extract private benefits from the company. The managers need a veil of opaque accounting numbers to pursue their own interests at the expense of shareholders. Therefore, if companies are required to release more accurate accounting information in a timely fashion, managers may be less tempted to take actions that are detrimental to the interests of shareholders. Basically, a greater accounting transparency will reduce the information asymmetry between corporate insiders and the public and discourage managerial self-dealings.

To achieve a greater transparency, however, it is important for (1) countries to reform the accounting rules and (2) companies to have an active and qualified audit committee. As we will discuss later in this chapter, the Sarbanes-Oxley Act of 2002 aims, among other things, to promote a greater accounting transparency in the United States.

Debt

对于拥有自由现金流的公司，债务机制比股票机制更能促进讲诚信的经理人向投资者发放现金。

Although managers have discretion over how much of a dividend to pay to shareholders, debt does not allow such managerial discretion. If managers fail to pay interest and principal to creditors, the company can be forced into bankruptcy and its managers may lose their jobs. Borrowing and the subsequent obligation to make interest payments on time can have a major disciplinary effect on managers, motivating them to curb private perks and wasteful investments and trim bloated organizations. In fact, debt can serve as a substitute for dividends by forcing managers to disgorge free cash flow to outside investors rather than wasting it. For firms with free cash flows, debt can be a stronger mechanism than stocks for credibly bonding managers to release cash flows to investors.[7]

Excessive debt, however, can create its own problem. In turbulent economic conditions, equities can buffer the company against adversity. Managers can pare down or skip dividend payments until the situation improves. With debt, however, managers do not have such flexibility and the company's survival can be threatened. Excessive debt may also induce the risk-averse managers to forgo profitable but risky investment projects, causing an underinvestment problem. For this reason, debt may not be such a desirable governance mechanism for young companies with few cash

---

[6]It is noted that the authors actually used "Tobin's *q*" to measure firm value. Tobin's *q* is the ratio of the market value of company assets to the replacement costs of the assets.

[7]Leveraged buy-outs (LBOs) can also be viewed as a remedy for the agency problem. LBOs involve managers or buyout partners acquiring controlling interests in public companies, usually financed by heavy borrowing. Concentrated ownership and high level of debt associated with LBOs can be effective in solving the agency problem.

reserves or tangible assets. In addition, companies can misuse debt to finance corporate empire building. Daewoo, a Korean *chaebol,* borrowed excessively to finance global expansion until it went into bankruptcy; its debt-to-equity ratio reached 600 percent before bankruptcy.

Overseas Stock Listings

一般来说，对于来自公司治理机制薄弱国家的公司来说，将股票在美国上市会获得更多好处。

Companies domiciled in countries with weak investor protection, such as Italy, Korea, and Russia, can bond themselves credibly to better investor protection by listing their stocks in countries with strong investor protection, such as the United States and the United Kingdom. In other words, foreign firms with weak governance mechanisms can opt to outsource a superior corporate governance regime available in the United States via cross-listings. Suppose that Benetton, an Italian clothier, announces its decision to list its stock on the New York Stock Exchange (NYSE).[8] Since the level of shareholder protection afforded by the U.S. Securities Exchange Commission (SEC) and the NYSE is much higher than that provided in Italy, the action will be interpreted as signaling the company's commitment to shareholder rights. Then, investors both in Italy and abroad will be more willing to provide capital to the company and value the company shares more. Generally speaking, the beneficial effects from U.S. listings will be greater for firms from countries with weaker governance mechanisms.

Studies confirm the effects of cross-border listings. Specifically, Doidge, Karolyi, and Stulz (2002) report that foreign firms listed in the United States are valued more than those from the same countries that are not listed in the United States. They argue that firms listed in the United States can take better advantage of growth opportunities and that controlling shareholders cannot extract as many private benefits. It is pointed out, however, that foreign firms in mature industries with limited growth opportunities are not very likely to seek U.S. listings, even though these firms face more serious agency problems than firms with growth opportunities that are more likely to seek U.S. listings. In other words, firms with more serious problems are less likely to seek the remedies.

Market for Corporate Control

公司控制权市场能对经理人产生约束效果并能提高公司的效率。

Suppose a company continually performs poorly and all of its internal governance mechanisms fail to correct the problem. This situation may prompt an outsider (another company or investor) to mount a takeover bid. In a hostile takeover attempt, the bidder typically makes a tender offer to the target shareholders at a price substantially exceeding the prevailing share price. The target shareholders thus have an opportunity to sell their shares at a substantial premium. If the bid is successful, the bidder will acquire the control rights of the target and restructure the company. Following a successful takeover, the bidder often replaces the management team, divests some assets or divisions, and trims employment in an effort to enhance efficiency. If these efforts are successful, the combined market value of the acquirer and target companies will become higher than the sum of stand-alone values of the two companies, reflecting the synergies created. The market for corporate control, if it exists, can have a disciplinary effect on managers and enhance company efficiency.

In the United States and the United Kingdom, hostile takeovers can serve as a drastic governance mechanism of the last resort. Under the potential threat of takeover, managers cannot take their control of the company for granted. In many other countries, however, hostile takeovers are quite rare. This is so partly because of concentrated ownership in these countries and partly because of cultural values and political environments disapproving hostile corporate takeovers. But even in these countries, the incidence of corporate takeovers has been gradually increasing. This can be due, in part, to the spreading of equity culture and the opening and deregulation of capital markets. In Germany, for instance, takeovers are carried out

---

[8]Benetton is actually listed on the New York Stock Exchange.

through transfer of block holdings. In Japan, as in Germany, interfirm cross-holdings of equities are loosening, creating capital market conditions that are more conducive to takeover activities. To the extent that companies with poor investment opportunities and excess cash initiate takeovers, it is a symptom, rather than a cure, of the agency problem.

Law and Corporate Governance

一旦外部投资者对公司进行了投资，他们也就可享有受法律保护的权利。

When outside investors entrust funds to the company, they receive certain rights that are legally protected. Among these are the rights to elect the board of directors, receive dividends on a pro-rata basis, participate in shareholders' meetings, and sue the company for expropriation. These rights empower investors to extract from management fair returns on their funds. However, the content of law protecting investors' rights and the quality of law enforcement vary a great deal across countries. According to the studies of La Porta, Lopez-de-Silanes, Shleifer, and Vishny (LLSV), many of the observed differences in international corporate governance systems arise from the differences in how well outside investors are protected by law from expropriation by managers and other corporate insiders. LLSV argue that the legal protection of investor rights systematically varies, depending on the historical origins of national legal systems.

法律渊源

Legal scholars show that the commercial legal systems (for example, company, security, bankruptcy, and contract laws) of most countries derive from relatively few **legal origins:**

- English common law
- French civil law
- German civil law
- Scandinavian civil law

The French and German civil laws derived from the Roman law, whereas the Scandinavian countries developed their own civil law tradition that is less derivative of Roman law. The civil law tradition, which is the most influential and widely spread, is based on the comprehensive *codification of legal rules*. In contrast, English common law is formed by the *discrete rulings* of independent judges on specific disputes and *judicial precedent*.

这些不同的法律系统，尤其是**英国普通法体系和法国大陆法体系**，通过占领地、殖民统治、自动采纳和细致模仿而遍及全球。

These distinct legal systems, especially **English common law** and **French civil law,** spread around the world through conquest, colonization, voluntary adoption, and subtle imitation. The United Kingdom and its former colonies, including Australia, Canada, India, Malaysia, Singapore, South Africa, New Zealand, and the United States, have the English common law system. France and the parts of Europe conquered by Napoleon, such as Belgium, the Netherlands, Italy, Portugal, and Spain, ended up with the French civil law tradition. Further, many former overseas colonies of France, the Netherlands, Portugal, and Spain, such as Algeria, Argentina, Brazil, Chile, Indonesia, Mexico, and the Philippines, also ended up with the French civil law system. The German civil law family comprises Germany and the Germanic countries of Europe, such as Austria and Switzerland, and a few East Asian countries such as Japan, Korea, The Scandinavian civil law family includes four Nordic countries: Denmark, Finland, Norway, and Sweden. Thus, in most countries, the national legal system did not indigenously develop but rather was transplanted from one of several legal origins. Although national legal systems have evolved and adapted to local conditions, it is still possible to classify them into a few distinct families. Such a classification is provided in Exhibit 4.2. The exhibit also provides the indexes for shareholder rights and rule of law for each country as computed by LLSV (1998).

EXHIBIT 4.2

Classification of Countries by Legal Origins

Legal Origin	Region or Country	Shareholder Rights Index	Rule of Law Index
1. English common law	Australia	4	10.00
	Canada	5	10.00
	Hong Kong SAR	5	8.22
	India	5	4.17
	Ireland	4	7.80
	Israel	3	4.82
	Kenya	3	5.42
	Malaysia	4	6.78
	New Zealand	4	10.00
	Nigeria	3	2.73
	Pakistan	5	3.03
	Singapore	4	8.57
	South Africa	5	4.42
	Sri Lanka	3	1.90
	Thailand	2	6.25
	United Kingdom	5	8.57
	United States	5	10.00
	Zimbabwe	3	3.68
	English-origin average	**4.00**	**6.46**
2. French civil law	Argentina	4	5.35
	Belgium	0	10.00
	Brazil	3	6.32
	Chile	5	7.02
	Colombia	3	2.08
	Ecuador	2	6.67
	Egypt	2	4.17
	France	3	8.98
	Greece	2	6.18
	Indonesia	2	3.98
	Italy	1	8.33
	Jordan	1	4.35
	Mexico	1	5.35
	Netherlands	2	10.00
	Peru	3	2.50
	Philippines	3	2.73
	Portugal	3	8.68
	Spain	4	7.80
	Turkey	2	5.18
	Uruguay	2	5.00
	Venezuela	1	6.37
	French-origin average	**2.33**	**6.05**
3. German civil law	Austria	2	10.00
	Germany	1	9.23
	Japan	4	8.98
	South Korea	2	5.35
	Switzerland	2	10.00
	China's Taiwan	3	8.52
	German-origin average	**2.33**	**8.68**
4. Scandinavian civil law	Denmark	2	10.00
	Finland	3	10.00
	Norway	4	10.00
	Sweden	3	10.00
	Scandinavian-origin average	**3.00**	**10.00**

Note: Shareholder rights index scales from 0 (lowest) to 6 (highest). Rule of law index scales from 0 (lowest) to 10 (highest).

Source: Rafael La Porta, Florencio Lopez-de-Silanes, Andrei Shleifer, Robert W. Vishny, "Law and Finance," *Journal of Political Economy* 106 (1998), pp. 1113–55.

Exhibit 4.2 shows that the average shareholder rights index is 4.00 for English common law countries, 2.33 for both French and German civil law countries, and 3.00 for Scandinavian civil law countries. Thus, English common law countries tend to offer the strongest protection for investors, French and German civil law countries offer the weakest, and Scandinavian civil law countries fall in the middle. The quality of law enforcement, as measured by the rule of law index, is the highest in Scandinavian and German civil law countries, followed by English common law countries; it is lowest in French civil law countries.

显然，在英国普通法和法国大陆法这两种影响最大的法律体系之间，对投资者的法律保护程度有着显著的差异。

Clearly, there is a marked difference in the legal protection of investors between the two most influential legal systems, namely, English common law and French civil law. A logical question is: Why is the English common law system more protective of investors than the French civil law system? According to the prevailing view, the state historically has played a more active role in regulating economic activities and has been less protective of property rights in civil law countries than in common law countries. In England, control of the court passed from the crown to Parliament and property owners in the seventeenth century. English common law thus became more protective of property owners, and this protection was extended to investors over time. This legal tradition in England allows the court to exercise its discretionary judgment or "smell test" over which managerial self-dealings are *unfair* to investors. In France as well as in Germany, parliamentary power was weak and commercial laws were codified by the state, with the role of the court confined to simply determining whether the codified rules were violated or not. Since managers can be creative enough to expropriate investors without obviously violating the codified rules, investors receive low protection in civil law countries.

在最近的研究中，Glaesser和Shleifer提出一项有意义的解释：法国和英国的法律起源是以中世纪盛行的不同政治体制为基础的。

In a recent study, Glaesser and Shleifer (2002) offer an intriguing explanation of the English and French legal origins based on the divergent political situations prevailing in the Middle Ages. In France, local feudal lords were powerful and there were incessant wars. Under this turbulent situation, there was a need for the protection of adjudicators from local powers, which can only be provided by the king. France came to adopt a royal judge-inquisitor model based on the *Justinian code* of the Roman Empire in the thirteenth century. According to this model, judges appointed by the king collect evidence, prepare written records, and determine the outcome of the case. Understandably, royal judges were mindful of the preferences of the king. The French legal tradition was formalized by the *Code Napoleon*. Napoleon extensively codified legal rules, *bright line rules* in legal terms, and required state-appointed judges to merely apply these rules. In England, in contrast, local lords were less powerful and war was less frequent. In a more peaceful England, which partly reflects the country's geographical isolation, local magnates were mainly afraid of royal power and preferred adjudication by a local jury that was not beholden to the preferences of the crown and was more knowledgeable about local facts and preferences. Initially, the jury consisted of 12 armed knights who were less likely to be intimidated by local bullies or special pressure groups. After the *Magna Carta* of 1215, local magnates basically paid the crown for the privilege of local, independent adjudication and other rights. The divergent legal developments in England and France came to have lasting effects on the legal systems of many countries.

Consequences of Law

Protection of investors' righs not only has interesting legal origins, but the concept is shown to have major economic consequences on the pattern of corporate ownership and valuation, the development of capital markets, economic growth, and others. To illustrate, let us consider two European countries, Italy and the United Kingdom. As shown in Exhibit 4.3, Italy has a French civil law tradition with weak shareholder

EXHIBIT 4.3

Does Law Matter? Italy versus the U.K.

	Italy	U.K.
Legal origin	French civil law	English common law
Shareholder rights	1 (low)	5 (high)
Ownership by three largest shareholders	58%	19%
Market cap/GDP	71%	248%
Listed stocks	247	2,292

Note: Shareholder rights refer to the antidirector rights index as computed by La Porta, Lopez-de-Silanes, Shleifer, and Vishny (1998). Both the ratio of stock market capitalization to GDP and the number of listed stocks are as of 1999.
Source: Various studies of LLSV and the CIA's World Factbook.

protection, whereas the United Kingdom, with its common law tradition, provides strong investor protection. In Italy (U.K.), the three largest shareholders own 58 percent (19 percent) of the company, on average. Company ownership is thus highly concentrated in Italy and more diffuse in the United Kingdom. In addition, as of 1999, only 247 companies are listed on the stock exchange in Italy, whereas 2,292 companies are listed in the United Kingdom. In the same year, the stock market capitalization as a proportion of the annual GDP was 71 percent in Italy but 248 percent in the United Kingdom. The stark contrast between the two countries suggests that protection of investors has significant economic consequences. Concentrated ownership can be viewed as a rational response to weak investor protection, but it may create a different agency conflict between large controlling shareholders and small outside shareholders. We now discuss some of the issues in detail.

Ownership and Control Pattern

Companies domiciled in countries with weak investor protection may need to have concentrated ownership as a substitute for legal protection. With concentrated ownership, large shareholders can control and monitor managers effectively and solve the agency problem. LLSV (1998) indeed found that corporate ownership tends to be more concentrated in countries with weaker investor protection. As can be seen from Exhibit 4.4, the three largest shareholders own 43 percent of companies on average in English common law countries, and 54 percent of companies on average in French civil law countries.

如果大股东的利益只能来自现金流量，那么，在大股东和小股东之间就不会发生冲突。

If large shareholders benefit only from pro-rata cash flows, there will be no conflicts between large shareholders and small shareholders. What is good for large shareholders should be good for small shareholders as well. Since investors may be able to derive private benefits from control, however, they may seek to acquire control rights exceeding cash flow rights. Dominant investors may acquire control through various schemes, such as:

1. Shares with superior voting rights
2. Pyramidal ownership structure
3. Interfirm cross-holdings

许多公司发行具有不同表决权的股票，而不是遵循一股一票的原则。

金字塔所有权

交叉持股

Many companies issue shares with differential voting rights, deviating from the one-share one-vote principle. By accumulating superior voting shares, investors can acquire control rights exceeding cash flow rights. In addition, large shareholders, who are often founders and their families, can use a **pyramidal** structure in which they control a holding company that owns a controlling block of another company, which in turn owns controlling interests in yet another company, and so on. Also, **equity cross-holdings** among a group of companies, such as *keiretsu* and *chaebols*, can be used to concentrate and leverage voting rights to acquire control. Obviously, a combination of these schemes may also be used to acquire control.

EXHIBIT 4.4	Consequences of Law: Ownership and Capital Markets		
Legal Origin	Region or Country	Ownership Concentration	External Cap/GNP	Domestic Firms/Population
1. English common law	Australia	0.28	0.49	63.55
	Canada	0.40	0.39	40.86
	Hong Kong SAR	0.54	1.18	88.16
	India	0.40	0.31	7.79
	Ireland	0.39	0.27	20.00
	Israel	0.51	0.25	127.60
	Kenya	na	na	2.24
	Malaysia	0.54	1.48	25.15
	New Zealand	0.48	0.28	69.00
	Nigeria	0.40	0.27	1.68
	Pakistan	0.37	0.18	5.88
	Singapore	0.49	1.18	80.00
	South Africa	0.52	1.45	16.00
	Sri Lanka	0.60	0.11	11.94
	Thailand	0.47	0.56	6.70
	United Kingdom	0.19	1.00	35.68
	United States	0.20	0.58	30.11
	Zimbabwe	0.55	0.18	5.81
	English-origin average	**0.43**	**0.60**	**35.45**
2. French civil law	Argentina	0.53	0.07	4.58
	Belgium	0.54	0.17	15.50
	Brazil	0.57	0.18	3.48
	Chile	0.45	0.80	19.92
	Colombia	0.63	0.14	3.13
	Ecuador	na	na	13.18
	Egypt	0.62	0.08	3.48
	France	0.34	0.23	8.05
	Greece	0.67	0.07	21.60
	Indonesia	0.58	0.15	1.15
	Italy	0.58	0.08	3.91
	Jordan	na	na	23.75
	Mexico	0.64	0.22	2.28
	Netherlands	0.39	0.52	21.13
	Peru	0.56	0.40	9.47
	Philippines	0.57	0.10	2.90
	Portugal	0.52	0.08	19.50
	Spain	0.51	0.17	9.71
	Turkey	0.59	0.18	2.93
	Uruguay	na	na	7.00
	Venezuela	0.51	0.08	4.28
	French-origin average	**0.54**	**0.21**	**10.00**
3. German civil law	Austria	0.58	0.06	13.87
	Germany	0.48	0.13	5.14
	Japan	0.18	0.62	17.78
	South Korea	0.23	0.44	15.88
	Switzerland	0.41	0.62	33.85
	China's Taiwan	0.18	0.86	14.22
	German-origin average	**0.34**	**0.46**	**16.79**
4. Scandinavian civil law	Denmark	0.45	0.21	50.40
	Finland	0.37	0.25	13.00
	Norway	0.36	0.22	33.00
	Sweden	0.28	0.51	12.66
	Scandinavian-origin average	**0.37**	**0.30**	**27.26**

Note: Ownership concentration measures the average share ownership by three largest shareholders. External Cap/GNP is the ratio of the stock market capitalization held by minority shareholders (other than three shareholders) to the gross national product for 1994. Domestic Firms/Population is the ratio of the number of domestic firms listed in a given country to its population (million) in 1994.
Source: Various studies of LLSV.

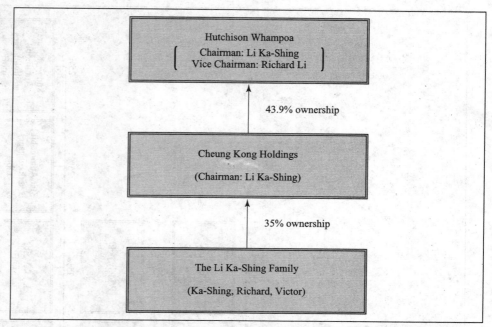

EXHIBIT 4.5

Hutchison Whampoa: The Chain of Control

Source: R. La Porta, F. Lopez-de-Silanes, A. Shleifer, and R. Vishny, "Corporate Ownership around the World," *Journal of Finance* 54 (1999), p. 483.

Hutchison Whampoa, the third most valuable public company in China-Hong Kong SAR, provides an interesting example of pyramidal control structure. The company is 43.9 percent controlled by another public company, Cheung Kong Holdings, which is the fifth-largest publicly traded company in China-Hong Kong SAR. Cheung Kong Holdings, in turn, is 35 percent controlled by the Li Ka-Shing family. The cash flow rights of the Li family in Hutchison Whampoa are thus 15.4 percent ($.35 \times .439 = .154$), but the family's control rights in Hutchson Whampoa is 43.9 percent. The chain of control of Hutchison Whampoa is illustrated in Exhibit 4.5. In Korea, the ownership structure can be more complicated. Take Samsung Electronics, Korea's most valuable company. Lee Keun-Hee, the chairman of the Samsung *chaebol* and the son of Samsung's founder, controls 8.3 percent of Samsung Electronics directly. In addition, Lee controls 15 percent of Samsung Life, which controls 8.7 percent of Samsung Electronics and 14.1 percent of Cheil Chedang, which controls 3.2 percent of Samsung Electronics and 11.5 percent of Samsung Life. This byzantine web of cross-holdings enables Lee to exercise an effective control of Samsung Electronics.[9]

与亚洲一样，所有权集中、控制权与现金流权利之间存在重大差异等现象在欧洲大陆也很普遍。

As in Asia, concentrated ownership and a significant wedge between control and cash flow rights are widespread in continental Europe. Exhibit 4.6 illustrates the pyramidal ownership structure for Daimler-Benz, a German company, at the beginning of the 1990s.[10] The company has three major block holders: Deutsche Bank (28.3 percent), Mercedes-Automobil Holding AG (25.23 percent), and the Kuwait government (14 percent). The remaining 32.37 percent of shares are widely held. The pyramidal ownership structure illustrated in Exhibit 4.6 makes it possible for large investors to acquire significant control rights with relatively small investments. For example, Robert Bosch GmbH controls 25 percent of Stella Automobil, which in turn owns 25 percent of Mercedes-Automobil Holding, which controls 25 percent of Daimler-

---

[9]Examples here are from R. La Porta, F. Lopez-de-Silanes, A. Shleifer, and R. Vishny, "Corporate Ownership around the World," *Journal of Finance* 54 (1999), pp. 471–517.

[10]This example is from Julian Franks and Colin Mayer, "Ownership and Control of German Corporations," *Review of Financial Studies* 14 (2001), pp. 943–77. Note that the ownership structure of Daimler-Benz has been significantly altered since 1990.

EXHIBIT 4.6   **Ownership Structure of Daimler-Benz AG, 1990**

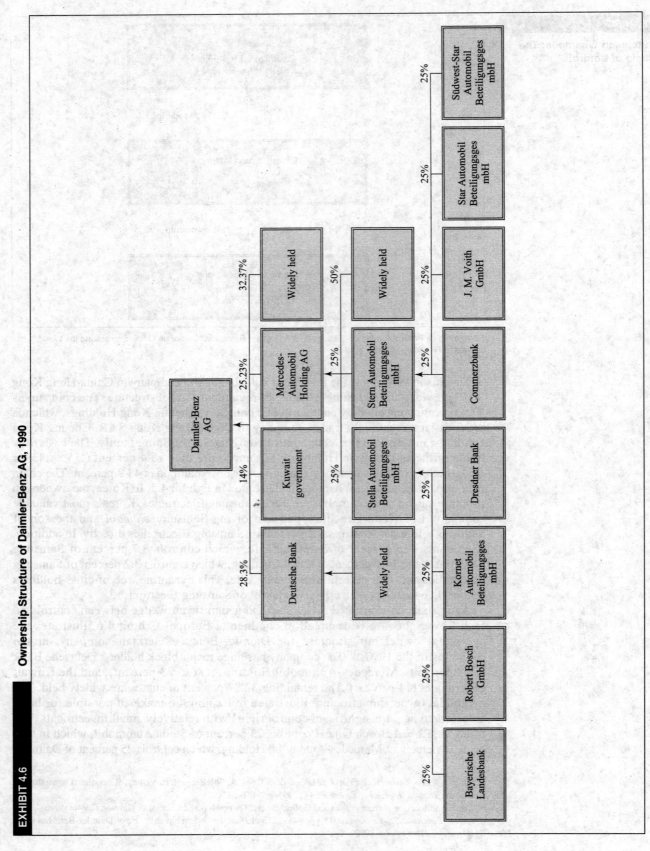

Source: Julian Franks and Colin Mayer, "Ownership and Control of German Corporation," Review of Financial Studies 14 (2001), p. 949.

Benz AG. Robert Bosch can possibly control up to 25 percent of the voting rights of Daimler-Benz AG with only 1.56 percent cash flow rights in the company.

Private Benefits of Control

一旦大股东拥有的控制权超过了现金流权利，就可获得**控制权的私有利益**——其他股东按照平均分摊原则所无法得到的利益。

Once large shareholders acquire control rights exceeding cash flow rights, they may extract **private benefits of control** that are not shared by other shareholders on a pro-rata basis. A few studies document the existence and magnitude of private benefits. Nenova (2001) computed the premium for voting shares relative to nonvoting shares in different countries. The voting premium, defined as the total vote value (value of a vote times the number of votes) as a proportion of the firm's equity market value is only about 2 percent in the United States and 2.8 percent in Canada. This implies that private benefits of control are not very significant in both countries. In contrast, the voting premium is 23 percent in Brazil, 9.5 percent in Germany, 29 percent in both Italy and Korea, and 36 percent in Mexico, suggesting that in these countries, dominant shareholders extract substantial private benefits of control. Unless investors can derive significant private benefits of control, they will not pay substantial premiums for voting shares over nonvoting shares.

Dyck and Zingales (2003), on the other hand, computed "block premium," that is, the difference between the price per share paid for the control block and the exchange price after the announcement of the control transaction, divided by the exchange price after the control transaction. Obviously, control blocks will command premiums only if block holders can extract private benefits of control. Similar to Nenova's findings, Dyck and Zingales report that during the period 1990–2000, the average block premium was only 1 percent in Canada, the United Kingdom, and the United States, and 2 percent in Australia and Finland. The average block premium, however, was much higher in other countries-65 percent in Brazil, 58 percent in the Czech Republic, 27 percent in Israel, 37 percent in Italy, 16 percent in Korea, and 34 percent in Mexico. Clearly, large shareholders extract significant private benefits of control in those countries where the rights of minority shareholders are not well protected.

Capital Markets and Valuation

The legal analysis of corporate governance predicts that investor protection promotes the development of external capital markets. When investors are assured of receiving fair returns on their funds, they will be willing to pay more for securities. To the extent that this induces companies to seek more funds from outside investors, strong investor protection will be conducive to large capital markets. LLSV (1997) empirically document that countries with strong shareholder protection tend to have more valuable stock markets and more companies listed on stock exchanges per capita than countries with weak protection. Also, a few studies report that higher insider cash flow rights are associated with higher valuation of corporate assets, whereas greater insider control rights are associated with lower valuation of corporate assets. Exhibit 4.4 shows that the stock market capitalization held by minority shareholders (excluding the three largest shareholders) as a proportion to the GNP for the year 1994 is 0.60 in English common law countries and 0.21 in French civil law countries. The exhibit also shows that the number of domestic firms listed on stock exchanges per population (million) is about 35 in English common law countries, compared with only 10 in French civil law countries.

在金融危机期间，对投资者保护的弱化也是导致市场直线下跌的一个重要因素。

Weak investor protection can also be a contributing factor to sharp market declines during a financial crisis. In countries with weak investor protection, insiders may treat outside investors reasonably well as long as business prospects warrant continued external financing. However, once future prospects dim, insiders may start to expropriate the outside investors as the need for external funding dissipates. The accelerated expropriation can induce sharp declines in security prices. Johnson, Boon, Breach, and Friedman (2000) provide evidence that during the Asian financial crisis of 1997–98, stock markets actually declined more in countries with weaker investor protection.

The existence of well-developed financial markets, promoted by strong investor protection, may stimulate economic growth by making funds readily available for investment at low cost. Earlier, Schumpeter (1934) argued that financial development promotes economic growth. Several studies now document the empirical link between financial development and economic growth, supporting the Schumpeter hypothesis.[11] According to Beck et al. (2000), financial development can contribute to economic growth in three major ways: (1) It enhances savings; (2) it channels savings toward real investments in productive capacities, thereby fostering capital accumulation; and (3) it enhances the efficiency of investment allocation through the monitoring and signaling functions of capital markets.

Corporate Governance Reform

In the wake of the Asian financial crisis of 1997–98 and the spectacular failure of several major companies like Daewoo, Enron, and WorldCom, scandal-weary investors around the world are demanding corporate governance reform. The failure of these companies hurts shareholders as well as other stakeholders, including workers, customers, and suppliers. Many employees who invested heavily in company stock for their retirement were dealt severe financial blows. It is not just the companies' internal governance mechanisms that failed; auditors, regulators, banks, and institutional investors also failed in their respective roles. Failure to reform corporate governance will damage investor confidence, stunt the development of capital markets, raise the cost of capital, distort capital allocation, and even shake confidence in capitalism itself.

公司治理制度不改革，会使投资者信心受挫，会阻碍资本市场的发展，会使资本成本上升，会扭曲资源配置并动摇对市场经济的信心。

Objectives of Reform

During the 1980s, when the economies of Germany and Japan were strong performers, the governance systems of the two countries received much attention and admiration. In both Germany and Japan, banks and a few permanent large shareholders play the central role in corporate governance. This "bank-centered" governance system was seen as guiding corporate managers to pursue long-term performance goals and also as effectively supporting companies when they were in financial distress. In contrast, the "market-centered" governance system of the United States was viewed as inducing short-term-oriented corporate decisions and being ineffectual in many ways. However, as the U.S. economy and its stock market surged ahead in the 1990s, with Germany and Japan lagging behind, the U.S.-style market-centered governance system replaced the German-Japanese system as a subject of admiration. The American market-oriented system seemed the wave of the future. But then, the subsequent slowdown of the U.S. economy and stock market and the shocking corporate scandals again dethroned the U.S. system. It seems fair to say that no country has a perfect system for other countries to emulate.

There is a growing consensus that corporate governance reform should be a matter of global concern. Although some countries face more serious problems than others, existing governance mechanisms have failed to effectively protect outside investors in many countries. What should be the objective of reform? Our discussion in this chapter suggests a simple answer: *Strengthen the protection of outside investors from expropriation by managers and controlling insiders.* Among other things, reform requires: (1) strengthening the independence of boards of directors with more outsiders, (2) enhancing the transparency and disclosure standard of financial statements, and (3) energizing the regulatory and monitoring functions of the SEC (in the United States) and stock exchanges. In many developing and transition countries, it may be necessary to first modernize the legal framework.

公司治理制度的改革必须：(1) 增加外部股东人数以提高董事会独立性；(2) 提高财务报告的透明度和披露标准；(3) 强化SEC和股票交易所的管理和监督职能。

---

[11]Examples include King and Levine (1993), Rajan and Zingales (1998), and Beck, Levine, and Loayza (2000).

Political Dynamics

www.brt.org/taskforces/

This site discusses the principles of corporate governance.

为了成功，改革者必须了解有关治理问题的政治因素，并从媒体、公众舆论、非政府机构（NGOs）处寻求帮助。

However, as we have seen from the experiences of many countries, governance reform is easier said than done. First of all, the existing governance system is a product of the historical evolution of the country's economic, legal, and political infrastructure. It is not easy to change historical legacies. Second, many parties have vested interests in the current system, and they will resist any attempt to change the status quo. For example, Arthur Levitt, chairman of the SEC during much of the 1990s, attempted to reform the accounting industry, but it successfully resisted the attempt through the use of lobbyists and advertising. In Levitt's words (*The Wall Street Journal,* June 17, 2002, p. C7): "The ferocity of the accounting profession's opposition to our attempt to reform the industry a few years ago is no secret. . . . They will do everything possible to protect their franchise, and will do so with little regard for the public interest." This earlier failure to reform the accounting industry contributed to the breakout of corporate scandals in the United States. It is noted that the former executives of WorldCom were indicted for allegedly orchestrating the largest accounting fraud in history, with the help of conniving auditors.[12] In another example, following the Asian financial crisis, the Korean government led efforts to reform the country's *chaebol* system but met with stiff resistance from the founding families, which were basically afraid of losing their private benefits of control. Nevertheless, reform efforts in Korea were partially successful, partly because the weight and prestige of the government were behind them and partly because public opinion was generally in favor of reform.

To be successful, reformers should understand the political dynamics surrounding governance issues and seek help from the media, public opinion, and nongovernmental organizations (NGOs). The role of NGOs and the media can be illustrated by the success of the People's Solidarity for Participatory Democracy (PSPD) in Korea, organized by Hasung Jang of Korea University. The PSPD and Professor Jang have utilized legal pressure and media exposure to create public opinion and shame corporate executives into changing their practices. For example, PSPD successfully challenged the transfer pricing of SK Telecom. Specifically, SK Telecom transferred huge profits to two subsidiaries, Sunkyung Distribution, which is 94.6 percent owned by SK Group Chairman Choi Jong-Hyun, and Daehan Telecom, fully owned by Choi's son and his son-in-law, thereby expropriating outside shareholders of SK Telecom. The PSPD exposed this practice to the media, and the episode was reported in the *Financial Times* as well as local newspapers and television. Facing unfavorable public opinion, SK Telecom finally agreed to stop the practice.[13]

The Sarbanes-Oxley Act

面对公众对美国公司丑闻的愤慨，政客们采取了纠正行动。美国国会在2002年7月通过了《萨班斯－奥克斯利法案》。

Facing public uproar following the U.S. corporate scandals, politicians took actions to remedy the problem. The U.S. Congress passed the **Sarbanes-Oxley Act** in July 2002. The major components of the Sarbanes-Oxley Act are:

- Accounting regulation-The creation of a public accounting oversight board charged with overseeing the auditing of public companies, and restricting the consulting services that auditors can provide to clients.

- Audit committee-The company should appoint independent "financial experts" to its audit committee.

- Internal control assessment-Public companies and their auditors should assess the effectiveness of internal control of financial record keeping and fraud prevention.

- Executive responsibility-Chief executive and finance officers (CEO and CFO) must sign off on the company's quarterly and annual financial statements. If fraud causes an overstatement of earnings, these officers must return any bonuses.

---

[12]*New York Times,* September 2, 2002, p. A16.

[13]Alexander Dyck and Luigi Zingales, "The Corporate Governance Role of the Media," working paper (2002).

The New York Stock Exchange (NYSE) is also currently considering various measures to protect investors. These measures call for, among other things: (1) listed companies to have boards of directors with a majority of independents; (2) the compensation, nominating, and audit committees to be entirely composed of independent directors; and (3) the publication of corporate governance guidelines and reporting of annual evaluation of the board and CEO. These measures, if properly implemented, should improve the corporate governance regime in the United States.

The implementation of the Sarbanes-Oxley Act, however, was not free from frictions. Many companies find the compliance with a particular provision of the act, that is, Section 404, onerous, costing millions of dollars. Section 404 requires public companies and their auditors to assess the effectiveness of internal control of financial record keeping and fraud prevention and file reports with the Securities and Exchange Commission (SEC). Clearly, the cost of compliance disproportionately affects smaller companies. In addition, many U.S.-listed foreign firms that have different governance structure at home also find it costly to comply with the Sarbanes-Oxley Act. Since the passage of the act, some foreign firms choose to list their shares on the London Stock Exchange and other European exchanges, instead of U.S. exchanges, to avoid the costly compliance.

自《萨班斯－奥克斯利法案》通过以来，为了避免昂贵的遵循成本，一些外国公司选择到伦敦股票交易所或欧洲其他交易所上市，而不是到美国的交易所上市。

The Cadbury Code of Best Practice

Like the United States, the United Kingdom was hit by a spate of corporate scandals in the 1980s and early 1990s, resulting in the bankruptcy of such high-profile companies as Ferranti, Colorol Group, BCCI, and Maxwell Group. The "scandalous" collapse of these prominent British companies was popularly attributed to their complete corporate control by a single top executive, weak governance mechanisms, and the failure of their boards of directors. Against this backdrop, the British government appointed the *Cadbury Committee* in 1991 with the broad mandate to address corporate governance problems in the United Kingdom. Sir Adrian Cadbury, CEO of Cadbury Company, chaired the committee.[14] The work of the committee led to successful governance reform in the United Kingdom.

In December 1992, the Cadbury Committee issued its report, including the *Code of Best Practice* in corporate governance. The code recommends that (1) boards of directors of public companies include at least three outside (nonexecutive) directors, and that (2) the positions of chief executive officer (CEO) and chairman of the board (COB) of these companies be held by two different individuals; boards of directors of most British companies were dominated by insiders, with the positions of CEO and COB often held by the same individuals. Specifically, the code prescribed that:

> The board should meet regularly, retain full and effective control over the company and monitor the executive management. There should be a clearly accepted division of responsibilities at the head of a company, which will ensure a balance of power and authority, such that no one individual has unfettered power of decisions. Where the chairman is also the chief executive, it is essential that there should be a strong and independent element on the board, with a recognized senior member. The board should include non-executive directors of significant calibre and number for their views to carry significant weight in the board's decisions.

《坎德伯里准则》尚未被立法，企业对该法规的遵循完全出于自愿。

The **Cadbury Code** has not been legislated into law, and compliance with the code is voluntary. However, the London Stock Exchange (LSE) currently requires that each listed company show whether the company is in compliance with the code and explain why if it is not. This "comply or explain" approach has apparently persuaded many companies to comply rather than explain; currently, 90 percent of all LSE-listed companies have adopted the Cadbury Code. According to a study by Dahya, McConnell, and Travlos (2002), the proportion of outside directors rose from

---

[14]For a detailed discussion of the Cadbury Committee and its effect on corporate governance in the U.K., refer to Dahya, McConnell, and Travlos (2002).

26 percent before the adoption to 47 percent afterwards among those companies newly complying with the code. On the other hand, joint CEO/COB positions declined from 37 percent of the companies before the adoption to 15 percent afterwards. This means that even though the compliance is voluntary, the Cadbury Code has made a significant impact on the internal governance mechanisms of U.K. companies. The Dahya et al. study further shows that the "negative" relationship between CEO turnover and the company performance became stronger after the introduction of the Cadbury Code. This means that the job security of chief executives has become more sensitive to the company performance, strengthening managerial accountability and weakening its entrenchment.

SUMMARY

随着美国和其他国家金融危机的不断爆发，以及知名公司丑闻和倒闭事件的连续发生，公司治理制度已引起了全球范围的关注。本章论述了公司治理问题的总体情况，并重点分析了各国间公司治理机制的差异。

1. 公众公司是经济发展所带来的一种主要的组织创新，这种公司为众多股东共同拥有并受有限责任所保护。有效的风险分摊机制使得公众公司能以较低的成本筹集到大量资本，并从事众多有利可图的投资项目。

2. 公众公司的一个致命弱点就是因公司经理人与股东之间的利益冲突而产生的代理问题。自利的经理人以牺牲股东的权利为代价来提高自己的利益。对于具有过剩自由现金流但又缺乏发展机遇的公司而言，代理问题似乎更为严重。

3. 必须通过加强公司治理来保护股东的权利、限制经理人的无节制行为并重拾投资者对资本市场的信心。公司治理是公司的控制权和现金流在公司股东、经理人员和公司的其他利益相关者之间进行分配所依赖的经济、法律和制度方面的框架。

4. 公司管理的核心问题是：如何最大限度地保护外部投资者的权利，以免受到经理人和内部控制者的剥削，从而获得公平的投资回报。

5. 代理问题可以通过多种方法来解决，包括：(1) 加强董事会成员的独立性，(2) 与经理人签订激励合约，如股票和股票期权等合约，从而更好地统一股东与经理人之间的利益，(3) 进行所有权集中，以便大股东可以控制经理人，(4) 利用负债来促使经理人将自由现金流归还给投资者，(5) 在股东权益受到较好保护的伦敦或纽约股票交易所上市，(6) 如果经理人浪费资金、剥削股东，那么就发起敌意收购行动。

6. 不同国家对投资者权利的法律保护存在系统性差别，这依赖于各国法律体系的历史渊源。英国普通法系国家能给投资者最强有力的保护，而法国大陆法系国家所提供

In the wake of recurrent financial crises and high-profile corporate scandals and failures in the United States and abroad, corporate governance has attracted a lot of attention worldwide. This chapter provides an overview of corporate governance issues, with the emphasis on intercountry differences in the governance mechanisms.

1. The public corporation, which is jointly owned by many shareholders with limited liability, is a major organizational innovation with significant economic consequences. The efficient risk-sharing mechanism allows the public corporation to raise large amounts of capital at low cost and profitably undertake many investment projects.

2. The public corporation has a major weakness: the agency problem associated with the conflicts of interest between shareholders and managers. Self-interested managers can take actions to promote their own interests at the expense of shareholders. The agency problem tends to be more serious for firms with excessive free cash flows but without growth opportunities.

3. To protect shareholder rights, curb managerial excesses, and restore confidence in capital markets, it is important to strengthen corporate governance, defined as the economic, legal, and institutional framework in which corporate control and cash flow rights are distributed among shareholders, managers, and other stakeholders of the company.

4. The central issue in corporate governance is: how to best protect outside investors from expropriation by managers and controlling insiders so that investors can receive fair returns on their funds.

5. The agency problem can be alleviated by various methods, including (a) strengthening the independence of boards of directors; (b) providing managers with incentive contracts, such as stocks and stock options, to better align the interests of managers with those of shareholders; (c) concentrated ownership so that large shareholders can control managers; (d) using debt to induce managers to disgorge free cash flows to investors; (e) listing stocks on the London or New York stock exchange where shareholders are better protected; and (f) inviting hostile takeover bids if the managers waste funds and expropriate shareholders.

6. Legal protection of investor rights systematically varies across countries, depending on the historical origin of the national legal system. English common law countries tend to provide the strongest protection, French civil law countries the weakest. The civil law tradition is based on the comprehensive codification of legal rules, whereas the common law tradition is based on the discrete rulings by independent judges on specific disputes and judicial precedent. The English common law tradition, based on independent judges and local juries, evolved

的保护最弱。大陆法惯例是通过对
法律裁决的综合汇编而形成的。相
反，普通法则完全是由关于个案的
裁决和判例所构成的。英国普通法
传统上以独立法官和地方陪审团为
基础，更倾向于对产权的保护，并
延伸至对投资者权利的保护。

7．对投资者权利的保护会对公司
的所有权模式、资本市场的发展、经
济增长等产生重要的经济影响。对投
资者保护的不足会导致所有权集中、
从控制权中谋取过多的私利、资本市
场发展的不健全和经济发展的缓慢。

8．在美国和英国之外的地区，大
股东——通常为创建者所在的家族——
倾向于对经理人进行控制并剥削外部
小股东。换言之，占主导地位的大股
东更倾向于从控制权中诈取私利。

9．公司治理改革的重点是如何更
好地保护外部投资者的权利免受内部
控制者的剥削。通常，内部控制者会
反对改革，因为他们不想失去控制权
带来的私利。改革者应该了解影响改
革的政治动因，并动员群众支持他们。

to be more protective of property rights, which were extended to the rights of investors.

7. Protecting the rights of investors has major economic consequences in terms of corporate ownership patterns, the development of capital markets, economic growth, and more. Poor investor protection results in concentrated ownership, excessive private benefits of control, underdeveloped capital markets, and slower economic growth.

8. Outside the United States and the United Kingdom, large shareholders, often founding families, tend to control managers and expropriate small outside shareholders. In other words, large, dominant shareholders tend to extract substantial private benefits of control.

9. Corporate governance reform efforts should be focused on how to better protect outside investors from expropriation by controlling insiders. Often, controlling insiders resist reform efforts, as they do not like to lose their private benefits of control. Reformers should understand political dynamics and mobilize public opinion to their cause.

KEY WORDS

agency problem, 81	equity cross-holdings, 91	private benefits of control, 95
Cadbury Code, 98	free cash flow, 81	
complete contract, 80	French civil law, 88	public corporation, 79
concentrated ownership, 85	incentive contracts, 83	pyramidal ownership, 91
	legal origin, 88	residual control rights, 81
corporate governance, 78	managerial entrenchment, 81	Sarbanes-Oxley Act, 97
English common law, 88		shareholder rights, 78

QUESTIONS

1. The majority of major corporations are franchised as public corporations. Discuss the key strength and weakness of the "public corporation." When do you think the public corporation as an organizational form is unsuitable?

2. The public corporation is owned by a multitude of shareholders but run by professional managers. Managers can take self-interested actions at the expense of shareholders. Discuss the conditions under which the so-called agency problem arises.

3. Following corporate scandals and failures in the United States and abroad, there is a growing demand for corporate governance reform. What should be the key objectives of corporate governance reform? What kind of obstacles can thwart reform efforts?

4. Studies show that the legal protection of shareholder rights varies a great deal across countries. Discuss the possible reasons why the English common law tradition provides the strongest protection of investors and the French civil law tradition the weakest.

5. Explain "the wedge" between control and cash flow rights and discuss its implications for corporate governance.

6. Discuss different ways that dominant investors may establish and maintain control of a company with relatively small investments.

7. The *Cadbury Code of Best Practice*, adopted in the United Kingdom, led to a successful reform of corporate governance in the country. Explain the key requirements of the code and discuss how it contributed to the success of reform.

8. Many companies grant stock or stock options to managers. Discuss the benefits and possible costs of using this kind of incentive compensation scheme.

9. It has been shown that foreign companies listed on U.S. stock exchanges are valued more than those from the same countries that are not listed in the United States. Explain why U.S.-listed foreign firms are valued more than those that are not. Also explain why not every foreign firm wants to list stocks in the United States.

10. Explain "free cash flows." Why do managers like to retain free cash flows instead of distributing it to shareholders? Discuss what mechanisms may be used to solve this problem.

INTERNET EXERCISES

It is often mentioned that the United States has a "market-centered" corporate governance system, whereas Germany has a "bank-centered" system. Review the website of OECD, www.oecd.org/daf/corporate-affairs/governance/ or any other relevant websites and answer the following questions:

(a) Compare and contrast the corporate governance systems of the two countries.

(b) How did the two countries come to have the particular governance systems?

(c) What are the consequences of the different governance systems in the two countries?

MINI CASE

Parmalat: Europe's Enron

Following such high-profile corporate scandals as Enron and WorldCom in the United States, European business executives smugly proclaimed that the same cannot happen on their side of the Atlantic as Europe does not share America's laissez-faire capitalism. Unfortunately, however, they proved wrong quickly when Parmalat, a jewel of Italian capitalism, collapsed spectacularly as a result of massive accounting frauds.

Parmalat was founded in 1961 as a dairy company. Calisto Tanzi, the founder, transformed Parmalat into a national player by embarking on an aggressive acquisition program in the 1980s when local governments of Italy privatized their municipal dairies. While solidifying its dominant position in the Italian home market, Parmalat aggressively ventured into international markets during the 1990s, establishing operations in 30 countries throughout the Americas, Asia/Pacific, and Southern Africa. To finance its rapid expansion, the company borrowed heavily from international banks and investors. Worldwide sales of Parmalat reached €7.6 billion in 2002 and its aspiration to become the Coca-Cola of milk seemed within reach. However, things began to unravel in 2003.

Parmalat first defaulted on a $185 million debt payment in November 2003, which prompted a scrutiny of the firm's finances. Auditors and regulators soon found out that a $4.9 billion cash reserve supposedly held in a Bank of America account of the Cayman Island subsidiary of Parmalat actually did not exist, and that the total debt of the company was around €16 billion—more than the double the amount (€7.2 billion) shown on the balance sheet. Italian investigators subsequently discovered that Parmalat managers simply "invented assets" to cover the company's debts and falsified accounts over a 15-year period. Following the discovery of massive frauds, Parmalat was forced into bankruptcy in December 2003. Calisto Tanzi, founder and former CEO, was arrested on suspicion of fraud, embezzlement, false accounting, and misleading investors. The Parmalat saga represents the largest and most brazen corporate fraud in European history and is widely dubbed as Europe's Enron.

Enrico Bondi, a new CEO of Parmalat, filed a $10 billion lawsuit against Citigroup, Bank of America, and former auditors Grant Thornton and Deloitte Touche Tohmatsu, for sharing responsibility for the company's collapse. He also filed legal actions against UBS of Switzerland and Deutsche Bank for the transactions that allegedly contributed to the collapse of Parmalat. Bondi has alleged that Parmalat's foreign "enablers," including international banks and auditors, were complicit in the frauds. He maintained that they knew about Parmalat's fraudulent finances and helped the company to disguise them in exchange for fat fees. Bondi effectively declared a war on Parmalat's international bankers and creditors.

Discussion Points

1. How was it possible for Parmalat managers to "cook the books" and hide it for so long?

2. Investigate and discuss the role that international banks and auditors might have played in Parmalat's collapse.

3. Study and discuss Italy's corporate governance regime and its role in the failure of Parmalat.

REFERENCES & SUGGESTED READINGS

Beck, T., R. Levine, and N. Loayza. "Finance and the Sources of Growth." *Journal of Financial Economics* 58 (2000), pp. 261–300.

Claessens, S., S. Djankov, and L. H. P. Lang. "The Separation of Ownership and Control in East Asian Corporations." *Journal of Financial Economics* 58 (2000), pp. 81–112.

Coase, Ronald. "The Nature of the Firm." *Economica* 4 (1937), pp. 386–405.

Dahya, Jay, John McConnell, and Nickolaos Travlos. "The Cadbury Committee, Corporate Performance, and Top Management Turnover." *Journal of Finance* 57 (2002), pp. 461–83.

Denis, D., and J. McConnell. "International Corporate Governance." Working Paper (2002).

Demsetz, H., and K. Lehn. "The Structure of Corporate Ownership: Causes and Consequences." *Journal of Political Economy* 93 (1985), pp. 1155–77.

Doidge, C., A. Karolyi, and R. Stulz. "Why Are Foreign Firms Listed in the U.S. Worth More?" Working Paper, NBER (2002).

Dyck, A., and L. Zingales. "The Corporate Governance Role of the Media." Working Paper (2002).

Dyck, A., and L. Zingales. "Private Benefits of Control: An International Comparison." *Journal of Finance* 59 (2004), pp. 537–600.

Franks, J. R., and C. Mayer. "Ownership and Control of German Corporations." *Review of Financial Studies* 14 (2001), pp. 943–77.

Glaesser, E., and A. Shleifer. "Legal Origin." *Quarterly Journal of Economics* 117 (2002), pp. 1193–1229.

Gorton, G., and F. A. Schmid. "Universal Banking and the Performance of German Firms." *Journal of Financial Economics* 58 (2000), pp. 28–80.

Holstrom, B., and S. N. Kaplan. "Corporate Governance and Merger Activity in the U.S.: Making Sense of the 1980s and 1990s." Working Paper, NBER (2001).

Jensen, M. "Eclipse of the Public Corporation." *Harvard Business Review* (1989), pp. 61–74.

Jensen, M., and W. Meckling. "Theory of the Firm: Managerial Behavior, Agency Cost, and Ownership Structure." *Journal of Financial Economics* 3 (1976), pp. 305–60.

Jensen, M., and K. Murphy. "Performance Pay and Top Management Incentives." *Journal of Political Economy* 98 (1990), pp. 225–63.

Johnson, S., P. Boon, A. Breach, and E. Friedman. "Corporate Governance in the Asian Financial Crisis." *Journal of Financial Economics* 58 (2000), pp. 141–86.

Johnson, S., R. La Porta, F. Lopez-de-Silanes, and A. Shleifer. "Tunneling." *American Economic Review* 90 (2000), pp. 22–27.

Kang, J., and A. Shivdasani. "Firm Performance, Corporate Governance, and Top Executive Turnover in Japan." *Journal of Financial Economics* 38 (1995), pp. 29–58.

King, R, and R. Levine. "Finance and Growth: Schumpeter Might Be Right." *Quarterly Journal of Economics* 108 (1993), pp. 717–38.

La Porta, R., F. Lopez-de-Silanes, A. Shleifer, and R. Vishny. "Legal Determinants of External Finance." *Journal of Finance* 52 (1997), pp. 1131–50.

———. "Law and Finance." *Journal of Political Economy* 106 (1998), pp. 1113–55.

———. "Corporate Ownership around the World." *Journal of Finance* 54 (1999), pp. 471–517.

———. "Investor Protection and Corporate Governance." *Journal of Financial Economics* 58 (2000), pp. 3–27.

———. "Investor Protection and Corporate Valuation." *Journal of Finance* 57 (2002), pp. 1147–69.

Lemmon, M. L., and K. V. Lins. "Ownership Structure, Corporate Governance, and Firm Value: Evidence from the East Asian Financial Crisis." Working Paper (2001).

Morck, R., A. Shleifer, and R. Vishny. "Management Ownership and Market Valuation: An Empirical Analysis." *Journal of Financial Economics* 20 (1988), pp. 293–315.

Nenova, T., "The Value of Corporate Votes and Control Benefits: A Cross-Country Analysis." Working Paper (2001).

Rajan, R., and L. Zingales. "Financial Dependence and Growth." *American Economic Review* 88 (1998), pp. 559–86.

Reese, W. A., Jr., and M. S. Weisbach. "Protection of Minority Shareholder Interests, Cross-listings in the United States, and Subsequent Equity Offerings." Working Paper, NBER (2001).

Shleifer, A., and R. Vishny. "A Survey of Corporate Governance." *Journal of Finance* 52 (1997), pp. 737–83.

Short, H., and K. Keasey. "Managerial Ownership and the Performance of Firms: Evidence from the UK." *Journal of Corporate Finance* 5 (1999), pp. 79–101.

Smith, Adam. *An Inquiry Into the Nature and Causes of the Wealth of Nations*. (1776).

Schumpeter, J. *The Theory of Economic Development*. Translated by R. Opie. Cambridge, MA: Harvard University Press, 1934.

Stulz, R., and R. Williamson. "Culture, Openness, and Finance." *Journal of Financial Economics* 10 (2003), pp. 313–49.

Zingales, L. "The Value of the Voting Right: A Study of the Milan Stock Exchange Experience." *Review of Financial Studies* 7 (1994), pp. 125–48.

PART TWO

The Foreign Exchange Market, Exchange Rate Determination, and Currency Derivatives

PART TWO begins with a discussion of the organization of the market for foreign exchange. Both spot and forward transactions are studied. The next chapter examines exchange rate determination. The discussion focuses on how changes in the exchange rate between two countries' currencies depend on the relative difference between the nominal interest rates and inflation rates between the two countries. The final chapter of this section introduces currency derivative contracts useful for managing foreign currency exposure.

CHAPTER 5 provides an introduction to the organization and operation of the spot and forward foreign exchange market. This chapter describes institutional arrangements of the foreign exchange market and details of how foreign exchange is quoted and traded worldwide.

CHAPTER 6 presents the fundamental international parity relationships among exchange rates, interest rates, and inflation rates. An understanding of these parity relationships is essential for practicing financial management in a global setting.

CHAPTER 7 provides an extensive treatment of exchange-traded currency futures and options contracts. Basic valuation models are developed.

5 The Market for Foreign Exchange

通常，人们会用自己的货币去购买外汇，此时外汇购买者已将他的购买力转换为外汇卖出国的购买力。

无论以何种标准来衡量，外汇市场事实上已成为世界上最大的金融市场。

外汇（FX）市场

www.bis.org.

This is the website of the Bank for International Settlements. Many interesting reports and statistics can be obtained here. The report titled Triennial Central Bank Survey can be downloaded for study.

MONEY REPRESENTS PURCHASING power. Possessing money from your country gives you the power to purchase goods and services produced (or assets held) by other residents of your country. However, to purchase goods and services produced by the residents of another country generally requires first purchasing the other country's currency. This is done by selling one's own currency for the currency of the country with whose residents you desire to transact. More formally, one's own currency has been used to buy *foreign exchange,* and in doing so the buyer has converted his purchasing power into the purchasing power of the seller's country.

The market for foreign exchange is the largest financial market in the world by virtually any standard. It is open somewhere in the world 365 days a year, 24 hours a day. The 2004 triennial central bank survey compiled by the Bank for International Settlements (BIS) places worldwide daily trading of spot and forward foreign exchange at $1.88 trillion dollars. This is equivalent to over $300 in transactions for every person on earth. This represents a 57 percent increase over 2001 at current exchange rates. The increase in turnover is likely due to the increased investor interest in foreign exchange, apart from equity and fixed income, as an asset class, and greater activity by asset managers and hedge fund managers. London remains the world's largest foreign exchange trading center. According to the 2004 triennial survey, daily trading volume in the U.K. is estimated at $753 billion, a 49 percent increase from 2001. The U.S. daily turnover was $461 billion, which represents an 81 percent increase from 2001. Exhibit 5.1 presents a pie chart showing the shares of global foreign exchange turnover.

Broadly defined, the **foreign exchange (FX) market** encompasses the conversion of purchasing power from one currency into another, bank deposits of foreign currency, the extension of credit denominated in a foreign currency, foreign trade financing, trading in foreign currency options and futures contracts, and currency swaps. Obviously, one chapter cannot adequately cover all these topics. Consequently, we confine the discussion in this chapter to the spot and forward market for foreign exchange.

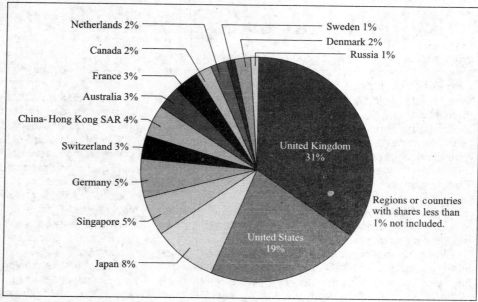

Note: Percent of total reporting foreign exchange turnover, adjusted for intracountry double-counting.
Source: Tabulated from data in Table E.4 in the Triennial Central Bank Survey, Bank for International Settlements, Basle, March 2005.

In Chapter 7, we examine currency futures and options contracts, and in Chapter 14, currency swaps are discussed.

This chapter begins with an overview of the function and structure of the foreign exchange market and the major market participants that trade currencies in this market. Following is a discussion of the spot market for foreign exchange. This section covers how to read spot market quotations, derives cross-rate quotations, and develops the concept of triangular arbitrage as a means of ensuring market efficiency. The chapter concludes with a discussion of the forward market for foreign exchange. Forward market quotations are presented, the purpose of the market is discussed, and the purpose of swap rate quotations is explained.

This chapter lays the foundation for much of the discussion throughout the remainder of the text. Without a solid understanding of how the foreign exchange market works, international finance cannot be studied in an intelligent manner. As authors, we urge you to read this chapter carefully and thoughtfully.

Function and Structure of the FX Market

外汇市场结构反映了商业银行主要功能的延伸，即帮助客户从事国际贸易。

场外（OTC）市场

The structure of the foreign exchange market is an outgrowth of one of the primary functions of a commercial banker: to assist clients in the conduct of international commerce. For example, a corporate client desiring to import merchandise from abroad would need a source of foreign exchange if the import was invoiced in the exporter's home currency. Alternatively, the exporter might need a way to dispose of foreign exchange if payment for the export was invoiced and received in the importer's home currency. Assisting in foreign exchange transactions of this type is one of the services that commercial banks provide for their clients, and one of the services that bank customers expect from their bank.

The spot and forward foreign exchange markets are **over-the-counter (OTC) markets;** that is, trading does not take place in a central marketplace where buyers and sellers congregate. Rather, the foreign exchange market is a worldwide linkage of bank

The Mouse Takes Over the Floor

When electronic trading first began to make a significant dent in the foreign exchange market traders, reportedly concerned about the loss of the human factor in dealing, were heard to grumble that a computer wasn't going to buy them a beer.

Ten years ago a deal was still done when somebody yelled "done" into one of their telephones amid the background noise of other traders doing the same while voice broker prices were constantly being pumped out via a Tannoy system known as the squawkbox or the "hoot'n holler."

"It was bloody noisy and bloody good fun," reminisced one ex-dealer, who felt the advent of technology had robbed the market of much of its personality.

Today, that roar is more of a steady hum as traders face banks of screens and hold electronic conversations while the "hoot'n holler" is used to spread analyst assessments of the latest economic data. The old noise level has been transplanted to bars where, it seems, plenty of beers are still being bought.

Reuters' first screen-based trading system was launched in 1982 for the interbank market, where the majority of foreign exchange dealing takes place. The company launched a conversational dealing product in 1989 and an anonymous "matching" platform in 1992, but faced its first stiff competition only in 1993 with the launch of Electronic Broking Services (EBS), a platform owned by a number of the big banks and designed with the express purpose of preventing Reuters gaining a monopoly position. Now, both platforms still dominate the interbank market but face competition from the internet, where a number of web-based portals are encouraging new participants to trade directly.

In simple volume terms the online platforms look like minnows. EBS reports average daily volumes worth about $100bn whereas the larger internet platforms have average volumes between $15bn–$20bn. But Justyn Trenner of Client-Knowledge calculates the combined value of all online trading is now worth $100bn a day and highlights the rapid growth in the sector.

Platforms such as FXAll, Hotspot FXi and e-Speed are quick to dismiss suggestions of direct competition with the giants. Instead, they say they offer different parties, such as corporate treasurers or fund managers, the opportunity to participate directly and trade outside their usual banking relationships.

If electronic technology in the interbank market helped smaller banks access price transparency in the interbank market, the latest generation of internet platforms is doing the same for those banks' clients.

"We're not going for the interbank market; we live in the space where banks face out to clients," says John Eley, chief executive of Hotspot foreign exchange, who says bank clients, who would previously call three or four dealers for quotes, can get the same range in seconds off a web-based platform, and then deal themselves.

"Multibank portals lower the barriers for third-party foreign exchange trades by cutting costs and reducing risk," adds Mark Warms, chief marketing officer at FXAll,

外汇市场可分为三大细分市场：澳大利亚、欧洲和北美外汇市场。

currency traders, nonbank dealers, and FX brokers, who assist in trades, connected to one another via a network of telephones, computer terminals, and automated dealing systems. Reuters and Electronic Broking Services (EBS) are the largest vendors of quote screen monitors used in trading currencies. The communications system of the foreign exchange market is second to none, including industry, government, the military, and national security and intelligence operations. The International Finance in Practice box "The Mouse Takes Over the Floor" describes the electronic nature of today's FX trading environment.

Twenty-four-hour-a-day currency trading follows the sun around the globe. Three major market segments can be identified: Australasia, Europe, and North America. Australasia includes the trading centers of Sydney, Tokyo, China-Hong Kong SAR, Singapore, and Bahrain; Europe includes Zurich, Frankfurt, Paris, Brussels, Amsterdam, and London; and North America includes New York, Montreal, Toronto, Chicago, San Francisco, and Los Angeles. Most trading rooms operate over a 9- to 12-hour working day, although some banks have experimented with operating three eight-hour shifts in order to trade around the clock. Especially active trading takes place when the trading hours of the Australasia centers and the European centers overlap and when the European and the North American centers overlap. More than half of the trading in the United States occurs between 8:00 A.M. and noon eastern who says the volumes traded by hedge funds have tripled on the platform.

Rick Sears, head of foreign exchange at the Chicago Mercantile Exchange, says volumes in its foreign exchange products had risen sharply since its electronic Globex platform allowed investors to trade its futures contracts 24 hours a day. Between 40 and 45 percent of CME's foreign exchange participants are commodity trading accounts (CTAs) and hedge funds.

"These groups are a lot more comfortable dealing electronically than before. They used to worry about execution risk but e-trading is increasingly popular," he says.

The considerable growth of online platforms, and the survival of a number of different models has surpassed most observers' expectations. Early predictions were that multibank portals such as FXAll, which offer prices from a wide range of banks, would surpass proprietary platforms owned by a single bank. Instead, both are growing rapidly. A recent survey by Greenwich Associates, the US consultancy group, listed both FXAll and UBS's proprietary platforms as leading online trading volumes.

There were also initial fears that the sudden surge in trading outlets could fragment liquidity, hampering trading, but this does not yet appeared to have happened. "Instead, it is more channels for the same market-a price on one platform or another is virtually the same," says Fabian Shey, global head of foreign exchange distribution at UBS.

Mr. Trenner suggested that overall, the shrinking of foreign exchange trading into a few global centers-Tokyo, London and New York-and banks' reorganization to follow suit had instead consolidated liquidity.

When EBS was first launched, dealers raised concerns about the demise of voice brokers' and dealers' market-making role, warning that removing the obligation to quote two-way prices could weaken liquidity in times of crisis with dealers happy to take prices and less prepared to quote them.

But 11 years on, the market has not suffered a significant problem and very little evidence of prices lurching through "grapping"-when the new bid-offer spread does not overlap with the last price posted.

The relative smoothness of price moves is proof, says Jack Jeffery, chief executive of EBS, that the marketplace has evolved with the development of trading technologies.

"The market is so liquid with so many diverse views and flows that marketmaking has changed," he said. "It is now about participation. If you participate, you are contributing to liquidity, not just taking it out."

Some still fret, however, that the market's current dependence on technology leaves it at the mercy of computer servers.

Outages are extremely rare, however, and long-time participants are sanguine about the risks posed.

"Yes, there's a risk, but the market is very adaptable," says Nick Beecroft, head of foreign exchange trading at Standard Chartered.

"In the event of a serious IT meltdown, there are plenty of lines from broking houses to dealing floors and it would just be a question of pulling all the ex-spot brokers back on to the phones, from other products. FX is a highly resilient marketplace."

It seems fears about the loss of the human factor are as yet groundless.

Source: Jennifer Hughes, Financial Times, Special Report: Foreign Exchange, May 27, 2004, p. 1.

standard time (1:00 P.M. and 5:00 P.M. Greenwich Mean Time [London]), when the European markets are still open. Certain trading centers have a more dominant effect on the market than others. For example, trading diminishes dramatically in the Australasian market segment when the Tokyo traders are taking their lunch break! Exhibit 5.2 provides a general indication of the participation level in the global FX market by showing electronic trades per hour.

FX Market Participants

批发市场（whole-sale market）

银行同业市场（Inter-bank market）

零售市场（retail market）

客户市场（client market）

国际银行构成了外汇市场的核心。

The market for foreign exchange can be viewed as a two-tier market. One tier is the **wholesale** or **interbank market** and the other tier is the **retail** or **client market.** FX market participants can be categorized into five groups: international banks, bank customers, nonbank dealers, FX brokers, and central banks.

International banks provide the core of the FX market. Approximately 100 to 200 banks worldwide actively "make a market" in foreign exchange, that is, they stand willing to buy or sell foreign currency for their own account. These international banks serve their retail clients, the *bank customers,* in conducting foreign commerce or making international investment in financial assets that require foreign exchange. Bank customers broadly include MNCs, money managers, and private speculators. According to 2004 BIS statistics, retail or bank client transactions account for approximately 14 percent of FX trading volume. The other 86 percent of trading

EXHIBIT 5.2

The Circadian Rhythms of the FX Market

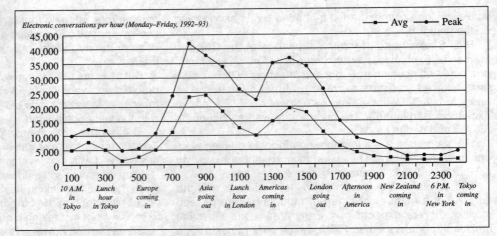

Note: Time (0100–2400 hours, Greenwich Mean Time).
Source: Sam Y. Cross, All About the Foreign Exchange Market in the United States, Federal Reserve Bank of New York, www.ny.frb.org.

国际银行间发生的银行同业交易中有一部分是用以调整它们所持有的外汇头寸的。

See the following websites that are examples of on-line FX trading platforms as discussed in the International Finance in Practice box "Where Money Talks Very Loudly."

www.espeed.com
www.currenex.com
www.forexsten.com

为了实现目标，干预外汇市场的中央银行通常得损失外汇储备。

volume is from interbank trades between international banks or nonbank dealers. *Nonbank dealers* are large nonbank financial institutions such as investment banks, mutual funds, pension funds, and hedge funds, whose size and frequency of trades make it cost-effective to establish their own dealing rooms to trade directly in the interbank market for their foreign exchange needs. In 2004, nonbank dealers accounted for 33 percent of interbank trading volume.

Part of the interbank trading among international banks involves adjusting the inventory positions they hold in various foreign currencies. However, most interbank trades are *speculative* or *arbitrage* transactions, where market participants attempt to correctly judge the future direction of price movements in one currency versus another or attempt to profit from temporary price discrepancies in currencies between competing dealers. Market psychology is a key ingredient in currency trading, and a dealer can often infer another's trading intention from the currency position being accumulated.

FX brokers match dealer orders to buy and sell currencies for a fee, but do not take a position themselves. Brokers have knowledge of the quotes offered by many dealers in the market. Today, however, only a few specialized broking firms still exist. The vast majority of interbank trades flows over Reuters and EBS platforms. The International Finance in Practice box "Where Money Talks Very Loudly" explains how FX trading has changed in the past 10 years and how nonbank dealers using electronic trading platforms can compete with bank traders and other nonbank dealers.

One frequently sees or hears news media reports that the *central bank* (national monetary authority) of a particular country has intervened in the foreign exchange market in an attempt to influence the price of its currency against that of a major trading partner, or a country that it "fixes" or "pegs" its currency against. *Intervention* is the process of using foreign currency reserves to buy one's own currency in order to decrease its supply and thus increase its value in the foreign exchange market, or alternatively, selling one's own currency for foreign currency in order to increase its supply and lower its price. For example, intervention that successfully increases the value of one's currency against a trading partner may reduce exports and increase imports, thus alleviating persistent trade deficits of the trading partner. Central bank traders intervening in the currency market often lose bank reserves in attempting to accomplish their goal. However, there is little evidence that even massive intervention can materially affect exchange rates.

Correspondent Banking Relationships
联行制度

银行同业往来账户体系为外汇市场有效运行提供了保障。

The interbank market is a network of **correspondent banking relationships,** with large commercial banks maintaining demand deposit accounts with one another, called correspondent banking accounts. The correspondent bank account network allows for the efficient functioning of the foreign exchange market.

EXAMPLE 5.1

Correspondent Banking Relationship   As an example of how the network of correspondent bank accounts facilitates international foreign exchange transactions, consider U.S. Importer desiring to purchase merchandise from Dutch Exporter invoiced in euros, at a cost of €750,000. U.S. Importer will contact his U.S. Bank and inquire about the $/€ exchange rate. Say U.S. Bank offers a price of $1.3112/€1.00. If U.S. Importer accepts the price, U.S. Bank will debit U.S. Importer's demand deposit account $983,400 = €750,000 × 1.3112 for the purchase of the euros. U.S. Bank will instruct its correspondent bank in the euro zone, EZ Bank, to debit its correspondent bank account €750,000 and to credit that amount to Dutch Exporter's bank account. U.S. Bank will then credit its books $983,400, as an offset to the $983,400 debit to U.S. Importer's account, to reflect the decrease in its correspondent bank account balance with EZ Bank.

This rather contrived example assumes that U.S. Bank and Dutch Exporter both have bank accounts at EZ Bank. A more realistic interpretation is to assume that EZ Bank represents the entire euro zone banking system. Additionally, the example implies some type of communication system between U.S. Bank and EZ Bank. The *Society for Worldwide Interbank Financial Telecommunication (SWIFT)* allows international commercial banks to communicate instructions of the type in this example to one another. SWIFT is a private nonprofit message transfer system with headquarters in Brussels, with intercontinental switching centers in the Netherlands and Virginia. The *Clearing House Interbank Payments System (CHIPS)* in cooperation with the U.S. Federal Reserve Bank System, called Fedwire, provides a clearinghouse for the interbank settlement for over 95 percent of U.S. dollar payments between international banks. Returning to our example, suppose U.S. Bank first needed to purchase euros in order to have them for transfer to Dutch Exporter. U.S. Bank can use CHIPS for settling the purchase of euros for dollars from, say, Swiss Bank, with instructions via SWIFT to Swiss Bank to deposit the euros in its account with EZ Bank and to EZ Bank to transfer ownership to Dutch Exporter. The transfer between Swiss Bank and EZ Bank would in turn be accomplished through correspondent bank accounts or through a European clearinghouse.

In August 1995, *Exchange Clearing House Limited (ECHO),* the first global clearinghouse for settling interbank FX transactions, began operation. ECHO was a multilateral netting system that on each settlement date netted a client's payments and receipts in each currency, regardless of whether they are due to or from multiple counterparties. Multilateral netting eliminates the risk and inefficiency of individual settlement. In 1997, ECHO merged with CLS Services Limited and operates currently as part of CLS Group. Fifteen currencies are currently eligible for settlement among 58 members.

www.swift.com

www.chips.com

www.cls-group.com

The Spot Market

即期外汇市场所涉及的几乎就是外汇的现货交易。

The **spot market** involves almost the immediate purchase or sale of foreign exchange. Typically, cash settlement is made two business days (excluding holidays of either the buyer or the seller) after the transaction for trades between the U.S. dollar and a non–North American currency. For regular spot trades between the U.S. dollar and the

Where Money Talks Very Loudly

Foreign exchange is the largest, most dynamic market in the world. About $1.88 trillion worth of currency is traded daily in a market that literally does not sleep. Centered in Tokyo, London and New York, traders deal smoothly across borders and time-zones, often in multiples of $1bn, in transactions that take less than a second.

The market's development into its current form has left it virtually unrecognizable from 10 years ago.

Then, banks dealt currencies on behalf of their clients via traders holding multiple telephone conversations or perhaps using the relatively new electronic systems offered by Reuters and Electronic Broking Services (EBS). Today, clients can deal alongside banks on a number of platforms and the quiet hum of computers has done much to reduce the noise level on trading floors.

Old timers complain that a lot of the "personality" has been drained from trading by the rise of faceless systems. But the marketplace itself is, if anything, more vigorous now than then. Many banks and trading platforms are reporting stiff rises in recent volumes traded and, allowing for some growth in market share, most believe overall trading activity has risen as the transparency of the market, and access to it, has improved.

EBS recently said that half of its top 35 busiest trading days since the launch of the company 10 years ago had been in the first two months of 2004. Reuters said it saw growth of 35 percent year-on-year in 2003 in spot market transactions and that year-to-date, it estimated spot volumes to be 50 percent higher from a year ago.

"FX has come of age as an asset class over the last five years," says Nick Beecroft, head of foreign exchange trading at Standard Chartered. "There is much more activity, from active hedgers and from asset managers in other classes who tend to worry about FX much more than they did five, let alone 10 years ago."

Then, the market largely consisted of deals between banks and the technologies being introduced were designed to replicate that. Roughly 50 percent of foreign exchange deals were conducted by conversations between two counterparties and a further 35 percent were conducted through voice brokers, who "matched" bids and offers without either side knowing who the counterparty was.

Reuters had launched its first screen-based system in 1982, and in 1989 followed it up with a conversational platform designed to mimic dealers' telephone trades. In 1992 it went live with a matching system aimed at reproducing the role played by voice brokers. EBS's matching platform was launched in 1993 in a bid by banks to curb Reuters' development of a monopoly position.

The advent of electronic broking for the interbank market gave smaller banks, which previously had little access to the best prices, the opportunity to deal alongside the bigger banks on an even basis because of the transparency afforded by electronic price provision.

Today, only a few specialist voice-broking firms still operate and the bulk of interbank business flows over Reuters and EBS's platforms.

Foreign Exchange Survey 2004

Overall Market share		Institutional investors Market share		Banks Market share	
Company	%	Company	%	Company	%
UBS	12.36	Deutsche Bank	11.99	UBS	19.09
Deutsche Bank	12.18	UBS	11.32	Deutsche Bank	15.01
Citigroup	9.37	Citigroup	9.84	RBS	5.95
JPMorgan	5.78	JPMorgan	6.83	Citigroup	5.94
HSBC	4.89	CSFB/Credit Suisse Group	5.63	Dresdner Kleinwort Wasserstein	5.70
Goldman Sachs	4.54	HSBC	5.38	JPMorgan	4.62
Barclays	4.08	Goldman Sachs	5.22	Merrill Lynch	3.76
CSFB/Credit Suisse Group	3.79	Morgan Stanley	4.72	Goldman Sachs	3.14
RBS	3.51	Merrill Lynch	4.24	Barclays	2.65
Merrill Lynch	3.49	Barclays	4.15	Danske Bank	2.39

Source: Euromoney.

Since then however, there has been another seismic shift in the foreign exchange (FX) marketplace; the extension of price transparency to clients outside the banking world.

Through an array of web-based platforms fund managers and hedge funds, for example, can rapidly view a series of quotes for a particular currency pair, and conduct the deal themselves. On some platforms, the counterparty could as easily be another fund manager as a bank.

"The market has changed more in the last three years than the previous seven," says John Nelson, global head of FX markets at ABN Amro. "One stroke of a key will send a trade from the back office of one counterparty and settle in the back of the other almost instantly."

Rapid price dissemination has, to a great extent, now levelled the playing field and extended the reach of FX trading well beyond the core investment bank market.

"What differentiated banks from customers then was that banks could see the real market prices and customers couldn't. Fast-forward to now, and I can see real-time market prices streaming over my desktop," says Justyn Trenner, chief executive of ClientKnowledge, an independent research firm. "This greatly facilitates the more sophisticated fund managers in actively trading FX as an asset class." The near instant dissemination of news, data and price information has led to what market theorists call "efficiency"—an accurate price at any given time. But it has affected the way in which currency pairs move.

"You get more zigs and zags within a trend than you used to see because everybody reacts to every piece of news at the same time," says Chris Furness, senior currencies strategist at 4Cast economic consultancy, who likened today's behaviour to a school of fish that all change direction at the same time. The upshot of more dramatic intraday price movement, particularly over the past two years, is greater overall volatility.

"Having absorbed the uncertainties around the launch of the euro and despite a contraction in the number of traders, this is a very healthy time for the market," says Mark Robson, head of treasury and fixed income at Reuters.

But although there are new direct players as a result of new trading opportunities and as the price playing field has been levelled, many of the smaller banks have been relegated to the sidelines.

Once more they may specialise in their regional currency but they are more usually clients of the bigger banks because of the expense of the new wave of trading technology.

The few banks with the deepest pockets have developed and operate successful e-trading platforms of their own that add to the volumes they trade and their profits. In turn, they can afford to offer clients the tailormade products that are becoming the norm.

"The intense competition in this space means everyone is trying to distinguish themselves through customisation," says Joe Noviello, chief information officer at e-speed, Cantor Fitzgerald's online platform, which expanded to offer FX trading last year.

Source: Excerpted from Jennifer Hughes, Financial Times, Special Report: Foreign Exchange, May 27, 2004, p. 2.

Hedge funds Market share		E-commerce, proprietary platforms Market share		E-COMMERCE, multi-bank share platforms Market share	
Company	%	Company	%	Company	%
Deutsche Bank	16.42	UBS	34.91	FXall	47.22
UBS	11.70	Deutsche Bank	25.08	FX Connect	35.66
CSFB/Credit Suisse Group	8.68	Dresdner Kleinwort Wasserstein	7.08	EBS Trader on Bloomberg	6.40
Citigroup	8.26	Barclays	4.69	HotspotFxi	4.66
JPMorgan	7.33	Citigroup	4.52	Currenex	2.81
Goldman Sachs	5.52	JPMorgan	3.94	Saxo Trader	1.58
HSBC	5.48	Goldman Sachs	2.51	BuyFX	0.45
Morgan Stanley	4.24	SEB	2.48	IFX Direct	0.32
Merrill Lynch	3.82	ABN Amro	2.35	360 Treasury Systems	0.30
ABN Amro	3.62	HSBC	2.13	Reuters Dealing 3000 Direct	0.27

EXHIBIT 5.3

Average Daily Foreign Exchange Turnover by Instrument and Counterparty

Instrument/Counterparty	Turnover in USD (million)		Percent
Spot		**$621,073**	**35**
With reporting dealers	300,399		17
With other financial institutions	212,529		12
With nonfinancial customers	107,552		6
Outright Forwards		**208,333**	**12**
With reporting dealers	72,833		4
With other financial institutions	79,897		5
With nonfinancial customers	55,603		3
Foreign Exchange Swaps		**943,869**	**53**
With reporting dealers	562,293		32
With other financial institutions	292,928		17
With nonfinancial customers	88,648		5
Total		$1,773,275	100

Note: Turnover is net of local and cross-border interdealer double-counting. Components do not always add due to incomplete counterparty breakdown. Estimated gaps in reporting of $106,725 million brings the total to approximately $1,880,000 million, the estimated daily average turnover figure.
Source: Tabulated from data in Table E.1 in the Triennial Central Bank Survey, Bank for International Settlements, Basle, March 2005.

Mexican peso or the Canadian dollar, settlement takes only one business day.[1] According to BIS statistics, spot foreign exchange trading accounted for 35 percent of FX trades in 2004. Exhibit 5.3 provides a detailed analysis of foreign exchange turnover by instrument and counterparty.

Spot Rate Quotations

即期汇率

直接标价

间接标价

全世界的外汇交易商普遍采用按美元报价和交易的手段。

在银行同业市场，大部分货币采用**欧式标价法**，即以外币表示单位美元的价格。

Spot rate currency quotations can be stated in direct or indirect terms. To understand the difference, let's refer to Exhibit 5.4. The exhibit shows currency quotations by bank dealers from Reuters and other sources as of 4:00 P.M. eastern time for Wednesday, March 2, and Thursday, March 3, 2005. The first two columns provide **direct quotations** from the U.S. perspective, that is, the price of one unit of the foreign currency in U.S. dollars. For example, the Thursday spot quote for one British pound was $1.9077. (Forward quotations for one-, three-, and six-month contracts, which will be discussed in a following section, appear directly under the spot quotations for four currencies.) The second two columns provide **indirect quotations** from the U.S. perspective, that is, the price of one U.S. dollar in the foreign currency. For example, in the third column, we see that the Thursday spot quote for one dollar in British pound sterling was £0.5242. Obviously, the direct quotation from the U.S. perspective is an indirect quote from the British viewpoint, and the indirect quote from the U.S. perspective is a direct quote from the British viewpoint.

It is common practice among currency traders worldwide to both price and trade currencies against the U.S. dollar. For example, BIS statistics indicate that in 2004, 89 percent of currency trading in the world involved the dollar on one side of the transaction. In recent years, however, the use of other currencies has been increasing, especially in dealing done by smaller regional banks. For example, in 2004, 37 percent of all currency trading worldwide involved the euro on one side of the transaction. With respect to other major currencies, 20 percent involved the Japanese yen, 17 percent the British pound, 6 percent the Swiss franc, and 4 percent the Canadian dollar. Exhibit 5.5 provides a detailed analysis of foreign exchange turnover by currency.

Most currencies in the interbank market are quoted in **European terms,** that is, the U.S. dollar is priced in terms of the foreign currency (an indirect quote from the

---

[1]The banknote market for converting small amounts of foreign exchange, which travelers are familiar with, is different from the spot market.

EXHIBIT 5.4   **Exchange Rates**

Exchange Rates   March 3, 2005

The foreign exchange mid-range rates below apply to trading among banks in amounts of $1 million and more, as quoted at 4 p.m. eastern time by Reuters and other sources. Retail transactions provide fewer units of foreign currency per dollar.

Region or Country	U.S. $ EQUIVALENT		CURRENCY PER U.S. $	
	Thu	Wed	Thu	Wed
Argentina (Peso)-y	.3388	.3383	2.9516	2.9560
Australia (Dollar)	.7830	.7836	1.2771	1.2762
Bahrain (Dinar)	2.6525	2.6524	.3770	.3770
Brazil (Real)	.3735	.3791	2.6774	2.6378
Canada (Dollar)	.8037	.8068	1.2442	1.2395
1 month forward	.8037	.8069	1.2442	1.2393
3-months forward	.8043	.8074	1.2433	1.2385
6-months forward	.8057	.8088	1.2412	1.2364
Chile (Peso)	.001690	.001699	591.72	588.58
China (Renminbi)	.1208	.1208	8.2765	8.2765
Colombia (Peso)	.0004267	.0004295	2343.57	2328.29
Czech, Rep. (Koruna)				
Commercial rate	.04432	.04431	22.563	22.568
Denmark (Krone)	.1761	.1765	5.6786	5.6657
Ecuador (US Dollar)	1.0000	1.0000	1.0000	1.0000
Egypt (Pound)-y	.1722	.1722	5.8089	5.8062
China-Hong Kong SAR (Dollar)	.1782	.1282	7.8003	7.8003
Hungary (Forint)	.005406	.005421	184.98	184.47
India (Rupee)	.02290	.02290	43.668	43.668
Indonesia (Rupiah)	.0001076	.0001078	9294	9276
Israel (Shekel)	.2304	.2307	4.3403	4.3346
Japan (Yen)	.009498	.009554	105.29	104.67
1-month forward	.009521	.009576	105.03	104.43
3-months forward	.009569	.009627	104.50	103.87
6-months forward	.009651	.009709	103.62	103.00
Jordan (Dinar)	1.4114	1.4104	.7085	.7090
Kuwait (Dinar)	3.4247	3.4245	.2920	.2920
Lebanon (Pound)	.0006605	.0006605	1514.00	1514.00
Malaysia (Ringgit)-b	.2632	.2632	3.7994	3.7994

Region or Country	U.S. $ EQUIVALENT		CURRENCY PER U.S. $	
	Thu	Wed	Thu	Wed
Malta (Lira)	3.0431	3.0491	.3286	.3280
Mexico (Peso)				
Floating rate	.0899	.0902	11.1185	11.0852
New Zealand (Dollar)	.7272	.7268	1.3751	1.3759
Norway (Krone)	.1595	.1600	6.2696	6.2500
Pakistan (Rupee)	.01685	.01685	59.347	59.347
Peru (new Sol)	.3066	.3065	3.2616	3.2626
Philippines (Peso)	.01822	.01827	54.885	54.735
Poland (Zloty)	.3333	.3334	3.0003	2.9994
Russia (Ruble)-a	.03606	.03605	27.732	27.739
Saudi Arabia (Riyal)	.2667	.2666	3.7495	3.7509
Singapore (Dollar)	.6140	.6152	1.6287	1.6255
Slovak Rep. (Koruna)	.03462	.03470	28.885	28.818
South Africa (Rand)	.1676	.1694	5.9666	5.9032
South Korea (Won)	.0009935	.0009926	1006.54	1007.46
Sweden (Krona)	.1450	.1448	6.8966	6.9061
Switzerland (Franc)	.8470	.8520	1.1806	1.1737
1-month forward	.8485	.8534	1.1786	1.1718
3-months forward	.8517	.8568	1.1741	1.1671
6-months forward	.8573	.8623	1.1665	1.1597
China's Taiwan (Dollar)	.03254	.03252	30.731	30.750
Thailand (Baht)	.02600	.02608	38.462	38.344
Turkey (New Lira)-d	.7800	.7785	1.2820	1.2845
U.K. (Pound)	1.9077	1.9135	.5242	.5226
1-month forward	1.9044	1.9101	.5251	.5235
3-months forward	1.8983	1.9038	.5268	.5253
6-months forward	1.8904	1.8959	.5290	.5275
United Arab (Dirham)	.2723	.2723	3.6724	3.6724
Uruguay (Peso)				
Financial	.03900	.03910	25.641	25.575
Venezuela (Bolivar)	.000466	.000521	2145.92	1919.39
SDR	1.5248	1.5238	.6558	.6563
Euro	1.3112	1.3136	.7627	.7613

Special Drawing Rights (SDR) are based on exchange rates for the U.S., British, and Japanese currencies. Source: International Monetary Fund.

a-Russian Central Bank rate. b-Government rate. d-Rebased as of Jan. 1, 2005, y-Floating rate.

Source: The Wall Street Journal, March 4, 2005, p. B6. Reprinted by permission of The Wall Street Journal, © 2005 Dow Jones & Company, Inc. All Rights Reserved Worldwide.

美式标价

U.S. perspective). By convention, however, it is standard practice to price certain currencies in terms of the U.S. dollar, or in what is referred to as **American terms** (a direct quote from the U.S. perspective). Prior to 1971, the British pound was a nondecimal currency; that is, a pound was not naturally divisible into 10 subcurrency units. Thus, it was cumbersome to price decimal currencies in terms of the pound. By necessity, the practice developed of pricing the British pound, as well as the Australian dollar and New Zealand dollar, in terms of decimal currencies, and this convention continues today. When the common euro currency was introduced, it was decided that it also would be quoted in American terms. To the uninitiated, this can be confusing, and it is something to bear in mind when examining currency quotations.

In this textbook, we will use the following notation for spot rate quotations. In general, $S(j/k)$ will refer to the price of one unit of currency k in terms of currency j. Thus, the American term quote from Exhibit 5.4 for the British (U.K.) pound on Thursday, March 3, is $S(\$/£) = 1.9077$. The corresponding European quote is $S(£/\$) = .5242$. When the context is clear as to what terms the quotation is in, the less cumbersome S will be used to denote the spot rate.

EXHIBIT 5.5

Average Daily Foreign Exchange Turnover by Currency against All Other Currencies

Currency	Turnover Stated in USD (millions)	Percent
U.S. dollar	$1,572,918	89
Euro	659,361	37
Japanese yen	359,231	20
Pound sterling	299,417	17
Swiss franc	107,705	6
Australian dollar	97,123	6
Canadian dollar	74,573	4
Other currencies	376,222	21
Total—double-counted	$3,546,550	200
Total—not double-counted	$1,773,275	100

Note: Since there are two sides to each transaction, each currency is reported twice. Turnover is net of local and cross-border interdealer double-counting. Estimated gaps in reporting of $106,725 million brings the total to approximately $1,880,000 million, the estimated daily average turnover figure.
Source: Tabulated from data in Table E.1 in the Triennial Central Bank Survey, Bank for International Settlements, Basle, March 2005.

It should be intuitive that the American and European term quotes are reciprocals of one another. That is,

$$S(\$/£) = \frac{1}{S(£/\$)}$$

(5.1)

$$1.9077 = \frac{1}{.5242}$$

and

$$S(£/\$) = \frac{1}{S(\$/£)}$$

$$.5242 = \frac{1}{1.9077}$$

(5.2)

The Bid-Ask Spread

买入报价
卖出报价

这里，欧式报价代
表的是银行同业买入价。

Up to this point in our discussion, we have ignored the bid-ask spread in FX transactions. Interbank FX traders buy currency for inventory at the **bid price** and sell from inventory at the higher **offer** or **ask price.** Consider the Reuters quotations from Exhibit 5.4. What are they, bid or ask? In a manner of speaking, the answer is both, depending on whether one is referring to the American or European term quotes. Note the wording directly under the *Exchange Rates* title. The key to our inquiry is the sentence that reads: "Retail transactions provide fewer units of foreign currency per dollar." The word "provide" implies that the quotes in the third and fourth columns under the "Currency per U.S. $" heading are buying, or bid quotes. Thus the European term quotations are interbank bid prices.

To be more specific about the £/$ quote we have been using as an example, we can specify that it is a bid quote by writing $S^b(£/\$) = .5242$, meaning the bank dealer will bid, or pay, £0.5242 for one U.S. dollar. However, if the bank dealer is buying dollars for British pounds, it must be selling British pounds for U.S. dollars. This implies that the $/£ quote we have been using as an example is an ask quote, which we can designate as $S^a(\$/£) = 1.9077$. That is, the bank dealer will sell one British pound for $1.9077.

Returning to the reciprocal relationship between European and American term quotations, the recognition of the bid-ask spread implies:

$$S^a(\$/£) = \frac{1}{S^b(£/\$)}$$

(5.3)

In American terms, the bank dealer is asking $1.9077 for one British pound; that means the bank dealer is willing to pay, or bid, less. Interbank bid-ask spreads are quite small. Let's assume the bid price is $0.0005 less than the ask; thus $S^b(\$/£) = 1.9072$. Similarly, the bank dealer will want an ask price in European terms greater than its bid price.

The reciprocal relationship between European and American term quotes implies:

$$S^a(£/\$) = \frac{1}{S^b(\$/£)}$$

$$= \frac{1}{1.9072}$$

$$= .5243$$

(5.4)

Thus, the bank dealer's ask price of £0.5243 per U.S. dollar is indeed greater than its bid price of £0.5242.

The following table summarizes the reciprocal relationship between American and European bid and ask quotations.

	Bid	Ask
$S(\$/£)$	1.9072	1.9077
	reciprocal equals	reciprocal equals
$S(£/\$)$	.5242	.5243

Note that in each row the quotations refer to buying or selling the denominator currency, in the first row £s and in the second row $s.

Spot FX Trading

Examination of Exhibit 5.4 indicates that for most currencies, quotations are carried out to four decimal places in both American and European terms. However, for some currencies (e.g., the Japanese yen, Slovakian koruna, South Korean won) quotations in European terms are carried out only to two or three decimal places, but in American terms the quotations may be carried out to as many as seven decimal places (see, for example, the Lebanese pound).

In the interbank market, the standard-size trade among large banks in the major currencies is for the U.S.-dollar equivalent of $10,000,000, or "ten dollars" in trader jargon. Dealers quote both the bid and the ask, willing to either buy or sell up to $10,000,000 at the quoted prices. Spot quotations are good for only a few seconds. If a trader cannot immediately make up his mind whether to buy or sell at the proffered prices, the quotes are likely to be withdrawn.

In conversation, interbank FX traders use a shorthand abbreviation in expressing spot currency quotations. Consider the $/£ bid-ask quotes from above, $1.9072–$1.9077. The "1.90" is known as the *big figure,* and it is assumed to be known by all traders. The second two digits to the right of the decimal place are referred to as the *small figure.* Since spot bid-ask spreads for the British pound sterling are typically around 5 "points," it is unambiguous for a trader to respond with "72–77" when asked what is his quote for British pound sterling. Similarly, "97 to 02" is a sufficient response for a quote of $1.9097–$1.9102, where the big figures are 1.90 and 1.91, respectively, for the bid and ask quotes.

买卖报价差制度使外汇存货买卖变得方便。

The establishment of the bid-ask spread will facilitate acquiring or disposing of inventory. Suppose most $/£ dealers are trading at $1.9072–$1.9077. A trader believing the pound will soon appreciate substantially against the dollar will desire to acquire a larger inventory of British pounds. A quote of "73–78" will encourage some traders to sell at the higher than market bid price, but also dissuade other traders from purchasing at the higher offer price. Analogously, a quote of "71–76" will allow a dealer to lower his pound inventory if he thinks the pound is ready to depreciate.

外汇零售的买卖价差幅度大于银行间的买卖报价差幅度。

The retail bid-ask spread is wider than the interbank spread; that is, lower bid and higher ask prices apply to the smaller sums traded at the retail level. This is necessary to cover the fixed costs of a transaction that exist regardless of which tier the trade is made in.

Interbank trading rooms are typically organized with individual traders dealing in a particular currency. The dealing rooms of large banks are set up with traders dealing against the U.S. dollar in all the major currencies: the Japanese yen, euro, Canadian dollar, Swiss franc, and British pound, plus the local currency if it is not one of the majors. Individual banks may also specialize by making a market in regional currencies or in the currencies of less-developed countries, again all versus the U.S. dollar. Additionally, banks will usually have a cross-rate desk where trades between two currencies not involving the U.S. dollar are handled. It is not uncommon for a trader of an active currency pair to make as many as 1,500 quotes and 400 trades in a day.[2] In smaller European banks accustomed to more regional trading, dealers will frequently quote and trade versus the euro.

Cross-Exchange Rate Quotations
套算汇率

Let's ignore the transaction costs of trading temporarily while we develop the concept of a cross-rate. A **cross-exchange rate** is an exchange rate between a currency pair where neither currency is the U.S. dollar. The cross-exchange rate can be calculated from the U.S. dollar exchange rates for the two currencies, using either European or American term quotations. For example, the €/£ cross-rate can be calculated from American term quotations as follows:

$$S(€/£) = \frac{S(\$/£)}{S(\$/€)} \tag{5.5}$$

where from Exhibit 5.4,

$$S(€/£) = \frac{1.9077}{1.3112} = 1.4549$$

That is, if £1.00 cost $1.9077 and €1.00 cost $1.3112, the cost of £1.00 in euros is €1.4549. In European terms, the calculation is

$$S(€/£) = \frac{S(€/\$)}{S(£/\$)} \tag{5.6}$$

$$= \frac{.7627}{.5242}$$

$$= 1.4550 \text{ where the difference from 1.4549 is due to rounding.}$$

Analogously,

$$S(£/€) = \frac{S(\$/€)}{S(\$/£)} \tag{5.7}$$

$$= \frac{1.3112}{1.9077}$$

$$= .6873$$

and

http://money.cnn.com/markets/currencies

This subsite at the CNN and Money magazine website provides a currency converter. As an example, use the converter to calculate the current S(€/£) and S(£/€) cross-exchange rates.

$$S(£/€) = \frac{S(£/\$)}{S(€/\$)} \tag{5.8}$$

$$= \frac{.5242}{.7627}$$

$$= .6873$$

Equations 5.5 to 5.8 imply that given N currencies, one can calculate a triangular matrix of the $N \times (N-1)/2$ cross-exchange rates. Daily in *The Wall Street Journal* appear the 21 cross-exchange rates for all pair combinations of seven currencies that are stated as $S(j/k)$ and $S(k/j)$. Exhibit 5.6 presents an example of the table for Thursday, March 3, 2005.

---

[2]These numbers were obtained during a discussion with the manager of the spot trading desk at the New York branch of UBS.

EXHIBIT 5.6		Key Currency Cross Rates					
	Dollar	**Euro**	**Pound**	**SFranc**	**Peso**	**Yen**	**CdnDlr**
Canada	1.2442	1.6315	2.3736	1.0539	.11191	.01182	–
Japan	105.29	138.05	200.85	89.177	9.469	–	84.618
Mexico	11.1185	14.5786	21.211	9.4174	–	.10560	8.9360
Switzerland	1.1806	1.5481	2.2523	–	.10619	.01121	.9489
U.K.	.52420	.6873	–	.4440	.04715	.00498	.42129
Euro	.76270	–	1.4549	.64597	.06859	.00724	.61295
U.S.	–	1.3112	1.9077	.84700	.08994	.00950	.80370

Late New York Trading Thursday, March 3, 2005.
Source: The Wall Street Journal, March 4, 2005, p. B6. Reprinted by permission of The Wall Street Journal, © 2005 Dow Jones & Company, Inc. All Rights Reserved Worldwide.

Alternative Expressions for the Cross-Exchange Rate

For some purposes, it is easier to think of cross-exchange rates calculated as the product of an American term and a European term exchange rate rather than as the quotient of two American term or two European term exchange rates. For example, substituting $S(€/\$)$ for $1/S(\$/€)$ allows Equation 5.5 to be rewritten as:

$$S(€/£) = S(\$/£) \times S(€/\$) \qquad (5.9)$$
$$= 1.9077 \times .7627$$
$$= 1.4550$$

In general terms,

$$S(j/k) = S(\$/k) \times S(j/\$) \qquad (5.10)$$

and taking reciprocals of both sides of Equation 5.10 yields

$$S(k/j) = S(k/\$) \times S(\$/j) \qquad (5.11)$$

Note the $ signs cancel one another out in both Equations 5.10 and 5.11.

The Cross-Rate Trading Desk

货币对货币互换

银行进行这种诸如为银行客户卖出英镑购入瑞士法郎的外汇对外汇的交易时，均使用套汇汇率。

Earlier in the chapter, it was mentioned that most interbank trading goes through the dollar. Suppose a bank customer wants to trade out of British pounds into Swiss francs. In dealer jargon, a nondollar trade such as this is referred to as a **currency against currency** trade. The bank will frequently (or effectively) handle this trade for its customer by selling British pounds for U.S. dollars and then selling U.S. dollars for Swiss francs. At first blush, this might seem ridiculous. Why not just sell the British pounds directly for Swiss francs? To answer this question, let's return to Exhibit 5.6 of the cross-exchange rates. Suppose a bank's home currency was one of the seven currencies in the exhibit and that it made markets in the other six currencies. The bank's trading room would typically be organized with six trading desks, each for trading one of the nondollar currencies against the U.S. dollar. A dealer needs to be concerned only with making a market in his nondollar currency against the dollar. However, if each of the seven currencies was traded directly with the others, the dealing room would need to accommodate 21 trading desks. Or worse, individual traders would be responsible for making a market in several currency pairs, say, the €/$, €/£, and €/SF, instead of just the €/$. As Grabbe (1996) notes, this would entail an informational complexity that would be virtually impossible to handle.

Banks handle currency against currency trades, such as for the bank customer who wants to trade out of British pounds into Swiss francs, at the cross-rate desk. Recall from Equation 5.10 that a $S(SF/£)$ quote can be obtained from the product of $S(\$/£)$ and $S(SF/\$)$. Recognizing transaction costs implies the following restatement of Equation 5.10:

$$S^b(SF/£) = S^b(\$/£) \times S^b(SF/\$) \qquad (5.12)$$

The bank will quote its customer a buying (bid) price for the British pounds in terms of Swiss francs determined by multiplying its American term bid price for British pounds and its European term bid price (for U.S. dollars) stated in Swiss francs.

Taking reciprocals of Equation 5.12 yields

$$S^a(£/SF) = S^a(£/\$) \times S^a(\$/SF) \qquad (5.13)$$

which is analogous to Equation 5.11. In terms of our example, Equation 5.13 says the bank could alternatively quote its customer an offer (ask) price for Swiss francs in terms of British pounds determined by multiplying its European term ask price (for U.S. dollars) stated in British pounds by its American term ask price for Swiss francs.

EXAMPLE 5.2

Calculating the Cross-Exchange Rate Bid-Ask Spread   Let's assume (as we did earlier) that the $/£ bid-ask prices are $1.9072–$1.9077 and the £/$ bid-ask prices are £0.5242–£0.5243. Let's also assume the $/€ bid-ask prices are $1.3108–$1.3112 and the €/$ bid-ask prices are €0.7627–€0.7629. These bid and ask prices and Equation 5.12 imply that $S^b(€/£) = 1.9072 \times .7627 = 1.4546$. The reciprocal of $S^b(€/£)$ implies that $S^a(£/€) = .6875$. Analogously, Equation 5.13 suggests that $S^a(€/£) = 1.9077 \times .7629 = 1.4554$, and its reciprocal implies that $S^b(£/€) = .6871$. That is, the €/£ bid-ask prices are €1.4546–€1.4554 and the £/€ bid-ask prices are £0.6871–0.6875. Note that the cross-rate bid-ask spreads are much larger than the American or European bid-ask spreads. For example, the €/£ bid-ask spread is €0.0008 versus a €/$ spread of $0.0002. The £/€ bid-ask spread is £0.0004 versus the $/€ spread of $0.0004, which is a sizable difference since a British pound is priced at nearly two dollars. The implication is that cross-exchange rates implicitly incorporate the bid-ask spreads of the two transactions that are necessary for trading out of one nondollar currency and into another. Hence, even when a bank makes a direct market in one nondollar currency versus another, the trade is effectively going through the dollar because the "currency against currency" exchange rate is consistent with a cross-exchange rate calculated from the dollar exchange rates of the two currencies. Exhibit 5.7 provides a more detailed presentation of cross-rate foreign exchange transactions.

EXHIBIT 5.7

Cross-Rate Foreign Exchange Transactions

Bank Quotations	American Terms		European Terms	
	Bid	Ask	Bid	Ask
British pounds	1.9072	1.9077	.5242	.5243
Euros	1.3108	1.3112	.7627	.7629

a. Bank Customer wants to sell £1,000,000 for euros. The Bank will sell U.S. dollars (buy British pounds) for $1.9072. The sale yields Bank Customer:
£1,000,000 × 1.9072 = $1,907,200.
The Bank will buy dollars (sell euros) for €0.7627. The sale of dollars yields Bank Customer:
$1,907,200 × €0.7627 = €1,454,621.
Bank Customer has effectively sold British pounds at a €/£ bid price of
€1,454,621/£1,000,000 = €1.4546/£1.00.

b. Bank Customer wants to sell €1,000,000 for British pounds. The Bank will sell U.S. dollars (buy euros) for €0.7629. The sale yields Bank Customer:
€1,000,000 ÷ .7629 = $1,310,788.
The Bank will buy dollars (sell British pounds) for $1.9077. The sale of dollars yields Bank Customer:
$1,310,788 ÷ 1.9077 = £687,104.
Bank Customer has effectively bought British pounds at a €/£ ask price of
€1,000,000/£687,104 = €1.4554/£1.00.
From parts (a) and (b), we see the currency against currency bid-ask spread for British pounds is €1.4546–€1.4554.

Triangular Arbitrage

三角套汇的目的是
通过第二种货币与第三
种货币的交易赚取套汇
利润，只要这两种货币
的直接外汇汇率与套算
汇率不一致。

Certain banks specialize in making a direct market between nondollar currencies, pricing at a narrower bid-ask spread than the cross-rate spread. Nevertheless, the implied cross-rate bid-ask quotations imposes a discipline on the nondollar market makers. If their direct quotes are not consistent with cross-exchange rates, a triangular arbitrage profit is possible. **Triangular arbitrage** is the process of trading out of the U.S. dollar into a second currency, then trading it for a third currency, which is in turn traded for U.S. dollars. The purpose is to earn an arbitrage profit via trading from the second to the third currency when the direct exchange rate between the two is not in alignment with the cross-exchange rate.

EXAMPLE 5.3

Taking Advantage of a Triangular Arbitrage Opportunity   To illustrate a triangular arbitrage, assume the cross-rate trader at Deutsche Bank notices that Crédit Lyonnais is buying dollars at $S^b(\text{€}/\$) = .7627$, the same as Deutsche Bank's bid price. Similarly, he observes that Barclays is buying British pounds at $S^b(\$/\text{£}) = 1.9072$, also the same as Deutsche Bank. He next finds that Crédit Agricole is making a direct market between the euro and the pound, with a current ask price of $S^a(\text{€}/\text{£}) = 1.4490$. Cross-rate Equation 5.12 implies that the €/£ bid price should be no lower than $S^b(\text{€}/\text{£}) = 1.9072 \times .7627 = 1.4546$. Yet Crédit Agricole is offering to sell British pounds at a rate of only 1.4490!

A triangular arbitrage profit is available if the Deutsche Bank traders are quick enough. A sale of $5,000,000 to Crédit Lyonnais for euros will yield €3,813,500 = $5,000,000 × .7627. The €3,813,500 will be resold to Crédit Agricole for £2,631,815 = €3,813,500/1.4490. Likewise, the British pounds will be resold to Barclays for $5,019,398 = £2,631,815 × 1.9072, yielding an arbitrage profit of $19,398.

Obviously, Crédit Agricole must raise its asking price above €1.4490/£1.00. The cross-exchange rates (from Exhibit 5.7) gave €/£ bid-ask prices of €1.4546−€1.4554. These prices imply that Crédit Agricole can deal inside the spread and sell for less than €1.4554, but not less than €1.4546. An ask price of €1.4550, for example, would eliminate the arbitrage profit. At that price, the €3,813,500 would be resold for £2,620,962 = €3,813,500/1.4550, which in turn would yield only $4,998,699 = £2,620,962 × 1.9072, or a loss of $1,301. In today's "high-tech" FX market, many FX trading rooms around the world have developed in-house software that receives a digital feed of real-time FX prices from the EBS Spot electronic broking system to explore for triangular arbitrage opportunities. Just a couple of years ago, prior to the development of computerized dealing systems, the FX market was considered too efficient to yield triangular arbitrage profits! Exhibit 5.8 presents a diagram and a summary of this triangular arbitrage example.

Spot Foreign Exchange Market Microstructure

总之，交易商的竞争
程度是决定即期外汇买
卖价差的一个基本因素。

Market microstructure refers to the basic mechanics of how a marketplace operates. Five recent empirical studies on FX market microstructure shed light on the operation of the spot FX marketplace. Huang and Masulis (1999) study spot FX rates on DM/$ trades over the October 1, 1992 to September 29, 1993, period. They find that bid-ask spreads in the spot FX market increase with FX exchange rate volatility and decrease with dealer competition. These results are consistent with models of market microstructure. They also find that the bid-ask spread decreases when the percentage of large dealers in the marketplace increases. They conclude that dealer competition is a fundamental determinant of the spot FX bid-ask spread.

Lyons (1998) tracks the trading activity of a DM/$ trader at a large New York bank over a period of five trading days. The dealer he tracks was extremely profitable over the study period, averaging profits of $100,000 per day on volume of $1 billion. Lyons is able to disentangle total trades into those that are speculative and those that are nonspeculative, or where the dealer acts as a financial intermediary for a retail client. He

EXHIBIT 5.8

Triangular Arbitrge Example

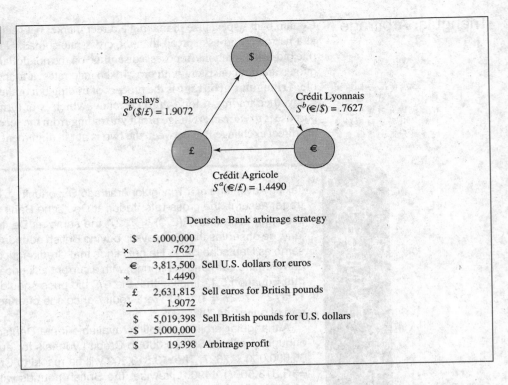

$$S^b(\$/£) = 1.9072 \quad \text{Barclays}$$

$$S^b(€/\$) = .7627 \quad \text{Crédit Lyonnais}$$

$$S^a(€/£) = 1.4490 \quad \text{Crédit Agricole}$$

Deutsche Bank arbitrage strategy

$	5,000,000	
×	.7627	
€	3,813,500	Sell U.S. dollars for euros
÷	1.4490	
£	2,631,815	Sell euros for British pounds
×	1.9072	
$	5,019,398	Sell British pounds for U.S. dollars
−$	5,000,000	
$	19,398	Arbitrage profit

determines that the dealer's profits come primarily from the dealer's role as an intermediary. This makes sense, since speculative trading is a zero-sum game among all speculators, and in the long-run it is unlikely that any one trader has a unique advantage. Interestingly, Lyons finds that the half-life of the dealer's position in nonspeculative trades is only 10 minutes! That is, the dealer typically trades or swaps out of a nonspeculative position within 20 minutes.

Ito, Lyons, and Melvin (1998) study the role of private information in the spot FX market. They examine ¥/$ and DM/$ between September 29, 1994, and March 28, 1995. Their study provides evidence against the common view that private information is irrelevant, since all market participants are assumed to possess the same set of public information. Their evidence comes from the Tokyo foreign exchange market, which prior to December 21, 1994, closed for lunch between noon and 1:30 P.M. After December 21, 1994, the variance in spot exchange rates increased during the lunch period relative to the period of closed trading. This was true for both ¥/$ and DM/$ trades, but more so for the ¥/$ data, which is to be expected since ¥/$ trading is more intensive in the Tokyo FX market. Ito, Lyons, and Melvin attribute these results to a greater revelation of private information in trades being allocated to the lunch hour. This suggests that private information is, indeed, an important determinant of spot exchange rates.

这表明内幕消息的确是决定即期汇率的重要因素。

Cheung and Chinn (2001) conducted a survey of U.S. foreign exchange traders and received 142 usable questionnaires. The purpose of their survey was to elicit information about several aspects of exchange rate dynamics not typically observable in trading data. In particular they are interested in traders' perceptions about news events—innovations in macroeconomic variables—that cause movements in exchange rates. The traders they survey respond that the bulk of the adjustment to economic announcements regarding unemployment, trade deficits, inflation, GDP, and the Federal funds rate takes place within one minute. In fact, "about one-third of the respondents claim that full price adjustment takes place in less than 10 seconds"! They also find that central bank intervention does not appear to have a substantial impact on exchange rates, but intervention does increase market volatility. Dominguez (1998) confirms this latter finding.

The Forward Market

远期外汇市场涉及
那些为了将来购买或出
售外汇而现在签署合约
的交易。

In conjunction with spot trading, there is also a forward foreign exchange market. The **forward market** involves contracting today for the future purchase or sale of foreign exchange. The forward price may be the same as the spot price, but usually it is higher (at a premium) or lower (at a discount) than the spot price. Forward exchange rates are quoted on most major currencies for a variety of maturities. Bank quotes for maturities of 1, 3, 6, 9, and 12 months are readily available. Quotations on nonstandard, or broken-term, maturities are also available. Maturities extending beyond one year are becoming more frequent, and for good bank customers, a maturity extending out to 5, and even as long as 10 years, is possible.

Forward Rate Quotations

远期汇率

To learn how to read forward exchange rate quotations, let's examine Exhibit 5.4. Notice that **forward rate** quotations appear directly under the spot rate quotations for four major currencies (the British pound, Canadian dollar, Japanese yen, and Swiss franc) for one-, three-, and six-month maturities. As an example, the settlement date of a three-month forward transaction is three calendar months from the spot settlement date for the currency. That is, if today is September 11, 2006, and spot settlement is September 13, then the forward settlement date would be December 13, 2006, a period of 91 days from September 13.

In this textbook, we will use the following notation for forward rate quotations. In general, $F_N(j/k)$ will refer to the price of one unit of currency k in terms of currency j for delivery in N months. N equaling 1 denotes a one-month maturity based on a 360-day banker's year. Thus, N equaling 3 denotes a three-month maturity. When the context is clear, the simpler notation F will be used to denote a forward exchange rate.

远期汇率标价可采
用直接标价或间接标价，
这两种标价互为倒数。

Forward quotes are either direct or indirect, one being the reciprocal of the other. From the U.S. perspective, a direct forward quote is in American terms. As an example, let's consider the American term Swiss franc forward quotations in relationship to the spot rate quotation for Thursday, March 3, 2005. We see that:

$$S(\$/SF) = .8470$$
$$F_1(\$/SF) = .8485$$
$$F_3(\$/SF) = .8517$$
$$F_6(\$/SF) = .8573$$

From these quotations, we can see that in American terms the Swiss franc is trading at a *premium* to the dollar, and that the premium increases out to six months, the further the forward maturity date is from March 3. As we will more formally learn in the next chapter, under certain conditions the forward exchange rate is an unbiased predictor of the expected spot exchange rate N months into the future. Thus, according to the forward rate, when the Swiss franc is trading at a premium to the dollar in American terms, we can say the market expects the dollar to **depreciate,** or become less valuable, relative to the Swiss franc. Consequently, it costs more dollars to buy a Swiss franc forward.

贬值

European term forward quotations are the reciprocal of the American term quotes. In European terms, the corresponding Swiss franc forward quotes to those stated above are:

$$S(SF/\$) = 1.1806$$
$$F_1(SF/\$) = 1.1786$$
$$F_3(SF/\$) = 1.1741$$
$$F_6(SF/\$) = 1.1665$$

From these quotations, we can see that in European terms the dollar is trading at a *discount* to the Swiss franc and that the discount increases out to six months, the further the forward maturity date is from March 3. Thus, according to the forward rate, when the dollar is trading at a discount to the Swiss franc in European terms,

EXHIBIT 5.9

Graph of Long and Short Position in the 3-Month Swiss Franc Contract

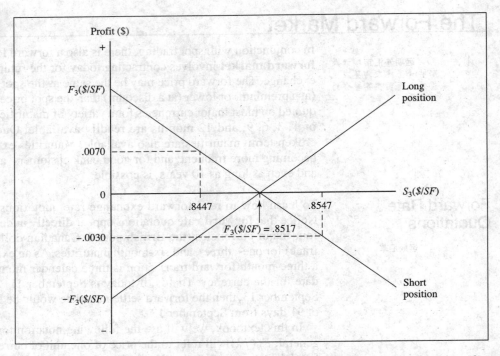

升值

we can say the market expects the Swiss franc to **appreciate,** or become more valuable, relative to the dollar. Consequently, it costs fewer Swiss francs to buy a dollar forward. This is exactly what we should expect, since the European term quotes are the reciprocals of the corresponding American term quotations.

Long and Short Forward Positions

如果使用远期合约，那么就锁定了将来按合约规定的价格购买或卖出外汇的交易。

One can buy (take a long position) or sell (take a short position) foreign exchange forward. Bank customers can contract with their international bank to buy or sell a specific sum of FX for delivery on a certain date. Likewise, interbank traders can establish a long or short position by dealing with a trader from a competing bank. Exhibit 5.9 graphs both the long and short positions for the three-month Swiss franc contract, using the American quote for March 3, 2005 from Exhibit 5.4. The graph measures profits or losses on the vertical axis. The horizontal axis shows the spot price of foreign exchange on the maturity date of the forward contract, $S_3(\$/SF)$. If one uses the forward contract, he has "locked in" the forward price for forward purchase or sale of foreign exchange. Regardless of what the spot price is on the maturity date of the

A Speculative Forward Position   It is March 3, 2005. Suppose the $/SF trader has just heard an economic forecast from the bank's head economist that causes him to believe that the dollar will likely appreciate in value against the Swiss franc over the next three months. If he decides to act on this information, the trader will short the three-month $/SF contract. We will assume that he sells SF5,000,000 forward against dollars. Suppose the forecast has proven correct, and on June 3, 2005, spot $/SF is trading at $0.8447. The trader can buy Swiss franc spot at $0.8447 and deliver it under the forward contract at a price of $0.8517. The trader has made a speculative profit of ($0.8517 − $0.8447) = $0.0070 per unit, as Exhibit 5.9 shows. The total profit from the trade is $35,000 = (SF5,000,000 × $0.0070). If the dollar depreciated and S_N was $0.8547, the speculator would have lost ($0.8517 − $0.8547) = −$0.0030 per unit, for a total loss of −$15,000 = (SF5,000,000)(−$0.0030).

forward contract, the trader buys (if he is long) or sells (if he is short) at $F_3(\$/SF) =$ .8517 per unit of FX. Forward contracts can also be used for speculative purposes, as Example 5.4 demonstrates.

Forward Cross-Exchange Rates

Forward cross-exchange rate quotations are calculated in an analogous manner to spot cross-rates, so it is not necessary to provide detailed examples. In generic terms,

$$F_N(j/k) = \frac{F_N(\$/k)}{F_N(\$/j)} \tag{5.14}$$

or

$$F_N(j/k) = \frac{F_N(j/\$)}{F_N(k/\$)} \tag{5.15}$$

and

$$F_N(k/j) = \frac{F_N(\$/j)}{F_N(\$/k)} \tag{5.16}$$

or

$$F_N(k/j) = \frac{F_N(k/\$)}{F_N(j/\$)} \tag{5.17}$$

Swap Transactions

直接远期交易

互换交易就是在进行一项远期买入（或卖出）操作的同时，对大约等量的外汇进行即期卖出（或买入）。

Forward trades can be classified as outright or swap transactions. In conducting their trading, bank dealers do take speculative positions in the currencies they trade, but more often traders offset the currency exposure inherent in a trade. From the bank's standpoint, an **outright forward transaction** is an uncovered speculative position in a currency, even though it might be part of a currency hedge to the bank customer on the other side of the transaction. Swap transactions provide a means for the bank to mitigate the currency exposure in a forward trade. A **swap transaction** is the simultaneous sale (or purchase) of spot foreign exchange against a forward purchase (or sale) of approximately an equal amount of the foreign currency.

Swap transactions account for approximately 53 percent of interbank FX trading, whereas outright trades are 12 percent. (See Exhibit 5.3.) Because interbank forward transactions are most frequently made as part of a swap transaction, bank dealers in conversation among themselves use a shorthand notation to quote bid and ask forward prices in terms of *forward points* that are either added to or subtracted from the spot bid and ask quotations.

EXAMPLE 5.5

Forward Point Quotations   Recall the $/£ spot bid-ask rates of $1.9072 – $1.9077 developed previously. With reference to these rates, forward prices might be displayed as:

Spot	1.9072–1.9077
One-Month	32–30
Three-Month	57–54
Six-Month	145–138

When the second number in a forward point "pair" is smaller than the first, the dealer "knows" the forward points are subtracted from the spot bid and ask prices to obtain the outright forward rates. For example, the spot bid price of $1.9072 minus .0032 (or 32 points) equals $1.9040, the one-month forward bid price. The spot ask

(continued)

EXAMPLE 5.5 (continued)

price of $1.9077 minus .0030 (or 30 points) equals $1.9047, the one-month ask price. Analogously, the three-month outright forward bid-ask rates are $1.9015–$1.9023 and the six-month outright forward bid-ask rates are $1.8927–$1.8939.[3] The following table summarizes the calculations.

Spot		1.9072–1.9077
	Forward Point Quotations	**Outright Forward Quotations**
One-Month	32–30	1.9040–1.9047
Three-Month	57–54	1.9015–1.9023
Six-Month	145–138	1.8927–1.8939

Three things are notable about the outright prices. First, the pound is trading at a forward discount to the dollar. Second, all bid prices are less than the corresponding ask prices, as they must be for a trader to be willing to make a market. Third, the bid-ask spread increases in time to maturity, as is typical. These three conditions prevail only because the forward points were subtracted from the spot prices. As a check, note that in points the spot bid-ask spread is 5 points, the one-month forward bid-ask spread is 7 points, the three-month spread is 8 points, and the six-month spread is 12 points.

If the forward prices were trading at a premium to the spot price, the second number in a forward point pair would be larger than the first, and the trader would know to add the points to the spot bid and ask prices to obtain the outright forward bid and ask rates. For example, if the three-month and six-month swap points were 54–57 and 138–145, the corresponding three-month and six-month bid-ask rates would be $1.9126–$1.9134 and $1.9210–$1.9222. In points, the three- and six-month bid-ask spreads would be 8 and 12, that is, increasing in term to maturity.

Quoting forward rates in terms of forward points is convenient for two reasons. First, forward points may remain constant for long periods of time, even if the spot rates fluctuate frequently. Second, in swap transactions where the trader is attempting to minimize currency exposure, the actual spot and outright forward rates are often of no consequence. What is important is the premium or discount differential, measured in forward points. To illustrate, suppose a bank customer wants to sell dollars three months forward against British pound sterling. The bank can handle this trade for its customer and simultaneously neutralize the exchange rate risk in the trade by selling (borrowed) dollars spot against British pounds. The bank will lend the pound sterling for three months until they are needed to deliver against the dollars it has purchased forward. The dollars received will be used to liquidate the dollar loan. Implicit in this transaction is the interest rate differential between the dollar borrowing rate and the pound sterling lending rate. The interest rate differential is captured by the forward premium or discount measured in forward points. As a rule, when the interest rate of the foreign currency is greater than the interest rate of the quoting currency, the outright forward rate is less than the spot exchange rate, and vice versa. This will become clear in the following chapter on international parity relationships.

通常, 当外币利率比标价货币的利率高时, 直接远期汇率将低于即期汇率, 反之亦然。

Forward Premium

It is common to express the premium or discount of a forward rate as an annualized percentage deviation from the spot rate. The forward premium (or discount) is useful for

---

[3]If the one-month forward points quotation were, say, 30–30, further elaboration from the market maker would be needed to determine if the forward points would be added to or subtracted from the spot prices. An electronic dealing system would state forward points as −30 −30 if they were to be subtracted.

远期升水/贴水可以
用美式或欧式标价法来
表示。

comparing against the interest rate differential between two countries, as we will see more clearly in Chapter 6 on international parity relationships. The **forward premium** or **discount** can be calculated using American or European term quotations.

EXAMPLE 5.6

Calculating the Forward Premium/Discount   The formula for calculating the forward premium or discount for currency j in American terms is:

$$f_{N,\,j} = \frac{F_N(\$/j) - S(\$/j)}{S(\$/j)} \times 360/\text{days} \tag{5.18}$$

When the context is clear, the forward premium will simply be stated as f.

As an example of calculating the forward premium, let's use the March 3 quotes from Exhibit 5.4 to calculate the three-month forward premium or discount for the Japanese yen versus the U.S. dollar. The calculation is:

$$f_{3,\,\yen} = \frac{.009569 - .009498}{.009498} \times \frac{360}{92} = .0293$$

We see that the three-month forward premium is .0293, or 2.93 percent. In words, we say that the Japanese yen is trading at a 2.93 percent premium versus the U.S. dollar for delivery in 92 days.

In European terms the forward premium or discount for the U.S. dollar is calculated as:

$$f_{N,\,\$} = \frac{F_N(j/\$) - S(j/\$)}{S(j/\$)} \times \frac{360}{\text{days}} \tag{5.19}$$

Using the March 3 three-month European term quotations for the Japanese yen from Exhibit 5.4 yields:

$$f_{3,\,\$} = \frac{104.50 - 105.29}{105.29} \times \frac{360}{92} = -.0294$$

We see that the three-month forward discount is −.0294, or −2.94 percent. In words, we say that the U.S. dollar is trading versus the Japanese yen at a 2.94 percent discount for delivery in 92 days.

SUMMARY

本章对外汇市场做了介绍。广
义而言，外汇交易市场涉及到货币
间购买力的转换、银行的外汇储备、
以外币标价的信用延期、对外贸易
融资以及外汇期权与期货合约的交
易等。本章仅讨论即期外汇市场和
远期外汇市场，其他议题在后面的
章节中再做讨论。

　　1. 外汇市场是世界上最大、最
活跃的金融市场。世界上每时每刻
总有某个外汇市场处于营业中。

　　2. 外汇市场可分为两个层次：
零售或客户市场和批发或银行同业
市场。零售市场是指国际性银行为
那些因进行国际贸易或国际金融资
产交易而需要外汇的客户提供服务
的市场。绝大部分外汇交易发生在
银行同业市场，目的是调整外汇存
货头寸或进行投机及套利操作。

　　3. 外汇市场的参与者包括国际
银行、银行客户、非银行的外汇交易

This chapter presents an introduction to the market for foreign exchange. Broadly defined, the foreign exchange market encompasses the conversion of purchasing power from one currency into another, bank deposits of foreign currency, the extension of credit denominated in a foreign currency, foreign trade financing, and trading in foreign currency options and futures contracts. This chapter limits the discussion to the spot and forward market for foreign exchange. The other topics are covered in later chapters.

1. The FX market is the largest and most active financial market in the world. It is open somewhere in the world 24 hours a day, 365 days a year.

2. The FX market is divided into two tiers: the retail or client market and the wholesale or interbank market. The retail market is where international banks service their customers who need foreign exchange to conduct international commerce or trade in international financial assets. The great majority of FX trading takes place in the interbank market among international banks that are adjusting inventory positions or conducting speculative and arbitrage trades.

3. The FX market participants include international banks, bank customers, nonbank FX dealers, FX brokers, and central banks.

商、外汇经纪人和中央银行。

　　4. 在即期外汇市场上，外汇的买卖几乎是瞬间完成的。在本章中，引入了定义即期汇率标价的符号。此外，还确定了套算汇率的概念。非美元外汇间的交易必须满足由套算公式决定的买卖价差，或者说要存在三角套利的机会。

　　5. 在远期市场上，买卖双方目前就商定好在未来某个时间买卖外汇的一个远期价格。这里引入了表示远期汇率标价的符号。运用远期点数这一简便方法来表示基于即期汇率标价的远期汇率标价。此外，还引入了远期升水的概念。

4. In the spot market for FX, nearly immediate purchase and sale of currencies take place. In the chapter, notation for defining a spot rate quotation was developed. Additionally, the concept of a cross-exchange rate was developed. It was determined that nondollar currency transactions must satisfy the bid-ask spread determined from the cross-rate formula or a triangular arbitrage opportunity exists.

5. In the forward market, buyers and sellers can transact today at the forward price for the future purchase and sale of foreign exchange. Notation for forward exchange rate quotations was developed. The use of forward points as a shorthand method for expressing forward quotes from spot rate quotations was presented. Additionally, the concept of a forward premium was developed.

KEY WORDS

American terms, *115*
appreciate, *124*
ask price, *116*
bid price, *116*
client market, *109*
correspondent banking
    relationships, *111*
cross-exchange rate, *118*
currency against
    currency, *119*
depreciate, *123*

direct quotation, *114*
European terms, *114*
foreign exchange
    (FX) market, *106*
forward market, *123*
forward premium/
    discount, *127*
forward rate, *123*
indirect quotation, *114*
interbank market, *109*
offer price, *116*

outright forward
    transaction, *125*
over-the-counter (OTC)
    market, *107*
retail market, *109*
spot market, *111*
spot rate, *114*
swap transaction, *125*
triangular
    arbitrage, *121*
wholesale market, *109*

QUESTIONS

1. Give a full definition of the market for foreign exchange.

2. What is the difference between the retail or client market and the wholesale or interbank market for foreign exchange?

3. Who are the market participants in the foreign exchange market?

4. How are foreign exchange transactions between international banks settled?

5. What is meant by a currency trading at a discount or at a premium in the forward market?

6. Why does most interbank currency trading worldwide involve the U.S. dollar?

7. Banks find it necessary to accommodate their clients' needs to buy or sell FX forward, in many instances for hedging purposes. How can the bank eliminate the currency exposure it has created for itself by accommodating a client's forward transaction?

8. A CD/$ bank trader is currently quoting a *small figure* bid-ask of 35–40, when the rest of the market is trading at CD1.3436–CD1.3441. What is implied about the trader's beliefs by his prices?

9. What is triangular arbitrage? What is a condition that will give rise to a triangular arbitrage opportunity?

PROBLEMS

1. Using Exhibit 5.4, calculate a cross-rate matrix for the euro, Swiss franc, Japanese yen, and the British pound. Use the most current American term quotes to calculate the cross-rates so that the triangular matrix resulting is similar to the portion above the diagonal in Exhibit 5.6.

2. Using Exhibit 5.4, calculate the one-, three-, and six-month forward cross-exchange rates between the Canadian dollar and the Swiss franc using the most current quotations. State the forward cross-rates in "Canadian" terms.

3. Restate the following one-, three-, and six-month outright forward European term bid-ask quotes in forward points.

Spot	1.3431–1.3436
One-Month	1.3432–1.3442
Three-Month	1.3448–1.3463
Six-Month	1.3488–1.3508

4. Using the spot and outright forward quotes in problem 3, determine the corresponding bid-ask spreads in points.

5. Using Exhibit 5.4, calculate the one-, three-, and six-month forward premium or discount for the Canadian dollar versus the U.S. dollar using American term quotations. For simplicity, assume each month has 30 days. What is the interpretation of your results?

6. Using Exhibit 5.4, calculate the one-, three-, and six-month forward premium or discount for the U.S. dollar versus the British pound using European term quotations. For simplicity, assume each month has 30 days. What is the interpretation of your results?

7. Given the following information, what are the NZD/SGD currency against currency bid-ask quotations?

Bank Quotations	American Terms		European Terms	
	Bid	Ask	Bid	Ask
New Zealand dollar	.7265	.7272	1.3751	1.3765
Singapore dollar	.6135	.6140	1.6287	1.6300

8. Assume you are a trader with Deutsche Bank. From the quote screen on your computer terminal, you notice that Dresdner Bank is quoting €0.7627/$1.00 and Credit Suisse is offering SF1.1806/$1.00. You learn that UBS is making a direct market between the Swiss franc and the euro, with a current €/SF quote of .6395. Show how you can make a triangular arbitrage profit by trading at these prices. (Ignore bid-ask spreads for this problem.) Assume you have $5,000,000 with which to conduct the arbitrage. What happens if you initially sell dollars for Swiss francs? What €/SF price will eliminate triangular arbitrage?

9. The current spot exchange rate is $1.95/£ and the three-month forward rate is $1.90/£. On the basis of your analysis of the exchange rate, you are pretty confident that the spot exchange rate will be $1.92/£ in three months. Assume that you would like to buy or sell £1,000,000.

   a. What actions do you need to take to speculate in the forward market? What is the expected dollar profit from speculation?

   b. What would be your speculative profit in dollar terms if the spot exchange rate actually turns out to be $1.86/£.

10. Omni Advisors, an international pension fund manager, plans to sell equities denominated in Swiss francs (CHF) and purchase an equivalent amount of equities denominated in South African rands (ZAR).

   Omni will realize net proceeds of 3 million CHF at the end of 30 days and wants to eliminate the risk that the ZAR will appreciate relative to the CHF during this 30-day period. The following exhibit shows current exchange rates between the ZAR, CHF, and the U.S. dollar (USD).

CFA®
PROBLEMS

Currency Exchange Rates

Maturity	ZAR/USD		CHF/USD	
	Bid	Ask	Bid	Ask
Spot	6.2681	6.2789	1.5282	1.5343
30-day	6.2538	6.2641	1.5226	1.5285
90-day	6.2104	6.2200	1.5058	1.5115

a. Describe the currency transaction that Omni should undertake to eliminate currency risk over the 30-day period.

b. Calculate the following:

- The CHF/ZAR cross currency rate Omni would use in valuing the Swiss equity portfolio.

- The current value of Omni's Swiss equity portfolio in ZAR.

- The annualized forward premium or discount at which the ZAR is trading versus the CHF.

INTERNET EXERCISES

1. A currency trader makes a market in a currency and attempts to generate speculative profits from dealing against other currency traders. Today electronic dealing systems are frequently used by currency traders. The most widely used spot trading system is EBS Spot. Go to their website, www.ebsp.com/products/spot/asp. Click on the sample view of the monitor screen to enlarge it. What is meant by the terms "ESB Best Price" and "Credit Screened Dealable Prices" that you see on the screen?

2. In addition to the historic currency symbols, such as, $, ¥, £, and €, there is an official three-letter symbol for each currency that is recognized worldwide. These symbols can be found at xe.com the Full Universal Currency Converter website: www.xe.com/ucc/full.shtml. Go to this site. What is the currency symbol for the Costa Rican colon? The Guyana dollar?

MINI CASE

Shrewsbury Herbal Products, Ltd.

Shrewsbury Herbal Products, located in central England close to the Welsh border, is an old-line producer of herbal teas, seasonings, and medicines. Its products are marketed all over the United Kingdom and in many parts of continental Europe as well.

Shrewsbury Herbal generally invoices in British pound sterling when it sells to foreign customers in order to guard against adverse exchange rate changes. Nevertheless, it has just received an order from a large wholesaler in central France for £320,000 of its products, conditional upon delivery being made in three months' time and the order invoiced in euros.

Shrewsbury's controller, Elton Peters, is concerned with whether the pound will appreciate versus the euro over the next three months, thus eliminating all or most of the profit when the euro receivable is paid. He thinks this an unlikely possibility, but he decides to contact the firm's banker for suggestions about hedging the exchange rate exposure.

Mr. Peters learns from the banker that the current spot exchange rate in €/£ is €1.4537; thus the invoice amount should be €465,184. Mr. Peters also learns that the three-month forward rates for the pound and the euro versus the U.S. dollar are $1.8990/£1.00 and $1.3154/€1.00, respectively. The banker offers to set up a forward hedge for selling the euro receivable for pound sterling based on the €/£ forward corss-exchange rate implicit in the forward rates against the dollar.

What would you do if you were Mr. Peters?

REFERENCES & SUGGESTED READINGS

Bank for International Settlements. *Triennial Central Bank Survey*. Basle, Switzerland: Bank for International Settlements, March 2005.

Cheung, Yin-Wong, and Menzie David Chinn. "Currency Traders and Exchange Rate Dynamics: A Survey of the US Market." *Journal of International Money and Finance* 20 (2001), pp. 439–71.

Dominguez, Kathryn M. "Central Bank Intervention and Exchange Rate Volatility." *Journal of International Money and Finance* 17 (1998), pp. 161–90.

Federal Reserve Bank of New York. *The Foreign Exchange and Interest Rate Derivatives Markets: Turnover in the United States*. New York: Federal Reserve Bank of New York, 2004.

Grabbe, J. Orlin. *International Financial Markets*, 3rd ed. Upper Saddle River, N.J.: Prentice Hall, 1996.

Huang, Roger D., and Ronald W. Masulis. "FX Spreads and Dealer Competition across the 24-Hour Trading Day." *Review of Financial Studies* 12 (1999) pp. 61–93.

International Monetary Fund. *International Capital Markets: Part I. Exchange Rate Management and International Capital Flows*. Washington, D.C.: International Monetary Fund, 1993.

Ito, Takatoshi, Richard K. Lyons, and Michael T. Melvin. "Is There Private Information in the FX Market? The Tokyo Experiment." *Journal of Finance* 53 (1998), pp. 1111–30.

Lyons, Richard K. "Profits and Position Control: A Week of FX Dealing." *Journal of International Money and Finance* 17 (1998), pp. 97–115.

UBS Warburg. *Foreign Exchange and Money Market Transactions*. This book can be found and downloaded at www.ubswarburg.com/fx_swiss/.

6 International Parity Relationships and Forecasting Foreign Exchange Rates

FOR COMPANIES AND investors alike, it is important to have a firm understanding of the forces driving exchange rate changes as these changes would affect investment and financing opportunities. To that end, this chapter examines several key international parity relationships, such as interest rate parity and purchasing power parity, that have profound implications for international financial management. Some of these are, in fact, manifestations of the *law of one price* that must hold in *arbitrage equilibrium*.[1] An understanding of these parity relationships provides insights into (1) how foreign exchange rates are determined, and (2) how to forecast foreign exchange rates.

套利是指为了谋取
无风险利润而同时买进
和卖出相同的或具有同
等价值的资产或商品的
行为。

Since **arbitrage** plays a critical role in the ensuing discussion, we should define it upfront. The term *arbitrage* can be defined as *the act of simultaneously buying and selling the same or equivalent assets or commodities for the purpose of making certain, guaranteed profits*. As long as there are profitable arbitrage opportunities, the market cannot be in equilibrium. The market can be said to be in equilibrium when no profitable arbitrage opportunities exist. Such well-known parity relationships as interest rate parity and purchasing power parity, in fact, represent arbitrage equilibrium conditions. Let us begin our discussion with interest rate parity.

Interest Rate Parity

利率平价（IRP）
是国际金融市场保持均
衡时的套利条件。

Interest rate parity (IRP) is an arbitrage condition that must hold when international financial markets are in equilibrium. Suppose that you have $1 to invest over, say, a one-year period. Consider two alternative ways of investing your fund: (1) invest

---

[1]The law of one price prevails when the same or equivalent things are trading at the same price across different locations or markets, precluding profitable arbitrage opportunities. As we will see, many equilibrium pricing relationships in finance are obtained from imposing the law of one price, i.e., the two things that are equal to each other must be selling for the same price.

domestically at the U.S. interest rate, or, alternatively, (2) invest in a foreign country, say, the U.K., at the foreign interest rate and hedge the exchange risk by selling the maturity value of the foreign investment forward. It is assumed here that you want to consider only default-free investments.

If you invest $1 domestically at the U.S. interest rate ($i_\$$), the maturity value will be

$$\$1(1 + i_\$)$$

Since you are assumed to invest in a default-free instrument like a U.S. Treasury note, there is no uncertainty about the future maturity value of your investment in dollar terms.

To invest in the U.K., on the other hand, you carry out the following sequence of transactions:

1. Exchange $1 for a pound amount, that is, £$(1/S)$, at the prevailing spot exchange rate (S).[2]

2. Invest the pound amount at the U.K. interest rate ($i_£$), with the maturity value of £$(1/S)(1 + i_£)$.

3. Sell the maturity value of the U.K. investment forward in exchange for a *predetermined dollar amount,* that is, $\$[(1/S)(1 + i_£)]F$, where F denotes the forward exchange rate.

Note that the exchange rate, S or F, represents the dollar price of one unit of foreign currency, i.e., British pound in the above example. When your British investment matures in one year, you will receive the full maturity value, £$(1/S)(1 + i_£)$. But since you have to deliver exactly the same amount of pounds to the counterparty of the forward contract, your net pound position is reduced to zero. In other words, the exchange risk is completely hedged. Since, as with the U.S. investment, you are assured a predetermined dollar amount, your U.K. investment coupled with forward hedging is a perfect substitute for the domestic U.S. investment. Because you've hedged the exchange risk by a forward contract, you've effectively *redenominated* the U.K. investment in dollar terms. The "effective" dollar interest rate from the U.K. investment alternative is given by

$$\frac{F}{S}(1 + i_£) - 1$$

Arbitrage equilibrium then would dictate that the future dollar proceeds (or, equivalently, the dollar interest rates) from investing in the two equivalent investments must be the same, implying that

$$(1 + i_\$) = \frac{F}{S}(1 + i_£), \quad \text{or alternatively}$$

$$F = S\left[\frac{1 + i_\$}{1 + i_£}\right] \tag{6.1}$$

显然，利率平价是
一价定律（LOP）在国
际金融市场中的表现。

which is a formal statement of IRP. It should be clear from the way we arrived at Equation 6.1 that IRP is a manifestation of the **law of one price (LOP)** applied to international money market instruments. The IRP relationship has been known among currency traders since the late 19th century. But it was only during the 1920s that the relationship became widely known to the public from the writings of John M. Keynes and other economists.[3]

---

[2]For notational simplicity, we delete the currency subscripts for the exchange rate notations, S and F. If the exchange rate, S or F, is expressed as the amount of foreign currency per dollar, IRP formula will become as follows: $(1 + i_\$) = (S/F)(1 + i_£)$.

[3]A systematic exposition of the interest rate parity is generally attributed to Keynes's *Monetary Reform* (1924).

EXHIBIT 6.1

Dollar Cash Flows to an Arbitrage Portfolio

Transactions	CF_0	CF_1
1. Borrow in the U.S.	$\$S$	$-S(1 + i_\$)$
2. Lend in the U.K.	$-\$S$	$S_1(1 + i_£)$
3. Sell the £ receivable forward*	0	$(1 + i_£)(F - S_1)$
Net cash flow	0	$(1 + i_£)F - (1 + i_\$)S$

*Selling the £ receivable "forward" will not result in any cash flow at the present time, that is, $CF_0 = 0$. But at the maturity, the seller will receive $\$(F - S_1)$ for each pound sold forward. S_1 denotes the future spot exchange rate.

换句话说，利率平价也可以通过构造套利组合来得到。这种组合不存在净投资和风险，在均衡时的净现金流为零。

Alternatively, IRP can be derived by constructing an **arbitrage portfolio,** which involves (1) no net investment, as well as (2) no risk, and then requiring that such a portfolio should not generate any net cash flow in equilibrium. Consider an arbitrage portfolio consisting of three separate positions:

1. Borrowing $\$S$ in the United States, which is just enough to buy £1 at the prevailing spot exchange rate (S).

2. Lending £1 in the U.K. at the U.K. interest rate.

3. Selling the maturity value of the U.K. investment forward.

Exhibit 6.1 summarizes the present and future (maturity date) cash flows, CF_0 and CF_1, from investing in the arbitrage portfolio.

Two things are noteworthy in Exhibit 6.1. First, the net cash flow at the time of investment is zero. This, of course, implies that the arbitrage portfolio is indeed fully self-financing; it doesn't cost any money to hold this portfolio. Second, the net cash flow on the maturity date is known with certainty. That is so because none of the variables involved in the net cash flow, that is, S, F, $i_\$$, and $i_£$, is uncertain. Since no one should be able to make certain profits by holding this arbitrage portfolio, market equilibrium requires that the net cash flow on the maturity date be zero for this portfolio:

$$(1 + i_£)F - (1 + i_\$)S = 0 \qquad (6.2)$$

which, upon simple rearrangement, is the same result as Equation 6.1.

The IRP relationship is sometimes approximated as follows:

$$(i_\$ - i_£) = \left[\frac{F - S}{S}\right](1 + i_£) \approx \left[\frac{F - S}{S}\right] \qquad (6.3)$$

显然，利率平价与两国的利率有关。

As can be seen clearly from Equation 6.1, IRP provides a linkage between interest rates in two different countries. Specifically, the interest rate will be higher in the United States than in the U.K. when the dollar is at a forward discount, that is, $F > S$. Recall that the exchange rates, S and F, represent the dollar prices of one unit of foreign currency. When the dollar is at a forward discount, this implies that the dollar is expected to depreciate against the pound. If so, the U.S. interest rate should be higher than the U.K. interest rate to compensate for the expected depreciation of the dollar. Otherwise, nobody would hold dollar-denominated securities. On the other hand, the U.S. interest rate will be lower than the U.K. interest rate when the dollar is at a forward premium, that is, $F < S$. Equation 6.1 indicates that the forward exchange rate will deviate from the spot rate as long as the interest rates of the two countries are not the same.[4]

当利率平价条件成立时，不管是在美国还是在英国进行远期套期保值，对投资者而言无所区别。

When IRP holds, you will be indifferent between investing your money in the United States and investing in the U.K. with forward hedging. However, if IRP is violated, you will prefer one to another. You will be better off by investing in the United

---

[4]To determine if there exists an arbitrage opportunity, one should use the exact version of IRP, not the approximate version.

当利率平价不成立时，就会产生**抵补套利**的机会。

States (U.K.) if $(1 + i_\$)$ is greater (less) than $(F/S)(1 + i_£)$. When you need to borrow, on the other hand, you will choose to borrow where the dollar interest is lower. When IRP doesn't hold, the situation also gives rise to **covered interest arbitrage** opportunities.

Covered Interest Arbitrage

To explain the covered interest arbitrage (CIA) process, it is best to work with a numerical example.

EXAMPLE 6.1

Suppose that the annual interest rate is 5 percent in the United States and 8 percent in the U.K., and that the spot exchange rate is \$1.50/£ and the forward exchange rate, with one-year maturity, is \$1.48/£. In terms of our notation, $i_\$ = 5\%$, $i_£ = 8\%$, $S = \$1.50$, and $F = \$1.48$. Assume that the arbitrager can borrow up to \$1,000,000 or £666,667, which is equivalent to \$1,000,000 at the current spot exchange rate.

Let us first check if IRP is holding under current market conditions. Substituting the given data, we find,

$$\left[\frac{F}{S}\right](1 + i_£) = \left[\frac{1.48}{1.50}\right](1.08) = 1.0656,$$

which is not exactly equal to $(1 + i_\$) = 1.05$. Specifically, we find that the current market condition is characterized by

$$(1 + i_\$) < \left[\frac{F}{S}\right](1 + i_£). \tag{6.4}$$

Clearly, IRP is not holding, implying that a profitable arbitrage opportunity exists. Since the interest rate is lower in the United States, an arbitrage transaction should involve borrowing in the United States and lending in the U.K.

The arbitrager can carry out the following transactions:

1. In the United States, borrow \$1,000,000. Repayment in one year will be \$1,050,000 = \$1,000,000 × 1.05.
2. Buy £666,667 spot using \$1,000,000.
3. Invest £666,667 in the U.K. The maturity value will be £720,000 = £666,667 × 1.08.
4. Sell £720,000 forward in exchange for \$1,065,600 = (£720,000)(\$1.48/£).

In one year when everything matures, the arbitrager will receive the full maturity value of his U.K. investment, that is, £720,000. The arbitrager then will deliver this pound amount to the counterparty of the forward contract and receive \$1,065,600 in return. Out of this dollar amount, the maturity value of the dollar loan, \$1,050,000, will be paid. The arbitrager still has \$15,600 (= \$1,065,600 − \$1,050,000) left in his account, which is his arbitrage profit. In making this certain profit, the arbitrager neither invested any money out of his pocket nor bore any risk. He indeed carried out "covered interest arbitrage," which means that he borrowed at one interest rate and simultaneously lent at another interest rate, with exchange risk fully covered via forward hedging.[5] Exhibit 6.2 provides a summary of CIA transactions.

---

[5]The arbitrage profit is, in fact, equal to the effective interest rate differential times the amount borrowed, i.e., \$15,600 = (1.0656 − 1.05)(\$1,000,000).

EXHIBIT 6.2

Covered Interest Arbitrage: Cash Flow Analysis

Transactions	CF_0	CF_1
1. Borrow $1,000,000	$1,000,000	−$1,050,000
2. Buy £ spot	−$1,000,000	
	£666,667	
3. Lend £666,667	−£666,667	£720,000
4. Sell 720,000 forward		−£720,000
		$1,065,600
Net cash flow	0	$15,600

套利机会到底能存
在多久? 答案是: 很短!

How long will this arbitrage opportunity last? A simple answer is: only for a short while. As soon as deviations from IRP are detected, informed traders will immediately carry out CIA transactions. As a result of these arbitrage activities, IRP will be restored quite quickly. To see this, let's get back to our numerical example, which induced covered interest arbitrage activities. Since every trader will (1) borrow in the United States as much as possible, (2) lend in the U.K., (3) buy the pound spot, and, at the same time, (4) sell the pound forward, the following adjustments will occur to the initial market condition described in Equation 6.4:

1. The interest rate will rise in the United States ($i_\$\uparrow$).
2. The interest rate will fall in the U.K. ($i_\pounds\downarrow$).
3. The pound will appreciate in the spot market ($S\uparrow$).
4. The pound will depreciate in the forward market ($F\downarrow$).

These adjustments will raise the left-hand side of Equation 6.4 and, at the same time, lower the right-hand side until both sides are equalized, restoring IRP.

The adjustment process is depicted in Exhibit 6.3. The initial market condition described by Equation 6.4 is represented by point A in the exhibit, substantially off the IRP line.[6] CIA activities will increase the interest rate differential (as indicated by the

EXHIBIT 6.3

The Interest Rate Parity Diagram

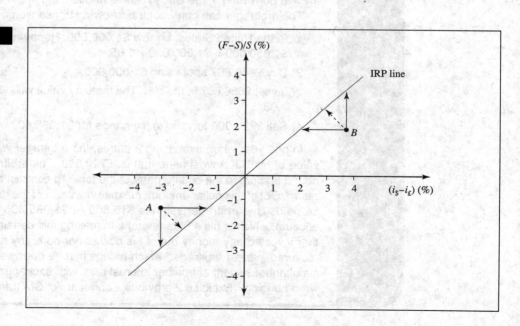

---

[6]Note that at point A, the interest rate differential is −3%, i.e., $i_\$ - i_\pounds = 5\% - 8\% = -3\%$, and the forward premium is −1.33%, i.e., $(F - S)/S = (1.48 - 1.50)/1.50 = -0.0133$, or −1.33%.

horizontal arrow) and, at the same time, lower the forward premium/discount (as indicated by the vertical arrow). Since the foreign exchange and money markets share the burden of adjustments, the actual path of adjustment to IRP can be depicted by the dotted arrow. When the initial market condition is located at point B, IRP will be restored partly by an increase in the forward premium, $(F - S)/S$, and partly by a decrease in the interest rate differential, $i_\$ - i_£$.

EXAMPLE 6.2

Before we move on, it would be useful to consider another CIA example. Suppose that the market condition is summarized as follows:

Three-month interest rate in the United States: 8.0% per annum.

Three-month interest rate in Germany: 5.0% per annum.

Current spot exchange rate: €0.800/$.

Three-month forward exchange rate: €0.7994/$.

The current example differs from the previous example in that the transaction horizon is three months rather than a year, and the exchange rates are quoted in *European* rather than American terms.

If we would like to apply IRP as defined in Equation 6.1, we should convert the exchange rates into American terms and use three-month interest rates, not annualized rates. In other words, we should use the following numerical values to check if IRP is holding:

$i_\$ = 8.0/4 = 2.0\%$ $i_€ = 5.0/4 = 1.25\%$

$S = 1/0.800 = \$1.250/€$ $F = 1/0.7994 = \$1.2510/€$

Now, we can compute the right-hand side of Equation 6.1:

$$\left[\frac{F}{S}\right](1 + i_€) = \left[\frac{1.2510}{1.2500}\right](1.0125) = 1.0133,$$

which is less than $(1 + i_\$) = 1.02$. Clearly, IRP is not holding and an arbitrage opportunity thus exists. Since the interest rate is lower in Germany than in the United States, the arbitrage transaction should involve borrowing in Germany and lending in the United States. Again, we assume that the arbitrager can borrow up to $1,000,000 or the equivalent € amount, €800,000.

The arbitrager can carry out the following transactions:

1. Borrow €800,000 in Germany. Repayment in three months will be €810,000 = €800,000 × 1.0125.

2. Buy $1,000,000 spot using €800,000.

3. Invest $1,000,000 in the United States. The maturity value will be $1,020,000 in three months.

4. Buy €810,000 forward in exchange for $1,013,310 = (€810,000)($1.2510/€).

In three months, the arbitrager will receive the full maturity value of the U.S. investment, $1,020,000. But then, the arbitrager should deliver $1,013,310 to the counterparty of the forward contract and receive €810,000 in return, which will be used to repay the euro loan. The arbitrage profit will thus be $6,690 (= $1,020,000−$1,013,310).[7]

---

[7]It is left to the readers to figure out how IRP may be restored in this example.

Interest Rate Parity and Exchange Rate Determination

Being an arbitrage equilibrium condition involving the (spot) exchange rate, IRP has an immediate implication for exchange rate determination. To see why, let us reformulate the IRP relationship in terms of the spot exchange rate:

$$S = \left[\frac{1+i_£}{1+i_\$}\right] F \tag{6.5}$$

Equation 6.5 indicates that given the forward exchange rate, the spot exchange rate depends on relative interest rates. All else equal, an increase in the U.S. interest rate will lead to a higher foreign exchange value of the dollar.[8] This is so because a higher U.S. interest rate will attract capital to the United States, increasing the demand for dollars. In contrast, a decrease in the U.S. interest rate will lower the foreign exchange value of the dollar.

除了相对利率之外，远期汇率是决定即期汇率的一个重要因素。

In addition to relative interest rates, the forward exchange rate is an important factor in spot exchange rate determination. Under certain conditions the forward exchange rate can be viewed as the expected future spot exchange rate conditional on all relevant information being available now, that is,

$$F = E(S_{t+1}|I_t) \tag{6.6}$$

where S_{t+1} is the future spot rate when the forward contract matures, and I_t denotes the set of information currently available.[9] When Equations 6.5 and 6.6 are combined, we obtain,

$$S = \left[\frac{1+i_£}{1+i_\$}\right] E(S_{t+1}/I_t) \tag{6.7}$$

Two things are noteworthy from Equation 6.7. First, "expectation" plays a key role in exchange rate determination. Specifically, the expected future exchange rate is shown to be a major determinant of the current exchange rate; when people "expect" the exchange rate to go up in the future, it goes up now. People's expectations thus become self-fulfilling. Second, exchange rate behavior will be driven by news events. People form their expectations based on the set of information (I_t) they possess. As they receive news continuously, they are going to update their expectations continuously. As a result, the exchange rate will tend to exhibit a *dynamic* and *volatile* short-term behavior, responding to various news events. By definition, news events are unpredictable, making forecasting future exchange rates an arduous task.

因此，汇率表现为一种动态的、波动的短期行为，会对各种新闻事件做出反应。

When the forward exchange rate F is replaced by the expected future spot exchange rate, $E(S_{t+1})$ in Equation 6.3, we obtain:

$$(i_\$ - i_£) \approx E(e) \tag{6.8}$$

无抵补利率平价

where $E(e)$ is the expected rate of change in the exchange rate, that is, $[E(S_{t+1}) - S_t]/S_t$. Equation 6.8 states that the interest rate differential between a pair of countries is (approximately) equal to the expected rate of change in the exchange rate. This relationship is known as the **uncovered interest rate parity**.[10] If, for instance, the annual interest rate is 5 percent in the United States and 8 percent in the U.K., as assumed in our numerical example, the uncovered IRP suggests that the pound is expected to depreciate against the dollar by about 3 percent, that is, $E(e) \approx -3\%$.

Reasons for Deviations from Interest Rate Parity

Although IRP tends to hold quite well, it may not hold precisely all the time for at least two reasons: transaction costs and capital controls.

In our previous examples of CIA transactions, we implicitly assumed, among other things, that no transaction costs existed. As a result, in our first CIA example, for each

---

[8]A higher U.S. interest rate ($i_\$ \uparrow$) will lead to a lower spot exchange rate ($S \downarrow$), which means a stronger dollar. Note that the variable S represents the number of U.S. dollars per pound.

[9]The set of relevant information should include money supplies, interest rates, trade balances, and so on that would influence the exchange rates.

[10]As we will discuss shortly, the same relationship is also known as the international Fisher effect.

EXHIBIT 6.4

Interest Rate Parity with Transaction Costs

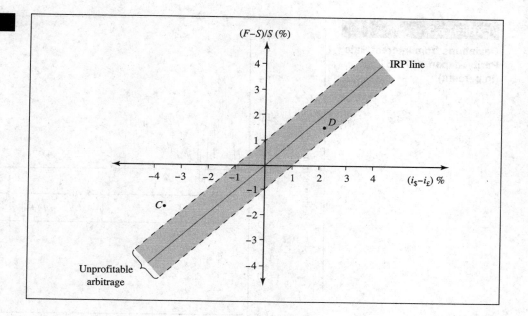

由于存在价差，所以单位借入美元的套利利润会小于零。

dollar borrowed at the U.S. interest rate ($i_\$$), the arbitrager could realize the following amount of positive profit:

$$(F/S)(1 + i_£) - (1 + i_\$) > 0 \tag{6.9}$$

In reality, transaction costs do exist. The interest rate at which the arbitrager borrows, i^a, tends to be higher than the rate at which he lends, i^b, reflecting the bid-ask spread. Likewise, there exist bid-ask spreads in the foreign exchange market as well. The arbitrager has to buy foreign exchanges at the higher ask price and sell them at the lower bid price. Each of the four variables in Equation 6.9 can be regarded as representing the midpoint of the spread.

Because of spreads, arbitrage profit from each dollar borrowed may become nonpositive:

$$(F^b/S^a)(1 + i_£^b) - (1 + i_\$^a) \le 0 \tag{6.10}$$

where the superscripts a and b to the exchange rates and interest rates denote the ask and bid prices, respectively. This is so because

$$(F^b/S^a) < (F/S)$$

$$(1 + i_£^b) < (1 + i_£)$$

$$(1 + i_£^a) > (1 + i_\$)$$

If the arbitrage profit turns negative because of transaction costs, the current deviation from IRP does not represent a profitable arbitrage opportunity. Thus, the IRP line in Exhibit 6.4 can be viewed as included within a band around it, and only IRP deviations outside the band, such as point C, represent profitable arbitrage opportunities. IRP deviations within the band, such as point D, would not represent profitable arbitrage opportunities. The width of this band will depend on the size of transaction costs.

另一个使利率平价偏离的原因是政府对资金流动的限制。

Another major reason for deviations from IRP is capital controls imposed by governments. For various macroeconomic reasons, governments sometimes restrict capital flows, inbound and/or outbound.[11] Governments achieve this objective by means of

---

[11]Capital controls were often imposed by governments in an effort to improve the balance-of-payments situations and to keep the exchange rate at a desirable level.

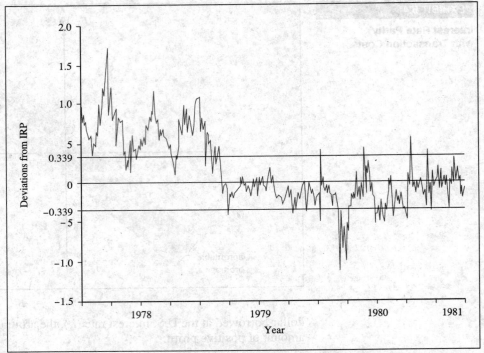

Note: Daily data were used in computing the deviations. The zone bounded by +0.339 and −0.339 represents the average width of the band around the IRP for the sample period.
Source: I. Otani and S. Tiwari, "Capital Controls and Interest Rate Parity: The Japanese Experience, 1978–81," *IMF Staff Papers* 28 (1981), pp. 793–816.

jawboning, imposing taxes, or even outright bans on cross-border capital movements. These control measures imposed by governments can effectively impair the arbitrage process, and, as a result, deviations from IRP may persist.

An interesting historical example is provided by Japan, where capital controls were imposed on and off until December 1980, when the Japanese government liberalized international capital flows. Otani and Tiwari (1981) investigated the effect of capital controls on IRP deviations during the period 1978–81. They computed deviations from interest rate parity (DIRP) as follows:[12]

$$\text{DIRP} = [(1 + i_{¥})S/(1 + i_{\$})F] - 1 \tag{6.11}$$

where:

$i_{¥}$ = interest rate on three-month Gensaki bonds.[13]
$i_{\$}$ = interest rate on three-month Euro-dollar deposits.
S = yen/dollar spot exchange rate in Tokyo.
F = yen/dollar three-month forward exchange rate in Tokyo.

如果利率平价成立，那么偏离程度呈期望值为 "0" 的随机分布。

Deviations from IRP computed as above are plotted in Exhibit 6.5. If IRP holds strictly, deviations from it would be randomly distributed, with the expected value of zero.

Exhibit 6.5, however, shows that deviations from IRP hardly hover around zero. The deviations were quite significant at times until near the end of 1980. They were the greatest during 1978. This can be attributed to various measures the Japanese government took

---

[12]Readers can convince themselves that DIRP in Equation 6.11 will be zero if IRP holds exactly.
[13]Gensaki bonds, issued in the Tokyo money market, are sold with a repurchase agreement. While interest rates on Gensaki bonds are determined by market forces, they can still be affected by various market imperfections.

to discourage capital inflows, which was done to keep the yen from appreciating. As these measures were removed in 1979, the deviations were reduced. They increased again considerably in 1980, however, reflecting an introduction of capital control; Japanese financial institutions were asked to discourage foreign currency deposits.

In December 1980, Japan adopted the new *Foreign Exchange and Foreign Trade Control Law,* which generally liberalized foreign exchange transactions. Not surprisingly, the deviations hover around zero in the first quarter of 1981. The empirical evidence presented in Exhibit 6.5 closely reflects changes in capital controls during the study period. This implies that deviations from IRP, especially in 1978 and 1980, do not represent unexploited profit opportunities; rather, they reflect the existence of significant barriers to cross-border arbitrage.

Purchasing Power Parity

购买力平价 (PPP) 理论认为，两国货币间的汇率应该等同于两国间价格水平的比。

When the law of one price is applied internationally to a *standard commodity basket,* we obtain the theory of **purchasing power parity** (PPP). This theory states that the exchange rate between currencies of two countries should be equal to the ratio of the countries' price levels. The basic idea of PPP was initially advanced by classical economists such as David Ricardo in the 19th century. But it is Gustav Cassel, a Swedish economist, who popularized the PPP in the 1920s. In those years, many countries, including Germany, Hungary, and the Soviet Union, experienced hyperinflation. As the purchasing power of the currencies in these countries sharply declined, the same currencies also depreciated sharply against stable currencies like the U.S. dollar. The PPP became popular against this historical backdrop.

Let $P_\$$ be the dollar price of the standard commodity basket in the United States and $P_\pounds$ the pound price of the same basket in the United Kingdom. Formally, PPP states that the exchange rate between the dollar and the pound should be

$$S = P_\$/P_\pounds \qquad (6.12)$$

where S is the dollar price of one pound. PPP implies that if the standard commodity basket costs \$225 in the United States and £150 in the U.K., then the exchange rate should be \$1.50 per pound:

$$\$1.50/\pounds = \$225/\pounds150$$

If the price of the commodity basket is higher in the United States, say, \$300, then PPP dictates that the exchange rate should be higher, that is, \$2.00/£.

To give an alternative interpretation to PPP, let us rewrite Equation 6.12 as follows:

$$P_\$ = S \times P_\pounds$$

This equation states that the dollar price of the commodity basket in the United States, $P_\$$, must be the same as the dollar price of the basket in the U.K., that is, $P_\pounds$ multiplied by S. In other words, PPP requires that the price of the standard commodity basket be the same across countries when measured in a common currency. Clearly, PPP is the manifestation of the law of one price applied to the standard consumption basket. As discussed in the International Finance in Practice box "Big MacCurrencies," PPP is a way of defining the equilibrium exchange rate.

换句话说，购买力平价理论要求用同一种货币表示的标准商品篮子的价格在国际间是相同的。

As a light-hearted guide to the "correct" level of exchange rate, *The Economist* each year compiles local prices of Big Macs around the world and computes the so-called "Big Mac PPP," the exchange rate that would equalize the hamburger prices between America and elsewhere. To compare this PPP and the actual exchange rate, a currency may be judged to be either undervalued or overvalued. In April 2002, a Big Mac cost (on average) \$2.49 in America and 2.50 pesos in Argentina. Thus, the Big Mac PPP would be about one peso per dollar. The actual exchange rate, however, is 3.13 pesos

Big MacCurrencies

Currency forecasters have had it hard in recent years. Most expected the euro to rise after its launch in 1999, yet it fell. When America went into recession last year, the dollar was tipped to decline; it rose. So to help forecasters really get their teeth into exchange rates, *The Economist* has updated its Big Mac index.

Devised 16 years ago as a light-hearted guide to whether currencies are at their "correct" level, the index is based on the theory of purchasing-power parity (PPP). In the long run, countries' exchange rates should move towards rates that would equalise the prices of an identical basket of goods and services. Our basket is a McDonald's Big Mac, produced in 120 countries. The Big Mac PPP is the exchange rate that would leave hamburgers costing the same in America as elsewhere. Comparing these with actual rates signals if a currency is under- or overvalued.

The first column of the table shows the local-currency prices of a Big Mac. The second converts these into dollars. The average American price has fallen slightly over the past year, to $2.49. The cheapest Big Mac is in Argentina (78 cents), after its massive devaluation; the most expensive ($3.81) is in Switzerland. (More countries are listed on our website.) By this measure, the Argentina peso is the most undervalued currency and the Swiss franc the most overvalued.

The third column calculates Big Mac PPPS. Dividing the Japanese price by the American price, for instance, gives a dollar PPP of ¥105, against an actual exchange rate of ¥130. This implies that the yen is 19% undervalued. The euro is only 5% undervalued relative to its Big Mac PPP, far less than many economists claim. The euro area may have a single currency, but the price of a Big Mac varies widely, from €2.15 in Greece to €2.95 in France. However, that range has narrowed from a year ago. And prices vary just as much within America, which is why we use the average price in four cities.

The Australian dollar is the most undervalued rich-world currency, 35% below McParity. No wonder the Australian economy was so strong last year. Sterling, by contrast, is one of the few currencies that is overvalued against the dollar, by 16%; it is 21% too strong against the euro.

Overall, the dollar now looks more overvalued against the average of the other big currencies than at any time in the life of the Big Mac index. Most emerging-market currencies also look cheap against the dollar. Over half the emerging-market currencies are more than 30% undervalued. That implies that any currency close to McParity (e.g., the Argentine peso last year, or the Mexican peso today) will be overvalued against other emerging-market rivals.

Adjustment back towards PPP does not always come through a shift in exchange rates. It can also come about partly through price changes. In 1995 the yen was 100% overvalued. It has since fallen by 35%; but the price of a Japanese burger has also dropped by one-third.

Every time we update our Big Mac index, readers complain that burgernomics does not cut the mustard. The Big Mac is an imperfect basket. Hamburgers cannot be traded across borders; prices may be distorted by taxes, different profit margins or differences in the cost of non-tradable goods and services, such as rents. Yet it seems to pay to follow burgernomics.

In 1999, for instance, the Big Mac index suggested that the euro was already overvalued at its launch, when nearly every economist predicted it would rise. Several studies confirm that, over the long run, purchasing-power parity—including the Big Mac PPP—is a fairly good guide to exchange-rate movements.

Still, currencies can deviate from PPP for long periods. In the early 1990s the Big Mac index repeatedly signaled that the dollar was undervalued, yet it continued to slide for several years until it flipped around. Our latest figures suggest that, sooner or later, the mighty dollar will tumble; relish for fans of burgernomics.

Source: "Economics Focus Big MacCurrencies," *The Economist,* April 27, 2002, p. 76.

---

per dollar, implying that the peso is vastly undervalued. In contrast, the Big Mac PPP for Switzerland is 2.53 Swiss francs per dollar, compared with the actual exchange rate of 1.66 francs per dollar. This implies that the Swiss franc is very much overvalued.

The PPP relationship of Equation 6.12 is called the *absolute* version of PPP. When the PPP relationship is presented in the "rate of change" form, we obtain the *relative* version:

$$e = \left[\frac{\pi_\$ - \pi_£}{1 + \pi_£} \right] \approx \pi_\$ - \pi_£ \tag{6.13}$$

where e is the rate of change in the exchange rate and $\pi_\$$ and $\pi_£$ are the inflation rates in the United States and U.K., respectively. For example, if the inflation rate is 6 percent

The hamburger standard					
	Big Mac prices		Implied	Actual dollar	Under (−)/over (+)
	in local currency	in dollars	PPP* of the dollar	exchange rate 23/04/02	valuation against the dollar, %
United States[†]	$2.49	2.49	–	–	–
Argentina	Peso 2.50	0.78	1.00	3.13	−68
Australia	A$3.00	1.62	1.20	1.86	−35
Brazil	*Real* 3.60	1.55	1.45	2.34	−38
Britain	£1.99	2.88	1.25[‡]	1.45[‡]	+16
Canada	C$3.33	2.12	1.34	1.57	−15
Chile	Peso 1,400	2.16	562	655	−14
China	Yuan 10.50	1.27	4.22	8.28	−49
Czech Rep	Koruna 56.28	1.66	22.6	34.0	−33
Denmark	DKr24.75	2.96	9.94	8.38	+19
Euro area	€2.67	2.37	0.93[§]	0.89[§]	−5
China-Hong Kong ASR	HK$11.20	1.40	4.50	7.80	−42
Hungary	Forint459	1.69	184	272	−32
Indonesia	Rupiah 16,000	1.71	6,426	9,430	−32
Israel	Shekel 12.00	2.51	4.82	4.79	+1
Japan	¥262	2.01	105	130	−19
Malaysia	M$5.04	1.33	2.02	3.8	−47
Mexico	Peso 21.90	2.37	8.80	9.28	−5
New Zealand	NZ$3.95	1.77	1.59	2.24	−29
Peru	New Sol 8.50	2.48	3.41	3.43	−1
Philippines	Peso 65.00	1.28	26.1	51.0	−49
Poland	Zloty 5.90	1.46	2.37	4.04	−41
Russia	Rouble 39.00	1.25	15.7	31.2	−50
Singapore	S$3.30	1.81	1.33	1.82	−27
South Africa	Rand 9.70	0.87	3.90	10.9	−64
South Korea	Won 3,100	2.36	1,245	1,304	−5
Sweden	SKr26.00	2.52	10.4	10.3	+1
Switzerland	SFr6.30	3.81	2.53	1.66	+53
China's Taiwan	NT$70.00	2.01	28.1	34.8	−19
Thailand	Baht 55.00	1.27	22.1	43.3	−49
Turkey	Lira 4,000,000	3.06	1,606,426	1,324,500	+21
Venezuela	Bolivar 2,500	2.92	1,004	857	+17

*Purchasing-power-parity: local price divided by price in United States.

[†]Average of New York, Chicago, San Francisco and Atlanta.

[‡]Dollars per pound.

[§]Dollars per euro.

Source: McDonald's; *The Economist*.

请注意，即使绝对购买力平价不成立，但相对购买力平价却总是成立的。

PPP Deviations and the Real Exchange Rate

per year in the United States and 4 percent in the U.K., then the pound should appreciate against the dollar by about 2 percent, that is, $e \approx 2$ percent, per year. It is noted that even if absolute PPP does not hold, relative PPP may hold.[14]

Whether PPP holds or not has important implications for international trade. If PPP holds and thus the differential inflation rates between countries are exactly offset by exchange rate changes, countries' competitive positions in world export markets will

[14]From Equation 6.12 we obtain $(1 + e) = (1 + \pi_s)/(1 + \pi_\pounds)$. Rearranging the above expression we obtain $e = (\pi_s - \pi_\pounds)/(1 + \pi_\pounds)$, which is approximated by $e = \pi_s + \pi_\pounds$ as in Equation 6.13.

然而，如果偏离了
购买力平价，名义汇率
的变化就会引起**实际汇
率**的变化，从而影响该
国的国际竞争力。

not be systematically affected by exchange rate changes. However, if there are deviations from PPP, changes in nominal exchange rates cause changes in the **real exchange rates,** affecting the international competitive positions of countries. This, in turn, would affect countries' trade balances.

The real exchange rate, q, which measures deviations from PPP, can be defined as follows:[15]

$$q = \frac{1 + \pi_s}{(1 + e)(1 + \pi_£)} \qquad \text{(6.14)}$$

First note that if PPP holds, that is, $(1 + e) = (1 + \pi_s)/(1 + \pi_£)$, the real exchange rate will be unity, $q = 1$. When PPP is violated, however, the real exchange rate will deviate from unity. Suppose, for example, the annual inflation rate is 5 percent in the United States and 3.5 percent in the U.K., and the dollar depreciated against the pound by 4.5 percent. Then the real exchange rate is .97:

$$q = (1.05)/(1.045)(1.035) = .97$$

In the above example, the dollar depreciated by more than is warranted by PPP, strengthening the competitiveness of U.S. industries in the world market. If the dollar depreciates by less than the inflation rate differential, the real exchange rate will be greater than unity, weakening the competitiveness of U.S. industries. To summarize,

$q = 1$: Competitiveness of the domestic country unaltered.
$q < 1$: Competitiveness of the domestic country improves.
$q > 1$: Competitiveness of the domestic country deteriorates.

Exhibit 6.6 plots the real "effective" exchange rates for the U.S. dollar, Japanese yen, Canadian dollar, Mexican peso, Chinese yuan, and British pound since 1980. The rates plotted in Exhibit 6.6 are, however, the real effective exchange rate "indices" computed using 2000 rates as the base, that is, 2000 = 100. The real effective exchange rate is a weighted average of bilateral real exchange rates, with the weight for each foreign currency determined by the country's share in the domestic country's international trade. The real effective exchange rate rises if domestic inflation exceeds inflation abroad and the nominal exchange rate fails to depreciate to compensate for the higher domestic inflation rate. Thus, if the real effective exchange rate rises (falls), the domestic country's competitiveness declines (improves). It is noted that the real effective exchange rate of the Chinese yuan has fallen sharply in the first half of the 1980s and stayed at a low level since then.

Evidence on Purchasing Power Parity

购买力平价成了一
系列检验的对象，但是
通常得到相反的结果。

As is clear from the above discussions, whether PPP holds in reality is a question of considerable importance. In view of the fact that PPP is the manifestation of the law of one price applied to a standard commodity basket, it will hold only if the prices of constituent commodities are equalized across countries in a given currency and if the composition of the consumption basket is the same across countries.

The PPP has been the subject of a series of tests, yielding generally negative results. For example, in his study of disaggregated commodity arbitrage between the United States and Canada, Richardson (1978) was unable to detect commodity arbitrage for a majority of commodity classes. Richardson reported: "The presence of commodity arbitrage could be rejected with 95 percent confidence for at least 13 out of the 22 commodity groups" (p. 346). Although Richardson did not directly test PPP, his findings can be viewed as highly negative news for PPP. If commodity arbitrage is imperfect between neighboring countries like the United States and Canada that have

---

[15]The real exchange rate measures the degree of deviations from PPP over a certain period of time, assuming that PPP held roughly at a starting point. If PPP holds continuously, the real exchange rate will remain unity.

EXHIBIT 6.6   **Real Effective Exchange Rates for Selected Currencies**

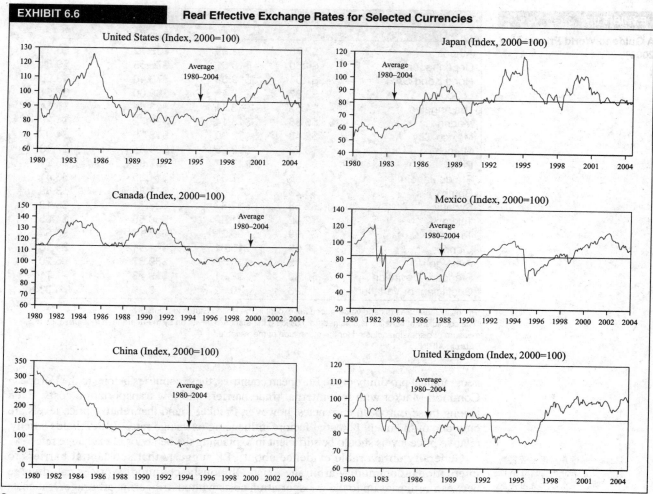

Source: Datastream.

relatively few trade restrictions, PPP is not likely to hold much better for other pairs of countries.

Exhibit 6.7, "A Guide to World Prices," also provides evidence against commodity price parity. The price of aspirin (100 units) ranges from $2.30 in Mexico City to $31.99 in Tokyo. Likewise, a cost of a man's haircut ranges from $13.75 in Mexico City to $79.58 in Copenhagen. It cost 6 times (!) more to have a haircut in Copenhagen than in Mexico City. The price differential, however, is likely to persist because haircuts are simply not tradable. In comparison, the price disparity for camera film is substantially less. This can be attributable to the fact that camera film is a highly standardized commodity that is actively traded across national borders.

Kravis和Lipsey (1978) 考察了通货膨胀率和汇率之间的关系，发现如果没有套汇带来的快速修正，价格水平差别可以变得相当大，这就否定了关于一体化的国际商品价格结构的看法。

Kravis and Lipsey (1978) examined the relationship between inflation rates and exchange rates and found that price levels can move far apart without rapid correction via arbitrage, thus rejecting the notion of integrated international commodity price structure. In a similar vein, Adler and Lehman (1983) found that deviations from PPP follow a random walk, without exhibiting any tendency to revert to PPP.

Frenkel (1981) reported that while PPP did very poorly in explaining the behavior of exchange rates between the U.S. dollar and major European currencies, it performed somewhat better in explaining the exchange rates between a pair of European currencies, such as the British pound versus the German mark, and the French franc versus the German mark. Frenkel's finding may be attributable to the fact that, in addition to the

EXHIBIT 6.7

A Guide to World Prices: May 2004[a]

Location	Fast Food (1 unit)	Aspirin (100 units)	Man's Haircut (1 unit)	Camera Film (24 exposures)
Athens	$2.75	$2.99	$37.72	$3.59
Copenhagen	$4.50	$13.61	$79.58	$9.64
Hong Kong-SAR	$1.54	$19.02	$73.40	$3.08
London	$3.37	$19.49	$69.00	$7.51
Los Angeles	$4.53	$13.11	$23.09	$5.64
Madrid	$3.35	$18.14	$25.72	$4.20
Mexico City	$2.48	$2.30	$13.75	$4.07
Munich	$3.29	$23.35	$24.55	$7.18
Paris	$3.59	$17.37	$37.92	$5.27
Rio de Janeiro	$1.86	$7.31	$14.83	$3.41
Rome	$3.23	$23.65	$31.88	$3.89
Sydney	$2.58	$12.87	$33.71	$5.12
Tokyo	$2.42	$31.99	$50.86	$4.95
Toronto	$2.99	$6.20	$37.17	$5.64
Vienna	$3.29	$15.81	$44.91	$4.78
Average	$3.05	$15.15	$39.87	$5.20
Standard Deviation	$0.80	$7.91	$19.73	$1.71
Coefficient of Variation[b]	0.26	0.52	0.49	0.33

[a]Prices include sales tax and value-added tax except in the United States location.
[b]The coefficient of variation is obtained from dividing the standard deviation by the average. It thus provides a measure of dispersion adjusted for the magnitude of the variable.
Source: AIRINC.

通常，那些否定购买力平价成立的证据说明：存在着大量阻碍国际商品套利的障碍。

不可贸易商品

即使购买力平价在实际中是不成立的，但对经济分析仍然有着重要作用。

geographical proximity of the European countries, these countries belong to the European Common Market with low internal trade barriers and low transportation costs. Even among these European currencies, however, Frenkel found that relative price levels are only one of the many potential factors influencing exchange rates. If PPP holds strictly, relative price levels should be sufficient in explaining the behavior of exchange rates.

Generally unfavorable evidence about PPP suggests that substantial barriers to international commodity arbitrage exist. Obviously, commodity prices can diverge between countries up to the transportation costs without triggering arbitrage. If it costs $50 to ship a ton of rice from Thailand to Korea, the price of rice can diverge by up to $50 in either direction between the two countries. Likewise, deviations from PPP can result from tariffs and quotas imposed on international trade.

As is well recognized, some commodities never enter into international trade. Examples of such **nontradables** include haircuts, medical services, housing, and the like. These items are either immovable or inseparable from the providers of these services. Suppose a quality haircut costs $20 in New York City, but the comparable haircut costs only $7 in Mexico City. Obviously, you cannot import haircuts from Mexico. Either you have to travel to Mexico or a Mexican barber must travel to New York City, both of which, of course, are impractical in view of the travel costs and the immigration laws. Consequently, a large price differential for haircuts will persist. As long as there are nontradables, PPP will not hold in its absolute version. If PPP holds for tradables and the relative prices between tradables and nontradables are maintained, then PPP can hold in its relative version. These conditions, however, are not very likely to hold.

Even if PPP may not hold in reality, it can still play a useful role in economic analysis. First, one can use the PPP-determined exchange rate as a benchmark in deciding if a country's currency is undervalued or overvalued against other currencies. Second, one can often make more meaningful international comparisons of economic data using PPP-determined rather than market-determined exchange rates. This point is highlighted in Exhibit 6.8, "How Large Is India's Economy?"

Suppose you want to rank countries in terms of gross national product (GNP). If you use market exchange rates, you can either underestimate or overestimate the true GNP values.

EXHIBIT 6.8

How Large Is India's Economy?

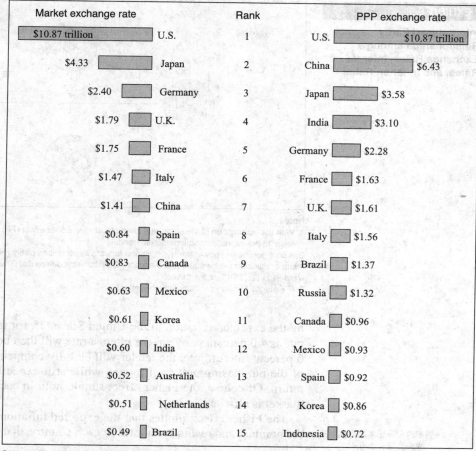

Source: The World Bank. All GNP figures are for 2003.

Exhibit 6.8 provides the GNP values of the major countries in 2003 computed using both PPP and market exchange rates. A country's ranking in terms of GNP value is quite sensitive to which exchange rate is used. India provides a striking example. When the market exchange rate is used, India ranks 12th, lagging behind such countries as Canada, Spain, and Mexico. However, when the PPP exchange rate is used, India moves up to fourth (!) after Japan, but ahead of Germany, France, and the U.K. China also moves up from seventh to second, ahead of Japan, when the PPP exchange rate is used. In contrast, countries like Canada and Spain move down in the GNP ranking when PPP exchange rates are used.

Fisher Effects

按照**费雪效应**的观点，一国预期通货膨胀率的上升（下降）将引起该国利率同比例的上升（下降）。

Another parity condition we often encounter in the literature is the **Fisher effect.** The Fisher effect holds that *an increase (decrease) in the expected inflation rate in a country will cause a proportionate increase (decrease) in the interest rate in the country.* Formally, the Fisher effect can be written for the United States as follows:

$$i_\$ = \rho_\$ + E(\pi_\$) + \rho_\$ E(\pi_\$) \approx \rho_\$ + E(\pi_\$) \tag{6.15}$$

where $\rho_\$$ denotes the equilibrium expected "real" interest rate in the United States.[16]

For example, suppose the expected real interest rate is 2 percent per year in the United States. Given this, the U.S. (nominal) interest rate will be entirely determined

[16]It is noted that Equation 6.15 obtains from the relationship: $(1 + i_\$) = (1 + \rho_\$)(1 + E(\pi_\$))$.

EXHIBIT 6.9

International Parity Relationships among Exchange Rates, Interest Rates, and Inflation Rates

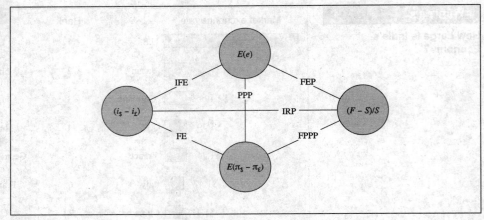

Notes:

1. With the assumption of the same real interest rate, the Fisher effect (FE) implies that the interest rate differential is equal to the expected inflation rate differential.

2. If both purchasing power parity (PPP) and forward expectations parity (FEP) hold, then the forward exchange premium or discount will be equal to the expected inflation rate differential. The latter relationship is denoted by the forward-PPP, i.e., FPPP in the exhibit.

3. IFE stands for the international Fisher effect.

by the expected inflation in the United States. If, for instance, the expected inflation rate is 4.0 percent per year, the interest rate will then be set at about 6 percent. With a 6 percent interest rate, the lender will be fully compensated for the expected erosion of the purchasing power of money while still expecting to realize a 2 percent real return. Of course, the Fisher effect should hold in each country as long as the bond market is efficient.

费雪效应意味着预期通货膨胀率只是名义利率和实际利率的差额。

The Fisher effect implies that the expected inflation rate is the difference between the nominal and real interest rates in each country, that is,

$$E(\pi_\$) = (i_\$ - \rho_\$)/(1 + \rho_\$) \approx i_\$ - \rho_\$$$
$$E(\pi_£) = (i_£ - \rho_£)/(1 + \rho_£) \approx i_£ - \rho_£$$

Now, let us assume that the real interest rate is the same between countries, that is, $\rho_\$ = \rho_£$, because of unrestricted capital flows. When we substitute the above results into the relative PPP in its expectational form in equation (6.13), we obtain

$$E(e) = (i_\$ - i_£)/(1 + i_£) \approx i_\$ - i_£ \tag{6.16}$$

国际费雪效应 (IFE)
表明两国名义利率差异表现为汇率变化的期望值。

which is known as the **international Fisher effect (IFE).**[17] IFE suggests that the nominal interest rate differential reflects the expected change in exchange rate. For instance, if the interest rate is 5 percent per year in the United States and 7 percent in the U.K., the dollar is expected to appreciate against the British pound by about 2 percent per year.

Lastly, when the international Fisher effect is combined with IRP, that is, $(F - S)/S = (i_\$ - i_£)/(1 + i_£)$, we obtain

远期预期平价
(FEP)

$$(F - S)/S = E(e) \tag{6.17}$$

which is referred to as **forward expectations parity (FEP).** Forward parity states that any forward premium or discount is equal to the expected change in the exchange rate. When investors are risk-neutral, forward parity will hold as long as

[17]The international Fisher effect is the same as the uncovered IRP previously discussed. While the Fisher effect should hold in an efficient market, the international Fisher effect need not hold even in an efficient market unless investors are risk-neutral. Generally speaking, the interest rate differential may reflect not only the expected change in the exchange rate but also a risk premium.

the foreign exchange market is informationally efficient. Otherwise, it need not hold even if the market is efficient. Exhibit 6.9 (on page 148) summarizes the parity relationships discussed so far.[18]

Forecasting Exchange Rates

Since the advent of the flexible exchange rate system in 1973, exchange rates have become increasingly more volatile and erratic. At the same time, the scope of business activities has become highly international. Consequently, many business decisions are now made based on forecasts, implicit or explicit, of future exchange rates. Understandably, forecasting exchange rates as accurately as possible is a matter of vital importance for currency traders who are actively engaged in speculating, hedging, and arbitrage in the foreign exchange markets. It is also a vital concern for multinational corporations that are formulating international sourcing, production, financing, and marketing strategies. The quality of these corporate decisions will critically depend on the accuracy of exchange rate forecasts.

汇率预测对跨国公司制定国际采购，生产融资和营销战略也有着要作用。

Some corporations generate their own forecasts, while others subscribe to outside services for a fee. While forecasters use a wide variety of forecasting techniques, most can be classified into three distinct approaches:

- Efficient market approach
- Fundamental approach
- Technical approach

Let us briefly examine each of these approaches.

Efficient Market Approach

有效市场假说(EMH)

Financial markets are said to be efficient if the current asset prices fully reflect all the available and relevant information. The **efficient market hypothesis** (EMH), which is largely attributable to Professor Eugene Fama of the University of Chicago, has strong implications for forecasting.[19]

Suppose that foreign exchange markets are efficient. This means that the current exchange rate has already reflected all relevant information, such as money supplies, inflation rates, trade balances, and output growth. The exchange rate will then change only when the market receives new information. Since news by definition is unpredictable, the exchange rate will change randomly over time. In a word, incremental changes in the exchange rate will be independent of the past history of the exchange rate. If the exchange rate indeed follows a random walk, the future exchange rate is expected to be the same as the current exchange rate, that is,

$$S_t = E(S_{t+1})$$

从某种意义上来说，**随机漫步假说**表明，应该用今天的汇率预测明天的汇率。

In a sense, the **random walk hypothesis** suggests that today's exchange rate is the best predictor of tomorrow's exchange rate.

While researchers found it difficult to reject the random walk hypothesis for exchange rates on empirical grounds, there is no theoretical reason why exchange rates should follow a pure random walk. The parity relationships we discussed previously indicate that the current forward exchange rate can be viewed as the market's consensus forecast of the future exchange rate based on the available information (I_t) if the

---

[18]Suppose that the Fisher effect holds both in the United States and in the U.K., and that the real interest rate is the same in both the countries. As shown in Exhibit 6.9, the Fisher effect (FE) then implies that the interest rate differential should be equal to the expected inflation differential. Furthermore, when forward parity and PPP are combined, we obtain what might be called "forward-PPP" (FPPP), i.e., the forward premium/discount is equal to the expected inflation differential.

[19]For a detailed discussion of the efficient market hypothesis, refer to Eugene Fama, "Efficient Capital Markets II," *Journal of Finance* 26 (1991), pp. 1575–1617.

foreign exchange markets are efficient, that is,

$$F_t = E(S_{t+1}/I_t)$$

To the extent that interest rates are different between two countries, the forward exchange rate will be different from the current spot exchange rate. This means that the future exchange rate should be expected to be different from the current spot exchange rate.

若赞成有效市场假说，那就可通过当前的即期汇率或远期汇率来预测未来的汇率。

Those who subscribe to the efficient market hypothesis may predict the future exchange rate using either the current spot exchange rate or the current forward exchange rate. But which one is better? Researchers like Agmon and Amihud (1981) compared the performance of the forward exchange rate with that of the random walk model as a predictor of the future spot exchange rate. Their empirical findings indicate that the forward exchange rate failed to outperform the random walk model in predicting the future exchange rate; the two prediction models that are based on the efficient market hypothesis registered largely comparable performances.[20]

Predicting the exchange rates using the efficient market approach has two advantages. First, since the efficient market approach is based on market-determined prices, it is costless to generate forecasts. Both the current spot and forward exchange rates are public information. As such, everyone has free access to it. Second, given the efficiency of foreign exchange markets, it is difficult to outperform the market-based forecasts unless the forecaster has access to private information that is not yet reflected in the current exchange rate.

Fundamental Approach

The fundamental approach to exchange rate forecasting uses various models. For example, the monetary approach to exchange rate determination suggests that the exchange rate is determined by three independent (explanatory) variables: (1) relative money supplies, (2) relative velocity of monies, and (3) relative national outputs.[21] One can thus formulate the monetary approach in the following empirical form:[22]

www.oecd.org/statsportal.html

Provides macroeconomic data useful for fundamental analysis.

$$s = \alpha + \beta_1(m - m^*) + \beta_2(v - v^*) + \beta_3(y^* - y) + u \tag{6.18}$$

where:

$$
\begin{aligned}
s &= \text{natural logarithm of the spot exchange rate.} \\
m - m^* &= \text{natural logarithm of domestic/foreign money supply.} \\
v - v^* &= \text{natural logarithm of domestic/foreign velocity of money.} \\
y^* - y &= \text{natural logarithm of foreign/domestic output.} \\
u &= \text{random error term, with mean zero.} \\
\alpha, \beta\text{'s} &= \text{model parameters.}
\end{aligned}
$$

Generating forecasts using the fundamental approach would involve three steps:

Step 1: Estimation of the structural model like Equation 6.18 to determine the numerical values for the parameters such as α and β's.

Step 2: Estimation of future values of the independent variables like $(m - m^*)$, $(v - v^*)$, and $(y^* - y)$.

Step 3: Substituting the estimated values of the independent variables into the estimated structural model to generate the exchange rate forecasts.

If, for example, the forecaster would like to predict the exchange rate one year into the future, he or she has to estimate the values that the independent variables will assume in one year. These values will then be substituted in the structural model that was fitted to historical data.

[20]For a detailed discussion, refer to Tamir Agmon and Yakov Amihud, "The Forward Exchange Rate and the Prediction of the Future Spot Rate," *Journal of Banking and Finance* 5 (1981), pp. 425–37.

[21]For a detailed discussion of the monetary approach, see Appendix 6A.

[22]For notational simplicity, we omit the time subscripts in the following equation.

The fundamental approach to exchange rate forecasting has three main difficulties. First, one has to forecast a set of independent variables to forecast the exchange rates. Forecasting the former will certainly be subject to errors and may not be necessarily easier than forecasting the latter. Second, the parameter values, that is, α and β's, that are estimated using historical data may change over time because of changes in government policies and/or the underlying structure of the economy. Either difficulty can diminish the accuracy of forecasts even if the model is correct. Third, the model itself can be wrong. For example, the model described by Equation 6.18 may be wrong. The forecast generated by a wrong model cannot be very accurate.

Not surprisingly, researchers found that the fundamental models failed to more accurately forecast exchange rates than either the forward rate model or the random walk model. Meese and Rogoff (1983), for example, found that the fundamental models developed based on the monetary approach did worse than the random walk model even if realized (true) values were used for the independent variables. They also confirmed that the forward rate did not do better than the random walk model. In the words of Meese and Rogoff:

> Ignoring for the present the fact that the spot rate does no worse than the forward rate, the striking feature . . . is that none of the models achieves lower, much less significantly lower, RMSE than the random walk model at any horizon. . . . The structural models in particular fail to improve on the random walk model in spite of the fact that their forecasts are based on realized values of the explanatory variables.[23] (p. 12)

果然，研究人员发现用基本分析模型预测汇率并不比远期汇率或随机漫步模型更准确。

Technical Approach

www.forexe.com

Provides information about technical analysis and currency charts.

The technical approach first analyzes the past behavior of exchange rates for the purpose of identifying "patterns" and then projects them into the future to generate forecasts. Clearly, the technical approach is based on the premise that *history repeats itself*. The technical approach thus is at odds with the efficient market approach. At the same time, it differs from the fundamental approach in that it does not use the key economic variables such as money supplies or trade balances for the purpose of forecasting. However, technical analysts sometimes consider various transaction data like trading volume, outstanding interests, and bid-ask spreads to aid their analyses.

An example of technical analysis is provided by the moving average crossover rule illustrated in Exhibit 6.10. Many technical analysts or chartists compute moving averages

EXHIBIT 6.10

Moving Average Crossover Rule: A Technical Analysis

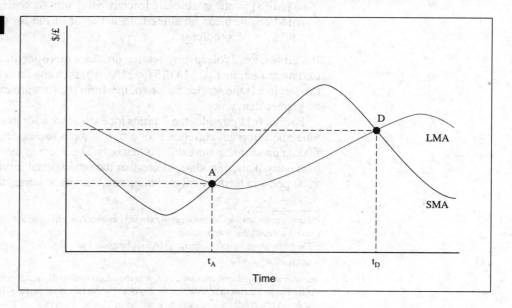

---

[23]RMSE, which stands for the root mean squared error, is the criterion that Meese and Rogoff used in evaluating the accuracy of forecasts.

as a way of separating short- and long-term trends from the vicissitudes of daily exchange rates. Exhibit 6.10 illustrates how exchange rates may be forecast based on the movements of short- and long-term moving averages. Since the short-term moving average (SMA) weighs recent exchange rate changes more heavily than the long-term moving average (LMA), the SMA will lie below (above) the LMA when the British pound is falling (rising) against the dollar. This implies that one can forecast exchange rate movements based on the crossover of the moving averages. According to this rule, a crossover of the SMA above the LMA at point A signals that the British pound is appreciating. On the other hand, a crossover of the SMA below the LMA at point D signals that the British pound is depreciating.

While academic studies tend to discredit the validity of **technical analysis,** many traders depend on technical analyses for their trading strategies. If a trader knows that other traders use technical analysis, it can be rational for the trader to use technical analysis too. If enough traders use technical analysis, the predictions based on it can become self-fulfilling to some extent, at least in the short run.

技术分析法

如果有足够的交易者使用技术分析法，那么所得到的预测结果至少在短期内会应验。

Performance of the Forecasters

Because predicting exchange rates is difficult, many firms and investors subscribe to professional forecasting services for a fee. Since an alternative to subscribing to professional forecasting services is to use a market-determined price such as the forward exchange rate, it is relevant to ask: *Can professional forecasters outperform the market?*

An answer to the above question was provided by Professor Richard Levich of New York University, who evaluated the performances of 13 forecasting services using the forward exchange rate as a benchmark. Under certain conditions, the forward exchange rate can be viewed as the market's consensus forecast of the future exchange rate.[24] These services use different methods of forecasting, such as econometric, technical, and judgmental. In evaluating the performance of forecasters, Levich computed the following ratio:

$$R = \text{MAE(S)}/\text{MAE(F)} \tag{6.19}$$

where:

  MAE(S) = mean absolute forecast error of a forecasting service.
  MAE(F) = mean absolute forecast error of the forward exchange rate as a predictor.[25]

If a professional forecasting service provides more accurate forecasts than the forward exchange rate, that is, MAE(S) < MAE(F), then the ratio R will be less than unity for the service. If the service fails to outperform the forward exchange rate, the ratio R will be greater than unity.

Exhibit 6.11 provides the R ratios for each service for the U.S. dollar exchange rates of nine major foreign currencies for a three-month forecasting horizon. The most striking finding presented in the exhibit is that only 24 percent of the entries, 25 out of 104, are less than unity. This, of course, means that the professional services as a whole clearly failed to outperform the forward exchange rate.[26] In other words, they failed to beat the market.

---

[24]These conditions are: (a) the foreign exchange markets are efficient, and (b) the forward exchange rate does not contain a significant risk premium.

[25]The mean absolute forecast error (MAE) is computed as follows:

  $$\text{MAE} = \Sigma_i |P_i - A_i|/n$$

where P is the predicted exchange rate, A is the actual (realized) exchange rate, and n is the number of forecasts made. The MAE criterion penalizes the over- and underestimation equally. If a forecaster has perfect foresight so that P = A always, then MAE will be zero.

[26]Levich found that the same qualitative result holds for different horizons like 1 month, 6 months, and 12 months.

EXHIBIT 6.11			Performance of Exchange Rate Forecasting Services										
	Forecasting Services												
Currency	1	2	3	4	5	6	7	8	9	10	11	12	13
Canadian dollar	1.29	1.13	1.00	1.59	0.99	1.08	n.a.	1.47	1.17	1.03	1.47	1.74	0.80
British pound	1.11	1.24	0.91	1.44	1.09	0.98	1.05	1.09	1.27	1.69	1.03	1.22	1.01
Belgian franc	0.95	1.07	n.a.	1.33	1.17	n.a.	n.a.	0.99	1.21	n.a.	1.06	1.01	0.77
French franc	0.91	0.98	1.02	1.43	1.27	n.a.	0.98	0.92	1.00	0.96	1.03	1.16	0.70
German mark	1.08	1.13	1.07	1.28	1.19	1.35	1.06	0.83	1.19	1.07	1.13	1.04	0.76
Italian lira	1.07	0.91	1.09	1.45	1.14	n.a.	1.12	1.12	1.00	1.17	1.64	1.54	0.93
Dutch guilder	0.80	1.10	n.a.	1.41	1.06	n.a.	n.a.	0.91	1.26	1.26	1.10	1.01	0.81
Swiss franc	1.01	n.a.	1.08	1.21	1.32	n.a.	n.a.	0.86	1.06	1.04	1.04	0.94	0.63
Japanese yen	1.42	1.05	1.02	1.23	1.08	1.45	1.09	1.24	0.94	0.47	1.31	1.30	1.79

Note: Each entry represents the R ratio defined in Equation 6.19. If a forecasting service outperforms (underperforms) the forward exchange rate, the R ratio will be less (greater) than unity.

Source: Richard Levich, "Evaluating the Performance of the Forecasters," in Richard Ensor, ed., *The Management of Foreign Exchange Risk,* 2nd ed. (Euromoney Publications, 1982).

但是，个人预测服务业存在着较大的预测业绩差异。

However, there are substantial variations in the performance records across individual services. In the cases of services 4 and 11, for instance, every entry is greater than unity. In contrast, for service 13, which is Wharton Econometric Forecasting Associates, the majority of entries, seven out of nine, are less than unity. It is also clear from the exhibit that the performance record of each service varies substantially across currencies. The R ratio for Wharton, for example, ranges from 0.63 for the Swiss franc to 1.79 for the Japanese yen. Wharton Associates clearly has difficulty in forecasting the dollar/yen exchange rate. Service 10, on the other hand, convincingly beat the market in forecasting the yen exchange rate, with an R ratio of 0.47! This suggests that consumers need to discriminate among forecasting services depending on what currencies they are interested in. Lastly, note that service 12, which is known to use technical analysis, outperformed neither the forward rate nor other services. This result certainly does not add credence to the technical approach to exchange rate forecasting.

In a more recent study, Eun and Sabherwal (2002) evaluated the forecasting performances of 10 major commercial banks from around the world. They used the data from *Risk*, a London-based monthly publication dealing with practical issues related to derivative securities and risk management. During the period April 1989 to February 1993, *Risk* published forecasts provided by the banks for exchange rates 3, 6, 9, and 12 months ahead. These forecasts were made for the U.S. dollar exchange rates of the British pound, German mark, Swiss franc, and Japanese yen on the same day of the month by all the banks. This is a rare case where banks' exchange rate forecasts were made available to the public. Since commercial banks are the market makers as well as key players in foreign exchange markets, they should be in a position to observe the order flows and the market sentiments closely. It is thus interesting to check how these banks perform.

在评价银行业绩时，Eun和Sabherwal以即期汇率作为基准。

In evaluating the performance of the banks, Eun and Sabherwal used the spot exchange rate as the benchmark. Recall that if you believe the exchange rate follows a random walk, today's spot exchange rate can be taken as the prediction of the future spot exchange rate. They thus computed the forecasting accuracy of each bank and compared it with that of the current spot exchange rate, that is, the rate prevailing on the day when forecast is made. In evaluating the performance of banks, they computed the following ratio:

$$R = \text{MSE(B)} / \text{MSE(S)}$$

EXHIBIT 6.12 Forecasting Exchange Rates: Do Banks Know Better?

Currency	Forecast Lead (months)	ANZ Bank (Australia)	Banque-Paribas (France)	Barclays Bank (U.K.)	Chemical Bank (U.S.)	Commerz Bank (Germany)	Generale Bank (France)	Harris Bank (U.S.)	Ind. Bank of Japan (Japan)	Midland-Montagu (U.K.)	Union Bank (Switzerland)	Forward Rate
British pound	3	2.09	1.31	1.08	1.33	1.31	1.41	1.95	1.10	1.10	0.98	1.02
	6	1.60	1.12	0.92	0.96	1.01	1.17	1.97	0.94	1.11	0.96	1.04
	9	1.42	1.04	0.81	0.88	0.78	0.97	1.65	0.81	0.99	1.09	0.83
	12	1.06	0.84	0.60	1.07	0.72	0.77	1.69	0.68	0.95	1.16	1.02
German mark	3	1.98	1.39	1.09	1.19	1.59	1.39	1.95	1.14	1.26	1.00	1.01
	6	1.15	1.53	1.16	1.03	1.21	1.21	1.97	1.07	1.27	1.05	1.00
	9	0.92	1.45	1.33	0.99	0.85	0.96	1.71	1.00	1.09	0.93	1.06
	12	0.80	1.19	1.14	1.16	0.62	0.97	1.51	1.00	0.87	1.16	0.96
Swiss franc	3	2.15	1.47	1.13	1.26	1.66	1.32	1.98	1.05	1.19	1.03	1.02
	6	1.18	1.58	1.30	0.98	1.29	1.35	1.88	1.04	1.24	1.05	1.00
	9	0.88	1.46	1.38	0.84	0.96	1.10	1.66	0.96	1.13	0.87	0.99
	12	0.67	1.16	1.15	0.88	0.74	1.01	1.40	0.91	0.98	1.01	0.94
Japanese yen	3	3.52	2.31	1.46	1.44	1.73	2.19	2.51	1.52	2.16	1.80	1.08
	6	2.32	2.43	1.55	1.39	1.59	1.62	2.31	1.62	1.68	1.70	1.06
	9	2.54	2.73	1.80	1.57	1.60	1.85	2.22	1.90	1.74	1.97	0.99
	12	2.70	2.61	1.83	1.79	1.44	1.97	1.89	1.93	1.68	2.00	1.10

Source: Cheol Eun and Sanjiv Sabherwal, "Forecasting Exchange Rates: Do Banks Know Better?" *Global Finance Journal*, 2002, pp. 195–215.

where:

MSE(B) = mean squared forecast error of a bank.
MSE(S) = mean squared forecast error of the spot exchange rate.

如果一家银行提供
的预测比即期汇率更加
准确，也就是说，
MSE(B)<MSE(S)，那么
比率R将小于1。

If a bank provides more accurate forecasts than the spot exchange rate, that is, MSE(B) < MSE(S), then the ratio R will be less than unity, that is, $R < 1$.

Exhibit 6.12 provides the computed R ratios for each of the 10 sample banks as well as the forward exchange rate. Overall, the majority of entries in the exhibit exceed unity, implying that these banks as a whole could not outperform the random walk model. However, some banks significantly outperformed the random walk model, especially in the longer run. For example, in forecasting the British pound exchange rate 12 months into the future, Barclays Bank ($R = 0.60$), Commerz Bank ($R = 0.72$), and Industrial Bank of Japan ($R = 0.68$) provided more accurate forecasts, on average, than the random walk model. Likewise, Commerz Bank outperformed the random walk model in forecasting the German mark and Swiss franc rates 12 months into the future. But these are more exceptional cases. It is noted that no bank, including the Japanese bank, could beat the random walk model in forecasting the Japanese yen rate at any lead. The last column of Exhibit 6.12 shows that the R-ratio for the forward exchange rate is about unity, implying that the performance of the forward rate is comparable to that of the spot rate.

SUMMARY

本章系统讨论了主要的国际平
价关系及两个相关问题：汇率决定
和汇率预测。有效的财务管理离不
开对平价关系的全面理解。

1. 如果利率平价（IRP）关系成
立，那么远期升水或贴水必须等于
两国间的利率差异。利率平价关系
表明，如果不存在影响国际资本自
由流动的壁垒，那么利率平价是套
利的均衡条件。

2. 如果利率平价关系不成立，
那么通过借入一种货币同时借出另
一种货币并利用远期合约来对汇率
风险进行套期保值，投资者就可确
保获利。借助于这种抵补套利活动，
利率平价将重新成立。

3. 利率平价关系表明，从短期
来看，汇率决定于两方面的因素：
（a）两国间的相对利率水平，（b）
预期的远期汇率。在其他条件相同的
情况下，较高（低）的本国利率将导致
本国货币的升（贬）值。人们对未来汇
率的预期往往是自我实现的。

4. 购买力平价（PPP）关系表明，
两国货币间的汇率应该等于两国的
物价水平之比。购买力平价关系反
映的是一价定律应用于国际一篮子
商品时的情形。相对购买力平价关
系表明，汇率的变化率必须等于两
国间的通货膨胀率差异。不过，现
有的实证研究大多否定了购买力平
价关系。这表明，进行国际商品套
利存在着许多壁垒。

5. 有三种不同的汇率预测方法：
（a）有效市场法；（b）基本分析
法；（c）技术分析法。有效市场法

This chapter provides a systematic discussion of the key international parity relationships and two related issues, exchange rate determination and prediction. A thorough understanding of parity relationships is essential for astute financial management.

1. Interest rate parity (IRP) holds that the forward premium or discount should be equal to the interest rate differential between two countries. IRP represents an arbitrage equilibrium condition that should hold in the absence of barriers to international capital flows.

2. If IRP is violated, one can lock in guaranteed profit by borrowing in one currency and lending in another, with exchange risk hedged via forward contract. As a result of this covered interest arbitrage, IRP will be restored.

3. IRP implies that in the short run, the exchange rate depends on (a) the relative interest rates between two countries, and (b) the expected future exchange rate. Other things being equal, a higher (lower) domestic interest rate will lead to appreciation (depreciation) of the domestic currency. People's expectations concerning future exchange rates are self-fulfilling.

4. Purchasing power parity (PPP) states that the exchange rate between two countries' currencies should be equal to the ratio of their price levels. PPP is a manifestation of the law of one price applied internationally to a standard commodity basket. The relative version of PPP states that the rate of change in the exchange rate should be equal to the inflation rate differential between countries. The existing empirical evidence, however, is generally negative on PPP. This implies that substantial barriers to international commodity arbitrage exist.

5. There are three distinct approaches to exchange rate forecasting: (a) the efficient market approach, (b) the fundamental approach, and (c) the technical approach. The efficient market approach uses such market-determined prices as the current exchange rate or the forward exchange rate to forecast the future exchange rate. The fundamental approach uses various formal models of exchange rate determination for forecasting purposes. The technical approach, on the other hand,

利用的是即期汇率或远期汇率等市
场价格来预测未来汇率。基本分析
法利用各种正式的汇率决定模型来
进行预测。技术分析法则利用历史
汇率数据来预测未来汇率。实证研
究表明，基本分析法和技术分析法
都不如有效市场法有用。

identifies patterns from the past history of the exchange rate and projects it into the future. The existing empirical evidence indicates that neither the fundamental nor the technical approach outperforms the efficient market approach.

KEY WORDS

arbitrage, *132*
arbitrage portfolio, *134*
covered interest
    arbitrage, *135*
efficient market
    hypothesis, *149*
Fisher effect, *147*
forward expectations
    parity, *148*

interest rate
    parity, *132*
international Fisher
    effect, *148*
law of one price, *133*
monetary approach, *161*
nontradables, *146*
purchasing power
    parity, *141*

quantity theory of
    money, *161*
random walk
    hypothesis, *149*
real exchange rate, *144*
technical
    analysis, *152*
uncovered interest rate
    parity, *138*

QUESTIONS

1. Give a full definition of *arbitrage*.

2. Discuss the implications of interest rate parity for exchange rate determination.

3. Explain the conditions under which the forward exchange rate will be an unbiased predictor of the future spot exchange rate.

4. Explain purchasing power parity, both the absolute and relative versions. What causes deviations from purchasing power parity?

5. Discuss the implications of the deviations from purchasing power parity for countries' competitive positions in the world market.

6. Explain and derive the international Fisher effect.

7. Researchers found that it is very difficult to forecast future exchange rates more accurately than the forward exchange rate or the current spot exchange rate. How would you interpret this finding?

8. Explain the random walk model for exchange rate forecasting. Can it be consistent with technical analysis?

9. Derive and explain the monetary approach to exchange rate determination.

10. Explain the following three concepts of purchasing power parity (PPP):

    a. The law of one price.

    b. Absolute PPP.

    c. Relative PPP.

11. Evaluate the usefulness of relative PPP in predicting movements in foreign exchange rates on:

    a. Short-term basis (for example, three months).

    b. Long-term basis (for example, six years).

CFA® PROBLEMS

CFA® PROBLEMS

PROBLEMS

1. Suppose that the treasurer of IBM has an extra cash reserve of $100,000,000 to invest for six months. The six-month interest rate is 8 percent per annum in the United States and 7 percent per annum in Germany. Currently, the spot exchange rate is €1.01 per dollar and the six-month forward exchange rate is €0.99 per dollar. The treasurer of IBM does not wish to bear any exchange risk. Where should he or she invest to maximize the return?

2. While you were visiting London, you purchased a Jaguar for £35,000, payable in three months. You have enough cash at your bank in New York City, which pays 0.35 percent interest per month, compounding monthly, to pay for the car.

Currently, the spot exchange rate is $1.45/£ and the three-month forward exchange rate is $1.40/£. In London, the money market interest rate is 2.0 percent for a three-month investment. There are two alternative ways of paying for your Jaguar.

a. Keep the funds at your bank in the United States and buy £35,000 forward.

b. Buy a certain pound amount spot today and invest the amount in the U.K. for three months so that the maturity value becomes equal to £35,000. Evaluate each payment method. Which method would you prefer? Why?

3. Currently, the spot exchange rate is $1.50/£ and the three-month forward exchange rate is $1.52/£. The three-month interest rate is 8.0 percent per annum in the U.S. and 5.8 percent per annum in the U.K. Assume that you can borrow as much as $1,500,000 or £1,000,000.

a. Determine whether interest rate parity is currently holding.

b. If IRP is not holding, how would you carry out covered interest arbitrage? Show all the steps and determine the arbitrage profit.

c. Explain how IRP will be restored as a result of covered arbitrage activities.

4. Suppose that the current spot exchange rate is €0.80/$ and the three-month forward exchange rate is €0.7813/$. The three-month interest rate is 5.6 percent per annum in the United States and 5.40 percent per annum in France. Assume that you can borrow up to $1,000,000 or €800,000.

a. Show how to realize a certain profit via covered interest arbitrage, assuming that you want to realize profit in terms of U.S. dollars. Also determine the size of your arbitrage profit.

b. Assume that you want to realize profit in terms of euros. Show the covered arbitrage process and determine the arbitrage profit in euros.

5. In the October 23, 1999, issue, *The Economist* reports that the interest rate per annum is 5.93 percent in the United States and 70.0 percent in Turkey. Why do you think the interest rate is so high in Turkey? On the basis of the reported interest rates, how would you predict the change of the exchange rate between the U.S. dollar and the Turkish lira?

6. As of November 1, 1999, the exchange rate between the Brazilian real and U.S. dollar was R$1.95/$. The consensus forecast for the U.S. and Brazil inflation rates for the next one-year period is 2.6 percent and 20.0 percent, respectively. What would you forecast the exchange rate to be at around November 1, 2000?

7. Omni Advisors, an international pension fund manager, uses the concepts of purchasing power parity (PPP) and the International Fisher Effect (IFE) to forecast spot exchange rates. Omni gathers the financial information as follows:

Base price level	100
Current U.S. price level	105
Current South African price level	111
Base rand spot exchange rate	$0.175
Current rand spot exchange rate	$0.158
Expected annual U.S. inflation	7%
Expected annual South African inflation	5%
Expected U.S. one-year interest rate	10%
Expected South African one-year interest rate	8%

Calculate the following exchange rates (ZAR and USD refer to the South African rand and U.S. dollar, respectively):

a. The current ZAR spot rate in USD that would have been forecast by PPP.

b. Using the IFE, the expected ZAR spot rate in USD one year from now.

c. Using PPP, the expected ZAR spot rate in USD four years from now.

8. Suppose that the current spot exchange rate is €1.50/£ and the one-year forward exchange rate is €1.60/£. The one-year interest rate is 5.4 percent in euros and 5.2 percent in pounds. You can borrow at most €1,000,000 or the equivalent pound amount, that is, £666,667, at the current spot exchange rate.

a. Show how you can realize a guaranteed profit from covered interest arbitrage. Assume that you are a euro-based investor. Also determine the size of the arbitrage profit.

b. Discuss how the interest rate parity may be restored as a result of the above transactions.

c. Suppose you are a pound-based investor. Show the covered arbitrage process and determine the pound profit amount.

9. Due to the integrated nature of their capital markets, investors in both the United States and U.K. require the same real interest rate, 2.5 percent, on their lending. There is a consensus in capital markets that the annual inflation rate is likely to be 3.5 percent in the United States and 1.5 percent in the U.K. for the next three years. The spot exchange rate is currently $1.50/£.

a. Compute the nominal interest rate per annum in both the United States and U.K., assuming that the Fisher effect holds.

b. What is your expected future spot dollar–pound exchange rate in three years from now?

c. Can you infer the forward dollar–pound exchange rate for one-year maturity?

CFA® PROBLEMS

10. After studying Iris Hamson's credit analysis, George Davies is considering whether he can increase the holding period return on Yucatan Resort's excess cash holdings (which are held in pesos) by investing those cash holdings in the Mexican bond market. Although Davies would be investing in a peso-denominated bond, the investment goal is to achieve the highest holding period return, measured in U.S. dollars, on the investment.

Davies finds the higher yield on the Mexican one-year bond, which is considered to be free of credit risk, to be attractive but he is concerned that depreciation of the peso will reduce the holding period return, measured in U.S. dollars. Hamson has prepared selected economic and financial data to help Davies make the decision.

Selected Economic and Financial Data for U.S. and Mexico	
Expected U.S. Inflation Rate	2.0% per year
Expected Mexican Inflation Rate	6.0% per year
U.S. One-year Treasury Bond Yield	2.5%
Mexican One-year Bond Yield	6.5%

Nominal Exchange Rates	
Spot	9.5000 Pesos = U.S. $1.00
One-year Forward	9.8707 Pesos = U.S. $1.00

Hamson recommends buying the Mexican one-year bond and hedging the foreign currency exposure using the one-year forward exchange rate. She concludes: "This transaction will result in a U.S. dollar holding period return that is equal to the holding period return of the U.S. one-year bond."

a. Calculate the U.S. dollar holding period return that would result from the transaction recommended by Hamson. Show your calculations. State whether

Hamson's conclusion about the U.S. dollar holding period return resulting from the transaction is correct or incorrect.

After conducting his own analysis of the U.S. and Mexican economies, Davies expects that both the U.S. inflation rate and the real exchange rate will remain constant over the coming year. Because of favorable political developments in Mexico, however, he expects that the Mexican inflation rate (in annual terms) will fall from 6.0 percent to 3.0 percent before the end of the year. As a result, Davies decides to invest Yucatan Resort's cash holdings in the Mexican one-year bond but not to hedge the currency exposure.

b. Calculate the expected exchange rate (pesos per dollar) one year from now. Show your calculations. Note: Your calculations should assume that Davies is correct in his expectations about the real exchange rate and the Mexican and U.S. inflation rates.

c. Calculate the expected U.S. dollar holding period return on the Mexican one-year bond. Show your calculations. Note: Your calculations should assume that Davies is correct in his expectations about the real exchange rate and the Mexican and U.S. inflation rates.

INTERNET EXERCISES

1. You provide foreign exchange consulting services based on technical (chartist) analysis. Your client would like to have a good idea about the U.S. dollar and Mexican peso exchange rate six months into the future. First plot the past exchange rates and try to identify patterns that can be projected into the future. What forecast exchange rate would you offer to your client? You may download exchange rate data from fx.sauder.ubc.ca.

MINI CASE

Turkish Lira and Purchasing Power Parity

Veritas Emerging Market Fund specializes in investing in emerging stock markets of the world. Mr. Henry Mobaus, an experienced hand in international investment and your boss, is currently interested in Turkish stock markets. He thinks that Turkey will eventually be invited to negotiate its membership in the European Union. If this happens, it will boost stock prices in Turkey. But, at the same time, he is quite concerned with the volatile exchange rates of the Turkish currency. He would like to understand what drives Turkish exchange rates. Since the inflation rate is much higher in Turkey than in the United States, he thinks that purchasing power parity may be holding at least to some extent. As a research assistant for him, you are assigned to check this out. In other words, you have to study and prepare a report on the following question: Does purchasing power parity hold for the Turkish lira–U.S. dollar exchange rate? Among other things, Mr. Mobaus would like you to do the following:

1. Plot past exchange rate changes against the differential inflation rates between Turkey and the United States for the last four years.

2. Regress the rate of exchange rate changes on the inflation rate differential to estimate the intercept and the slope coefficient, and interpret the regression results.

Data sources: You may download consumer price index data for the United States and Turkey from the following website: http://ifs.apdi.net/imf/logon.aspx. You may download exchange rate data from the website: fx.sauder.ubc.ca.

REFERENCES & SUGGESTED READINGS

Abuaf, N., and P. Jorion. "Purchasing Power Parity in the Long Run." *Journal of Finance* 45 (1990), pp. 157–74.

Aliber, R. "The Interest Rate Parity: A Reinterpretation." *Journal of Political Economy* (1973), pp. 1451–59.

Adler, Michael, and Bruce Lehman. "Deviations from Purchasing Power Parity in the Long Run." *Journal of Finance* 38 (1983), pp. 1471–87.

Eun, Cheol, and Sanjiv Sabherwal. "Forecasting Exchange Rates: Do Banks Know Better?" *Global Finance Journal* (2002), pp. 195–215.

Fisher, Irving. *The Theory of Interest,* rpt. ed. New York: Macmillan, 1980.

Frenkel, Jacob. "Flexible Exchange Rates, Prices and the Role of News: Lessons from the 1970s." *Journal of Political Economy* 89 (1981), pp. 665–705.

Frenkel, Jacob, and Richard Levich. "Covered Interest Arbitrage: Unexploited Profits?" *Journal of Political Economy* 83 (1975), pp. 325–38.

Keynes, John M. *Monetary Reform.* New York: Harcourt, Brace, 1924.

Kravis, I., and R. Lipsey. "Price Behavior in the Light of Balance of Payment Theories." *Journal of International Economics* (1978), pp. 193–246.

Larsen, Glen, and Bruce Resnick. "International Party Relationships and Tests for Risk Premia in Forward Foreign Exchange Rates." *Journal of International Financial Markets, Institutions and Money* 3 (1993), pp. 33–56.

Levich, Richard. "Evaluating the Performance of the Forecasters." *The Management of Foreign Exchange Risk,* 2nd ed. In ed. Richard Ensor. Euromoney Publication, 1982, pp. 121–34.

Meese, Richard, and Kenneth Rogoff. "Empirical Exchange Rate Models of the Seventies: Do They Fit Out of Sample?" *Journal of International Economics* 14 (1983), pp. 3–24.

Otani, Ichiro, and Siddharth Tiwari. "Capital Controls and Interest Rate Parity: The Japanese Experience, 1978–81." *International Monetary Fund Staff Papers* 28 (1981), pp. 793–815.

Richardson, J. "Some Empirical Evidence on Commodity Arbitrage and the Law of One Price." *Journal of International Economics* 8 (1978), pp. 341–52.

6A Purchasing Power Parity and Exchange Rate Determination

货币分析法

Although PPP itself can be viewed as a theory of exchange rate determination, it also serves as a foundation for a more complete theory, namely, the **monetary approach.** The monetary approach, associated with the Chicago School of Economics, is based on two basic tenets: purchasing power parity and the quantity theory of money.

货币数量理论

From the **quantity theory of money,** we obtain the following identity that must hold in each country:

$$P_\$ = M_\$ V_\$/y_\$ \tag{6A.1A}$$

$$P_£ = M_£ V_£/y_£ \tag{6A.1B}$$

where M denotes the money supply, V the velocity of money, measuring the speed at which money is being circulated in the economy, y the national aggregate output, and P the general price level; the subscripts denote countries. When the above equations are substituted for the price levels in the PPP Equation 6.12, we obtain the following expression for the exchange rate:

$$S = (M_\$/M_£)(V_\$/V_£)(y_£/y_\$) \tag{6A.2}$$

According to the monetary approach, what matters in the exchange rate determination are

1. The relative money supplies.

2. The relative velocities of money.

3. The relative national outputs.

All else equal, an increase in the U.S. money supply will result in a proportionate depreciation of the dollar against the pound. So will an increase in the velocity of the dollar, which has the same effect as an increased supply of dollars. But an increase in U.S. output will result in a proportionate appreciation of the dollar.

The monetary approach, which is based on PPP, can be viewed as a long-run theory, not a short-run theory, of exchange rate determination. This is so because the monetary approach does not allow for price rigidities. It assumes that prices adjust fully and completely, which is unrealistic in the short run. Prices of many commodities and services are often fixed over a certain period of time. A good example of short-term price rigidity is the wage rate set by a labor contract. Despite this apparent shortcoming, the monetary approach remains an influential theory and serves as a benchmark in modern exchange rate economics.

7 Futures and Options on Foreign Exchange

ON FEBRUARY 27, 1995, Barings PLC, the oldest merchant bank in the United Kingdom, was placed in "administration" by the Bank of England because of losses that exceeded the bank's entire $860 million in equity capital. The cause of these losses was a breakdown in Barings' risk-management system that allowed a single rogue trader to accumulate and conceal an unhedged $27 billion position in various exchange-traded futures and options contracts, primarily the Nikkei 225 stock index futures contract traded on the Singapore International Monetary Exchange. The losses occurred when the market moved unfavorably against the trader's speculative positions. The trader recently completed a prison term in Singapore for fraudulent trading. Barings was taken over by ING Group, the Dutch banking and insurance conglomerate.

As this story implies, futures and options contracts can be very risky investments, indeed, when used for speculative purposes. Nevertheless, they are also important risk-management tools. In this chapter, we introduce exchange-traded currency futures contracts, options contracts, and options on currency futures that are useful for both speculating on foreign exchange price movements and hedging exchange rate uncertainty. These contracts make up part of the foreign exchange market that was introduced in Chapter 5, where we discussed spot and forward exchange rates.

The discussion begins by comparing forward and futures contracts, noting similarities and differences between the two. We discuss the markets where futures are traded, the currencies on which contracts are written, and contract specifications for the various currency contracts. We also discuss Eurodollar interest rate futures contracts, which are useful for hedging short-term dollar interest rate risk.

Next, options contracts on foreign exchange are introduced, comparing and contrasting the options and the futures markets. The exchanges where options are traded are identified and contract terms are specified. The over-the-counter options market is also discussed. Basic option-pricing boundary relationships are illustrated using actual

本章介绍交易所交易的外汇期货合约、期权合约和外汇期货期权。其中外汇期货期权可用来对外汇价格走势的投机和对汇率的不确定性进行套期保值。

本章从比较远期合约和期货合约开始，讨论它们的异同。

market prices. Additionally, illustrations of how a speculator might use currency options are also provided. The chapter closes with the development of a currency option-pricing model. This chapter and the knowledge gained about forward contracts in Chapters 5 and 6 set the stage for Chapters 8, 9, and 10, which explain how these vehicles can be used for hedging foreign exchange risk.

Futures Contracts: Some Preliminaries

远期合约和期货合约都是**衍生证券** (derivative)，也称**或有债权证券** (contingent claim securities)，因为其合约价值均来源于标的证券价值。

期货（futures）

标准化（standardized）

场内交易（exchange-traded）

合约规模（contract size）

到期日（maturity date）

交割月份（delivery months）

初始保证金（initial performance bond）

In Chapter 5, a *forward contract* was defined as a vehicle for buying or selling a stated amount of foreign exchange at a stated price per unit at a specified time in the future. Both forward and futures contracts are classified as **derivative** or **contingent claim securities** because their values are derived from or contingent upon the value of the underlying security. But while a **futures** contract is similar to a forward contract, there are many distinctions between the two. A forward contract is tailor-made for a client by his international bank; in contrast, a futures contract has **standardized** features and is **exchange-traded,** that is, traded on organized exchanges rather than over the counter. A client desiring a position in futures contracts contacts his broker, who transmits the order to the exchange floor where it is transferred to the trading pit. In the trading pit, the price for the order is negotiated by open outcry between floor brokers or traders.

The main standardized features are the **contract size** specifying the amount of the underlying foreign currency for future purchase or sale and the **maturity date** of the contract. A futures contract is written for a specific amount of foreign currency rather than for a tailor-made sum. Hence, a position in multiple contracts may be necessary to establish a sizable hedge or speculative position. Futures contracts have specific **delivery months** during the year in which contracts mature on a specified day of the month.

An **initial performance bond** (formerly called *margin*) must be deposited into a collateral account to establish a futures position. The initial performance bond is generally equal to about 2 percent of the contract value. Either cash or Treasury bills may be used to meet the performance bond requirement. The account balance will fluctuate through daily settlement, as illustrated by the following discussion. The performance bond put up by the contract holder can be viewed as "good-faith" money that he will fulfill his side of the financial obligation.

远期合约和期货合约的最大差异在于对将来买进或卖出的标的资产的定价方法的不同。

逐日结算（settled-up）

钉市操作（marked-to-market）

结算价格（settlement price）

多头（long）

空头（short）

The major difference between a forward contract and a futures contract is the way the underlying asset is priced for future purchase or sale. A forward contract states a price for the future transaction. By contrast, a futures contract is **settled-up,** or **marked-to-market,** daily at the settlement price. The **settlement price** is a price representative of futures transaction prices at the close of daily trading on the exchange. It is determined by a settlement committee for the commodity, and it may be somewhat arbitrary if trading volume for the contract has been light for the day. A buyer of a futures contract (one who holds a **long** position) in which the settlement price is higher (lower) than the previous day's settlement price has a positive (negative) settlement for the day. Since a long position entitles the owner to purchase the underlying asset, a higher (lower) settlement price means the futures price of the underlying asset has increased (decreased). Consequently, a long position in the contract is worth more (less). The change in settlement prices from one day to the next determines the settlement amount. That is, the change in settlement prices per unit of the underlying asset, multiplied by the size of the contract, equals the size of the daily settlement to be added to (or subtracted from) the long's performance bond account. Analogously, the seller of the futures contract (**short** position) will have his performance bond account increased (or decreased) by the amount the long's performance bond account is decreased (or increased). Thus, futures trading between the long and the short is a

---

EXHIBIT 7.1

Differences between Futures and Forward Contracts

Trading Location
Futures: Traded competitively on organized exchanges.
Forward: Traded by bank dealers via a network of telephones and computerized dealing systems.

Contractual Size
Futures: Standardized amount of the underlying asset.
Forward: Tailor-made to the needs of the participant.

Settlement
Futures: Daily settlement, or marking-to-market, done by the futures clearinghouse through the participant's performance bond account.
Forward: Participant buys or sells the contractual amount of the underlying asset from the bank at maturity at the forward (contractual) price.

Expiration Date
Futures: Standardized delivery dates.
Forward: Tailor-made delivery date that meets the needs of the investor.

Delivery
Futures: Delivery of the underlying asset is seldom made. Usually a reversing trade is transacted to exit the market.
Forward: Delivery of the underlying asset is commonly made.

Trading Costs
Futures: Bid-ask spread plus broker's commission.
Forward: Bid-ask spread plus indirect bank charges via compensating balance requirements.

零和博弈
维持保证金

zero-sum game; that is, the sum of the long and short's daily settlement is zero. If the investor's performance bond account falls below a **maintenance performance bond** level (roughly equal to 75 percent of the initial performance bond), additional funds must be deposited into the account to bring it back to the initial performance bond level in order to keep the position open. An investor who suffers a liquidity crunch and cannot deposit additional funds will have his position liquidated by his broker.

The marking-to-market feature of futures markets means that market participants realize their profits or suffer their losses on a day-to-day basis rather than all at once at maturity as with a forward contract. At the end of daily trading, a futures contract is analogous to a new forward contract on the underlying asset at the new settlement price with a one-day-shorter maturity. Because of the daily marking-to-market, the futures price will converge through time to the spot price on the last day of trading in the contract. That is, the final settlement price at which any transaction in the underlying asset will transpire is the spot price on the last day of trading. The effective price is, nevertheless, the original futures contract price, once the profit or loss in the performance bond account is included. Exhibit 7.1 summarizes the differences between forward and futures contracts.

要使衍生品市场能
最有效运作，必须要有
两类市场参与者：投机
者和套期保值者。

投机者
套期保值者

Two types of market participants are necessary for a derivatives market to operate most efficiently: **speculators** and **hedgers.** A speculator attempts to profit from a change in the futures price. To do this, the speculator will take a long or short position in a futures contract depending upon his expectations of future price movement. A hedger, on the other hand, wants to avoid price variation by locking in a purchase price of the underlying asset through a long position in the futures contract or a sales price through a short position. In effect, the hedger passes off the risk of price variation to the speculator, who is better able, or at least more willing, to bear this risk.

外汇远期和外汇期
货市场都富有流动性。

对冲交易

佣金

清算所

通 常，期 货 交 易 所
对期货价格有一个**日价格**
变动限额，即与上一日的
结算价格相比，结算价格
增加或减少的限制。

Both forward and futures markets for foreign exchange are very liquid. A **reversing trade** can be made in either market that will close out, or neutralize, a position.[1] In forward markets, approximately 90 percent of all contracts result in the short making delivery of the underlying asset to the long. This is natural given the tailor-made terms of forward contracts. By contrast, only about 1 percent of currency futures contracts result in delivery. While futures contracts are useful for speculation and hedging, their standardized delivery dates are unlikely to correspond to the actual future dates when foreign exchange transactions will transpire. Thus, they are generally closed out in a reversing trade. The **commission** that buyers and sellers pay to transact in the futures market is a single amount paid up front that covers the *round-trip* transactions of initiating and closing out the position. These days, through a discount broker, the commission charge can be as little as $15 per currency futures contract.

In futures markets, a **clearinghouse** serves as the third party to all transactions. That is, the buyer of a futures contract effectively buys from the clearinghouse and the seller sells to the clearinghouse. This feature of futures markets facilitates active secondary market trading because the buyer and the seller do not have to evaluate one another's creditworthiness. The clearinghouse is made up of *clearing members*. Individual brokers who are not clearing members must deal through a clearing member to clear a customer's trade. In the event of default of one side of a futures trade, the clearing member stands in for the defaulting party, and then seeks restitution from that party. The clearinghouse's liability is limited because a contractholder's position is marked-to-market daily. Given the organizational structure, it is only logical that the clearinghouse maintains the futures performance bond accounts for the clearing members.

Frequently, a futures exchange may have a **daily price limit** on the futures price, that is, a limit as to how much the settlement price can increase or decrease from the previous day's settlement price. Forward markets do not have this. Obviously, when the price limit is hit, trading will halt as a new market-clearing equilibrium price cannot be obtained. Exchange rules exist for expanding the daily price limit in an orderly fashion until a market-clearing price can be established.

Currency Futures Markets

www.cme.com

This is the website of the Chicago Mercantile Exchange. It provides detailed information about the futures contracts and futures options contracts traded on it.

www.phlx.com

This is the website of the Philadelphia Stock Exchange and the Philadelphia Board of Trade. It provides detailed information about the stocks and derivative products that trade on the exchanges.

On May 16, 1972, trading in currency futures contracts began at the Chicago Mercantile Exchange (CME). Trading activity in currency futures has expanded rapidly at the CME. In 1978, only 2 million contracts were traded; this figure stood at over 48 million contracts in 2004. Most CME currency futures trade in a March, June, September, and December expiration cycle, with the delivery date being the third Wednesday of the expiration month. The last day of trading for most contracts is the second business day prior to the delivery date. Regular trading in CME currency futures contracts takes place each business day from 7:20 A.M. to 2:00 P.M. Chicago time. Additional CME currency futures trading takes place Monday through Thursday on the GLOBEX trading system from 5:00 P.M. to 4:00 P.M. Chicago time the next day. On Sundays trading begins at 5:00 P.M. GLOBEX is a worldwide automated order-entry and matching system for futures and options that facilitates nearly 24-hour trading after the close of regular exchange trading. Exhibit 7.2 summarizes the basic CME currency contract specifications. The International Finance in Practice box "CME Ramping

---

[1]In the forward market, the investor holds offsetting positions after a reversing trade; in the futures market the investor actually exits the marketplace.

CME Ramping Up FOREX Support, Targets OTC Business

The modern era of futures markets can be traced to 1972 when the Chicago Mercantile Exchange (CME) created the International Monetary Market (IMM) to begin trading foreign currency futures benchmarked against the U.S. dollar. Those first significant financial futures contracts set into motion a series of innovations that were the blueprint for today's markets that are dominated by contracts based on financial futures. Until recently, however, the grand-daddy currency contracts had produced volume more reflective of their agricultural predecessors while trillion dollar volume days became standard place in the OTC interbank currency markets.

Currency futures began coming into their own, however, when the CME listed the currency complex virtually 24 hours on its electronic matching engine, GLOBEX. That move made currency futures more attractive to retail clientele. Now, an agreement with global information firm Reuters is literally making the currency futures available from thousands of institutional traders' desktops. Under the agreement, Reuters will offer the CME's electronic foreign exchange markets to its worldwide customers through the Reuters FX Dealing 3000 platform in a spot equivalent format. That means that the 3,500 institutions located in 123 countries—many large currency dealing banks—that trade cash and forward foreign exchange rates will be able to trade currency futures off of the same platform priced in the same format.

Leo Melamed, CME chairman emeritus and senior policy advisor, who shepherded the creation of the IMM while serving as exchange chairman, sees the move as completing his original vision.

"I would rate the agreement with Reuters as the culmination of 30 years worth of growth and proof that these future markets are intertwined with the cash markets of the world," Melamed says. "Right from the beginning, what I was trying to do was make sure that the Merc's currency markets were connected to the interbank markets."

CME Chairman Terry Duffy says the foreign exchange area has huge growth potential. "The FX market is a $1.2 trillion dollar a day market with about a $500 billion a day spot market. The notional value is staggering and while the CME having the lions share of the exchange-traded FX we think that our [market share]—we are 2% to 3% of the total [cash volume]—can grow. If we can increase that by a couple of percentage points it is big volume to the CME."

The move comes amid other efforts by the CME to make its currency complex more attractive, including adding additional crossrate products and reducing fees.

Despite these moves, some veteran FOREX market participants doubt whether large dealers will move to the listed market.

Osman Ghandour, who writes a FX newsletter and has traded the interbank market for years, says interbank trading offers unique benefits that will make it unlikely dealers would switch to an exchange-listed market.

"If I have 100 contracts to buy in the futures, there is no way they can guarantee [a fill]. . . . That quality is an advantage for the interbank market," Ghandour says. "If a hedge fund wants to buy or sell $1 billion worth of euros, I don't think he is going to go to the CME. He is going to pick up his phone and place on order with a bank and get one single unit price and be assured of that."

That said, there is little doubt the extra visibility does put the CME on more equal footing with the interbank market.

"The fact that the CME currency futures are now on the Reuters' platform is proof that the market truly is homogenous. Whether you are trading cash FX or futures, the exposures are identical," says CME President Phupinder Gill.

Up FOREX Support, Targets OTC Business" provides a discussion of how CME currency futures will also be traded on the Reuters FX Dealing 3000 platform discussed in Chapter 5 on trading spot and forward foreign exchange.

The Philadelphia Board of Trade (PBOT), a subsidiary of the Philadelphia Stock Exchange, introduced currency futures trading in July 1986. The PBOT contracts trade in the same expiration cycle as the CME currency futures, plus two additional near-term months. The delivery date is also the third Wednesday of the expiration month, with the last day of trading being the preceding Friday. The trading hours of the

费城股票交易所下属的费城期货交易所于1986年7月引进外汇期货交易的业务。

EXHIBIT 7.2

Currency Futures Contract Specifications*

Currency	Contract Size	Exchange
Price Quoted in U.S. Dollars		
Australian dollar	AD100,000	CME, PBOT
Brazilian real	BR100,000	CME
British pound	£62,500	CME, PBOT
Canadian dollar	CD100,000	CME, PBOT
Czech Koruna	CZK4,000,000	CME
Euro FX	EUR125,000	CME, PBOT
Hungarian Forint	HUF30,000,000	CME
Japanese yen	¥12,500,000	CME, PBOT
Mexican peso	MP500,000	CME
New Zealand dollar	NE100,00	CME
Norwegian Krone	NKR2,000,000	CME
Polish Zloty	PLZ500,000	CME
Russian ruble	RU2,500,000	CME
South African rand	RA500,000	CME
Swiss franc	SF125,000	CME, PBOT
Cross-Rate Futures *(Underlying Currency/Price Currency)*		
Euro FX/British pound	EUR125,000	CME
Euro FX/Japanese yen	EUR125,000	CME
Euro FX/Swiss franc	EUR125,000	CME

*CME denotes Chicago Mercantile Exchange; PBOT denotes Philadelphia Board of Trade.
Sources: Chicago Mercantile Exchange website, www.cme.com and Philadelphia PBOT Board of Trade website, www.phlx.com.

www.numa.com/ref/exchange.htm

This is the website of Numa Directory. It provides the website address of most of the stock and derivative exchanges in the world.

PBOT contracts are 2:30 A.M. to 2:30 P.M. ET, except for the Canadian dollar, which trades between 7:00 A.M. and 2:30 P.M. ET. Exhibit 7.2 shows the currencies and the size of the contracts traded on the PBOT.

In addition to the CME and the PBOT, currency futures trading takes place on the New York Board of Trade, the Mexican Derivatives Exchange, the BM&F Exchange in Brazil, the Budapest Commodity Exchange, and the Futures Market Division of the Korea Exchange.

Basic Currency Futures Relationships

未平仓合约

近期月份合约

一般地，未平仓合约（一个并不严格的需求指示器）随大部分期货合约到期日的来临而减少。

Exhibit 7.3 shows quotations for CME futures contracts. For each delivery month for each currency, we see the opening price quotation, the high and the low quotes for the trading day (in this case March 3, 2005), and the settlement price. Each is presented in American terms, that is, $F(\$/i)$. (We use the same symbol F for futures prices as for forward prices, and explain why shortly.) For each contract, the **open interest** is also presented. This is the total number of short or long contracts outstanding for the particular delivery month. Note that the open interest is greatest for each currency in the **nearby** contract, in this case the March 2005 contract. Since few of these contracts will actually result in delivery, if we were to follow the open interest in the March contracts through time, we would see the number for each different currency decrease as the last day of trading (March 11, 2005) approaches as a result of reversing trades. Additionally, we would note increased open interest in the June 2005 contract as trading interest in the soon-to-be nearby contract picks up. In general, open interest (loosely an indicator of demand) typically decreases with the term-to-maturity of most futures contracts.

| EXHIBIT 7.3 | Chicago Mercantile Exchange Currency Futures Contract Quotations | | | | | | | |

	Open	High	Low	Settle	Change	Lifetime High	Lifetime Low	Open Interest
Japanese Yen (CME)-¥12,500,000; $ per ¥								
Mar	.9553	.9556	.9492	.9505	−.0049	.9885	.8873	128,958
June	.9628	.9628	.9565	.9576	−.0050	.9930	.9040	23,603
Est vol 42,196; vol Wed 32,510; open int 152,733, −898.								
Canadian Dollar (CME)-CAD 100,000; $ per CAD								
Mar	.8069	.8075	.8002	.8046	−.0022	.8526	.7150	86,462
June	.8078	.8084	.8012	.8054	−.0023	.8495	.7150	8,742
Sept	.8050	.8060	.8040	.8070	−.0023	.8490	−7160	1,370
Dec	.8085	.8085	.8070	.8088	−.0023	.8515	.7480	766
Est vol 31,547; vol Wed 18,889; open int 97, 375, +1,731.								
British Pound (CME)-£62,500; $ per £								
Mar	1.9121	1.9129	1.9046	1.9063	−.0056	1.9446	1.7321	78,706
Est vol 19,566; vol Wed 15,190; open int 80,754, +844.								
Swiss Franc (CME)-CHF 125,000; $ per CHF								
Mar	.8525	.8527	.8458	.8474	−.0051	.8892	.7853	58,881
June	.8571	.8574	.8507	.8522	−.0051	.8920	.7880	2,101
Est vol 20,232; vol Wed 23,355; open int 61,107, −849.								
Australian Dollar (CME)-AUD 100,00; $ per AUD								
Mar	.7821	.7845	.7797	.7828	−.0002	.7945	.6400	91,185
June	.7760	.7791	.7746	.7775	−.0002	.7891	.6670	7,011
Sept	.7720	.7730	.7720	.7726	−.0002	.7838	.6600	745
Est vol 12,053; vol Wed 23,806; open int 99,053, −5,046.								
Mexican Peso (CME)-MXN 500,000; $ per MXN								
Mar	.09002	.09045	.8977	.08990	−00007	.09050	.08200	98,990
June	.08900	.08900	.08837	.08845	−00007	.08905	.08160	4,719
Est vol 27,106; vol Wed 10,751; open int 104,533, +2,147.								
Euro/US Dollar (CME)- 125,000; $ per €								
Mar	1.3136	1.3167	1.3098	1.3112	−.0025	1.3687	1.1363	159,822
June	1.3170	1.3193	1.3126	1.3140	−.0025	1.3699	1.1750	10,096
Sept	1.3202	1.3225	1.3175	1.3182	−.0025	1.3711	1.1750	600
Est vol 85,606; vol Wed 112,457; open int 171,598, +1,656.								
Euro/US Dollar (NYBOT)- €200,000; $ per €								
Mar	1.3135	1.3153	1.3101	1.3116	−.0023	1.3643	1.2780	543
Est vol 248; vol Wed 357; open int 548, −12.								
Euro/Japanese Yen (NYBOT)-€100,000; ¥ per €								
Mar	137.59	138.05	137.59	137.90	.43	140.94	132.74	14,765
Est vol 1,639; vol Wed 546; open int 16,746, +36.								
Euro/British Pound (NYBOT)-€100,000; £ per €								
Mar	.6879	.6892	.6879	.6880	.0008	.7140	.6871	5,399
Est vol 406; vol Wed 187; open int 5,429, +65.								

EXAMPLE 7.1

Reading Futures Quotations   As an example of reading futures quotations, let's use the June 2005 Canadian dollar contract. From Exhibit 7.3, we see that on Thursday, March 3, 2005, the contract opened for trading at a price of $0.8078/CD, and traded in the range of $0.8012 CD/(low) to $0.8084/CD (high) throughout the day. During its lifetime, the June 2005 contract has traded in the range of $0.7150/CD (low) to $0.8495/CD (high). The settlement ("closing") price was $0.8054/CD. The open interest, or the number of June 2005 contracts outstanding, was 8,742.

At the settlement price of $0.8054, the holder of a long position in one contract is committing himself to paying $80,540 for CD100,000 on the delivery day, June 15, 2005, if he actually takes delivery. Note that the settlement price decreased $.0023 from the previous day. That is, it fell from $0.8077/CD to $0.8054/CD. Both the buyer and the seller of the contract would have their accounts marked-to-market by the change in the settlement prices. That is, one holding a long position from the previous day would have $230 (= $.0023 × CD100,000) subtracted from his performance bond account and the short would have $230 added to his account.

Even though marking-to-market is an important economic difference between the operation of the futures market and the forward market, it has little effect on the pricing of futures contracts as opposed to the way forward contracts are priced. To see this, note the pattern of CD forward prices from the *Exchange Rates* presented in Exhibit 5.4 in Chapter 5. They go from a spot price of $0.8037/CD to $0.8037 (1-month) to $0.8043 (3-months) to $0.8057 (6-months). To the extent that forward prices are an unbiased predictor of future spot exchange rates, the market is anticipating the U.S. dollar to depreciate over the next six months relative to the Canadian dollar. Similarly, we see a depreciating pattern of the U.S. dollar from the pattern of settlement prices for the CD futures contracts: $0.8046 (March) to $0.8054 (June) to $0.8070 (September) to $0.8088 (December). It is also noteworthy that both the forward and the futures contracts together display a chronological depreciating pattern. For example, the 1-month forward price (with a value date of April 5) and the 6-month forward price (with a value date of September 6) surround the June futures contract price (with a delivery date of June 15); these coupled with the September futures contract price (with a delivery date of September 21) and the December futures contract price (with a delivery date of December 21) display a consistent depreciating pattern: $0.8037, $0.8054, $0.8057, $0.8070, and $0.8088, respectively. Thus, both the forward market and the futures market are useful for **price discovery**, or obtaining the market's forecast of the spot exchange rate at different future dates.

价格发现

Example 7.1 implies that futures are priced very similarly to forward contracts. In Chapter 6, we developed the Interest Rate Parity (IRP) model, which states that the forward price for delivery at time T is

$$F_T(\$/i) = S_0(\$/i)\frac{(1+r_\$)^T}{(1+r_i)^T} \tag{7.1}$$

这是一个很好的解决办法，因为假如期货市场和远期市场的价格很不一致，两个市场之间的相似性就会提供套利机会。

We will use the same equation to define the futures price. This should work well since the similarities between the forward and the futures markets allow arbitrage opportunities if the prices between the markets are not roughly in accord.[2]

---
[2]As a theoretical proposition, Cox, Ingersoll, and Ross (1981) show that forward and futures prices should not be equal unless interest rates are constant or can be predicted with certainty. For our purposes, it is not necessary to be theoretically specific.

价格趋同

EXAMPLE 7.2

Speculating and Hedging with Currency Futures   Suppose a trader takes a position on March 3, 2005, in one June 2005 CD futures contract at $0.8054/CD. The trader holds the position until the last day of trading when the spot price is $0.7900/CD. This will also be the final settlement price because of **price convergence**. The trader's profit or loss depends upon whether he had a long or short position in the June CD contract. If the trader had a long position, and he was a speculator with no underlying position in Canadian dollars, he would have a cumulative loss of − $1,540 [= ($0.7900 − $0.8054) × CD100,000] from March 3 through June 15. This amount would be subtracted from his margin account as a result of daily marking-to-market. If he takes delivery, he will pay out-of-pocket $79,000 for the CD100,000 (which have a spot market value of $79,000). The effective cost, however, is $80,540 (= $79,000 + $1,540), including the amount subtracted from the margin money. Alternatively, as a hedger desiring to acquire CD100,000 on June 15 for $0.8054/CD, our trader has locked in a purchase price of $80,540 from a long position in the June CD futures contract.

   If the trader had taken a short position, and he was a speculator with no underlying position in Canadian dollars, he would have a cumulative profit of $1,540 [= $0.8054 − $0.7900) × CD100,000] from March 3 through June 15. This amount would be added to his margin account as a result of daily marking-to-market. If he makes delivery, he will receive $79,000 for the CD100,000 (which also cost $79,000 in the spot market). The effective amount he receives, however, is $80,540 ($79,000 + $1,540), including the amount added to his margin account. Alternatively, as a hedger desiring to sell CD100,000 on June 15 for $0.8054/CD, our trader has locked in a sales price of $80,540 from a short position in the June CD futures contract. Exhibit 7.4 graphs these long and short futures positions.

EXHIBIT 7.4

Graph of Long and Short Positions in the June 2005 Canadian Dollar Futures Contract

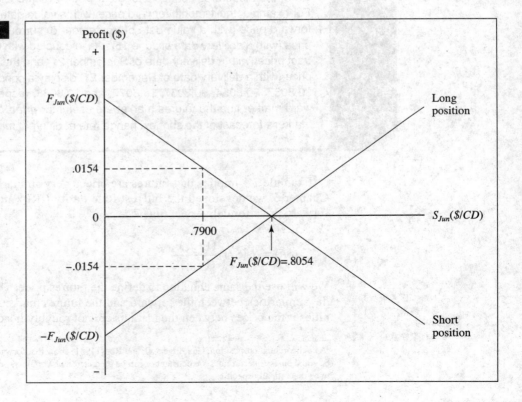

Eurodollar Interest Rate Futures Contracts

To this point, we have considered only futures contracts written on foreign exchange. Nevertheless, future contracts are traded on many different underlying assets. One particularly important contract is the Eurodollar interest rate futures traded on the Chicago Mercantile Exchange and the Singapore Exchange. The Eurodollar contract has become the most widely used futures contract for hedging short-term U.S. dollar interest rate risk. Other Eurocurrency futures contracts that trade are the Euroyen, EuroSwiss, and the EURIBOR contract, which began trading after the introduction of the euro.

芝加哥商品交易
所的欧洲美元期货合
约的标的被假定为是
1 000 000美元90天的欧
洲美元定期存款。

The CME Eurodollar futures contract is written on a hypothetical $1,000,000 ninety-day deposit of Eurodollars. The contract trades in the March, June, September, and December cycle. The hypothetical delivery date is the third Wednesday of the delivery month. The last day of trading is two business days prior to the delivery date. The contract is a cash settlement contract. That is, the delivery of a $1,000,000 Eurodollar deposit is not actually made or received. Instead, final settlement is made through realizing profits or losses in the performance bond account on the delivery date based on the final settlement price on the last day of trading. Exhibit 7.5 presents an example of CME Eurodollar futures quotations. Note that contracts trade out many years into the future.

EXHIBIT 7.5

Chicago Mercantile Exchange Eurodollar Futures Contract Quotations

	Open	High	Low	Settle	Chg	Yld	Chg	Open Int
Eurodollar (CME)-$1,000,000; pts of 100%								
Mar	96.99	96.99	96.99	96.99	...	3.01	...	840,069
Apr	96.81	96.82	96.81	96.81	...	3.19	...	7,167
June	96.56	96.58	96.55	96.56	...	3.44	...	1,398,959
Sept	96.21	96.24	96.20	96.20	−.01	3.80	.01	1,414,354
Dec	96.00	96.03	95.98	95.99	−.01	4.01	.01	1,056,200
Mr06	95.88	95.90	95.85	95.86	−.01	4.14	.01	776,378
June	95.77	95.80	95.75	95.75	−.01	4.25	.01	555,590
Sept	95.69	95.72	95.66	95.67	−.02	4.33	.02	403,156
Dec	95.60	95.63	95.58	95.59	−.01	4.41	.01	363,025
Mr07	95.56	95.59	95.54	95.54	−.01	4.46	.01	242,504
June	95.51	95.53	95.48	95.49	−.01	4.51	.01	201,962
Sept	95.45	95.48	95.43	95.43	−.01	4.57	.01	154,074
Dec	95.39	95.42	95.37	95.37	−.01	4.63	.01	144,440
Mr08	95.35	95.37	95.33	95.33	−.01	4.67	.01	118,033
June	95.30	95.31	95.28	95.28	−.01	4.72	.01	112,774
Sept	95.26	95.25	95.22	95.22	...	4.78	...	106,465
Dec	95.17	95.19	95.16	95.16	...	4.84	...	93,526
Mr09	95.14	95.15	95.11	95.12	...	4.88	...	79,185
June	95.09	95.10	95.05	95.07	...	4.93	...	72,900
Sept	95.04	95.05	95.02	95.02	...	4.98	...	61,891
Dec	94.98	94.99	94.96	94.96	...	5.04	...	40,158
Mr10	94.92	94.94	94.92	94.92	...	5.08	...	16,265
June	94.88	94.90	94.87	94.88	...	5.12	...	11,220
Sept	94.83	94.85	94.83	94.83	...	5.17	...	8,546
Dec	94.78	94.80	94.77	94.78	...	5.22	...	8,333
Mr11	94.75	94.76	94.75	94.75	...	5.25	...	6,046
June	94.71	94.72	94.70	94.71	...	5.29	...	4,983
Sept	94.65	94.68	94.65	94.66	...	5.34	...	3,119
Dec	94.60	94.62	94.60	94.61	...	5.39	...	2,531
Est vol 1,437,937; vol Wed 1,559,507; open int 8,319,646, +5,539.								

Source: *The Wall Street Journal*, March 4, 2005, p. B6. Reprinted by permission of *The Wall Street Journal*, © 2005 Dow Jones & Company, Inc: All Rights Reserved Woldwide.

EXAMPLE 7.3

Reading Eurodollar Futures Quotations   Eurodollar futures prices are stated as an index number of three-month LIBOR, calculated as: $F = 100 - LIBOR$. For example, from Exhibit 7.5 we see that the June 2005 contract (with hypothetical delivery on June 15, 2005) had a settlement price of 96.56 on Thursday, March 3, 2005. The implied three-month LIBOR yield is thus 3.44 percent. The minimum price change is one basis point (bp). On $1,000,000 of face value, a one-basis-point change represents $100 on an annual basis. Since the contract is for a 90-day deposit, one basis point corresponds to a $25 price change.

EXAMPLE 7.4

Eurodollar Futures Hedge   As an example of how this contract can be used to hedge interest rate risk, consider the treasurer of a MNC, who on March 3, 2005, learns that his firm expects to receive $20,000,000 in cash from a large sale of merchandise on June 15, 2005. The money will not be needed for a period of 90 days. Thus, the treasurer should invest the excess funds for this period in a money market instrument such as a Eurodollar deposit.

The treasurer notes that three-month LIBOR is currently 2.91 percent. (See *Money Rates* in the inside back cover.) The implied three-month LIBOR rate in the June 2005 contract is considerably higher at 3.44 percent. Additionally, the treasurer notes that the pattern of future expected three-month LIBOR rates implied by the pattern of Eurodollar futures prices suggests that it is expected to increase through time. Nevertheless, the treasurer believes that a 90-day rate of return of 3.44 percent is a decent rate to "lock in," so he decides to hedge against lower three-month LIBOR in June 2005. By hedging, the treasurer is locking in a certain return of $172,000 (= $20,000,000 × .0344 × 90/360) for the 90-day period the MNC has $20,000,000 in excess funds.

To construct the hedge, the treasurer will need to buy, or take a long position, in Eurodollar futures contracts. At first it may seem counterintuitive that a long position is needed, but remember, a decrease in the implied three-month LIBOR yield causes the Eurodollar futures price to increase. To hedge the interest rate risk in a $20,000,000 deposit, the treasurer will need to buy 20 June 2005 contracts.

Assume that on the last day of trading in the June 2005 contract three-month LIBOR is 3.10 percent. The treasurer is indeed fortunate that he chose to hedge. At 3.10 percent, a 90-day Eurodollar deposit of $20,000,000 will generate only $155,000 of interest income, or $17,000 less than at a rate of 3.44 percent. In fact, the treasurer will have to deposit the excess funds at a rate of 3.10 percent. But the shortfall will be made up by profits from the long futures position. At a rate of 3.10 percent, the final settlement price on the June 2005 contract is 96.90 (= 100 − 3.10). The profit earned on the futures position is calculated as: [96.90 − 96.56] × 100 bp × $25 × 20 contracts = $17,000. This is precisely the amount of the shortfall.

Options Contracts: Some Preliminaries

期权是一种允许拥
有者在将来某一时间以
某一规定的价格买进或

An **option** is a contract giving the owner the right, but not the obligation, to buy or sell a given quantity of an asset at a specified price at some time in the future. Like a futures or forward contract, an option is a derivative, or contingent claim, security. Its value is derived from its definable relationship with the underlying asset—in this chapter, foreign currency, or some claim on it. An option to buy the underlying asset is a **call**, and an option to sell the underlying asset is a **put**. Buying or selling the underlying asset via the option is known as exercising the option. The stated price paid (or received) is known as the **exercise** or **striking price**. In options terminology, the buyer of an option is frequently referred to as the long and the seller of an option is referred to as the **writer** of the option, or the short.

Because the option owner does not have to exercise the option if it is to his disadvantage, the option has a price, or **premium**. There are two types of options, American and European. The names do not refer to the continents where they are traded, but rather to their exercise characteristics. A **European option** can be exercised only at the maturity or expiration date of the contract, whereas an **American option** can be exercised at any time during the contract. Thus, the American option allows the owner to do everything he can do with a European option, and more.

Currency Options Markets

Prior to 1982, all currency option contracts were over-the-counter options written by international banks, investment banks, and brokerage houses. Over-the-counter options are tailor-made according to the specifications of the buyer in terms of maturity length, exercise price, and the amount of the underlying currency. Generally, these contracts are written for large amounts, at least $1,000,000 of the currency serving as the underlying asset. Frequently, they are written for U.S. dollars, with the euro, British pound, Japanese yen, Canadian dollar, and Swiss franc serving as the underlying currency, though options are also available on less actively traded currencies. Over-the-counter options are typically European style.

In December 1982, the Philadelphia Stock Exchange (PHLX) began trading European- and American-style options on foreign currency. Currently, trading is in six major currencies against the U.S. dollar. These options trade in a March, June, September, and December expiration cycle with original maturities of 3, 6, 9, and 12 months, plus two near-term months so that there are always options with one-, two-, and three-month expirations. These options mature on the Friday before the third Wednesday of the expiration month. Exhibit 7.6 shows the currencies on which options are traded at the PHLX and the amount, or size, of underlying currency per contract. Note that the size of PHLX option contracts are half the corresponding futures contract size, as noted in Exhibit 7.2. The trading hours of these contracts are 2:30 A.M. to 2:30 P.M. Philadelphia time.

The PHLX also trades European-style currency options with custom-made contractual terms. Customized options allow users to customize the exercise price, expiration date up to two years, and the premium quotation in either units of currency or percent of underlying value for 56 currency pairs.

EXHIBIT 7.6

Philadelphia Stock Exchange Option Contract Specifications

Currency	Contract Size
Premium Quoted in U.S. Dollars	
Australian dollar	AD50,000
British pound	£31,250
Canadian dollar	CD50,000
Euro	EUR62,500
Japanese yen	¥6,250,000
Swiss franc	SF62,500

Source: Philadelphia Stock Exchange, *Standardized Currency Options*, www.phlx.com

场外外汇期权的交易量比有组织的交易所期权交易量大得多。

The volume of OTC currency options trading is much larger than that of organized-exchange option trading. According to the Bank for International Settlements, in 2004 the OTC volume was approximately $117 billion per day. By comparison exchange-traded currency option volume was approximately $2.5 billion per day, or about 5 million contracts per year. Nevertheless, the market for exchange-traded options is very important, even to the OTC market. As Grabbe (1996) notes, international banks and brokerage houses frequently buy or sell standardized exchange-traded options, which they then repackage in creating the tailor-made options desired by their clients.

Currency Futures Options

The Chicago Mercantile Exchange trades American options on the currency futures contracts it offers. With these options, the underlying asset is a futures contract on the foreign currency instead of the physical currency. Options trade on each of the currency futures contracts offered by the CME (refer to Exhibit 7.2). One futures contract underlies one options contract.

Most CME futures options trade with expirations based on the most current month of the March, June, September, December expiration cycle of the underlying futures contract and two noncycle months plus four weekly expirations. For example, in January, options with expirations in January, February, and March would trade on futures with a March expiration. Monthly options expire on the second Friday prior to the third Wednesday of the options contract month. Weekly options expire on Friday. Regular trading takes place each business day from 7:20 A.M. to 2:00 P.M. Chicago time. For most contracts, extended-hour trading on the GLOBEX system begins at 2:00 P.M. and continues until 7:05 A.M. Chicago time. On Sundays, GLOBEX trading begins at 5:00 P.M.

Options on currency futures behave very similarly to options on the physical currency since the futures price converges to the spot price as the futures contract nears maturity. Exercise of a futures option results in a long futures position for the call buyer or the put writer and a short futures position for the put buyer or call writer. If the futures position is not offset prior to the futures expiration date, receipt or delivery of the underlying currency will, respectively, result or be required. In addition to the PHLX and the CME, there is some limited exchange-traded currency options trading at the BM&F Exchange in Brazil, on Euronext, and at the Tel-Aviv Stock Exchange.

Basic Option-Pricing Relationships at Expiration

At expiration, a European option and an American option (which has not been previously exercised), both with the same exercise price, will have the same terminal value. For call options the time T expiration value per unit of foreign currency can be stated as:

$$C_{aT} = C_{eT} = Max \, [S_T - E, 0], \qquad (7.2)$$

价内（in-the-money）
平价（at-the-momey）
价外（out-of-the-money）

where C_{aT} denotes the value of the American call at expiration, C_{eT} is the value of the European call at expiration, E is the exercise price per unit of foreign currency, S_T is the expiration date spot price, and Max is an abbreviation for denoting the maximum of the arguments within the brackets. A call (put) option with $S_T > E \, (E > S_T)$ expires **in-the-money** and it will be exercised. If $S_T = E$ the option expires **at-the-money**. If $S_T < E \, (E < S_T)$ the call (put) option expires **out-of-the-money** and it will not be exercised.

Expiration Value of an American Call Option   As an illustration of pricing Equation 7.2, consider the PHLX 130 Jun EUR American call option from Exhibit 7.7. This option has a current premium, C_a, of 4.59 cents per EUR. The exercise price is 130 cents per EUR and it expires on June 10, 2005. Suppose that at expiration the spot rate is $1.3425/EUR. In this event, the call option has an exercise value of $134.25 - 130 = 4.25$ cents per each of the EUR62,500 of the contract, or $2,656.25. That is, the call owner can buy EUR62,500, worth $83,906.25 (= EUR62,500 × $1.3425) in the spot market, for $81,250 (= EUR62,500 × $1.30). On the other hand, if the spot rate is $1.2807/EUR at expiration, the call option has a negative exercise value, $128.07 - 130 = -1.93$ cents per EUR. The call buyer is under no obligation to exercise the option if it is to his disadvantage, so he should not. He should let it expire worthless, or with zero value.

Exhibit 7.8A graphs the 130 Jun EUR call option from the buyer's perspective and Exhibit 7.8B graphs it from the call writer's perspective at expiration. Note that the two graphs are mirror-images of one another. The call buyer can lose no more than the call premium but theoretically has an unlimited profit potential. The call writer can profit by no more than the call premium but theoretically can lose an unlimited amount. At an expiration spot price of $S_T = E + C_a = 130 + 4.59 = 134.59$ cents per EUR, both the call buyer and writer break even, that is, neither earns nor loses anything.

The speculative possibilities of a long position in a call are clearly evident from Exhibit 7.8. Anytime the speculator believes that S_T will be in excess of the breakeven point, he will establish a long position in the call. The speculator who is correct realizes a profit. If the speculator is incorrect in his forecast, the loss will be limited to the premium paid. Alternatively, if the speculator believes that S_T will be less than the breakeven point, a short position in the call will yield a profit, the largest amount being the call premium received from the buyer. If the speculator is incorrect, very large losses can result if S_T is much larger than the breakeven point.

EXHIBIT 7.7

Philadelphia Stock Exchange American Currency Options Quotations

Options Philadelphia Exchange

		Calls	Puts	
Euro				133.39
62,500 Euro-cents per unit.				
120	Mar	13.42	–	
126	Mar	–	.03	
126	Jun	–	.26	
126	Sep	–	.73	
130	Mar	3.43	.03	
130	Jun	4.59	.94	
130	Sep	–	1.81	
130	Dec	6.76	2.43	
Japanese Yen				95.80
6,250,000 J.Yen-100ths of a cent per unit.				
95	Mar	.97	.05	
95	Jun	–	1.04	
95	Sep	–	1.48	
96	Mar	.31	.39	
96	Jun	2.00	1.53	
96	Sep	3.22	1.96	
96	Dec	–	2.21	
97	Mar	.05	–	
97	Jun	1.53	2.05	
97	Sep	2.08	2.47	
97	Dec	–	2.70	

Source: Mid-prices complied from bid and ask quotations obtained from Bloomberg on Tuesday, March 8, 2005.

EXHIBIT 7.8A

**Graph of 130 June EUR Call
Option: Buyer's Perspective**

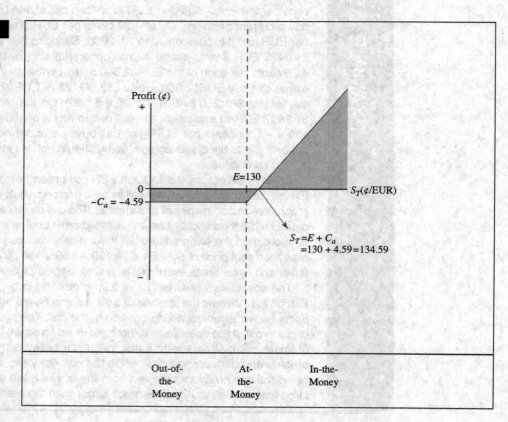

EXHIBIT 7.8B

**Graph of 130 June EUR Call
Option: Writer's Perspective**

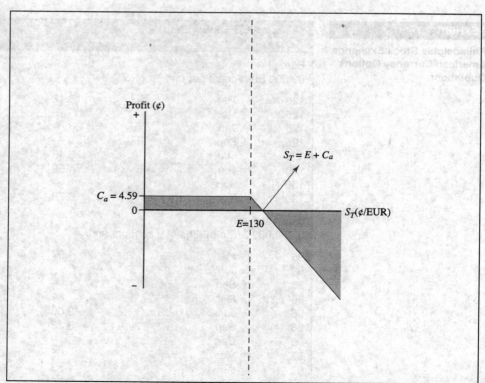

Analogously, at expiration a European put and an American put will have the same value. Algebraically, the expiration value can be stated as:

$$P_{aT} = P_{eT} = Max\ [E - S_T, 0] \tag{7.3}$$

where P denotes the value of the put at expiration.

EXAMPLE 7.6

Expiration Value of an American Put Option   As an example of pricing Equation 7.3, consider the 130 Jun EUR American put, which has a current premium, P_a, of .94 cents per EUR. If S_T is $1.2807/EUR, the put contract has an exercise value of 130 − 128.07 = 1.93 cents per EUR for each of the EUR62,500 of the contract, or $1,206.25. That is, the put owner can sell EUR62,500, worth $80,043.75 (= EUR62,500 × $1.2807) in the spot market, for $81,250 (= EUR62,500 × $1.30). If S_T = $1.3025/EUR, the exercise value is 130 −130.25 = −.25 cents per EUR. The put buyer would rationally not exercise the put; in other words, he should let it expire worthless with zero value.

Exhibit 7.9A graphs the 130 Jun EUR put from the buyer's perspective and Exhibit 7.9B graphs it from the put writer's perspective at expiration. The two graphs are mirror-images of one another. The put buyer can lose no more than the put premium and the put writer can profit by no more than the premium. The put buyer can earn a maximum profit of $E - P_a$ = 130 − .94 = 129.06 cents per EUR if the terminal spot exchange rate is an unrealistic $0/EUR. The put writer's maximum loss is 129.06 cents per EUR. Additionally, at $S_T = E - P_a$ = 129.06 cents per EUR, the put buyer and writer both break even; neither loses nor earns anything.

The speculative possibilities of a long position in a put are clearly evident from Exhibit 7.9. Anytime the speculator believes that S_T will be less than the breakeven point, he will establish a long position in the put. If the speculator is correct, he will realize a profit. If the speculator is incorrect in his forecast, the loss will be limited to the premium paid. Alternatively, if the speculator believes that S_T will be in excess of the breakeven point, a short position in the put will yield a profit, the largest amount being the put premium received from the buyer. If the speculator is incorrect, very large losses can result if S_T is much smaller than the breakeven point.

American Option-Pricing Relationships

An American call or put option can be exercised at any time prior to expiration. Consequently, in a rational marketplace, American options will satisfy the following basic pricing relationships at time t prior to expiration:

$$C_a \geq Max\ [S_t - E, 0] \tag{7.4}$$

and

$$P_a \geq Max\ [E - S_t, 0] \tag{7.5}$$

内在价值

Verbally, these equations state that the American call and put premiums at time t will be at least as large as the immediate exercise value, or **intrinsic value,** of the call or put option. (The t subscripts are deleted from the call and put premiums to simplify the notation.) Since the owner of a long-maturity American option can exercise it on any date that he could exercise a shorter maturity option he held on a currency, or at some later date after the shorter maturity option expires, it follows that all else remaining the same, the longer-term American option will have a market price at least as large as the shorter-term option.

EXHIBIT 7.9A

**Graph of 130 June EUR Put
Option: Buyer's Perspective**

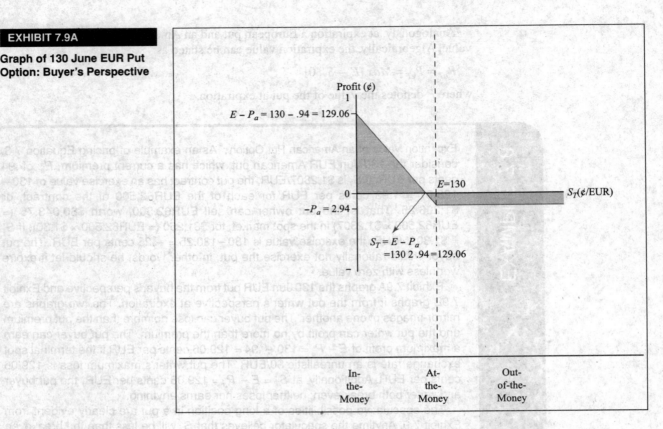

EXHIBIT 7.9B

**Graph of 130 June EUR Put
Option: Writer's Perspective**

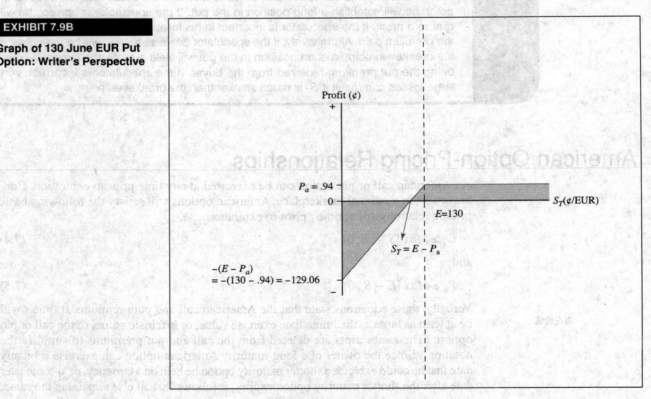

EXHIBIT 7.10

Market Value, Time Value, and Intrinsic Value of an American Call Option

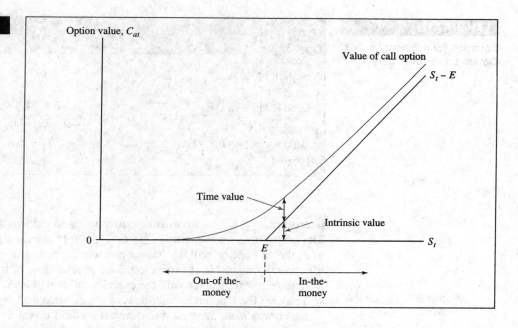

A call (put) option with $S_t > E (E > S_t)$ is referred to as trading in-the-money. If $S_t \cong E$ the option is trading at-the-money. If $S_t < E (E < S_t)$ the call (put) option is trading out-of-the-money. The difference between the option premium and the option's intrinsic value is nonnegative and sometimes referred to as the option's **time value.** For example, the time value for an American call is $C_a - Max[S_t - E, 0]$. The time value exists, meaning investors are willing to pay more than the immediate exercise value, because the option may move more in-the-money, and thus become more valuable, as time elapses. Exhibit 7.10 graphs the intrinsic value and time value for an American call option.

时间价值

EXAMPLE 7.7

American Option-Pricing Valuation   Let's see if Equations 7.4 and 7.5 actually hold for the 130 Jun EUR American call and the 130 Jun EUR American put options we considered. For the 130 Jun EUR call,

$$4.59 \geq Max[133.39 - 130, 0] = Max[3.39, 0] = 3.39.$$

Thus, the lower boundary relationship on the American call premium holds. (The spot price of 133.39 cents per EUR is obtained from the beginning of the EUR PHLX quotation section.) For the 130 Jun EUR put,

$$.94 \geq Max[130 - 133.39, 0] = Max[-3.39, 0] = 0.$$

Thus, the lower boundary relationship on the American put premium holds as well.

European Option-Pricing Relationships

欧式看跌和看涨期权的期权费的上下限更复杂，因为它们只能在到期日执行。

The pricing boundaries for European put and call premiums are more complex because they can only be exercised at expiration. Hence, there is a time value element to the boundary expressions. Exhibit 7.11 develops the lower boundary expression for a European call.

Exhibit 7.11 compares the costs and payoffs of two portfolios a U.S. dollar investor could make. Portfolio A involves purchasing a European call option and lending (or investing) an amount equal to the present value of the exercise price, E, at the U.S.

	Current Time	Expiration	
		$S_T \leq E$	$S_T > E$
Portfolio A:			
Buy Call	$-C_e$	0	$S_T - E$
Lend PV of E in U.S	$-E/(1+r_\$)$	E	E
	$-C_e - E/(1+r_\$)$	E	S_T
Portfolio B:			
Lend PV of one unit of currency i at rate r_i	$-S_t/(1+r_i)$	S_T	S_T

interest rate $r_\$$, which we assume corresponds to the length of the investment period. The cost of this investment is $C_e + E/(1 + r_\$)$. If at expiration, S_T is less than or equal to E, the call option will not have a positive exercise value and the call owner will let it expire worthless. If at expiration, S_T is greater than E, it will be to the call owner's advantage to exercise the call; the exercise value will be $S_T - E > 0$. The risk-free loan will pay off the amount E regardless of which state occurs at time T.

不管在时刻T发生何种情况，无风险贷款的回报是E。

By comparison, the U.S. dollar investor could invest in portfolio B, which consists of lending the present value of one unit of foreign currency i at the foreign interest rate r_i, which we assume corresponds to the length of the investment period. In U.S. dollar terms, the cost of this investment is $S_t/(1 + r_i)$. Regardless of which state exists at time T, this investment will pay off one unit of foreign currency, which in U.S. dollar terms will have value S_T.

It is easily seen from Exhibit 7.11 that if $S_T > E$, portfolios A and B pay off the same amount, S_T. However, if $S_T \leq E$, portfolio A has a larger payoff than portfolio B. It follows that in a rational marketplace, portfolio A will be priced to sell for at least as much as portfolio B, that is, $C_e + E/(1 + r_\$) \geq S_t/(1 + r_i)$. This implies that

$$C_e \geq Max\left[\frac{S_t}{(1+r_i)} - \frac{E}{(1+r_\$)}, 0\right] \qquad (7.6)$$

since the European call can never sell for a negative amount.

Similarly, it can be shown that the lower boundary pricing relationship for a European put is:

$$P_e \geq Max\left[\frac{E}{(1+r_\$)} - \frac{S_t}{(1+r_i)}, 0\right] \qquad (7.7)$$

The derivation of this formula is left as an exercise for the reader. (Hint: Portfolio A involves buying a put and lending spot, portfolio B involves lending the present value of the exercise price.)

Note that both C_e and P_e are functions of only five variables: $S_t, E, r_i, r_\$$, and implicitly the term-to-maturity. From Equations 7.6 and 7.7, it can be determined that, when all else remains the same, the call premium C_e (put premium P_e) will increase:

1. The larger (smaller) is S_t,
2. The smaller (larger) is E,
3. The smaller (larger) is r_i,
4. The larger (smaller) is $r_\$$, and
5. The larger (smaller) $r_\$$ is relative to r_i.

这里的隐含意义是：期权的执行期越长，r_s和r_i就越大。

Implicitly, both $r_\$$ and r_i will be larger the longer the length of the option period. When $r_\$$ and r_i are not too much different in size, a European FX call and put will increase in price when the option term-to-maturity increases. However, when $r_\$$ is very much larger than r_i, a European FX call will increase in price, but the put premium will decrease, when the option term-to-maturity increases. The opposite is true when r_i is very much greater than $r_\$$.

Recall that IRP implies $F_T = S_t[(1 + r_\$)/(1 + r_i)]$, which in turn implies that $F_T/(1 + r_\$) = S_t/(1 + r_i)$. Hence, European call and put prices on spot foreign exchange, Equations 7.6 and 7.7 can be, respectively, restated as:[3]

$$C_e \geq Max\left[\frac{(F_T - E)}{(1 + r_\$)}, 0\right]$$ (7.8)

and

$$P_e \geq Max\left[\frac{(E - F_T)}{(1 + r_\$)}, 0\right]$$ (7.9)

Binomial Option-Pricing Model

The option pricing relationships we have discussed to this point have been lower boundaries on the call and put premiums, instead of exact equality expressions for the premiums. The binomial option-pricing model provides an exact pricing formula for an American call or put.[4] We will examine only a simple one-step case of the binomial model to better understand the nature of option pricing.

We want to use the binomial model to value the PHLX 130 Jun EUR American call from Exhibit 7.7. We see from the exhibit that the option is quoted at a premium of 4.59 cents. The current spot price of the EUR in American terms is $S_0 = 133.39$ cents. Our estimate of the option's volatility (annualized standard deviation of the change in the spot rate) is $\sigma = 9$ percent, which was obtained from the Federal Reserve Bank of New York at www.ny.frb.org. This call option expires in 94 days on June 10, 2005, or in $T = 94/365 = .2575$ years. The one-step binomial model assumes that at the end of the option period the EUR will have appreciated to $S_{uT} = S_0 \cdot u$ or depreciated to $S_{dT} = S_0 \cdot d$, where $u = e^{\sigma \cdot \sqrt{T}}$ and $d = 1/u$. The spot rate at T will be either $139.62 = 133.39$ (1.04673) or $127.44 = 133.39 (.95536)$, where $u = e^{.09 \cdot \sqrt{.2575}} = 1.04673$ and $d = 1/u = .95536$. At the exercise price of $E = 130$, the option will only be exercised at time T if the EUR appreciates; its exercise value would be $C_{uT} = 9.62 = 139.62 - 130$. If the EUR depreciates it would not be rational to exercise the option; its value would be $C_{dT} = 0$.

二项式期权定价模型只要求：$u > 1 + r_s > d$。

The binominal option-pricing model only requires that $u > 1 + r_\$ > d$. The three-month Eurodollar bid rate is 2.97 percent. Thus, $1 + r_\$ = (1.0297)^T = 1.00756$. We see that $1.04673 > 1.00756 > .95536$.

The binomial option-pricing model relies on the risk-neutral probabilities of the underlying asset increasing and decreasing in value. For our purposes, the risk-neutral probability of the EUR appreciating is calculated as:

$$q = (F_T - S_0 \cdot d)/S_0(u - d),$$

where F_T is the forward (or futures) price that spans the option period. We will use the June EUR futures price on March 8, 2005, as our estimate of $F_T(\$/EUR) = \$1.3373$. Therefore,

---

[3] An American option can be exercised at any time during its life. If it is not advantageous for the option owner to exercise it prior to maturity, the owner can let it behave as a European option, which can only be exercised at maturity. It follows from Equations 7.4 and 7.8 (for calls) and 7.5 and 7.9 (for puts) that a more restrictive lower boundary relationship for American call and put options are, respectively:

$C_a \geq Max [S_t - E, (F - E)/(1 + r_\$), 0]$ and $P_a \geq Max [E - S_t, (E - F)/(1 + r_\$), 0]$

[4] The binomial option-pricing model was independently derived by Sharpe (1978), Rendleman and Bartter (1979), and Cox, Ross, and Rubinstein (1979).

$$q = (133.73 - 127.44)/(139.62 - 127.44) = .5164.$$

It follows that the risk-neutral probability of the EUR depreciating is $1 - q = 1 - .5164 = .4836$.

Because the American call option can be exercised at any time, including time 0, the binomial call option premium is determined by:

$$C_0 = Max \, [qC_{uT} + (1 - q)C_{dT}]/(1 + r_\$), S_0 - E] \qquad (7.10)$$
$$= Max \, [.5164(9.62) + .4836(0)]/(1.00756), 133.39 - 130 \,]$$
$$= Max \, [4.93, 3.39] = 4.93 \text{ cents per EUR.}$$

Alternatively, (if C_{uT} is positive) the binomial call price can be expressed as:

$$C_0 = \, Max\{[F_T \cdot h - E((S_0 \cdot u/E)(h - 1) + 1)]/(1 + r_\$), S_0 - E\}, \qquad (7.11)$$

where $h = (C_{uT} - C_{dT})/S_0(u - d)$ is the risk-free hedge ratio. The *hedge ratio* is the size of the long (short) position the investor must have in the underlying asset per option the investor must write (buy) to have a risk-free offsetting investment that will result in the investor receiving the same terminal value at time T regardless of whether the underlying asset increases or decreases in value. For our example numbers, we see that

$$h = (9.62 - 0)/(139.62 - 127.44) = .7898.$$

Thus, the call premium is:

$$C_0 = \, Max \, \{[133.73(.7898) - 130((139.62/130)(.7898 - 1) + 1)]/$$
$$(1.00756), 133.39 - 130\}$$
$$= Max \, [4.93, 3.39] = 4.93 \text{ cents per EUR.}$$

Equation 7.11 is more intuitive than Equation 7.10 because it is in the same general form as Equation 7.8. In an analogous manner, a binomial put option-pricing model can be developed. Nevertheless, for our example, the binomial call option-pricing model yielded a price that was too large compared to the actual market price of 4.59 cents. This is what we might expect with such a simple model, and when using such an arbitrary value for the option's volatility. In the next section, we consider a more refined option-pricing model.

European Option-Pricing Formula

In the last section, we examined a simple one-step version of binomial option-pricing model. Instead, we could have assumed the stock price followed a multiplicative binomial process by subdividing the option period into many subperiods. In this case, S_T and C_T could be many different values. When the number of subperiods into which the option period is subdivided goes to infinity, the European call and put pricing formulas presented in this section are obtained. Exact European call and put pricing formulas are:[5]

$$C_e = S_t e^{-r_i T} N(d_1) - E e^{-r_\$ T} N(d_2) \qquad (7.12)$$

and

$$P_e = E e^{-r_\$ T} N(-d_2) - S_t e^{-r_i T} N(-d_1) \qquad (7.13)$$

The interest rates r_i and $r_\$$ are assumed to be annualized and constant over the term-to-maturity T of the option contract, which is expressed as a fraction of a year.

---

[5]The European option-pricing model was developed by Biger and Hull (1983), Garman and Kohlhagen (1983), and Grabbe (1983). The evolution of the model can be traced back to European option-pricing models developed by Merton (1973) and Black (1976).

Invoking IRP, where with continuous compounding $F_T = S_t e^{(r_\$ - r_i)T}$, C_e and P_e in Equations 7.12 and 7.13 can be, respectively, restated as:

$$C_e = [F_T N(d_1) - E N(d_2)]\, e^{r_\$ T} \tag{7.14}$$

and

$$P_e = [E N(-d_2) - F_T N(-d_1)]\, e^{r_\$ T} \tag{7.15}$$

where

$$d_1 = \frac{ln(F_T / E) + .5\sigma^2 T}{\sigma\sqrt{T}}$$

and

$$d_2 = d_1 - \sigma\sqrt{T}\,.$$

$N(d)$ denotes the cumulative area under the standard normal density function from $-\infty$ to d_1 (or d_2). The variable σ is the annualized volatility of the change in exchange rate $ln(S_{t+1}/S_t)$. Equations 7.14 and 7.15 indicate that C_e and P_e are functions of only five variables: F_T, E, $r_\$$, T, and σ. It can be shown that both C_e and P_e increase when σ becomes larger.

The value $N(d)$ can be calculated using the NORMSDIST function of Microsoft Excel.

Equations 7.14 and 7.15 are widely used in practice, especially by international banks in trading OTC options.

EXAMPLE 7.8

The European Option-Pricing Model   As an example of using the European options-pricing model, consider the PHLX 130 Jun EUR American call option from Exhibit 7.7. We will use the European model even though the call is an American option. This is frequently done in practice, and the prices between the two option styles vary very little.[6]

The option has a premium of 4.59 U.S. cents per EUR. The option will expire on June 10, 2005–94 days from the quotation date, or $T = 94/365 = .2575$. We will use the June futures price on March 8, 2005, as our estimate of $F_T(\$/EUR) = \$1.3373$. The rate $r_\$$ is estimated as the annualized three-month Eurodollar bid rate of 2.97 percent on the same day. The estimated volatility is 9.0 percent and was obtained from the Federal Reserve Bank of New York at www.ny.frb.org.

The values d_1 and d_2 are:

$$d_1 = \frac{ln(133.73/130) + .5(.09)^2(.2575)}{(.09)\sqrt{.2575}} = .6422$$

and

$$d_2 = .6422 - (.09)\sqrt{.2575} = .5965$$

Consequently, it can be determined that $N(.6422) = .7396$ and $N(.5965) = .7246$. We now have everything we need to compute the model price:

$$C_e = [133.73(.7396) - 130(.7246)]e^{-(.0297)(.2575)}$$
$$= [98.9067 - 94.1980](.9924)$$
$$= 4.67 \text{ cents per EUR vs. the actual market mid-price of 4.59 cents.}$$

As we see, the model has done a good job of valuing the EUR call.

---

[6]Barone-Adesi and Whaley (1987) have developed an approximate American call option-pricing model that has roved quite accurate in valuing American currency call options.

Empirical Tests of Currency Options

然而，当他们使用同步的价格数据并考虑交易费用时，他们得出的结论是：PHLX的美式期权定价是有效的。

Shastri and Tandon (1985) empirically test the American boundary relationships we developed in this chapter (Equations 7.4, 7.5, 7.6, 7.7, 7.8, and 7.9) using PHLX put and call data. They discover many violations of the boundary relationships, but conclude that nonsimultaneous data could account for most of the violations. Bodurtha and Courtadon (1986) test the immediate exercise boundary relationships (Equations 7.4 and 7.5) for PHLX American put and call options. They also find many violations when using last daily trade data. However, when they use simultaneous price data and incorporate transaction costs, they conclude that the PHLX American currency options are efficiently priced.

Shastri and Tandon (1986) also test the European option-pricing model using PHLX American put and call data. They determine that a nonmember of the PHLX could not earn abnormal profits from the hedging strategies they examine. This implies that the European option-pricing model works well in pricing American currency options. Barone-Adesi and Whaley (1987) also find that the European option-pricing model works well for pricing American currency options that are *at* or *out-of-the money,* but does not do well in pricing *in-the-money* calls and puts. For *in-the-money* options, their approximate American option-pricing model yields superior results.

SUMMARY

本章介绍了外汇期货和外汇期权。这两种工具对投机和规避汇率波动风险都很有用。后面各章将讨论如何使用这些工具来达到套期保值的目的。

　　1. 远期合约、期货合约以及期权合约属于衍生的或或有的债券。也就是说，其价值取决于这些证券的标的资产的价值。

　　2. 作为金融工具，远期合约和期货合约具有相似性，但也有差异性。两者都约定在未来可按某个价格买进或卖出一定数量的某种标的资产。不过，期货合约是在交易所交易的，具有标准化特征，不同于可以量身定做的远期合约。期货合约的两种标准化特征是合约规模和割期日期。

　　3. 此外，期货合约每天按新的结算价格进行钉市操作。因此，期货头寸拥有者的个人保证金账户每天会发生增减变化，以反映因期货结算价格相对于前一天所发生的变动而产生的利润或亏损。

　　4. 期货市场的有效运作需要有投机者和套期保值者的参与。套期保值者的目的是避免因标的资产价格的变动而产生的风险，而投机者的目的是通过预测期货价格变化趋势来获取利润。

　　5. 芝加哥商品交易所和费城交易所是两家最大的外汇期货交易所。

　　6. 利率平价关系常被用做对外汇期货的定价，也可用做对外汇远期合约的定价。

　　7. 欧元利率期货合约可用做规避短期利率风险的工具。

　　8. 期权是指以特定的价格在约定的时期里买卖标的资产的一种权利而非义务。看涨期权赋予其所有

This chapter introduced currency futures and options on foreign exchange. These instruments are useful for speculating and hedging foreign exchange rate movements. In later chapters, it will be shown how to use these vehicles for hedging purposes.

1. Forward, futures, and options contracts are derivative, or contingent claim, securities. That is, their value is derived or contingent upon the value of the asset that underlies these securities.

2. Forward and futures contracts are similar instruments, but there are differences. Both are contracts to buy or sell a certain quantity of a specific underlying asset at some specific price in the future. Futures contracts, however, are exchange-traded, and there are standardized features that distinguish them from the tailor-made terms of forward contracts. The two main standardized features are contract size and maturity date.

3. Additionally, futures contracts are marked-to-market on a daily basis at the new settlement price. Hence, the performance bond account of an individual with a futures position is increased or decreased, reflecting daily realized profits or losses resulting from the change in the futures settlement price from the previous day's settlement price.

4. A futures market requires speculators and hedgers to effectively operate. Hedgers attempt to avoid the risk of price change of the underlying asset, and speculators attempt to profit from anticipating the direction of future price changes.

5. The Chicago Mercantile Exchange and the Philadelphia Board of Trade are the two largest currency futures exchanges.

6. The pricing equation typically used to price currency futures is the IRP relationship, which is also used to price currency forward contracts.

7. Eurodollar interest rate futures contracts were introduced as a vehicle for hedging short-term interest-rate risk.

8. An option is the right, but not the obligation, to buy or sell the underlying asset for a stated price over a stated time period. Call options give the owner the right to buy, put options the right to sell. American options can be exercised at any time during their life; European options can only be exercised at maturity.

者购买的权利，而看跌期权赋予所
有者卖出的权利。美式期权可以在
期权存续期间的任何时候执行，而
欧式期权只能在到期日执行。

9. 在两家交易所交易的期权具
有标准化特征。即期外汇期权在费
城交易所进行交易，而外汇期货期
权在芝加哥商品交易所进行交易。

10. 看涨期权和看跌期权的基本
价格界限表达式可通过实际期权价
格数据来加以确定和检验。

11. 看涨期权和看跌期权的欧式
定价模型同样可通过实际的市场价
格数据来推出并解释。

9. Exchange-traded options with standardized features are traded on two exchanges. Options on spot foreign exchange are traded at the Philadelphia Stock Exchange, and options on currency futures are traded at the Chicago Mercantile Exchange.

10. Basic boundary expressions for put and call option prices were developed and examined using actual option-pricing data.

11. A European option-pricing model for put and call options was also presented and explained using actual market data.

KEY WORDS

American option, *173*	futures, *163*	premium, *173*
at-the-money, *174*	hedger, *164*	price convergence, *170*
call, *173*	in-the-money, *174*	price discovery, *169*
clearinghouse, *165*	initial performance	put, *173*
commission, *165*	bond, *163*	reversing trade, *165*
contingent claim	intrinsic value, *177*	settled-up, *163*
security, *163*	long, *163*	settlement price, *163*
contract size, *163*	marked-to-market, *163*	short, *163*
daily price limit, *165*	maintenance	speculator, *164*
delivery month, *163*	performance bond, *164*	standardized, *163*
derivative	maturity date, *163*	striking price, *173*
security, *163*	nearby, *167*	time value, *179*
European option, *173*	open interest, *167*	writer, *173*
exchange-traded, *163*	option, *172*	zero-sum game, *164*
exercise price, *173*	out-of-the-money, *174*	

QUESTIONS

1. Explain the basic differences between the operation of a currency forward market and a futures market.

2. In order for a derivatives market to function most efficiently, two types of economic agents are needed: hedgers and speculators. Explain.

3. Why are most futures positions closed out through a reversing trade rather than held to delivery?

4. How can the FX futures market be used for price discovery?

5. What is the major difference in the obligation of one with a long position in a futures (or forward) contract in comparison to an options contract?

6. What is meant by the terminology that an option is in-, at-, or out-of-the-money?

7. List the arguments (variables) of which an FX call or put option model price is a function. How does the call and put premium change with respect to a change in the arguments?

PROBLEMS

1. Assume today's settlement price on a CME EUR futures contract is $1.3140/EUR. You have a short position in one contract. Your performance bond account currently has a balance of $1,700. The next three days' settlement prices are $1.3126, $1.3133, and $1.3049. Calculate the changes in the performance bond account from daily marking-to-market and the balance of the performance bond account after the third day.

2. Do problem 1 again assuming you have a long position in the futures contract.

3. Using the quotations in Exhibit 7.3, calculate the face value of the open interest in the June 2005 Swiss franc futures contract.

4. Using the quotations in Exhibit 7.3, note that the June 2005 Mexican peso futures contract has a price of $0.08845. You believe the spot price in June will be $0.09500. What speculative position would you enter into to attempt to profit from your beliefs? Calculate your anticipated profits, assuming you take a position in three contracts. What is the size of your profit (loss) if the futures price is indeed an unbiased predictor of the future spot price and this price materializes?

5. Do problem 4 again assuming you believe the June 2005 spot price will be $0.07500.

6. George Johnson is considering a possible six-month $100 million LIBOR-based, floating-rate bank loan to fund a project at terms shown in the table below. Johnson fears a possible rise in the LIBOR rate by December and wants to use the December Eurodollar futures contract to hedge this risk. The contract expires December 20, 1999, has a US$ 1 million contract size, and a discount yield of 7.3 percent.

Johnson will ignore the cash flow implications of marking-to-market, initial performance bond requirements, and any timing mismatch between exchange-traded futures contract cash flows and the interest payments due in March.

	Loan Terms	
September 20, 1999	**December 20, 1999**	**March 20, 2000**
• Borrow $100 million at September 20 LIBOR + 200 basis points (bps)	• Pay interest for first three months	• Pay back principal plus interest
• September 20 LIBOR = 7%	• Roll loan over at December 20 LIBOR + 200 bps	

Loan initiated	First loan payment (9%) and futures contract expires	Second payment and principal
↓	↓	↓
•	•	•
9/20/99	12/20/99	3/20/00

a. Formulate Johnson's September 20 floating-to-fixed-rate strategy using the Eurodollar future contracts discussed in the text above. Show that this strategy would result in a fixed-rate loan, assuming an increase in the LIBOR rate to 7.8 percent by December 20, which remains at 7.8 percent through March 20. Show all calculations.

Johnson is considering a 12-month loan as an alternative. This approach will result in two additional uncertain cash flows, as follows:

Loan initiated	First payment (9%)	Second payment	Third payment	Fourth payment and principal
↓	↓	↓	↓	↓
•	•	•	•	•
9/20/99	12/20/99	3/20/00	6/20/00	9/20/00

b. Describe the strip hedge that Johnson could use and explain how it hedges the 12-month loan (specify number of contracts.) No calculations are needed.

7. Jacob Bower has a liability that:
   • has a principal balance of $100 million on June 30, 1998,
   • accrues interest quarterly starting on June 30, 1998,
   • pays interest quarterly,
   • has a one-year term to maturity, and
   • calculates interest due based on 90-day LIBOR (the London Interbank Offered Rate).

Bower wishes to hedge his remaining interest payments against changes in interest rates. Bower has correctly calculated that he needs to sell (short) 300 Eurodollar futures contracts to accomplish the hedge. He is considering the alternative hedging strategies outlined in the following table.

Initial Position (6/30/98) in 90-Day LIBOR Eurodollar Contracts

Contract Month	Strategy A (contracts)	Strategy B (contracts)
September 1998	300	100
December 1998	0	100
March 1999	0	100

   a. Explain why strategy B is a more effective hedge than strategy A when the yield curve undergoes an instantaneous nonparallel shift.

   b. Discuss an interest rate scenario in which strategy A would be superior to strategy B.

8. Use the quotations in Exhibit 7.7 to calculate the intrinsic value and the time value of the 97 September Japanese yen American call and put options.

9. Assume the spot Swiss franc is $0.7000 and the six-month forward rate is $0.6950. What is the minimum price that a six-month American call option with a striking price of $0.6800 should sell for in a rational market? Assume the annualized six-month Eurodollar rate is 3 1/2 percent.

10. Do problem 9 again assuming an American put option instead of a call option.

11. Use the European option-pricing models developed in the chapter to value the call of problem 9 and the put of problem 10. Assume the annualized volatility of the Swiss franc is 14.2 percent. This problem can be solved using the FXOPM.xls spreadsheet.

12. Use the binomial option-pricing model developed in the chapter to value the call of problem 9. The volatility of the Swiss franc is 14.2 percent.

INTERNET EXERCISES

1. Data on currency futures can be found at the Chicago Mercantile Exchange website, www.cme.com. Go the the "Market Data" section at this website and determine in which currency there is the most trading volume today. Click on the currency name to determine in which contract expiration there is the most trading volume. Is it the near-term contract or a deferred delivery contract?

MINI CASE

The Options Speculator

A speculator is considering the purchase of five three-month Japanese yen call options with a striking price of 96 cents per 100 yen. The premium is 1.35 cents per 100 yen. The spot price is 95.28 cents per 100 yen and the 90-day forward rate is 95.71 cents. The speculator believes the yen will appreciate to $1.00 per 100 yen over the next three months. As the speculator's assistant, you have been asked to prepare the following:

1. Graph the call option cash flow schedule.

2. Determine the speculator's profit if the yen appreciates to $1.00/100 yen.

3. Determine the speculator's profit if the yen appreciates only to the forward rate.

4. Determine the future spot price at which the speculator will only break even.

REFERENCES & SUGGESTED READINGS

Barone-Adesi, Giovanni, and Robert Whaley. "Efficient Analytic Approximation of American Option Values." *Journal of Finance* 42 (1987), pp. 301–20.

Biger, Nahum, and John Hull. "The Valuation of Currency Options." *Financial Management* 12 (1983), pp. 24–28.

Black, Fischer. "The Pricing of Commodity Contracts." *Journal of Financial Economics* 3 (1976), pp. 167–79.

——and Myron Scholes. "The Pricing of Options and Corporate Liabilities." *Journal of Political Economy* 81 (1973), pp. 637–54.

Bodurtha, James, Jr., and George Courtadon. "Efficiency Tests of the Foreign Currency Options Market." *Journal of Finance* 41 (1986), pp. 151–62.

Cox, John C., Jonathan E. Ingersoll, and Stephen A. Ross. "The Relation between Forward Prices and Futures Prices." *Journal of Financial Economics* 9 (1981), pp. 321–46.

Cox, John C., Stephen A. Ross, and Mark Rubinstein. "Option Pricing: A Simplified Approach." *Journal of Financial Economics* 7 (1979), pp. 229–63.

Garman, Mark, and Steven Kohlhagen. "Foreign Currency Option Values." *Journal of International Money and Finance* 2 (1983), pp. 231–38.

Grabbe, J. Orlin. "The Pricing of Call and Put Options on Foreign Exchange." *Journal of International Money and Finance* 2 (1983), pp. 239–54.

——*International Financial Markets,* 3rd ed. Upper Saddle River, N.J.: Prentice Hall, 1996.

Merton, Robert. "Theory of Rational Option Pricing." *The Bell Journal of Economics and Management Science* 4 (1973), pp. 141–83.

Rendleman, Richard J., Jr., and Brit J. Bartter. "Two-State Option Pricing." *Journal of Finance* 34 (1979), pp. 1093–1110.

Sharpe, William F. "Chapter 14." *Investments*. Englewood Cliffs, N.J.: Prentice Hall, 1978.

Shastri, Kuldeep, and Kishore Tandon. "Arbitrage Tests of the Efficiency of the Foreign Currency Options Market." *Journal of International Money and Finance* 4 (1985), pp. 455–68.

——"Valuation of Foreign Currency Options: Some Empirical Tests." *Journal of Financial and Quantitative Analysis* 21 (1986), pp. 145–60.

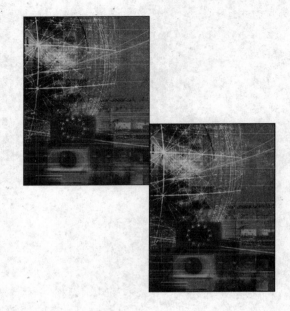

PART THREE

OUTLINE

Foreign Exchange Exposure and Management

PART THREE is composed of three chapters covering the topics of transaction, economic, and translation exposure management, respectively.

CHAPTER 8 covers the management of transaction exposure that arises from contractual obligations denominated in a foreign currency. Several methods for hedging this exposure are compared and contrasted. The chapter also includes a discussion of why a MNC should hedge, a debatable subject in the minds of both academics and practitioners.

CHAPTER 9 covers economic exposure, that is, the extent to which the value of the firm will be affected by unexpected changes in exchange rates. The chapter provides a way to measure economic exposure, discusses its determinants, and presents methods for managing and hedging economic exposure.

CHAPTER 10 covers translation exposure or, as it is sometimes called, accounting exposure. Translation exposure refers to the effect that changes in exchange rates will have on the consolidated financial reports of a MNC. The chapter discusses, compares, and contrasts the various methods for translating financial statements denominated in foreign currencies, and includes a discussion of managing translation exposure using funds adjustment and the pros and cons of using balance sheet and derivatives hedges.

8 Management of Transaction Exposure

AS THE NATURE OF BUSINESS becomes international, many firms are exposed to the risk of fluctuating exchange rates. Changes in exchange rates may affect the settlement of contracts, cash flows, and the firm valuation. It is thus important for financial managers to know the firm's foreign currency exposure and properly manage the exposure. By doing so, managers can stabilize the firm's cash flows and enhance the firm value.

这样，经营者就能稳定公司的现金流并提高公司的价值。

Three Types of Exposure

习惯上，外币风险暴露分为交易风险暴露、经济风险暴露与换算风险暴露。

Before we get into the important issue of how to manage transaction exposure, let us briefly discuss different types of exposure. It is conventional to classify foreign currency exposures into three types:

- Transaction exposure
- Economic exposure
- Translation exposure

交易风险暴露

Transaction exposure, a subject to be discussed in this chapter, can be defined as the sensitivity of "realized" domestic currency values of the firm's contractual cash flows *denominated* in foreign currencies to unexpected exchange rate changes. Since settlements of these contractual cash flows affect the firm's domestic currency cash flows, transaction exposure is sometimes regarded as a short-term economic exposure. Transaction exposure arises from fixed-price contracting in a world where exchange rates are changing randomly.

www.stern.nyu.edu/~igiddy/fxrisk.htm   经济风险暴露

Provides an overview of exchange risk management issues.

Economic exposure, a subject to be discussed in Chapter 9, can be defined as the extent to which the value of the firm would be affected by unanticipated changes in exchange rates. Any anticipated changes in exchange rates would have been already discounted and reflected in the firm's value. As we will discuss later, changes in exchange rates can have a profound effect on the firm's competitive position in the world market and thus on its cash flows and market value.

换算风险暴露

On the other hand, **translation exposure,** which will be discussed in Chapter 10, refers to the potential that the firm's consolidated financial statements can be affected by changes in exchange rates. Consolidation involves translation of subsidiaries' financial statements from local currencies to the home currency. Consider a U.S. multinational firm that has subsidiaries in the United Kingdom and Japan. Each subsidiary will produce financial statements in local currency. To consolidate financial statements worldwide, the firm must translate the subsidiaries' financial statements in local currencies into the U.S. dollar, the home currency. As we will see later, translation involves many controversial issues. Resultant translation gains and losses represent the accounting system's attempt to measure economic exposure *ex post*. It does not provide a good measure of *ex ante* economic exposure. In the remainder of this chapter, we will focus on how to manage transaction exposure.

如前所述，当公司发生固定的外币现金流时，公司就面临着交易风险暴露。

As discussed above, the firm is subject to transaction exposure when it faces *contractual* cash flows that are fixed in foreign currencies. Suppose that a U.S. firm sold its product to a German client on three-month credit terms and invoiced €1 million. When the U.S. firm receives €1 million in three months, it will have to convert (unless it hedges) the euros into dollars at the spot exchange rate prevailing on the maturity date, which cannot be known in advance. As a result, the dollar receipt from this foreign sale becomes uncertain; should the euro appreciate (depreciate) against the dollar, the dollar receipt will be higher (lower). This situation implies that if the firm does nothing about the exposure, it is effectively speculating on the future course of the exchange rate.

For another example of transaction exposure, consider a Japanese firm entering into a loan contract with a Swiss bank that calls for the payment of SF100 million for principal and interest in one year. To the extent that the yen/Swiss franc exchange rate is uncertain, the Japanese firm does not know how much yen it will take to buy SF100 million spot in one year's time. If the yen appreciates (depreciates) against the Swiss franc, a smaller (larger) yen amount will be needed to pay off the SF-denominated loan.

这些例子说明，只要公司有外币记账的收支，就面临着交易风险暴露。

These examples suggest that whenever the firm has foreign-currency-denominated receivables or payables, it is subject to transaction exposure, and their settlements are likely to affect the firm's cash flow position. Furthermore, in view of the fact that firms are now more frequently entering into commercial and financial contracts denominated in foreign currencies, judicious management of transaction exposure has become an important function of international financial management. Unlike economic exposure, transaction exposure is well defined: The magnitude of transaction exposure is the same as the amount of foreign currency that is receivable or payable. This chapter will thus focus on alternative ways of hedging transaction exposure using various financial contracts and *operational techniques:*

本章重点介绍利用各种金融合约和操作技巧来对交易风险暴露进行套期保值的方法。

Financial contracts

- Forward market hedge
- Money market hedge
- Option market hedge
- Swap market hedge

Operational techniques

- Choice of the invoice currency
- Lead/lag strategy
- Exposure netting

Before we discuss how to manage transaction exposure, however, it is useful to introduce a particular business situation that gives rise to exposure. Suppose that Boeing Corporation exported a Boeing 747 to British Airways and billed £10 million payable in one year. The money market interest rates and foreign exchange rates are given as follows:

The U.S. interest rate:	6.10% per annum.
The U.K. interest rate:	9.00% per annum.
The spot exchange rate:	$1.50/£.
The forward exchange rate:	$1.46/£ (1-year maturity).

Let us now look at the various techniques for managing this transaction exposure.

Forward Market Hedge 远期市场套期保值

也许最直接、最普遍的对外币交易风险暴露进行套期保值的方法是货币远期合约。

Perhaps the most direct and popular way of hedging transaction exposure is by currency forward contracts. Generally speaking, the firm may sell (buy) its foreign currency receivables (payables) forward to eliminate its exchange risk exposure. In the above example, in order to hedge foreign exchange exposure, Boeing may simply sell forward its pounds receivable, £10 million for delivery in one year, in exchange for a given amount of U.S. dollars. On the maturity date of the contract, Boeing will have to deliver £10 million to the bank, which is the counterparty of the contract, and, in return, take delivery of $14.6 million ($1.46 × 10 million), regardless of the spot exchange rate that may prevail on the maturity date. Boeing will, of course, use the £10 million that it is going to receive from British Airways to fulfill the forward contract. Since Boeing's pound receivable is exactly offset by the pound payable (created by the forward contract), the company's net pound exposure becomes zero.

Since Boeing is assured of receiving a given dollar amount, $14.6 million, from the counterparty of the forward contract, the dollar proceeds from this British sale will not be affected at all by future changes in the exchange rate. This point is illustrated in Exhibit 8.1. Once Boeing enters into the forward contract, exchange rate uncertainty becomes irrelevant for Boeing. Exhibit 8.1 also illustrates how the dollar proceeds from the British sale will be affected by the future spot exchange rate when exchange exposure is not hedged. The exhibit shows that the dollar proceeds under the forward

EXHIBIT 8.1

Dollar Proceeds from the British Sale: Forward Hedge versus Unhedged Position

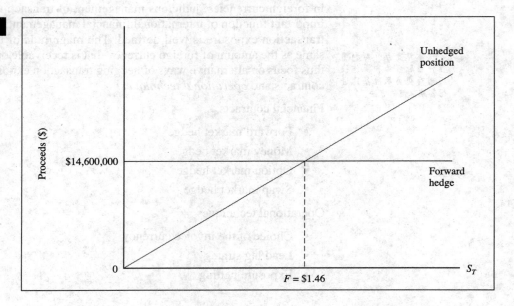

EXHIBIT 8.2

Gains/Losses from Forward Hedge

Spot Exchange Rate on the Maturity Date (S_T)	Receipts from the British Sale		Gains/Losses from Hedge[b]
	Unhedged Position	Forward Hedge	
$1.30	$13,000,000	$14,600,000	$1,600,000
$1.40	$14,000,000	$14,600,000	$ 600,000
$1.46[a]	$14,600,000	$14,600,000	0
$1.50	$15,000,000	$14,600,000	–$ 400,000
$1.60	$16,000,000	$14,600,000	–$1,400,000

[a]The forward exchange rate (F) is $1.46/£ in this example.
[b]The gains/losses are computed as the proceeds under the forward hedge minus the proceeds from the unhedged position at the various spot exchange rates on the maturity date.

hedge will be higher than those under the unhedged position if the future spot exchange rate turns out to be less than the forward rate, that is, $F = \$1.46/£$, and the opposite will hold if the future spot rate becomes higher than the forward rate. In the latter case, Boeing forgoes an opportunity to benefit from a strong pound.

Suppose that on the maturity date of the forward contract, the spot rate turns out to be $\$1.40/£$, which is less than the forward rate, $\$1.46/£$. In this case, Boeing would have received $14.0 million, rather than $14.6 million, had it not entered into the forward contract. Thus, one can say that Boeing gained $0.6 million from forward hedging. Needless to say, Boeing will not always gain in this manner. If the spot rate is, say, $\$1.50/£$ on the maturity date, then Boeing could have received $15.0 million by remaining unhedged. Thus, one can say *ex post* that forward hedging cost Boeing $0.40 million.

The gains and losses from forward hedging can be illustrated as in Exhibits 8.2 and 8.3. The gain/loss is computed as follows:

$$\text{Gain} = (F - S_T) \times £10 \text{ million} \tag{13.1}$$

显然，只要在到期日时远期汇率高于即期汇率，收益就是正的，即当$F > S_T$时，收益为正；反之，收益为负。

Obviously, the gain will be positive as long as the forward exchange rate is greater than the spot rate on the maturity date, that is, $F > S_T$, and the gain will be negative (that is, a loss will result) if the opposite holds. As Exhibit 8.3 shows, the firm theoretically can gain as much as $14.6 million when the pound becomes worthless, which, of course, is unlikely, whereas there is no limit to possible losses.

EXHIBIT 8.3

Illustration of Gains and Losses from Forward Hedging

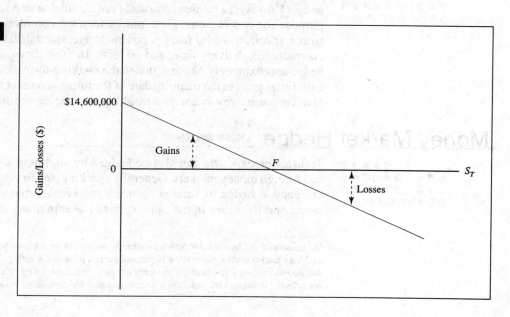

It is important, however, to note that the above analysis is *ex post* in nature, and that no one can know for sure what the future spot rate will be beforehand. The firm must decide whether to hedge or not to hedge *ex ante*. To help the firm decide, it is useful to consider the following three alternative scenarios:

1. $\overline{S}_T \approx F$
2. $\overline{S}_T < F$
3. $\overline{S}_T > F$

where $\overline{S}_T$ denotes the firm's expected spot exchange rate for the maturity date.

Under the first scenario, where the firm's expected future spot exchange rate, $\overline{S}_T$, is about the same as the forward rate, F, the "expected" gains or losses are approximately zero. But forward hedging eliminates exchange exposure. In other words, the firm can eliminate foreign exchange exposure without sacrificing any expected dollar proceeds from the foreign sale. Under this scenario the firm would be inclined to hedge as long as it is averse to risk. Note that this scenario becomes valid when the forward exchange rate is an unbiased predictor of the future spot rate.[1]

Under the second scenario, where the firm's expected future spot exchange rate is less than the forward rate, the firm expects a positive gain from forward hedging. Since the firm expects to increase the dollar proceeds while eliminating exchange exposure, it would be even more inclined to hedge under this scenario than under the first scenario. The second scenario, however, implies that the firm's management dissents from the market's consensus forecast of the future spot exchange rate as reflected in the forward rate.

Under the third scenario, on the other hand, where the firm's expected future spot exchange rate is more than the forward rate, the firm can eliminate exchange exposure via the forward contract only at the cost of reduced expected dollar proceeds from the foreign sale. Thus, the firm would be less inclined to hedge under this scenario, other things being equal. Despite lower expected dollar proceeds, however, the firm may still end up hedging. Whether the firm actually hedges or not depends on the degree of risk aversion; the more risk averse the firm is, the more likely it is to hedge. From the perspective of a hedging firm, the reduction in the expected dollar proceeds can be viewed implicitly as an "insurance premium" paid for avoiding the hazard of exchange risk.

公司可以用货币期货合约而不是远期合约来进行套期保值。

The firm can use a currency futures contract, rather than a forward contract, to hedge. However, a futures contract is not as suitable as a forward contract for hedging purpose for two reasons. First, unlike forward contracts that are tailor-made to the firm's specific needs, futures contracts are standardized instruments in terms of contract size, delivery date, and so forth. In most cases, therefore, the firm can only hedge approximately. Second, due to the marking-to-market property, there are interim cash flows prior to the maturity date of the futures contract that may have to be invested at uncertain interest rates. As a result, exact hedging again would be difficult.

Money Market Hedge   货币市场套期保值

交易风险暴露也可以通过在国内或国外货币市场上借入和贷出资金来进行套期保值。

Transaction exposure can also be hedged by lending and borrowing in the domestic and foreign money markets. Generally speaking, the firm may borrow (lend) in foreign currency to hedge its foreign currency receivables (payables), thereby matching its assets and liabilities in the same currency. Again using the same example presented

---

[1]As mentioned in Chapter 6, the forward exchange rate will be an unbiased predictor of the future spot rate if the exchange market is informationally efficient and the risk premium is not significant. Empirical evidence indicates that the risk premium, if it exists, is generally not very significant. Unless the firm has private information that is not reflected in the forward rate, it would have no reason for disagreeing with the forward rate.

EXHIBIT 8.4

Cash Flow Analysis of a Money Market Hedge

Transaction	Current Cash Flow	Cash Flow at Maturity
1. Borrow pounds	£ 9,174,312	−£10,000,000
2. Buy dollar spot	$13,761,468	
with pounds	−£ 9,174,312	
3. Invest in the United States	−$13,761,468	$14,600,918
4. Collect pound receivable		£10,000,000
Net cash flow	0	$14,600,918

进行货币市场套期保值的第一步是决定英镑的借入量。

above, Boeing can eliminate the exchange exposure arising from the British sale by first borrowing in pounds, then converting the loan proceeds into dollars, which then can be invested at the dollar interest rate. On the maturity date of the loan, Boeing is going to use the pound receivable to pay off the pound loan. If Boeing borrows a particular pound amount so that the maturity value of this loan becomes exactly equal to the pound receivable from the British sale, Boeing's net pound exposure is reduced to zero, and Boeing will receive the future maturity value of the dollar investment.

The first important step in money market hedging is to determine the amount of pounds to borrow. Since the maturity value of borrowing should be the same as the pound receivable, the amount to borrow can be computed as the discounted present value of the pound receivable, that is, £10 million/(1.09) = £9,174,312. When Boeing borrows £9,174,312, it then has to repay £10 million in one year, which is equivalent to its pound receivable. The step-by-step procedure of money market hedging can be illustrated as follows:

Step 1: Borrow £9,174,312 in the U.K.

Step 2: Convert £9,174,312 into $13,761,468 at the current spot exchange rate of $1.50/£.

Step 3: Invest $13,761,468 in the United States.

Step 4: Collect £10 million from British Airways and use it to repay the pound loan.

Step 5: Receive the maturity value of the dollar investment, that is, $14,600,918 = $13,761,468(1.061), which is the guaranteed dollar proceeds from the British sale.

Exhibit 8.4 provides a cash flow analysis of money market hedging. The table shows that the net cash flow is zero at the present time, implying that, apart from possible transaction costs, the money market hedge is fully self-financing. The table also clearly shows how the 10 million receivable is exactly offset by the 10 million payable (created by borrowing), leaving a net cash flow of $14,600,918 on the maturity date.[2]

The maturity value of the dollar investment from the money market hedge turns out to be nearly identical to the dollar proceeds from forward hedging. This result is no coincidence. Rather, this is due to the fact that the interest rate parity (IRP) condition is approximately holding in our example. If the IRP is not holding, the dollar proceeds from money market hedging will not be the same as those from forward hedging. As a result, one hedging method will dominate another. In a competitive and

在一个充满竞争的有效国际金融市场下，对利率平价的任何偏离都不可能持续。

---

[2]In the case where the firm has an account payable denominated in pounds, the money market hedge calls for borrowing in dollars, buying pounds spot, and investing at the pound interest rate.

efficient world financial market, however, any deviations from IRP are not likely to persist.

Options Market Hedge 期权市场套期保值

远期市场和货币市场的一个可能缺陷，就是这些方法完全排除了汇率风险。

One possible shortcoming of both forward and money market hedges is that these methods completely eliminate exchange exposure. Consequently, the firm has to forgo the opportunity to benefit from favorable exchange rate changes. To elaborate on this point, let us assume that the spot exchange rate turns out to be $1.60 per pound on the maturity date of the forward contract. In this instance, forward hedging would cost the firm $1.4 million in terms of forgone dollar receipts (see Exhibit 8.2). If Boeing had indeed entered into a forward contract, it would regret its decision to do so. With its pound receivable, Boeing ideally would like to protect itself only if the pound weakens, while retaining the opportunity to benefit if the pound strengthens. Currency options provide such a *flexible* "optional" hedge against exchange exposure. Generally speaking, the firm may buy a foreign currency call (put) option to hedge its foreign currency payables (receivables).

To show how the options hedge works, suppose that in the over-the-counter market Boeing purchased a put option on 10 million British pounds with an exercise price of $1.46 and a one-year expiration. Assume that the option premium (price) was $0.02 per pound. Boeing thus paid $200,000 (= $0.02 × 10 million) for the option. This transaction provides Boeing with the right, but not the obligation, to sell up to £10 million for $1.46/£, regardless of the future spot rate.

Now assume that the spot exchange rate turns out to be $1.30 on the expiration date. Since Boeing has the right to sell each pound for $1.46, it will certainly exercise its put option on the pound and convert £10 million into $14.6 million. The main advantage of options hedging is that the firm can decide whether to exercise the option based on the realized spot exchange rate on the expiration date. Recall that Boeing paid $200,000 upfront for the option. Considering the time value of money, this upfront cost is equivalent to $212,200 (= $200,000 × 1.061) as of the expiration date. This means that under the options hedge, the net dollar proceeds from the British sale become $14,387,800:

$$\$14,387,800 = \$14,600,000 - \$212,200$$

Since Boeing is going to exercise its put option on the pound whenever the future spot exchange rate falls below the exercise rate of $1.46, it is assured of a "minimum" dollar receipt of $14,387,800 from the British sale.

Next, consider an alternative scenario where the pound appreciates against the dollar. Assume that the spot rate turns out to be $1.60 per pound on the expiration date. In this event, Boeing would have no incentive to exercise the option. It will rather let the option expire and convert £10 million into $16 million at the spot rate. Subtracting $212,200 for the option cost, the net dollar proceeds will become $15,787,800 under the option hedge. As suggested by these scenarios, the options hedge allows the firm to *limit the downside risk while preserving the upside potential.* The firm, however, has to pay for this flexibility in terms of the option premium. There rarely exist free lunches in finance! Note that neither the forward nor the money market hedge involves any upfront cost.

值得注意的是，无论是远期市场还是货币市场的套期保值都不需要事先支付任何费用。

Exhibit 8.5 provides the net dollar proceeds from the British sale under options hedging for a range of future spot exchange rates. The same results are illustrated in Exhibit 8.6. As Exhibit 8.6 shows, the options hedge sets a "floor" for the dollar proceeds. The future dollar proceeds will be at least $14,387,800 under the option hedge. Boeing thus can be said to have an insurance policy against the exchange risk hazard; the upfront option cost, $200,000, Boeing incurred can be explicitly regarded as an insurance premium. When a firm has an account payable rather than a receivable,

EXHIBIT 8.5

Dollar Proceeds from Options Hedge

Future Spot Exchange Rate (S_T)	Exercise Decision	Gross Dollar Proceeds	Option Cost	Net Dollar Proceeds
$1.30	Exercise	$14,600,000	$212,200	$14,387,800
$1.40	Exercise	$14,600,000	$212,200	$14,387,800
$1.46	Neutral	$14,600,000	$212,200	$14,387,800
$1.50	Not exercise	$15,000,000	$212,200	$14,787,800
$1.60	Not exercise	$16,000,000	$212,200	$15,787,800

Note: The exercise exchange rate (E) is $1.46 in this example.

in terms of a foreign currency, the firm can set a "ceiling" for the future dollar cost of buying the foreign currency amount by buying a call option on the foreign currency amount.

Exhibit 8.6 also compares the dollar proceeds from forward and options hedges. As indicated in the exhibit, the options hedge dominates the forward hedge for future spot rates greater than $1.48 per pound, whereas the opposite holds for spot rates lower than $1.48 per pound. Boeing will be indifferent between the two hedging methods at the "break-even" spot rate of $1.48 per pound.

The break-even spot rate, which is useful for choosing a hedging method, can be determined as follows:

$$\$(10,000,000)S_T - \$212,200 = \$14,600,000$$

By solving the equation for S_T, we obtain the break-even spot rate, $S_T^* = \$1.48$. The break-even analysis suggests that if the firm's expected future spot rate is greater (less) than the break-even rate, then the options (forward) hedge might be preferred.

与远期合约在合约到期日只有一个远期汇率不同，期权合约有多种执行汇率。

Unlike the forward contract, which has only one forward rate for a given maturity, there are multiple exercise exchange rates (prices) for the options contract. In the preceding discussion, we worked with an option with an exercise price of $1.46. Considering that Boeing has a pound receivable, it is tempting to think that it would be a good idea for Boeing to buy a put option with a higher exercise price, thereby increasing the minimum dollar receipt from the British sale. But it becomes immediately clear that the firm has to pay for it in terms of a higher option premium.

EXHIBIT 8.6

Dollar Proceeds from the British Sale: Option versus Forward Hedge

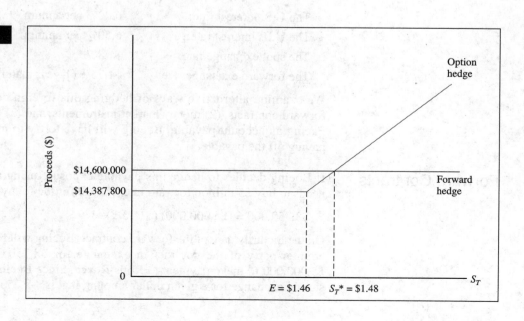

EXHIBIT 8.7	Boeing's Alternative Hedging Strategies: A Summary	
Strategy	**Transactions**	**Outcomes**
Forward market hedge	1. Sell £10,000,000 forward for U.S dollars now. 2. In one year, receive £10,000,000 rate from the British client and deliver it to the counterparty of the forward contract.	Assured of receiving $14,600,000 in one year; future spot exchange becomes irrelevant.
Money market hedge	1. Borrow £9,174,312 and buy $13,761,468 spot now. 2. In one year, collect £10,000,000 from the British client and pay off the pound loan using the amount.	Assured of receiving $13,761,468 now or $14,600,918 in one year; future spot exchange rate becomes irrelevant.
Options market hedge	1. Buy a put option on £10,000,000 for an upfront cost of $200,000. 2. In one year, decide whether to exercise the option upon observing the prevailing spot exchange rate.	Assured of receiving at least $14,387,800 or more if the future spot exchange rate exceeds the exercise exchange rate; Boeing controls the downside risk while retaining the upside potential.

选择怎样的期权执
行价最终取决于公司愿
意承受风险的程度。

Again, there is no free lunch. Choice of the exercise price for the options contract ultimately depends on the extent to which the firm is willing to bear exchange risk. For instance, if the firm's objective is only to avoid very unfavorable exchange rate changes (that is, a major depreciation of the pound in Boeing's example), then it should consider buying an out-of-money put option with a low exercise price, saving option costs. The three alternative hedging strategies are summarized in Exhibit 8.7.

Hedging Foreign Currency Payables

So far, we have discussed how to hedge foreign currency transaction exposure using Boeing's receivable as an example. In this section, we are going to discuss how to hedge foreign currency "payables." Suppose Boeing imported a Rolls-Royce jet engine for £5 million payable in one year. The market condition is summarized as follows:

The U.S. interest rate:	6.00% per annum.
The U.K. interest rate:	6.50% per annum.
The spot exchange rate:	$1.80/£.
The forward exchange rate:	$1.75/£ (1-year maturity)

We examine alternative ways of hedging this foreign currency payable using (1) forward contracts, (2) money market instruments, and (3) currency options contracts. Facing an account payable, Boeing will have to try to minimize the dollar cost of paying off the payable.

Forward Contracts

If Boeing decides to hedge this payable exposure using a forward contract, it only needs to buy £5 million forward in exchange for the following dollar amount:

$8,750,000 = (£5,000,000) ($1.75/£).

On the maturity date of the forward contract, Boeing will receive £5,000,000 from the counter-party of the contract in exchange for $8,750,000. Boeing then can use £5,000,000 to make payment to Rolls-Royce. Since Boeing will have £5,000,000 for sure in exchange for a given dollar amount, that is, $8,750,000, regardless of the spot exchange rate that may prevail in one year, Boeing's foreign currency payable is fully hedged.

Money Market Instruments

If Boeing first computes the present value of its foreign currency payable, that is

$$£4,694,836 = £5,000,000/1.065,$$

and immediately invests exactly the same pound amount at the British interest rate of 6.5 percent per annum, it is assured of having £5,000,000 in one year. Boeing then can use the maturity value of this investment to pay off its pound payable. Under this money market hedging, Boeing has to outlay a certain dollar amount today in order to buy spot the pound amount that needs to be invested:

$$\$8,450,705 = (£4,694,836)(\$1.80/£).$$

The future value of this dollar cost of buying the necessary pound amount is computed as follows:

$$\$8,957,747 = (\$8,450,705)(1.06),$$

which exceeds the dollar cost of securing £5,000,000 under forward hedging, $8,750,000. Since Boeing will have to try to minimize the dollar cost of securing the pound amount, forward hedge would be preferable to money market hedge.

Currency Options Contracts

If Boeing decides to use a currency options contract to hedge its pound payable, it needs to buy "call" options on £5,000,000. Boeing also will have to decide on the exercise or strike price for the call options. We assume that Boeing chooses the exercise price at $1.80/£ with the premium of $0.018 per pound. The total cost of options as of the maturity date (considering the time value of money) then can be computed as follows:

$$\$95,400 = (\$0.018/£)(£5,000,000)(1.06).$$

If the British pound appreciates against the dollar beyond $1.80/£, the strike price of the options contract, Boeing will choose to exercise its options and purchase £5,000,000 for $9,000,000 = (£5,000,000)($1.80/£). If the spot rate on the maturity date turns out to be below the strike price, on the other hand, Boeing will let the option expire and purchase the pound amount in the spot market. Thus, Boeing will be able to secure £5,000,000 for a maximum of $9,095,400 (= $9,000,000 + $95,400), or less.

比较远期套期保值和期权套期保值是非常有用的。

It would be useful to compare the forward hedge and options hedge. Exhibit 8.8 illustrates the dollar costs of securing £5,000,000 under the two alternative hedging approaches for different levels of spot exchange rate on the maturity date. As can be seen from Exhibit 8.8, options hedge would be preferable if the spot exchange rate turns out to be less than $1.731/£ as the options hedge involves a lower dollar cost. On the other hand, if the spot exchange rate turns out to be higher than $1.731/£, the forward hedge would be preferable. The break-even spot exchange rate, that is, S_T^*, can be computed from the following equation:

$$\$8,750,000 = (5,000,000)S_T + \$95,400,$$

where the dollar cost of securing £5,000,00 under the forward hedge is equated to that under the options hedge. When we solve the above equation for S_T, we obtain the break-even spot exchange rate.

Cross-Hedging Minor Currency Exposure

If a firm has receivables or payables in major currencies such as the British pound, euro, and Japanese yen, it can easily use forward, money market, or options contracts to manage its exchange risk exposure. In contrast, if the firm has positions in minor

| EXHIBIT 8.8 | Dollar Costs of Securing the Pound Payable: Option versus Forward Hedge |

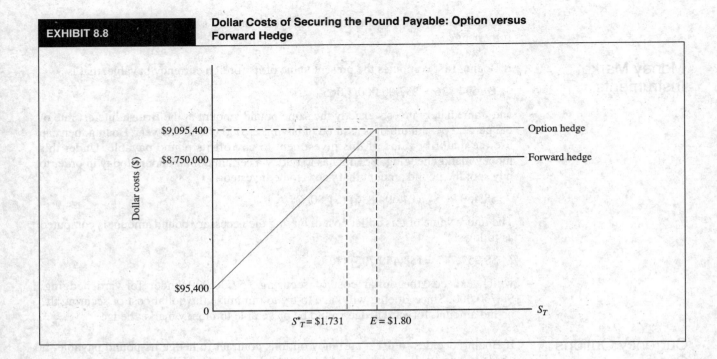

www.florin.com/v4/
valore4.html

Discusses issues related to
currency risk management.

交叉套期保值(cross-
hedging)

currencies such as the Korean won, Thai bhat, and Czech koruna, it may be either very costly or impossible to use financial contracts in these currencies. This is because financial markets of developing countries are relatively underdeveloped and often highly regulated. Facing this situation, the firm may consider using **cross-hedging** techniques to manage its minor currency exposure. Cross-hedging involves hedging a position in one asset by taking a position in another asset.

Suppose a U.S. firm has an account receivable in Korean won and would like to hedge its won position. If there were a well-functioning forward market in won, the firm would simply sell the won receivable forward. But the firm finds it impossible to do so. However, since the won/dollar exchange rate is highly correlated with the yen/dollar exchange rate, the U.S. firm may sell a yen amount, which is equivalent to the won receivable, forward against the dollar thereby cross-hedging its won exposure. Obviously, the effectiveness of this cross-hedging technique would depend on the stability and strength of the won/yen correlation. A study by Aggarwal and Demaskey (1997) indicates that Japanese yen derivative contracts are fairly effective in cross-hedging exposure to minor Asian currencies such as the Indonesian rupiah, Korean won, Philippine peso, and Thai bhat. Likewise, German mark derivatives can be effective in cross-hedging exposures in some Central and East European currencies such as the Czech koruna, Estonian kroon, and Hungarian forint.

Benet (1990)的另一
项研究表明，商品期货
合约可以用来有效地对
非主流货币进行交叉套
期保值交易。

Another study by Benet (1990) suggests that commodity futures contracts may be used effectively to cross-hedge some minor currency exposures. Suppose the dollar price of the Mexican peso is positively correlated to the world oil price. Note that Mexico is a major exporter of oil, accounting for roughly 5 percent of the world market share. Considering this situation, a firm may use oil futures contracts to manage its peso exposure. The firm can sell (buy) oil futures if it has peso receivables (payables). In the same vein, soybean and coffee futures contracts may be used to cross-hedge a Brazilian real exposure. Again, the effectiveness of this cross-hedging technique would depend on the strength and stability of the relationship between the exchange rate and the commodity futures prices.

Hedging Contingent Exposure

或有风险暴露是指
公司可能不遭受汇率风
险的情况。

In addition to providing a flexible hedge against exchange exposure, options contracts can also provide an effective hedge against what might be called **contingent exposure.** Contingent exposure refers to a situation in which the firm may or may not be subject to exchange exposure. Suppose General Electric (GE) is bidding on a hydroelectric project in Quebec Province, Canada. If the bid is accepted, which will be known in three months, GE is going to receive C$100 million to initiate the project. Since GE may or may not face exchange exposure depending on whether its bid will be accepted, it faces a typical contingent exposure situation.[3]

It is difficult to deal with contingent exposure using traditional hedging tools like forward contracts. Suppose that GE sold C$100 million forward to hedge the contingent exposure. If GE's bid is accepted, then GE will have no problem because it will have C$100 million to fulfill the forward contract. However, if the bid is rejected, GE now faces an unhedged short position in Canadian dollars. Clearly, a forward contract does not provide a satisfactory hedge against contingent exposure. A "do-nothing" policy does not guarantee a satisfactory outcome either. The problem with this policy is that if GE's bid is accepted, the firm ends up with an unhedged long position in Canadian dollars.

An alternative approach is to buy a three-month put option on C$100 million. In this case, there are four possible outcomes:

1. The bid is accepted and the spot exchange rate turns out to be less than the exercise rate: In this case, the firm will simply exercise the put option and convert C$100 million at the exercise rate.

2. The bid is accepted and the spot exchange rate turns out to be greater than the exercise rate: In this case, the firm will let the put option expire and convert C$100 million at the spot rate.

3. The bid is rejected and the spot exchange rate turns out to be less than the exercise rate: In this case, although the firm does not have Canadian dollars, it will exercise the put option and make a profit.

4. The bid is rejected and the spot rate turns out to be greater than the exercise rate: In this case, the firm will simply let the put option expire.

The above scenarios indicate that when the put option is purchased, each outcome is adequately covered; the firm will not be left with an unhedged foreign currency position. Again, it is stressed that the firm has to pay the option premium upfront. The preceding discussion is summarized in Exhibit 8.9.

Hedging Recurrent Exposure with Swap Contracts

因此，互换合约就
像是一连串有不同到期
日的远期合约构成的组
合。

Firms often have to deal with a "sequence" of accounts payable or receivable in terms of a foreign currency. Such recurrent cash flows in a foreign currency can best be hedged using a currency swap contract, which is an agreement to exchange one currency for another at a predetermined exchange rate, that is, the swap rate, on a sequence of future dates. As such, a swap contract is like a portfolio of forward

---

[3]These days, it is not unusual for the exporter to let the importer choose the currency of payment. For example, Boeing may allow British Airways to pay either $15 million or £10 million. To the extent that Boeing does not know in advance which currency it is going to receive, it faces a contingent exposure. Given the future spot exchange rate, British Airways will choose to pay with a cheaper currency. It is noteworthy that in this example, Boeing provided British Airways with a free option to buy up to $15 million using pounds (which is equivalent to an option to sell pounds for dollars) at the implicit exercise rate of $1.50/£.

EXHIBIT 8.9

**Contingent Exposure
Management: The Case of GE
Bidding
for a Quebec
Hydroelectric Project**

	Bid Outcome	
Alternative Strategies	**Bid Accepted**	**Bid Rejected**
Do nothing	An unhedged long position in C$100 million	No exposure
Sell C$ forward	No exposure	An unhedged short position in C$100 million
Buy a put option on C$[a]	If the future spot rate becomes less than the exercise rate, $(S_T < E)$	
	Convert C$100 million at the exercise price	Exercise the option and make a profit
	If the future spot rate becomes greater than the exercise rate, $(S_T > E)$	
	Let the option expire and convert C$100 million at the spot exchange rate	Simply let the option expire

[a]If the future spot rate turns out to be equal to the exercise price, i.e. $S_T = E$, GE will be indifferent between
(i) exercising the option and (ii) letting the option expire and converting C$100 million at the spot rate.

contracts with different maturities. Swaps are very flexible in terms of amount and maturity; the maturity can range from a few months to 20 years.

Suppose that Boeing is scheduled to deliver an aircraft to British Airways at the beginning of each year for the next five years, starting in 1996. British Airways, in turn, is scheduled to pay £10,000,000 to Boeing on December 1 of each year for five years, starting in 1996. In this case, Boeing faces a sequence of exchange risk exposures. As previously mentioned, Boeing can hedge this type of exposure using a swap agreement by which Boeing delivers £10,000,000 to the counterparty of the contract on December 1 of each year for five years and takes delivery of a predetermined dollar amount each year. If the agreed swap exchange rate is $1.50/£, then Boeing will receive $15 million each year, regardless of the future spot and forward rates. Note that a sequence of five forward contracts would not be priced at a uniform rate, $1.50/£; the forward rates will be different for different maturities. In addition, longer-term forward contracts are not readily available.

Hedging through Invoice Currency   通过发票货币的套期保值

公司可以通过选择
适当的记账货币来转移、
共担或分散汇率风险。

While such financial hedging instruments as forward, money market, swap, and options contracts are well known, hedging through the choice of invoice currency, an operational technique, has not received much attention. The firm can *shift, share*, or *diversify* exchange risk by appropriately choosing the currency of invoice. For instance, if Boeing invoices $15 million rather than £10 million for the sale of the aircraft, then it does not face exchange exposure anymore. Note, however, that the exchange exposure has not disappeared; it has merely shifted to the British importer. British Airways now has an account payable denominated in U.S. dollars.

Instead of shifting the exchange exposure entirely to British Airways, Boeing can share the exposure with British Airways by, for example, invoicing half of the bill in U.S. dollars and the remaining half in British pounds, that is, $7.5 million and £5 million. In this case, the magnitude of Boeing's exchange exposure is reduced by half. As a practical matter, however, the firm may not be able to use risk shifting or sharing

还要说明一点，如果进出口双方的货币都不适合用来清算国际贸易，那么双方都不能用风险转移/共担来管理汇率风险。

as much as it wishes to for fear of losing sales to competitors. Only an exporter with substantial market power can use this approach. In addition, if the currencies of both the exporter and the importer are not suitable for settling international trade, neither party can resort to risk shifting/sharing to deal with exchange exposure.

The firm can diversify exchange exposure to some extent by using currency basket units such as the SDR as the invoice currency. Often, multinational corporations and sovereign entities are known to float bonds denominated either in the SDR or in the ECU prior to the introduction of the euro. For example, the Egyptian government charges for the use of the Suez Canal using the SDR. Obviously, these currency baskets are used to reduce exchange exposure. As previously noted, the SDR now comprises four individual currencies, the U.S. dollar, the euro, the Japanese yen, and the British pound. Because the SDR is a portfolio of currencies, its value should be substantially more stable than the value of any individual constituent currency. Currency basket units can be a useful hedging tool especially for long-term exposure for which no forward or options contracts are readily available. The International Finance in Practice box "Riding Shifting Waves of Currency" shows how companies deal with exchange risk exposure using various operational techniques.

Hedging via Lead and Lag

公司可用来降低交易风险的另一种方法是提前/延后外币的收入和支出。

Another operational technique the firm can use to reduce transaction exposure is leading and lagging foreign currency receipts and payments. To "lead" means to pay or collect early, whereas to "lag" means to pay or collect late. The firm would like to lead soft currency receivables and lag hard currency receivables to avoid the loss from depreciation of the soft currency and benefit from the appreciation of the hard currency. For the same reason, the firm will attempt to lead the hard currency payables and lag soft currency payables.

超前/延后支付策略

To the extent that the firm can effectively implement the **lead/lag strategy,** the transaction exposure the firm faces can be reduced. However, a word of caution is in order. Suppose, concerned with the likely depreciation of sterling, Boeing would like British Airways to prepay £10 million. Boeing's attempt to lead the pound receivable may encounter difficulties. First of all, British Airways would like to lag this payment, which is denominated in the soft currency (the pound), and thus has no incentive to prepay unless Boeing offers a substantial discount to compensate for the prepayment. This, of course, reduces the benefits of collecting the pound receivable early. Second, pressing British Airways for prepayment can hamper future sales efforts by Boeing. Third, to the extent that the original invoice price, £10 million, incorporates the expected depreciation of the pound, Boeing is already partially protected against the depreciation of the pound.

The lead/lag strategy can be employed more effectively to deal with intrafirm payables and receivables, such as material costs, rents, royalties, interests, and dividends, among subsidiaries of the same multinational corporation. Since managements of various subsidiaries of the same firm are presumably working for the good of the entire firm, the lead/lag strategy can be applied more aggressively.

Exposure Netting 风险暴露的净额结算

In 1984, Lufthansa, a German airline, signed a contract to buy $3 billion worth of aircraft from Boeing and entered into a forward contract to purchase $1.5 billion forward for the purpose of hedging against the expected appreciation of the dollar against the German mark. This decision, however, suffered from a major flaw: A significant portion of Lufthansa's cash flows was also dollar-denominated. As a result,

Riding Shifting Waves of Currency

Most companies love nothing more than locking in customers for a good long time. But when LuxCel Group Inc. set up shop to sell paging devices in the Crimean city of Yalta last month, it adamantly refused to sign long-term service contracts for them.

With local currencies in the former Soviet Union spiraling downward, there was nothing that LuxCel wanted less than a customer boasting a three-year contract. Instead, the 30-employee company, based in Paramus, N.J., limits ruble-denominated service pacts to three months.

As small and midsized companies such as LuxCel increasingly operate abroad, they are busy honing techniques to protect themselves against falling foreign currencies. The task is rapidly gaining urgency.

In recent days, monetary turmoil in Europe has exposed American companies operating there to greater foreign-exchange risk than they ordinarily face. While violent currency swings may be unlikely, American business can count on continued volatility because European countries have agreed to allow far more fluctuation in their exchange rates now.

Losses from Plunging Currency

Meanwhile, currencies plunge in value in the former Soviet Union, Brazil and elsewhere. It all means that fortunes can be lost by holding the wrong currency at the wrong time.

"We're just as worried as the big companies," says Mitchell Reback, director of finance for Neutrogena Corp., a 700-employee Los Angeles concern that derives 25% of its revenue from overseas.

The most common danger: A local currency may lose value between a sale's close in a local currency and payment of the bill. When payment day arrives, the American business owner could end up with currency worth much less in dollars than anticipated.

For companies that can get away with it, the preferred way is to bill in dollars and let customers bear the brunt of shifting exchange rates. "If you have a strong marketing position, you can play the hardball game of saying, 'I want to be paid in my own currency,'" says Robert Bush, controller of Wedco Technology Inc.

Wedco, which custom-grinds plastics and other materials for companies in the U.S. and Europe, is the dominant player in its small niche. The Bloomsbury, N.J., concern earned about a third of its $30.3 million in revenue in Western Europe last year.

European customers sometimes balk at paying dollars, Mr. Bush says. "But we say, 'I'm sorry, this is the way we do it.' Obviously, we could lose some sales, but it [billing in dollars] takes a tremendous worry off our shoulders."

Wedco's market dominance also allows it to eliminate currency-fluctuation risk connected to inventory. Some manufacturers purchase raw materials in one country to

实际中，一家典型的跨国公司会持有多种货币的头寸。

Lufthansa's net exposure to the exchange risk might not have been significant. Lufthansa had a so-called "natural hedge." In 1985, the dollar depreciated substantially against the mark and, as a result, Lufthansa experienced a major foreign exchange loss from settling the forward contract. This episode shows that when a firm has both receivables and payables in a given foreign currency, it should consider hedging only its net exposure.

So far, we have discussed exposure management on a currency-by-currency basis. In reality, a typical multinational corporation is likely to have a portfolio of currency positions. For instance, a U.S. firm may have an account payable in euros and, at the same time, an account receivable in Swiss francs. Considering that the euro and franc move against the dollar almost in lockstep, the firm can just wait until these accounts become due and then buy euros spot with francs. It can be wasteful and unnecessary to buy euros forward and sell francs forward. In other words, if the firm has a portfolio of currency positions, it makes sense to hedge residual exposure rather than hedge each currency position separately.

如果想要更加积极地进行风险冲销，公司可以把它的汇率风险集中到一个部门来管理。

内部发票中心

If the firm would like to apply exposure netting aggressively, it helps to centralize the firm's exchange exposure management function in one location. Many multinational corporations are using a **reinvoice center,** a financial subsidiary, as a mechanism for centralizing exposure management functions. All the invoices arising from intrafirm transactions are sent to the reinvoice center, where exposure is netted. Once the residual exposure is determined, then foreign exchange experts at the center determine optimal hedging methods and implement them.

sell, in processed form, in another. If currency fluctuations suddenly make materials more expensive, the manufacturer must pass on the higher cost to customers— or swallow it. To avoid this trap, many companies try to buy raw materials in the country where they sell finished goods, or shift purchases to countries with weakening currencies.

Wedco's own solution: Force the customer to supply its own raw materials. Again, some balk. Faced with a recession in Europe causing slackening demand, Wedco acquiesces in cases involving "longstanding customers," the controller says.

'Short Term of Payment'

Circon Corp., a Santa Barbara, Calif., maker of medical endoscopes and video systems, collects dollars for about 50% of its European sales. If the company can't get payment in greenbacks, it tries to minimize risk by negotiating a "very short term of payment, 10 or 15 days," says Richard Auhll, chairman.

American businesses buying from European vendors also seek shelter. Suprema Specialties Inc., Paterson, N.J., buys cheese from Italian cooperatives. Commonly ordering six months in advance, it negotiates a price in dollars to be due upon shipment. Because the cooperatives have an oversupply of cheese, "they'll take any kind of payment possible," says Paul Lauriero, executive vice president.

Many companies achieve the same effect—locking in dollar-denominated prices—by buying "forward contracts" from banks. These contracts obligate the parties to exchange one currency for another at a future date and at a pre-determined rate. Some companies also purchase "option contracts," which give concerns the right, but not the obligation, to exchange one currency for another at a future date at a set rate. Even for small companies, this protection generally costs well under 1% of the amount involved.

Some companies, such as Neutrogena, say big banks are often reluctant to spend the time necessary to counsel small or midsize players on appropriate hedging strategies. But Checkpoint Systems Inc., a maker of surveillance systems, scanning equipment and antitheft tags, says it finds banks eager to help. The Thorofare, N.J., concern is now talking to banks about hedging payables and receivables abroad, says Steven Selfridge, chief financial officer.

Solution in Financial Hedging

Telematics International Inc., a Fort Lauderdale, Fla., computer-networking systems company that gets about half its $67.3 million in sales overseas, turned to financial hedging seven months ago. That was after the company recorded $632,000 in losses for 1992 because it didn't hedge its currency exposure. "We were exposed" to the plummeting British pound, says John Dooley, an assistant treasurer.

Should the Firm Hedge?

www.sec.gov/edgar.shtml

Company files with SEC show how companies deal with exchange risk exposure.

We have discussed how the firm can hedge exchange exposure if it wishes. We have not discussed whether the firm should try to hedge to begin with. As can be seen from the International Finance in Practice box "To Hedge or Not to Hedge," there hardly exists a consensus on whether the firm should hedge. Some would argue that exchange exposure management at the corporate level is redundant when stockholders can manage the exposure themselves. Others would argue that what matters in the firm valuation is only systematic risk; corporate risk management may only reduce the total risk. These arguments suggest that corporate exposure management would not necessarily add to the value of the firm.

While the above arguments against corporate risk management may be valid in a "perfect" capital market, one can make a case for it based on various market imperfections:

1. Information asymmetry: Management knows about the firm's exposure position much better than stockholders. Thus, the management of the firm, not its stockholders, should manage exchange exposure.

2. Differential transaction costs: The firm is in a position to acquire low-cost hedges; transaction costs for individual stockholders can be substantial. Also, the firm has hedging tools like the reinvoice center that are not available to stockholders.

To Hedge or Not to Hedge

"Most value-maximising firms do not hedge." Thus Merton Miller and Christopher Culp, two economists at the University of Chicago, said in a recent article[1] about Metallgesellschaft, a firm that saw its value plunge after its oil-price hedging strategy came a cropper. Yet the vast majority of firms that use derivatives do so to hedge. Last year's survey of big American non-financial companies by the Wharton School and Chase Manhattan bank found that, of those firms that used derivatives (about one-third of the sample), some 75% said they did so to hedge commitments. As many as 40% of the derivatives users said they sometimes took a view on the direction of markets, but only 8% admitted to doing so frequently.

To justify speculation, managers ought to have good reason to suppose that they can consistently outwit firms for which playing the financial markets is a core business. Commodity businesses, such as oil or grain companies taking positions on the direction of their related commodity markets, may have such reason, but non-financial firms taking bets on interest rates or foreign-exchange rates almost certainly do not—though some claim to make a profit on it. But why might hedging be wrong?

In the 1950s, Merton Miller and Franco Modigliani, another financial economist, demonstrated that firms make money only if they make good investments—the kind that increase their operating cash flows. Whether those investments are financed through debt, equity or retained earnings is irrelevant. Different methods of financing simply determine how a firm's value is divided between its various sorts of investors (e.g., shareholders or bondholders), not the value itself. This surprising insight helped win each of them a Nobel prize. If they are right, it has crucial implications for hedging. For if methods of financing and the character of financial risks do not matter, managing them is pointless. It cannot add to the firm's value; on the contrary, as derivatives do not come free, using them for hedging might actually lower that value. Moreover, as Messrs. Miller and Modigliani showed, if investors want to avoid the financial risks attached to holding shares in a firm, they can diversify their portfolio of holdings. Firms need not manage their financial risks; investors can do it for themselves.

In recent years, other academics have challenged the Miller-Modigliani thesis—at least in its pure form—and demonstrated that hedging can sometimes add value. That is because firms may be able to manage certain risks internally in ways that cannot be replicated by outside investors. Some investors may not want, or be able, to hold diversified share portfolios (for instance, if the firm is family-owned). It may be possible to use derivatives to reduce profits in good years and raise them in bad years in order to cut the firm's average tax bill. Hedging can also be used to prevent the firm getting into financial difficulties, or even going bust.

Recently, another view has been winning converts. According to Kenneth Froot, David Sharfstein and Jeremy Stein, three Boston-based economists, firms should hedge to ensure they always have sufficient cash flow to fund their planned investment programme.[2] Otherwise some potentially profitable investments may be missed because of inefficiencies in the bond and equity markets that prevent the firm raising the funds, or the reluctance of managers to tap these markets when internal cash is tight. Merck, an American pharmaceuticals firm, has helped to pioneer the use of derivatives to ensure that investment plans—particularly in R&D—can always be financed. In a paper explaining the firm's strategy, Judy Lewent and John Kearney observed that "our experience, and that of the [drugs] industry in general, has been that cash-flow and earnings uncertainty caused by exchange-rate volatility leads to a reduction in research spending."[3]

Though apparently simple, such a strategy has some intriguing implications. As Messrs Froot, Scharfstein and Stein point out, the factors that cause cash flow to fall below expectations may also cut the number of profitable investment opportunities, so lessening the need to hedge.

3. Default costs: If default costs are significant, corporate hedging would be justifiable because it will reduce the probability of default. Perception of a reduced default risk, in turn, can lead to a better credit rating and lower financing costs.

4. Progressive corporate taxes: Under progressive corporate tax rates, stable before-tax earnings lead to lower corporate taxes than volatile earnings with the same average value. This happens because under progressive tax rates, the firm pays more taxes in high-earning periods than it saves in low-earning periods.

The last point merits elaboration. Suppose the country's corporate income tax system is such that a tax rate of 20 percent applies to the first $10 million of corporate earnings and a 40 percent rate applies to any earnings exceeding $10 million. Firms

For instance, an oil company's cash flow may suffer due to a fall in oil prices. However, that fall in prices also reduces the value of investing in developing new oil fields. With fewer profitable projects to invest in, the firm will need less cash to finance investment.

All about Cash Flow

Rene Stulz, an economist at Ohio State University, sees even more powerful implications.[4] He says that there are only a couple of good reasons why a firm should hedge. One is to cut its tax bills, which is likely to happen only if the firm's profits tend to yo-yo between lower and higher tax bands. The other one is being unable to get cash when it needs it, or facing a serious risk of running short. By this rule, reckons Mr. Stulz, a firm with little debt or with highly-rated debt has no need to hedge, as the risk of it getting into financial trouble is tiny. If he is right, many of America's biggest hedgers—including some of those that have revealed losses on derivatives, such as Procter & Gamble—may be wasting their energies, or worse. By contrast, Mr. Stulz thinks that if a firm is highly geared, hedging can boost its value significantly. Indeed, during the leveraged buy-out craze of the 1980s, when firms were taken over by buying off shareholders and loading up on debt, tough risk-management requirements were standard in any borrowing arrangement.

Messrs. Culp and Miller, of the University of Chicago, take this argument a step further in defending the management of Metallgesellschaft from some of the wilder accusations of recklessness (a matter that is now before the American courts). Instead of analysing the firm's hedging strategy (which involved selling oil for up to ten years ahead and hedging this exposure with futures contracts) in terms of its effectiveness in reducing risk, Messrs. Culp and Miller argue that the company had no need to reduce its risk-exposure because it had no reason to suppose it could not get hold of cash if needed. After all, the mighty Deutsche Bank, as its principal creditor and controlling shareholder, was behind the firm, ensuring that it could not go bust; and, as it turned out, it did not. Rather, the aim of the hedging strategy was to exploit what

Metallgesellschaft thought was its superior understanding of the relationship between spot prices and futures prices—risky but not obviously foolish.

Not everyone agrees that firms with little debt should not hedge. Myron Scholes, an economist at Stanford University, reaches the opposite conclusion: firms with little debt could reduce their riskiness by hedging, and so be able to borrow more and rely less on equity. Equity can be expensive compared with debt; it is inherently riskier, offering no guaranteed payout, so investors require a higher average return on it than they do on bonds. Ultimately, through risk-reducing hedging and borrowing, more firms might be able to remain (or become) privately owned, reckons Mr. Scholes. But to do this well, managers will need a very good understanding of the risks to which their firm is exposed, and of opportunities to hedge.

However, the way firms typically use derivatives to reduce the cost of capital is different from that described above. Rather than hedge and borrow more, they substitute for traditional debt a hybrid of bonds and options and/or futures that will pay off in certain circumstances, thus lowering capital costs. This is speculation dressed up as prudence, because if events take an unexpected turn, capital costs go up by at least the cost of the options.

[1]"Hedging in the Theory of Corporate Finance: A Reply to Our Critics." By Christopher Culp and Merton Miller. Journal of Applied Corporate Finance; Spring 1995.

[2]"A Framework for Risk Management." By Kenneth Froot, David Scharfstein and Jeremy Stein. Harvard Business Review; November 1994.

[3]"Identifying, Measuring and Hedging Currency Risk at Merck." By Judy Lewent and John Kearney. In The New Corporate Finance, edited by Donald Chew, McGraw-Hill; 1993.

[4]"Rethinking Risk Management." By Rene Stulz. Ohio State University working paper; 1995.

thus face a simple progressive tax structure. Now consider an exporting firm that expects to earn $15 million if the dollar depreciates, but only $5 million if the dollar appreciates. Let's assume that the dollar may appreciate or depreciate with equal chances. In this case, the firm's expected tax will be $2.5 million:

$$\text{Expected tax} = \frac{1}{2}[(.20)(\$5,000,000)] + \frac{1}{2}[(.20)(\$10,000,000) \\ + (.40)(\$5,000,000)] \\ = \$2,500,000$$

Now consider another firm, B, that is identical to firm A in every respect except that, unlike firm A, firm B aggressively and successfully hedges its risk exposure and, as a result, it can expect to realize certain earnings of $10,000,000, the same as firm A's expected earnings. Firm B, however, expects to pay only $2 million as taxes. Obviously, hedging results in a $500,000 tax saving. Exhibit 8.10 illustrates this situation.

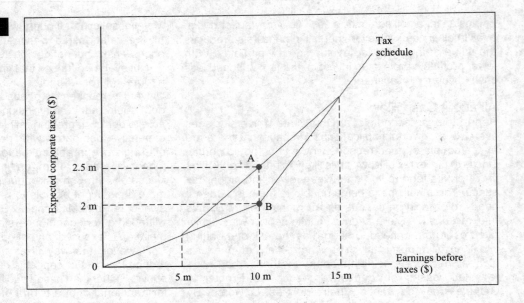

EXHIBIT 8.10

Tax Savings from Hedging Exchange Risk Exposure

尽管不是所有的公司都在进行汇率风险的套期保值，但许多公司还是或多或少地在进行套期保值活动，这说明风险管理与公司价值的最大化有关。

While not every firm is hedging exchange exposure, many firms are engaged in hedging activities, suggesting that corporate risk management is relevant to maximizing the firm's value. To the extent that for various reasons, stockholders themselves cannot properly manage exchange risk, the firm's managers can do it for them, contributing to the firm's value. Some corporate hedging activities, however, might be motivated by managerial objectives; managers may want to stabilize cash flows so that the risk to their human capital can be reduced.

A study by Allayannis and Weston (2001) provides direct evidence on the important issue of whether hedging actually adds to the value of the firm. Specifically, they examine whether firms with currency exposure that use foreign currency derivative contracts, such as currency forward and options, increase their valuation. The authors find that U.S. firms that face currency risk and use currency derivatives for hedging have, on average, about 5 percent higher value than firms that do not use currency derivatives. For firms that have no direct foreign involvement but may be exposed to exchange rate movements via export/import competition, they find a small hedging valuation premium. In addition, they find that firms that stop hedging experience a decrease in firm valuation compared with those firms that continue to hedge. Their study thus clearly suggests that corporate hedging contributes to firm value.

What Risk Management Products Do Firms Use?

这些结果显示绝大多数美国公司通过远期合约、互换协议、期权合约来管理汇率风险。

In an extensive survey, Jesswein, Kwok, and Folks (1995) documented the extent of knowledge and use of foreign exchange risk management products by U.S. corporations. On the basis of a survey of *Fortune* 500 firms, they found that the traditional forward contract is the most popular product. As Exhibit 8.11 shows, about 93 percent of respondents of the survey used forward contracts. This old, traditional instrument has not been supplanted by recent "fancy" innovations. The next commonly used instruments are foreign currency swaps (52.6 percent) and over-the-counter currency options (48.8 percent). Such recent innovations as compound options (3.8 percent) and lookback options (5.1 percent) are among the least extensively used instruments. These findings seem to indicate that most U.S. firms meet their exchange risk management needs with forward, swap, and options contracts.

EXHIBIT 8.11

A Survey of Knowledge and Use of Foreign Exchange Risk Management Products[a]

Type of Product	Heard of (Awareness)	Used (Adoption)
Forward contracts	100.0%	93.1%
Foreign currency swaps	98.8	52.6
Foreign currency futures	98.8	20.1
Exchange-traded currency options	96.4	17.3
Exchange-traded futures options	95.8	8.9
Over-the-counter currency options	93.5	48.8
Cylinder options	91.2	28.7
Synthetic forwards	88.0	22.0
Synthetic options	88.0	18.6
Participating forwards, etc.	83.6	15.8
Forward exchange agreements, etc.	81.7	14.8
Foreign currency warrants	77.7	4.2
Break forwards, etc.	65.3	4.9
Compound options	55.8	3.8
Lookback options, etc.	52.1	5.1
Average across products	84.4%	23.9%

[a]The products are ranked by the percentages of respondents who have heard of products. There are 173 respondents in total.

Source: Kurt Jesswein, Chuck Kwok, and William Folks, Jr., "Corporate Use of Innovative Foreign Exchange Risk Management Products," Columbia Journal of World Business (Fall 1995).

The Jesswein, Kwok, and Folks survey also shows that, among the various industries, the finance/insurance/real estate industry stands out as the most frequent user of exchange risk management products. This finding is not surprising. This industry has more finance experts who are skillful at using derivative securities. In addition, this industry handles mainly financial assets, which tend to be exposed to exchange risk. The survey further shows that the corporate use of foreign exchange risk management products is positively related to the firm's degree of international involvement. This finding is not surprising either. As the firm becomes more internationalized through cross-border trade and investments, it is likely to handle an increasing amount of foreign currencies, giving rise to a greater demand for exchange risk hedging.

随着公司通过跨国贸易和投资变得更加国际化，它就要处理更多的外汇业务，因此对汇率风险管理也提出了更高的要求。

SUMMARY

1. 如果公司发生以外币表示的契约性现金流，那么该公司就面临着交易风险暴露。交易风险暴露可以通过远期合约、货币市场合约、期权合约等金融合约来套期保值，也可以通过诸如发票货币选择、超前或延后支付策略以及风险暴露净额结算等操作性方法来套期保值。

2. 如果公司拥有一笔外币收入（支出），它可以通过卖出（买入）该外币收入（支出）的远期合约来进行套期保值。在远期利率是未来即期汇率的无偏估计的情况下，公司就可无成本地消除风险暴露。公司还可通过在本国或外国货币市场上借入和贷出资金来达到同样的套期保值效果。

3. 与远期合约和货币市场套期保值不同，货币期权是一种更为灵活的套期保值方法。借助于货币期权

1. The firm is subject to a transaction exposure when it faces contractual cash flows denominated in foreign currencies. Transaction exposure can be hedged by financial contracts like forward, money market, and options contracts, as well as by such operational techniques as the choice of invoice currency, lead/lag strategy, and exposure netting.

2. If the firm has a foreign-currency-denominated receivable (payable), it can hedge the exposure by selling (buying) the foreign currency receivable (payable) forward. The firm can *expect* to eliminate the exposure without incurring costs as long as the forward exchange rate is an unbiased predictor of the future spot rate. The firm can achieve equivalent hedging results by lending and borrowing in the domestic and foreign money markets.

3. Unlike forward and money market hedges, currency options provide flexible hedges against exchange exposure. With the options hedge, the firm can limit the downside risk while preserving the upside potential. Currency options also provide the firm with an effective hedge against contingent exposure.

套期保值，公司能控制亏损的程度，而对盈利则没有限制。货币期权也是对付或有风险的一种常用套期保值工具。

　　4. 公司通过适当地选择发票货币就可实现汇率风险的转移、共担和分散。在无法使用金融工具来对长期风险进行套期保值时，可通过选用特别提款权、欧元等货币篮子单位来实现部分套期保值。

　　5. 公司可以通过超前/延后收付外币来降低交易风险暴露，该方法特别适用于公司内部子公司间的交易。

　　6. 当公司持有多种外币头寸时，仅需对剩余风险暴露进行套期保值，而无需对各种货币分别进行套期保值。内部发票中心有助于通过组合投资来管理汇率风险暴露。

　　7. 在完善的资本市场上，股东都能够对汇率风险暴露和公司进行套期保值，因此公司层面的风险暴露管理几乎没有必要。不过，实际资本市场并不完善，公司比股东在实施套期保值策略时更具有优势。因此，完全有可能通过风险暴露管理来增加公司的价值。

4. The firm can shift, share, and diversify exchange exposure by appropriately choosing the invoice currency. Currency basket units such as the SDR and ECU can be used as an invoice currency to partially hedge long-term exposure for which financial hedges are not readily available.

5. The firm can reduce transaction exposure by leading and lagging foreign currency receipts and payments, especially among its own affiliates.

6. When a firm has a portfolio of foreign currency positions, it makes sense only to hedge the residual exposure rather than hedging each currency position separately. The reinvoice center can help implement the portfolio approach to exposure management.

7. In a perfect capital market where stockholders can hedge exchange exposure as well as the firm, it is difficult to justify exposure management at the corporate level. In reality, capital markets are far from perfect, and the firm often has advantages over the stockholders in implementing hedging strategies. There thus exists room for corporate exposure management to contribute to the firm value.

KEY WORDS

contingent exposure, *203*
cross-hedging, *202*
economic exposure, *192*
exposure netting, *205*
forward market
　hedge, *194*

hedging through invoice
　currency, *204*
lead/lag strategy, *205*
money market hedge, *196*
options market
　hedge, *198*

reinvoice center, *206*
transaction
　exposure, *192*
translation
　exposure, *193*

QUESTIONS

1. How would you define *transaction exposure*? How is it different from economic exposure?

2. Discuss and compare hedging transaction exposure using the forward contract versus money market instruments. When do alternative hedging approaches produce the same result?

3. Discuss and compare the costs of hedging by forward contracts and options contracts.

4. What are the advantages of a currency options contract as a hedging tool compared with the forward contract?

5. Suppose your company has purchased a put option on the euro to manage exchange exposure associated with an account receivable denominated in that currency. In this case, your company can be said to have an "insurance" policy on its receivable. Explain in what sense this is so.

6. Recent surveys of corporate exchange risk management practices indicate that many U.S. firms simply do not hedge. How would you explain this result?

7. Should a firm hedge? Why or why not?

8. Using an example, discuss the possible effect of hedging on a firm's tax obligations.

9. Explain *contingent exposure* and discuss the advantages of using currency options to manage this type of currency exposure.

10. Explain cross-hedging and discuss the factors determining its effectiveness.

PROBLEMS

The spreadsheet TRNSEXP.xls may be used in solving parts of problems 2, 3, 4, and 6.

1. Cray Research sold a supercomputer to the Max Planck Institute in Germany on credit and invoiced €10 million payable in six months. Currently, the six-month

forward exchange rate is $1.10/€ and the foreign exchange adviser for Cray Research predicts that the spot rate is likely to be $1.05/€ in six months.

a. What is the expected gain/loss from a forward hedge?

b. If you were the financial manager of Cray Research, would you recommend hedging this euro receivable? Why or why not?

c. Suppose the foreign exchange adviser predicts that the future spot rate will be the same as the forward exchange rate quoted today. Would you recommend hedging in this case? Why or why not?

2. IBM purchased computer chips from NEC, a Japanese electronics concern, and was billed ¥250 million payable in three months. Currently, the spot exchange rate is ¥105/$ and the three-month forward rate is ¥100/$. The three-month money market interest rate is 8 percent per annum in the United States and 7 percent per annum in Japan. The management of IBM decided to use a money market hedge to deal with this yen account payable.

a. Explain the process of a money market hedge and compute the dollar cost of meeting the yen obligation.

b. Conduct a cash flow analysis of the money market hedge.

3. You plan to visit Geneva, Switzerland, in three months to attend an international business conference. You expect to incur a total cost of SF5,000 for lodging, meals, and transportation during your stay. As of today, the spot exchange rate is $0.60/SF and the three-month forward rate is $0.63/SF. You can buy the three-month call option on SF with an exercise price of $0.64/SF for the premium of $0.05 per SF. Assume that your expected future spot exchange rate is the same as the forward rate. The three-month interest rate is 6 percent per annum in the United States and 4 percent per annum in Switzerland.

a. Calculate your expected dollar cost of buying SF5,000 if you choose to hedge by a call option on SF.

b. Calculate the future dollar cost of meeting this SF obligation if you decide to hedge using a forward contract.

c. At what future spot exchange rate will you be indifferent between the forward and option market hedges?

d. Illustrate the future dollar cost of meeting the SF payable against the future spot exchange rate under both the options and forward market hedges.

4. Boeing just signed a contract to sell a Boeing 737 aircraft to Air France. Air France will be billed €20 million payable in one year. The current spot exchange rate is $1.05/€ and the one-year forward rate is $1.10/€. The annual interest rate is 6 percent in the United States and 5 percent in France. Boeing is concerned with the volatile exchange rate between the dollar and the franc and would like to hedge exchange exposure.

a. It is considering two hedging alternatives: sell the euro proceeds from the sale forward or borrow euros from Crédit Lyonnaise against the euro receivable. Which alternative would you recommend? Why?

b. Other things being equal, at what forward exchange rate would Boeing be indifferent between the two hedging methods?

5. Suppose that Baltimore Machinery sold a drilling machine to a Swiss firm and gave the Swiss client a choice of paying either $10,000 or SF15,000 in three months.

a. In the example, Baltimore Machinery effectively gave the Swiss client a free option to buy up to $10,000 using Swiss francs. What is the "implied" exercise exchange rate?

b. If the spot exchange rate turns out to be $0.62/SF, which currency do you think the Swiss client will choose to use for payment? What is the value of this free option for the Swiss client?

c. What is the best way for Baltimore Machinery to deal with exchange exposure?

6. Princess Cruise Company (PCC) purchased a ship from Mitsubishi Heavy Industry for 500 million yen payable in one year. The current spot rate is ¥124/$ and the one-year forward rate is 110/$. The annual interest rate is 5 percent in Japan and 8 percent in the United States. PCC can also buy a one-year call option on yen at the strike price of $.0081 per yen for a premium of .014 cents per yen.

a. Compute the future dollar costs of meeting this obligation using the money market and forward hedges.

b. Assuming that the forward exchange rate is the best predictor of the future spot rate, compute the expected future dollar cost of meeting this obligation when the option hedge is used.

c. At what future spot rate do you think PCC may be indifferent between the option and forward hedge?

INTERNET EXERCISES

Bankware, a Boston-based company specializing in banking-related softwares, exported its software for automatic teller machines (ATM) to Oslo Commerce Bank, which is trying to modernize its operation. Facing competition from European software vendors, Bankware decided to bill the sales in the client's currency, Norwegian krone 500,000, payable in one year. Since there are no active forward currency markets for the Norwegian currency, Bankware is considering selling a euro or British pound amount forward for cross-hedging purpose. Assess the hedging effectiveness of selling the euro versus pound amount forward to cover the company's exposure to the Norwegian currency. In solving this problem, consult exchange rate data available from the following website: fx.sauder.ubc.ca. You may consult other websites.

MINI CASE

Airbus' Dollar Exposure

Airbus sold an A400 aircraft to Delta Airlines, a U.S. company, and billed $30 million payable in six months. Airbus is concerned about the euro proceeds from international sales and would like to control exchange risk. The current spot exchange rate is $1.05/€ and the six-month forward exchange rate is $1.10/€. Airbus can buy a six-month put option on U.S. dollars with a strike price of €0.95/$ for a premium of €0.02 per U.S. dollar. Currently, six-month interest rate is 2.5 percent in the euro zone and 3.0 percent in the United States.

1. Compute the guaranteed euro proceeds from the American sale if Airbus decides to hedge using a forward contract.

2. If Airbus decides to hedge using money market instruments, what action does Airbus need to take? What would be the guaranteed euro proceeds from the American sale in this case?

3. If Airbus decides to hedge using put options on U.S. dollars, what would be the "expected" euro proceeds from the American sale? Assume that Airbus regards the current forward exchange rate as an unbiased predictor of the future spot exchange rate.

4. At what future spot exchange do you think Airbus will be indifferent between the option and money market hedge?

CASE APPLICATION	Chase Options, Inc.: Hedging Foreign Currency Exposure through Currency Options

Harvey A. Poniachek

This case study briefly reviews the foreign currency options market and hedging. It presents several international transactions that require currency options hedging strategies by the corporations involved.

The Currency Options Market

Foreign currency options include options on spot exchange, options on foreign currency futures, and futures-style options.[1] Foreign currency options can be transacted over-the-counter and on organized exchanges.

The market for currency options is comprised of an interbank market that consists of London, New York, and Tokyo. Markets for over-the-counter (OTC) currency options began to develop in the early 1980s. Transactions over-the-counter mainly involve the U.S. dollar against the major currencies, including the pound sterling, the German mark, the Japanese yen, and others. Over-the-counter options offer corporations tailor-made accommodation transactions in terms of size and maturity.

The main currency traded on the exchange-based markets include the DM, the yen, the Australian dollar, the Canadian dollar, the ECU, and the Swiss franc. Currency options in the United States are traded in standardized contracts that generally correspond to the features of the International Money Market (IMM) of the Chicago Mercantile Exchange currency futures contracts. Option prices are usually quoted in cents (or a fraction thereof) per unit of foreign currency. Currency options are listed on the Philadelphia Stock Exchange, the IMM, the CBOE (Chicago Board Options Exchange), the LIFFE (London International Financial Futures Exchange), and several other exchanges.

American-style currency options on spot exchange are traded over-the-counter at the Philadelphia Stock Exchange (PHLX) in the amount of one-half the size of the IMM futures contracts. Options on currency futures—traded on the Chicago Mercantile Exchange (CME)—provide options on exchange traded currency futures contracts. All currency traded options on currency futures are American-type contracts.

Markets for foreign exchange options increased in breadth in recent years. International activity has expanded due to the high volatility of exchange rates, which has created a continuing need for hedging. The proliferation of market activity in currency options around the world led to the emergence of new centers and the establishment of links among different exchanges in different time zones. See Appendix on pages 219–220 for information on where currency options are traded, contract size, and volume of business.

Fundamentals of Options

A foreign currency option contract is an agreement between the buyer and the seller, where the seller grants the buyer the right to buy or sell a currency under certain conditions. The buyer of a call or put pays the seller a price, called the premium, for the right of buying or selling a specific amount of a currency at a pre-agreed upon price, known as the exercise price or strike price, during a specific period of time, or on a specific date, called the expiration date or maturity date. Foreign currency options limit the risk of

[1]See for instance J. Orlin Grabbe, International Financial Markets, 2nd Ed., Elsevier, New York, 1991, Ch. 6, "Foreign Currency Options."

the options buyer to the premium paid, but provide the buyer with unlimited potential gain. The option seller's gain is limited to its premium, but its loss is unlimited.

There are American and European options. Exchange traded currency options are all American style, whereas over-the-counter currency options are primarily European-style options. An American option affords the holder the right to exercise at any time before maturity, whereas a European option allows the holder the right to exercise only at maturity. In an option on a futures currency contract, the underlying asset is not a spot asset, but a futures contract on the currency. Acquiring an option on the futures implies that the holder obtains a long position in the currency futures.

In summary, currency options are characterized by several features: the currency option type (American or European), the expiration date, the strike price, premium, and the type of underlying instrument (spot or future). Option valuation or pricing is determined by models that are based on the Black-Scholes principles, and by the application of several variables:

1. The spot price of the underlying currency (e.g., the price of dollar per yen),
2. The strike price of the option,
3. The maturity,
4. The volatility of the underlying currency, and
5. The interest rates in both countries (e.g., in the U.S. and Japan when the option price on yen is determined).

Hedging with Currency Options

The currency options market is rapidly becoming the preferred venue for corporations wishing to hedge their foreign currency exposure. The surge in demand for currency options has come from translation exposure—as defined according to Financial Accounting Standards Board (FASB) 52 requirements. In addition, the increased internationalization of the U.S. economy in the late 1980s has given rise to greater international involvement and currency exposure. These factors contributed to the growth of the over-the-counter options markets. Unlike organized exchange markets traded options, OTC options offer customized maturities, contract size and strike prices, do not involve the extra cost and inconvenience of posting and satisfying minimum margin requirements, and have no brokerage fees.

Foreign currency forwards and options are imperfect substitutes for hedging of currency exposure. Forward currency hedging locks the firm into a rigid position, whereby the firm needs to perform the forward contract or else be in default. By entering into a forward contract the hedger could not enjoy favorable future developments in the currency market. Options are most suitable for hedging foreign currency denominated transactions that might not occur (e.g., competitive bidding for a construction project abroad that might not be awarded). In addition, hedging through options provides the potential for enjoying favorable market circumstances. Currency options have the advantage over forward exchange contracts because they allow corporations to benefit from favorable currency movements and limit the extent of currency losses. The option markets allow the trading of volatility; that is, taking a view on how volatile the underlying currency will be.

Currency options can be used to hedge foreign currency exposure under a variety of circumstances that involve transactions denominated in foreign currencies or attempts to enhance international competitiveness:

1. Anticipated currency transactions where the company seeks to take a view on the exchange rate trend (e.g., account payables or account receivables denominated in foreign exchange, dividend flows from foreign subsidiaries or investments). If the company doesn't have a view it should use forward exchange hedging.

2. Uncertain currency transactions (e.g., bids on international projects denominated in a foreign currency, portfolio hedges where the timing of the sale of securities due to interest rate conditions is difficult to determine ahead of time).

3. Economic exposure (e.g., circumstances where a company's market position stands to be hurt by foreign competition if its currency rises in value in relation to others).

The three most favored currency options strategies include:

1. BUYING AN OPTION. Allows unlimited upside potential and caps downside exposure.

2. SELLING AN OPTION. Caps upside potential but allows unlimited downside exposure.

   Buying an option and selling a put provides the hedger with a comparable outcome. For instance, buying a dollar call against a yen implies that the buyers could exercise the option by buying dollars and paying yen. Alternatively, by buying a yen put against dollars, the hedger could exercise by delivering yen and getting paid dollars. Both options require that the hedger pays yen and obtains dollars.

3. BUY-SELL OPTIONS. Caps upside potential and downward exposure, and it is generally obtained at zero cost.

Devising Hedging Strategies

The Assignment

You are a member of Chase Options, Inc., who was asked to participate in designing hedging strategies for the following transactions:

Anticipated Currency Transactions

1. A U.S. company expects DM 100 million in repatriated profits from its German subsidiary on March 20, 1991. The company believes that the dollar has reached a long-term low at the current level DM/$1.6700; however, it doesn't want to lock in a forward exchange contract because of uncertainty concerning the impact of the German reunification on the currency market. The company doesn't want to exchange at greater than DM/$1.7000 (e.g., 1.7200). Design a hedging strategy by using currency options and utilizing the rates available in Table 1 (Row 1). Examine the implications of hedging instead with a forward contract. Consider whether strategy (III) B (3) listed below is applicable for this transaction. Utilize the data in Table 1 (Row 2).

2. A U.S. firm has bought industrial equipment from a U.K. firm for £5 million payable in 60 days. The firm believes that U.K.'s political and economic uncertainty might drive the pound sterling down significantly. Design a hedging strategy for the corporation by employing either forward currency contracts or currency options and utilizing the data listed in Table 1 (Row 3).

Uncertain Currency Transactions

3. A U.S. fund manager who bought 100 million in Australian dollar (A$) bonds when the A$ was at US$/A$0.72 is worried that the A$ might depreciate because of disappointing Australian economic performance. He decides to set A$/$0.72 as the maximum downside loss that he wants to risk from the current level of A$/$0.7850 (spot). The fund manager doesn't mind foregoing profit opportunities from a further upward move in the A$ and is uncertain how long he will hold the bonds. He sets the year end as his time horizon. By utilizing

| TABLE 1 | | | | | | | |

Currency Options Quotations

Row	Contract	Currency Exchange Rates		Interest Rate		Option Type	Strike Price
		Spot	Forward	U.S.	Foreign		
1	DM/$	1.67	1.6725	8.3	8.5106	PUT	1.7
2	DDM/$	1.67	1.6725	8.3	8.5106	CALL	1.647
3	$/STG	1.7	1.6818	8.2	14.8657	CALL	1.7
4	A$/$	0.785	0.76	8.25	14.7892	PUT	0.72
5	A$/$	0.785	0.76	8.25	14.7892	CALL	0.8025
6	DM/STG	2.8921	2.8845	7.9091	14.8811	PUT	2.8845
7	YEN/$	120.0	116.5	8.7	7.1318	PUT	128.15

Row	Maturity	Premium per FC	Premium per Dollar	Hedging Ratio		
				Delta	Gamma	Theta
1	272	0.0164	0.0466	0.3387	0.039	0.00003
2	272	0.0164	0.0452	0.423	0.041	0.00003
3	60	0.0176	0.006105	0.388	0.098	0.00008
4	195	0.007211	0.0128	0.206	0.037	0.00007
5	195	0.007234	0.0115			
6	14	0.0161	0.001936	0.494	0.281	0.00085
7	731	0.000127	1.9595	0.188	0.019	N.A.

Table 1 (Rows 4 and 5) data, which hedging strategy should the fund manager adopt?

4. A German company is bidding on a contract in the U.K. The bid is estimated at £40 million and they anticipate a profit margin of 30 percent on the project. Hence, they will need to repatriate £12 million in profit, but they worry that the new U.K. economic trends could hurt the pound sterling exchange rate. Determine how the German company could hedge their potential exposure. Utilize Table 1 (Row 6) for data.

Economic Hedging

5. In late 1987 American Motors Corporation (AMC) believed that with the yen exchange rate at ¥/$120 the corporation was competitive vis-à-vis its Japanese rivals. However, if the dollar is to rise again, AMC believed that it could lose 5–10 percent of its sales for every 10 percent strengthening of the dollar. Propose a hedging policy for AMC by utilizing the data in Table 1 (Row 7). What is the cost of your recommendation and what is the company's break-even point?

Cross Hedging

6. Multinational corporation B has borrowed DM to finance expansion of its German subsidiary. The German subsidiary sells 89 percent of its products to an Italian customer who pays in lira. Company B is exposed to the depreciation of the lira and the appreciation of the DM. Design a hedging strategy for the parent.

7. Multinational corporation B has lira sales, but because of high interest rates on lira denominated funds, hedging with lira options could be less favorable than hedging with DM options. Which hedging strategy would you consider as the most feasible?

| APPENDIX | **Currency Futures and Options**
Currency Futures and Options: Exchanges, Contracts, and Volume of Trades (1988–89) |

| | | Volume of Contracts Traded | |
| | Face Value | | 1989 |
Exchange/Type	of Contract	1988	Jan.–Oct.
		(in thousands of contracts)	
United States			
Chicago Mercantile Exchange (CME)			
Currency			
Futures			
Eurodollar (three months)[a]	$1,000,000	21,705	35,862
Pound sterling[a]	£25,000	2,616	2,148
Canadian dollar	Can$100,000	1,409	1,108
Deutsche mark[a]	DM 125,000	5,662	6,729
Japanese yen[a]	¥12,500,000	6,433	6,762
Swiss franc	Sw F 125,000	5,283	5,194
French franc	F250,000	4	2
Australian dollar	$A 100,000	76	104
Options			
Eurodollar	$1,000,000	2,600	5,181
Pound sterling	£25,000	543	350
Deutsche mark	DM 125,000	2,734	3,164
Swiss franc	Sw F 125,000	1,070	1,305
Japanese yen	¥12,500,000	2,945	2,780
Canadian dollar	Can$100,000	314	246
Australian dollar	$A 100,000	7	21
Philadelphia Stock Exchange (PHLX)			
Currency[b]			
Options			
Australian dollar	$A 100,000	351	673
Canadian dollar	CAN$100,000	317	424
European currency unit	ECU 125,000	1	9
French franc	F 500,000	252	86
Japanese yen	¥12,500,000	2,921	2,876
Pound sterling	£62,500	1,283	409
Swiss franc	Sw F 125,000	1,067	919
United Kingdom			
London International Financial Futures Exchange (LIFFE)			
Currency			
Futures			
Eurodollar (three-month)	$1,000,000	1,662	1,850
Pound sterling (three-month)	£500,000	3,555	6,049
Japanese yen	¥12,500,000	3	3
Swiss franc	Sw F 125,000	3	1
Pound sterling	£25,000	7	5
Deutsche mark	DM 125,000	4	2
Euromark		n.t.	712
Options			
Eurodollar (three-month)	$1,000,000	77	71
Pound sterling (three-month)	£500,000	446	709
Pound/U.S. dollar		10	1
Pound sterling	£25,000	446	709

(continued)

APPENDIX

Currency Futures and Options
Currency Futures and Options: Exchanges, Contracts, and Volume of Trades (1988–89) (continued)

Exchange/Type	Face Value of Contract	Volume of Contracts Traded	
		1988	**1989** Jan.–Oct.
		(in thousands of contracts)	
France			
March} © Terme d'Instruments Financiers (MATIF)			
Currency			
Futures			
Euro-deutsche mark		n.t.	481
The Netherlands			
European Options Exchange (EOE)			
Currency			
Options			
U.S. dollar/guilder and	$10,000		412
pound sterling/guilder	£10,000		
Australia			
Sydney Futures Exchange			
Currency			
Futures			
Australian dollar		22	5
Options			
Australian dollar		3	—
New Zealand			
New Zealand Futures Exchange			
Currency			
Futures			
U.S. Dollar	$50,000	19	4
N.Z. dollar	$NZ 100,000	n.t.	2
Singapore			
Singapore International Monetary Exchange (SIMEX)			
Currency			
Futures			
Deutsche mark	DM 125,000	98	23
Eurodollar	$1,000,000	1,881	3,406
Euro-yen		n.t.	58
Japanese yen	¥23,500,000	221	275
Pound sterling	£62,500	3	3
Options			
Deutsche mark	DM 125,000	12	1
Eurodollar	$1,000,000	11	10
Japanese yen	¥12,500,000	61	2

[a]CME Eurodollar, pound sterling, deutsche mark, and Japanese yen contracts are listed on a mutual offset link with SIMEX in Singapore.
[b]American volume.

n.t. = not traded; $A = Australian dollar; Can$ = Canadian dollar; DM = deutsche mark; ECU = European Currency Unit; F = French franc; HK$ = China-Hong kong SAR dollar; ¥ = Japanese yen; $NZ = New Zealand dollar; f. = Netherland guilder; £ = pound sterling; SKr = Swedish krone; and $ = U.S. dollar. Options volume is puts and calls combined. 1989 covers January to October.
Sources: International Monetary Fund, International Capital Markets; Developments and Prospects, Washington, D.C., April 1990.

REFERENCES & SUGGESTED READINGS

Aggarwal, R., and A. Demaskey. "Cross-Hedging Currency Risks in Asian Emerging Markets Using Derivatives in Major Currencies." *Journal of Portfolio Management,* Spring (1997), pp. 88–95.

Allayannis, George, and James Weston. "The Use of Foreign Currency Derivatives and Firm Market Value." *Review of Financial Studies* 14 (2001), pp. 243–76.

Aubey, R., and R. Cramer. "Use of International Currency Cocktails in the Reduction of Exchange Rate Risk." *Journal of Economics and Business,* Winter (1977), pp. 128–34.

Benet, B. "Commodity Futures Cross-Hedging of Foreign Exchange Exposure." *Journal of Futures Markets,* Fall (1990), pp. 287–306.

Beidelman, Carl, John Hillary, and James Greenleaf. "Alternatives in Hedging Long-Date Contractual Foreign Exchange Exposure." *Sloan Management Review,* Summer (1983), pp. 45–54.

Dufey, Gunter, and S. Srinivasulu. "The Case for Corporate Management of Foreign Exchange Risk." *Financial Management,* Winter (1983), pp. 54–62.

Folks, William. "Decision Analysis for Exchange Risk Management." *Financial Management,* Winter (1972), pp. 101–12.

Giddy, Ian. "The Foreign Exchange Option as a Hedging Tool." *Midland Corporate Finance Journal,* Fall (1983), pp. 32–42.

Jesswein, Kurt, Chuck C. Y. Kwok, and William Folks, Jr. "Corporate Use of Innovative Foreign Exchange Risk Management Products." *Columbia Journal of World Business,* Fall (1995), pp. 70–82.

Khoury, Sarkis, and K. H. Chan. "Hedging Foreign Exchange Risk: Selecting the Optimal Tool." *Midland Corporate Finance Journal,* Winter (1988), pp. 40–52.

Levi, Maurice. *International Finance.* New York: McGraw-Hill, 1990.

Smithson, Charles. "A LEGO Approach to Financial Engineering: An Introduction to Forwards, Futures, Swaps and Options." *Midland Corporate Finance Journal,* Winter (1987), pp. 16–28.

Stulz, Rene, and Clifford Smith. "The Determinants of Firms' Hedging Policies." *Journal of Financial and Quantitative Analysis,* December 1985, pp. 391–405.

9 Management of Economic Exposure

随着经济的不断全球化，越来越多的公司有必要关注外汇风险并制定和实施相应的套期保值措施。

AS BUSINESS BECOMES increasingly global, more and more firms find it necessary to pay careful attention to foreign exchange exposure and to design and implement appropriate hedging strategies. Suppose, for example, that the U.S. dollar substantially depreciates against the Japanese yen, as it often has since the mideighties. This change in the exchange rate can have significant economic consequences for both U.S. and Japanese firms. For example, it can adversely affect the competitive position of Japanese car makers in the highly competitive U.S. market by forcing them to raise dollar prices of their cars by more than their U.S. competitors do. The same change in exchange rate, however, will tend to strengthen the competitive position of import-competing U.S. car makers. On the other hand, should the dollar appreciate against the yen, it would bolster the competitive position of Japanese car makers at the expense of U.S. makers. A real-world example of the effect of exchange rate changes is provided in the International Finance in Practice box on page 224, "U.S. Firms Feel the Pain of Peso's Plunge." The box explains how U.S. companies were adversely affected by the collapse of the Mexican peso during the period 1994–95.

汇率变化不仅影响直接从事国际贸易的企业，还影响单纯从事国内贸易的企业。

Changes in exchange rates can affect not only firms that are directly engaged in international trade but also purely domestic firms. Consider, for example, a U.S. bicycle manufacturer that sources only domestic materials and sells exclusively in the U.S. market, with no foreign-currency receivables or payables in its accounting book. This seemingly purely domestic U.S. firm can be subject to foreign exchange exposure if it competes against imports, say, from a Chinese bicycle manufacturer. When the Chinese Yuan depreciates against the U.S. dollar, this is likely to lead to a lower U.S. dollar price of Chinese bicycles, boosting their sales in the United States, thereby hurting the U.S. manufacturer.

Changes in exchange rates may affect not only the operating cash flows of a firm by altering its competitive position but also dollar (home currency) values of the firm's assets and liabilities. Consider a U.S. firm that has borrowed Swiss francs.

Since the dollar amount needed to pay off the franc debt depends on the dollar/franc exchange rate, the U.S. firm can gain or lose as the Swiss franc depreciates or appreciates against the dollar. A classic example of the peril of facing currency exposure is provided by Laker Airways, a British firm founded by Sir Freddie Laker, which pioneered the concept of mass-marketed, low-fare air travel. The company heavily borrowed U.S. dollars to finance acquisitions of aircraft while it derived more than half of its revenue in sterling. As the dollar kept appreciating against the British pound (and most major currencies) throughout the first half of the 1980s, the burden of servicing the dollar debts became overwhelming for Laker Airways, forcing it to default.

上面的例子表明汇率变化通过影响企业的现金流和资产负债的本币价值而影响其公司价值。

The preceding examples suggest that exchange rate changes can systematically affect the value of the firm by influencing its operating cash flows as well as the domestic currency values of its assets and liabilities. In a study examining the exposure of U.S. firms to currency risk, Jorion (1990) documented that a significant relationship exists between stock returns and the dollar's value. Recent studies, such as Choi and Prasad (1995), Simkins and Laux (1996), and Allayannis and Ofek (2001), also document that U.S. stock returns are sensitive to exchange rate movements.

Exhibit 9.1, which is excerpted from the Simkins and Laux study, provides an estimate of the U.S. industries' market betas as well as the "forex" betas. The market and forex betas measure the sensitivities of an industry portfolio against the U.S. stock market index and the dollar exchange rate index, respectively. As Exhibit 9.1 shows, the forex

EXHIBIT 9.1

Exchange Rate Exposure of U.S. Industry Portfolios[a]

Industry	Market Beta[b]	Forex Beta[c]
1. Aerospace	0.999	0.034
2. Apparel	1.264	0.051
3. Beverage	1.145	−0.437
4. Building materials	1.107	0.604
5. Chemicals	1.074	−0.009
6. Computers, office equipment	0.928	0.248
7. Electronics, electrical equipment	1.202	0.608*
8. Food	1.080	−0.430
9. Forest and paper products	1.117	0.445
10. Furniture	0.901	1.217*
11. Industrial and farm equipment	1.125	0.473
12. Metal products	1.081	−0.440
13. Metals	1.164	0.743*
14. Mining and crude oil	0.310	−0.713
15. Motor vehicles and parts	0.919	1.168*
16. Petroleum refining	0.515	−0.746*
17. Pharmaceuticals	1.124	−1.272*
18. Publishing and printing	1.154	0.567
19. Rubber and plastics	1.357	0.524
20. Science, photo, and control equipment	0.975	−0.437*
21. Cosmetics	1.051	0.417
22. Textiles	1.279	1.831*
23. Tobacco	0.898	−0.768*
24. Toys, sporting goods	1.572	−0.660
25. Transportation equipment	1.613	1.524*

[a]The market and forex (foreign exchange) betas are obtained from regressing the industry portfolio (monthly) returns, constructed from the Fortune 500 companies, on the U.S. stock market index returns and the rate of change in the dollar exchange rate index over the sample period 1.1989–12.93.
[b]For every industry portfolio the market beta is statistically significant at the 1% level.
[c]The forex beta is significant for some industry portfolios and insignificant for others. Those forex betas that are significant at 10% or higher are denoted by (*).
Source: Betty Simkins and Paul Laux, "Derivatives Use and the Exchange Rate Risk of Investing in Large U.S. Corporations," Case Western Reserve University Working Paper (1996).

U.S. Firms Feel the Pain of Peso's Plunge

Foreign-exchange traders and investors aren't the only Americans feeling the pain of the two-week plunge in the value of the Mexican peso.

For U.S. companies that are paid in pesos or that own substantial assets in Mexico, the recent 37% decline in the currency's value is a vivid example of just how quickly and substantially changes in the value of foreign currency can affect sales and profits.

And for the hundreds of companies that see Mexico as a ticket for expansion, the peso's fall is another reminder that foreign markets aren't anything like those at home. The Mexican financial crisis forces U.S. companies to "pay attention to the direction of the economy in any country they invest in," says Serge Ratmiroff, senior manager, international services, at Deloitte & Touche in Chicago.

The impact of the peso's fall on those that do business in the Mexican currency is striking. A U.S. company that sold widgets for 345 pesos early last month received about $100. Now, 345 pesos is valued at between $60 and $65. Meanwhile, as the value of the peso declines, prices of U.S. exports will rise, making them less affordable for Mexican buyers.

Ford Motor Co., for instance, said the peso's problems could dent its growth in exports to Mexico next year. Ford sent 27,000 to 28,000 vehicles to Mexico in 1994, up from a few hundred in 1992. It had hoped those sales would double over time with the aid of the North American Free Trade Agreement. But the auto maker's chairman and chief executive officer, Alexander Trotman, noted Tuesday that the cost of Ford autos "in peso terms has gone up enormously." Ford continues to build more than 200,000 vehicles a year in Mexico, but its Mexican output excludes such hot-sellers as the Mustang sports coupe, which is imported from the U.S. While wages should fall at its Mexican plants, at least in dollar terms, a spokesman said the company wouldn't see much gain from that because most of the parts used to assemble cars in Mexico actually are made in the U.S.

Other companies are feeling the impact immediately. Toy maker Mattel Inc. said yesterday that it will take an eight-cent-a-share charge for the fourth quarter because the peso's decline has reduced the value of its Mexican inventory and receivables. The charge means that despite a 35% jump in world-wide sales, Mattel's record earnings for the year will be on the "conservative" side of analysts' estimates.

Metalclad Corp., a Newport Beach, Calif., company with waste-oil recycling and landfill operations in Mexico, said the peso's plunge may wipe out its hopes for a profitable fiscal third quarter, ending Feb. 28. And Pilgrim's Pride, a Pittsburg, Texas, chicken producer, expects to take a substantial write-down for its first quarter ended Dec. 31, as it marks down its $120 million in assets in Mexico. A spokesman for Goodyear Tire & Rubber Co. in Akron, Ohio, said the company has "seen tire business fall off in Mexico because dealers don't want to sell the product at less than what they bought it for."

For many big U.S. companies, however, the swings are just another day in the currency markets. Mexico is a relatively small international market, though it accounts for about 9% of U.S. exports. Many companies say they do business in dollars or have otherwise hedged against currency changes, and won't feel any immediate financial impact. Further, those who manufacture there should see lower labor costs while some businesses, like trucking and hotels, contend they will benefit from increasing U.S. imports and tourism.

Still, some firms are putting expansion plans on hold and even large companies expect exports to Mexico to fall off this year as Mexican buyers adjust to the higher prices of U.S. goods. After all, that's part of Mexico's goal in letting the peso's value fall in relation to the dollar. "The whole purpose of what they're doing is to try to reduce the level of imports and increase Mexican exports," says Sidney Weintraub of the Center for Strategic and International Studies, a Washington think tank.

A drop in product sales to Mexico would be felt particularly in Texas, which exported about $20.38 billion in goods to its southern neighbor in 1993—nearly half the U.S. exports to Mexico. The state comptroller's office is predicting that exports will grow another 5% to 7% this year, but rise just 3% a year in 1996 and beyond, in part, because currency changes will curtail demand.

beta varies greatly across industry lines; it ranges from -1.272 for pharmaceuticals to 1.831 for textiles. A negative (positive) forex beta means that stock returns tend to move down (up) as the dollar appreciates. Out of the 25 total industries studied, 10 were found to have a significant exposure to exchange rate movements.

This chapter is devoted to the management of economic exposure to currency risk. But we need to first discuss how to measure economic exposure.

How to Measure Economic Exposure

外汇风险或不确定
性表现为汇率的随机变
化，而外汇风险暴露用
于衡量什么东西暴露在
风险下。二者并不相同。

Currency risk or uncertainty, which represents random changes in exchange rates, is not the same as the currency exposure, which measures "what is at risk." Under certain conditions, a firm may not face any exposure at all, that is, nothing is at risk, even if the exchange rates change randomly. Suppose your company maintains a vacation home for employees in the British countryside and the local price of this property is always moving together with the pound price of the U.S. dollar. As a result, whenever the pound depreciates against the dollar, the local currency price of this property goes up by the same proportion. In this case, your company is not exposed to currency risk even if the pound/dollar exchange rate fluctuates randomly. The British asset your company owns has an embedded hedge against exchange risk, rendering the dollar price of the asset *insensitive* to exchange rate changes.

Consider an alternative situation in which the local (pound) price of your company's British asset barely changes. In this case, the dollar value of the asset will be highly *sensitive* to the exchange rate since the former will change as the latter does. To the extent that the dollar price of the British asset exhibits "sensitivity" to exchange rate movements, your company is exposed to currency risk. Similarly, if your company's operating cash flows are sensitive to exchange rate changes, the company is again exposed to currency risk.

类似地，如果公司
的经营现金流对外汇变
化敏感，该公司也面临
着外汇风险暴露。

Exposure to currency risk thus can be properly measured by the *sensitivities* of (1) the future home currency values of the firm's assets (and liabilities) and (2) the firm's operating cash flows to random changes in exchange rates. The same point is illustrated by Exhibit 9.2; assets include the tangible assets (property, plant and equipment, inventory) as well as financial assets. Let us first discuss the case of asset exposure. For expositional convenience, assume that dollar inflation is nonrandom. Then, from the perspective of the U.S. firm that owns an asset in Britain, the exposure can be measured by the coefficient (b) in regressing the dollar value (P) of the British asset on the dollar/pound exchange rate (S).[1]

$$P = a + b \times S + e \tag{9.1}$$

EXHIBIT 9.2

Channels of Economic Exposure

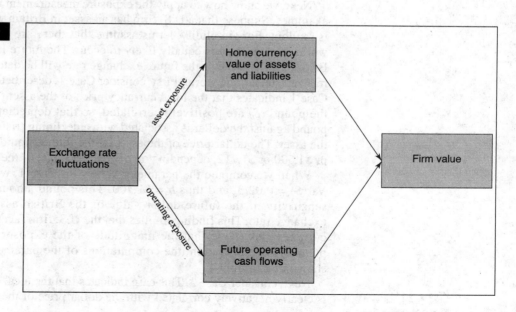

---

[1]Our discussion in this section draws on Adler and Dumas (1984) who clarified the notion of currency exposure.

EXHIBIT 9.3

Measurement of Currency Exposure

State	Probability	P*	S	P(=SP*)	Parameters
A. Case 1					
1	1/3	£ 980	$1.40	$1,372	Cov(P,S) = 34/3
2	1/3	£1,000	$1.50	$1,500	Var(S) = .02/3
3	1/3	£1,070	$1.60	$1,712	**b = £1,700**
Mean			$1.50	$1,528	
B. Case 2					
1	1/3	£1,000	$1.40	$1,400	Cov(P,S) = 0
2	1/3	£ 933	$1.50	$1,400	Var(S) = .02/3
3	1/3	£ 875	$1.60	$1,400	**b = 0**
Mean			$1.50	$1,400	
C. Case 3					
1	1/3	£1,000	$1.40	$1,400	Cov(P,S) = 20/3
2	1/3	£1,000	$1.50	$1,500	Var(S) = .02/3
3	1/3	£1,000	$1.60	$1,600	**b = £1,000**
Mean			$1.50	$1,500	

风险暴露系数

where a is the regression constant and e is the random error term with mean zero, that is, $E(e) = 0$; $P = SP^*$, where P^* is the local currency (pound) price of the asset.[2] It is obvious from the above equation that the regression coefficient b measures the sensitivity of the dollar value of the asset (P) to the exchange rate (S). If the regression coefficient is zero, that is, $b = 0$, the dollar value of the asset is independent of exchange rate movements, implying no exposure. On the basis of the above analysis, one can say that *exposure is the regression coefficient*. Statistically, the **exposure coefficient, b**, is defined as follows:

$$b = \frac{\text{Cov}(P,S)}{\text{Var}(S)}$$

where $\text{Cov}(P,S)$ is the covariance between the dollar value of the asset and the exchange rate, and $\text{Var}(S)$ is the variance of the exchange rate.

Next, we show how to apply the exposure measurement technique using numerical examples. Suppose that a U.S. firm has an asset in Britain whose local currency price is random. For simplicity, let us assume that there are three possible states of the world, with each state equally likely to occur. The future local currency price of this British asset as well as the future exchange rate will be determined, depending on the realized state of the world. First, consider Case 1, described in Panel A of Exhibit 9.3. Case 1 indicates that the local currency price of the asset (P^*) and the dollar price of the pound (S) are positively correlated, so that depreciation (appreciation) of the pound against the dollar is associated with a declining (rising) local currency price of the asset. The dollar price of the asset on the future (liquidation) date can be $1,372, or $1,500 or $1,712, depending on the realized state of the world.

When we compute the parameter values for Case 1, we obtain $\text{Cov}(P,S) = 34/3$, $\text{Var}(S) = 0.02/3$, and thus $b = £1,700$. This pound amount, £1,700, represents the sensitivity of the future dollar value of the British asset to random changes in exchange rate. This finding implies that the U.S. firm faces a substantial exposure to currency risk. Note that the magnitude of the exposure is expressed in British pounds. For illustration, the computations of the parameter values for Case 1 are shown in Exhibit 9.4.

Next, consider Case 2. This case indicates that the local currency value of the asset is clearly negatively correlated with the dollar price of the British pound. In fact, the

事实上，汇率变化的
影响会被资产的当地货币
价格的变化而完全抵消，
表现为资产的美元价格对
汇率变化完全不敏感。

---

[2]In addition, the covariance between the random error (residual) term and the exchange rate is zero, i.e., $\text{Cov}(S,e) = 0$, by construction.

Computations of Regression Parameters: Case 1

1. Computation of Means

$$\bar{P} = \sum_i q_i P_i = \frac{1}{3}(1,372 + 1,500 + 1,712) = 1,528$$

$$\bar{S} = \sum_i q_i S_i = \frac{1}{3}(1.40 + 1.50 + 1.60) = 1.50$$

2. Computation of Variance and Covariance

$$\text{Var}(S) = \sum_i q_i (S_i = \bar{S})^2$$

$$= \frac{1}{3}[(1.40-1.50)^2 + (1.50-1.50)^2 + (1.60-1.50)^2]$$

$$= 0.02/3$$

$$\text{Cov}(P_iS) = \sum_i q_i (P_i - \bar{P})(S_i - \bar{S})$$

$$= \frac{1}{3}[(1,372 - 1,528)(1.40 - 1.50) + (1,500 - 1,528)$$

$$(1.50 - 1.50) + (1,712-1,528)(1.60-1.50)]$$

$$= 34/3$$

3. Computation of the Exposure Coefficient

$$b = \text{Cov}(P,S)/\text{Var}(S) = (34/3)/(0.02/3) = 1,700$$

Note: q_i denotes the probability for the i th state.

effect of exchange rate changes is exactly offset by movements of the local currency price of the asset, rendering the dollar price of the asset totally insensitive to exchange rate changes. The future dollar price of the asset will be uniformly $1,400 across the three states of the world. One thus can say that the British asset is effectively *denominated* in terms of the dollar. Although this case is clearly unrealistic, it shows that uncertain exchange rates or exchange risk does not necessarily constitute exchange exposure. Despite the fact that the future exchange rate is uncertain, the U.S. firm has nothing at risk in this case. Since the firm faces no exposure, no hedging will be necessary.

We now turn to Case 3, where the local currency price of the asset is fixed at £1,000. In this case, the U.S. firm faces a "contractual" cash flow that is *denominated* in pounds. This case, in fact, represents an example of the special case of **economic exposure, transaction exposure.** Intuitively, what is at risk is £1,000, that is, the exposure coefficient, b, is £1,000. Readers can confirm this by going through the same kind of computations as shown in Exhibit 9.4. Measurement of transaction exposure is thus very simple. The exposure coefficient, b, is the same as the magnitude of the contractual cash flow fixed in terms of foreign currency.

Once the magnitude of exposure is known, the firm can hedge the exposure by simply selling the exposure forward. In Case 3, where the asset value is fixed in terms of local currency, it is possible to completely eliminate the variability of the future dollar price of the asset by selling £1,000 forward. In Case 1, however, where the local currency price of the asset is random, selling £1,700 forward will not completely eliminate the variability of the future dollar price; there will be a residual variability that is independent of exchange rate changes.

On the basis of regression Equation 9.1, we can decompose the variability of the dollar value of the asset, Var(P), into two separate components: exchange rate-related and residual. Specifically,

$$\text{Var}(P) = b^2\text{Var}(S) + \text{Var}(e) \tag{9.2}$$

The first term in the right-hand side of the equation, $b^2\text{Var}(S)$, represents the part of the variability of the dollar value of the asset that is related to random changes in the

这里，美国公司拥有以英镑计量的契约性现金流。这种情况实际上代表了**经济风险暴露**的特例——**交易风险暴露。**

一旦风险暴露大小已知，公司就可以简单地通过提前卖出远期风险暴露来对风险进行套期保值。

EXHIBIT 9.5

Consequences of Hedging Currency Exposure

Future Quantities	State 1	State 2	State 3	Variance
A. Case 1 (B$_i$ = £1,700)				
Local currency asset price (P*)	980	1,000	1,070	
Exchange rate (S)	1.40	1.50	1.60	
Dollar value (P = SP*)	1,372	1,500	1,712	19,659
Proceeds from forward contract	170	0	−170	
Dollar value of hedged position (HP)	1,542	1,500	1,542	392
B. Case 3 (b = £1,000)				
Local currency asset price (P*)	1,000	1,000	1,000	
Exchange rate (S)	1.40	1.50	1.60	
Dollar value (P = SP*)	1,400	1,500	1,600	6,667
Proceeds from forward contract	100	0	−100	
Dollar value of hedged position (HP)	1,500	1,500	1,500	0

Note: In both cases, the forward exchange rate (F) is assumed to be \$1.50/£. Proceeds from the forward contract are computed as \$b(F − S). Recall that each of the three states is equally likely to happen, i.e., q_i = 1/3 for each state.

exchange rate, whereas the second term, Var(e), captures the residual part of the dollar value variability that is independent of exchange rate movements.

The consequences of hedging the exposure by forward contracts are illustrated in Exhibit 9.5. Consider Case 1, where the firm faces an exposure coefficient (b) of £1,700. If the firm sells £1,700 forward, the dollar proceeds that the firm will receive are given by

$$\$1,700(F - S)$$

where F is the forward exchange rate and S is the spot rate realized on the maturity date. Note that for each pound sold forward, the firm will receive a dollar amount equal to $(F - S)$. In Exhibit 9.5, the forward exchange rate is assumed to be \$1.50, which is the same as the expected future spot rate. Thus, if the future spot rate turns out to be \$1.40 under state 1, the dollar proceed from the forward contract will be \$170 = 1,700(1.50−1.40). Since the dollar value (P) of the asset is \$1,372 under state 1, the dollar value of the hedged position (HP) will be \$1,542 (= \$1,372 + \$170) under state 1.

As shown in part A of Exhibit 9.5, the variance of the dollar value of the hedged position is only 392($)², whereas that of the unhedged position is 19,659($)². This result implies that much of the uncertainty regarding the future dollar value of the asset is associated with exchange rate uncertainty. As a result, once the exchange exposure is hedged, most of the variability of the dollar value of the asset is eliminated. The residual variability of the dollar value of the asset that is independent of exchange rate changes, Var(e), is equal to 392($)².

Let us now turn to Case 3 where the local currency price of the asset is fixed. In this case, complete hedging is possible in the specific sense that there will be no residual variability. As shown in part B of Exhibit 9.5, the future dollar value of the asset, which is totally dependent upon the exchange rate, has a variance of 6,667($)². Once the firm hedges the exposure by selling £1,000 forward, the dollar value of the hedged position (HP) becomes nonrandom, and is \$1,500 across the three states of the world. Since the asset now has a constant dollar value, it is effectively *redenominated* in terms of the dollar.

因此，一旦外汇风险被套期保值，资产的美元价值波动就会被大大削弱。

在这种情况下，由于没有残差项，表明完全套期保值是可能的。

Operating Exposure: Definition

While many managers understand the effects of random exchange rate changes on the dollar value of their firms' assets and liabilities denominated in foreign currencies, they often do not fully understand the effect of volatile exchange rates on operating

汇率的波动会严重
影响这些公司在国内外
市场的竞争地位，从而
影响公司的现金流。

cash flows. As the economy becomes increasingly globalized, more firms are subject to international competition. Fluctuating exchange rates can seriously alter the relative competitive positions of such firms in domestic and foreign markets, affecting their operating cash flows.

经营风险暴露
资产风险暴露

Unlike the exposure of assets and liabilities (such as accounts payable and receivable, loans denominated in foreign currencies, and so forth) that are listed in accounting statements, the exposure of operating cash flows depends on the effect of random exchange rate changes on the firm's competitive position, which is not readily measurable. This difficulty notwithstanding, it is important for the firm to properly manage **operating exposure** as well as **asset exposure.** In many cases, operating exposure may account for a larger portion of the firm's total exposure than contractual exposure. Formally, operating exposure can be defined as the *extent to which the firm's operating cash flows would be affected by random changes in exchange rates*.

Illustration of Operating Exposure

在讨论经营风险暴
露的决定因素及如何管
理它之前，有必要用一
个简单的例子来说明这
种风险暴露。

Before we discuss what determines operating exposure and how to manage it, it is useful to illustrate the exposure using a simple example. Suppose that a U.S. computer company has a wholly owned British subsidiary, Albion Computers PLC, that manufactures and sells personal computers in the U.K. market. Albion Computers imports microprocessors from Intel, which sells them for $512 per unit. At the current exchange rate of $1.60 per pound, each Intel microprocessor costs £320. Albion Computers hires British workers and sources all the other inputs locally. Albion faces a 50 percent income tax rate in the U.K.

Exhibit 9.6 summarizes projected operations for Albion Computers, assuming that the exchange rate will remain unchanged at $1.60 per pound. The company expects to sell 50,000 units of personal computers per year at a selling price of £1,000 per unit. The unit variable cost is £650, which comprises £320 for the imported input and £330 for the locally sourced inputs. Needless to say, the pound price of the imported input will change as the exchange rate changes, which, in turn, can affect the selling price in the U.K. market. Each year, Albion incurs fixed overhead costs of £4 million for rents, property taxes, and the like, regardless of output level. As the exhibit shows, the projected operating cash flow is £7,250,000 per year, which is equivalent to $11,600,000 at the current exchange rate of $1.60 per pound.

Now, consider the possible effect of a depreciation of the pound on the projected dollar operating cash flow of Albion Computers. Assume that the pound may depreciate

EXHIBIT 9.6		
Projected Operations for Albion Computers PLC: Benchmark Case ($1.60/£)	Sales (50,000 units at £1,000/unit)	£50,000,000
	Variable costs (50,000 units at £650/unit)[a]	32,500,000
	Fixed overhead costs	4,000,000
	Depreciation allowances	1,000,000
	Net profit before tax	£12,500,000
	Income tax (at 50%)	6,250,000
	Profit after tax	6,250,000
	Add back depreciation	1,000,000
	Operating cash flow in pounds	£ 7,250,000
	Operating cash flow in dollars	$11,600,000

[a]The unit variable cost, £650, comprises £330 for the locally sourced inputs and £320 for the imported input, which is priced in dollars, i.e., $512. At the exchange rate of $1.60/£ the imported part costs £320.

EXHIBIT 9.7

Projected Operations for Albion Computers PLC: Case 1 ($1.40/£)

Sales (50,000 units at £1,000/unit)	£50,000,000
Variable costs (50,000 units at £696/unit)	34,800,000
Fixed overhead costs	4,000,000
Depreciation allowances	1,000,000
Net profit before tax	£10,200,000
income tax (at 50%)	5,100,000
Profit after tax	5,100,000
Add back depreciation	1,000,000
Operating cash flow in pounds	£ 6,100,000
Operating cash flow in dollars	$ 8,540,000

from $1.60 to $1.40 per pound. The dollar operating cash flow may change following a pound depreciation due to:

竞争效应

1. The **competitive effect:** A pound depreciation may affect operating cash flow in pounds by altering the firm's competitive position in the marketplace.

兑换效应

2. The **conversion effect:** A given operating cash flow in pounds will be converted into a lower dollar amount after the pound depreciation.

To get a feel of how the dollar operating cash flow may change as the exchange rate changes, consider the following cases with varying degrees of realism:

Case 1: No variables change, except the price of the imported input.

Case 2: The selling price as well as the price of the imported input changes, with no other changes.

Case 3: All the variables change.

In Case 1, which is illustrated in Exhibit 9.7, the unit variable cost of the imported input rises to £366 (= $512/$1.40) following the pound depreciation, with no other changes. Following the depreciation, the total variable costs become £34.8 million, lowering the firm's before-tax profit from £12.5 million (for the benchmark case) to £10.2 million. Considering that the firm faces a 50 percent income tax rate, depreciation of the pound will lower the net operating cash flow from £7.25 million (for the benchmark case) to £6.1 million. In terms of dollars, Albion's projected net operating cash flow changes from $11.6 million to $8.54 million as the exchange rate changes from $1.60 per pound to $1.40 per pound. Albion may be forced not to raise the pound selling price because it faces a British competitor that manufactures similar products using only locally sourced inputs. An increase in selling price can potentially lead to a sharp decline in unit sales volume. Under this kind of competitive environment, Albion's costs are responsive to exchange rate changes, but the selling

EXHIBIT 9.8

Projected Operations for Albion Computers PLC: Case 2 ($1.40/£)

Sales (50,000 units at £1,143/unit)	£57,150,000
Variable costs (50,000 units at £696/unit)	34,800,000
Fixed overhead costs	4,000,000
Depreciation allowances	1,000,000
Net profit before tax	£17,350,000
Income tax (at 50%)	8,675,000
Profit after tax	8,675,000
Add back depreciation	1,000,000
Operating cash flow in pounds	£ 9,675,000
Operating cash flow in dollars	$13,545,000

EXHIBIT 9.9

Projected Operations for Albion Computers PLC: Case 3 ($1.40/£)

Sales (40,000 units at £1,080/unit)	£43,200,000
Variable costs (40,000 units at £722/unit)	28,880,000
Fixed overhead costs	4,000,000
Depreciation allowances	1,000,000
Net profit before tax	£ 9,320,000
Income tax (at 50%)	4,660,000
Profit after tax	4,660,000
Add back depreciation	1,000,000
Operating cash flow in pounds	£ 5,660,000
Operating cash flow in dollars	$ 7,924,000

这种不对称性使得公司的经营现金流对汇率变化敏感，从而产生经营风险暴露。

price is not. This asymmetry makes the firm's operating cash flow sensitive to exchange rate changes, giving rise to operating exposure.

In Case 2, which is analyzed in Exhibit 9.8, the selling price as well as the price of the imported input increases following the pound depreciation. In this case, Albion Computers does not face any serious competition in the British market and faces a highly inelastic demand for its products. Thus, Albion can raise the selling price to £1,143 (to keep the dollar selling price at $1,600 after the pound depreciation) and still maintain the sales volume at 50,000 units. Computations presented in Exhibit 9.8 indicate that the projected operating cash flow actually increases to £9,675,000, which is equivalent to $13,545,000. Compared with the benchmark case, the dollar operating cash flow is higher when the pound depreciates. This case shows that a pound depreciation need not always lead to a lower dollar operating cash flow.

这个例子说明英镑贬值未必总会导致以美元计量的经营现金流的下降。

We now turn to Case 3 where the selling price, sales volume, and the prices of both locally sourced and imported inputs change following the pound depreciation. In particular, we assume that both the selling price and the price of locally sourced inputs increase at the rate of 8 percent, reflecting the underlying inflation rate in the U.K. As a result, the selling price will be £1,080 per unit and the unit variable cost of locally sourced inputs will be £356. Since the price of the imported input is £366, the combined unit variable cost will be £722. Facing an **elastic demand** for its products, sales volume declines to 40,000 units per year after the price increase. As Exhibit 9.9 shows, Albion's projected operating cash flow is £5.66 million, which is equivalent to $7.924 million. The projected dollar cash flow under Case 3 is lower than that of the benchmark case by $3.676 million.

需求弹性

Exhibit 9.10 summarizes the projected operating exposure effect of the pound depreciation on Albion Computers PLC. For expositional purposes it is assumed here

EXHIBIT 9.10 Summary of Operating Exposure Effect of Pound Depreciation on Albion Computers PLC

Variables	Benchmark Case	Case 1	Case 2	Case 3
Exchange rate ($/£)	1.60	1.40	1.40	1.40
Unit variable cost (£)	650	696	696	722
Unit sales price (£)	1,000	1,000	1,143	1,080
Sales volume (units)	50,000	50,000	50,000	40,000
Annual cash flow (£)	7,250,000	6,100,000	9,675,000	5,660,000
Annual cash flow ($)	11,600,000	8,540,000	13,545,000	7,924,000
Four-year present value ($)[a]	33,118,000	24,382,000	38,671,000	22,623,000
Operating gains/losses ($)[b]		−8,736,000	5,553,000	−10,495,000

[a]The discounted present value of dollar cash flows was computed over a four-year period using a 15 percent discount rate. A constant cash flow is assumed for each of four years.
[b]Operating gains or losses represent the present value of change in cash flows, which is due to pound depreciation, from the benchmark case.

that a change in exchange rate will have effects on the firm's operating cash flow for four years. The exhibit provides, among other things, the four-year present values of operating cash flows for each of the three cases as well as for the benchmark case. The proper discount rate for Albion's cash flow is assumed to be 15 percent. The exhibit also shows the operating gains or losses computed as the present value of changes in operating cash flows (over a four-year period) from the benchmark case that are due to the exchange rate change. In Case 3, for instance, the firm expects to experience an operating loss of $10,495,000 due to the pound depreciation.

Determinants of Operating Exposure

公司的经营风险暴露由以下因素决定：(1) 公司取得劳动力、原材料等投入品的市场和销售产品的市场的结构，(2) 公司通过调整市场结构、产品结构和原料来源地来减轻汇率变化影响的能力。

Unlike contractual (i.e., transaction) exposure, which can readily be determined from the firm's accounting statements, operating exposure cannot be determined in the same manner. A firm's operating exposure is determined by (1) the structure of the markets in which the firm sources its inputs, such as labor and materials, and sells its products, and (2) the firm's ability to mitigate the effect of exchange rate changes by adjusting its markets, product mix, and sourcing.

To highlight the importance of market structure in determining operating exposure, consider a hypothetical company, Ford Mexicana, a subsidiary of Ford, which imports cars from the parent and distributes them in Mexico. If the dollar appreciates against the Mexican peso, Ford Mexicana's costs go up in peso terms. Whether this creates operating exposure for Ford critically depends on the structure of the car market in Mexico. For example, if Ford Mexicana faces competition from Mexican car makers whose peso costs did not rise, it will not be able to raise the peso price of imported Ford cars without risking a major reduction in sales. Facing a highly elastic demand for its products, Ford Mexicana cannot let the **exchange rate pass-through** the peso price. As a result, an appreciation of the dollar will squeeze the profit of Ford Mexicana, subjecting the parent firm to a high degree of operating exposure.

汇率传递

In contrast, consider the case in which Ford Mexicana faces import competition only from other U.S. car makers like General Motors and Chrysler rather than from local producers. Since peso costs of those other imported U.S. cars will be affected by a dollar appreciation in the same manner, the competitive position of Ford Mexicana will not be adversely affected. Under this market structure, the dollar appreciation is likely to be reflected in higher peso prices of imported U.S. cars pretty quickly. As a result, Ford will be able to better maintain its dollar profit, without being subject to a major operating exposure.

Generally speaking, a firm is subject to high degrees of operating exposure when *either* its cost *or* its price is sensitive to exchange rate changes. On the other hand, when *both* the cost *and* the price are sensitive or insensitive to exchange rate changes, the firm has no major operating exposure.

Given the market structure, however, the extent to which a firm is subject to operating exposure depends on the firm's ability to stabilize cash flows in the face of exchange rate changes. Even if Ford faces competition from local car makers in Mexico, for example, it can reduce exposure by starting to source Mexican parts and materials, which would be cheaper in dollar terms after the dollar appreciation. Ford can even start to produce cars in Mexico by hiring local workers and sourcing local inputs, thereby making peso costs relatively insensitive to changes in the dollar/peso exchange rate. In other words, the firm's flexibility regarding production locations, sourcing, and financial hedging strategy is an important determinant of its operating exposure to exchange risk.

在讨论如何对经营风险暴露进行套期保值之前，有必要知道：名义汇率的变化并不一定总是影响公司的竞争地位。

Before we discuss how to hedge operating exposure, it is important to recognize that changes in nominal exchange rates may not always affect the firm's competitive position. This is the case when a change in exchange rate is exactly offset by the inflation differential. To show this point, let us again use the example of Ford Mexicana competing against local car makers. Suppose that the annual inflation rate is 4 percent in the United States and 15 percent in Mexico. For simplicity, we assume that car prices appreciate at the same pace as the general domestic inflation rate in both the United States and Mexico. Now, suppose that the dollar appreciates about 11 percent against the peso, offsetting the inflation rate differential between the two countries. This, of course, implies that purchasing power parity is holding.

Under this situation the peso price of Ford cars appreciates by about 15 percent, which reflects a 4 percent increase in the dollar price of cars and an 11 percent appreciation of the dollar against the peso. Since the peso prices of both Ford and locally produced cars rise by the same 15 percent, the 11 percent appreciation of the dollar will not affect the competitive position of Ford vis-à-vis local car makers. Ford thus does not have operating exposure.

If, however, the dollar appreciates by more than 11 percent against the peso, Ford cars will become relatively more expensive than locally produced cars, adversely affecting Ford's competitive position. Ford is thus exposed to exchange risk. Since purchasing power parity does not hold very well, especially in the short run, exchange rate changes are likely to affect the competitive positions of firms that are sourcing from different locations but selling in the same markets.

在考虑下一个议题之前，必须考虑汇率变化和商品价格调整之间的关系。

Before we move on, it would be useful to examine the relationship between exchange rate changes and the price adjustments of goods. Facing exchange rate changes, a firm may choose one of the following three pricing strategies: (1) pass the cost shock fully to its selling prices (complete pass-through), (2) fully absorb the shock to keep its selling prices unaltered (no pass-through), or (3) do some combination of the two strategies described above (partial pass-through). Import prices in the United States do not fully reflect exchange rate changes, exhibiting a partial pass-through phenomenon.

在一份综合研究中，杨(1997)调查了1980~1991年美国制造业的汇率传递情况，发现外国出口公司的定价行为通常表现为部分传递。

In a comprehensive study, Yang (1997) investigated exchange rate pass-through in U.S. manufacturing industries during the sample period 1980–1991 and found that the pricing behavior of foreign exporting firms is generally consistent with partial pass-through. Exhibit 9.11, constructed based on the Yang study, provides

EXHIBIT 9.11

Exchange Rate Pass-Through Coefficients for U.S. Manufacturing Industries

Industry Code (SIC)	Industry	Pass-Through Coefficient
20	Food and kindred products	0.2485
22	Textile mill products	0.3124
23	Apparels	0.1068
24	Lumber and wood products	0.0812
25	Furniture and fixtures	0.3576
28	Chemicals and allied products	0.5312
30	Rubber and plastic products	0.5318
31	Leather products	0.3144
32	Stone, glass, concrete products	0.8843
33	Primary metal industries	0.2123
34	Fabricated metal products	0.3138
35	Machinery, except electrical	0.7559
36	Electrical and electronic machinery	0.3914
37	Transportation equipment	0.3583
38	Measurement instruments	0.7256
39	Miscellaneous manufacturing	0.2765
Average		0.4205

Source: Jiawen Yang. "Exchange Rate Pass-Through in U.S. Manufacturing Industries," Review of Economics and Statistics 79 (1997), pp. 95–104.

the pass-through coefficients for different industries; the coefficient would be 1 for complete pass-through and 0 for no pass-through. As can be seen from the exhibit, the pass-through coefficient ranges from 0.0812 for SIC 24 (lumber and wood products) to 0.8843 for SIC 32 (stone, glass, and concrete products). The average coefficient is 0.4205, implying that when the U.S. dollar appreciates or depreciates by 1 percent, import prices of foreign products change, on average, by about 0.42 percent. It is noteworthy that partial pass-through is common but varies a great deal across industries. Import prices would be affected relatively little by exchange rate changes in industries with low product differentiation and thus high demand elasticities. In contrast, in industries with a high degree of product differentiation and thus low demand elasticities, import prices will tend to change more as the exchange rates change.

Managing Operating Exposure

管理经营风险暴露的目的就是在汇率波动时维持公司现金流的稳定。

As the economy becomes increasingly globalized, many firms are engaged in international activities such as exports, cross-border sourcing, joint ventures with foreign partners, and establishing production and sales affiliates abroad. The cash flows of such firms can be quite sensitive to exchange rate changes. The objective of managing operating exposure is to stabilize cash flows in the face of fluctuating exchange rates.

Since a firm is exposed to exchange risk mainly through the effect of exchange rate changes on its competitive position, it is important to consider exchange exposure management in the context of the firm's long-term strategic planning. For example, in making such strategic decisions as choosing where to locate production facilities, where to purchase materials and components, and where to sell products, the firm should consider the currency effect on its overall future cash flows. Managing operating exposure is thus not a short-term tactical issue. The firm can use the following strategies for managing operating exposure:

1. Selecting low-cost production sites.
2. Flexible sourcing policy.
3. Diversification of the market.
4. Product differentiation and R&D efforts.
5. Financial hedging.

Selecting Low-Cost Production Sites

公司也可以在多个国家设立生产基地以应对汇率变化。

When the domestic currency is strong or expected to become strong, eroding the competitive position of the firm, it can choose to locate production facilities in a foreign country where costs are low due to either the undervalued currency or underpriced factors of production. Recently, Japanese car makers, including Nissan and Toyota, have been increasingly shifting production to U.S. manufacturing facilities in order to mitigate the negative effect of the strong yen on U.S. sales. German car makers such as Daimler Benz and BMW also decided to establish manufacturing facilities in the United States for the same reason. A real-world example is provided by the International Finance in Practice box, "The Strong Yen and Toyota's Choice."

Also, the firm can choose to establish and maintain production facilities in multiple countries to deal with the effect of exchange rate changes. Consider Nissan, which has manufacturing facilities in the United States and Mexico, as well as in Japan. Multiple manufacturing sites provide Nissan with a great deal of flexibility regarding where to produce, given the prevailing exchange rates. While the yen appreciated substantially against the dollar, the Mexican peso depreciated against the dollar in recent years. Under this sort of exchange rate development, Nissan may choose to increase production in the United States, and especially in Mexico, in order to serve the U.S.

The Strong Yen and Toyota's Choice

Facing a strong yen in recent years that made Japanese exports more expensive, Toyota, Japan's biggest car maker, chose to shift production from Japan to U.S. manufacturing facilities, where the cost of production is lower. Toyota plans to boost U.S. production by about 50 percent by 1996 compared with 1993. Consequently, Toyota expects that its exports to the United States will decline by about 30 percent over the same period. The car maker also plans to double its production of engines at its Georgetown, Kentucky, plant. In addition to substantially boosting car production at its Georgetown factory, Toyota is also shifting production of all its pickup trucks sold in the United States from Japan to Fremont, California.

As a result, American-built vehicles will account for more than 60 percent of Toyota's U.S. sales in 1996 (about 800,000 units) compared with 46 percent in 1993. Toyota also will boost its exports from America to about 80,000 vehicles by 1996, an increase of about 60 percent from the 50,000 units exported in 1993. The company expects U.S. jobs will grow by 23 percent to 6,000 workers by 1996 at its Georgetown plant. At the same time, procurement of U.S. parts and materials will rise about 40 percent to $6.45 billion from $4.65 billion in 1993.

In addition to shifting production and sourcing to the United States, Toyota is using attractive lease deals to help close the price gap on imports. Since the company doesn't have to raise monthly leasing fees in step with the rising yen, the cars remain more attractive to U.S. consumers, although the company risks taking losses upon resale.

Although shifting production to the United States helps Toyota to get out of the dollar/yen problem and maintain its market share in the United States, it adds to the excess capacity problem of Toyota and leads to underutilization of domestic plants and job losses. A persistent strong yen can result in hollowing out of the Japanese economy, as some worry.

market. This is, in fact, how Nissan has reacted to the rising yen in recent years. Maintaining multiple manufacturing sites, however, may prevent the firm from taking advantage of economies of scale, raising its cost of production. The resultant higher cost can partially offset the advantages of maintaining multiple production sites.

Flexible Sourcing Policy 弹性采购政策

在20世纪80年代初期，美元比大多数主要货币要强势，美国跨国公司经常从外国供应商手中购入低成本的原材料和零部件，以避免因价格高而被挤出市场的厄运。

Even if the firm has manufacturing facilities only in the domestic country, it can substantially lessen the effect of exchange rate changes by sourcing from where input costs are low. In the early 1980s when the dollar was very strong against most major currencies, U.S. multinational firms often purchased materials and components from low-cost foreign suppliers in order to keep themselves from being priced out of the market.

Facing the strong yen in recent years, many Japanese firms are adopting the same practices. It is well known that Japanese manufacturers, especially in the car and consumer electronics industries, depend heavily on parts and intermediate products from such low-cost countries as Thailand, Malaysia, and China. Flexible sourcing need not be confined just to materials and parts. Firms can also hire low-cost guest workers from foreign countries instead of high-cost domestic workers in order to be competitive. For example, Japan Airlines is known to heavily hire foreign crews to stay competitive in international routes in face of a strong yen.

Diversification of the Market 市场分散化

另一种应对外汇风险暴露的方法是尽可能使产品销售市场分散化。

Another way of dealing with exchange exposure is to diversify the market for the firm's products as much as possible. Suppose that General Electric (GE) is selling power generators in Mexico as well as in Germany. Reduced sales in Mexico due to the dollar appreciation against the peso can be compensated by increased sales in Germany due to the dollar depreciation against the euro. As a result, GE's overall cash flows will be much more stable than would be the case if GE sold only in one foreign market, either Mexico or Germany. As long as exchange rates do not always move in the same direction, the firm can stabilize its operating cash flows by diversifying its export market.

Porsche Powers Profit With Currency Plays

Stephen Power

Frankfurt

The weak dollar is denting many European car makers, but Porsche AG may have found a way of using the ailing buck to rev up its results.

Investment analysts believe sophisticated currency bets—not sports cars like the 911—are turbo-charging Porsche's profits. Goldman Sachs, for one, estimates that as much as 75% of the company's pretax profits—or up to 800 million ($1.07 billion) of the €1.1 billion Porsche reported for the fiscal year that ended July 31—came from skillfully executing currency options. Other analysts say that percentage is too high, but most European auto watchers agree that Porsche probably racks up a big chunk of its operating profit from crafty currency plays.

The company declined to make Chief Financial Officer Holger Haerter available to comment on its foreign-exchange profits. A spokesman, Manfred Ayasse, acknowledges that Porsche's hedging generates a profit and is an important part of its overall strategy. Porsche currency exposure is fully hedged through July 31, 2007, and the auto maker is working to extend its protection well beyond that date, he adds. "Fully hedged" refers to taking currency positions that aim to protect all of a company's earnings from movements in the foreign-exchange market, but currency options and other derivatives can also become profit centers depending on how well a company makes its bets.

Without elaborating, Mr. Ayasse says Goldman's estimate of Porsche's currency earnings is "far too high," and "by far the majority" of Porsche's profits come from selling cars.

Among other analysts, Michael Raab at Sal. Oppenheim & Cie. in Frankfurt and Stephen Cheetham at Sanford C. Bernstein in London believe Porsche is getting 40% to 50% of its pretax profit from hedging.

Porsche's apparent success in turning a profit while weathering the dollar's dips is rare these days, though auto makers have been able to do so in the past. For example, even as its North American unit struggled last year, Daimler-Chrysler AG earned hundreds of millions of euros on currency hedges.

Typically, however, the strong euro makes German cars, French wines or British drugs more expensive for customers who pay in dollars and harms European manufacturers.

Among car makers, Volkswagen AG expects a $1.3 billion loss in North America this year, largely as a result of the euro's strength. Ford Motor Co.'s Jaguar unit has cited

---

有时，人们认为公司可以通过在不同行业的分散化经营来降低外汇风险暴露。

It is sometimes argued that the firm can reduce currency exposure by diversifying across different business lines. The idea is that although each individual business may be exposed to exchange risk to some degree, the firm as a whole may not face a significant exposure. It is pointed out, however, that the firm should not get into new lines of business solely to diversify exchange risk because conglomerate expansion can bring about inefficiency and losses. Expansion into a new business should be justified on its own right.

R&D Efforts and Product Differentiation

Investment in R&D activities can allow the firm to maintain and strengthen its competitive position in the face of adverse exchange rate movements. Successful R&D efforts allow the firm to cut costs and enhance productivity. In addition, R&D efforts can lead to the introduction of new and unique products for which competitors offer no close substitutes. Since the demand for unique products tends to be highly inelastic (i.e., price insensitive), the firm would be less exposed to exchange risk. At the same time, the firm can strive to create a perception among consumers that its product is indeed different from those offered by competitors. Once the firm's product acquires a unique identity, its demand is less likely to be price-sensitive.

一旦公司的产品获得惟一认可，对该产品的需求就不易受价格变化的影响。

Volvo, a Swedish automobile manufacturer, provides a good example here. The company has invested heavily in strengthening safety features of its cars and successfully established its reputation as the producer of safe cars. This reputation, reinforced by a focused marketing campaign, "Volvo for Life," helped the company to carve out a niche among safety-minded consumers in highly competitive world automobile markets.

the dollar's slide as contributing to its decision this year to cut output by 12%. BMW AG and Daimler Chrysler's Mercedes division have been hurt less because, unlike Porsche and Volkswagen, both operate U.S. plants that export cars in Europe, providing a natural hedge against exchange-rate swings.

At late afternoon in New York yesterday, the dollar was trading at $1.347, near its all-time low, against the euro. (See related article on page C2.)

Pinpointing how much Porsche makes from currency options is difficult, because the family-controlled company reports earnings only twice a year. The company also provides fewer details about its accounting practices than other automakers.

But in its report, Goldman points out that Porsche books hedging profits in the cost-of-materials line in its profit-and-loss statement. The investment bank notes that in fiscal 2002–03 Porsche's raw material costs fell 7%—even though the company built 33% more cars than the year before. Goldman says falling development costs and other savings are "insufficient" to generate such a drop.

Porsche won't describe its hedging technique, but Goldman Sachs believes the car maker essentially bets on a weak dollar, by buying from another party-presumably a bank-an option to exchange dollars for euros at an artificially low exchange rate for the euro-for example, 96 U.S. cents to one euro.

If the dollar's value on the open market falls below that level-to, say, $1.20 for one euro—Porsche gets a hefty cash payout, Goldman writes. Conversely, if the dollar strengthens, the only losses Porsche incurs are the premiums it has paid for buying those options. Although those premiums are high—around 2% annually of the total amount Porsche wants to hedge, or $20 million on hypothetical U.S. revenues of $1 billion—Porsche can afford them, since its profit margins are among the highest in the industry.

Goldman Sachs says Porsche's profit levels are unsustainable. Mr. Cheetham, the Bernstein analyst, agrees. "Hedging is just a short-run thing," he says.

Predicting the dollar's swings is critical for Porsche. It makes its cars entirely in Europe, but generates 40% or 45% of its sales in the U.S. During the late 1980s and early 1990s, Porsche made little effort to shield itself from currency effects, raising prices as often as three times a year in response to a weak dollar. The result: Porsche's U.S. sales slid from 30,000 cars in 1986 to 4,500 in 1992.

Mr. Ayasse acknowledges the company raised its prices too often, but says other car makers "made this error, too." "We don't want to see negative surprises in the forthcoming years," he adds.

Source: The Wall Street Journal (December 8, 2004), p. C3. Reprinted with permission.

Financial Hedging

经营套期保值
金融套期保值

金融套期保值虽然不能取代上面讨论的长期的经营套期保值方法，但也可用来稳定公司的现金流。

While not a substitute for the long-term, **operational hedging** approaches discussed above, **financial hedging** can be used to stabilize the firm's cash flows. For example, the firm can lend or borrow foreign currencies on a long-term basis. Or, the firm can use currency forward or options contracts and roll them over if necessary. It is noted that existing financial contracts are designed to hedge against nominal, rather than real, changes in exchange rates. Since the firm's competitive position is affected by real changes in exchange rates, financial contracts can at best provide an approximate hedge against the firm's operating exposure. However, if operational hedges, which involve redeployment of resources, are costly or impractical, financial contracts can provide the firm with a flexible and economical way of dealing with exchange exposure. The International Finance in Practice box, "Porsche Powers Profit With Currency Plays," explains how the German car maker deals with currency exposure with financial hedging.

| CASE APPLICATION | Exchange Risk Management at Merck[3] |

To further examine how companies actually manage exchange risk exposure, we choose Merck & Co. Incorporated, a major U.S. pharmaceutical company, and study its approach to overall exchange exposure management. While Merck's actual hedging decision reflects its own particular business situation, the basic framework for dealing with currency exposure can be informative for other firms.

[3]This case is adopted from Lewent and Kearney (1990).

Merck & Co. primarily develops, produces, and markets health care pharmaceuticals. As a multinational company that operates in more than 100 countries, Merck had worldwide sales of $6.6 billion in 1989, and it controlled about a 4.7 percent market share worldwide. Merck's major foreign competitors are European firms and emerging Japanese firms. Merck is among the most internationally oriented U.S. pharmaceutical companies, with overseas assets accounting for about 40 percent of the firm's total and with roughly 50 percent of its sales overseas.

As is typical in the pharmaceutical industry, Merck established overseas subsidiaries. These subsidiaries number about 70 and are responsible for finishing imported products and marketing in the local markets of incorporation. Sales are denominated in local currencies, and thus the company is directly affected by exchange rate fluctuations. Costs are incurred partly in the U.S. dollar for basic manufacturing and research and partly in terms of local currency for finishing, marketing, distribution, and so on. Merck found that costs and revenues were not matched in individual currencies mainly because of the concentration of research, manufacturing, and headquarters operations in the United States.

To reduce the currency mismatch, Merck first considered the possibility of redeploying resources in order to shift dollar costs to other currencies. The company, however, decided that relocating employees and manufacturing and research sites was not a practical and cost-effective way of dealing with exchange exposure. Having decided that operational hedging was not appropriate, Merck considered the alternative of financial hedging. Merck developed a five-step procedure for financial hedging:

1. Exchange forecasting.

2. Assessing strategic plan impact.

3. Hedging rationale.

4. Financial instruments.

5. Hedging program.

Step 1: Exchange Forecasting
The first step involves reviewing the likelihood of adverse exchange movements. The treasury staff estimates possible ranges for dollar strength or weakness over the five-year planning horizon. In doing so, the major factors expected to influence exchange rates, such as the U.S. trade deficit, capital flows, the U.S. budget deficit, and government policies regarding exchange rates, are considered. Outside forecasters are also polled on the outlook for the dollar over the planning horizon.

Step 2: Assessing Strategic Plan Impact
Once the future exchange rate ranges are estimated, cash flows and earnings are projected and compared under the alternative exchange rate scenarios, such as strong dollar and weak dollar. These projections are made on a five-year cumulative basis rather than on a year-to-year basis because cumulative results provide more useful information concerning the magnitude of exchange exposure associated with the company's long-range plan.

Step 3: Deciding Whether to Hedge
In deciding whether to hedge exchange exposure, Merck focused on the objective of maximizing long-term cash flows and on the potential effect of exchange rate movements on the firm's ability to meet its strategic objectives. This focus is ultimately intended to maximize shareholder wealth. Merck decided to hedge for two main reasons. First, the company has a large portion of earnings generated overseas while a disproportionate share of costs is incurred in dollars. Second, volatile cash flows can adversely affect the

EXHIBIT 9.12

Cash Flows Unhedged versus Hedged

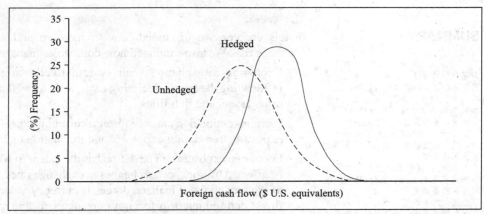

Source: J. Lewent and J. Kearney, "Identifying, Measuring, and Hedging Currency Risk at Merck." Reprinted with permission from the Bank of America Journal of Applied Corporate Finance, Winter 1990.

firm's ability to implement the strategic plan, especially investments in R&D that form the basis for future growth. To succeed in a highly competitive industry, the company needs to make a long-term commitment to a high level of research funding. But the cash flow uncertainty caused by volatile exchange rates makes it difficult to justify a high level of research spending. Management decided to hedge in order to reduce the potential effect of volatile exchange rates on future cash flows.

Step 4: Selecting the Hedging Instruments

The objective was to select the most cost-effective hedging tool that accommodated the company's risk preference. Among various hedging tools, such as forward currency contracts, foreign currency borrowing, and currency options, Merck chose currency options because it was not willing to forgo the potential gains if the dollar depreciated against foreign currencies as it has been doing against major currencies since the mid-eighties. Merck regarded option costs as premiums for the insurance policy designed to preserve its ability to implement the strategic plan.

Step 5: Constructing a Hedging Program

Having selected currency options as the key hedging vehicle, the company still had to formulate an implementation strategy regarding the term of the hedge, the strike price of the currency options, and the percentage of income to be covered. After simulating the outcomes of alternative implementation strategies under various exchange rate scenarios, Merck decided to (1) hedge for a multiyear period using long-dated options contracts, rather than hedge year-by-year, to protect the firm's strategic cash flows, (2) not use far out-of-money options to save costs, and (3) hedge only on a partial basis, with the remainder self-insured.

To help formulate the most cost-effective hedging program, Merck developed a computer-based model that simulates the effectiveness of various hedging strategies. Exhibit 9.12 provides an example of simulation results, comparing distributions of hedged and unhedged cash flows. Obviously, the hedged cash flow distribution has a higher mean and a lower standard deviation than the unhedged cash flow distribution. As we discuss in Chapter 8, hedging may not only reduce risk but also increase cash flows if a reduced risk lowers the firm's cost of capital and tax liabilities. In this scenario, hedging is preferred to no hedging.

SUMMARY

本章我们讨论了如何度量和管理汇率风险的经济风险暴露，也考察了实际中公司是如何管理外汇风险的。

1. 汇率变化会影响企业的现金流和以本币计量的资产和负债的价值，从而对企业的价值产生系统影响。

2. 外汇风险暴露常常被分为三类：经济风险暴露、交易风险暴露和换算风险暴露。

3. 经济风险暴露是指汇率的不可预期变化对企业价值的影响程度。交易风险暴露是指公司的契约性外币现金流的本币价值对不可预期的汇率变化的敏感程度。换算风险暴露是指汇率变化对公司合并财务报表的潜在影响程度。

4. 若公司在国外拥有资产，其外汇风险暴露可用外国资产的美元价值对汇率的回归系数来衡量。如果风险大小已知，公司就可简单地通过卖出远期外汇来对风险进行套期保值。

5. 资产和负债的风险暴露可明确地体现在会计报表中，但经营风险暴露取决于汇率的随机变化对公司未来现金流的影响。不过，这种影响很难度量。尽管如此，对经营风险暴露的管理常常十分重要，因为在公司的全部风险暴露中，经营风险比契约性风险占有更大的比例。

6. 公司的经营风险暴露由以下因素决定：(1) 公司的原材料市场和产品销售市场的结构，(2) 公司通过调整市场、产品组合和资源获取渠道来降低汇率变化影响的能力。

7. 由于公司的汇率风险主要来自汇率变化对其竞争地位的影响，因此，汇率风险管理在公司的长期战略计划中占有非常重要的地位。风险暴露管理的目的就是在汇率波动时维持现金流的稳定。

8. 公司可以通过各种策略来管理经营风险暴露，例如：(1) 选择低成本生产基地，(2) 灵活的原材料采购政策，(3) 市场多元化，(4) 产品差异化，(5) 利用货币期权和远期合约的金融套期保值。

In this chapter, we discussed how to measure and manage economic exposure to exchange risk. We also examined how companies manage currency risk in the real world.

1. Exchange rate changes can systematically affect the value of the firm by influencing the firm's operating cash flows as well as the domestic currency values of its assets and liabilities.

2. It is conventional to classify foreign currency exposure into three classes: economic exposure, transaction exposure, and translation exposure.

3. Economic exposure can be defined as the extent to which the value of the firm would be affected by unexpected changes in exchange rates. Transaction exposure is defined as the sensitivity of realized domestic currency values of the firm's contractual cash flows denominated in foreign currencies to unexpected exchange rate changes. Translation exposure, on the other hand, refers to the potential that the firm's consolidated financial statements can be affected by changes in exchange rates.

4. If the firm has an asset in a foreign country, its exposure to currency risk can be properly measured by the coefficient in regressing the dollar value of the foreign asset on the exchange rate. Once the magnitude of exposure is known, the firm can hedge the exposure simply by selling the exposure forward.

5. Unlike the exposure of assets and liabilities that are listed in accounting statements, operating exposure depends on the effect of random exchange rate changes on the firm's future cash flows, which are not readily measurable. Despite this difficulty, it is important to properly manage operating exposure since operating exposure may account for a larger portion of the firm's total exposure than contractual exposure.

6. A firm's operating exposure is determined by (a) the structure of the markets in which the firm sources its inputs and sells its products, and (b) the firm's ability to mitigate the effect of exchange rate changes on its competitive position by adjusting markets, product mix, and sourcing.

7. Since a firm is exposed to exchange risk mainly via the effect of exchange rate changes on its competitive position, it is important to consider exchange exposure management in the context of the firm's overall long-term strategic plan. The objective of exposure management is to stabilize cash flow in the face of fluctuating exchange rates.

8. To manage operating exposure, the firm can use various strategies, such as (a) choosing low-cost production sites, (b) maintaining flexible sourcing policy, (c) diversification of the market, (d) product differentiation, and (e) financial hedging using currency options and forward contracts.

KEY WORDS

asset exposure, *229*
competitive effect, *230*
conversion effect, *230*
diversification of the market, *235*
economic exposure, *227*
elasticity of demand, *231*

exchange rate pass-through, *232*
exposure coefficient, *226*
financial hedges, *237*
flexible sourcing policy, *235*

operating exposure, *229*
operational hedges, *237*
product differentiation, *236*
transaction exposure, *227*

QUESTIONS

1. How would you define economic exposure to exchange risk?

2. Explain the following statement: "Exposure is the regression coefficient."

3. Suppose that your company has an equity position in a French firm. Discuss the condition under which dollar/euro exchange rate uncertainty does not constitute exchange exposure for your company.

4. Explain the competitive and conversion effects of exchange rate changes on the firm's operating cash flow.

5. Discuss the determinants of operating exposure.

6. Discuss the implications of purchasing power parity for operating exposure.

7. General Motors exports cars to Spain, but the strong dollar against the euro hurts sales of GM cars in Spain. In the Spanish market, GM faces competition from Italian and French car makers, such as Fiat and Renault, whose operating currencies are the euro. What kind of measures would you recommend so that GM can maintain its market share in Spain?

8. What are the advantages and disadvantages to a firm of financial hedging of its operating exposure compared to operational hedges (such as relocating its manufacturing site)?

9. Discuss the advantages and disadvantages of maintaining multiple manufacturing sites as a hedge against exchange rate exposure.

10. Evaluate the following statement: "A firm can reduce its currency exposure by diversifying across different business lines."

11. Exchange rate uncertainty may not necessarily mean that firms face exchange risk exposure. Explain why this may be the case.

PROBLEMS

1. Suppose that you hold a piece of land in the city of London that you may want to sell in one year. As a U.S. resident, you are concerned with the dollar value of the land. Assume that if the British economy booms in the future, the land will be worth £2,000, and one British pound will be worth $1.40. If the British economy slows down, on the other hand, the land will be worth less, say, £1,500, but the pound will be stronger, say, $1.50/£. You feel that the British economy will experience a boom with a 60 percent probability and a slowdown with a 40 percent probability.

   a. Estimate your exposure (*b*) to the exchange risk.

   b. Compute the variance of the dollar value of your property that is attributable to exchange rate uncertainty.

   c. Discuss how you can hedge your exchange risk exposure and also examine the consequences of hedging.

2. A U.S. firm holds an asset in France and faces the following scenario:

	State 1	State 2	State 3	State 4
Probability	25%	25%	25%	25%
Spot rate	$1.20/€	$1.10/€	$1.00/€	$0.90/€
P*	€ 1,500	€ 1,400	€ 1,300	€ 1,200
P	$1,800	$1,540	$1,300	$1,080

In the above table, P^* is the euro price of the asset held by the U.S. firm and P is the dollar price of the asset.

   a. Compute the exchange exposure faced by the U.S. firm.

   b. What is the variance of the dollar price of this asset if the U.S. firm remains unhedged against this exposure?

   c. If the U.S. firm hedges against this exposure using a forward contract, what is the variance of the dollar value of the hedged position?

3. Suppose you are a British venture capitalist holding a major stake in an e-commerce start-up in Silicon Valley. As a British resident, you are concerned with the pound value of your U.S. equity position. Assume that if the American economy booms in the future, your equity stake will be worth $1,000,000, and the exchange rate will be $1.40/£. If the American economy experiences a recession, on the other hand, your American equity stake will be worth $500,000, and the exchange rate will be $1.60/£. You assess that the American economy will experience a boom with a 70 percent probability and a recession with a 30 percent probability.

   a. Estimate your exposure to the exchange risk.

   b. Compute the variance of the pound value of your American equity position that is attributable to the exchange rate uncertainty.

   c. How would you hedge this exposure? If you hedge, what is the variance of the pound value of the hedged position?

INTERNET EXERCISES

Coca-Cola, a well-known U.S. multinational company, derives about three-quarters of its revenue from overseas markets. It is thus highly likely that the company is exposed to currency risks. Investigate the company's exchange risk management policies and practices from its Annual Report (10-K) filed with the Securities and Exchange Commission (SEC) of the United States, especially the "Financial Risk Management" section, which are available from the following website: www.sec.gov/edgar.

How would you evaluate Coca-Cola's approach to exchange risk management?

MINI CASE

Economic Exposure of Albion Computers PLC

Consider Case 3 of Albion Computers PLC discussed in the chapter. Now, assume that the pound is expected to depreciate to $1.50 from the current level of $1.60 per pound. This implies that the pound cost of the imported part, that is, Intel's microprocessors, is £341 (=$512/$1.50). Other variables, such as the unit sales volume and the U.K. inflation rate, remain the same as in Case 3.

   a. Compute the projected annual cash flow in dollars.

   b. Compute the projected operating gains/losses over the four-year horizon as the discounted present value of change in cash flows, which is due to the pound depreciation, from the benchmark case presented in Exhibit 9.6.

   c. What actions, if any, can Albion take to mitigate the projected operating losses due to the pound depreciation?

REFERENCES & SUGGESTED READINGS

Adler, Michael, and Bernard Dumas. "Exposure to Currency Risk: Definition and Measurement." *Financial Management,* Spring (1984), pp. 41–50.

Allayannis, George, and Eli Ofek. "Exchange Rate Exposure, Hedging, and the Use of Foreign Currency Derivatives." *Journal of International Money and Finance* 20 (2001), pp. 273–96.

Bartov, Eli, and Gordon Bodnar. "Firm Valuation, Earnings Expectations, and the Exchange-Rate Exposure Effect." *Journal of Finance* 49, 1994, pp. 1755–85.

Choi, Jongmoo, and Anita Prasad. "Exchange Rate Sensitivity and Its Determinants: A Firm and Industry Analysis of U.S. Multinationals." *Financial Management* 23 (1995), pp. 77–88.

Dornbusch, Rudiger. "Exchange Rates and Prices." *American Economic Review* 77, 1987, pp. 93–106.

Dufey, Gunter, and S. L. Srinivasulu. "The Case for Corporate Management of Foreign Exchange Risk." *Financial Management,* Winter (1983), pp. 54–62.

Eaker, Mark. "The Numeraire Problem and Foreign Exchange Risk." *Journal of Finance,* May 1981, pp. 419–27.

Flood, Eugene, and Donald Lessard. "On the Measurement of Operating Exposure to Exchange Rates: A Conceptual Approach." *Financial Management* 15, Spring (1986), pp. 25–36.

Glaum, M., M. Brunner, and H. Himmel. "The DAX and the Dollar: The Economic Exchange Rate Exposure of German Corporations." Working Paper, Europa-Universitat Viadrina, 1998.

Hekman, Christine R. "Don't Blame Currency Values for Strategic Errors." *Midland Corporate Finance Journal,* Fall (1986), pp. 45–55.

Jacque, Laurent. "Management of Foreign Exchange Risk: A Review Article." *Journal of International Business Studies,* Spring (1981), pp. 81–100.

Jorion, Philippe. "The Exchange-Rate Exposure of U.S. Multinationals." *Journal of Business* 63 (1990), pp. 331–45.

Lessard, Donald, and S. B. Lightstone. "Volatile Exchange Rates Can Put Operations at Risk." *Harvard Business Review,* July/August 1986, pp. 107–14.

Lewent, Judy, and John Kearney. "Identifying, Measuring and Hedging Currency Risk at Merck." *Journal of Applied Corporate Finance,* Winter (1990), pp. 19–28.

Pringle, John, and Robert Connolly. "The Nature and Causes of Foreign Currency Exposure." *Journal of Applied Corporate Finance,* Fall (1993), pp. 61–72.

Simkins, Berry, and Paul Laux. "Derivatives Use and the Exchange Rate Risk of Investing in Large U.S. Corporations." Case Western Reserve University Working Paper (1996).

Wihlborg, Clas. "Economics of Exposure Management of Foreign Subsidiaries of Multinational Corporations." *Journal of International Business Studies,* Winter (1980), pp. 9–18.

Williamson, Rohan. "Exchange Rate Exposure and Competition: Evidence from the Automotive Industry." *Journal of Financial Economics* 59 (2001), pp. 441–75.

Yang, Jiawen. "Exchange Rate Pass-through in U.S. Manufacturing Industries." *Review of Economics and Statistics* 79 (1997), pp. 95–104.

10 Management of Translation Exposure

换算风险暴露常称做会计风险暴露，指汇率发生的预期外变化对跨国公司合并财务报表所产生的影响。

THIS CHAPTER CONCLUDES our discussion of foreign exchange exposure and management. In it we discuss translation exposure. **Translation exposure,** also frequently called *accounting exposure,* refers to the effect that an unanticipated change in exchange rates will have on the consolidated financial reports of a MNC. When exchange rates change, the value of a foreign subsidiary's assets and liabilities denominated in a foreign currency change when they are viewed from the perspective of the parent firm. Consequently, there must be a mechanical means for handling the consolidation process for MNCs that logically deals with exchange rate changes.

本章介绍了处理换算调整的基本方法。

This chapter presents the basic methods of handling translation adjustments. We present an example of a simple consolidation using the different methods for handling translation adjustments so that the effects of the various methods can be compared. Special consideration is given to recently prescribed methods of the Financial Accounting Standards Board (FASB), the authoritative body in the United States that specifies accounting policy for U.S. business firms and certified public accounting firms. However, translation methods used in other major developed countries are also briefly examined.

We use a case application to explore at length the impact of exchange rate changes on the consolidation process according to the currently prescribed FASB statement. Following this, the relationships between translation exposure and economic exposure and translation exposure and transaction exposure are addressed. Next, the need for, and methods for, managing translation exposure are examined. The chapter concludes with a discussion of an empirical analysis of the effect on firm value of a change in translation methods.

Translation Methods

近年来，企业主要采用四种外币换算方法：流动和非流动法、货币和非货币法、时态法和现行汇率法。

Four methods of foreign currency translation have been used in recent years: the current/noncurrent method, the monetary/nonmonetary method, the temporal method, and the current rate method.

Current/Noncurrent Method 流动及非流动法

www.fasb.org

This is the website of the Financial Accounting Standards Board. Information about FASB and FASB statements can be found here.

若使用流动和非流动法，大多数利润表项目则要按照会计期间内的平均汇率进行换算。

The **current/noncurrent method** of foreign currency translation was generally accepted in the United States from the 1930s until 1975, when FASB 8 became effective. The underlying principle of this method is that assets and liabilities should be translated based on their maturity. Current assets and liabilities, which by definition have a maturity of one year or less, are converted at the current exchange rate. Noncurrent assets and liabilities are translated at the historical exchange rate in effect at the time the asset or liability was first recorded on the books. Under this method, a foreign subsidiary with current assets in excess of current liabilities will cause a translation gain (loss) if the local currency appreciates (depreciates). The opposite will happen if there is negative net working capital in local terms in the foreign subsidiary.

Most income statement items under this method are translated at the average exchange rate for the accounting period. However, revenue and expense items that are associated with noncurrent assets or liabilities, such as depreciation expense, are translated at the historical rate that applies to the applicable balance sheet item.

Monetary/ Nonmonetary Method 货币及非货币法

According to the **monetary/nonmonetary** method, all monetary balance sheet accounts (for example, cash, marketable securities, accounts receivable, notes payable, accounts payable) of a foreign subsidiary are translated at the current exchange rate. All other (nonmonetary) balance sheet accounts, including stockholders' equity, are translated at the historical exchange rate in effect when the account was first recorded. In comparison to the current/noncurrent method, this method differs substantially with respect to accounts such as inventory, long-term receivables, and long-term debt. The underlying philosophy of the monetary/nonmonetary method is that monetary accounts have a similarity because their value represents a sum of money whose currency equivalent after translation changes each time the exchange rate changes. This method classifies accounts on the basis of similarity of attributes rather than similarity of maturities.

按照时态法，大多数利润表账户按当期平均汇率进行换算。

Under this method, most income statement accounts are translated at the average exchange rate for the period. However, revenue and expense items associated with nonmonetary accounts, such as cost of goods sold and depreciation, are translated at the historical rate associated with the balance sheet account.

Temporal Method 时态法

Under the **temporal** method, monetary accounts such as cash, receivables, and payables (both current and noncurrent) are translated at the current exchange rate. Other balance sheet accounts are translated at the current rate, if they are carried on the books at current value; if they are carried at historical costs, they are translated at the rate of exchange on the date the item was placed on the books. Since fixed assets and inventory are usually carried at historical costs, the temporal method and the monetary/nonmonetary method will typically provide the same translation. Nevertheless, the underlying philosophies of the two methods are entirely different. Under current value accounting, all balance sheet accounts are translated at the current exchange rate.

Under the temporal method, most income statement items are translated at the average exchange rate for the period. Depreciation and cost of goods sold, however, are translated at historical rates if the associated balance sheet accounts are carried at historical costs.

Current Rate Method

采用**现行汇率法**时，全部利润表项目按各项目被确认日的汇率进行换算。

www.duni.com

This website illustrates translation and transaction exposure as reported in the current annual report of a Swedish multinational firm.

累积换算调整数 (CTA)

Under the **current rate** method, all balance sheet accounts are translated at the current exchange rate, except for stockholders' equity. This is the simplest of all translation methods to apply. The common stock account and any additional paid-in capital are carried at the exchange rates in effect on the respective dates of issuance. Year-end retained earnings equal the beginning balance of retained earnings plus any additions for the year. A "plug" equity account named **cumulative translation adjustment (CTA)** is used to make the balance sheet balance, since translation gains or losses do not go through the income statement according to this method.

Under the current rate method, income statement items are to be translated at the exchange rate at the dates the items are recognized. Since this is generally impractical, an appropriately weighted average exchange rate for the period may be used for the translation.

EXAMPLE 10.1

Comparison of Translation Methods   Exhibits 10.1A and 10.1B use examples to present a comparison of the effects of the different translation methods on financial statement preparation. The examples assume that the balance sheet and income statement of a Swiss subsidiary, which keeps its books in Swiss francs, is translated into U.S. dollars, the reporting currency of the MNC.

Exhibit 10.1A first presents the balance sheet and income statement in Swiss francs, from which it can be seen that both additions to retained earnings and accumulated retained earnings are SF900,000. (The example assumes that the subsidiary is at the end of its first year of operation.) The historical exchange rate is SF3.00/$1.00. The next four columns show the translated statements after an assumed appreciation of the Swiss franc to SF2.00/$1.00. The average exchange for the period is thus SF2.50/$1.00. As one can see from the exhibit, total assets vary from $2,550,000 under the monetary/nonmonetary method, which has a foreign exchange loss of $550,000 passed through the income statement, to $3,300,000 under the current rate method, which has an effective foreign exchange gain of $540,000 carried in the cumulative translation adjustment (CTA) account.

Under the temporal method, it is assumed that the firm carries its inventory at the current market value of SF1,800,000 instead of at the historical value of SF1,500,000. Note that the temporal method and the monetary/nonmonetary methods would both translate inventory to a value of $500,000 if the subsidiary was assumed to carry inventory at its historical value under the temporal method.

Exhibit 10.1B also shows the translated balance sheet and income statements after an assumed depreciation of the Swiss franc from SF3.00/$1.00 to SF4.00/$1.00. The average exchange rate for the period is thus SF3.50/$1.00. As the exhibit shows, total assets vary from $1,650,000 under the current rate method, which has an effective foreign exchange loss of $257,000 carried in the CTA account, to $2,025,000 under the monetary/nonmonetary method, which has a foreign exchange gain of $361,000.

EXHIBIT 10.1A	Comparison of Effects of Translation Methods on Financial Statement Preparation after Appreciation from SF 3.00 to SF 2.00 = $1.00 (in 000 Currency Units)				
	Local Currency	Current/ Noncurrent	Monetary/ Nonmonetary	Temporal	Current Rate
Balance Sheet					
Cash	SF 2,100	$1,050	$1,050	$1,050	$1,050
Inventory					
(Current value = SF1,800)	1,500	750	500	900	750
Net fixed assets	3,000	1,000	1,000	1,000	1,500
Total assets	SF 6,600	$2,800	$2,550	$2,950	$3,300
Current liabilities	SF 1,200	$ 600	$ 600	$ 600	$ 600
Long-term debt	1,800	600	900	900	900
Common stock	2,700	900	900	900	900
Retained earnings	900	700	150	550	360
CTA	—	—	—	—	540
Total liabilities and equity	SF 6,600	$2,800	$2,550	$2,950	$3,300
Income Statement					
Sales revenue	SF10,000	$4,000	$4,000	$4,000	$4,000
COGS	7,500	3,000	2,500	3,000	3,000
Depreciation	1,000	333	333	333	400
Net operating income	1,500	667	1,167	667	600
Income tax (40%)	600	267	467	267	240
Profit after tax	900	400	700	400	360
Foreign exchange gain (loss)	—	300	(550)	150	—
Net income	900	700	150	550	360
Dividends	0	0	0	0	0
Addition to retained earnings	SF 900	$ 700	$ 150	$ 550	$ 360

EXHIBIT 10.1B	Comparison of Effects of Translation Methods on Financial Statement Preparation after Depreciation from SF 3.00 to SF 4.00 = $1.00 (in 000 Currency Units)				
	Local Currency	Current/ Noncurrent	Monetary/ Nonmonetary	Temporal	Current Rate
Balance Sheet					
Cash	SF 2,100	$ 525	$ 525	$ 525	$ 525
Inventory					
(Current value = SF1,800)	1,500	375	500	450	375
Net fixed assets	3,000	1,000	1,000	1,000	750
Total assets	SF 6,600	$1,900	$2,025	$1,975	$1,650
Current liabilities	SF 1,200	$ 300	$ 300	$ 300	$ 300
Long-term debt	1,800	600	450	450	450
Common stock	2,700	900	900	900	900
Retained earnings	900	100	375	325	257
CTA	—	—	—	—	(257)
Total liabilities and equity	SF 6,600	$1,900	$2,025	$1,975	$1,650
Income Statement					
Sales revenue	SF10,000	$2,857	$2,857	$2,857	$2,857
COGS	7,500	2,143	2,500	2,143	2,143
Depreciation	1,000	333	333	333	286
Net operating income	1,500	381	24	381	428
Income tax (40%)	600	152	10	152	171
Profit after tax	900	229	14	229	257
Foreign exchange gain (loss)	—	(129)	361	96	—
Net income	900	100	375	325	257
Dividends	0	0	0	0	0
Addition to retained earnings	SF 900	$ 100	$ 375	$ 325	$ 257

Financial Accounting Standards Board Statement 8

《财务会计准则第8号公告》于1976年1月1日生效，其目标是根据公认会计准则，用美元计量跨国公司国外子公司用外币报告的资产、负债、收入及费用。

FASB 8 became effective on January 1, 1976. Its objective was to measure in dollars an enterprise's assets, liabilities, revenues, or expenses that are denominated in a foreign currency according to generally accepted accounting principles. FASB 8 is essentially the temporal method of translation as previously defined, but there are some subtleties. For example, according to the temporal method, revenues and expenses are to be measured at the average exchange rate for the period. In practice, MNCs prepare monthly statements. What is done is to cumulate the monthly figures to obtain the total for the year.

FASB 8 ran into acceptance problems from the accounting profession and MNCs from the very beginning. The temporal method requires taking foreign exchange gains or losses through the income statement, as was demonstrated in Example 10.1. Consequently, reported earnings could, and did, fluctuate substantially from year to year, which was irritating to corporate executives.

Additionally, many MNCs did not like translating inventory at historical rates, which was required if the firm carried the inventory at historical values, as most did, and do. It was felt that it would be much simpler to translate at the current rate.

Financial Accounting Standards Board Statement 52

www.iasb.org.

This is the website of the International Accounting Standards Board. Information about the organization and its mission can be found at this site.

Given the controversy surrounding FASB 8, a proposal was put on the agenda of the FASB in January 1979 to consider all features of FASB 8. Subsequently, in February 1979, a task force was established with representatives of the board, the International Accounting Standards Committee (now the International Accounting Standards Board), and the accounting standards bodies from Canada and the United Kingdom. After many meetings and hearings, FASB 52 was issued in December 1981, and all U.S. MNCs were required to adopt the statement for fiscal years beginning on or after December 15, 1982.

The stated objectives of FASB 52 are to:

a. Provide information that is generally compatible with the expected economic effects of a rate change on an enterprise's cash flows and equity; and
b. Reflect in consolidated statements the financial results and relationships of the individual consolidated entities as measured in their functional currencies in conformity with U.S. generally accepted accounting principles.[1]

本位币

Many discussions of FASB 52 claim that it is a current rate method of translation. This, however, is a misnomer, as FASB 52 requires the current rate method of translation in some circumstances and the temporal method in others. Which method of translation is prescribed by FASB 52 depends upon the functional currency used by the foreign subsidiary whose statements are to be translated. The **functional currency** is defined in FASB 52 as "the currency of the primary economic environment in which the entity operates."[2] Normally, that is the local currency of the country in which the entity conducts most of its business. However, under certain circumstances, the functional currency may be the parent firm's home country currency or some third-country currency. Exhibit 10.2 summarizes the method for determining the functional currency.

报告货币是指跨国公司在编制合并财务报表时所采用的货币。

The **reporting currency** is defined as the currency in which the MNC prepares its consolidated financial statements. That currency is usually the currency in which the parent firm keeps its books, which in turn is usually the currency of the country in

---

[1]See FASB 52, paragraph 4.
[2]See FASB 52, paragraph 5.

Cash Flow Indicators
Foreign Currency: Foreign entity's cash flows are primarily in foreign currency and they do not directly affect the parent firm's cash flows.
Parent's Currency: Foreign entity's cash flows directly affect the parent's cash flows and are readily available for remittance to the parent firm.

Sales Price Indicators
Foreign Currency: Sales prices for the foreign entity's products are generally not responsive on a short-term basis to exchange rate changes, but are determined more by local competition and government regulation.
Parent's Currency: Sales prices for the foreign entity's products are responsive on a short-term basis to exchange rate changes, where sales prices are determined through worldwide competition.

Sales Market Indicators
Foreign Currency: There is an active local sales market for the foreign entity's products.
Parent's Currency: The sales market is primarily located in the parent's country or sales contracts are denominated in the parent's currency.

Expense Indicators
Foreign Currency: Factor of production costs of the foreign entity are primarily local costs.
Parent's Currency: Factor of production costs of the foreign entity are primarily, and on a continuing basis, costs for components obtained from the parent's country.

Financing Indicators
Foreign Currency: Financing of the foreign entity is primarily denominated in the foreign currency and the debt service obligations are normally handled by the foreign entity.
Parent's Currency: Financing of the foreign entity is primarily from the parent, with debt service obligations met by the parent, or the debt service obligations incurred by the foreign entity are primarily made by the parent.

Intercompany Transactions and Arrangements Indicators
Foreign Currency: There is a low volume of intercompany transactions and a minor interrelationship of operations between the foreign entity and the parent. However, the foreign entity may benefit from competitive advantages of the parent, such as patents or trademarks.
Parent's Currency: There is a large volume of intercompany transactions and an extensive interrelationship of operations between the foreign entity and the parent. Moreover, if the foreign entity is only a shell company for carrying accounts that could be carried on the parent's books, the functional currency would generally be the parent's currency.

Source: Excerpted from *Foreign Currency Translation, Statement of Financial Accounting Standards No. 52*, Paragraph 42, Financial Accounting Standards Board, Stamford, CT, October 1981. Used by permission.

which the parent is located and conducts most of its business. However, the reporting currency could be some third currency. For our purposes in this chapter, the terms reporting currency and parent currency will be used synonymously, and will be assumed to be the U.S. dollar.

The Mechanics of the FASB 52 Translation Process

The actual translation process prescribed by FASB 52 is a two-stage process. First, it is necessary to determine in which currency the foreign entity keeps its books. If the local currency in which the foreign entity keeps its books is not the functional currency (and, as shown in Exhibit 10.3, it does not have to be), remeasurement into the functional currency is required. *Remeasurement* is intended "to produce the same result as if the entity's books had been maintained in the functional currency."[3] The temporal method of translation is used to accomplish the remeasurement. Second, when the

---
[3]See FASB 52, paragraph 10.

EXHIBIT 10.3

FASB 52 Two-Stage
Translation Process[a]

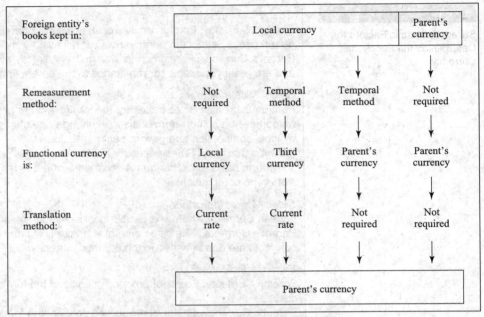

[a]The translation process prescribed by FASB 52 is a two-stage process. First, if the local currency in which the foreign entity keeps its books is not the functional currency, remeasurement by the temporal method is required. Second, when the foreign entity's functional currency is not the same as the parent's currency, the foreign entity's books are translated from the functional currency into the reporting currency using the current rate method. If the foreign entity is in a highly inflationary economy, FASB 52 requires that the local currency be remeasured into the parent's currency.
Source: Derived from J. S. Arpan and L. H. Radenbaugh, *International Accounting and Multinational Enterprises,* 2nd ed. (New York: Wiley, 1985), Exhibit 5.2, p. 136, and Andrew A. Haried, Leroy F. Imdieke, and Ralph E. Smith, *Advanced Accounting,* 6th ed. (New York: Wiley, 1994), Illustration 15-3, p. 562.

foreign entity's functional currency is not the same as the parent's currency, the foreign entity's books are *translated* from the functional currency into the reporting currency using the current rate method. Obviously, translation is not required if the foreign entity's functional currency is the same as the reporting currency.

Highly Inflationary Economies

高通货膨胀经济是指"三年内的累计通货膨胀率达到约100%或以上"。

In highly inflationary economies, FASB 52 requires that the foreign entity's financial statements be remeasured from the local currency "as if the functional currency were the reporting currency" using the temporal translation method.[4] A highly inflationary economy is defined as "one that has cumulative inflation of approximately 100 percent or more over a 3-year period."[5] The purpose of this requirement is to prevent large important balance sheet accounts, carried at historical values, from having insignificant values once translated into the reporting currency at the current rate. We know that according to relative purchasing power parity a currency from a higher inflationary economy will depreciate relative to the currency of a lower inflationary economy by approximately the differential of the two countries' inflation rates. Hence, for example, the fixed asset account of a foreign entity in a highly inflationary economy, carried on the books in the local currency, would soon lose value relative to the reporting currency, and translate into a relatively insignificant amount in comparison to its true book value. Exhibit 10.3 presents a diagram of the two-stage translation process prescribed by FASB 52. For comparison purposes, Exhibit 10.4 presents foreign-currency translation methods used in other major developed countries.

[4]See FASB 52, paragraph 11.
[5]See FASB 52, paragraph 11.

| **EXHIBIT 10.4** | **Foreign-Currency Translation Methods Used in Other Major Developed Countries** |

Japan

Receivables and payables in foreign currencies must be translated into yen at the end of the accounting period. Both translation gains or losses and realized foreign exchange gains or losses are treated as taxable income or loss and flow through earnings. Historical exchange rates that existed at the transaction date are generally used to record revenue, costs, and expenses resulting from foreign currency transactions.

Short-term foreign currency receivables and payables are translated at the prevailing year-end rate. Long-term foreign currency receivables and payables are translated at the historical rate, except in unusual circumstances. Securities, inventories, and fixed assets are translated at the rate in effect when they were acquired (historical rate).

Any change in the method of translating foreign currencies requires prior approval by tax regulators.

Germany

As of year-end 1992, a common treatment of foreign-currency translation had not been implemented. All translation methods are, in principle, acceptable.

A broad variety of practices are followed, including the (1) current/noncurrent, (2) monetary/nonmonetary, (3) temporal, (4) closing, and (5) current rate methods. Some companies flow translation gains or losses through stockholders' equity, while others flow the impact of foreign-currency translation through the profit and loss account.

France

Many different methods of foreign-currency translation are followed.

GROUP ACCOUNTS:

Most companies appear to use the closing exchange rate for balance sheet translations (translation gains and losses impact shareholders' equity) and the average exchange rate for the income statement.

Differences between income statement and balance sheet translation gains and losses (if different exchange rates are used) would flow through shareholders' equity.

INDIVIDUAL ACCOUNTS:

Detailed rules govern foreign-currency translation in individual company accounts. These give rise to long-term deferred charges and credits.

Unsettled monetary assets and liabilities denominated in a foreign currency must be restated to their closing value at the balance sheet date. Foreign exchange gains are recorded as long-term deferred credits and released when the account is settled.

Foreign exchange losses result in the following entries: (1) The original account is adjusted and a deferred charge appears on the balance sheet; (2) a balance sheet provision is set up, and the income statement is debited.

Foreign-currency translation policies may differ. Some firms only provide against unrealized foreign exchange losses if they exceed unrealized foreign exchange gains. These deferred exchange gains and losses could be offset against each other with the difference applied to the risk provision.

Canada

Foreign exchange gains and losses may be treated differently for book and tax purposes.

REALIZED GAINS AND LOSSES:

The excess of realized foreign exchange gains of a capital nature over realized losses is treated as a capital gain; three-quarters of this capital gain is included in taxable income.

In cases where foreign exchange losses exceed gains, three-quarters of the loss is deductible from other taxable gains. Foreign exchange gains and losses arising from current business transactions of a taxpayer are fully included in income or fully deductible on an accrual basis.

UNREALIZED GAINS AND LOSSES:

Unrealized gains and losses resulting from foreign currency translation are ignored for tax purposes.

However, for accounting purposes (1) unrealized gains or losses related to short-term assets or liabilities are recognized in the current period, and (2) unrealized gains or losses related to long-term assets or liabilities are deferred and amortized over the remaining life of the assets or liability.

Italy

REALIZED GAINS AND LOSSES:

Income, receipts, and expenditures in foreign currency are translated at the exchange rates that existed on the transaction date. These realized gains and losses flow through the income statement.

UNREALIZED GAINS AND LOSSES:

The average exchange rate of the last month of the accounting period is used for foreign-currency translation. Items denominated in foreign currency are originally recorded at the exchange rate that existed on the transaction date.

Unrealized foreign currency translation gains and losses flow through a special provision, impacting shareholders' equity.

United Kingdom

Foreign-currency translation adjustments are disclosed for both individual and group (consolidated) accounts. In cases of consolidation, companies prepare a set of translation accounts for (1) the individual firms within the group and (2) the group as a whole.

(continued)

| EXHIBIT 10.4 | Foreign-Currency Translation Methods Used in Other Major Developed Countries
(concluded) |

INDIVIDUAL COMPANY:
Foreign-currency transactions are generally translated into the home currency of each company using the average rate method. Nonmonetary assets are not restated.

Currency differences flow through the profit and loss account (separately from ongoing businesses) and are shown as discontinued operations. Exchange rate gains and losses related to foreign currency hedging pass through reserves.

GROUP ACCOUNTS:
The average rate/net investment method is commonly used, although the temporal method is also acceptable. Consolidated accounts are prepared in the currency in which the parent company is based.

Investments in the foreign enterprises are represented by the net worth held by the parent. Exchange rate gains or losses that impact the group accounts pass through reserves, with no impact on the group profit and loss account.

Source: © 1993 by Goldman Sachs. By Gabrielle Napolitano, an employee of Goldman Sachs.

CASE APPLICATION

Consolidation of Accounts according to FASB 52: The Centralia Corporation

We use a case application to illustrate consolidating the balance sheet of a MNC according to FASB 52. The basic information is provided in Exhibit 10.5, which shows the unconsolidated balance sheets for Centralia Corporation, a U.S. parent firm, and its two wholly owned affiliates located in Mexico and Spain. Centralia Corporation is a midwestern manufacturer of small kitchen electrical appliances. The Mexican manufacturing affiliate has been established to cater to the Mexican market, which is expected to expand rapidly under NAFTA. Similarly, the Spanish manufacturing affiliate was established to handle demand in the European Union. The functional currency of the Mexican affiliate is the peso, and the euro is the functional currency for the Spanish affiliate. The reporting currency is the U.S. dollar. The initial exchange rates assumed in the example are: $1.00 = CD1.3333 = Ps10.00 = €1.10 = SF1.50.

The nonconsolidated balance sheets and the footnotes to the statements indicate that the Mexican affiliate owes the parent firm Ps3,000,000, which is carried on the parent's books as a $300,000 accounts receivable at the current exchange rate of Ps10.00/$1.00. Additionally, the $2,200,000 investment of the parent firm in the Mexican affiliate is the translated amount of Ps22,000,000 of equity on the Mexican affiliate's books. Similarly, the $1,660,000 investment of the parent in the Spanish affiliate is the translated amount of €1,826,000 of equity on the Spanish affiliate's books. The footnotes also show that the parent firm has CD200,000 deposited in a Canadian bank, carried as $150,000 in the cash account, and the Spanish affiliate has a SF375,000 loan outstanding from a Swiss bank, translated at SF1.3636/€1.00, and carried at €275,000 as part of its €1,210,000 of notes payable.

必须注意：合并时公司内负债和投资进行了抵消。

Exhibit 10.6 shows the process of consolidating the balance sheets for Centralia Corp. and its affiliates. Of importance is to note that *both* intracompany debt *and* investment net out in the consolidation. That is, the Ps3,000,000 owed by the Mexican affiliate to the parent is not reflected in the consolidated accounts receivable nor in the accounts payable. When this debt is eventually paid, in effect it will be the same as taking money out of one company pocket and putting it into another. In a similar vein, the investment of the parent in each affiliate cancels with the net worth of each affiliate. The parent owns the affiliates, and, in turn, the shareholders' investment represents ownership of the parent firm. In this manner, the shareholders own the entire MNC.

因此，合并产生的合并资产负债表在汇率改变后并不一定能平衡。

The consolidation presented in Exhibit 10.6 is rather simplistic. It is nice and neat from the standpoint that the consolidated balance sheet, in fact, balances. That is, total assets

EXHIBIT 10.5	Nonconsolidated Balance Sheet for Centralia Corporation and Its Mexican and Spanish Affiliates, December 31, 2005 (in 000 Currency Units)		
	Centralia Corp. (Parent)	Mexican Affiliate	Spanish Affiliate
Assets			
Cash	$ 950[a]	Ps 6,000	€ 825
Accounts receivable	1,750[b]	9,000	1,045
Inventory	3,000	15,000	1,650
Investment in Mexican affiliate	2,200[c]	—	—
Investment in Spanish affiliate	1,660[d]	—	—
Net fixed assets	9,000	46,000	4,400
Total assets	$18,560	Ps 76,000	€7,920
Liabilities and Net Worth			
Accounts payable	$ 1,800	Ps 10,000[b]	€1,364
Notes payable	2,200	17,000	1,210[e]
Long-term debt	7,110	27,000	3,520
Common stock	3,500	16,000[c]	1,320[d]
Retained earnings	3,950	6,000[c]	506[d]
Total liabilities and net worth	$18,560	Ps 76,000	€7,920

[a]The parent firm has a deposit of CD200,000 in a Canadian bank. This sum is carried on the parent firm's books at $150,000, translated at CD1.3333/$1.00.
[b]The parent firm is owed Ps3,000,000 by the Mexican affiliate. This sum is included in the parent's accounts receivable as $300,000. The remainder of the parent's (Mexican affiliate's) accounts receivable (payable) is denominated in dollars (pesos).
[c]The Mexican affiliate is wholly owned by the parent firm. It is carried on the parent firm's books at $2,200,000. This represents the sum of the common stock (Ps16,000,000) and retained earnings (Ps6,000,000) on the Mexican affiliate's books, translated at Ps10.00/$1.00.
[d]The Spanish affiliate is wholly owned by the parent firm. It is carried on the parent firm's books at $1,660,000. This represents the sum of the common stock (€1,320,000) and the retained earnings (€506,000) on the Spanish affiliate's books, translated at €1.10/$1.00.
[e]The Spanish affiliate has outstanding notes payable of SF375,000 (+SF1.3636/€1.00 = €275,000) from a Swiss bank. This loan is carried on the Spanish affiliate's books as part of the €1,210,000 = €27 5,000 +€935,000.

EXHIBIT 10.6	Consolidated Balance Sheet for Centralia Corporation and Its Mexican and Spanish Affiliates, December 31, 2005: Pre-Exchange Rate Change (in 000 Dollars)			
	Centralia Corp. (Parent)	Mexican Affiliate	Spanish Affiliate	Consolidated Balance Sheet
Assets				
Cash	$ 950[a]	$ 600	$ 750	$ 2,300
Accounts receivable	1,450[b]	900	950	3,300
Inventory	3,000	1,500	1,500	6,000
Investment in Mexican affiliation	—[c]	—	—	—
Investment in Spanish affiliation	—[d]	—	—	—
Net fixed assets	9,000	4,600	4,000	17,600
Total assets				$29,200
Liabilities and Net Worth				
Accounts payable	$1,800	$ 700[b]	$1,240	$ 3,740
Notes payable	2,200	1,700	1,100[e]	5,000
Long-term debt	7,110	2,700	3,200	13,010
Common stock	3,500	—[c]	—[d]	3,500
Retained earnings	3,950	—[c]	—[d]	3,950
Total liabilities and net worth				$29,200

[a]This sum includes CD200,000 the parent firm has on deposit in a Canadian bank, carried on the books as $150,000. CD200,000/(CD1.3333/$1.00) = $150,000.
[b]$1,750,000 − $300,000 (= Ps3,000,000/(Ps10.00/$1.00)) intracompany loan = $1,450,000.
[c,d]The investment in the affiliates cancels with the net worth of the affiliates in the consolidation.
[e]The Spanish affiliate owes a Swiss bank SF375,000 (+ SF1.3636/€1.00 = €275,000). This is carried on the books as part of the €1,210,000 = €275,000 + €935,000. €1,210,000/(€1.10/$1.00) = $1,100,000.

EXHIBIT 10.7	Translation Exposure Report for Centralia Corporation and Its Mexican and Spanish Affiliates, December 31, 2005 (in 000 Currency Units)			
	Canadian Dollar	Mexican Peso	Euro	Swiss Franc
Assets				
Cash	CD200	Ps 6,000	€ 825	SF 0
Accounts receivable	0	9,000	1,045	0
Inventory	0	15,000	1,650	0
Net fixed assets	0	46,000	4,400	0
Exposed assets	CD200	Ps 76,000	€ 7,920	SF 0
Liabilities				
Accounts payable	CD 0	Ps 7,000	€ 1,364	SF 0
Notes payable	0	17,000	935	375
Long-term debt	0	27,000	3,520	0
Exposed liabilities	CD 0	Ps 51,000	€ 5,819	SF 375
Net exposure	CD200	Ps 25,000	€ 2,101	(SF375)

要确定汇率变化对
跨国公司合并财务报告
的影响，有必要编制换
算风险暴露报告。

equal total liabilities and net worth. Implicit in the example are that the current exchange rates used are the same as those used when the affiliates were originally established; that is, they have not changed from that time. Thus, the example is not very realistic even though it properly presents the mechanics of the consolidation process under FASB 52. After all, the central purpose of a translation method is to deal in some systematic way with exchange rate *changes*.

To determine the effect that exchange rate changes will have on the consolidated balance sheet of a MNC, it is useful to prepare a translation exposure report. A **translation exposure report** shows, for each account that is included in the consolidated balance sheet, the amount of foreign exchange exposure that exists for each foreign currency in which the MNC has exposure. Continuing with our example of Centralia Corporation and its affiliates, we know from Exhibit 10.5 that the MNC has foreign exchange exposure from the Mexican peso, euro, Canadian dollar, and Swiss franc. A change in any one of these currency exchange rates versus the reporting currency will have an effect on the consolidated balance sheet if there exists a net translation exposure for that currency.

Exhibit 10.7 presents the translation exposure report for Centralia. The report shows, for each exposure currency, the amount of exposed assets and exposed liabilities denominated in that currency, and the net difference, or net exposure. For the Canadian dollar the net exposure is a positive CD200,000; for the Mexican peso a positive Ps25,000,000; for the euro a positive €2,101,000; and for the Swiss franc a negative SF375,000. A positive net exposure means there are more exposed assets than liabilities, and vice versa for negative net exposure. When the exchange rate of an exposure currency depreciates against the reporting currency, exposed assets fall in translated value by a greater (smaller) amount than exposed liabilities if there is positive (negative) net exposure. Analogously, when an exposure currency appreciates against the reporting currency, exposed assets increase in translated value by a smaller (greater) amount than exposed liabilities if there is negative (positive) net exposure. Consequently, the consolidation process will not result in a consolidated balance sheet that balances after an exchange rate change.

To show the effect on the consolidation process after an exchange rate change, let's perform the consolidation of the nonconsolidated balance sheets from Exhibit 10.5 once again, assuming this time that exchange rates have changed from $1.00 = CD1.3333 = Ps10.00 = €1.10 = SF1.50 to $1.00 = CD1.3333 = Ps10.00 = €1.1786 = SF1.50. We are assuming that only the euro has changed (depreciated) versus all other currencies in order to keep the example simple so as to better decipher the effect of an exchange rate change.

EXHIBIT 10.8	**Consolidated Balance Sheet for Centralia Corporation and Its Mexican and Spanish Affiliates, December 31, 2005: Post-Exchange Rate Change** (in 000 Dollars)			

	Centralia Corp. (Parent)	Mexican Affiliate	Spanish Affiliate	Consolidated Balance Sheet
Assets				
Cash	$ 950[a]	$ 600	$ 700	$ 2,250
Accounts receivable	1,450[b]	900	887	3,237
Inventory	3,000	1,500	1,400	5,900
Investment in Mexican affiliate	—[c]	—		
Investment in Spanish affiliate	—[d]			
Net fixed assets	9,000	4,600	3,733	17,333
Total Assets				$28,720
Liabilities and Net Worth				
Accounts payable	$1,800	$ 700[b]	$1,157	$ 3,657
Notes payable	2,200	1,700	1,043[e]	4,943
Long-term debt	7,110	2,700	2,987	12,797
Common stock	3,500	—[c]	—[d]	3,500
Retained earnings	3,950	—[c]	—[d]	3,950
CTA	—	—	—	(127)
Total liabilities and net worth				$28,720

[a]This includes CD200,000 the parent firm has in a Canadian bank, carried as $150,000. CD200,000/(CD1.3333/$1.00) = $150,000.
[b]$1,750,000 − $300,000 (= Ps3,000,000/(Ps10.00/$1.00)) intracompany loan = $1,450,000.
[c,d]Investment in affiliates cancels with the net worth of the affiliates in the consolidation.
[e]The Spanish affiliate owes a Swiss bank SF375,000 (÷ SF1.2727/€1.00 = €294,649). This is carried on the books, after the exchange rate change, as part of €1,229,649 = €294,649 + €935,000. €1,229,649/(€1.1786/$1.00) = $1,043,313.

To get an overview of the effect of the exchange rate change, recall from Exhibit 10.7 that there is a positive net exposure of €2,101,000. This implies that after the 7.145 percent depreciation from €1.1000/$1.00 to €1.1786/$1.00, the exposed assets denominated in euros will fall in translated value by $127,377 more than the exposed liabilities denominated in euros. This can be calculated as follows:

$$\frac{\text{Net exposure currency } i}{S_{new}[i/\text{reporting}]} - \frac{\text{Net exposure currency } i}{S_{old}[i/\text{reporting}]}$$

= Reporting currency imbalance.

For our example,

$$\frac{€2,101,000}{€1.1786/\$1.00} - \frac{€2,101,000}{€1.1000/\$1.00} = -\$127,377$$

In other words, the net translation exposure of €2,101,000 in dollars is $1,910,000 when translated at the exchange rate of €1.1000/$1.00. A 7.145 percent depreciation of the euro to €1.1786/$1.00 will result in a translation loss of $127,377 = €2,101,000 ÷ 1.1786 × .07145.

Exhibit 10.8 shows the consolidation process and consolidated balance sheet for Centralia Corporation and its two foreign affiliates after the depreciation of the euro. Note that the values for the accounts are the same as in Exhibit 10.6 for the parent firm and the Mexican affiliate. However, the values of the accounts of the Spanish affiliate are different because of the exchange rate change. In order for the consolidated balance sheet to now balance, it is necessary to have a "plug" equity account with a balance of −$127,377. As before, we referred to this special equity account as the cumulative translation adjustment account, or CTA account. The balance of this account at any time represents the accumulated total of all past translation adjustments. FASB 52 handles the effect of exchange rate changes as an adjustment to equity rather than as an adjustment to net income because "exchange rate changes have an indirect effect on the net investment that may be realized upon sale or liquidation, but . . . prior to sale or liquidation, that effect is so uncertain and remote as to require that translation adjustments arising currently should not be reported as part of operating results."[6]

Management of Translation Exposure

Translation Exposure versus Transaction Exposure

需要注意的是，有些项目既会产生交易风险暴露，也会产生换算风险暴露。

总的来说，要完全消除交易风险暴露和换算风险暴露是不可能的。

In Chapter 8, we discussed transaction exposure and ways to manage it. It is interesting to note that some items that are a source of transaction exposure are also a source of translation exposure, and some are not. Exhibit 10.9 presents a transaction exposure report for Centralia Corporation and its two affiliates. Items that create transaction exposure are receivables or payables that are denominated in a currency other than the currency in which the unit transacts its business, or cash holdings denominated in a foreign currency. From the exhibit, it can be seen that the parent firm has two sources of transaction exposure. One is the CD200,000 deposit that it has in a Canadian bank. Obviously, if the Canadian dollar depreciates, the deposit will be worth less to Centralia Corporation once converted to U.S. dollars. Previously, it was noted that this deposit was also a translation exposure; it is, in fact, for the same reason that it is a transaction exposure. The Ps3,000,000 accounts receivable the parent holds on the Mexican affiliate is also a transaction exposure, but it is not a translation exposure because of the netting of intracompany payables and receivables. The SF375,000 notes payable the Spanish affiliate owes the Swiss bank is both a transaction and a translation exposure.

It is, generally, not possible to eliminate both translation and transaction exposure. In some cases, the elimination of one exposure will also eliminate the other. But in other cases, the elimination of one exposure actually creates the other. Since transaction exposure involves real cash flows, we believe it should be considered the most important of the two. That is, the financial manager would not want to legitimately create transaction exposure at the expense of minimizing or eliminating translation exposure. As previously noted, the translation process has no direct effect on reporting currency cash flows, and will only have a realizable effect on net investment upon the sale or liquidation of the assets. Actual practitioners appear to concur. In a recent survey of exchange risk management practices of U.K., U.S., and Asia Pacific multinational firms, Marshall (2000) found that 83 percent placed a "significant" or the "most" amount of emphasis on managing transaction exposure, whereas only 37 percent placed that much emphasis on managing translation exposure.

EXHIBIT 10.9			
Affiliate	**Amount**	**Account**	**Translation Exposure**
Parent	CD200,000	Cash	Yes
Parent	Ps3,000,000	Accounts receivable	No
Spanish	SF375,000	Notes payable	Yes

Transaction Exposure Report for Centralia Corporation and Its Mexican and Spanish Affiliates, December 31, 2005

[6]See FASB 52, paragraph 111.

Revised Translation Exposure Report for Centralia Corporation and Its Mexican and Spanish Affiliates, December 31, 2005
(in 000 Currency Units)

	Canadian Dollar	Mexican Peso	Euro	Swiss Franc
Assets				
Cash	CD0	Ps 3,000	€ 550	SF0
Accounts receivable	0	9,000	1,045	0
Inventory	0	15,000	1,650	0
Net fixed assets	0	46,000	4,400	0
Exposed assets	CD0	Ps 73,000	€7,645	SF0
Liabilities				
Accounts payable	CD0	Ps 7,000	€1,364	SF0
Notes payable	0	17,000	935	0
Long-term debt	0	27,000	3,520	00
Exposed liabilities	CD0	Ps 51,000	€5,819	SF0
Net exposure	CD0	Ps 22,000	€1,826	SF0

Centralia公司及其子公司可以采取某些措施，在降低交易风险暴露的同时，使换算风险暴露得到控制。

Centralia Corporation and its affiliates can take certain measures to reduce its transaction exposure and to simultaneously reduce its translation exposure. One step the parent firm can take is to convert its Canadian dollar cash deposits into U.S. dollar deposits. Secondly, the parent firm can request payment of the Ps3,000,000 owed to it by the Mexican affiliate. Third, the Spanish affiliate has enough cash to pay off the SF375,000 loan to the Swiss bank. If these three steps are taken, all transaction exposure for the MNC will be eliminated. Moreover, translation exposure will be reduced. This can be seen from Exhibit 10.10, which presents a revision of Exhibit 10.7, the translation exposure report for Centralia Corporation and its affiliates. Exhibit 10.10 shows that there is no longer any translation exposure associated with the Canadian dollar or the Swiss franc. Additionally, the exhibit shows that the net exposure has been reduced from Ps25,000,000 to Ps22,000,000 for the peso and from €2,101,000 to €1,826,000 for the euro.

Hedging Translation Exposure

Exhibit 10.10 indicates that there is still considerable translation exposure with respect to changes in the exchange rate of the Mexican peso and the euro against the U.S. dollar. There are two methods for dealing with this remaining exposure, if one desires to attempt to control accounting changes in the historical value of net investment. These methods are a balance sheet hedge or a derivatives hedge.

Balance Sheet Hedge

资产负债表套期保值能够消除以同一货币计量的净资产与净负债间的不匹配风险。

Note that translation exposure is not entity specific; rather, it is currency specific. Its source is a mismatch of net assets and net liabilities denominated in the same currency. A **balance sheet hedge** eliminates the mismatch. Using the euro as an example, Exhibit 10.10 shows that there are €1,826,000 more exposed assets than liabilities. If the Spanish affiliate, or more practically the parent firm or the Mexican affiliate, had €1,826,000 more liabilities, or less assets, denominated in euros, there would not be any translation exposure with respect to the euro. A perfect balance sheet hedge would have been created. A change in the €/$ exchange rate would no longer have any effect on the consolidated balance sheet since the change in value of the assets denominated in euros would completely offset the change in value of the liabilities denominated in euros. Nevertheless, if the parent firm or the Mexican affiliate increased its liabilities through, say, euro-denominated borrowings to affect the balance sheet hedge, it would simultaneously be creating transaction exposure in the euro, if the new liability could not be covered from euro cash flows generated by the Spanish affiliate.

Derivatives Hedge

我们之所以用"试着"这个词，是因为采用**衍生工具套期保值**来控制换算风险暴露时，实际上是对汇率变化的一种投机。

According to Exhibit 10.7, we determined that when the net exposure for the euro was €2,101,000, a depreciation from €1.1000/$1.00 to €1.1786/$1.00 would create a paper loss of stockholders' equity equal to $127,377. According to the revised translation exposure report shown as Exhibit 10.10, the same depreciation in the euro will result in an equity loss of $110,704, still a sizable amount. (The calculation of this amount is left as an exercise for the reader.) If one desires, a derivative product, such as a forward contract, can be used to attempt to hedge this potential loss. We use the word "attempt" because as the following example demonstrates, using a **derivatives hedge** to control translation exposure really involves speculation about foreign exchange rate changes.

EXAMPLE 10.2

Hedging Translation Exposure with a Forward Contract To see how a forward contract can be used to hedge the $110,704 potential translation loss in equity, assume that the forward rate coinciding with the date of the consolidation is €1.1393/$1.00. If the expected spot rate on the consolidation date is forecast to be €1.1786/$1.00, a forward sale of €3,782,468 will "hedge" the risk:

$$\frac{\text{Potential translation loss}}{F(\text{reporting/functional}) - \text{Expected}[S(\text{reporting/functional})]}$$

= forward contract position in functional currency,

$$\frac{\$110,704}{1/(€1.1393/\$1.00) - 1/(€1.1786/\$1.00)} = €3,782,468$$

The purchase of €3,782,468 at the expected spot price will cost $3,209,289. The delivery of €3,782,468 under the forward contract will yield $3,319,993, for a profit of $110,704. If everything goes as expected, the $110,704 profit from the forward hedge will offset the equity loss from the translation adjustment. Note, however, that the hedge will not provide a certain outcome because the size of the forward position is based on the expected future spot rate. Consequently, the forward position taken in euros is actually a speculative position. If the realized spot rate turns out to be less than €1.1393/$1.00, a loss from the forward position will result. Moreover, the hedging procedure violates the hypothesis of the forward rate being the market's unbiased predictor of the future spot rate.

In 1988, FASB 133 was issued. This statement establishes accounting and reporting standards for derivative instruments. According to the statement, the gain or loss from a derivative designated as hedging the foreign currency exposure of a net investment in a foreign operation is reported as part of the CTA. Consequently, as in Example 10.2, if everything goes as expected, the gain from the derivatives hedge will fully offset the translation loss, resulting in a cumulative translation adjustment of zero.

Translation Exposure versus Operating Exposure

As noted, an unhedged depreciation in the euro will result in an equity loss. Such a loss, however, would only be a paper loss. It would not have any direct effect on reporting currency cash flows. Moreover, it would only have a realizable effect on net investment in the MNC if the affiliate's assets were sold or liquidated. However, as was discussed in Chapter 9, the depreciation of the local currency may, under certain circumstances, have a favorable operating effect. A currency depreciation may, for example, allow the affiliate to raise its sales price because the prices of imported competitive goods are now relatively higher. If costs do not rise proportionately and unit demand remains the same, the affiliate would realize an operating profit as a result of the currency depreciation. It is substantive issues such as these, which result in realizable changes in operating profit, that management should concern itself with.

Empirical Analysis of the Change from FASB 8 to FASB 52

因此，换算过程的变化会影响跨国公司的报告损益。

Garlicki, Fabozzi, and Fonfeder (1987) empirically tested a sample of MNCs to determine if there was a change in value when the firms were required to switch from FASB 8 to FASB 52. FASB 8 calls for recognizing translation gains or losses immediately in net income. FASB 52 calls for recognizing translation gains or losses in the cumulative translation adjustment account on the balance sheet. Consequently, the change in the translation process had an effect on reported earnings. "Despite the impact of the change . . . on reported earnings, the actual cash flow of multinationals would not be affected *if managers were not making suboptimal decisions based on accounting rather than economic considerations under Statement 8.* In such circumstances, the mandated switch . . . should not change the value of the firm."[7]

研究结果表明，如果收益的表面变动不影响企业的价值，市场就不会对这些表面性收益变动做出反应。

The researchers tested their hypothesis concerning a change in value on the initial exposure draft date and on the date FASB 52 was adopted. They found that there was no significant positive reaction to the change or perceived change in the foreign currency translation process. The results suggest that market agents do not react to cosmetic earnings changes that do not affect value. Other researchers have found similar results when investigating other accounting changes that had only a cosmetic effect on earnings. The results of Garlicki, Fabozzi, and Fonfeder also underline the futility of attempting to manage translation gains and losses.

SUMMARY

在本章中，我们讨论了换算风险暴露的本质及管理。换算风险暴露是指汇率的非预期变动对跨国公司合并财务报表所带来的影响。

1. 跨国公司在合并财务报告时所采用的四种公认的方法是：流动及非流动法、货币及非货币法、时态法和现行汇率法。

2. 在假设外国货币升值或贬值的情况下，本章通过实例对四种换算方法进行了比较。值得注意的是，按照现行汇率法进行的换算调整所引起的换算损益不会影响所报告的现金流，同样，其他三种方法所引起的换算损益也不会影响所报告的现金流。

3. 本章讨论了由财务会计准则委员会出台的《财务会计准则第8号公告》中所规定的换算方法，并将其与《财务会计准则第52号公告》中的相关规定进行了比较。

4. 在执行《财务会计准则第52号公告》时，国外子公司所采用的本位币必须换算成合并财务报表所采用的报告货币。国外子公司所在地货币不一定就是其本位币。在这种情况下，就要通过时态法并采用本位币来重新计量国外子公司的

In this chapter, we have discussed the nature and management of translation exposure. Translation exposure relates to the effect that an unanticipated change in exchange rates will have on the consolidated financial reports of a MNC.

1. The four recognized methods for consolidating the financial reports of a MNC include the current/noncurrent method, the monetary/nonmonetary method, the temporal method, and the current rate method.

2. An example comparing and contrasting the four translation methods was presented under the assumptions that the foreign currency had appreciated and depreciated. It was noted that under the current rate method the gain or loss due to translation adjustment does not affect reported cash flows, as it does with the other three translation methods.

3. The old translation method prescribed by the Financial Accounting Standards Board, FASB 8, was discussed and compared with the present prescribed process, FASB 52.

4. In implementing FASB 52, the functional currency of the foreign entity must be translated into the reporting currency in which the consolidated statements are reported. The local currency of a foreign entity may not always be its functional

[7]Garlicki, Fabozzi, and Fonfeder (1987).

财务报表。在将本位币换算成报告货币时，可以使用现行汇率法。在有些情况下，国外子公司的本位币可能是报告货币，这时也就没有必要进行换算了。

　　5. 图10-4简要概括了其他主要发达国家所采用的外币换算方法。如图所示，实际操作中采用各种换算方法。

　　6. 本章通过一家拥有两家全资子公司的跨国公司的小案例说明了该如何按照《财务会计准则第52号公告》对资产负债表进行换算。为此，首先讨论自公司开业以来汇率未发生过变动情况下的处理方法，接下来讨论了假设汇率发生了预期变动时的处理方法，以便全面反映《财务会计准则第52号公告》对合并资产负债表的影响。如果存在净换算风险暴露，就需要用累计换算调整账户来平衡汇率变化后的合并资产负债表。

　　7. 本章介绍了控制换算风险暴露的两种方法：资产负债表套期保值和衍生工具套期保值。因为换算风险暴露不会对经营现金流立刻产生直接影响，因此，与控制交易风险暴露（它涉及到港在的实际现金流损失）相比，对换算风险暴露的控制显得相对不太重要。一般而言，要在实际操作中同时消除交易风险和换算风险暴露几乎是不可能的。合乎逻辑的做法是，对交易风险暴露进行有效管理，即便这是以发生换算风险暴露为代价。

currency. If it is not, the temporal method of translation is used to remeasure the foreign entity's books into the functional currency. The current rate method is used to translate from the functional currency to the reporting currency. In some cases, a foreign entity's functional currency may be the same as the reporting currency, in which case translation is not necessary.

5. Foreign-currency translation methods used in other major developed countries were briefly summarized in Exhibit 10.4. As the exhibit shows, a broad variety of methods are used in practice.

6. A case application illustrating the translation process of the balance sheet of a parent firm with two foreign wholly owned affiliates according to FASB 52 was presented. This was done assuming the foreign exchange rates had not changed since the inception of the businesses, and again after an assumed change, to more thoroughly show the effects of balance sheet consolidation under FASB 52. When a net translation exposure exists, a cumulative translation adjustment account is necessary to bring balance to the consolidated balance sheet after an exchange rate change.

7. Two ways to control translation risk were presented: a balance sheet hedge and a derivatives "hedge." Since translation exposure does not have an immediate direct effect on operating cash flows, its control is relatively unimportant in comparison to transaction exposure, which involves potential real cash flow losses. Since it is, generally, not possible to eliminate both translation and transaction exposure, it is more logical to effectively manage transaction exposure, even at the expense of translation exposure.

KEY WORDS

balance sheet hedge, *257*	current rate method, *246*	reporting currency, *248*
cumulative translation	derivatives hedge, *258*	temporal method, *245*
adjustment	functional	translation
(CTA), *246*	currency, *248*	exposure, *244*
current/noncurrent	monetary/nonmonetary	translation exposure
method, *245*	method, *245*	report, *254*

QUESTIONS

1. Explain the difference in the translation process between the monetary/nonmonetary method and the temporal method.

2. How are translation gains and losses handled differently according to the current rate method in comparison to the other three methods, that is, the current/noncurrent method, the monetary/nonmonetary method, and the temporal method?

3. Identify some instances under FASB 52 when a foreign entity's functional currency would be the same as the parent firm's currency.

4. Describe the remeasurement and translation process under FASB 52 of a wholly owned affiliate that keeps its books in the local currency of the country in which it operates, which is different than its functional currency.

5. It is, generally, not possible to completely eliminate both translation exposure and transaction exposure. In some cases, the elimination of one exposure will also eliminate the other. But in other cases, the elimination of one exposure actually creates the other. Discuss which exposure might be viewed as the most important to effectively manage, if a conflict between controlling both arises. Also, discuss and critique the common methods for controlling translation exposure.

PROBLEMS

1. Assume that FASB 8 is still in effect instead of FASB 52. Construct a translation exposure report for Centralia Corporation and its affiliates that is the counterpart to Exhibit 10.7 in the text. Centralia and its affiliates carry inventory and fixed assets on the books at historical values.

2. Assume that FASB 8 is still in effect instead of FASB 52. Construct a consolidated balance sheet for Centralia Corporation and its affiliates after a depreciation of the euro from €1.1000/$1.00 to €1.1786/$1.00 that is the counterpart to Exhibit 10.8 in the text. Centralia and its affiliates carry inventory and fixed assets on the books at historical values.

3. In Example 10.2, a forward contract was used to establish a derivatives "hedge" to protect Centralia from a translation loss if the euro depreciated from €1.1000/$1.00 to €1.1786/$1.00. Assume that an over-the-counter put option on the euro with a strike price of €1.1393/$1.00 (or $0.8777/€1.00) can be purchased for $0.0088 per euro. Show how the potential translation loss can be "hedged" with an option contract.

INTERNET EXERCISES

Ford Motor Company manufactures and sells motor vehicles worldwide. Through their worldwide operations they are exposed to all types of foreign currency risk. Their website is www.ford.com. Go to this website and access their 2003 annual report. Scroll through the report until you find the section "Quantitative and Qualitative Disclosures about Market Risk" on page 62. In the subsections titled "Automotive Market and Counterparty Risk" and "Foreign Currency Risk" is a discussion of how Ford uses earnings at risk (EAR) analysis in evaluating foreign currency exposure for hedging. Note from the discussion that Ford hedges economic and transaction exposure but not translation exposure. This is consistent with the discussion in the chapter mentioning that the translation process does not have a direct effect on reporting currency cash flows, and will only have a realizable effect on net investment upon the sale or liquidation of exposed assets.

MINI CASE

Sundance Sporting Goods, Inc.

Sundance Sporting Goods, Inc., is a U.S. manufacturer of high-quality sporting goods—principally golf, tennis, and other racquet equipment, and also lawn sports, such as croquet and badminton—with administrative offices and manufacturing facilities in Chicago, Illinois. Sundance has two wholly owned manufacturing affiliates, one in Mexico and the other in Canada. The Mexican affiliate is located in Mexico City and services all of Latin America. The Canadian affiliate is in Toronto and serves only Canada. Each affiliate keeps its books in its local currency, which is also the functional currency for the affiliate. The current exchange rates are: $1.00 = CD1.25 = Ps3.30 = A1.00 = ¥105 = W800. The nonconsolidated balance sheets for Sundance and its two affiliates appear in the accompanying table.

You joined the International Treasury division of Sundance six months ago after spending the last two years receiving your MBA degree. The corporate treasurer has asked you to prepare a report analyzing all aspects of the translation exposure faced by Sundance as a MNC. She has also asked you to address in your analysis the relationship between the firm's translation exposure and its transaction exposure. After performing a forecast of future spot rates of exchange, you decide that you must do the following before any sensible report can be written.

a. Using the current exchange rates and the nonconsolidated balance sheets for Sundance and its affiliates, prepare a consolidated balance sheet for the MNC according to FASB 52.

b. i. Prepare a translation exposure report for Sundance Sporting Goods, Inc., and its two affiliates.

ii. Using the translation exposure report you have prepared, determine if any reporting currency imbalance will result from a change in exchange rates to which the firm has currency exposure. Your forecast is that exchange rates will change from $1.00 = CD1.25 = Ps3.30 = A1.00 = ¥105 = W800 to $1.00 = CD1.30 = Ps3.30 = A1.03 = ¥105 = W800.

c. Prepare a second consolidated balance sheet for the MNC using the exchange rates you expect in the future. Determine how any reporting currency imbalance will affect the new consolidated balance sheet for the MNC.

d. i. Prepare a transaction exposure report for Sundance and its affiliates. Determine if any transaction exposures are also translation exposures.

ii. Investigate what Sundance and its affiliates can do to control its transaction and translation exposures. Determine if any of the translation exposure should be hedged.

Nonconsolidated Balance Sheet for Sundance Sporting Goods, Inc. and Its Mexican and Canadian Affiliates, December 31, 2005
(in 000 currency units)

	Sundance, Inc. (Parent)	Mexican Affiliate	Canadian Affiliate
Assets			
Cash	$ 1,500	Ps 1,420	CD 1,200
Accounts receivable	2,500[a]	2,800[e]	1,500[f]
Inventory	5,000	6,200	2,500
Investment in Mexican affiliate	2,400[b]	—	—
Investment in Canadian affiliate	3,600[c]	—	—
Net fixed assets	12,000	11,200	5,600
Total assets	$27,000	Ps21,620	CD10,800
Liabilities and Net Worth			
Accounts payable	$ 3,000	Ps 2,500[a]	CD 1,700
Notes payable	4,000[d]	4,200	2,300
Long-term debt	9,000	7,000	2,300
Common stock	5,000	4,500[b]	2,900[c]
Retained earnings	6,000	3,420[b]	1,600[c]
Total liabilities and net worth	$27,000	Ps21,620	CD10,800

[a]The parent firm is owed Ps1,320,000 by the Mexican affiliate. This sum is included in the parent's accounts receivable as $400,000, translated at Ps3.30/$1.00. The remainder of the parent's (Mexican affiliate's) accounts receivable (payable) is denominated in dollars (pesos).

[b]The Mexican affiliate is wholly owned by the parent firm. It is carried on the parent firm's books at $2,400,000. This represents the sum of the common stock (Ps4,500,000) and retained earnings (Ps3,420,000) on the Mexican affiliate's books, translated at Ps3.30/$1.00.

[c]The Canadian affiliate is wholly owned by the parent firm. It is carried on the parent firm's books at $3,600,000. This represents the sum of the common stock (CD2,900,000) and the retained earnings (CD1,600,000) on the Canadian affiliate's books, translated at CD1.25/$1.00.

[d]The parent firm has outstanding notes payable of ¥126,000,000 due a Japanese bank. This sum is carried on the parent firm's books as $1,200,000, translated at ¥105/$1.00. Other notes payable are denominated in U.S. dollars.

[e]The Mexican affiliate has sold on account A120,000 of merchandise to an Argentine import house. This sum is carried on the Mexican affiliate's books as Ps396,000, translated at A1.00/Ps3.30. Other accounts receivable are denominated in Mexican pesos.

[f]The Canadian affiliate has sold on account W192,000,000 of merchandise to a Korean importer. This sum is carried on the Canadian affiliate's books as CD300,000, translated at W800/CD1.25. Other accounts receivable are denominated in Canadian dollars.

REFERENCES & SUGGESTED READINGS

Arpan, J. S., and L. H. Radenbaugh. *International Accounting and Multinational Enterprises,* 2nd ed. New York: Wiley, 1985.

Coopers & Lybrand. *Foreign Currency Translation and Hedging.* New York: Coopers & Lybrand, February 1994.

Financial Accounting Standards Board. *Accounting for the Translation of Foreign Currency Transactions and Foreign Currency Financial Statements, Statement of Financial Accounting Standards No. 8.* Stamford, CT: Financial Accounting Standards Board, October 1975.

Financial Accounting Standards Board. *Foreign Currency Translation, Statement of Financial Accounting Standards No. 52.* Stamford, Conn.: Financial Accounting Standards Board, December 1981.

Financial Accounting Standards Board. "Summary of Statement No. 133." www.fasb.org.

Garlicki, T. Dessa, Frank J. Fabozzi, and Robert Fonfeder. "The Impact of Earnings under FASB 52 on Equity Returns." *Financial Management* 16 (1987), pp. 36-44.

Haried, Andrew A., Leroy F. Imdieke, and Ralph E. Smith. *Advanced Accounting,* 6th ed. New York: Wiley, 1994.

Marshall, Andrew P. "Foreign Exchange Risk Management in UK, USA, and Asia Pacific Multinational Companies." *Journal of Multinational Financial Management* 10 (2000), pp. 185–211.

Napolitano, Gabrielle. *International Accounting Standards: A Primer.* New York: Goldman, Sachs & Co., November 24, 1993.

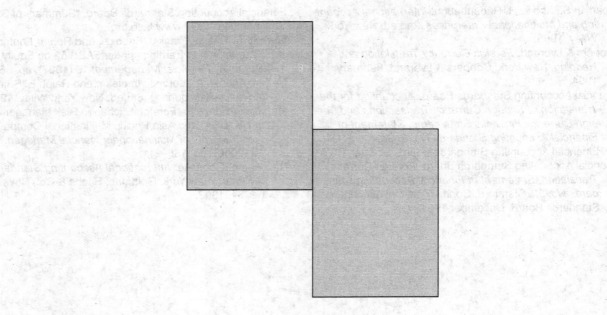

PART FOUR

World Financial Markets and Institutions

PART FOUR provides a thorough discussion of international financial institutions, assets, and marketplaces, and develops the tools necessary to manage exchange rate uncertainty.

CHAPTER 11 differentiates between international bank and domestic bank operations and examines the institutional differences of various types of international banking offices. International banks and their clients constitute the Eurocurrency market and form the core of the international money market.

CHAPTER 12 distinguishes between foreign bonds and Eurobonds, which together make up the international bond market. The advantages of sourcing funds from the international bond market as opposed to raising funds domestically are discussed. A discussion of the major types of international bonds is included in the chapter.

CHAPTER 13 covers international equity markets. The chapter begins with a statistical documentation of the size of equity markets in both developed and developing countries. Various methods of trading equity shares in the secondary markets are discussed. Additionally, the chapter provides a discussion of the advantages to the firm of cross-listing equity shares in more than one country.

CHAPTER 14 covers interest rate and currency swaps, useful tools for hedging, long-term interest rate and currency risk.

CHAPTER 15 covers international portfolio investment. It documents that the potential benefits from international diversification are available to all national investors.

11 International Banking and Money Market

本章介绍的国际金融市场与组织涉及三大主题：国际银行、国际货币市场运作（其中，银行起着重要作用）、国际债务危机。

WE BEGIN OUR discussion of world financial markets and institutions in this chapter, which takes up three major topics: international banking; international money market operations, in which banks are dominant players; and the international debt crisis. The chapter starts with a discussion of the services international banks provide to their clients. This is appropriate since international banks and domestic banks are characterized by different service mixes. Statistics that show the size and financial strength of the world's largest international banks are presented next. The first part of the chapter concludes with a discussion of the different types of bank operations that encompass international banking. The second part begins with an analysis of the Eurocurrency market, the creation of Eurocurrency deposits by international banks, and the Eurocredit loans they make. These form the foundation of the international money market. Euronotes, Eurocommercial paper, and forward rate agreements are other important money market instruments that are discussed. The chapter concludes with a history of the severe international debt crisis of only a few years ago and the dangers of private bank lending to sovereign governments.

International Banking Services

国际银行的特点在于它们所提供的区别于国内银行的服务类型。

International banks can be characterized by the types of services they provide that distinguish them from domestic banks. Foremost, international banks facilitate the imports and exports of their clients by arranging trade financing. Additionally, they serve their clients by arranging for foreign exchange necessary to conduct cross-border transactions and make foreign investments. In conducting foreign exchange transactions, banks often assist their clients in hedging exchange rate risk in foreign currency receivables and payables through forward and options contracts. Since international banks have the facilities to trade foreign exchange, they generally also trade foreign exchange products for their own account.

The major features that distinguish international banks from domestic banks are the types of deposits they accept and the loans and investments they make. Large international banks both borrow and lend in the Eurocurrency market. Additionally, they are frequently members of international loan syndicates, participating with other international banks to lend large sums to MNCs needing project financing and sovereign governments needing funds for economic development. Moreover, depending on the regulations of the country in which it operates and its organizational type, an international bank may participate in the underwriting of Eurobonds and foreign bonds. Banks that both perform traditional commercial banking functions, the subject of this chapter, and engage in investment banking activities are often called **merchant banks.**

International banks frequently provide consulting services and advice to their clients. Areas in which international banks typically have expertise are foreign exchange hedging strategies, interest rate and currency swap financing, and international cash management services. All of these international banking services and operations are covered in depth in this and other chapters of the text. Not all international banks provide all services, however. Banks that do provide a majority of these services are commonly known as **universal banks** or **full service banks.**

The World's Largest Banks

Exhibit 11.1 lists the world's 30 largest banks ranked by total assets as of fiscal year-end 2003. The exhibit shows the shareholder equity of each bank, its total assets, net income stated in millions of U.S. dollars, and Tier I bank capital ratio (discussed later in the chapter). The exhibit indicates that 8 of the world's 30 largest banks are from the United States, 4 each are from Japan and the U.K., 3 each are from France and the Netherlands, 2 each are from China, Spain, and Switzerland, and 1 each is from Germany and Italy.

From Exhibit 11.1, one might correctly surmise that the world's major international finance centers are New York, Tokyo, London, Paris, Frankfurt, and Zurich. London, New York, and Tokyo, however, are by far the most important international finance centers because of the relatively liberal banking regulations of their respective countries. These three financial centers are frequently referred to as *full service centers* because the major banks that operate in them usually provide a full range of services.

Reasons for International Banking

The opening discussion on the services international banks provide implied some of the reasons why a bank may establish multinational operations. Rugman and Kamath (1987) provide a more formal list:

1. *Low marginal costs*—Managerial and marketing knowledge developed at home can be used abroad with low marginal costs.

2. *Knowledge advantage*—The foreign bank subsidiary can draw on the parent bank's knowledge of personal contacts and credit investigations for use in that foreign market.

3. *Home country information services*—Local firms may be able to obtain from a foreign subsidiary bank operating in their country more complete trade and financial market information about the subsidiary's home country than they can obtain from their own domestic banks.

4. *Prestige*—Very large multinational banks have high perceived prestige, liquidity, and deposit safety that can be used to attract clients abroad.

EXHIBIT 11.1	**The World's 30 Largest Banks** (in Millions of U.S. Dollars, as of fiscal year-end 2003)					
Rank	Bank	Country	Shareholder Equity	Total Assets	Net Income	Tier I Capital Ratio (%)
1	Citigroup	United States	98,014	1,264,032	17,853	8.9%
2	HSBC	UK	85,354	1,034,216	8,774	8.9%
3	Groupe Crédit Agricole	France	59,140	1,098,669	3,461	7.6%
4	Royal Bank of Scotland	UK	54,781	809,433	7,181	7.4%
5	Bank of America	United States	47,980	736,487	10,810	7.8%
6	JPMorgan Chase	United States	46,154	770,912	6,719	8.5%
7	BNP Paribas	France	42,929	982,917	4,721	9.4%
8	Santander Central Hispano	Spain	38,284	406,946	3,277	8.3%
9	Mizuho Financial Group	Japan	36,864	1,223,478	−20,499	—
10	Deutsche Bank	Germany	35,399	1,008,696	1,713	10.0%
11	Wells Fargo	United States	34,469	387,798	6,202	8.4%
12	Wachovia Corp	United States	32,428	401,032	4,264	8.5%
13	HBOS	UK	31,965	726,117	3,853	7.6%
14	UBS	Switzerland	31,827	1,116,215	5,142	11.8%
15	Barclays	UK	29,790	788,252	4,879	7.9%
16	Rabobank Nederland	Netherlands	29,564	506,228	1,761	10.8%
17	Banco Bilbao Vizcaya Argentaria	Spain	29,380	361,755	2,795	8.5%
18	Mitsubishi Tokyo FG	Japan	28,412	836,358	−1,362	5.7%
19	Credit Suisse Group	Switzerland	27,939	774,879	4,026	11.7%
20	Sumitomo Mitsui Banking	Japan	26,714	863,507	−3,621	5.4%
21	Société Générale	France	26,640	677,039	3,128	8.7%
22	Bank of China	China	26,539	434,216	1,141	7.9%
23	Bank One	United States	23,419	326,563	3,535	10.0%
24	UFJ Holdings	Japan	22,477	679,215	−5,124	—
25	ABN Amro	Netherlands	22,472	703,461	3,968	8.2%
26	Industrial & Commercial Bank of China (ICBC)	China	21,531	577,130	789	5.5%
27	ING	Netherlands	20,964	679,809	1,807	7.6%
28	Banca Intesa	Italy	19,793	326,622	1,524	7.8%
29	Washington Mutual	United States	19,742	275,178	3,880	—
30	US Bancorp	United States	19,242	189,286	3,733	9.1%

Source: Excerpted from Euromoney, June 2004, p. 178.

5. *Regulation advantage*—Multinational banks are often not subject to the same regulations as domestic banks. There may be reduced need to publish adequate financial information, lack of required deposit insurance and reserve requirements on foreign currency deposits, and the absence of territorial restrictions (that is, U.S. banks may not be restricted to state of origin).

6. *Wholesale defensive strategy*—Banks follow their multinational customers abroad to prevent the erosion of their clientele to foreign banks seeking to service the multinational's foreign subsidiaries.

7. *Retail defensive strategy*—Multinational banking operations help a bank prevent the erosion of its traveler's check, tourist, and foreign business markets from foreign bank competition.

8. *Transaction costs*—By maintaining foreign branches and foreign currency balances, banks may reduce transaction costs and foreign exchange risk on currency conversion if government controls can be circumvented.

9. *Growth*—Growth prospects in a home nation may be limited by a market largely saturated with the services offered by domestic banks.

10. *Risk reduction*—Greater stability of earnings is possible with international diversification. Offsetting business and monetary policy cycles across nations reduces the country-specific risk of any one nation.

Types of International Banking Offices

国际银行的服务和
运作是关于银行经营的
制度环境和所建立的银
行设施类型的函数。

The services and operations of international banks are a function of the regulatory environment in which the bank operates and the type of banking facility established. Following is a discussion of the major types of international banking offices, detailing the purpose of each and the regulatory rationale for its existence. The discussion moves from correspondent bank relationships, through which minimal service can be provided to a bank's customers, to a description of offices providing a fuller array of services, to those that have been established by regulatory change for the purpose of leveling the worldwide competitive playing field.[1]

Correspondent Bank
代理银行关系

代理银行主要是为
跨国公司的国际交易所引
起的外汇兑换提供服务。

The large banks in the world will generally have a correspondent relationship with other banks in all the major financial centers in which they do not have their own banking operation. A **correspondent bank relationship** is established when two banks maintain a correspondent bank account with one another. For example, a large New York bank will have a correspondent bank account in a London bank, and the London bank will maintain one with the New York bank.

The correspondent banking system enables a bank's MNC client to conduct business worldwide through his local bank or its contacts. Correspondent banking services center around foreign exchange conversions that arise through the international transactions the MNC makes. However, correspondent bank services also include assistance with trade financing, such as honoring letters of credit and accepting drafts drawn on the correspondent bank. Additionally, a MNC needing foreign local financing for one of its subsidiaries may rely on its local bank to provide it with a letter of introduction to the correspondent bank in the foreign country.

The correspondent bank relationship is beneficial because a bank can service its MNC clients at a very low cost and without the need of having bank personnel physically located in many countries. A disadvantage is that the bank's clients may not receive the level of service through the correspondent bank that they would if the bank had its own foreign facilities to service its clients.

Representative Offices
代表处

A **representative office** is a small service facility staffed by parent bank personnel that is designed to assist MNC clients of the parent bank in dealings with the bank's correspondents. It is a way for the parent bank to provide its MNC clients with a level of service greater than that provided through merely a correspondent relationship. The parent bank may open a representative office in a country in which it has many MNC clients or at least an important client. Representative offices also assist MNC clients with information about local business practices, economic information, and credit evaluation of the MNC's foreign customers.

Foreign Branches
国外分行

A **foreign branch bank** operates like a local bank, but legally it is a part of the parent bank. As such, a branch bank is subject to both the banking regulations of its home country and the country in which it operates. U.S. branch banks in foreign countries are regulated from the United States by the Federal Reserve Act and Federal Reserve Regulation K: International Banking Operations, which covers most of the regulations relating to U.S. banks operating in foreign countries and foreign banks operating within the United States.

---

[1]Much of the discussion in this section follows Hultman (1990).

母银行设立国外分行的原因有很多。最重要的一个原因是通过设立外国分行可以比设立代表处向其跨国公司客户提供更全面、更完善的服务。

There are several reasons why a parent bank might establish a branch bank. The primary one is that the bank organization can provide a much fuller range of services for its MNC customers through a branch office than it can through a representative office. For example, branch bank loan limits are based on the capital of the parent bank, not the branch bank. Consequently, a branch bank will likely be able to extend a larger loan to a customer than a locally chartered subsidiary bank of the parent. Additionally, the books of a foreign branch are part of the parent bank's books. Thus, a branch bank system allows customers much faster check clearing than does a correspondent bank network because the debit and credit procedure is handled internally within one organization.

Another reason a U.S. parent bank may establish a foreign branch bank is to compete on a local level with the banks of the host country. Branches of U.S. banks are not subject to U.S. reserve requirements on deposits and are not required to have Federal Deposit Insurance Corporation (FDIC) insurance on deposits. Consequently, branch banks are on the same competitive level as local banks in terms of their cost structure in making loans.

Branch banking is the most popular way for U.S. banks to expand operations overseas. Most branch banks are located in Europe, in particular the United Kingdom. Many branch banks are operated as "shell" branches in offshore banking centers, a topic covered later in this section.

The most important piece of legislation affecting the operation of foreign banks in the United States is the International Banking Act of 1978 (IBA). In general, the act specifies that foreign branch banks operating in the United States must comply with U.S. banking regulations just like U.S. banks. In particular, the IBA specifies that foreign branch banks must meet the Fed reserve requirements on deposits and make FDIC insurance available for customer deposits.

Subsidiary and Affiliate Banks
子银行和联营银行

A **subsidiary bank** is a locally incorporated bank that is either wholly owned or owned in major part by a foreign parent. An **affiliate bank** is one that is only partially owned but not controlled by its foreign parent. Both subsidiary and affiliate banks operate under the banking laws of the country in which they are incorporated. U.S. parent banks find subsidiary and affiliate banking structures desirable because they are allowed to underwrite securities.

Foreign-owned subsidiary banks in the United States tend to locate in the states that are major centers of financial activity, as do U.S. branches of foreign parent banks. In the United States, foreign bank offices tend to locate in the highly populous states of New York, California, Illinois, Florida, Georgia, and Texas.[2]

Edge Act Banks
为了绕开关于州际银行交易的限制,《埃奇法案》银行一般设立在母公司所在州以外的州。

Edge Act banks are federally chartered subsidiaries of U.S. banks that are physically located in the United States and are allowed to engage in a full range of international banking activities. Senator Walter E. Edge of New Jersey sponsored the 1919 amendment to Section 25 of the Federal Reserve Act to allow U.S. banks to be competitive with the services foreign banks could supply their customers. Federal Reserve Regulation K allows Edge Act banks to accept foreign deposits, extend trade credit, finance foreign projects abroad, trade foreign currencies, and engage in investment banking activities with U.S. citizens involving foreign securities. As such, Edge Act banks do not compete directly with the services provided by U.S. commercial banks.

An Edge Act bank is typically located in a state different from that of its parent in order to get around the prohibition on interstate branch banking. However, since 1979, the Federal Reserve has permitted interstate banking by Edge Act banks. Moreover, the IBA permits foreign banks operating in the United States to establish Edge Act

---

[2]See Goldberg and Grosse (1994).

banks. Thus, both U.S. and foreign Edge Act banks operate on an equally competitive basis.

Edge Act banks are not prohibited from owning equity in business corporations, unlike domestic commercial banks. Thus, it is *through* the Edge Act that U.S. parent banks own foreign banking subsidiaries and have ownership positions in foreign banking affiliates.

Offshore Banking Centers

离岸金融中心

A significant portion of the external banking activity takes place through offshore banking centers. An **offshore banking center** is a country whose banking system is organized to permit external accounts beyond the normal economic activity of the country. The International Monetary Fund recognizes the Bahamas, Bahrain, the Cayman Islands, China-Hong Kong SAR, the Netherlands Antilles, Panama, and Singapore as major offshore banking centers.

Offshore banks operate as branches or subsidiaries of the parent bank. The principal features that make a country attractive for establishing an offshore banking operation are virtually total freedom from host-country governmental banking regulations—for example, low reserve requirements and no deposit insurance, low taxes, a favorable time zone that facilitates international banking transactions, and, to a minor extent, strict banking secrecy laws. It should not be inferred that offshore host governments tolerate or encourage poor banking practices, as entry is usually confined to the largest and most reputable international banks.

离岸银行所从事的主要活动是吸收非东道国政府货币存款并发放相应的贷款。

The primary activities of offshore banks are to seek deposits and grant loans in currencies other than the currency of the host government. Offshore banking was spawned in the late 1960s when the Federal Reserve authorized U.S. banks to establish "shell" branches, which needs to be nothing more than a post office box in the host country. The actual banking transactions were conducted by the parent bank. The purpose was to allow smaller U.S. banks the opportunity to participate in the growing Eurodollar market without having to bear the expense of setting up operations in a major European money center. Today there are hundreds of offshore bank branches and subsidiaries, about one-third operated by U.S. parent banks.[3] Most offshore banking centers continue to serve as locations for shell branches, but China-Hong Kong SAR and Singapore have developed into full service banking centers that now rival London, New York, and Tokyo.

International Banking Facilities

国际银行便利(IBF)

In 1981, the Federal Reserve authorized the establishment of **International Banking Facilities (IBF).** An IBF is a separate set of asset and liability accounts that are segregated on the parent bank's books; it is not a unique physical or legal entity. Any U.S.-chartered depository institution, a U.S. branch or subsidiary of a foreign bank, or a U.S. office of an Edge Act bank may operate an IBF. IBFs operate as foreign banks in the United States. They are not subject to domestic reserve requirements on deposits, nor is FDIC insurance required on deposits. IBFs seek deposits from non-U.S. citizens and can make loans only to foreigners. All nonbank deposits must be nonnegotiable time deposits with a maturity of at least two business days and be of a size of at least $100,000.

在很大程度上，IBF是离岸金融中心获得成功后的产物。

IBFs were established largely as a result of the success of offshore banking. The Federal Reserve desired to return a large share of the deposit and loan business of U.S. branches and subsidiaries to the United States. IBFs have been successful in capturing a large portion of the Eurodollar business that was previously handled offshore. However, offshore banking will never be completely eliminated because IBFs are restricted from lending to U.S. citizens, while offshore banks are not.

Exhibit 11.2 summarizes the organizational structure and characteristics of international banking offices from the perspective of the United States.

---

[3]See Chapter 10 of Hultman (1990) for an excellent discussion of the development of offshore banking and international banking facilities.

EXHIBIT 11.2	Organizational Structure of International Banking Offices from the U.S. Perspective					
Type of Bank	Physical Location	Accept Foreign Deposits	Make Loans to Foreigners	Subject to Fed Reserve Requirements	FDIC Insured Deposits	Separate Legal Equity from Parent
Domestic bank	U.S.	No	No	Yes	Yes	No
Correspondent bank	Foreign	N/A	N/A	No	No	N/A
Representative office	Foreign	No	No	Yes	Yes	No
Foreign branch	Foreign	Yes	Yes	No	No	No
Subsidiary bank	Foreign	Yes	Yes	No	No	Yes
Affiliate bank	Foreign	Yes	Yes	No	No	Yes
Edge Act bank	U.S.	Yes	Yes	No	No	Yes
Offshore banking center	Technically Foreign	Yes	Yes	No	No	No
International banking facility	U.S.	Yes	Yes	No	No	No

Capital Adequacy Standards

银行资本充足率指的是银行为防范风险资产和银行倒闭而持有的作为储备的权益资本及其他证券。

www.bis.org.

This is the official website of the Bank for International Settlements. It is quite extensive. One can download many papers on international bank policies and reports containing statistics on international banks, capital markets, and derivative securities markets. There is also a web page that provides a link to the websites of most central banks in the world.

《巴塞尔协议》
(Basel Accord)

1988年的《巴塞尔协议》被全球各国银行监管者所接纳。

A concern of bank regulators worldwide and of bank depositors is the safety of bank deposits. **Bank capital adequacy** refers to the amount of equity capital and other securities a bank holds as reserves against risky assets to reduce the probability of a bank failure. In a 1988 agreement known as the **Basel Accord,** after the Swiss city in which it is headquartered, the Bank for International Settlements (BIS) established a framework for measuring bank capital adequacy for banks in the Group of Ten (G-10) countries and Luxembourg. The BIS is the central bank for clearing international transactions between national central banks, and also serves as a facilitator in reaching international banking agreements among its members.

The Basel Accord called for a minimum bank capital adequacy ratio of 8 percent of risk-weighted assets for internationally active banks. The accord divides bank capital into two categories: Tier I Core capital, which consists of shareholder equity and retained earnings, and Tier II Supplemental capital, which consists of internationally recognized nonequity items such as preferred stock and subordinated bonds. Supplemental capital is allowed to count for no more than 50 percent of total bank capital, or no more than 4 percent of risk-weighted assets. In determining risk-weighted assets, four categories of risky assets are each weighted differently. More risky assets receive a higher weight. Government obligations are weighted at zero percent, short-term interbank assets are weighted at 20 percent, residential mortgages at 50 percent, and other assets at 100 percent. Thus, a bank with $100 million in each of the four asset categories would have the equivalent of $170 million in risk-weighted assets. It would need to maintain $13.6 million in capital against these investments, of which no more than one-half, or $6.8 million, could be Tier II capital.

The 1988 Basel Capital Accord primarily addressed banking in the context of deposit gathering and lending. Thus, its focus was on *credit* risk. The accord was widely adopted throughout the world by national bank regulators. Nevertheless, it had its problems and its critics. One major criticism concerned the arbitrary nature in which the accord was implemented. The 8 percent minimum capital requirement assigned to risk-weighted assets was unchanging regardless of whether the degree of credit risk fluctuated throughout the business cycle, regardless of whether the bank was located in a developed or a developing country, and regardless of the types of risks in which banks were engaged. Bank trading in equity, interest rate, and exchange rate derivative products escalated throughout the 1990s. Many of these products were not even in existence when the Basel Accord was drafted. Consequently, even if the accord was satisfactory in safeguarding bank depositors from traditional credit risks, the capital adequacy requirements were not sufficient to safeguard against the *market* risk from derivatives trading. For example, Barings Bank, which collapsed in 1995 due in part to the activities of a rogue derivatives trader, was considered to be a safe bank by the Basel capital adequacy standards.

Given the shortcomings of the 1988 accord, the Basel Committee concluded in the early 1990s that an updated capital accord was needed. A 1996 amendment, which went into effect in 1998, required commercial banks engaging in significant trading activity to set aside additional capital under the 8 percent rule to cover the market risks inherent in their trading accounts. A new Tier III capital comprised of short-term subordinated debt could be used to satisfy the capital requirement on market risk. By this time additional shortcomings of the original accord were becoming evident. *Operational* risk, which includes such matters as computer failure, poor documentation, and fraud, was becoming evident as a significant risk. This expanded view of risk reflects the type of business in which banks now engage and the business environment in which banks operate. In 1999, the Basel Committee proposed a new capital accord. In June 2004, after an extensive consultative process, the new capital adequacy framework commonly referred to as Basel II was endorsed by central bank governors and bank supervisors in the G-10 countries. It is expected to be available for implementation by year-end 2006.

《巴塞尔协议II》建立在三条相互强化的原则之上：最低资本金率要求、监管评价程序及对市场规则的有效应用。

Basel II is based on three mutually reinforcing pillars: minimum capital requirements, a supervisory review process, and the effective use of market discipline. The new framework sets out the details for adopting more risk-sensitive minimum capital requirements that are extended up to the holding company level of diversified bank groups. With respect to the first pillar, bank capital is defined as per the 1988 accord, but the minimum 8 percent capital ratio is calculated on the sum of the bank's credit, market, and operational risk. In determining adequate capital, the new framework provides a range of options open to banks for valuing credit risk and operational risk. For valuing credit risk, banks may choose among the *standardized approach,* the *internal rating-based (IRB) approach,* and the *securitization approach.* The standardized approach provides for risk-weighting assets from five categories based on external credit agencies assessments of the credit risk inherent in the asset. For example, AAA claims on sovereigns have a risk-weighting of zero percent, AAA claims on corporates and single A claims on sovereigns have a risk-weighting of 20 percent, single A claims on corporates and BBB claims on sovereigns have a risk-weighting of 50 percent, whereas corporate claims below BB- have a risk-weighting of 150 percent. The IRB approach allows banks that have received supervisory approval to rely on their own internal estimates of risk in determining the capital requirement for a given exposure. The key variables the bank must estimate to value credit risk under this approach are the *probability of default* and the *loss given default* for each asset. The securitization approach provides for determining the securitized value of a cash flow stream and then risk-weighting the value according to the standardized approach or (if the bank has received supervisory approval) by applying the IRB approach to determine the capital requirement. Operational risk is valued by one of three methods of increasing sophistication. The less sophisticated methods involve applying a fixed percentage to gross income from operations. Banks are encouraged to move along the spectrum of approaches as they develop more sophisticated operational risk measurement systems. Market risk is determined by marking-to-market the value of the bank's trading account, or if that is not possible, marking to a model determined value.

第二条原则旨在确保每家银行都有健全的内部程序，以便在全面估算风险的基础上正确评估其资本充足率。

The second pillar is designed to ensure that each bank has a sound internal process in place to properly assess the adequacy of its capital based on a thorough evaluation of its risks. For example, banks adopting the IRB approach for valuing credit risk are required to conduct meaningful stress tests designed to estimate the extent that capital requirements could increase in an adverse economic scenario. Banks and supervisors are to use the results of these tests to ensure that banks hold sufficient capital. The third pillar is designed to complement the other two. It is believed that public disclosure of key information will bring greater market discipline to bear on banks and supervisors to better manage risk and improve bank stability.[4]

International Money Market

Eurocurrency Market

欧洲货币是指货币发行国之外的国际银行所拥有的该货币的定期存款。

The core of the international money market is the Eurocurrency market. A **Eurocurrency** is a *time* deposit of money in an international bank located in a country different from the country that issued the currency. For example, Eurodollars are deposits of U.S. dollars in banks located outside of the United States, Eurosterling are deposits of British pound sterling in banks outside of the United Kingdom, and Euroyen are deposits of Japanese yen in banks outside of Japan. The prefix *Euro* is somewhat of a misnomer, since the bank in which the deposit is made does not have to be located in Europe. The depository bank could be located in Europe, the Caribbean, or Asia. Indeed, as we saw in the previous section, Eurodollar deposits can be made in offshore shell branches or IBFs, where the physical dollar deposits are actually with the U.S. parent bank. An "Asian dollar" market exists, with headquarters in Singapore, but it can be viewed as a major division of the Eurocurrency market.

The origin of the Eurocurrency market can be traced back to the 1950s and early 1960s, when the former Soviet Union and Soviet-bloc countries sold gold and commodities to raise hard currency. Because of anti-Soviet sentiment, these Communist countries were afraid of depositing their U.S. dollars in U.S. banks for fear that the deposits could be frozen or taken. Instead they deposited their dollars in a French bank whose telex address was EURO-BANK. Since that time, dollar deposits outside the United States have been called Eurodollars and banks accepting Eurocurrency deposits have been called **Eurobanks**.[5]

欧洲银行

欧洲货币市场是一种外部银行系统，与货币发行国的国内银行系统并行运行。

The Eurocurrency market is an *external* banking system that runs parallel to the *domestic* banking system of the country that issued the currency. Both banking systems seek deposits and make loans to customers from the deposited funds. In the United States, banks are subject to the Federal Reserve Regulation D, specifying reserve requirements on bank time deposits. Additionally, U.S. banks must pay FDIC insurance premiums on deposited funds. Eurodollar deposits, on the other hand, are not subject to these arbitrary reserve requirements or deposit insurance; hence the cost of operations is less. Because of the reduced cost structure, the Eurocurrency market, and in particular the Eurodollar market, has grown spectacularly since its inception.

欧洲货币市场在银行同业和/或货币批发市场上运作。

The Eurocurrency market operates at the *interbank* and/or *wholesale* level. The majority of Eurocurrency transactions are interbank transactions, representing sums of $1,000,000 or more. Eurobanks with surplus funds and no retail customers to lend to will lend to Eurobanks that have borrowers but need loanable funds. The rate charged by banks with excess funds is referred to as the *interbank offered rate;* they will accept interbank deposits at the *interbank bid rate*. The spread is generally 1/8 of 1 percent for most major Eurocurrencies.

伦敦银行同业拆借利率（LIBOR）

London has historically been, and remains, the major Eurocurrency financial center. These days, most people have heard of the **London Interbank Offered Rate (LIBOR),** the reference rate in London for Eurocurrency deposits. To be clear, there is a LIBOR for Eurodollars, Euro–Canadian dollars, Euroyen, and even euros. In other financial centers, other reference rates are used. For example, *SIBOR* is the Singapore Interbank Offered

---

[4]The information in this section is from *International Convergence of Capital Measurement and Capital Standards: A Revised Framework,* Bank for International Settlements, June 2004.

[5]See Rivera-Batiz and Rivera-Batiz (1994) for an account of the historical origin of the Eurocurrency market.

EXHIBIT 11.3 **Eurocurrency Interest Rate Quotations: March 3, 2005**

	Short Term	7 Days' Notice	One Month	Three Months	Six Months	One Year
Euro	$2\frac{1}{18}-2\frac{1}{32}$	$2\frac{1}{8}-2\frac{1}{32}$	$2\frac{1}{8}-2\frac{1}{16}$	$2\frac{5}{32}-2\frac{5}{32}$	$2\frac{3}{16}-2\frac{1}{8}$	$2\frac{5}{16}-2\frac{1}{4}$
Danish Krone	$2\frac{1}{4}-2\frac{3}{32}$	$2\frac{1}{4}-2\frac{1}{32}$	$2\frac{7}{32}-2\frac{1}{32}$	$2\frac{7}{32}-2\frac{1}{16}$	$2\frac{1}{4}-2\frac{3}{32}$	$2\frac{13}{32}-2\frac{1}{4}$
Sterling	$5\frac{9}{16}-5\frac{11}{32}$	$4\frac{3}{4}-4\frac{5}{8}$	$4\frac{13}{16}-4\frac{11}{16}$	$4\frac{15}{16}-4\frac{13}{16}$	$5\frac{1}{16}-4\frac{15}{16}$	$5\frac{5}{32}-5\frac{1}{32}$
Swiss Franc	$\frac{11}{16}-\frac{17}{32}$	$\frac{3}{4}-\frac{5}{8}$	$\frac{3}{4}-\frac{5}{8}$	$\frac{3}{4}-\frac{5}{8}$	$\frac{13}{16}-\frac{11}{16}$	$\frac{31}{32}-\frac{7}{8}$
Canadian Dollar	$2\frac{3}{4}-2\frac{19}{32}$	$2\frac{5}{8}-2\frac{17}{32}$	$2\frac{5}{8}-2\frac{17}{32}$	$2\frac{5}{8}-2\frac{17}{32}$	$2\frac{11}{16}-2\frac{19}{32}$	$2\frac{29}{32}-2\frac{13}{16}$
US Dollar	$2\frac{17}{32}-2\frac{15}{32}$	$2\frac{19}{32}-2\frac{1}{2}$	$2\frac{3}{4}-2\frac{11}{16}$	$2\frac{31}{32}-2\frac{7}{8}$	$3\frac{3}{16}-3\frac{1}{8}$	$3\frac{17}{32}-3\frac{1}{2}$
Japanese Yen	$\frac{1}{32}-\frac{1}{16}$	$\frac{1}{32}-\frac{1}{16}$	$\frac{1}{32}-\frac{1}{8}$	$\frac{1}{16}-\frac{1}{32}$	$\frac{1}{16}-\frac{1}{32}$	$\frac{1}{8}-\frac{1}{32}$
Singapore $	$1\frac{13}{16}-1\frac{9}{16}$	$1\frac{15}{16}-1\frac{11}{16}$	$1\frac{15}{16}-1\frac{11}{16}$	$2-1\frac{3}{4}$	$2\frac{1}{15}-1\frac{13}{16}$	$2\frac{1}{8}-1\frac{7}{8}$

Note: Short term rates are call for the U.S. Dollar and Yen, others: two day's notice.
Source: Financial Times, March 4, 2005, p. 25.

www.euribor.org

This website provides a brief history of the euro common currency and a discussion of EURIBOR.

欧元银行同业拆借利率（EURIBOR）

在货币批发市场，欧洲银行接受欧洲货币的定期存款并发行可转让定期存单（NCD）。

大约90%的大额欧洲银行存款属于固定存款，其余的为可转让定期存单。

Rate, and *TIBOR* is the Tokyo Interbank Offered Rate. Obviously, competition forces the various interbank rates for a particular Eurocurrency to be close to one another.

The advent of the common euro currency on January 1, 1999, among the 11 countries of the European Union making up the Economic and Monetary Union created a need for a new interbank offered rate designation. It also creates some confusion as to whether one is referring to the common euro currency or another Eurocurrency, such as Eurodollars. Because of this, it is starting to become common practice to refer to *international* currencies instead of Eurocurrencies and *prime* banks instead of Eurobanks. **EURIBOR** is the rate at which interbank deposits of the euro are offered by one prime bank to another in the euro zone.

In the wholesale money market, Eurobanks accept Eurocurrency fixed time deposits and issue **negotiable certificates of deposit (NCDs).** In fact, these are the preferable ways for Eurobanks to raise loanable funds, as the deposits tend to be for a lengthier period and the acquiring rate is often slightly less than the interbank rate. Denominations are at least $500,000, but sizes of $1,000,000 or larger are more typical. Rates on Eurocurrency deposits are quoted for maturities ranging from one day to several years; however, more standard maturities are for 1, 2, 3, 6, 9, and 12 months. Exhibit 11.3 shows sample Eurocurrency interest rates. Appendix 11A illustrates the creation of the Eurocurrency.

Exhibit 11.4 shows the year-end values of international bank external liabilities (Eurodeposits and other Euro liabilities) in billions of U.S. dollars for the years 1999–2003. The 2003 column shows that total external liabilities were $15,328.8 billion and that interbank liabilities accounted for $11,094.7 billion of this amount, whereas nonbank deposits were $4,234.1 billion. The major currencies denominating these were the U.S. dollar, the euro, and the British pound sterling.

Approximately 90 percent of wholesale Eurobank external liabilities come from fixed time deposits, the remainder from NCDs. There is an interest penalty for the early with-

EXHIBIT 11.4

International Bank External Liabilities (at Year-End in Billions of U.S. Dollars)

Type Liability	1999	2000	2001	2002	2003
Interbank	7,311.2	7,909.2	8,330.0	9,543.9	11,094.7
Nonbank	2,306.8	2,512.7	2,859.8	3,311.5	4,234.1
Total	9,618.0	10,421.8	11,189.8	12,855.4	15,328.8

Source: International Banking and Financial Market Developments, Bank for International Settlements, Tables 1, p. A7, June 2002, 2003, 2004.

EXHIBIT 11.5

Comparison of U.S. Lending and Borrowing Rates with Eurodollar Rates on March 3, 2005

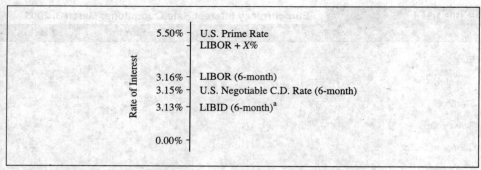

5.50%	U.S. Prime Rate
	LIBOR + X%
3.16%	LIBOR (6-month)
3.15%	U.S. Negotiable C.D. Rate (6-month)
3.13%	LIBID (6-month)[a]
0.00%	

Rate of Interest

[a]LIBID denotes the London Interbank Bid rate.

drawal of funds from a fixed time deposit. NCDs, on the other hand, being negotiable, can be sold in the secondary market if the depositor suddenly needs his funds prior to scheduled maturity. The NCD market began in 1967 in London for Eurodollars. EuroCDs for currencies other than the U.S. dollar are offered by banks in London and in other financial centers, but the secondary market for nondollar NCDs is not very liquid.

Eurocredits

欧洲信贷是欧洲银行提供给企业、主权政府、一些非主要银行或国际组织的短期或中期欧洲货币贷款。

这些贷款的信贷风险比在银行同业市场拆借的风险要大。

辛迪加(syndicate)

Eurocredits are short- to medium-term loans of Eurocurrency extended by Eurobanks to corporations, sovereign governments, nonprime banks, or international organizations. The loans are denominated in currencies other than the home currency of the Eurobank. Because these loans are frequently too large for a single bank to handle, Eurobanks will band together to form a bank lending **syndicate** to share the risk.

The credit risk on these loans is greater than on loans to other banks in the interbank market. Thus, the interest rate on Eurocredits must compensate the bank, or banking syndicate, for the added credit risk. On Eurocredits originating in London the base lending rate is LIBOR. The lending rate on these credits is stated as LIBOR + X percent, where X is the lending margin charged depending upon the creditworthiness of the borrower. Additionally, rollover pricing was created on Eurocredits so that Eurobanks do not end up paying more on Eurocurrency time deposits than they earn from the loans. Thus, a Eurocredit may be viewed as a series of shorter-term loans, where at the end of each time period (generally three or six months), the loan is rolled over and the base lending rate is repriced to current LIBOR over the next time interval of the loan.

Exhibit 11.5 shows the relationship among the various interest rates we have discussed in this section. The numbers come from the *Money Rates* section of *The Wall Street Journal* (see inside back cover). On March 3, 2005, U.S. domestic banks were paying 3.15 percent for six-month NCDs and the prime lending rate, the base rate charged the bank's most creditworthy corporate clients, was 5.50 percent. This appears to represent a spread of 2.35 percent for the bank to cover operating costs and earn a profit. By comparison, Eurobanks will accept six-month Eurodollar time deposits, say, Eurodollar NCDs, at a rate of 3.13 percent. (We use the London Late Eurodollar bid rate, which is the afternoon closing rate in London on large deposits.) The rate charged for Eurodollar credits is LIBOR + X percent, where any lending margin less than 2.34 percent appears to make the Eurodollar loan more attractive than the prime rate loan. Since lending margins typically fall in the range of ¼ percent to 3 percent, with the median rate being ½ percent to 1½ percent, the exhibit shows the narrow borrowing-lending spreads of Eurobankers in the Eurodollar credit market. This analysis seems to suggest that borrowers can obtain funds more cheaply in the Eurodollar market. However, international competition in recent years has forced U.S. commercial banks to lend domestically at subprime rates.

Rollover Pricing of a Eurocredit   Teltrex International can borrow $3,000,000 at LIBOR plus a lending margin of .75 percent per annum on a three-month rollover basis from Barclays in London. Suppose that three-month LIBOR is currently $5\frac{17}{32}$ percent. Further suppose that over the second three-month interval LIBOR falls to $5\frac{1}{8}$ percent. How much will Teltrex pay in interest to Barclays over the six-month period for the Eurodollar loan?

Solution: $3,000,000 × (.0553125 + .0075)/4 + $3,000.000 × (.05125 + .0075)/4 = $47,109.38 + $44,062.50 = $91,171.88

Forward Rate Agreements

欧洲银行在接受欧洲存款和扩张欧洲信贷时所面对的一个主要风险是存贷款到期期限长短不匹配所引起的利率风险。

远期利率协议 (FRA)是一种银行间协议,欧洲银行可以利用远期利率协议规避借贷期限不匹配产生的利率风险。

A major risk Eurobanks face in accepting Eurodeposits and in extending Eurocredits is interest rate risk resulting from a mismatch in the maturities of the deposits and credits. For example, if deposit maturities are longer than credit maturities, and interest rates fall, the credit rates will be adjusted downward while the bank is still paying a higher rate on deposits. Conversely, if deposit maturities are shorter than credit maturities, and interest rates rise, deposit rates will be adjusted upwards while the bank is still receiving a lower rate on credits. Only when deposit and credit maturities are perfectly matched will the rollover feature of Eurocredits allow the bank to earn the desired deposit-loan rate spread.

A forward rate agreement (FRA) is an interbank contract that allows the Eurobank to hedge the interest rate risk in mismatched deposits and credits. The size of the market is enormous. At June 2004, the notional value of FRAs outstanding was $13,144 billion. An FRA involves two parties, a buyer and a seller, where:

1. the buyer agrees to pay the seller the increased interest cost on a notional amount if interest rates fall below an agreement rate, or

2. the seller agrees to pay the buyer the increased interest cost if interest rates increase above the agreement rate.

Exhibit 11.6 graphs the payoff profile of a FRA. *SR* denotes the settlement rate and *AR* denotes the agreement rate.

EXHIBIT 11.6

Forward Rate Agreement Payoff Profile

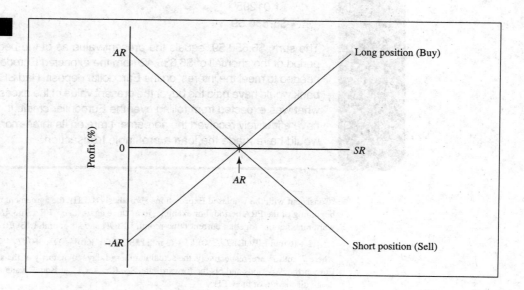

远期利率协议的目
的是解决标准期限的欧洲
存贷款协议因到期期限不
匹配而产生的问题。

FRAs are structured to capture the maturity mismatch in standard-length Eurodeposits and credits. For example, the FRA might be on a six-month interest rate for a six-month period beginning three months from today and ending nine months from today; this would be a "three against nine" FRA. The following time line depicts this FRA example.

Start	Agreement Period (3 Months)	Cash Settlement	FRA Period (6 Months)	End

The payment amount under an FRA is calculated as the absolute value of:

$$\frac{\text{Notional Amount} \times (SR - AR) \times days/360}{1 + (SR \times days/360)}$$

where *days* denotes the length of the FRA period.

EXAMPLE 11.2

Three against Six Forward Rate Agreement   As an example, consider a bank that has made a three-month Eurodollar loan of $3,000,000 against an offsetting six-month Eurodollar deposit. The bank's concern is that three-month LIBOR will fall below expectations and the Eurocredit is rolled over at the new lower base rate, making the six-month deposit unprofitable.[6] To protect itself, the bank could sell a $3,000,000 "three against six" FRA. The FRA will be priced such that the agreement rate is the expected three-month dollar LIBOR in three months.

Assume AR is 6 percent and the actual number of days in the three-month FRA period is 91. Thus, the bank expects to receive $45,500 (= $3,000,000 × .06 × 91/360) as the base amount of interest when the Eurodollar loan is rolled over for a second three-month period. If SR (i.e., three-month market LIBOR) is 5⅛ percent, the bank will receive only $38,864.58 in base interest, or a shortfall of $6,635.42. Since SR is less than AR, the bank will profit from the FRA it sold. It will receive from the buyer in three months a cash settlement at the beginning of the 91-day FRA period equaling the present value of the absolute value of [$3,000,000 × (.05125 − .06) × 91/360] = $6,635.42. This absolute present value is:

$$\frac{\$3,000,000 \times (.05125 - .06) \times 91/360}{1 + (.05125 \times 91/360)}$$

$$= \frac{\$6,635.42}{1.01295}$$

$$= \$6,550.59$$

The sum, $6,550.59, equals the present value as of the beginning of the 91-day FRA period of the shortfall of $6,635.42 from the expected Eurodollar loan proceeds that are needed to meet the interest on the Eurodollar deposit. Had SR been greater than AR, the bank would have paid the buyer the present value of the excess amount of interest above what was expected from rolling over the Eurodollar credit. In this event, the bank would have effectively received the agreement rate on its three-month Eurodollar loan, which would have made the loan a profitable transaction.

---

[6]Consistent with the Unbiased Expectations Hypothesis (UEH), the agreement rate *AR* is the expected rate at the beginning of the FRA period. For example, in a "three against six" FRA, the *AR* can be calculated from the forward rate that ties together current three-month LIBOR and six-month LIBOR:

$$([1 + (6 \text{ mth LIBOR})(T_2/360)]/[1 + (3 \text{ mth LIBOR})(T_1/360)] - 1) \times 360/(T_2 - T_1) = f \times 360/(T_2 - T_1) = AR,$$

where T_2 and T_1 are, respectively, the actual number of days to maturity of the six-month and three-month Eurocurrency periods and f is the forward rate. See Chapter 15 of Bodie, Kane, and Marcus (2005) for an in-depth discussion of the UEH.

EXHIBIT 11.7

Size of the Euronote Market at Year-End (in Billions of U.S. Dollars)

Instrument	1999	2000	2001	2002	2003
Euronotes	84.8	270.5	154.6	145.6	151.7
Eurocommercial Paper	175.2	223.3	243.1	292.2	417.6
Total	260.0	493.8	397.7	437.7	569.3

Source: International Banking and Financial Market Developments, Bank for International Settlements, Table 13A, p. 70, June 2000; Table 13A, p. A86, June 2002; Table 13A, p. 86, June 2004.

FRAs can be used for speculative purposes also. If one believes rates will be less than the AR, the sale of an FRA is the suitable position. In contrast, the purchase of an FRA is the suitable position if one believes rates will be greater than the AR.

Euronotes

欧洲票据 是由统称资金融通机构的一组国际投资银行或商业银行所承销的短期票据。

Euronotes are short-term notes underwritten by a group of international investment or commercial banks called a "facility." A client-borrower makes an agreement with a facility to issue Euronotes in its own name for a period of time, generally 3 to 10 years. Euronotes are sold at a discount from face value and pay back the full face value at maturity. Euronotes typically have maturities from three to six months. Borrowers find Euronotes attractive because the interest expense is usually slightly less—typically LIBOR plus ⅛ percent—in comparison to syndicated Eurobank loans. The banks find them attractive to issue because they earn a small fee from the underwriting or supply the funds and earn the interest return.

Eurocommercial Paper 欧洲商业票据

大多数欧洲商业票据都是以美元来标价的。

Eurocommercial paper, like domestic commercial paper, is an unsecured short-term promissory note issued by a corporation or a bank and placed directly with the investment public through a dealer. Like Euronotes, Eurocommercial paper is sold at a discount from face value. Maturities typically range from one to six months.

The vast majority of Eurocommercial paper is U.S. dollar-denominated. There are, however, a number of differences between the U.S. and Eurocommercial paper markets. The maturity of Eurocommercial paper tends to be about twice as long as U.S. commercial paper. For this reason, the secondary market is more active than for U.S. paper. Additionally, Eurocommercial paper issuers tend to be of much lower quality than their U.S. counterparts; consequently, yields tend to be higher.[7]

Exhibit 11.7 shows the year-end value of the Euronote and Eurocommercial paper market in billions of U.S. dollars for the years 1999 through 2003.

International Debt Crisis

国际债务危机

欠发达国家(LDC)

Certain principles define sound banking behavior. "At least five of these principles—namely, avoid an undue concentration of loans to single activities, individuals, or groups; expand cautiously into unfamiliar activities; know your counterparty; control mismatches between assets and liabilities; and beware that your collateral is not vulnerable to the same shocks that weaken the borrower—remain as relevant today as in earlier times."[8] Nevertheless, violation of the first two of these principles by some of the largest international banks in the world was responsible for the **international debt crisis** (sometimes called the Third World debt crisis), which was caused by lending to the sovereign governments of some **less-developed countries** (LDCs).

History

The international debt crisis began on August 20, 1982, when Mexico asked more than 100 U.S. and foreign banks to forgive its $68 billion in loans. Soon Brazil, Argentina, and more than 20 other developing countries announced similar problems in making

---

[7]See Dufey and Giddy (1994) for a list of the differences between the U.S. and Eurocommercial paper markets.
[8]The quotation is from *International Capital Markets: Part II. Systematic Issues in International Finance* (International Monetary Fund, Washington, D.C.), August 1993, p. 2.

the debt service on their bank loans. At the height of the crisis, Third World countries owed $1.2 trillion!

For years it appeared as if the crisis might bring down some of the world's largest banks. On average in 1989, the World Bank estimated that 19 LDCs had debt outstanding equivalent to 53.6 percent of their GNP. Interest payments alone amounted to 22.3 percent of export income. The international banking community was obviously shaken.

国际债务危机的根源是石油。

The source of the international debt crisis was oil. In the early 1970s, the Organization of Petroleum Exporting Countries (OPEC) became the dominant supplier of oil worldwide. Throughout this time period, OPEC raised oil prices dramatically. As a result of these price increases, OPEC amassed a tremendous amount of U.S. dollars, which was the currency generally demanded as payment from the oil-importing countries.

OPEC deposited billions in Eurodollar deposits; by 1976 the deposits amounted to nearly $100 billion. Eurobanks were faced with a huge problem of lending these funds in order to generate interest income to pay the interest on the deposits. Third World countries were only too eager to assist the eager Eurobankers in accepting Eurodollar loans that could be used for economic development *and* for payment of oil imports. The lending process became circular and known as *petrodollar recycling:* Eurodollar loan proceeds were used to pay for new oil imports; some of the oil revenues from developed and LDCs were redeposited, and the deposits were re-lent to Third World borrowers.

OPEC raised oil prices again in the late 1970s. The high oil prices were accompanied by high inflation and high unemployment in the industrialized countries. Tight monetary policies instituted in a number of the major industrialized countries led to a global recession and a decline in the demand for commodities, such as oil, and in commodity prices. The same economic policies led to higher real interest rates, which increased the borrowing costs of the LDCs, since most of the bank borrowing was denominated in U.S. dollars and had been made on a floating-rate basis. The collapse of commodity prices and the resultant loss of income made it impossible for the LDCs to meet their debt service obligations. As an indication of the magnitude of the involvement of some of the banks in LDC loans at the height of the crisis, Exhibit 11.8 lists the 10 largest U.S. bank lenders *just* to Mexico.

一个显而易见的原因是，银行持有巨额欧洲美元存款，必须尽快使这些存款产生利息收入。

Why would the international banks make such risky loans to LDC sovereign governments in the first place? One reason obviously was that they held vast sums of money in Eurodollar deposits that needed to be quickly placed to start producing interest income. Banks were simply too eager and not careful enough in analyzing the risks they were undertaking in lending to unfamiliar borrowers. Additionally, many U.S.

EXHIBIT 11.8

Ten Biggest U.S. Bank Lenders to Mexico
(in Billions of U.S. Dollars as of September 30, 1987)

Bank	Outstanding Loans to Mexico	Loan Loss Reserves for Developing Country Loans
Citicorp	$2.900	$3.432
BankAmerica Corp.	2.407	1.808
Manufacturers Hanover Corp.	1.883	1.833*
Chemical New York Corp.	1.733	1.505*
Chase Manhattan Corp.	1.660	1.970
Bankers Trust New York Corp.	1.277	1.000
J. P. Morgan & Co.	1.137	1.317
First Chicago Corp.	0.898	0.930
First Interstate Bancorp.	0.689	0.500
Wells Fargo & Co.	0.587	0.760

*As of June 30, 1987.
Source: The Wall Street Journal, December 30, 1987. Reprinted by permission of The Wall Street Journal, © 1987 Dow Jones & Company, Inc. All Rights Reserved Worldwide.

EXHIBIT 11.9

Debt-for-Equity Swap
Illustration

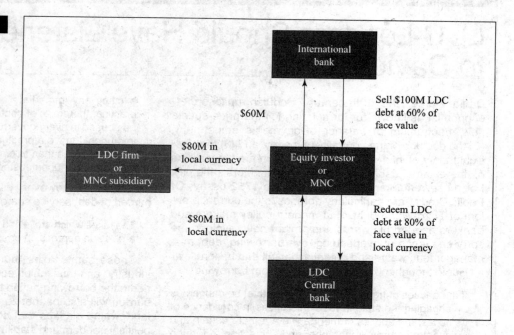

banks claim that there was official *arm-twisting* from Washington to assist the economic development of the Third World countries. Nevertheless, had the bankers and Washington policymakers been better versed in economic history, perhaps the LDC debt crisis might have been avoided, or at least mitigated. The International Finance in Practice box "LDC Lenders Should Have Listened to David Hume" presents an article documenting a clear warning by David Hume, the 18th-century Scottish economist, about the dangers of sovereign lending.

Debt-for-Equity Swaps

债权股权互换

In the midst of the LDC debt crisis, a secondary market developed for LDC debt at prices discounted significantly from face value. The secondary market consisted of approximately 50 creditor banks, investment banks, and boutique market makers. The LDC debt was purchased for use in **debt-for-equity swaps.** As part of debt rescheduling agreements among the bank lending syndicates and the debtor nations, creditor banks would sell their loans for U.S. dollars at discounts from face value to MNCs desiring to make equity investment in subsidiaries or local firms in the LDCs. An LDC central bank would buy the bank debt from a MNC at a smaller discount than the MNC paid, but in local currency. The MNC would use the local currency to make preapproved new investment in the LDC that was economically or socially beneficial to the LDC and its populace.

Exhibit 11.9 diagrams a hypothetical debt-for-equity swap. The exhibit shows a MNC purchasing $100 million of Mexican debt (either directly or through a market maker) from a creditor bank for $60 million, that is, at a 40 percent discount from face value. The MNC then redeems the $100 million note from the Mexican central bank for the equivalent of $80 million in Mexican pesos at the current exchange rate. The Mexican pesos are invested in a Mexican subsidiary of the MNC or in an equity position in an LDC firm. The MNC has paid $60 million for $80 million in Mexican pesos.

During the midst of the LDC debt crisis, Latin American debt was going at an average discount of approximately 70 percent. The September 10, 1990, issue of *Barron's* quotes Brazilian sovereign debt at 21.75 cents per dollar, Mexican debt at 43.12 cents, and Argentinean debt at only 14.25 cents.

现实生活中债权股
权互换的例子很多。

Real-life examples of debt-for-equity swaps abound. Chrysler invested $100 million in pesos in Chrysler de Mexico from money obtained from buying Mexican debt at a 56 percent discount. Volkswagen paid $170 million for $283 million in Mexican

LDC Lenders Should Have Listened to David Hume

David Hume, the 18th-century Scottish philosopher-economist, is known for formulating (1) the price-specie flow mechanism of balance-of-payments adjustment, (2) the doctrine of the neutrality of money, and (3) the classical theory of interest. Not so well known are his remarks on the external debt of sovereign nations. More's the pity. For those remarks, as contained in his 1752 essay "Of Public Credit," are particularly apropos to the current problem of Third World debt. Had modern policy makers and bankers heeded his words, they might have avoided the sorry sequence of overlending, overborrowing, debt mismanagement, waste and potential default that he foresaw.

Hume thought no good could result from borrowing:

If the abuses of treasures [held by the state] be dangerous by engaging the state in rash enterprizes in confidence of its riches; the abuses of mortgaging are more certain and inevitable; poverty, impotence, and subjection to foreign powers.

Nations, presuming they can find the necessary lenders, are tempted to borrow without limit and to squander the funds on unproductive projects:

It is very tempting to a minister to employ such an expedient as enables him to make a great figure during his administration without overburthening the people with taxes or exciting any immediate clamorous against himself. The practice, therefore, of contracting debt will almost infallibly be abused in every government. It would scarcely be more imprudent to give a prodigal son a credit in every banker's shop in London than to empower a statesman to draw bills in this manner upon posterity.

Eventually, however, interest must be paid and the burden of debt service charges will fall heavily on the poor:

The taxes which are levied to pay the interest of these debts are . . . an oppression on the poorer sort.

Those same taxes "hurt commerce and discourage industry" and thus inhibit economic development and condemn the borrowing nation to continuing poverty. The debt burden will also pauperize the prosperous merchant and landowning classes that constitute the main bulwark of political freedom and stability. With the pauperization of the middle class:

No expedient at all remains for resisting tyranny: Elections are swayed by bribery and corruption alone: And the middle power between king and people being totally removed, a grievous despotism must infallibly prevail. The landowners [and merchants] despised for their oppressions, will be utterly unable to make any opposition to it.

---

debt, which it swapped for the equivalent of $260 million of pesos. In a more complicated deal, CitiBank, acting as a market maker, paid $40 million to another bank for $60 million of Mexican debt, which was swapped with Banco de Mexico, the Mexican central bank, for $54 million worth of pesos later used by Nissan to expand a truck plant outside of Mexico City.

谁可以从债权股权互换中获利呢？理论上讲，所有参与者都有利可图，否则互换就难以形成。

Who benefits from a debt-for-equity swap? All parties are presumed to, or else the swap would not have taken place. The creditor bank benefits from getting an unproductive loan off its books and at least a portion of the principal repaid. The market maker obviously benefits from earning the bid-ask spread on the discounted loan amount. The LDC benefits in two ways. The first benefit comes from being able to pay off a "hard" currency loan (generally at a discount from face value) on which it cannot meet the debt service with its own local currency. The second benefit comes from the new productive investment made in the country, which was designed to foster economic growth. The equity investor benefits from the purchase of LDC local currency needed to make the investment at a discount from the current exchange rate.

现实生活中债权股权互换的例子很多。

Third World countries have only been open to allowing debt-for-equity swaps for certain types of investment. The LDC obtains the local currency to redeem the hard currency loan by printing it. This obviously increases the country's money supply and is inflationary. Thus, LDCs have only allowed swaps where the benefits of the new equity investment were expected to be greater than the harm caused to the economy by increased inflation. Acceptable types of investments have been in:

Can one imagine a more accurate assessment of the political situation in many Third World debtor nations?

Hume even foresaw the emigration of capital and labor to escape the burden of servicing debt held by foreign banks. Referring to England, then an underdeveloped nation, he said:

> As foreigners possess a great share of our national funds, they render the public, in a manner tributary to them, and may in time occasion by transport of our people and our industry.

As a country's debt expands, it eventually exceeds the taxable capacity to service it. Once this constraint is reached, Hume foresaw attempts to repudiate the debt. Contrary to Walter Wriston's dictum that sovereign nations never default, Hume argued that they would act on the belief that "either the nation must destroy public credit, or public credit will destroy the nation."

Such default, he thought, would hurt a nation's credit only temporarily. So forgetful and gullible are foreign banks that they would soon offer loans on the same generous terms and debt would flourish as before:

> So great dupes are the generality of mankind that notwithstanding such a violent shock to public credit as a voluntary bankruptcy in England would occasion, it would not probably be long ere credit would again revive in as flourishing a condition as before.

Forget rational expectations, said Hume; nobody behaves rationally all the time. People are destined to be fooled over and over again:

> Mankind are in all ages caught by the same baits: The same tricks played over and over again still trepan them. The heights of popularity and patriotism are still the beaten road to power and tyranny; flattery to treachery; standing armies to arbitrary governments; and the glory of God to the temporal interest of the clergy.

Because of the gullibility of lenders, "the fear of an everlasting destruction of credit . . . is a needless bugbear." In fact, a nation that has just defaulted may be a better credit risk than one that has not yet done so:

> A opulent knave . . . is a preferable debtor to an honest bankrupt: For the former, in order to carry on business, may find it his interest to discharge his debts where they are not exorbitant: The latter has it not in his power.

Hume's advice to would-be creditors: Lend sparingly. For once a country has borrowed beyond its taxable capacity, it will be tempted to default. From the debtor's viewpoint, debt repudiation may seem less costly than bleeding the nation dry in a vain effort to service the debt.

Hume, although prescient, was hardly infallible. He predicted that England would default on its large and rising debt within 50 years. His prediction was never realized. England's debt-service capacity exceeded his estimate.

Source: The Wall Street Journal, February 21, 1989, p. A20. Reprinted by permission of The Wall Street Journal, © 1989 Dow Jones & Company, Inc. All Rights Reserved Worldwide.

1. Export-oriented industries, such as automobiles, that will bring in hard currency.

2. High-technology industries that will lead to larger exports, improve the technological base of the country, and develop the skills of its people.

3. Tourist industry, such as resort hotels, that will increase tourism and visitors bringing hard currency.

4. Low-income housing developments that will improve the standard of living of some of the populace.

The Solution: Brady Bonds

解决方案：布雷迪债券

www.bradynet.com

This website offers current market information about Brady bonds.

Today, most debtor nations and creditor banks would agree that the international debt crisis is effectively over. U.S. Treasury Secretary Nicholas F. Brady of the first Bush administration is largely credited with designing a strategy in the spring of 1989 to resolve the problem. Brady's solution was to offer creditor banks one of three alternatives: (1) convert their loans to marketable bonds with a face value equal to 65 percent of the original loan amount; (2) convert the loans into collateralized bonds with a reduced interest rate of 6.5 percent; or, (3) lend additional funds to allow the debtor nations to get on their feet. As one can imagine, few banks chose the third alternative. The second alternative called for extending the debt maturities by 25 to 30 years and the purchase by the debtor nation of zero-coupon U.S. Treasury bonds with a corresponding maturity to guarantee the bonds and make them marketable. These bonds have come to be called **Brady bonds.**

By 1992, Brady bond agreements had been negotiated in many countries, including Argentina, Brazil, Mexico, Uruguay, Venezuela, Nigeria, and the Philippines. By August of 1992, 12 of 16 major debtor nations had reached refinancing agreements accounting for 92 percent of their outstanding private bank debt. In total, over $100 billion in bank debt has been converted to Brady bonds.

Japanese Banking Crisis

日本银行业危机的历史起因于日本金融系统的组织机构与一系列事件间的复杂关系。

The Japanese banking system ended fiscal year 2003 with its seventh deficit in nine years.[9] Cumulative losses over the nine-year period total ¥20 trillion (US$190 billion), an amount equivalent to approximately 80 percent of shareholders' capital at the beginning of the period. Superficially, the Japanese banking system looks healthy, with a capital ratio of nearly 12 percent. This figure, however, disguises the fact that a large percentage of bank capital comes from a combination of public funds and deferred tax credits that can only be realized as offsets against profit within a three-year time period. However, the profit potential for Japanese banks is questionable. A fundamental problem is the low margin charged on loans, resulting from strong competition from government-sponsored loans, government pressure to provide loans to small businesses on favorable terms, and the hesitation of bankers to charge an adequate rate to borrowers with whom they have close relationships.

The history of the Japanese banking crisis is a result of a complex combination of events and the structure of the Japanese financial system. In Japan, commercial banks have historically served as the financing arm and the center of a collaborative group of business firms known as *keiretsu*. Keiretsu members have cross-holdings of one another's equity and ties of trade and credit. Typically these equity shares are not traded. Additionally, Japanese banks frequently hold large equity positions in keiretsu members, which in turn tend to be highly levered in comparison to U.S. business firms. The robust Japanese economy of the late 1980s, fueled by large trade surpluses, created an economic environment of rapidly accelerating financial and real asset prices. Japanese banks, flush with cash and a desire to gain worldwide market share, engaged in tremendous lending both at home and abroad. A significant amount of this was in the form of real estate loans. During this time, Japanese firms had little trouble in servicing their bank loans.

日本股市的崩溃引发了整个日本经济，尤其是日本银行业的螺旋式衰退。

The collapse of the Japanese stock market set in motion a downward spiral for the entire Japanese economy, and, in particular, Japanese banks. The Japanese stock market bubble burst at year-end 1989. As of March 2005 it stands at less than a third of its value at the peak. The downturn in the Japanese economy and the drop in Japanese real estate values put in jeopardy massive amounts of bank loans to corporations. Additionally, the concurrent downturn in the U.S. economy resulted in a drop in value of real estate investments there.

The state of the Japanese banking system is indeed dire, but appears to be improving. In 2002, nonperforming loans stood at ¥32 trillion (US$245 billion). Major banks have stepped up efforts to reduce this amount by half by March 2005. At current low interest rates it is not too difficult for bank customers to meet periodic interest payments. Moreover, today's low rates have reduced the cost for banks to continue carrying nonperforming loans on their books. However, it is questionable whether these same customers will be able to make debt service obligations when interest rates turn up or whether they have the incentive or means to eventually pay off the loans. It is unlikely that the Japanese banking crisis will be rectified anytime soon. At least two important factors make this true. First, the Japanese financial system does not have a legal infrastructure that allows for an expedient method to restructure bad bank loans. Secondly, Japanese bank managers have little incentive to change outdated business practices because of the interrelations that exist between bank shareholders and bank customers.

---

[9]Much of this discussion follows from the BIS 72nd and 74th *Annual Reports*.

The Asian Crisis

有趣的是，在亚洲
金融危机爆发前，该地
区经济发展一度是靠创
纪录的私人资本输入来
筹集资金的。

As noted in Chapter 2, the Asian crisis began in mid-1997 when Thailand devalued the baht. Subsequently other Asian countries devalued their currencies by letting them float—ending their pegged value with the U.S. dollar. Not since the LDC debt crisis have international financial markets experienced such widespread turbulence. The troubles, which began in Thailand, soon affected other countries in the region and also emerging markets in other regions.[10]

Interestingly, the Asian crisis followed a period of economic expansion in the region financed by record private capital inflows. Bankers from the G-10 countries actively sought to finance the growth opportunities in Asia by providing businesses in the region with a full assortment of products and services. Domestic price bubbles in East Asia, particularly in real estate, were fostered by these capital inflows. The simultaneous liberalization of financial markets contributed to bubbles in financial asset prices as well. Additionally, the close interrelationships common among commercial firms and financial institutions in Asia resulted in poor investment decision making.

在东亚，债权银行
的风险暴露基本只涉及
当地银行和商业企业，
并不像欠发达国家债务危
机那样牵涉到主权政府。

The risk exposure of the lending banks in East Asia was primarily to local banks and commercial firms, and not to sovereignties, as in the LDC debt crisis. It may have been implicitly assumed, however, that the governments would come to the rescue of their private banks should financial problems develop. The history of managed growth in the region at least suggested that the economic and financial system, as an integral unit, could be managed in an economic downturn. This did not turn out to be the case. The Asian crisis is the most recent, but yet another, example of banks making a multitude of poor loans.

政治风险

It is doubtful if the international debt crisis or the Asian crisis has taught banks a lasting lesson about the risks of lending to sovereign governments or large amounts of funds targeted to specific regions of the world. For some reason, bankers always seem willing to lend huge amounts to borrowers with a limited potential to repay. Regardless, there is no excuse for not properly evaluating the potential risks of an investment or loan. In lending to a sovereign government or making loans to private parties in distant parts of the world, the risks are unique, and a proper analysis of the economic, political, and social factors that constitute **political risk** is warranted. While this subject might fit nicely with the current discussion, we leave it instead for the next chapter on the international bond market and Chapter 16 on direct foreign investment.

SUMMARY

本章介绍了国际银行业、国际
货币市场以及第三世界债务危机等
问题。本章是接着第5章关于世界金
融市场和机构进行介绍的。
    1. 国际银行的特点可以根据所
提供的服务类型来说明。国际银行
通过提供贸易融资为其客户提供进
出口业务方面的便利。国际银行也
提供外汇兑换服务，帮助客户规避
汇率风险，自营外汇交易业务，并
创造货币衍生品市场等。一些国际
银行还吸收外汇存款，向非国内银
行客户发放外币贷款。此外，如果
银行业规章许可，一些国际银行也
可能参与承销国际债券。
    2. 国际银行机构有各种类型，包
括代理银行、代表处、国外分行、子
银行及联营银行、《埃奇法案》银
行、离岸金融中心和国际银行便利。国

In this chapter, the topics of international banking, the international money market, and the Third World debt crisis were discussed. This chapter begins the textbook's five-chapter sequence on world financial markets and institutions.

1. International banks can be characterized by the types of services they provide. International banks facilitate the imports and exports of their clients by arranging trade financing. They also arrange foreign currency exchange, assist in hedging exchange rate exposure, trade foreign exchange for their own account, and make a market in currency derivative products. Some international banks seek deposits of foreign currencies and make foreign currency loans to nondomestic bank customers. Additionally, some international banks may participate in the underwriting of international bonds if banking regulations allow.

---

[10]The discussion in this section closely follows the discussion on the Asian crisis found in *International Capital Markets: Developments, Prospects, and Key Policy Issues* (International Monetary Fund, Washington, D.C.), September 1998, pp. 1–6 and the Bank for International Settlements working paper titled "Supervisory Lessons to Be Drawn from the Asian Crisis," June 1999.

际银行设立各类机构以及提供各种服务的原因各不相同。

3. 欧洲货币市场是国际货币市场的核心。欧洲货币是指存放在位于货币发行国之外国家的国际银行的该种货币的定期存款。例如，占货币市场很大份额的欧洲美元是指存放在美国境外的银行中的美元存款。欧洲货币市场的总部位于伦敦。欧洲银行是指吸收欧洲货币存款并发放欧洲货币贷款的国际银行。本章讲述了欧洲货币的产生过程并介绍了欧洲信贷即欧洲货币贷款的性质。

4. 其他主要的欧洲货币市场工具包括：远期利率协议、欧洲票据和欧洲商业票据。

5. 资本充足率是指银行为防范风险资产以降低经营失败概率而持有的权益资本和其他证券的数量。1988年的《巴塞尔协议》对从事国际交易业务的银行制定了确定资本充足率的框架。《巴塞尔协议》所针对的主要是银行吸收存款和发放贷款这一业务。因此，《巴塞尔协议》所关注的就是信贷风险问题。该协定已经为全球各地的银行监管部门所广泛采纳。在20世纪90年代，银行在权益、利率和汇率等衍生品方面的交易逐渐增多，而其中的许多衍生品在制定《巴塞尔协议》时甚至根本不存在，因而《巴塞尔协议》关于资本充足率的规定也就不足以防范市场风险。此外，包括电脑错误、文件管理失误和欺诈在内的经营风险也是最初的协定所未曾考虑的。2004年，"十国集团"的中央银行和银行监管机构签订了被称为《巴塞尔协议II》的新的资本充足率方案。《巴塞尔协议II》所要求的最低资本充足率为8%，以应对银行所面临的信贷、市场和经营风险。据估计，该新协定会在2006年年底得到正式实施。

6. 国际债务危机的起因在于国际银行对第三世界主权国家政府的过度放贷。危机始于20世纪70年代，当时石油输出国家组织的成员国将大量欧洲美元存入银行，而银行必须将这些存款借出以支付存款的利息。随后因石油价格的暴涨导致了高失业率和通货膨胀，使得很多欠发达国家不堪负担偿还贷款的义务。债务数额之大使得全球很多大银行，特别是借出大部分存款的美国银行濒于危险境地。虽然一些银行采用了债权股权互换方式来处理第三世界国家的债务问题，但最为主要的解决方法是采用抵押性的布雷迪债券，允许欠发达国家减少偿还金额并可延期偿还。

7. 亚洲金融危机爆发于1997年年中期。该危机始于泰国，迅速蔓延到该地区的其他国家或地区，并波及到其他地区的一些新兴市场。自欠发达国家债务危机爆发以来，国际金融市场从未遭受过这样大范围的动荡。就在亚洲金融危机爆发之前，该地区因大量私人资本的流入而一度出现了经济扩张。当时，来自工业化国家的银行竞相为该地区的成长机会提供资金。在东亚地区，银行信贷的风险暴露主要来自于当地的银行和企业，而不像欠发达国家的债务危机那样来自于主权政府。不过，人们很难准确计量政治风险和经济风险。亚洲金融危机是商业银行因提供大量不良贷款而发生危机的一个近例。

2. Various types of international banking offices include correspondent bank relationships, representative offices, foreign branches, subsidiaries and affiliates, Edge Act banks, offshore banking centers, and International Banking Facilities. The reasons for the various types of international banking offices and the services they provide vary considerably.

3. The core of the international money market is the Eurocurrency market. A Eurocurrency is a time deposit of money in an international bank located in a country different from the country that issued the currency. For example, Eurodollars, which make up the largest part of the market, are deposits of U.S. dollars in banks outside of the United States. The Eurocurrency market is headquartered in London. Eurobanks are international banks that seek Eurocurrency deposits and make Eurocurrency loans. The chapter illustrated the creation of Eurocurrency and discussed the nature of Eurocredits, or Eurocurrency loans.

4. Other main international money market instruments include forward rate agreements, Euronotes, and Eurocommercial paper.

5. Capital adequacy refers to the amount of equity capital and other securities a bank holds as reserves against risky assets to reduce the probability of a bank failure. The 1988 Basel Capital Accord established a framework for determining capital adequacy requirements for internationally active banks. The Basel Accord primarily addressed banking in the context of deposit gathering and lending. Thus, its focus was on credit risk. The accord has been widely adopted throughout the world by national bank regulators. Bank trading in equity, interest rate, and exchange rate derivative products escalated throughout the 1990s. Many of these products were not even in existence when the Basel Accord was drafted. Consequently, the capital adequacy requirements were not sufficient to safeguard against market risk. Additionally, operational risk, which includes such matters as computer failure, poor documentation, and fraud, was not covered by the original accord. In 2004, a new capital adequacy framework commonly referred to as Basel II was endorsed by central bank governors and bank supervisors in the G-10 countries. It requires 8 percent minimum capital to be held against a bank's credit, market, and operational risk. It is expected to be available for implementation by year-end 2006.

6. The international debt crisis was caused by international banks lending more to Third World sovereign governments than they should have. The crisis began during the 1970s when OPEC countries flooded banks with huge sums of Eurodollars that needed to be lent to cover the interest being paid on the deposits. Because of a subsequent collapse in oil prices, high unemployment, and high inflation, many less-developed countries could not afford to meet the debt service on their loans. The huge sums involved jeopardized some of the world's largest banks, in particular, U.S. banks that had lent most of the money. Debt-for-equity swaps were one means by which some banks shed themselves of problem Third World debt. But the main solution was collateralized Brady bonds, which allowed the less-developed countries to reduce the debt service on their loans and extend the maturities far into the future.

7. The Asian crisis began in mid-1997. The troubles, which began in Thailand, soon affected other countries in the region and also emerging markets in other regions. Not since the LDC debt crisis have international financial markets experienced such widespread turbulence. The crisis followed a period of economic expansion in the region financed by record private capital inflows. Bankers from industrialized countries actively sought to finance the growth opportunities. The risk exposure of the lending banks in East Asia was primarily to local banks and commercial firms, and not to sovereignties, as in the LDC debt crisis. Nevertheless, the political and economic risks were not correctly assessed. The Asian crisis is the most recent example of commercial banks making a multitude of poor loans.

KEY WORDS

affiliate bank, *270*
bank capital
  adequacy, *272*
Basel Accord, *272*
Brady bonds, *283*
correspondent bank
  relationship, *269*
debt-for-equity
  swap, *281*
Edge Act bank, *270*
Eurobank, *274*
Eurocommercial
  paper, *279*
Eurocredit, *276*

Eurocurrency, *274*
Euronote, *279*
Euro Interbank Offered
  Rate (EURIBOR), *275*
foreign branch bank, *269*
forward rate agreement
  (FRA), *277*
full service bank, *267*
International Banking
  Facility (IBF), *271*
international debt
  crisis, *279*
less-developed countries
  (LDCs), *279*

London Interbank
  Offered Rate
  (LIBOR), *274*
merchant bank, *267*
negotiable certificate of
  deposit (NCD), *275*
offshore banking
  center, *271*
political risk, *285*
representative office, *269*
subsidiary bank, *270*
syndicate, *276*
universal bank, *267*

QUESTIONS

1. Briefly discuss some of the services that international banks provide their customers and the marketplace.

2. Briefly discuss the various types of international banking offices.

3. How does the deposit-loan rate spread in the Eurodollar market compare with the deposit-loan rate spread in the domestic U.S. banking system? Why?

4. What is the difference between the Euronote market and the Eurocommercial paper market?

5. Briefly discuss the cause and the solution(s) to the international bank crisis involving less-developed countries.

6. What warning did David Hume, the 18th-century Scottish philosopher-economist, give about lending to sovereign governments?

7. What are the approaches available to an internationally active bank for valuing its credit risk under Basel II?

PROBLEMS

1. Grecian Tile Manufacturing of Athens, Georgia, borrows $1,500,000 at LIBOR plus a lending margin of 1.25 percent per annum on a six-month rollover basis from a London bank. If six-month LIBOR is 4½ percent over the first six-month interval and 5⅜ percent over the second six-month interval, how much will Grecian Tile pay in interest over the first year of its Eurodollar loan?

2. A bank sells a "three against six" $3,000,000 FRA for a three-month period beginning three months from today and ending six months from today. The purpose of the FRA is to cover the interest rate risk caused by the maturity mismatch from having made a three-month Eurodollar loan and having accepted a six-month Eurodollar deposit. The agreement rate with the buyer is 5.5 percent. There are actually 92 days in the three-month FRA period. Assume that three months from today the settlement rate is 4⅞ percent. Determine how much the FRA is worth and who pays who—the buyer pays the seller or the seller pays the buyer.

3. Assume the settlement rate in problem 2 is 6⅛ percent. What is the solution now?

4. A "three against nine" FRA has an agreement rate of 4.75 percent. You believe six-month LIBOR in three months will be 5.125 percent. You decide to take a speculative position in a FRA with a $1,000,000 notional value. There are 183 days in the FRA period. Determine whether you should buy or sell the FRA and what your expected profit will be if your forecast is correct about the six-month LIBOR rate.

5. Recall the FRA problem presented as Example 11.2. Show how the bank can alternatively use a position in Eurodollar futures contracts (Chapter 7) to hedge the interest rate risk created by the maturity mismatch it has with the $3,000,000 six-month Eurodollar deposit and rollover Eurocredit position indexed to three-month LIBOR. Assume that the bank can take a position in Eurodollar futures contracts that mature in three months and have a futures price of 94.00.

6. The Fisher effect (Chapter 6) suggests that nominal interest rates differ between countries because of differences in the respective rates of inflation. According to the Fisher effect and your examination of the one-year Eurocurrency interest rates presented in Exhibit 11.3, order the currencies from the eight countries from highest to lowest in terms of the size of the inflation premium embedded in the nominal interest rates for March 3, 2005.

7. An internationally active bank has a $500 million portfolio of investments and bank credits. $100 million are claims on sovereigns with a AAA credit rating, $100 million are claims on corporates with a AAA credit rating, $100 million are claims on sovereigns with a single A credit rating, $100 million are claims on corporates with a single A credit rating, and $100 million are claims on corporates with a single B credit rating. What is the minimum level of capital according to Basel II the bank must maintain using the standardized approach for valuing credit risk? Be sure to show both the value of the risk-weighted assets and the amount of bank capital.

INTERNET EXERCISES

1. Exhibit 11.5 compares the spread between the prime borrowing rate and dollar LIBOR. Go to the Bloomberg website www.bloomberg.com/markets/rates.index.html to see the current spread and the spread for one month to one year prior.

2. In this chapter, we noted that universal banks provide a host of services to corporate clients. Bank of America, one of the world's largest banks, is an example of a universal bank. Go to its website www.corp.bankofamerica.com to view the global services they provide.

3. Go to the Brady Net, Inc. website at www.bradynet.com. Click on the "Ratings" link and then click on "General Ratings and History." Compare and contrast the credit ratings assigned to various countries by the rating services.

MINI CASE

Detroit Motors' Latin American Expansion

It is September 1990 and Detroit Motors of Detroit, Michigan, is considering establishing an assembly plant in Latin America for a new utility vehicle it has just designed. The cost of the capital expenditures has been estimated at $65,000,000. There is not much of a sales market in Latin America, and virtually all output would be exported to the United States for sale. Nevertheless, an assembly plant in Latin America is attractive for at least two reasons. First, labor costs are expected to be half what Detroit Motors would have to pay in the United States to union workers. Since the assembly plant will be a new facility for a newly designed vehicle, Detroit Motors does not expect any hassle from its U.S. union in establishing the plant in Latin America. Secondly, the chief financial officer (CFO) of Detroit Motors believes that a debt-for-equity swap can be arranged with at least one of the Latin American countries that has not been able to meet its debt service on its sovereign debt with some of the major U.S. banks.

The September 10, 1990, issue of Barron's indicated the following prices (cents on the dollar) on Latin American bank debt:

Brazil	21.75
Mexico	43.12
Argentina	14.25
Venezuela	46.25
Chile	70.25

The CFO is not comfortable with the level of political risk in Brazil and Argentina, and has decided to eliminate them from consideration. After some preliminary discussions with the central banks of Mexico, Venezuela, and Chile, the CFO has learned that all three countries would be interested in hearing a detailed presentation about the type of facility Detroit Motors would construct, how long it would take, the number of locals that would be employed, and the number of units that would be manufactured per year. Since it is time-consuming to prepare and make these presentations, the CFO would like to approach the most attractive candidate first. He has learned that the central bank of Mexico will redeem its debt at 80 percent of face value in a debt-for-equity swap, Venezuela at 75 percent, and Chile 100 percent. As a first step, the CFO decides an analysis based purely on financial considerations is necessary to determine which country looks like the most viable candidate. You are asked to assist in the analysis. What do you advise?

REFERENCES & SUGGESTED READINGS

Bank for International Settlements. "Supervisory Lessons to Be Drawn from the Asian Crisis." Basel: Bank for International Settlements, June 1999.

Bank for International Settlements. *72nd Annual Report*. Basel: Bank for International Settlements, July 2002.

Bank for International Settlements. *74th Annual Report*. Basel: Bank for International Settlements, July 2004.

Bank for International Settlements. *International Convergence of Capital Measurement and Capital Standards: A Revised Framework*. Basel: Bank for International Settlements, July 2004.

Bodie, Zvi, Alex Kane, and Alan J. Marcus. *Investments*, 6th ed. New York: McGraw-Hill/Irwin, 2005.

Dufey, Gunter, and Ian Giddy. *The International Money Market*, 2nd ed. Upper Saddle River, N.J.: Prentice Hall, 1994.

Goldberg, Lawrence G., and Robert Grosse. "Location Choice of Foreign Banks in the United States." *Journal of Economics and Business* 46 (1994), pp. 367–79.

Hultman, Charles W. *The Environment of International Banking*. Englewood Cliffs, N.J.: Prentice Hall, 1990.

International Monetary Fund. *International Capital Markets: Part II. Systemic Issues in International Finance*. Washington, D.C.: International Monetary Fund, August 1993.

International Monetary Fund. *International Capital Markets: Developments, Prospects, and Key Policy Issues*. Washington, D.C.: International Monetary Fund, September 1998.

Rivera-Batiz, Francisco L., and Luis Rivera-Batiz. *International Finance and Open Economy Macroeconomics*. 2nd ed. Upper Saddle River, N.J.: Prentice Hall, 1994.

Rugman, Alan M., and Shyan J. Kamath. "International Diversification and Multinational Banking." In Sarkis J. Khoury and Alo Ghosh, eds.. *Recent Developments in International Banking and Finance*. Lexington, Mass.: Lexington Books, 1987.

11A   Eurocurrency Creation

As an illustration, consider the following simplified example of the creation of Eurodollars. Assume a U.S. Importer purchases $100 of merchandise from a German Exporter and pays for the purchase by drawing a $100 check on his U.S. checking account (demand deposit). Further assume the German Exporter deposits the $100 check received as payment in a demand deposit in the U.S. bank (which in actuality represents the entire U.S. commercial banking system). This transaction can be represented by T accounts, where changes in assets are on the left and changes in liabilities are on the right side of the T, as follows:

U.S. Commercial Bank

	Demand Deposits	
	U.S. Importer	−$100
	German Exporter	+$100

At this point, all that has changed in the U.S. banking system is that ownership of $100 of demand deposits has been transferred from domestic to foreign control.

The German Exporter is not likely to leave his deposit in the form of a demand deposit for long, as no interest is being earned on this type account. If the funds are not needed for the operation of the business, the Germany Exporter can deposit the $100 in a time deposit in a bank outside the United States and receive a greater rate of interest than if the funds were put in a U.S. time deposit. Assume the German Exporter closes out his demand deposit in the U.S. Bank and redeposits the funds in a London Eurobank. The London Eurobank credits the German Exporter with a $100 time deposit and deposits the $100 into its correspondent bank account (demand deposit) with the U.S. Bank (banking system). These transactions are represented as follows by T accounts:

U.S. Commercial Bank

	Demand Deposits	
	German Exporter	−$100
	London Eurobank	+$100

London Eurobank

Demand Deposits		*Time Deposits*	
U.S. Bank	+$100	German Exporter	+$100

Two points are noteworthy from these transactions. First, ownership of $100 of demand deposits has again been transferred (from the German Exporter to the London Eurobank), but the entire $100 still remains on deposit in the U.S. Bank. Second, the $100 time deposit of the German Exporter in the London Eurobank represents the creation of Eurodollars. This deposit exists in *addition* to the dollars deposited in the United States. Hence, no dollars have flowed out of the U.S. banking system in the creation of Eurodollars.

The London Eurobank will soon lend out the dollars, as it cannot afford to pay interest on a time deposit on which it is not earning a return. To whom will the London Eurobank lend the dollars? Most obviously to a party needing dollars for a dollar-denominated business transaction or to an investor desiring to invest in the United States. Let's assume that a Dutch Importer borrows $100 from the London Eurobank for the purpose of purchasing merchandise from a U.S. Exporter for resale in the Netherlands. The T accounts representing these transactions are as follows:

London Eurobank

Demand Deposits			
U.S. Bank	−$100		
Loans			
Dutch Importer	+$100		

U.S. Commercial Bank

		Demand Deposits	
		London Eurobank	−$100
		Dutch Importer	+$100

Dutch Importer

Demand Deposits		Loan from	
in U.S. Bank	+$100	London Eurobank	+$100

Note from these transactions that the London Eurobank transfers ownership of $100 of its demand deposits held in the U.S. Commercial Bank to the Dutch Exporter in exchange for the $100 loan.

The Dutch Exporter will draw a check on its demand deposit in the U.S. Bank to pay the U.S. Exporter for the merchandise shipment. The U.S. Exporter will deposit the check in his U.S. Bank demand deposit. These transactions are represented as follows:

Dutch Importer

Demand Deposit			
in U.S. Bank	−$100		
Inventory	+$100		

U.S. Exporter

Inventory	−$100		
Demand Deposit			
in U.S. Bank	+$100		

U.S. Commercial Bank

		Demand Deposit	
		Dutch Importer	−$100
		U.S. Exporter	+$100

The T accounts show that $100 of demand deposits in the U.S. Bank have changed ownership, going from the control of the Dutch Importer to the U.S. Exporter— or from foreign to U.S. ownership. The original $100, however, never left the U.S. banking system.

QUESTION   Explain how Eurocurrency is created.

12 International Bond Market

本章继续讨论国际资本市场及组织，但重点是国际债券市场。

国际债券市场可以分为两类基本市场：外国债券市场和欧洲债券市场。

THIS CHAPTER CONTINUES the discussion of international capital markets and institutions, focusing on the international bond market. The chapter is designed to be useful for the financial officer of a MNC interested in sourcing new debt capital in the international bond market, as well as for the international investor interested in international fixed-income securities.

The chapter opens with a brief statistical presentation showing the size of the world's bond markets and the major currencies in which bonds are denominated. The next section presents some useful definitions that describe exactly what is meant by the international bond market. The accompanying discussion elaborates on the features that distinguish these market segments and the various types of bond instruments traded in them. An examination of the currency distribution of the international bond market and the nationality and the type of borrower follows. Trading practices in the Eurobond market are discussed next. The chapter concludes with a discussion of international bond credit ratings and bond market indexes that are useful for performance analysis.

The World's Bond Markets: A Statistical Perspective

Exhibit 12.1 presents an overview of the world's bond markets. It shows the amounts of domestic and international bonds outstanding denominated in the major currencies. The exhibit shows that at year-end 2003 the face value of bonds outstanding in the world was approximately $51,395.8 billion. Domestic bonds account for the largest share of outstanding bonds, equaling $ 40,293.3 billion, or 78 percent, of the total.

EXHIBIT 12.1	Amounts of Domestic and International Bonds Outstanding (As of Year-End 2003 in Billions of U.S. Dollars)					
Currency	Domestic	Percent	International	Percent	Total	Percent
U.S. dollar	17,930.7	44.5	4,492.5	40.5	22,423.2	43.6
Euro	8,436.4	20.9	4,834.5	43.5	13,270.9	25.8
Pound sterling	1,274.6	3.2	778.7	7.0	2,053.3	4.0
Yen	8,145.0	20.2	488.6	4.4	8,633.6	16.8
Other	4,506.6	11.2	508.2	4.6	5,014.8	9.8
Total	40,293.3	100.0	11,102.5	100.0	51,395.8	100.0

Source: Derived from data in Tables 13B and 16A, pp. A87 and A92, respectively, in International Banking and Financial Market Developments, Bank for International Settlements, June 2004.

Exhibit 12.1 shows that the U.S. dollar, the euro, the pound sterling, and the yen are the four currencies in which the majority of domestic and international bonds are denominated. Proportionately more domestic bonds than international bonds are denominated in the dollar (44.5 percent versus 40.5 percent) and the yen (20.2 percent versus 4.4 percent) while more international bonds than domestic bonds are denominated in the euro (43.5 percent versus 20.9 percent) and the pound sterling (7.0 percent versus 3.2 percent).

Foreign Bonds and Eurobonds

外国债券

欧洲债券

The international bond market encompasses two basic market segments: foreign bonds and Eurobonds. A **foreign bond** issue is one offered by a foreign borrower to the investors in a national capital market and denominated in that nation's currency. An example is a German MNC issuing dollar-denominated bonds to U.S. investors. A **Eurobond** issue is one denominated in a particular currency but sold to investors in national capital markets other than the country that issued the denominating currency. An example is a Dutch borrower issuing dollar-denominated bonds to investors in the U.K., Switzerland, and the Netherlands. The markets for foreign bonds and Eurobonds operate in parallel with the domestic national bond markets, and all three market groups compete with one another.[1]

Exhibit 12.2 presents the year-end amounts of international bonds outstanding for 1999 through 2003. The exhibit classifies the amounts by type of issue. As the exhibit shows, the amounts of international bonds have increased steadily each year. At year-end 1999, $5,105.5 billion in bonds were outstanding; in 2003 the amount was $11,102.5 billion, a 117 percent increase.

EXHIBIT 12.2		1999	2000	2001	2002	2003
International Bond Amounts Outstanding Classified by Major Instruments (At Year-End in Billions of U.S. Dollars)	Instrument					
	Straight-fixed rate	3,633.6	4,158.3	5,015.8	6,253.9	7,891.6
	Floating-rate notes	1,235.8	1,478.9	1,822.5	2,192.0	2,849.3
	Convertible issues	218.3	230.9	264.1	298.5	351.5
	With equity warrants	17.8	11.4	10.3	10.5	10.0
	Total	5,105.5	5,879.4	7,112.7	8,754.9	11,102.5

Source: Derived from International Banking and Financial Market Developments, Bank for International Settlements, Table 13B, p. 71, June 2000; p. A87, June 2002, 2003, 2004.

---

[1]In this chapter the terms *market segment, market group,* and *market* are used interchangeably when referring to the foreign bond and Eurobond divisions of the international bond market.

在任何年份，新发
行的国际债券中几乎有
80％是欧洲债券而不是
外国债券。

In any given year, roughly 80 percent of new international bonds are likely to be Eurobonds rather than foreign bonds. Eurobonds are known by the currency in which they are denominated, for example, U.S. dollar Eurobonds, yen Eurobonds, and Swiss franc Eurobonds, or, correspondingly, Eurodollar bonds, Euroyen bonds, and EuroSF bonds. Foreign bonds, on the other hand, frequently have colorful names that designate the country in which they are issued. For example, *Yankee* bonds are dollar-denominated foreign bonds originally sold to U.S. investors, *Samurai* bonds are yen-denominated foreign bonds sold in Japan, and *Bulldogs* are pound sterling–denominated foreign bonds sold in the U.K.

Bearer Bonds and Registered Bonds
不记名债券与记名
债券

美国的证券法规要
求向美国公民销售的扬
基债券和美国公司债券
必须是记名债券。

Eurobonds are usually bearer bonds. With a **bearer bond,** possession is evidence of ownership. The issuer does not keep any records indicating who is the current owner of a bond. With **registered bonds,** the owner's name is on the bond and it is also recorded by the issuer, or else the owner's name is assigned to a bond serial number recorded by the issuer. When a registered bond is sold, a new bond certificate is issued with the new owner's name, or the new owner's name is assigned to the bond serial number.

U.S. security regulations require Yankee bonds and U.S. corporate bonds sold to U.S. citizens to be registered. Bearer bonds are very attractive to investors desiring privacy and anonymity. One reason for this is that they enable tax evasion. Consequently, investors will generally accept a lower yield on bearer bonds than on registered bonds of comparable terms, making them a less costly source of funds for the issuer to service.

National Security Regulations

Foreign bonds must meet the security regulations of the country in which they are issued. This means that publicly traded Yankee bonds must meet the same regulations as U.S. domestic bonds. The U.S. Securities Act of 1933 requires full disclosure of relevant information relating to a security issue. The U.S. Securities Exchange Act of 1934 established the Securities and Exchange Commission (SEC) to administer the 1933 Act. Securities sold in the United States to public investors must be registered with the SEC, and a prospectus disclosing detailed financial information about the issuer must be provided and made available to prospective investors. The expense of the registration process, the time delay it creates in bringing a new issue to market (four additional weeks), and the disclosure of information that many foreign borrowers consider private historically have made it more desirable for foreign borrowers to raise U.S. dollars in the Eurobond market. The shorter length of time in bringing a Eurodollar bond issue to market, coupled with the lower rate of interest that borrowers pay for Eurodollar bond financing in comparison to Yankee bond financing, are two major reasons why the Eurobond segment of the international bond market is roughly four times the size of the foreign bond segment. Because Eurobonds do not have to meet national security regulations, name recognition of the issuer is an extremely important factor in being able to source funds in the international capital market.

Eurobonds sold in the United States may not be sold to U.S. citizens. To prevent this, the initial purchaser receives the bearer bond only after a 90-day waiting period and presentation of identification that one is not a U.S. citizen. Of course, nothing prevents a U.S. investor from repurchasing bearer bonds in the secondary market after 90 days.

Withholding Taxes

Prior to 1984, the United States required a 30 percent withholding tax on interest paid to nonresidents who held U.S. government or corporate bonds. Moreover, U.S. firms issuing Eurodollar bonds from the United States were required to withhold the tax on interest paid to foreigners. In 1984, the withholding tax law was repealed. Additionally, U.S. corporations were allowed to issue domestic bearer bonds to nonresidents, but Congress would not grant this privilege to the Treasury.

预提税法案的废止
会引起美国政府债券与
欧洲美元债券相对收益
的重大变化。

The repeal of the withholding tax law caused a substantial shift in the relative yields on U.S. government and Eurodollar bonds. Prior to 1984, top-quality Eurodollar bonds sold overseas traded at lower yields than U.S. Treasury bonds of similar maturities that were subject to the withholding tax. Afterwards the situation was reversed; foreign investors found the safety of registered U.S. Treasury bonds without the withholding tax more attractive than higher yields on corporate Eurodollar bond issues.

Other Recent Regulatory Changes
上架登记

Two other recent changes in U.S. security regulations have had an effect on the international bond market. One is *Rule 415,* which the SEC instituted in 1982 to allow shelf registration. **Shelf registration** allows an issuer to preregister a securities issue, and then shelve the securities for later sale when financing is actually needed. Shelf registration has thus eliminated the time delay in bringing a foreign bond issue to market in the United States, but it has not eliminated the information disclosure that many foreign borrowers find too expensive and/or objectionable. In 1990, the SEC instituted *Rule 144A,* which allows qualified institutional investors in the United States to trade in private placement issues that do not have to meet the strict information disclosure requirements of publicly traded issues. Rule 144A was designed to make the U.S. capital markets more competitive with the Eurobond market. A large portion of the 144A market is composed of Yankee bonds.

Global Bonds

全球债券 是由单个借款人同时在北美、欧洲和亚洲出售的大型国际债券。

Global bond issues were first offered in 1989. **A global bond** issue is a very large international bond offering by a single borrower that is simultaneously sold in North America, Europe, and Asia. Global bonds denominated in U.S. dollars and issued by U.S. corporations trade as Eurobonds overseas and domestic bonds in the U.S. domestic market. Global bond offerings enlarge the borrower's opportunities for financing at reduced costs. Miller and Puthenpurackal (2002) document that U.S. issuers are able to borrow at 15 basis points lower using global bonds relative to domestic bonds, all other things being the same. Purchasers, mainly institutional investors to date, desire the increased liquidity of the issues and have been willing to accept lower yields. The largest corporate global bond issue to date is the $14.6 billion Deutsche Telekom multicurrency offering. The issue includes three U.S. dollar tranches with 5-, 10-, and 30-year maturities totaling $9.5 billion, two euro tranches with 5- and 10-year maturities totaling €3 billion, two British pound sterling tranches with 5- and 30-year maturities totaling £950 million, and one 5-year Japanese yen tranche of ¥90 billion. Another large global bond issue is the AT&T package of $2 billion of 5.625 percent notes due 2004, $3 billion of 6.000 percent notes due 2009, and $3 billion of 6.500 percent notes due 2029 issued in March 1999. The Republic of Italy issued one of the largest sovereign global bond issues in September 1993, a package of $2 billion of 6.000 percent notes due 2003 and $3.5 billion of 6.875 percent debentures due 2023. One of the largest emerging markets global bond issues to date is the Republic of Korea package issued April 1998 of $1 billion of 8.750 percent notes due 2003 and $3 billion of 8.875 percent bonds due 2008. SEC Rule 415 and Rule 144A have likely facilitated global bond offerings, and more offerings in the future can be expected.

Types of Instruments

The international bond market has been much more innovative than the domestic bond market in the types of instruments offered to investors. In this section, we examine the major types of international bonds. We begin with a discussion of the more standard types of instruments and conclude with the more exotic innovations that have appeared in recent years.

Straight Fixed-Rate Issues 固定利率债券

Straight fixed-rate bond issues have a designated maturity date at which the principal of the bond issue is promised to be repaid. During the life of the bond, fixed coupon payments, which are a percentage of the face value, are paid as interest to the bondholders. In contrast to many domestic bonds, which make semiannual coupon payments, coupon interest on Eurobonds is typically paid annually. The reason is that the Eurobonds are usually bearer bonds, and annual coupon redemption is more convenient for the bondholders and less costly for the bond issuer because the bondholders are scattered geographically. Exhibit 12.2 shows that the vast majority of new international bond offerings in any year are straight fixed-rate issues. The U.S. dollar, euro, British pound sterling, and Japanese yen have been the most common currencies denominating straight fixed-rate bonds in recent years.

Euro-Medium-Term Notes

与固定利率债券一样，欧洲中期票据（一般）有固定的到期日，并定期支付息票利息。

Euro-Medium-Term Notes (Euro MTNs) are (typically) fixed-rate notes issued by a corporation with maturities ranging from less than a year to about 10 years. Like fixed-rate bonds, Euro-MTNs have a fixed maturity and pay coupon interest on periodic dates. Unlike a bond issue, in which the entire issue is brought to market at once, a Euro-MTN issue is partially sold on a continuous basis through an issuance facility that allows the borrower to obtain funds only as needed on a flexible basis. This feature is very attractive to issuers. Euro-MTNs have become a very popular means of raising medium-term funds since they were first introduced in 1986. All the statistical exhibits in this chapter include the amounts outstanding of MTNs.

An example of straight-fixed rate bonds is the EUR 2,000,000 of 5.00 percent notes due in 2008, issued in March 1998 by the European Investment Bank.

Floating-Rate Notes

浮动利率票据（FRN）一般是中期债券，它参照某个参考利率支付息票利息。

The first floating-rate notes were introduced in 1970. **Floating-rate notes (FRNs)** are typically medium-term bonds with coupon payments indexed to some reference rate. Common reference rates are either three-month or six-month U.S. dollar LIBOR. Coupon payments on FRNs are usually quarterly or semiannual and in accord with the reference rate. For example, consider a five-year FRN with coupons referenced to six-month dollar LIBOR paying coupon interest semiannually. At the beginning of every six-month period, the next semiannual coupon payment is *reset* to be $.5 \times$ (LIBOR + X percent) of face value, where X represents the default risk premium above LIBOR the issuer must pay based on its creditworthiness. The premium is typically no larger than 1/8 percent for top-quality issuers. As an example, if X equals 1/8 percent and the current six-month LIBOR is 6.6 percent, the next period's coupon rate on a $1,000 face value FRN will be $.5 \times (.066 + .00125) \times \$1,000 = \$33.625$. If on the next reset date six-month LIBOR is 5.7 percent, the following semiannual coupon will be set at $29.125.

Obviously, FRNs behave differently in response to interest rate risk than straight fixed-rate bonds. All bonds experience an inverse price change when the market rate of interest changes. Accordingly, the price of straight fixed-rate bonds may vary significantly if interest rates are extremely volatile. FRNs, on the other hand, experience only mild price changes between reset dates, over which time the next period's coupon payment is fixed (assuming, of course, that the reference rate corresponds to the market rate applicable to the issuer). On the reset date, the market price will gravitate back close to par value when the next period's coupon payment is reset to the new market value of the reference rate, and subsequent coupon payments are repriced to market expectations of future values of the reference rate. (The actual FRN market price may deviate somewhat from exact par value because the default risk premium portion of the coupon payment is fixed at inception, whereas the credit quality of the borrower may change through time.) FRNs make attractive investments for investors with a strong need to preserve the principal value of the investment should they need to liquidate the investment prior to the maturity of the bonds. Exhibit 12.2 shows that FRNs are the second most common type of international bond issue. The euro and the U.S. dollar are the two currencies denominating most outstanding FRNs.

As an example of FRNs, in February 2002 the National Bank of Kuwait issued at par $450,000,000 of FRNs due 2005 indexed to 3-month LIBOR plus 25 basis points.

Equity-Related Bonds
与权益相关的债券

权益型债券有两类：
可转换债券和附认股权
证债券。

There are two types of **equity-related bonds:** convertible bonds and bonds with equity warrants. A **convertible bond** issue allows the investor to exchange the bond for a predetermined number of equity shares of the issuer. The *floor-value* of a convertible bond is its straight fixed-rate bond value. Convertibles usually sell at a premium above the larger of their straight debt value and their conversion value. Additionally, investors are usually willing to accept a lower coupon rate of interest than the comparable straight fixed coupon bond rate because they find the conversion feature attractive. **Bonds with equity warrants** can be viewed as straight fixed-rate bonds with the addition of a call option (or warrant) feature. The warrant entitles the bondholder to purchase a certain number of equity shares in the issuer at a prestated price over a predetermined period of time.

Zero-Coupon Bonds
零息债券

更一般地讲，零息
债券很能吸引那些想要
避免利息再投资风险的
投资者。

拆分债券

Zero-coupon bonds are sold at a discount from face value and do not pay any coupon interest over their life. At maturity the investor receives the full face value. Alternatively, some zero-coupon bonds originally sell for face value and at maturity the investor receives an amount in excess of face value to compensate the investor for the use of the money, but this is really nothing more than a semantic difference as to what constitutes "face value." Zero-coupon bonds have been denominated primarily in the U.S. dollar and the Swiss franc. Japanese investors are particularly attracted to zero-coupon bonds because their tax law treats the difference between face value and the discounted purchase price of the bond as a tax-free capital gain, whereas coupon interest is taxable. More generally, zero-coupon bonds are attractive to investors who desire to avoid the reinvestment risk of coupon receipts at possibly lower interest rates.

Examples of zero-coupon bond issues are the DM300,000,000 due in 1995 at 50 percent of face value and DM300,000,000 due in 2000 at 33⅓ percent of face value, issued in 1985 by Commerzbank Overseas Finance B. V., chartered in the Netherlands Antilles.

Another form of zero-coupon bonds are stripped bonds. A **stripped bond** is a zero-coupon bond that results from stripping the coupons and principal from a coupon bond. The result is a series of zero-coupon bonds represented by the individual coupon and principal payments. This practice began in the early 1980s when several investment banks created stripped bonds to satisfy the demand for zero-coupon U.S. Treasury securities with various maturity dates. For example, Salomon Brothers offered CATS, which is an acronym for Certificates of Accrual for Treasury Securities. The stripped bonds are actually *receipts* representing a portion of the Treasury security held in trust. In 1985, the U.S. Treasury introduced its own product called STRIPS, for Separate Trading of Registered Interest and Principal of Securities. Investment firms are allowed under Treasury regulations to sell the stripped bonds in bearer form to non-U.S. citizens, but, as previously mentioned, the Treasury does not have this privilege. Nevertheless, the Treasury's STRIPS dominate the stripped-bond market.

Dual-Currency Bonds
双币债券

Dual-currency bonds became popular in the mid-1980s. A **dual-currency bond** is a straight fixed-rate bond issued in one currency, say, Swiss francs, that pays coupon interest in that same currency. At maturity, the principal is repaid in another currency, say, U.S. dollars. Coupon interest is frequently at a higher rate than comparable straight fixed-rate bonds. The amount of the dollar principal repayment at maturity is set at inception; frequently, the amount allows for some appreciation in the exchange rate of

EXHIBIT 12.3

Typical Characteristics of International Bond Market Instruments

Instrument	Frequency of Interest Payment	Size of Coupon Payment	Payoff at Maturity
Straight fixed-rate	Annual	Fixed	Currency of issue
Floating-rate note	Quarterly or semiannual	Variable	Currency of issue
Convertible bond	Annual	Fixed	Currency of issue or conversion to equity shares
Straight fixed-rate with equity warrants	Annual	Fixed	Currency of issue plus equity shares from exercised warrants
Zero-coupon bond	None	Zero	Currency of issue
Dual-currency bond	Annual	Fixed	Dual currency

the stronger currency. From the investor's perspective, a dual-currency bond includes a long-term forward contract. If the dollar appreciates over the life of the bond, the principal repayment will be worth more than a return of principal in Swiss francs. The market value of a dual-currency bond in Swiss francs should equal the sum of the present value of the Swiss franc coupon stream discounted at the Swiss market rate of interest plus the dollar principal repayment, converted to Swiss francs at the expected future exchange rate, and discounted at the Swiss market rate of interest.

日本公司一直是双币债券的主要发行者。 Japanese firms have been large issuers of dual currency bonds. These bonds were issued and pay coupon interest in yen with the principal reimbursement in U.S. dollars. Yen/dollar dual currency bonds could be an attractive financing method for Japanese MNCs desiring to establish or expand U.S. subsidiaries. The yen proceeds can be converted to dollars to finance the capital investment in the United States, and during the early years the coupon payments can be made by the parent firm in yen. At maturity, the dollar principal repayment can be made from dollar profits earned by the subsidiary.

Exhibit 12.3 summarizes the typical characteristics of the international bond market instruments discussed in this section.

Currency Distribution, Nationality, and Type of Issuer

Exhibit 12.4 provides the distribution of the amounts of international bonds outstanding by currency for 1999 through 2003. The exhibit shows that the U.S. dollar, euro, yen, British pound sterling, Swiss franc, and Canadian dollar have been the most frequently used currencies to denominate issues.

EXHIBIT 12.4

Currency Distribution of International Bond Amounts Outstanding (At Year-End in Billions of U.S. Dollars)

	1999	2000	2001	2002	2003
Currency					
U.S. dollar	2,399.4	2,911.4	3,613.0	4,045.9	4,492.5
Euro	1,474.8	1,771.0	2,290.2	3,283.1	4,834.5
Yen	530.6	454.7	413.2	433.3	488.6
Pound sterling	394.3	453.1	506.4	618.6	778.7
Swiss franc	136.8	132.0	123.6	159.1	195.6
Canadian dollar	56.0	51.7	47.6	51.5	79.3
Other	113.6	105.5	118.7	163.4	233.3
Total	5,105.5	5,879.4	7,112.7	8,754.9	11,102.5

Source: Derived from International Banking and Financial Market Developments, Bank for International Settlements, Table 13B, p. 71, June 2000; p. A87, June 2002, 2003, 2004.

EXHIBIT 12.5

International Bond Amounts Outstanding Classified by Nationality and Type of Issuer (At Year-End in Billions of U.S. Dollars)

	1999	2000	2001	2002	2003
Nationality					
Australia	75.6	90.8	103.6	120.0	162.0
Canada	217.1	202.7	220.1	230.5	267.2
France	298.0	294.9	374.2	485.3	700.8
Germany	623.7	767.5	975.2	1,350.3	1,810.3
Italy	147.9	196.8	261.8	357.8	510.5
Japan	332.3	277.5	249.5	235.6	255.2
Netherlands	196.3	259.7	294.6	390.5	532.8
United Kingdom	436.7	505.1	575.4	755.6	1,032.1
United States	1,286.7	1,681.9	2,286.2	2,667.1	3,011.8
Other developed countries	658.3	714.1	815.4	1,084.0	1,559.0
Off-shore centers	56.9	67.5	96.0	108.0	128.9
Developing countries	400.9	446.8	482.9	538.1	630.8
International institutions	375.2	374.1	377.9	432.1	501.0
Total	5,105.5	5,879.4	7,112.7	8,754.9	11,102.5
Type					
Financial institutions	2,397.2	3,470.1	4,968.3	6,241.5	8,032.5
Governments[a]	1,032.1	1,173.3	692.4	855.6	1,122.3
International institutions	375.2	374.1	377.9	432.1	501.1
Corporate issuers	1,301.0	861.8	1,074.0	1,224.7	1,446.6
Total	5,105.5	5,879.4	7,112.7	8,754.9	11,102.5

[a]Includes central banks and state and local governments.
Source: Derived from International Banking and Financial Market Developments, Bank for International Settlements, Table 13B and 15B, pp. 71 and 75, June 2000; pp. A87 and A91, June 2002, 2003, 2004.

Exhibit 12.5 is divided into two panels that show the nationality and type of issuer of international bonds. The top panel indicates that the United States, Germany, the United Kingdom, France, and the Netherlands have been major issuers of international bonds during the past several years. In terms of type of issuer, the bottom panel of Exhibit 12.5 shows that financial institutions and governments have been the largest issuers of international bonds in recent years.

The International Finance in Practice box, "Heineken Refreshes Euromarket with Spectacular Unrated Bonds," discusses a Eurobond offering issued by Heineken.

International Bond Market Credit Ratings

www.fitchibca.com

This is the website of Fitch Ratings, an international bond rating service. Information about Fitch and its philosophy can be found here.

www.moodys.com

This is the website of Moody's Investors Service. Information about the investment services that Moody's provides and their bond ratings can be found here.

Fitch Ratings, Moody's Investors Service, and Standard & Poor's (S&P) have for years provided credit ratings on domestic and international bonds and their issuers. These three credit-rating organizations classify bond issues into categories based upon the creditworthiness of the borrower. The ratings are based on an analysis of current information regarding the likelihood of default and the specifics of the debt obligation. The ratings both reflect creditworthiness and exchange rate uncertainty.

Moody's rates bond issues (and issuers) into nine categories, from Aaa, Aa, A, Baa, and Ba down to C. Ratings of Aaa to Baa are known as *investment grade* ratings. These issues are judged not to have any speculative elements; interest payments and principal safety appear adequate at present. The future prospects of lower-rated issues cannot be considered as well assured. Within categories Aa through Caa, Moody's has three numeric modifiers, 1, 2, or 3, to place an issue, respectively, at the upper, middle, or lower end of the category.

INTERNATIONAL FINANCE IN PRACTICE

Heineken Refreshes Euromarket with Spectacular Unrated Bonds

Heineken launched the euro market's largest unrated bond this week with a spectacular two tranche Eu1.1bn debut transaction. The deal, in 6- and 10-year tranches, was more than four times oversubscribed and priced well inside price guidance. Heineken's success demonstrates the depth of demand for unrated credits in the Eurobond market, despite the growing prevalence of ratings and well publicized investor calls for borrowers to have at least two ratings. The major factor in Heineken's favour was the global reach of its brand—the brewer has operations in over 170 countries.

The 10 year bond—the first from an unrated corporate—was five times oversubscribed, enabling bookrunners Barclays Capital, Citigroup, Credit Suisse First Boston and JP Morgan to increase it from Eu500m to Eu600m. "There was no clear guidance in the market about what we could achieve for Heineken or where they could be positioned as a credit—we had to convince people," said Chris Tuffey, head of corporate syndicate at CSFB in London. "Unrated issues are typically tough to sell investors on, but the Heineken transaction was exactly the opposite—both tranches were heavily oversubscribed." Although the lead managers looked at brand names such as Louis Vuitton Moet Hennessy, McDonald's and Carlsberg in pricing the transaction, the price was decided by investors' perception of the credit. Heineken was priced as a single-A credit, although it paid a small premium for the absence of a rating.

Rene Hooft Graafland, a member of Heineken's executive board, said the Heineken family retains a controlling interest in the company and maintains a very conservative approach in running it. He said the diversity of the company's cashflows and profit sources made Heineken an attractive credit. Explaining why Heineken is not rated, Hooft Graafland said the bond was a one-off issue to partially finance the Eu1.9bn acquisition of Brau-Beteiligung AG, Austria's largest brewer, which was completed on October 15. Heineken does not intend to become a regular bond issuer.

"The decision not to obtain a rating was not taken lightly but there were clear indications that there was demand among investors for the Heineken name on an unrated basis," said Hooft Graafland. "The Heineken business model is relatively straightforward and there is high transparency in the way the company is run."

The acquisition of BBAG makes Heineken the leading regional player in central eastern Europe, with a market share of 27%. Besides its lack of a rating, investors were concerned by the level of subsidiary indebtedness and the possibility that the new bonds would be subordinated to the company's outstanding debt. Both issues were tackled by management on the five-day roadshow—and successfully so, judging by the level of oversubscription.

The reason that Heineken's previous debt had been concentrated in the operating subsidiaries rather than the holding company was simply that it was more cost effective under Dutch tax law, which has changed in the last month. "However, we made it clear that the debt level is modest and is historically concentrated in the three big operating companies," said Hooft Graafland. "In addition to the standard covenant package, the bond has a covenant that limits the level of subsidiary indebtedness at 35% of the total consolidated group assets." The main buyers of the 2010s were investors in Switzerland taking 25%, the UK with 22%, and France and the Benelux each with 17%. There was a large retail bid for the shorter maturity at 38%, while fund managers and insurance companies took 32% and 26% respectively. UK investors were by far the largest players in the 2013s, accounting for 36%, followed by French accounts with 14%, while Switzerland and Austria each took 10%. Fund managers predominated by taking 39% of the book, the retail bid was strong at 31%, and insurance companies followed closely with 28%.

Source: Excerpted from Euroweek. London: Oct 26, 2003, p. 1

人们已经注意到，与本国债券和外国债券相比，高信用级别的欧洲债券的比例要高得多。

Standard & Poor's rates bond issues (and issuers) into 10 categories. For bond issuers, the categories are AAA, AA, A, BBB, and BB down to CC and R, SD, and D. Categories AAA to BBB are investment grade ratings. An obligor rated R is under regulatory supervision owing to its financial condition. An obligor rated SD on D has failed to pay one or more of its financial obligations when due. Ratings for Categories AA to CCC may be modified with a plus (+) or minus (−) to reflect the relative standing of an issue to others in the category. Fitch uses ratings symbols and definitions similar to S&P's.

It has been noted that a disproportionate share of Eurobonds have high credit ratings in comparison to domestic and foreign bonds. For example, Claes, DeCeuster,

EXHIBIT 12.6   **S&P Long-Term Issuer Credit Ratings Definitions**

A Standard & Poor's Issuer Credit Rating is a current opinion of an obligor's overall financial capacity (its creditworthiness) to pay its financial obligations. This opinion focuses on the obligor's capacity and willingness to meet its financial commitments as they come due. It does not apply to any specific financial obligation, as it does not take into account the nature of and provisions of the obligation, its standing in bankruptcy or liquidation, statutory preferences, or the legality and enforceability of the obligation. In addition, it does not take into account the creditworthiness of the guarantors, insurers, or other forms of credit enhancement on the obligation. The Issuer Credit Rating is not a recommendation to purchase, sell, or hold a financial obligation issued by an obligor, as it does not comment on market price or suitability for a particular investor. Counterparty Credit Ratings, ratings assigned under the Corporate Credit Rating Service (formerly called the Credit Assessment Service) and Sovereign Credit Ratings are all forms of Issuer Credit Ratings.

Issuer Credit Ratings are based on current information furnished by obligors or obtained by Standard & Poor's from other sources it considers reliable. Standard & Poor's does not perform an audit in connection with any Issuer Credit Rating and may, on occasion, rely on unaudited financial information. Issuer Credit Ratings may be changed, suspended, or withdrawn as a result of changes in, or unavailability of, such information, or based on other circumstances. Issuer Credit Ratings can be either long-term or short-term. Short-Term Issuer Credit Ratings reflect the obligor's creditworthiness over a short-term time horizon.

Long-Term Issuer Credit Ratings

AAA An obligor rated 'AAA' has EXTREMELY STRONG capacity to meet its financial commitments. 'AAA' is the highest Issuer Credit Rating assigned by Standard & Poor's.

AA An obligor rated 'AA' has VERY STRONG capacity to meet its financial commitments. It differs from the highest rated obligors only in small degree.

A An obligor rated 'A' has STRONG capacity to meet its financial commitments but is somewhat more susceptible to the adverse effects of changes in circumstances and economic conditions than obligors in higher-rated categories.

BBB An obligor rated 'BBB' has ADEQUATE capacity to meet its financial commitments. However, adverse economic conditions or changing circumstances are more likely to lead to a weakened capacity of the obligor to meet its financial commitments.

Obligors rated 'BB', 'B', 'CCC', and 'CC' are regarded as having significant speculative characteristics. 'BB' indicates the least degree of speculation and 'CC' the highest. While such obligors will likely have some quality and protective characteristics, these may be outweighed by large uncertainties or major exposures to adverse conditions.

BB An obligor rated 'BB' is LESS VULNERABLE in the near term than other lower-rated obligors.

However, it faces major ongoing uncertainties and exposure to adverse business, financial, or economic conditions which could lead to the obligor's inadequate capacity to meet its financial commitments.

B An obligor rated 'B' is MORE VULNERABLE than the obligors rated 'BB', but the obligor currently has the capacity to meet its financial commitments. Adverse business, financial, or economic conditions will likely impair the obligor's capacity or willingness to meet its financial commitments.

CCC An obligor rated 'CCC' is CURRENTLY VULNERABLE, and is dependent upon favorable business, financial, and economic conditions to meet its financial commitments.

CC An obligor rated 'CC' is CURRENTLY HIGHLY-VULNERABLE.

Plus (+) or minus (−) The ratings from 'AA' to 'CCC' may be modified by the addition of a plus or minus sign to show relative standing within the major rating categories.

R An obligor rated 'R' is under regulatory supervision owing to its financial condition. During the pendency of the regulatory supervision the regulators may have the power to favor one class of obligations over others or pay some obligations and not others. Please see Standard & Poor's issue credit ratings for a more detailed description of the effects of regulatory supervision on specific issues or classes of obligations.

SD and D An obligor rated 'SD' (Selective Default) or 'D' has failed to pay one or more of its financial obligations (rated or unrated) when it came due. A 'D' rating is assigned when Standard & Poor's believes that the default will be a general default and that the obligor will fail to pay all or substantially all of its obligations as they come due. An 'SD' rating is assigned when Standard & Poor's believes that the obligor has selectively defaulted on a specific issue or class of obligations but it will continue to meet its payment obligations on other issues or classes of obligations in a timely manner. Please see Standard & Poor's issue credit ratings for a more detailed description of the effects of a default on specific issues or classes of obligations.

N.R. An issuer designated N.R. is not rated.

Local Currency And Foreign Currency Risks
Country risk considerations are a standard part of Standard & Poor's analysis for credit ratings on any issuer or issue. Currency of repayment is a key factor in this analysis. An obligor's capacity to repay Foreign Currency obligations may be lower than its capacity to repay obligations in its local currency due to the sovereign government's own relatively lower capacity to repay external versus domestic debt. These sovereign risk considerations are incorporated in the debt ratings assigned to specific issues. Foreign Currency issuer ratings are also distinguished from local currency issuer ratings to identify those instances where sovereign risks make them different for the same issuer.

and Polfliet (2002) report that approximately 40 percent of Eurobond issues are rated AAA and 30 percent are AA. One explanation is that the issuers receiving low credit ratings invoke their publication rights and have had them withdrawn prior to dissemination. Kim and Stulz (1988) suggest another explanation that we believe is more likely. That is, the Eurobond market is accessible only to firms that have good credit ratings and name recognition to begin with; hence, they are rated highly. Regardless, it is beneficial to know about the ratings Fitch, Moody's, and S&P assign to international bond issues.

Gande and Parsley (2005) study cross-border financial market linkages by examining changes in foreign U.S. dollar denominated sovereign debt yield spreads (i.e., sovereign yield above comparable U.S. Treasury yield) associated with ratings events abroad. They find an asymmetrical relationship. They find that positive ratings events in one country have no impact on sovereign spreads in other countries; however, negative ratings events are associated with a significant increase in spreads. On average, a one-notch downgrade of a sovereign bond is associated with a 12 basis point increase in spreads of sovereign bonds of other countries. They attribute the spillover among countries to highly positively correlated capital and trade flows.

一国所获得的信用等级特别重要，因为它通常就是标准普尔公司给予注册地在该国的企业债务的标准普尔评级上限。

Exhibit 12.6 presents a guide to S&P's Long-Term Issuer Credit Ratings for sovereigns, municipalities, corporations, utilities, and supranationals. As noted in Exhibit 12.5, sovereigns issue a sizable portion of all international bonds. In rating a sovereign government, S&P's analysis centers around an examination of ten factors profiled in Exhibit 12.7. The rating assigned to a sovereign is particularly important because it usually represents the ceiling for ratings S&P will assign to an obligation of an entity domiciled within that country.

Eurobond Market Structure and Practices

Given that in any year the Eurobond segment of the international bond market accounts for approximately 80 percent of new offerings, it is beneficial to know something about the Eurobond market structure and practices.

Primary Market

主承销商
承销银团

承销团

A borrower desiring to raise funds by issuing Eurobonds to the investing public will contact an investment banker and ask it to serve as the **lead manager** of an underwriting syndicate that will bring the bonds to market. The **underwriting syndicate** is a group of investment banks, merchant banks, and the merchant banking arms of commercial banks that specialize in some phase of a public issuance. The lead manager will sometimes invite comanagers to form a **managing group** to help negotiate terms with the borrower, ascertain market conditions, and manage the issuance. Exhibit 12.8 provides the 2003 and 2004 rankings for the top debt arrangers (underwriters) of international bonds and medium-term notes. Separate rankings are provided for the top underwriters of straight bonds and FRNs denominated in the dollars and the euro.

承销团以及其他银行一起成为债券发行商的**承销商**，也就是说，它们要用自己的资金从债券发行商处按照债券面额折价买进债券。这种折价称做**承销差价**。
销售团 (selling group)

The managing group, along with other banks, will serve as **underwriters** for the issue, that is, they will commit their own capital to buy the issue from the borrower at a discount from the issue price. The discount, or **underwriting spread,** is typically in the 2 to 2.5 percent range. By comparison, the spread averages about 1 percent for domestic issues. Most of the underwriters, along with other banks, will be part of a **selling group** that sells the bonds to the investing public. The various members of the underwriting syndicate receive a portion of the spread, depending on the number and type of functions they perform. The lead manager will obviously receive the full spread, but a bank serving as only a member of the selling group will receive a smaller portion. The total elapsed time from the decision date of the borrower to issue Eurobonds until the net proceeds from the sale are received is typically five to six weeks. Exhibit

EXHIBIT 12.7

Standard and Poor's
Sovereign Ratings
Methodology Profile

Political Risk
- Stability and legitimacy of political institutions
- Popular participation in political processes
- Orderliness of leadership succession
- Transparency in economic policy decisions and objectives
- Public security
- Geopolitical risk

Income and Economic Structure
- Prosperity, diversity, and degree to which economy is market-oriented
- Income disparities
- Effectiveness of financial sector in intermediating funds; availability of credit
- Competitiveness and profitability of nonfinancial private sector
- Efficiency of public sector
- Protectionism and other nonmarket influences
- Labor flexibility

Economic Growth Prospects
- Size and composition of savings and investment
- Rate and pattern of economic growth

Fiscal Flexibility
- General government revenue, expenditure, and surplus/deficit trends
- Revenue-raising flexibility and efficiency
- Expenditure effectiveness and pressures
- Timeliness, coverage, and transparency in reporting
- Pension obligations

General Government Debt Burden
- General government gross and net (of assets) debt as a percent of GDP
- Share of revenue devoted to interest
- Currency composition and maturity profile
- Depth and breadth of local capital markets

Offshore and Contingent Liabilities
- Size and health of nonfinancial public-sector enterprises
- Robustness of financial sector

Monetary Flexibility
- Price behavior in economic cycles
- Money and credit expansion
- Compatibility of exchange-rate regime and monetary goals
- Institutional factors such as central bank independence
- Range and efficiency of monetary policy tools

External Liquidity
- Impact of fiscal and monetary policies on external accounts
- Structure of the current account
- Composition of capital flows
- Reserve adequacy

Public-Sector External Debt Burden
- Gross and net public-sector external debt, including structured debt, as a percent of current account receipts
- Maturity profile, currency composition, and sensitivity to interest rate changes
- Access to concessional funding
- Debt service burden

Private-Sector External Debt Burden
- Gross and net financial-sector external debt, including deposits and structured debt, as a percent of current account receipts
- Gross and net nonfinancial private-sector external debt, including structured debt, as a percent of current account receipts
- Maturity profile, currency composition, and sensitivity to interest-rate changes
- Access to concessional funding
- Debt service burden

Source: www.standardandpoors.com. By David T. Beers, May 15, 2004. Reproduced with permission of Standard & Poor's, a division of The McGraw-Hill Companies, Inc.

EXHIBIT 12.8

Ranking of Top International
Bond and MTN Underwriters

		Bond Issues Overall	
2004	**2003**	**Bank**	**Score**
1	2	Citigroup	207
2	1	Deutsche Bank	171
3	3	JPMorgan	114
4	5	Barclays	105
5	4	UBS	100
6	11	Goldman Sachs	66
7	10	CSFB/Credit Suisse	63
8	12	Lehman Brothers	62
9	8=	ABN Amro	58
10	7	Morgan Stanley	55
11	13	Merrill Lynch	49
12	6	HSBC	48
13	8=	BNP Paribas	23
14	18=	RBS	15
15	16	Nomura Securities	12

		Best EMTN Dealer	
2004	**2003**	**Bank**	**Score**
1	2	Citigroup	112
2	1	Deutsche Bank	108
3	5	Barclays	58
4	3	UBS	53
5	7	Morgan Stanley	33
6	18=	Dresdner Bank	24
7	10=	Lehman Brothers	23
8	8=	Goldman Sachs	22
9	6	HSBC	21
10	4	JPMorgan	19

		Bond Instruments Dollar Straights	
2004	**2003**	**Bank**	**Score**
1	1	Citigroup	164
2	3	JPMorgan	94
3	7	Lehman Brothers	53
4	5	Goldman Sachs	49
5	6	Merrill Lynch	47
6	2	UBS	46
7	11	Morgan Stanley	42
8	4	Deutsche Bank	40
9=	9	Barclays	24
9=	12	Bank of America	24

		Dollar FRNs	
2004	**2003**	**Bank**	**Score**
1	1	Citigroup	78
2	6	Barclays	49
3	9	Goldman Sachs	32
4=	10=	Merrill Lynch	27
4=	14	CSFB/Credit Suisse	27
6	8	Morgan Stanley	25
7=	7	HSBC	23
7=	5	Lehman Brothers	23
7=	3	JPMorgan	23
10	2	UBS	20

(continued)

EXHIBIT 12.8

Ranking of Top International Bond and MTN Underwriters (continued)

Euro Straights			
2004	2003	Bank	Score
1	1	Deutsche Bank	178
2	3	Barclays	99
3	5	Citigroup	90
4	2	UBS	57
5	6	ABN Amro	51
6	12	CSFB/Credit Suisse	50
7	7	BNP Paribas	41
8	8	HSBC	40
9	4	JPMorgan	32
10	26=	Lehman Brothers	23

Euro FRNs			
2004	2003	Bank	Score
1	1	Deutsche Bank	77
2	6	Barclays	66
3	4	UBS	61
4	5	BNP Paribas	48
5	12	CSFB/Credit Suisse	31
6	8=	HSBC	29
7	2	Citigroup	27
8	3	ABN Amro	23
9	7	JPMorgan	22
10	13=	Lehman Brothers	20

Source: Euromoney, October 2004, pp. 46–47.

12.9 presents a tombstone (announcement) for a dollar-denominated Euro-medium-term note issue and the underwriting syndicate that brought the issue to market.

Secondary Market

一级市场（primary market）
二级市场（secondary market）

二级市场包括做市商和经纪人，他们通过一系列电信设备相互联系。
做市商(market makers)

买入价（bid prices）
卖出价（ask prices）

经纪人（broker）

Eurobonds initially purchased in the **primary market** from a member of the selling group may be resold prior to their maturities to other investors in the secondary market. The **secondary market** for Eurobonds is an over-the-counter market with principal trading in London. However, important trading is also done in other major European money centers, such as Zurich, Luxembourg, Frankfurt, and Amsterdam.

The secondary market comprises market makers and brokers connected by an array of telecommunications equipment. **Market makers** stand ready to buy or sell for their own account by quoting two-way **bid** and **ask** prices. Market makers trade directly with one another, through a broker, or with retail customers. The bid-ask spread represents their only profit; no other commission is charged.

Eurobond market makers and dealers are members of the International Securities Market Association (ISMA), a self-regulatory body based in Zurich. Market makers tend to be the same investment banks, merchant banks, and commercial banks that serve as lead managers in the underwriting process. **Brokers,** on the other hand, accept buy or sell orders from market makers and then attempt to find a matching party for the other side of the trade; they may also trade for their own account. Brokers charge a small commission for their services to the market maker that engaged them. They do not deal directly with retail clients.

Clearing Procedures

www.euroclear.com

www.clearstream.com

Eurobond transactions in the secondary market require a system for transferring ownership and payment from one party to another. Two major clearing systems, Euroclear and Clearstream International, have been established to handle most Eurobond trades. Euroclear is based in Brussels and is operated by Euroclear Bank. Clearstream, located in Luxembourg, was established in 2000 through a merger of Deutsche Börse Clearing and Cedel International, two other clearing firms.

Both clearing systems operate in a similar manner. Each clearing system has a group of depository banks that physically store bond certificates. Members of either system

EXHIBIT 12.9

Eurobond Tombstone

This announcement appears as a matter of record only

Hamburgische Landesbank

Hamburgische Landesbank – Girozentrale –
(incorporated as a credit institution under public law in the Federal Republic of Germany)

Hamburgische Landesbank London Branch

Hamburgische LB Finance (Guernsey) Limited
(incorporated in Guernsey)

U.S.$2,000,000,000

Euro Medium Term Note Programme
Guaranteed in respect of Notes issued by
Hamburgische LB Finance (Guernsey) Limited by
Hamburgische Landesbank – Girozentrale –

The Programme is rated Aa1 by Moody's and AAA by Fitch IBCA

Arrangers

Merrill Lynch International

Merrill Lynch Capital Markets Bank Limited,   Merrill Lynch Finance SA
Frankfurt/Main Branch

Dealers

Credit Suisse First Boston   Deutsche Morgan Grenfell
Hamburgische Landesbank – Girozentrale –   Merrill Lynch Finance SA
Merrill Lynch International   J.P. Morgan Securities Ltd.
Morgan Stanley Dean Witter   Nomura International
Salomon Smith Barney   Warburg Dillon Read

NOW RATED Aa1 BY MOODY'S

Source: Euromoney, January 1999, p. 11.

很少发生实物债券
转让的情况。

hold cash and bond accounts. When a transaction is conducted, electronic book entries are made that transfer book ownership of the bond certificates from the seller to the buyer and transfer funds from the purchaser's cash account to the seller's. Physical transfer of the bonds seldom takes place.

Euroclear and Clearstream perform other functions associated with the efficient operation of the Eurobond market. (1) The clearing systems will finance up to 90 percent of the inventory that a Eurobond market maker has deposited within the system. (2) Additionally, the clearing systems will assist in the distribution of a new bond issue. The clearing systems will take physical possession of the newly printed bond certificates in the depository, collect subscription payments from the purchasers, and record ownership of the bonds. (3) The clearing systems will also distribute coupon payments. The borrower pays to the clearing system the coupon interest due on the portion of the issue held in the depository, which in turn credits the appropriate amounts to the bond owners' cash accounts.

International Bond Market Indexes

国际债券市场指数
有好几种，其中知名度
最高的为J.P.摩根公司的
"本国政府债券指数" 和
"全球政府债券指数"。

www.jpmorgan.com

This is the website of J.P. Morgan and Company, an international investment banking firm. This is an extensive website detailing products and services of the firm.

There are several international bond market indexes. Some of the best known are the J.P. Morgan and Company Domestic Government Bond Indices and their Global Government Bond Index. J.P. Morgan publishes a government bond index for 18 individual countries: Australia, Belgium, Canada, Denmark, France, Germany, Italy, Japan, the Netherlands, Spain, Sweden, the United Kingdom, the United States, New Zealand, Ireland, Finland, Portugal, and South Africa. Each bond index includes only government bonds in five maturity categories: 1–3 years, 3–5 years, 5–7 years, 7–10 years, and 10-plus years. The Global Government Bond Index is a value-weighted representation of the 18 government bond indexes.

The J.P. Morgan Domestic and Global Government Bond Indices are widely referenced and used frequently as benchmarks of international bond market performance. The index values for six of the Domestic Government Indices, European Monetary Union Government Bond Index (EMU), the 18-country Global Government Bond Index, and an Emerging Market Government Bond Index (EMBI) appear daily in *The Wall Street Journal*. Exhibit 12.10 provides an example of these indexes. Note that the index values are provided in local currency terms and in U.S. dollar terms. Additionally, 1-day, 1-month, and 3-month total rates of return are provided for each index in local and U.S. dollar terms.

EXHIBIT 12.10 International Bond Market Data Provided Daily in The Wall Street Journal

International Government Bonds

Coupon	Maturity Mo/Yr	Price	Change	Yield*	Coupon	Maturity Mo/Yr	Price	Change	Yield*
Japan (3 p.m. Tokyo)					Germany (5 p.m. London)				
2.60%	03/07	105.02	−0.01	0.13%	2.25%	12/06	99.65	+ 0.05	2.451%
1.80	03/10	105.53	−0.08	0.67	3.50	10/09	101.80	+ 0.15	3.069
1.50	03/15	99.74	n.a.	1.53	3.75	01/15	99.95	+ 0.20	3.753
2.40	12/34	98.46	−0.17	2.49	4.00	01/37	95.66	+ 0.22	4.251
United Kingdom (5 p.m. London)					Canada (3 p.m. Eastern Time)				
7.75%	09/06	104.31	−0.01	4.764%	3.25%	12/06	100.48	−0.03	2.964%
5.75	12/09	103.95	+ 0.09	4.811	4.25	09/09	102.46	−0.03	3.651
5.00	09/14	101.42	+ 0.23	4.813	5.00	06/14	105.38	+ 0.02	4.289
4.25	06/32	93.75	+ 0.27	4.657	5.75	06/33	115.48	+ 0.07	4.748

*Equivalent to semi-annual compounded yields to maturity.

Total Rates of Return on International Bonds
In percent, based on J.P. Morgan Government Bond Index, Dec. 31, 1987 = 100

	Local Currency Terms				U.S. Dollar Terms			
	Index Value	1 Day	1 Mo	3 Mos	Since 12/31	Index Value	1 Day	1 Mo	3 Mos	Since 12/31
Japan	220.63	−0.07	−0.83	−0.13	−0.19	254.30	−0.22	−1.16	−2.52	−2.61
Britain	447.44	+ 0.11	−1.19	−0.31	−1.07	452.74	+ 0.02	+ 0.33	−1.80	−1.67
Germany	306.03	+ 0.13	−0.82	+ 0.80	+ 0.36	322.24	+ 0.22	+ 0.51	−1.03	−3.07
France	408.65	+ 0.13	−0.76	+ 0.83	+ 0.36	434.86	+ 0.22	+ 0.56	−1.00	−3.07
Canada	452.61	+ 0.03	+ 0.18	+ 1.49	+ 0.95	471.82	−0.39	−0.12	−2.42	−2.99
Netherlands	327.85	+ 0.13	−0.64	+ 0.77	+ 0.35	344.69	+ 0.22	+ 0.68	−1.07	−3.09
EMU-d	217.19	+ 0.13	−0.84	+ 0.89	+ 0.39	232.48	+ 0.22	+ 0.49	−0.94	−3.04
Global-a	351.12	+ 0.03	−0.79	+ 0.51	+ 0.05	361.23	+ 0.03	−0.17	−1.00	−2.15
EMBI+-b	334.92	+ 0.10	+ 0.84	+ 3.64	+ 1.63	334.92	+ 0.10	+ 0.84	+ 3.64	+ 1.63

a-18 int'l govt. markets. b-external-currency emerging mkt. debt, Dec. 31, 1993 = 100. d-Jan. 2, 1995 = 100.
Source: The Wall Street Journal, March 4, 2005, p. B7. Reprinted by permission of The Wall Street Journal, © 2005 Dow Jones & Company, Inc. All Rights Reserved Worldwide.

EXHIBIT 12.11

BENCHMARK GOVERNMENT BONDS

Mar 3	Redemption Date	Coupon	Bid Price	Bid Yield	Day Chg Yield	Wk Chg Yield	Month Chg Yld	Year Chg Yld
Australia	10/07	10.00	110.8110	5.48	− 0.03	+ 0.03	+ 0.22	+ 0.22
	04/15	6.25	105.0740	5.59	+ 0.01	+ 0.12	+ 0.24	− 0.03
Austria	10/07	5.60	107.0300	2.68	− 0.02	− 0.01	+ 0.07	+ 0.16
	07/14	4.30	104.4100	3.73	− 0.02	+ 0.02	+ 0.19	− 0.46
Belgium	03/07	6.25	107.3820	2.52	− 0.02	− 0.02	+ 0.04	+ 0.28
	09/14	4.25	103.9100	3.75	− 0.02	+ 0.03	+ 0.19	− 0.44
Canada	12/06	3.25	100.4600	2.98	+ 0.03	+ 0.01	+ 0.03	+ 0.52
	06/14	5.00	105.3300	4.29	—	− 0.02	+ 0.03	− 0.09
Denmark	11/06	3.00	100.8500	2.48	− 0.01	+ 0.01	+ 0.06	− 0.06
	11/15	4.00	101.3400	3.84	− 0.02	+ 0.06	+ 0.19	− 0.42
Finland	07/07	5.00	105.3800	2.58	− 0.04	− 0.04	+ 0.27	+ 0.09
	07/15	4.25	104.2500	3.74	− 0.03	+ 0.02	+ 0.18	− 0.32
France	01/07	3.75	102.2900	2.47	− 0.02	− 0.03	+ 0.02	+ 0.13
	01/10	3.00	99.4600	3.12	− 0.03	—	+ 0.12	− 0.14
	04/15	3.50	97.6100	3.79	− 0.02	+ 0.03	+ 0.24	− 0.31
	04/35	4.75	108.0300	4.27	—	+ 0.05	+ 0.24	− 0.58
Germany	12/06	2.25	99.6400	2.46	− 0.02	− 0.02	+ 0.04	+ 0.18
	10/09	3.50	101.7600	3.08	− 0.02	—	+ 0.12	− 0.22
	01/15	3.75	99.8900	3.76	− 0.02	+ 0.03	+ 0.20	− 0.32
	01/37	4.00	95.5400	4.26	—	+ 0.06	+ 0.25	− 0.57
Greece	06/08	2.90	100.0280	2.88	− 0.03	− 0.01	+ 0.09	+ 0.34
	07/15	3.70	97.9360	3.94	− 0.02	+ 0.03	+ 0.29	− 0.36
Ireland	04/09	3.25	101.0000	2.99	− 0.02	—	+ 0.12	+ 0.06
	04/13	5.00	110.0200	3.56	− 0.01	+ 0.02	+ 0.18	− 0.46
Italy	01/07	2.75	100.5440	2.46	− 0.03	− 0.04	+ 0.01	+ 0.13
	04/09	3.00	100.0100	3.02	− 0.03	− 0.01	+ 0.10	− 0.25
	02/15	4.25	103.4300	3.87	− 0.02	+ 0.03	+ 0.20	− 0.34
	08/34	5.00	109.6600	4.46	—	+ 0.05	+ 0.26	− 0.62
Japan	03/07	2.60	104.9970	0.14	—	+ 0.03	+ 0.05	+ 0.04
	03/10	1.80	105.4810	0.68	+ 0.02	+ 0.09	+ 0.14	+ 0.11
	03/15	1.50	99.6100	1.55	+ 0.04	+ 0.14	+ 0.22	+ 0.14
	12/24	2.10	99.6510	2.13	+ 0.01	+ 0.10	+ 0.19	+ 0.20
Netherlands	07/06	3.00	100.8500	2.35	− 0.02	− 0.02	—	− 0.17
	07/14	3.75	100.1400	3.73	− 0.02	+ 0.03	+ 0.19	− 0.35
New Zealand	11/06	8.00	102.4800	6.42	+ 0.03	+ 0.07	+ 0.07	+ 0.82
	04/13	6.50	102.0700	6.17	+ 0.01	+ 0.08	+ 0.12	+ 0.22
Norway	05/09	5.50	108.5600	3.28	− 0.01	+ 0.05	+ 0.22	− 0.17
	05/15	5.00	108.1500	4.01	− 0.01	+ 0.07	+ 0.18	− 0.13
Portugal	07/06	3.00	100.8370	2.36	− 0.02	− 0.05	+ 0.01	+ 0.12
	06/14	4.38	104.9800	3.73	− 0.01	+ 0.02	+ 0.20	− 0.41
Spain	10/06	4.80	103.8120	2.41	− 0.04	− 0.05	—	+ 0.23
	01/15	4.40	105.1100	3.77	− 0.02	+ 0.03	+ 0.20	− 0.31
Sweden	08/07	8.00	112.6530	2.57	− 0.02	− 0.01	+ 0.02	− 0.49
	08/15	4.50	104.8230	3.93	− 0.01	+ 0.04	+ 0.17	− 0.64
Switzerland	06/07	4.50	107.2900	1.20	− 0.05	− 0.01	+ 0.09	+ 0.43
	06/15	3.75	112.7300	2.34	− 0.02	+ 0.01	+ 0.16	− 0.22
UK	12/06	8.50	102.7800	4.72	—	+ 0.02	+ 0.26	+ 0.60
	12/09	5.75	103.9000	4.82	− 0.02	+ 0.02	+ 0.26	+ 0.11
	09/14	5.00	101.3200	4.83	− 0.01	+ 0.04	+ 0.22	− 0.02
	06/32	4.25	93.4600	4.68	+ 0.01	+ 0.09	+ 0.17	− 0.05
US	02/07	3.38	99.5938	3.59	+ 0.03	+ 0.10	+ 0.25	+ 1.87
	02/10	3.50	97.7109	4.01	+ 0.01	+ 0.11	+ 0.25	+ 1.01
	02/15	4.00	96.8750	4.39	+ 0.01	+ 0.11	+ 0.22	+ 0.36
	02/31	5.38	109.3750	4.74	+ 0.01	+ 0.07	+ 0.15	− 0.14

London close. New York Close.

Yields: Local market standard Annualised yield basis. Yields shown for Italy exclude withholding tax at 12.5 percent payable by nonresidents.

Source: Financial Times, March 4, 2005, p. 25.

Exhibit 12.10 shows that *The Wall Street Journal* also publishes daily values of yields to maturity for Japanese, German, British, and Canadian Government Bonds of various terms to maturity. These data allow for a comparison of the term structures of interest rates of these major industrial countries with one another and with the term structure of U.S. Treasury bonds that can be found elsewhere in the *WSJ*. Another source of international bond data is the coupon rates, prices, and yields to maturity found in the daily "Benchmark Government Bonds" table in the *Financial Times*. Exhibit 12.11 on the previous page provides an example.

SUMMARY

本章介绍并讨论了国际债券市场，并就国际债券市场的规模、各细分债券市场、各种债券工具、国际债券的主要标价货币、主要借款国的类型等进行了统计分析。本章还考察了国际债券市场的交易实务，也考察了国际债券的信用等级和国际债券市场指数。

1. 截至2003年年末，美国未清偿的国内债券为近40.3万亿美元，国际债券超过11.1万亿美元。四种主要债券标价货币分别是美元、欧元、英镑和日元。

2. 外国债券发行是指外国借款者向某国资本市场的投资者发行以该国货币标价的债券。欧洲债券发行是指以某国货币为标价，向该货币发行国以外国家的资本市场的投资者出售债券。

3. 在国际债券市场中，欧洲债券市场的规模约为外国债券市场的四倍。造成这种情况的原因主要有两个，不过，这两个原因都与美元是国际债券市场上最常用的融资货币有关。一方面，欧洲债券能较"扬基债券"更快地投放市场，这是因为欧洲债券并不面向美国国内的投资者发行，因此就不必遵循美国证监会严格的登记要求。另一方面，欧洲债券常常为不记名债券，持有者的匿名性为避免利息税提供了便利。由于这一原因，与记名的"扬基债券"相比，投资者通常更愿意接受收益率较低的欧洲债券。对于借款者而言，投资者的低收益率意味着他的低债务负担。

4. 固定利率债券是最常见的国际债券类型，其次是浮动利率债券。国际债券市场上的其他债券类型还有：可转换债券、附认股权证债券、零息债券、拆分债券和双币债券。

5. 惠誉国际评级、穆迪投资服务、标准普尔为大多数国际债券提供评级服务。人们已经注意到，欧洲债券中高信用等级的比例非常高。产生这种现象的合理解释是因为只有信用等级高和信誉好的公司才能发行欧洲债券。实体的信用等级通常不会高于其所在地主权政府的等级。在对主权政府进行信用评级时，标准普尔公司通常会考虑该国的政治风险和经济风险。

6. 目前，欧洲债券是在一级市场发行的，由受雇于借款者的承销银团负责向市场出售。欧洲债券的二级市场属于场外交易市场，大多数交易发生在伦敦。

7. 作为投资银行的摩根大通公司开发了一些最好的国际债券市场指数。这些指数常常被用于绩效评估。

This chapter introduces and discusses the international bond market. The chapter presents a statistical perspective of the market, noting its size, an analysis of the market segments, the types of instruments issued, the major currencies used to denominate international bonds, and the major borrowers by nationality and type. Trading practices of the Eurobond market are examined, as are credit ratings for international bonds and international bond market indexes.

1. At year-end 2003, there were nearly $40.3 trillion in domestic bonds outstanding and over $11.1 trillion in international bonds. The four major currencies that are used to denominate bonds are the U.S. dollar, euro, pound sterling, and yen.

2. A foreign bond issue is one offered by a foreign borrower to investors in a national capital market and denominated in that nation's currency. A Eurobond issue is one denominated in a particular currency but sold to investors in national capital markets other than the country that issues the denominating currency.

3. The Eurobond segment of the international bond market is roughly four times the size of the foreign bond segment. The two major reasons for this stem from the fact that the U.S. dollar is the currency most frequently sought in international bond financing. First, Eurodollar bonds can be brought to market more quickly than Yankee bonds because they are not offered to U.S. investors and thus do not have to meet the strict SEC registration requirements. Second, Eurobonds are typically bearer bonds that provide anonymity to the owner and thus allow a means for avoiding taxes on the interest received. Because of this feature, investors are generally willing to accept a lower yield on Eurodollar bonds in comparison to registered Yankee bonds of comparable terms, where ownership is recorded. For borrowers, the lower yield means a lower cost of debt service.

4. Straight fixed-rate bonds are the most frequent type of international bond issue, and floating-rate notes are the second. Other types of issues found in the international bond market are convertible bonds, bonds with equity warrants, zero-coupon bonds, stripped bonds, and dual-currency bonds.

5. Fitch Ratings, Moody's Investors Service, and Standard & Poor's provide credit ratings on most international bond issues. It has been noted that a disproportionate share of Eurobonds have high credit ratings. The evidence suggests that a logical reason for this is that the Eurobond market is accessible only to firms that have good credit ratings to begin with. An entity's credit rating is usually never higher than the rating assigned the sovereign government of the country in which it resides. S&P's analysis of a sovereign includes an examination of political risk and economic risk.

6. New Eurobond issues are offered in the primary market through an underwriting syndicate hired by the borrower to bring the bonds to market. The secondary market for Eurobonds is an over-the-counter arrangement with principal trading done in London.

7. The investment banking firm of J.P. Morgan and Company provides some of the best international bond market indexes that are frequently used for performance

摩根大通公布的债券指数包括18个
国家的国别债券指数、欧元区政府
债券指数、全球政府债券指数以及
新兴市场债券指数。

evaluations. J.P. Morgan publishes a Domestic Government Bond Index for 18 individual countries, a euro zone Government Index, a Global Government Bond Index, and an Emerging Market Bond Index.

KEY WORDS

ask price, *306*	Euro-medium-term note	secondary market, *306*
bearer bond, *295*	(Euro-MTN), *297*	selling group, *303*
bid price, *306*	floating-rate note	shelf registration, *296*
bond with equity	(FRN), *297*	straight fixed-rate
warrants, *298*	foreign bond, *294*	bond, *297*
broker, *306*	global bond, *296*	stripped bond, *298*
convertible bond, *298*	lead manager, *303*	underwriters, *303*
dual-currency	managing group, *303*	underwriting spread, *303*
bond, *298*	market makers, *306*	underwriting
equity-related bond, *298*	primary market, *306*	syndicate, *303*
Eurobond, *294*	registered bond, *295*	zero-coupon bond, *298*

QUESTIONS

1. Describe the differences between foreign bonds and Eurobonds. Also discuss why Eurobonds make up the lion's share of the international bond market.

2. Briefly define each of the major types of international bond market instruments, noting their distinguishing characteristics.

3. Why do most international bonds have high Moody's or Standard & Poor's credit ratings?

4. What factors does Standard & Poor's analyze in determining the credit rating it assigns to a sovereign government?

5. Discuss the process of bringing a new international bond issue to market.

6. You are an investment banker advising a Eurobank about a new international bond offering it is considering. The proceeds are to be used to fund Eurodollar loans to bank clients. What type of bond instrument would you recommend that the bank consider issuing? Why?

7. What should a borrower consider before issuing dual-currency bonds? What should an investor consider before investing in dual-currency bonds?

PROBLEMS

1. Your firm has just issued five-year floating-rate notes indexed to six-month U.S. dollar LIBOR plus 1/4 percent. What is the amount of the first coupon payment your firm will pay per U.S. $1,000 of face value, if six-month LIBOR is currently 7.2 percent?

2. The discussion of zero-coupon bonds in the text gave an example of two zero-coupon bonds issued by Commerzbank. The DM300,000,000 issue due in 1995 sold at 50 percent of face value, and the DM300,000,000 due in 2000 sold at 33⅓ percent of face value; both were issued in 1985. Calculate the implied yield to maturity of each of these two zero-coupon bond issues.

3. Consider 8.5 percent Swiss franc/U.S. dollar dual-currency bonds that pay $666.67 at maturity per SF1,000 of par value. What is the implicit SF/$ exchange rate at maturity? Will the investor be better or worse off at maturity if the actual SF/$ exchange rate is SF1.35/$1.00?

INTERNET EXERCISES

BondMarkets.com is the website of the Bond Market Association, a trade association representing the world bond market. A newsletter can be found at the website. Go to the website www.bondmarkets.com to see what current events are of concern in the global bond market.

MINI CASE

Sara Lee Corporation's Eurobonds

Sara Lee Corp. is serving up a brand name and a shorter maturity than other recent corporate borrowers to entice buyers to its first-ever dollar Eurobonds. The U.S. maker of consumer products, from Sara Lee cheesecake to Hanes pantyhose and Hillshire Farm meats, is selling $100 million in bonds with a 6 percent coupon. These are three-year bonds; other corporate bond sellers including Coca-Cola Co., Unilever NV, and Wal-Mart Stores Inc., have concentrated on its five-year maturities.

"It is a well-known name and it is bringing paper to a part of the maturity curve where there is not much there," said Noel Dunn of Goldman Sachs International. Goldman Sachs expects to find most buyers in the Swiss retail market, where "high-quality American corporate paper is their favorite buy," Dunn said.

These are the first bonds out of a $500 million Eurobond program that Sara Lee announced in August, 1995, and the proceeds will be used for general corporate purposes, said Jeffrey Smith, a spokesman for the company.

The bond is fairly priced, according to Bloomberg Fair Value analysis, which compared a bond with similar issues available in the market. The bond offers investors a yield of 5.881 percent annually or 5.797 percent semiannually. That is 22 basis points more than they can get on the benchmark five-year U.S. Treasury note.

BFV analysis calculates that the bond is worth $100,145 on a $100,000 bond, compared with the re-offer price of $100,320. Anything within a $500 range on a $100,000 bond more or less than its BFV price is deemed fairly priced. Sara Lee is rated "AA–" by Standard & Poor's Corp. and "A1," one notch lower, by Moody's Investors Service.

In July 1994, Sara Lee's Netherlands division sold 200 million Dutch guilders ($127 million) of three-year bonds at 35 basis points over comparable Netherlands government bonds. In January, its Australian division sold 51 million British pounds ($78 million) of bonds maturing in 2004, to yield 9.43 percent.

What thoughts do you have about Sara Lee's debt-financing strategy?

Source: Excerpted from Bloomberg News.

REFERENCES & SUGGESTED READINGS

Claes, A., Marc J. K. DeCeuster, and R. Polfliet. "Anatomy of the Eurobond Market." *European Financial Management* 8, no. 3 (2002).

Gande, Amar, and David C. Parsley. "News Spillovers in the Soverign Debt Market." *Journal of Financial Economics* 75 (2005), pp. 691–734.

Kim, Yong Cheol, and Rene M. Stultz. "The Eurobond Market and Corporate Financial Policy: A Test of the Clientele Hypothesis." *Journal of Financial Economics* 22 (1988), pp. 189–205.

Miller, Darius P., and John J. Puthenpurackal. "Do Multi-Market Offerings Lower the Cost of Capital? Evidence from Global Bond Issuance by U.S. Firms." Indiana University, Kelley School of Business working paper, March 2002.

13 International Equity Markets

本章重点讨论权益市场，即讨论公众持股公司的所有权是如何在全球进行交易的。

THIS CHAPTER FOCUSES on equity markets, or how ownership in publicly owned corporations is traded throughout the world. It discusses both the *primary* sale of new common stock by corporations to initial investors and how previously issued common stock is traded between investors in the *secondary* markets. This chapter is useful for understanding how companies source new equity capital and provides useful institutional information for investors interested in diversifying their portfolio internationally.

The chapter begins with an overview of the world's equity markets. Statistics are provided that show the comparative sizes and trading opportunities in various secondary equity marketplaces in both developed and developing countries. Differences in market structures are also explored, and comparative transaction costs of equity trading are presented. Following this, the discussion moves to the benefits of multiple listing of a corporation's stock on more than one national stock exchange. The related issue of sourcing new equity capital from primary investors in more than the home national market is also examined. The chapter concludes with a discussion of the factors that affect equity valuation. An examination of the historical market performances and the risks of investing in foreign national equity markets are not presented here, but rather in Chapter 15, where a strong case is made for international diversification of investment funds.

A Statistical Perspective

本节主要介绍背景知识以及东欧、中东、非洲、拉丁美洲、亚洲等地的新兴股票市场。

Before we can intelligently discuss international equity markets, it is helpful to understand where the major national equity markets are located, some information about their relative sizes, and the opportunities for trading and ownership. This section provides these background data, along with a statistical summary of emerging equity markets in Eastern Europe, the Middle East, Africa, Latin America, and Asia.

Market Capitalization of Equity Markets in Developed Countries (in Billions of U.S. Dollars)

Region or Country	1999	2000	2001	2002	2003
Europe	9,877	9,297	7,451	6,234	8,609
Austria	33	30	25	32	55
Belgium	185	182	166	128	174
Denmark	105	108	95	77	128
Finland	349	294	190	139	170
France	1,475	1,447	1,174	967	1,356
Germany	1,432	1,270	1,072	686	1,079
Greece	204	111	87	69	107
Iceland	5	4	4	6	9
Ireland	69	82	75	60	85
Italy	728	768	527	477	615
Luxembourg	36	34	24	25	37
Netherlands	695	640	458	401	489
Norway	64	65	69	67	95
Portugal	66	61	46	43	58
Spain	432	504	468	462	726
Sweden	373	328	233	177	288
Switzerland	693	792	521	554	726
United Kingdom	2,933	2,577	2,217	1,864	2,412
Middle East/Africa	40	36	11	1	1
Cyprus	7	4	3	1	1
Kuwait	19	21	—	—	—
Qatar	6	5	—	—	—
UAE	8	6	8	—	—
Far East	5,810	4,325	3,267	3,094	4,519
Australia	428	373	374	381	585
China-Hong Kong SAR	609	623	506	463	715
Japan	4,547	3,157	2,252	2,126	3,041
New Zealand	28	19	18	22	33
Singapore	198	153	117	102	145
Atlantic	2	3	3	2	3
Bermuda	1	2	2	—	3
Cayman Islands	<1	<1	<1	<1	—
North America	17,436	15,945	14,511	11,627	15,160
Canada	801	841	701	575	894
United States	16,635	15,104	13,810	11,052	14,266
Total Developed Markets[a]	33,166	29,607	25,243	20,958	28,291

[a]Column total may not sum due to rounding error.
Source: Global Stock Markets Factbook, Standard & Poor's, 2004.

Market Capitalization of Developed Countries

在发达国家，市场资本化的下降情况基本一致。

At year-end 2003, total market capitalization of the world's equity markets stood at $31,948 billion. Of this amount, 89 percent is accounted for by the market capitalization of the major equity markets from 31 developed countries. Exhibit 13.1 shows the market capitalizations for these 31 developed countries for 1999 through 2003. As the exhibit indicates, because of the stock market decline in 2000, their total market capitalization decreased 15 percent over the five-year period, from $33,166 billion to $28,291 billion.

The decline in market capitalization was fairly evenly spread among the developed countries. For example, the United States registered a decline of 14 percent over the five-year period and the decline in European markets was 12 percent. The Far East registered a 22 percent decline.

EXHIBIT 13.2	Region or Country	1999	2000	2001	2002	2003
Market Capitalization of Equity Markets in Selected Developing Countries (in Billions of U.S. Dollars)	Latin America					
	Argentina	84	166	192	103	39
	Brazil	228	226	186	124	235
	Chile	68	60	56	48	86
	Colombia	12	10	13	10	14
	Mexico	154	125	126	103	123
	Peru	13	11	11	13	16
	Venezuela	7	8	6	4	4
	Asia					
	China	331	581	524	463	681
	India	185	148	110	131	279
	Indonesia	64	27	23	30	55
	Korea	396	172	234	250	330
	Malaysia	145	117	120	124	168
	Pakistan	7	7	5	10	17
	Philippines	48	52	42	39	24
	Sri Lanka	2	1	1	2	3
	China's Taiwan	376	248	293	261	379
	Thailand	58	29	36	46	119
	Europe					
	Czech Republic	12	11	9	16	18
	Hungary	16	12	10	13	17
	Poland	30	31	26	29	37
	Russia	72	39	76	124	231
	Slovakia	1	1	2	2	3
	Turkey	113	70	47	34	68
	Mideast/Africa					
	Bahrain	7	7	7	7	10
	Egypt	33	29	24	26	27
	Israel	64	64	70	45	76
	Jordan	6	5	6	7	11
	Morocco	14	11	9	9	13
	Nigeria	3	4	5	6	9
	Oman	4	4	5	10	17
	Saudi Arabia	60	67	73	75	157
	South Africa	262	205	140	185	268
	Zimbabwe	3	2	8	16	5

Source: Global Stock Markets Factbook, Standard & Poor's, 2004.

Market Capitalization of Developing Countries

Exhibit 13.2 presents the market capitalization of 33 emerging secondary equity markets from developing countries. In general, Standard & Poor's Emerging Markets Data Base classifies a stock market as "emerging" if it meets at least one of two general criteria: (1) it is located in a low- or middle-income economy as defined by the World Bank, and/or (2) its investable market capitalization is low relative to its most recent GNI figures.

Exhibit 13.2 shows market capitalizations for 1999 through 2003. The table indicates that many emerging markets have grown significantly over the five-year period. The 2003 market capitalizations indicate that presently there are several tiny national equity markets in Latin America, Europe, the Middle East, and Africa. However, many of the national equity markets in Latin America (principally Brazil and Mexico) and in Asia (Korea) have market capitalizations far in excess of the size of some of the smaller equity markets in the developed countries presented in Exhibit 13.1. This is indicative of investment opportunities in these emerging national markets.

这说明新兴股票市场存在着投资机会。

EXHIBIT 13.3

Turnover Ratio of Equity Markets in Developed Countries (Transactions in U.S. $/Year-End Market Capitalization in U.S. $)

Region or Country	1999	2000	2001	2002	2003
Europe					
Austria	38	30	28	21	25
Belgium	28	21	24	26	25
Denmark	60	86	67	60	65
Finland	44	64	76	107	106
France	62	74	85	88	86
Germany	108	79	125	141	130
Greece	133	60	39	26	44
Iceland	4	51	37	73	94
Ireland	91	19	30	51	61
Italy	83	104	88	109	122
Luxembourg	3	3	2	2	1
Netherlands	145	101	192	124	104
Norway	90	93	75	68	86
Portugal	63	86	53	52	42
Spain	179	211	177	211	158
Sweden	73	111	113	96	114
Switzerland	78	82	47	101	90
United Kingdom	52	67	78	135	101
Middle East/Africa					
Cyprus	39	57	40	11	6
Kuwait	33	21	NA	NA	NA
Qatar	7	5	NA	NA	NA
UAE	NA	<1	4	NA	NA
Far East					
Australia	28	57	67	77	77
China-Hong Kong SAR	51	61	35	44	56
Japan	53	70	68	71	88
New Zealand	45	46	48	38	38
Singapore	67	52	47	39	71
Atlantic					
Bermuda	5	8	10	4	2
North America					
Canada	54	77	60	68	64
United States	124	201	201	203	123

Source: Various issues of Global Stock Markets Factbook, Standard & Poor's.

在20世纪80年代，投资外国权益市场已经成为常事，因为投资者开始意识到国际组合投资分散化的好处。

Investment in foreign equity markets became common practice in the 1980s as investors became aware of the benefits of international portfolio diversification (our topic in Chapter 15). However, during the 1980s, cross-border equity investment was largely confined to the equity markets of developed countries. Only in the 1990s did world investors start to invest sizable amounts in the emerging equity markets, as the economic growth and prospects of the developing countries improved. For example, Thompson Financial's 2001 *Investment Companies Yearbook* reports that at year-end 2000 there were 170 emerging equity funds and 27 emerging fixed income funds, collectively representing .38 of one percent of investment in U.S.-based mutual funds. Only three years prior, emerging market fund categories did not exist as separate mutual fund classifications.

Measures of Liquidity
流动性

A liquid stock market is one in which investors can buy and sell stocks quickly at close to the current quoted prices. A measure of **liquidity** for a stock market is the turnover ratio; that is, the ratio of stock market transactions over a period of time divided by the

EXHIBIT 13.4

Turnover Ratio of Emerging Equity Markets in Selected Developing Countries
(Transactions in U.S. $/Year-End Market Capitalization in U.S. $)

Region or Country	1999	2000	2001	2002	2003
Latin America					
Argentina	12	5	2	2	6
Brazil	45	45	35	32	32
Chile	11	10	8	6	10
Colombia	6	4	3	2	3
Mexico	29	33	32	24	21
Peru	18	13	8	9	6
Venezuela	10	9	6	3	4
Asia					
China	134	158	81	68	83
India	84	307	191	165	139
Indonesia	46	32	39	48	34
Korea	347	376	380	322	237
Malaysia	40	45	18	23	34
Pakistan	340	487	227	346	497
Philippines	47	16	7	8	9
Sri Lanka	13	11	13	21	35
China's Taiwan	286	315	199	226	185
Thailand	89	53	109	114	117
Europe					
Czech Republic	76	58	34	49	53
Hungary	95	86	44	52	58
Poland	45	48	26	22	27
Russia	6	37	39	36	46
Slovakia	56	122	141	46	29
Turkey	111	197	162	170	192
Mideast/Africa					
Bahrain	6	4	3	3	3
Egypt	32	36	14	10	14
Israel	30	37	45	99	68
Jordan	9	8	17	20	29
Morocco	17	9	10	7	7
Nigeria	5	7	10	8	11
Oman	12	14	15	16	28
Saudi Arabia	29	27	32	48	137
South Africa	34	33	37	50	45
Zimbabwe	12	11	29	21	26

Source: Various issues of Global Stock Markets Factbook, Standard & Poor's.

一般来说，周转率越高，二级股票市场的流动性越强，股票也就越容易转手。

size, or market capitalization, of the stock market. Generally, the higher the turnover ratio, the more liquid the secondary stock market, indicating ease in trading.

Exhibit 13.3 presents turnover ratio percentages for 30 equity markets of developed countries for the five years beginning with 1999. The table indicates that the turnover ratio varies considerably over time for most national equity markets. The table also indicates that most national equity markets had very high turnover ratios, with the great majority in excess of 50 percent turnover per year.

Exhibit 13.4 presents the turnover ratio percentages for 33 emerging stock markets for the five years from 1999 through 2003. The exhibit indicates a considerable difference in turnover ratios among the developing countries. Many of the small equity markets in each region (e.g., Chile, Colombia, Sri Lanka, Jordan, Morocco, and Zimbabwe) have relatively low turnover ratios, indicating poor liquidity at present. Nevertheless, the larger emerging equity markets (India, Korea, and Chian's Taiwan) demonstrate fairly strong liquidity. For many countries, the turnover ratio

EXHIBIT 13.5

Percentage of Market Capitalization Represented by the 10 Largest Stocks: Emerging Equity Markets in Selected Developing Countries

Region or Country	1999	2000	2001	2002	2003
Latin America					
Argentina	24	7	4	5	34
Brazil	32	32	33	34	38
Chile	42	34	41	45	48
Colombia	48	32	31	47	44
Mexico	53	54	57	51	57
Peru	50	37	44	54	62
Venezuela	56	38	40	50	61
Asia					
China	30	25	27	27	27
India	31	26	40	43	37
Indonesia	47	19	54	56	53
Korea	58	50	50	48	44
Malaysia	33	38	38	35	31
Pakistan	55	52	45	52	45
Philippines	42	27	29	28	63
Sri Lanka	38	37	37	39	46
China's Taiwan	35	35	39	31	34
Thailand	46	39	42	41	42
Europe					
Czech Republic	75	76	76	54	72
Hungary	83	68	87	87	84
Poland	58	62	59	68	64
Russia	46	73	85	83	80
Slovakia	65	68	98	41	51
Turkey	59	51	56	51	54
Mideast/Africa					
Bahrain	72	64	66	68	66
Egypt	32	35	16	13	24
Israel	38	47	47	52	48
Jordan	69	63	66	58	63
Morocco	65	69	70	69	69
Nigeria	41	50	51	59	63
Oman	53	54	52	46	60
Saudi Arabia	68	70	67	75	81
South Africa	23	27	27	29	28
Zimbabwe	60	50	46	45	40

Source: Various issues of Global Stock Markets Factbook, Standard & Poor's.

decreased following the stock market decline in 2000. Since then turnover ratios have in general stayed low.

Measures of Market Concentration

As was previously mentioned, Chapter 15 will examine the benefits of constructing a diversified international portfolio. In order to construct a diversified portfolio, however, there must be opportunities for making foreign investment. The more concentrated a national equity market is in a few stock issues, the less opportunity a global investor has to include shares from that country in an internationally diversified portfolio.

Exhibit 13.5 presents the concentration ratios for 33 emerging stock markets for 1999 through 2003. The smaller the concentration percentage, the less concentrated a market is in a few stock issues. In 1999, 23 stock markets had concentration ratios of 40 percent or more, 16 had 50 percent or more, and 8 had 60 percent or more. By comparison, in 2003, 25 stock markets had concentration ratios of 40 percent or more, 17 had 50 percent or more, and 13 had 60 percent or more. Thus, one must conclude

因此，可以得出结论：近年来发展中国家与地区新兴股票市场上的权益投资机会并未增加。

that the number of equity investment opportunities in emerging stock market countries has not been improving in recent years.

Market Structure, Trading Practices, and Costs

二级市场

一级市场

在二级市场交易中，一般通过代表公众买方和卖方的所谓经纪人来完成。

经纪人 (broker)
市价指令 (market order)
限价指令 (limit order)
限价指令簿 (limit order book)
自营商市场 (dealer market)
代理商市场 (agency market)

www.nasdaq.com

This is the official website of the NASDAQ stock exchange. It provides information about the exchange, portfolio-monitoring software, and price quotations.

场外交易 (OTC)
买入价 (bid price)
卖出价 (ask price)

www.nyse.com

This is the website of the New York Stock Exchange. Information about the NYSE, its operation, membership, and listed companies is provided here. U.S. stock price quotations are available at this site.

专营商 (specialist)

美国的场外市场和交易所市场都是连续型市场，在营业时间内，市价指令和限价指令可以随即得到执行。

The **secondary** equity markets of the world serve two major purposes. They provide *marketability* and *share valuation*.[1] Investors or traders who buy shares from the issuing firm in the **primary** market may not want to hold them indefinitely. The secondary market allows share owners to reduce their holdings of unwanted shares and purchasers to acquire the stock. Firms would have a difficult time attracting buyers in the primary market without the marketability provided through the secondary market. Additionally, competitive trading between buyers and sellers in the secondary market establishes fair market prices for existing issues.

In conducting a trade in a secondary market, public buyers and sellers are represented by an agent, known as a **broker.** The order submitted to the broker may be a market order or a limit order. **A market order** is executed at the best price available in the market when the order is received, that is, the *market price*. A **limit order** is an order *away from the market* price that is held in a **limit order book** until it can be executed at the desired price.

There are many different designs for secondary markets that allow for efficient trading of shares between buyers and sellers. Generally, however, a secondary market is structured as a dealer or agency market. In a **dealer market,** the broker takes the trade through the dealer, who participates in trades as a principal by buying and selling the security for his own account. Public traders do not trade directly with one another in a dealer market. In an **agency market,** the broker takes the client's order through the agent, who matches it with another public order. The agent can be viewed as a *broker's broker*. Other names for the agent are *official broker* and *central broker*.

Both dealer and agency structures exist in the United States. The **over-the-counter (OTC)** market is a dealer market. Almost all OTC stocks trade on the National Association of Security Dealers Automated Quotation System (NASDAQ), which is a computer-linked system that shows the **bid** (buy) and **ask** (sell) prices of all dealers in a security. As many as 20 dealers may make a market in the most actively traded issues.

In the United States, firms must meet certain listing requirements in order to have their stock traded on one of several organized stock exchanges. The two largest of these exchanges, the New York Stock Exchange (NYSE) and the American Stock Exchange (AMEX), are both national exchanges on which the stocks of the largest companies of most interest to investors are traded. Shares of firms of regional interest are traded on several regional exchanges.

The exchange markets in the United States are agency/auction markets. Each stock traded on the exchange is represented by a **specialist,** who makes a market by holding an inventory of the security. Each specialist has a designated station (desk) on the exchange trading floor where trades in his stock are conducted. Floor brokers bring the flow of public market orders for a security to the specialist's desk for execution. Serving as a dealer, the specialist is obligated to post bid and ask prices for the stock he represents and to stand willing to buy or sell for his own account at these prices. Through an auction process, the "crowd" of floor brokers may arrive at a more favorable market price for their clients between the specialist's bid and ask prices and thus transact among themselves. The specialist also holds the limit order book. In executing these orders, the specialist serves as an agent. Limit order prices receive preference in establishing the posted bid and ask prices if they are more favorable than the specialist's, and he must fill a limit order, if possible, from the flow of public orders before trading for his own account. Both the OTC and the exchange markets in the

---

[1]Much of the discussion in this section follows from Chapter 2 of Schwartz (1988).

EXHIBIT 13.6

Characteristics of Major Equity Trading Systems

Equity Trading System	Market Characteristics		
	Public Orders	**Order Flow**	**Example**
Dealer	Trade with dealer	Continuous	NASDAQ OTC
Agency	Agent assists with matching of public orders	Continuous or periodic	NYSE specialist system[a] (continuous) Old Paris Bourse (noncontinuous)
Fully automated	Electronic matching of public orders	Continuous	Toronto Stock Exchange

[a]As noted in the text, a specialist may at times also serve as a dealer.

连续交易市场

www.tse.com

This is the website of the Toronto Stock Exchange. Information about the exchange, its operation, membership, and listed companies is provided here. Canadian stock and mutual fund prices are available at this site.

在**短期同业拆放市场**，代理商在一段时间内累积一批指令，然后在交易日通过书面或口头竞价的方式定期执行这些指令。

集合交易

活跃的股票交易所非常需要连续交易系统，然而短期同行业拆放市场和大众交易为那些交易少的股票提供了便利，因为这样做减少了短期内出现指令稀少的可能性。

United States are **continuous markets** where market and limit orders can be executed at any time during business hours.

In recent years, most national stock markets have become automated for at least some of the issues traded on them. The first was the Toronto Stock Exchange (TSE), which in 1977 instituted the Computer Assisted Trading System (CATS). An automated trading system electronically stores and displays public orders on a continuous basis, and allows public traders to cross orders with one another to execute a trade without the assistance of exchange personnel. Automated systems are successful largely because orders can be filled faster and fewer exchange personnel are needed. Indeed, in some countries the exchange trading floor has been completely eliminated.

Not all stock market systems provide continuous trading. For example, the Paris Bourse was traditionally a call market. In a **call market,** an agent of the exchange accumulates, over a period of time, a batch of orders that are periodically executed by written or verbal auction throughout the trading day. Both market and limit orders are handled in this way. The major disadvantage of a call market is that traders are not certain about the price at which their orders will transact because bid and ask quotations are not available prior to the call. On September 22, 2000, the Paris Bourse merged with the Brussels and Amsterdam exchanges to form Euronext, discussed in a later section in this chapter.

A second type of noncontinuous exchange trading system is **crowd trading.** Typically, crowd trading is organized as follows. In a trading ring, an agent of the exchange periodically calls out the name of the issue. At this point, traders announce their bid and ask prices for the issue, and seek counterparts to a trade. Between counterparts a deal may be struck and a trade executed. Unlike a call market in which there is a common price for all trades, several bilateral trades may take place at different prices. Crowd trading was once the system of trading on the Zurich Stock Exchange, but the Swiss exchange moved to an automated system in August 1996. At present, crowd trading is practiced at the Madrid Stock Exchange for a small percentage of trading.

Continuous trading systems are desirable for actively traded issues, whereas call markets and crowd trading offer advantages for thinly traded issues because they mitigate the possibility of sparse order flow over short time periods. Exhibit 13.6 provides a summary of the major equity trading systems found worldwide.

Exhibit 13.7 provides a brief summary of the location and the market trading systems used at various major equity markets of the world. The exhibit also shows the typical taxes applicable to equity trades and the number of business days required to settle a trade.

International Equity Market Benchmarks

二级市场的股票交易指数是用来衡量一个国家股票市场活跃程度或绩效表现的基准。

As a benchmark of activity or performance of a given national equity market, an index of the stocks traded on the secondary exchange (or exchanges) of a country is used. Several national equity indexes are available for use by investors.

EXHIBIT 13.7		Trading Practices and Costs of Major Equity Markets		
Region or Country	**Primary Market**	**System**	**Taxes**	**Settlement**
Argentina	Buenos Aires	Auction market; automated	.0951% + VAT of 21% on commission	Trade date + 3 days
Australia	National market	Automated	Off shore: none; domestic: 10% of commission	Trade date + 3 days
Austria	Vienna	Automated quote and market-making	None	Trade date + 3 days
Belgium	Brussels	Euronext	None	Trade date + 3 days
Brazil	Sao Paulo	Crowd trading; automated	Fee: .035%	Trade date + 3 days
Canada	Toronto	Automated	None	Trade date + 3 days
Czech Republic	Prague	Automated and OTC	.080–.125%; OTC: 0%	Trade date + 3 days
Chile	Santiago	Automated and crowd trading	Cumulative schedule from .50%–0%	Trade date + 2 days
China	Shenzhen and Shanghai	Automated	Shenzhen: .1841% Shanghai: .18%	A shares: Trade date +1 day B shares: Trade date + 3 days
Colombia	National market	Automated	None	Trade date + 3 days
Denmark	Copenhagen	Norex	None	Trade date + 3 days
Egypt	Cairo, Alexandria	Automated	.025%	Trade date + 1 day (2 days) for sell (buy)
Finland	Helsinki	Norex	None	Trade date + 3 days
France	Paris	Euronext	VAT on commission; None for foreigners	Trade date + 3 days
Germany	Frankfurt	Automated and floor trading	None	Trade date + 2 days
Greece	Athens	Automated	Fees: .06% +.15% on sales	Trade date + 3 days
China-Hong Kong SAR	China-Hong Kong	Automated	.112%	Trade date + 2 days
Hungary	Budapest	Automated	None	Trade date + 3 days
India	National Stock Exchange; Bombay Stock Exchange	Automated	.075% +10.2% of commission	Trade date + 2 days
Indonesia	Jakarta	Automated	.111%+VAT on commission	Trade date + 3 days
Ireland	Dublin	Automated	1.00% on purchases	Trade date + 3 days
Israel	Tel Aviv	Automated	None	Trade date + 0(2) days (Foreign)
Italy	Milan	Automated	None	Trade date + 3 days
Japan	Tokyo, Osaka, JASDAQ	Automated	None	Trade date + 3 days
Malaysia	Kuala Lumpur	Automated	.04%	Trade date + 3 days
Mexico	Mexico City	Automated	.04%	Trade date + 2 days
Netherlands	Amsterdam	Euronext	None	Trade date + 3 days
New Zealand	Wellington	Automated	None	Trade date + 3 days
Norway	Oslo	Norex	None	Trade date + 3 days
Peru	Lima	Automated	.2356%	Trade date + 3 days
Philippines	Pasig, Makati	Automated	.50%(sales)+VAT on commission	Trade date + 3 days
Poland	Warsaw	Automated	.04%	Trade date + 3 days
Portugal	Lisbon	Euronext	None	Trade date + 3 days

(Continued)

EXHIBIT 13.7		Trading Practices and Costs of Major Equity Markets (continued)		
Region or Country	Primary Market	System	Taxes	Settlement
Russia	Moscow	Automated	None	Trade date + 5 to 10 days; Depository Receipt: Trade date + 3 days
Singapore	Singapore	Automated	.05% (Max SGD200) + 5% on commission and fees	Trade date + 3 days
South Africa	Johannesburg	Automated	.25% on buys + VAT on commission	Trade date + 5 days
South Korea	Seoul	Automated	.30% on sales	Trade date + 2 days
Spain	Madrid	Automated and crowd trading(<3%)	None	Trade date + 3 days
Sweden	Stockholm	Norex	None	Trade date + 3 days
Switzerland	Zurich	Automated	.085%	Trade date + 3 days
China's Taiwan	Taipei	Automated	.30% on sells	Trade date + 1 day
Thailand	Bangkok	Automated	VAT .0175%	Trade date + 3 days
Turkey	Istanbul	Automated	None	Trade date + 2 days
United Kingdom	London	Automated and automated dealer quotation system	.50% on purchases	Trade date + 3 days
United States	New York and OTC	Specialist: NYSE and AMEX; Automated quotation: NASDAQ OTC	USD 32.90 per USD 1 million sale value	Trade date + 3 days

Note: Euronext is a merger of the Amsterdam, Brussels, Paris, and Lisbon stock exchanges where trading is conducted over a single automated platform. Norex is an alliance of Nordic and Baltic stock exchanges where trading is conducted over a common automated trading system.
Source: Excerpted from Guide to Global Equity Markets, 14th ed., UBS Investment Bank, February 2005.

关于这一点，本章的一些图表给出了一些摘自标准普尔公司编制的股票市场指数的资料。

www.msci.com

This is the website of Morgan Stanley Capital International. Detailed information about the construction of MSCI's international stock market indexes is provided, as is information about index performance. One can also download index data at this site to an Excel spreadsheet.

To this point, the exhibits of this chapter have presented data from stock market indexes prepared by Standard & Poor's. Each year S&P publishes its *Global Stock Markets Factbook*, which provides a variety of statistical data on both emerging and developed country stock markets. The *Factbook* is an excellent source that is carried by many university libraries and provides annual comparative statistics in an easy-to-read format.

The indexes constructed and published by Morgan Stanley Capital International (MSCI) are an excellent source of national stock market performance. MSCI presents return and price level data for 24 national stock market indexes from developed countries. In constructing each of these indexes, an attempt is made to include equity issues representing at least 60 percent of the market capitalization of each industry within the country. The stocks in each country index are market-value weighted, that is, the proportion of the index a stock represents is determined by its proportion of the total market capitalization of all stocks in the index. Additionally, MSCI publishes a market-value-weighted World Index comprising 23 of its country indexes. The World Index includes approximately 2,600 stock issues of major corporations in the world. MSCI also publishes several regional indexes: the European, Australasia, Far East (EAFE) Index comprising approximately 1,000 stocks from 21 countries; the North American Index composed of the United States and Canada; the Far East Index (three countries); several Europe Indexes (depending upon whether individual constituent countries are included); the Nordic Countries Index (four countries); and the Pacific Index (five countries). The EAFE Index is widely followed, and it is representative of World Index excluding North American stock market performance. Daily values of several of the MSCI country indexes and the World Index can be found in *The Wall Street Journal*. MSCI also publishes dozens of industry indexes, each of which includes equity issues from the respective industry from the countries it follows.

EXHIBIT 13.8   **Example of Dow Jones Country Stock Market Indexes**

Dow Jones Country Indexes
March 3, 2005 5:15 p.m. ET
In U.S. dollar terms

Region or Country	Index	Chg	%Chg	YTD %Chg	Region or Country	Index	Chg	%Chg	YTD %Chg
Australia	292.69	+ 1.39	+ 0.48	+ 4.29	Mexico	275.94	+ 0.84	+ 0.31	+ 7.27
Austria	295.49	+ 4.25	+ 1.46	+ 6.49	Netherlands	294.21	+ 0.39	+ 0.13	+ 5.29
Belgium	317.87	− 0.39	− 0.12	+ 2.25	New Zealand	247.26	+ 0.76	+ 0.31	+ 5.18
Brazil	565.02	+ 4.43	+ 0.79	+ 11.18	Norway	243.55	+ 3.30	+ 1.37	+ 6.74
Canada	298.89	+ 0.59	+ 0.20	+ 2.65	Philippines	96.29	+ 1.18	+ 1.24	+ 14.39
Chile	265.75	+ 0.83	+ 0.31	− 2.16	Portugal	196.30	− 0.07	− 0.04	− 0.27
Denmark	326.40	+ 2.40	+ 0.74	+ 6.05	Singapore	164.30	+ 0.44	+ 0.27	+ 3.58
Finland	861.37	+ 1.85	+ 0.22	+ 3.29	South Africa	214.93	+ 0.96	− 0.44	− 1.74
France	258.46	+ 0.21	+ 0.08	+ 3.19	South Korea	155.76	+ 0.96	+ 0.62	+ 18.02
Germany	205.74	− 0.67	− 0.32	− 0.50	Spain	280.51	+ 0.47	− 0.17	+ 0.29
Greece	209.30	+ 0.10	+ 0.05	+ 7.81	Sweden	352.90	+ 1.66	+ 0.47	+ 1.15
China-Hong Kong SAR	251.88	+ 0.58	+ 0.23	− 1.54	Switzerland	401.55	− 1.76	− 0.44	+ 1.96
Indonesia	79.15	+ 0.47	+ 0.60	+ 9.16	China's Taiwan	129.59	− 0.51	− 0.39	+ 3.93
Ireland	452.09	+ 0.08	+ 0.02	− 3.98	Thailand	79.80	− 0.33	− 0.41	+ 9.38
Italy	216.85	+ 0.03	+ 0.01	− 0.58	U.K.	214.73	+ 0.68	+ 0.32	+ 3.59
Japan	91.27	+ 0.14	+ 0.15	+ 0.74	U.S.	288.87	+ 0.04	+ 0.01	− 0.17
Malaysia	118.97	− 0.27	− 0.23	− 1.43	Venezuela	41.63	− 1.69	− 3.90	− 5.80

Source: The Wall Street Journal, March 4, 2005, p. C14. Reprinted by permission of The Wall Street Journal, © 2005 Dow Jones & Company, Inc. All Rights Reserved Worldwide.

摩根士丹利资本国
际也发布来自27个发展
中国家新兴股票市场、
大概涉及这些国家1700
种证券的指数。

MSCI also publishes 27 national emerging stock market indexes for developing countries covering approximately 1,700 securities. Additionally, MSCI publishes several regional emerging markets indexes. MSCI recognizes that some countries impose ownership restrictions on stocks by foreigners. In this case, the constituent national indexes are excluded or underweighted to recognize the particular restriction in order to provide an index representative of investments that can be freely made.

The Dow Jones Company (DJ) provides stock market index values for a number of countries. The values and percentage changes of these indexes can be found daily in *The Wall Street Journal*. The data are presented in local currency terms and for comparative purposes in U.S. dollars. Exhibit 13.8 presents an example of the daily report of these indexes as found in *The Wall Street Journal*.

In addition to their own Dow Jones country stock market indexes, *The Wall Street Journal* also reports values and percentage changes in local currency values of the major stock market indexes of the national exchanges or markets from various countries in the world. Many of these indexes are prepared by the stock markets themselves or well-known investment advisory firms. Exhibit 13.9 presents a list of the indexes that appear daily in *The Wall Street Journal*.

iShares MSCI

www.ishares.com

This website describes the iShares MSCI created by Barclays Global Investors.

Barclays Global Investors introduced iShares MSCI as vehicles to facilitate investment in country funds. iShares MSCI are country-specific baskets of stocks designed to replicate the MSCI country indexes of 21 countries and four regions. iShares are exchange-traded funds that trade on the American Stock Exchange.

iShares are subject to U.S. SEC and Internal Revenue Service diversification requirements. These requirements prohibit the investment of more than 50 percent of the fund in five or fewer securities, or 25 percent of the fund in a single security. Thus, for some countries, the fund does not perfectly replicate the MSCI country index. Nevertheless, iShares are a low-cost, convenient way for investors to hold diversified investments in several different countries.

EXHIBIT 13.9		
Major National Stock Market Indexes	**Region or Country**	**Index**
	Argentina	Merval
	Australia	S&P/ASX 200
	Belgium	Bel-20
	Brazil	Sao Paulo Bovespa
	Canada	S&P/TSX Composite
	Chile	Santiago IPSA
	China	Dow Jones CBN China 600
	China	Dow Jones China 88
	Europe	DJ STOXX 600
	Europe	DJ STOXX 50
	Euro Zone	DJ Euro STOXX
	Euro Zone	DJ Euro STOXX 50
	France	Paris CAC 40
	Germany	Frankfurt Xetra DAX
	China-Hong Kong SAR	Hang Seng
	India	Bombay Sensex
	Israel	Tel Aviv 25
	Italy	S&P/MIB
	Japan	Tokyo Nikkei Stock Average
	Japan	Tokyo Nikkei 300
	Japan	Tokyo Topix Index
	Mexico	I.P.C. All-Share
	Netherlands	Amsterdam AEX
	Russia	DJ Russia Titans 10
	Singapore	Straits Times
	South Africa	Johannesburg All Share
	South Korea	KOSPI
	Spain	IBEX 35
	Sweden	SX All Share
	Switzerland	Zurich Swiss Market
	China's Taiwan	Weighted
	Turkey	Istanbul National 100
	U.K.	London FTSE 100-share
	U.K.	London FTSE 250-share
	United States	
	American Stock Exchange Composite	
	Dow Jones Industrial Average	
	National Association of Security Dealers	
	Automated Quotation Composite	
	New York Stock Exchange Composite	
	Russell 2000	
	Standard & Poor's 500	
	Wilshire 5000	
	Value-Line	

Source: The Wall Street Journal, March 4, 2005, p. C14. Reprinted by permission of The Wall Street Journal, © 2005 Dow Jones & Company, Inc. All Rights Reserved Worldwide.

The International Finance in Practice box "Foreign Interest In South Africa Takes Off" discusses investing in South Africa via the iShares MSCI South Africa exchange-traded fund.

Trading In International Equities

在20世纪80年代，世界资本市场开始向更广阔的全球一体化道路迈进。

During the 1980s world capital markets began a trend toward greater global integration. Several factors account for this movement. First, investors began to realize the benefits of international portfolio diversification. Second, major capital markets

Foreign Interest In South Africa Takes Off

For the past three years South Africa's equity market has been among the world's strongest performers, with returns to foreign investors boosted substantially by a strengthening currency. For most of this period, however, foreign interest was modest, and it is only during the last quarter of 2004 that this began to change as net foreign purchases of South African shares on the Johannesburg Securities Exchange (JSE) soared to ZAR21 billion ($3.74 billion), the highest quarterly level ever.

Fourth quarter net equity purchases were up from a five-year average of ZAR3.7 billion per quarter, or $895 million at the average exchange rate over the period. Andre Roux, Investec's chief economist in South Africa, says: "There appears to be a concerted move by foreign investors to reduce what has been a protracted period of holding an underweight position in South Africa [SA] equity."

Unlike past foreign buying, this time it is not confined to resource stocks. "They are buying into a buoyant domestic economic story and are including banks, local industrials and telecoms in their buying programmes," says Roux. "In a global context, SA shares offer reasonable value and buyers also appear satisfied that the country is in a period of higher growth with more currency and interest rate stability."

Unfortunately, scope is limited for investment in pure South African-asset mutual funds denominated in dollars, euros or sterling. Currently, the two largest investment vehicles are Barclays Global Investor's $127 million iShares MSCI South Africa Index (iShares SA), an exchange-traded fund (ETF) listed on the American Stock Exchange, and Old Mutual's Bermuda-based pound 65 million South Africa Trust (SAT), an investment company listed on the London Stock Exchange.

As an ETF, iShares SA is an index tracking product; SAT is actively managed and has as its benchmark the FTSE/JSE All Share Index. Portfolios of both products are dominated by big-cap, blue-chip stocks, but SAT has a lower exposure to resources at 41.3 percent and to financials at 24.6 percent than does iShares SA (48.1 percent and 27.0 percent, respectively). By contrast, SAT has a considerably higher exposure to industrials at 34.1 percent (versus 24.9 percent).

Lower exposure to resources, which suffered in 2004 as a result of the rand's strength, and a higher industrial content which includes top-performing retailers such as Truworths and Massmart, gave SAT the performance edge in 2004. SAT ended the year with a 49.9 percent gain, while iShares SA advanced 43.6 percent in sterling terms. However, in dollar terms iShares SA was ahead with a gain of 55.4 percent.

Source: Excerpted from Funds International. London: January 2005, p. P. 1. Reprinted by kind permission of VRL Publishing, Ltd. © 2005. All rights reserved.

became more liberalized through the elimination of fixed trading commissions, the reduction in governmental regulation, and measures taken by the European Union to integrate their capital markets. Third, new computer and communications technology facilitated efficient and fair securities trading through order routing and execution, information dissemination, and clearance and settlement. Fourth, MNCs realized the benefits of sourcing new capital internationally. In this section, we explore some of the major effects that greater global integration has had on the world's equity markets. We begin by examining the cross-listing of shares.

Cross-Listing of Shares

境外上市是指发行股票的公司除了在自己国家的股票交易所挂牌交易股票外，还在一个或更多的外国股票交易所挂牌交易股票。

Cross-listing refers to a firm having its equity shares listed on one or more foreign exchanges, in addition to the home country stock exchange. Cross-listing is not a new concept; however, with the increased globalization of world equity markets, the amount of cross-listing has exploded in recent years. In particular, MNCs often cross-list their shares, but non-MNCs also cross-list.

Exhibit 13.10 presents the total number of companies listed on various national stock exchanges in the world and the breakdown of the listings between domestic and foreign for 2003.[2] The exhibit also shows the number of new listings and the domestic-foreign split for 2003. The exhibit shows that some foreign companies are listed on virtually all national stock exchanges from developed countries. Several exchanges

---

[2]For the purpose of this discussion, NASDAQ OTC stocks will be referred to as listed shares.

EXHIBIT 13.10	Total, Domestic, and Foreign Company Listings on Major National Stock Exchanges for 2003					
	Total Listings			**New Listings**		
Exchange	Total	Domestic	Foreign	Total	Domestic	Foreign
Americas						
Amex	557	502	55	76	60	16
Bermuda	55	22	33	3	0	3
Buenos Aires	110	106	4	0	0	0
Lima	227	195	32	7	7	0
Mexico	237	158	79	78	1	77
Nasdaq	3,294	2,951	343	55	NA	NA
NYSE	2,308	1,842	466	107	91	16
Santiago	241	240	1	2	2	0
Sao Paulo	391	389	2	10	10	0
TSX Group	3,599	3,561	38	204	199	5
Europe, Africa, Middle East						
Athens	332	331	1	13	13	0
Borsa Italiana	279	271	8	11	10	1
Budapest	49	48	1	2	2	0
Copenhagen	194	187	7	2	2	0
Deutsche Börse	866	684	182	0	0	0
Euronext	1,392	1,046	346	24	14	10
Helsinki	145	142	3	1	0	1
Irish	66	55	11	0	0	0
Istanbul	285	285	0	4	4	0
JSE South Africa	411	390	21	7	7	0
Ljubilana	134	134	0	15	15	0
London	2,692	2,311	381	201	194	7
Luxembourg	242	44	198	24	0	24
Malta	13	13	0	0	0	0
Oslo	178	156	22	5	5	0
Spanish Exchanges (BME)	3,223	3,191	32	275	272	3
Stockholm	282	268	16	5	4	1
Swiss Exchange	419	289	130	2	1	1
Tehran	345	345	0	38	38	0
Tel Aviv	577	573	4	6	4	2
Warsaw	203	202	1	6	5	1
Wiener Börse	125	104	21	9	8	1
Asia, Pacific						
Australian	1,471	1,405	66	107	101	6
Colombo	244	244	0	8	8	0
China-Hong Kong	1,037	1,027	10	73	72	1
Jakarta	333	333	0	6	6	0
Korea	684	684	0	13	13	0
Kuala Lumpur	902	898	4	58	58	0
Mumbai	5,644	5,644	0	24	24	0
National Stock Exchange India	911	911	0	35	35	0
New Zealand	196	153	43	16	12	4
Osaka	1,140	1,140	0	26	26	0
Philippine	236	234	2	5	5	0
Shanghai	780	780	0	67	67	0
Shenzhen	505	505	0	0	0	0
Singapore	551	475	76	59	49	10
Taiwan	674	669	5	47	45	2
Thailand	418	418	0	27	27	0
Tokyo	2,206	2,174	32	120	120	0

Source: Table I.3, p. 83 and Table I.4., p. 84 from Annual Report and Statistics 2003, World Federation of Exchanges.

have a large proportion of foreign listings. In fact, the Luxembourg Stock Exchange has more foreign than domestic listings, while on the Swiss bourse the foreign listings are over 30 percent.

A firm may decide to cross-list its shares for many reasons:

1. Cross-listing provides a means for expanding the investor base for a firm's stock, thus potentially increasing its demand. Increased demand for a company's stock may increase the market price. Additionally, greater market demand and a broader investor base improves the price liquidity of the security.

2. Cross-listing establishes name recognition of the company in a new capital market, thus paving the way for the firm to source new equity or debt capital from local investors as demands dictate. This is an especially important reason for firms from emerging market countries with limited capital markets to cross-list their shares on exchanges in developed countries with enhanced capital market access.

3. Cross-listing brings the firm's name before more investor and consumer groups. Local consumers (investors) may more likely become investors in (consumers of) the company's stock (products) if the company's stock is (products are) locally available. International portfolio diversification is facilitated for investors if they can trade the security on their own stock exchange.

4. Cross-listing into developed capital markets with strict securities regulations and information disclosure requirements may be seen as a signal to investors that improved corporate governance is forthcoming.

5. Cross-listing may mitigate the possibility of a hostile takeover of the firm through the broader investor base created for the firm's shares.

将股票境外上市的公司必须遵守本国的证券法规，同时还要遵守上市所在地国家或地区相应的规章制度。

Cross-listing of a firm's stock obligates the firm to adhere to the securities regulations of its home country as well as the regulations of the countries in which it is cross-listed. Cross-listing in the United States means the firm must meet the accounting and disclosure requirements of the U.S. Securities and Exchange Commission. Reconciliation of a company's financial statements to U.S. standards can be a laborious process, and some foreign firms are reluctant to disclose hidden reserves. For foreign firms desiring to have their shares traded only among large institutional investors rather than listed on an exchange, less rigorous accounting and disclosure requirements apply under SEC Rule 144A. Rule 144A share sales are often acceptable to family-owned companies, which for privacy or tax reasons operate their business with generally unacceptable accounting standards.

Yankee Stock Offerings

自20世纪90年代初以来，许多外国公司，尤其是拉丁美洲的公司，开始在美国的股票交易所上市，这为未来在美国股票市场上发行**扬基股票**奠定了基础。

The introduction to this section indicated that in recent years U.S. investors have bought and sold a large amount of foreign stock. Since the beginning of the 1990s, many foreign companies, Latin American in particular, have listed their stocks on U.S. exchanges to prime the U.S. equity market for future **Yankee stock** offerings, that is, the direct sale of new equity capital to U.S. public investors. This was a break from the past for the Latin American companies, which typically sold restricted 144A shares to large investors. Three factors appear to be fueling the sale of Yankee stocks. One is the push for privatization by many Latin American and Eastern European government-owned companies. A second factor is the rapid growth in the economies of the developing countries. The third reason is the expected large demand for new capital by Mexican companies now that the North American Free Trade Agreement has been approved (and despite the meltdown of the peso in late 1994).

The European Stock Market

Western and Eastern Europe once had more than 20 national equity markets where at least 15 different languages were spoken. Several combinations and trading arrangements have been formed among these national stock exchanges in recent years, but as yet there is not a single European stock market that comprises all national markets, and it does not appear as if one will exist in the near future.

The closest arrangement to date that can be characterized as approaching a European stock market is Euronext. Euronext N.V. Shareholders was formed on September 22, 2000, as a result of a merger of the Amsterdam Exchanges, Brussels Exchanges, and the Paris Bourse. The three markets are wholly owned subsidiaries of Euronext N.V., doing business as Euronext Amsterdam, Euronext Brussels, and Euronext Paris. Euronext creates a single trading platform serving all members at each of the three subsidiary exchanges. Access to all shares and products is provided. Additionally, a single order book exists for each stock, allowing for transparency and liquidity. A single clearinghouse and payment and delivery system facilitates trading. In June 2001, the Portuguese stock exchange merged with Euronext. Additionally, in 2001, a cross-access and cross-trading agreement was signed between Euronext and the Luxembourg and Warsaw stock exchanges. Thus, it appears that over time a European stock exchange will eventually develop. However, a lack of common securities regulations, even among the countries of the European Union, is hindering this development.

Another noteworthy European trading arrangement is Norex. Norex is an alliance among the Nordic and Baltic exchanges in Denmark, Finland, Estonia, Iceland, Norway, Latvia, and Sweden. Trading on Norex exchanges is carried out through the Stockholm Automated Exchange (SAXESS), a state-of-the-art computerized and electronic trading system capable of handing 2,000 orders per second.

American Depository Receipts

美国存托凭证(ADR)
是指由美国银行发行的外国公司存托凭证，用于证明持有人在外国公司的股权。

www.euronext.com
This is the official website of Euronext.

www.norex.com
This is the official website of Norex.

Foreign stocks can be traded directly on a national stock market, but most often they are traded in the form of a *depository receipt*. For example, Yankee stock issues often trade on the U.S. exchanges as **American Depository Receipts (ADRs).** An ADR is a receipt representing a number of foreign shares that remain on deposit with the U.S. depository's custodian in the issuer's home market. The bank serves as the transfer agent for the ADRs, which are traded on the listed exchanges in the United States or in the OTC market. The first ADRs began trading in 1927 as a means of eliminating some of the risks, delays, inconveniences, and expenses of trading the actual shares. The ADR market has grown significantly over the years; at year-end 2004 there were 1,858 ADR programs, representing issuers from more than 73 countries. Approximately 500 ADRs trade on U.S. exchanges. Similarly, *Singapore Depository Receipts* trade on the Singapore Stock Exchange. *Global Depository Receipts (GDRs)* allow a foreign firm to simultaneously cross-list on several national exchanges. Many GDRs are traded on the London and Luxembourg stock exchanges. Exhibit 13.11 shows a tombstone for a Global Depository Receipt.

ADRs offer the U.S. investor many advantages over trading directly in the underlying stock on the foreign exchange. Non-U.S. investors can also invest in ADRs, and frequently do so rather than invest in the underlying stock because of the investment advantages. These advantages include:

1. ADRs are denominated in dollars, trade on a U.S. stock exchange, and can be purchased through the investor's regular broker. By contrast, trading in the underlying shares would likely require the investor to: set up an account with a broker from the country where the company issuing the stock is located; make a currency exchange; and arrange for the shipment of the stock certificates or the establishment of a custodial account.

2. Dividends received on the underlying shares are collected and converted to dollars by the custodian and paid to the ADR investor, whereas investment in the underlying shares requires the investor to collect the foreign dividends and make a currency conversion. Moreover, tax treaties between the United States and some countries lower the dividend tax rate paid by nonresident investors. Consequently, U.S. investors in the underlying shares need to file a form to get a refund on the tax difference withheld. ADR investors, however, receive the full dollar equivalent dividend, less only the applicable taxes.

EXHIBIT 13.11

Global Depository Receipt Tombstone

COMMERCIAL INTERNATIONAL BANK
(EGYPT) S.A.E.

International Offering of
9,999,000 Global Depository Receipts

corresponding to
999,900 Shares (nominal Value of E£100 per Share)

at an
Offer price of US$11.875 per Global Depository Receipt

Seller
National Bank of Egypt

Global Co-ordinator
Co Lead Managers
Robert Fleming & Co. Limited Salomon Brothers International Limited
UBS Limited

Domestic Advisor
Commercial International Investment Company S.A.E.

ING BARINGS

July 1996

Source: Euromoney, October 1998, p. 127.

3. ADR trades clear in three business days as do U.S. equities, whereas settlement practices for the underlying stock vary in foreign countries.

4. ADR price quotes are in U.S. dollars.

5. ADRs (except Rule 144A issues) are registered securities that provide for the protection of ownership rights, whereas most underlying stocks are bearer securities. Exhibit 13.12 describes the various types of ADR programs.

EXHIBIT 13.12

Types of ADRs

	Level I	Level II	Level III	Rule 144A
Description	Unlisted program in the U.S.	Listed on a U.S. exchange	Shares offered and listed on a U.S. exchange	Private placement to Qualified Institutional Buyers
Trading	OTC	NASDAQ, AMEX, NYSE	NASDAQ, AMEX, NYSE	U.S. private placement
SEC Registration	Form F-6	Form F-6	Forms F-1 and F-6	None
U.S. Reporting Requirements	Exempt under Rule 12g3-2(b)	Form 20-F*	Form 20-F*	Exempt under Rule 12g3-2(b)

*Financial statements must be partially reconciled to U.S. GAAP.
Level I: The most basic type of ADR program. The issuer is not seeking to raise new equity capital in the U.S. and/or cannot list on NASDAQ.
Level II: The issuer is not seeking to raise new equity capital in the U.S. and ADRs can be listed on NASDAQ, AMEX, or NYSE.
Level III: The issuer floats a public offering of new equity in the U.S. and lists the ADRs on NASDAQ, AMEX, or NYSE.
Rule 144A: This type of ADR program is a private placement of equity to Qualified Institutional Buyers (QIBs).
It can only be traded among QIBs.
Source: Excerpted from www.adr.com.

| EXHIBIT 13.13 | Mechanics of Issuance and Cancellation of ADRs |

A broker-dealer can purchase existing ADRs in the United States or purchase underlying shares in an issuer's home market and have new ADRs created, or issued, by the depositary bank. While the pool of available ADRs is constantly changing, the broker-dealer decides whether to purchase existing ADRs or have new ones issued, depending on such factors as availability, pricing, and market conditions in the United States and the issuer's home market.

To create new ADRs, underlying shares are deposited with a custodian bank in the issuer's home market. The depositary then issues ADRs representing those shares. The process for canceling ADRs is similar to the issuance process, but the steps are reversed. The following chart and description provide a more detailed explanation, including the parties and steps involved.

The ADR purchase and issuance process: two scenarios

EXISTING ADRS

A1   Investor places order with broker in the United States.

A2   Broker in the United States purchases ADRs in the applicable market.

A3   Settlement and delivery of the ADRs (in book-entry or certificate form).

NEW ADRS

B1   Investor places order with broker in the United States.

B2   Broker in the United States places order with local broker (outside U.S.) for equivalent shares.

B3   Local broker purchases shares in local market.

B4   Local shares are deposited with the depository's custodian.

B5   Depository receives confirmation of share deposit.

B6   Depository issues new ADRs and delivers them to broker in the US.

B7   Settlement and delivery of the ADRs (in book-entry or certificate form).

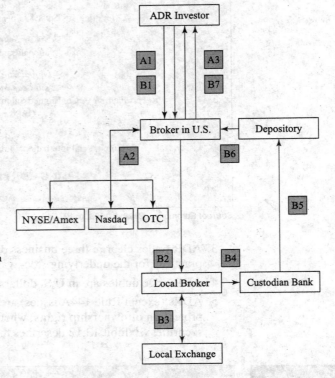

Source: Excerpted from www.adr.com.

6. An ADR investment can be sold by trading the depository receipt to another investor in the U.S. stock market, or the underlying shares can be sold in the local stock market. In this case the ADR is delivered for cancellation to the bank depository, which delivers the underlying shares to the buyer. Exhibit 13.13 charts the mechanics of issuance and cancellation of ADRs.

7. ADRs frequently represent a multiple of the underlying shares, rather than a one-for-one correspondence, to allow the ADR to trade in a price range customary for U.S. investors. A single ADR may represent more or less than one underlying share, depending upon the underlying share value.

8. ADR holders give instructions to the depository bank as to how to vote the rights associated with the underlying shares. Voting rights are not exercised by the depository bank in the absence of specific instructions from the ADR holders.

美国存托凭证有两
种类型：有担保存托凭
证和无担保存托凭证。

There are two types of ADRs: sponsored and unsponsored. *Sponsored* ADRs are created by a bank at the request of the foreign company that issued the underlying security. The sponsoring bank often offers ADR holders an assortment of services, including investment information and portions of the annual report translated into English. Sponsored ADRs are the only ones that can be listed on the U.S. stock markets. All new ADR programs must be sponsored. *Unsponsored* ADRs—some dating back prior to 1980 still exist—were usually created at the request of a U.S. investment banking firm without direct involvement by the foreign issuing firm. Consequently, the foreign company may not provide investment information or financial reports to the depository on a regular basis or in a timely manner. The depository fees of sponsored ADRs are paid by the foreign company. ADR investors pay the depository fees on unsponsored ADRs. Unsponsored ADRs may have several issuing banks, with the terms of the offering varying from bank to bank. In general, only sponsored ADRs trade on NASDAQ or the major stock exchanges.

一些实证研究就美
国存托凭证市场得出了
一些重要发现。

Several empirical studies document important findings about the ADR market. Rosenthal (1983), using a time series of weekly, biweekly, and monthly rates of return over the time period of 1974 through 1978 for 54 ADRs, found that the ADR market was weak-form efficient. That is, abnormal trading profits are not likely from studying historical price data.

Park (1990) found that a substantial portion of the variability in (i.e., change in) ADR returns is accounted for by variation in the share price of the underlying security in the home market; however, information observed in the U.S. market is also an important factor in the ADR return-generating process.

Officer and Hoffmeister (1987) and Kao, Wei, and Vu (1991) examined ADRs as vehicles for constructing diversified equity portfolios. Officer and Hoffmeister used a sample of 45 ADRs and 45 domestic stocks. For each, they had monthly rates of return for the period 1973 through 1983. They found that as few as four ADRs combined with four domestic stocks allowed the investor to reduce portfolio risk by as much as 25 percent without any reduction in expected return.

Kao, Wei, and Vu (1991) used 10 years of monthly return data covering the time period 1979 through 1989 for ADRs with underlying shares from the U.K., Australia, Japan, the Netherlands, and Sweden. They found that an internationally diversified portfolio of ADRs outperformed both a U.S. stock market and a world stock market benchmark on a risk-adjusted basis. Country ADR portfolios from all countries except Australia also outperformed the U.S. and world benchmarks, but only country ADR portfolios from the U.K., Japan, and the Netherlands outperformed their home country stock market benchmark.

Jayaraman, Shastri, and Tandon (1993) examine the effect of the listing of ADRs on the risk and return of the underlying stock. They find positive abnormal performance (i.e., return in excess of the expected equilibrium return) of the underlying security on the initial listing date. They interpret this result as evidence that an ADR listing provides the issuing firm with another market from which to source new equity capital. Additionally, they find an increase in the volatility of (change in) returns of the underlying stock. They interpret this result as consistent with the theory that traders with proprietary information will attempt to profit from their knowledge by taking advantage of price discrepancies caused by information differentials between the ADR and underlying security markets.

Gagnon and Karolyi (2004) compare synchronous intraday prices of ADRs and other types of cross-listed shares in U.S. markets relative to home-market prices after currency adjustment for 581 companies from 39 countries. They discover that for most stocks, prices of cross-listed shares are within 20 to 85 basis points of the home-market shares, thus limiting arbitrage opportunities after transaction costs. However, when institutional barriers that limit arbitrage exist, prices can deviate by as much as a 66 percent premium and an 87 percent discount. Large deviations seldom exist for more than a day. They also discover that cross-listed shares trading in the U.S. are relatively more (less) correlated with the U.S. market index than with the home market when there is proportionately more (less) trading in the U.S. market.

Global Registered Shares

全球记名的股票 (GRS) 是一种可以在全球各地进行交易的股票，而美国存托凭证则只能在外国市场上交易。

The merger of Daimler Benz AG and Chrysler Corporation on November 17, 1998, created DaimlerChrysler AG, a German firm. The merger was hailed as a landmark event for global equity markets because it simultaneously created a new type of equity share called Global Registered Shares (GRS). GRS are one share traded globally, unlike ADRs, which are receipts for bank deposits of home-market shares and traded on foreign markets. The primary exchanges for DaimlerChrysler GRS are the Frankfurt Stock Exchange and the NYSE; however, they are traded on a total of 20 exchanges worldwide. The shares are fully fungible—a GRS purchased on one exchange can be sold on another. They trade in both U.S. dollars and euros. A new global share registrar that links the U.S. and German transfer agents and registrars needed to be created to facilitate clearing. The main advantages of GRS over ADRs appear to be that all shareholders have equal status and direct voting rights. The main disadvantage of GRS appears to be the greater expense in establishing the global registrar and clearing facility. GRS have met with limited success; many companies that considered them opted instead for ADRs.[3]

EXAMPLE 13.1

DaimlerChrysler AG   Stock in DaimlerChrysler AG, the result of the merger of Daimler Benz AG, the famous German automobile manufacturer, and Chrysler Corporation trades on both the Frankfurt Stock Exchange in Germany and on the New York Stock Exchange. On the Frankfurt bourse, DaimlerChrysler closed at a price of EUR34.96 on Thursday, March 3, 2005. On the same day, DaimlerChrysler closed in New York at $45.85 per share. To prevent arbitrage trading between the two exchanges, the shares have to trade at the same price when adjusted for the exchange rate. We see that this is true. The $/EUR exchange rate on March 3 was $1.3112/EUR1.00. Thus, EUR34.96 × $1.3112 = $45.84, an amount very close to the closing price in New York of $45.85. The difference is easily explainable by the fact that the New York market closes several hours after the Frankfurt exchange, and thus market prices had changed slightly.

Factors Affecting International Equity Returns

Before closing this chapter, it is beneficial to explore some of the empirical evidence about which factors influence equity returns. After all, to construct an efficiently diversified international portfolio of stocks, one must estimate the expected return and the variance of returns for each security in the investment set plus the pairwise correlation structure. It may be easier to accurately estimate these parameters if a common set of factors affect equity returns. Some likely candidates are: macroeconomic variables that influence the overall economic environment in which the firm issuing the security conducts its business; exchange rate changes between the currency of the country issuing the stock and the currency of other countries where suppliers, customers, and investors of the firm reside; and the industrial structure of the country in which the firm operates.

这些参数可能包括：影响股票发行企业开展运营活动的整体经济环境中的宏观经济变量；股票发行企业所在国与该企业的供应商、客户、投资者所在国之间汇率的变化；企业经营所在国的产业结构。

---

[3]Much of the information in this section is from the 2002 clinical study by G. Andrew Karolyi.

Macroeconomic Factors

Two studies have tested the influence of various macroeconomic variables on stock returns. Solnik (1984) examined the effect of exchange rate changes, interest rate differentials, the level of the domestic interest rate, and changes in domestic inflation expectations. He found that international monetary variables had only weak influence on equity returns in comparison to domestic variables. In another study, Asprem (1989) found that changes in industrial production, employment, and imports, the level of interest rates, and an inflation measure explained only a small portion of the variability of equity returns for 10 European countries, but that substantially more of the variation was explained by an international market index.

Exchange Rates

他们发现，一般而言，汇率变化对外国股票市场收益率变化的影响比对外国债券指数收益率的影响更有解释力，但也有些国家的权益市场收益率比相应的债券市场面临更大的汇率变化风险暴露。

Adler and Simon (1986) examined the exposure of a sample of foreign equity and bond index returns to exchange rate changes. They found that changes in exchange rates generally explained a larger portion of the variability of foreign bond indexes than foreign equity indexes, but that some foreign equity markets were more exposed to exchange rate changes than were the respective foreign bond markets. Additionally, their results suggest that it would likely be beneficial to hedge (i.e., protect) foreign stock investment against exchange rate uncertainty.

In another study, Eun and Resnick (1988) find that the cross-correlations among major stock markets and exchange markets are relatively low, but positive. This result implies that the exchange rate changes in a given country reinforce the stock market movements in that country as well as in the other countries examined.

Industrial Structure

关于产业结构对外国权益收益率影响的研究并没有得到确定的结论。

Studies examining the influence of industrial structure on foreign equity returns are inconclusive. In a study examining the correlation structure of national equity markets, Roll (1992) concluded that the industrial structure of a country was important in explaining a significant part of the correlation structure of international equity index returns. He also found that industry factors explained a larger portion of stock market variability than did exchange rate changes.

In contrast, Eun and Resnick (1984) found for a sample of 160 stocks from eight countries and 12 industries that the pairwise correlation structure of international security returns could be better estimated from models that recognized country factors rather than industry factors. Similarly, using individual stock return data for 829 firms, from 12 countries, and representing seven broad industry groups, Heston and Rouwenhorst (1994) conclude "that industrial structure explains very little of the cross-sectional difference in country return volatility, and that the low correlation between country indices is almost completely due to country specific sources of variation."

Both Rouwenhorst (1999) and Beckers (1999) examine the effect of the EMU on European equity markets and come up with opposite conclusions. Rouwenhorst concludes that country effects in stock returns have been larger than industry effects in Western Europe since 1982 and that this situation continued throughout the 1993–98 period when interest rates were converging and fiscal and monetary policies were being harmonized in the countries entering the EMU. On the other hand, Beckers finds an increase in correlations between markets and between the same sector in different markets arising from the European integration of fiscal, monetary, and economic policies. He concludes that the increase in pairwise correlations in these countries represents a reduction in the diversification benefits from investing in the euro zone.

Griffin and Karolyi (1998) examine the effect of industrial structure on covariances by studying whether a difference exists in the effect between traded-goods industries and nontraded-goods industries. They find that the cross-country covariances are larger for firms within a given industry than the cross-country covariances across firms in different industries in traded-goods industries. In contrast, for nontraded-goods industries, there is little difference in cross-country covariances between firms in the same industry and those in different industries.

SUMMARY

本章对国际股票市场做了概要介绍。这里所介绍的内容不仅可以帮助读者理解跨国公司如何在国内一级市场之外筹集新的权益资本，也为那些对国际投资组合分散化感兴趣的投资者提供了关于制度方面的有用信息。

1. 本章首先介绍了发达国家主要股票市场及发展中国家新兴股票市场的统计概况，还提供了各个股票市场的市价总值和交易额方面的资料。显然，自2000年以来，发达国家的大多数股票市场发生了下跌。此外，许多新兴股票市场的交易换手率有所下降，而市场集中率仍然保持较高的状态，这表明这些市场的投资机会并未得到改善。

2. 本章还介绍了各种衡量国际股票市场的基准。了解从何处获得具有对比意义的股票市场绩效资料是很有用的。本章还专门讨论了标准普尔、摩根士丹利资本国际以及道琼斯国家股票市场等指数。此外，还给出了各国交易所或主要投资咨询机构所发布的主要国家的股票市场指数情况。

3. 本章还重点讨论了二级股票市场结构的差异性。传统上，二级市场被分为自营商市场或代理商市场。这两种市场结构虽然都能实现股票市场的连续交易，但非连续交易市场常常为代理商市场。场外交易市场、专营商市场及自动化市场都能做到连续的市场交易。短期同业拆放市场和集合交易都属于非连续交易形式。本章用表格形式总结了不同国家股票市场的交易费用情况（包括佣金和税金），并比较了各个市场的特征。值得注意的是，绝大多数国家的股票市场现在都已实现自动交易，至少有部分交易是这样的。

4. 本章还深入讨论了公司股票在国外交易所境外上市的情况。公司将其股票境外上市的目的在于：扩大其股票的投资者人数，在国外资本市场树立声誉；为向这些市场上的投资者筹集新的权益资本和债务资本铺平道路。本章还对发行扬基股票以及向美国投资者出售外国股票进行了讨论。在美国市场上，扬基股票可像美国存托凭证一样在美国市场上进行交易。美国存托凭证是美国银行存单，代表的是存放在外国银行的各种外国股份。美国存托凭证消除了进行实际股票交易时发生的风险、延误、不便以及费用。

5. 一些实证研究对可能影响股票收益率的因素进行了检验。结果表明，与国际货币市场因素相比，本国利率水平及本国通货膨胀的预期变化等因素对本国股票收益率有着更大的影响。产业结构似乎并不是最为重要的因素。实证研究还发现，股票收益率对本币的汇率变动较为敏感。

This chapter provides an overview of international equity markets. The material is designed to provide an understanding of how MNCs source new equity capital outside of their own domestic primary market and to provide useful institutional information to investors interested in diversifying their portfolio internationally.

1. The chapter began with a statistical perspective of the major equity markets in developed countries and of emerging equity markets in developing countries. Market capitalization and turnover figures were provided for each marketplace. It was seen that most national equity markets in developed countries declined since 2000. Additionally, turnover ratios in many emerging markets declined and market concentration ratios remained high, indicating that investment opportunities in these markets has not been improving.

2. A variety of international equity benchmarks were also presented. Knowledge of where to find comparative equity market performance data is useful. Specifically, Standard & Poor's, Morgan Stanley Capital International, and the Dow Jones Country Stock Market indexes were discussed. Also, a list of the major national stock market indexes prepared by the national exchanges or major investment advisory services was presented.

3. A considerable amount of discussion was devoted to differences in secondary equity market structures. Secondary markets have historically been structured as dealer or agency markets. Both of these types of market structure can provide for continuous market trading, but noncontinuous markets tended to be agency markets. Over-the-counter trading, specialist markets, and automated markets allow for continuous market trading. Call markets and crowd trading are each types of noncontinuous trading market systems. Trading systems on various national equity markets were summarized in a table comparing market characteristics. It was noted that most national stock markets are now automated for at least some of the issues traded on them.

4. Cross-listing of a company's shares on foreign exchanges was extensively discussed. A firm may cross-list its shares to: establish a broader investor base for its stock; establish name recognition in foreign capital markets; and pave the way for sourcing new equity and debt capital from investors in these markets. Yankee stock offerings, or sale of foreign stock to U.S. investors, were also discussed. Yankee shares trade on U.S. markets as American depository receipts (ADRs), which are bank receipts representing a multiple of foreign shares deposited in a foreign bank. ADRs eliminate some of the risks, delays, inconveniences, and expenses of trading actual shares.

5. Several empirical studies that tested for factors that might influence equity returns indicate that domestic factors, such as the level of domestic interest rates and expected changes in domestic inflation, as opposed to international monetary variables, had the greatest effect on national equity returns. Industrial structure did not appear to be of primary importance. Equity returns were also found to be sensitive to own-currency exchange rate changes.

KEY WORDS

agency market, *319*	continuous market, *320*	market order, *319*
American depository receipt (ADR), *328*	cross-listing, *325*	over-the-counter (OTC), *319*
ask price, *319*	crowd trading, *320*	primary market, *319*
bid price, *319*	dealer market, *319*	secondary market, *319*
broker, *319*	limit order, *319*	specialist, *319*
call market, *320*	limit order book, *319*	Yankee stock, *327*
	liquidity, *316*	

QUESTIONS

1. Get a current copy of *The Wall Street Journal* and find the *Dow Jones Country Indexes* listing in Section C of the newspaper. Examine the year-to-date percentage changes in U.S. dollars for the various national indexes. How do the changes from your table compare with the year-to-date percentage changes from the sample provided in the textbook as Exhibit 13.8? Are the same national indexes positive and negative in both listings? Discuss your findings.

2. As an investor, what factors would you consider before investing in the emerging stock market of a developing country?

3. Compare and contrast the various types of secondary market trading structures.

4. Discuss any benefits you can think of for a company to (a) cross-list its equity shares on more than one national exchange, and (b) to source new equity capital from foreign investors as well as domestic investors.

5. Why might it be easier for an investor desiring to diversify his portfolio internationally to buy depository receipts rather than the actual shares of the company?

6. Why do you think the empirical studies about factors affecting equity returns basically showed that domestic factors were more important than international factors, and, secondly, that industrial membership of a firm was of little importance in forecasting the international correlation structure of a set of international stocks?

PROBLEMS

1. On the Milan bourse, Fiat stock closed at EUR5.84 per share on Thursday, March 3, 2005. Fiat trades as an ADR on the NYSE. One underlying Fiat share equals one ADR. On March 3, the $/EUR spot exchange rate was $1.3112/EUR1.00.
   a. At this exchange rate, what is the no-arbitrage U.S. dollar price of one ADR?
   b. By comparison, Fiat ADRs closed at $7.61. Do you think an arbitrage opportunity exists?

2. If Fiat ADRs were trading at $7 when the underlying shares were trading in Milan at EUR5.84, what could you do to earn a trading profit? Use the information in problem 1, above, to help you and assume that transaction costs are negligible.

INTERNET EXERCISES

1. The Bloomberg website provides current values of many of the international stock indexes presented in Exhibit 13.9 at the website http://quote.bloomberg.com. Go to this website and determine what country's stock markets are trading higher and lower today. Is there any current news event that might influence the way different national markets are trading today?

2. The J.P. Morgan website www.adr.com provides on-line data on trading in ADRs. Go to this website to view today's total trading volume in ADRs and the year-to-date trading volume. What are the top 10 individual ADRs by trading volume? By dollar value? Does there seem to be a similarity in industry (such as telecom) represented by the top ADRs, or are they from a variety of different industries? Recall from the chapter that the effect of industrial structure on international stock returns is an unresolved issue.

MINI CASE

San Pico's New Stock Exchange

San Pico is a rapidly growing Latin American developing country. The country is blessed with miles of scenic beaches that have attracted tourists by the thousands in recent years to new resort hotels financed by joint ventures of San Pico businessmen and moneymen from the Middle East, Japan, and the United States. Additionally, San Pico has good natural harbors that are conducive for receiving imported merchandise from abroad and exporting merchandise produced in San Pico and other surrounding countries that lack access to the sea. Because of these advantages, many new businesses are being started in San Pico.

Presently, stock is traded in a cramped building in La Cobijio, the nation's capital. Admittedly, the San Pico Stock Exchange system is rather archaic. Twice a day an official of the exchange will call out the name of each of the 43 companies whose stock trades on the exchange. Brokers wanting to buy or sell shares for their clients then attempt to make a trade with one another. This crowd trading system has worked well for over one hundred years, but the government desires to replace it with a new modern system that will allow greater and more frequent opportunities for trading in each company, and will allow for trading the shares of the many new start-up companies that are expected to trade in the secondary market. Additionally, the government administration is rapidly privatizing many state-owned businesses in an attempt to foster their efficiency, obtain foreign exchange from the sale, and convert the country to a more capitalist economy. The government believes that it could conduct this privatization faster and perhaps at more attractive prices if it had a modern stock exchange facility where the shares of the newly privatized companies will eventually trade.

You are an expert in the operation of secondary stock markets and have been retained as a consultant to the San Pico Stock Exchange to offer your expertise in modernizing the stock market. What would you advise?

REFERENCES & SUGGESTED READINGS

Adler, Michael, and David Simon. "Exchange Rate Surprises in International Portfolios." *The Journal of Portfolio Management* 12 (1986), pp. 44–53.

Asprem, Mads. "Stock Prices, Assets Portfolios and Macroeconomic Variables in Ten European Countries." *Journal of Banking and Finance* 13 (1989), pp. 589–612.

Beckers, Stan. "Investment Implications of a Single European Capital Market." *Journal of Portfolio Management,* Spring (1999), pp. 9–17.

Eun, Cheol S., and Bruce G. Resnick. "Estimating the Correlation Structure of International Share Prices." *Journal of Finance* 39 (1984), pp. 1311–24.

Eun, Cheol S., and Bruce G. Resnick. "Exchange Rate Uncertainty, Forward Contracts, and International Portfolio Selection." *Journal of Finance* 43 (1988), pp. 197–215.

Gagnon, Louis, and G. Andrew Karolyi. "Multi-Market Trading and Arbitrage." Ohio State University working paper (July 200).

Griffin, John M., and G. Andrew Karolyi. "Another Look at the Role of the Industrial Structure of Markets for International Diversification Strategies." *Journal of Financial Economics* 50 (1998), pp. 351–73.

Heston, Steven L., and K. Geert Rouwenhorst. "Does Industrial Structure Explain the Benefits of International Diversification?" *Journal of Financial Economics* 36 (1994), pp. 3–27.

Jayaraman, Narayanan, Kuldeep Shastri, and Kishore Tandon. "The Impact of International Cross-Listings on Risk and Return: The Evidence from American Depository Receipts." *Journal of Banking and Finance* 17 (1993), pp. 91–103.

Kao, G., K. C. Wenchi, John Wei, and Joseph Vu. "Risk-Return Characteristics of the American Depository Receipts," unpublished working paper, 1991.

Karolyi, G. Andrew. "DaimlerChrysler AG, The First Truly Global Share." Ohio State University working paper (May 2002).

Miller, Darius P. "The Market Reaction to International Cross-Listings: Evidence from Depository Receipts." *Journal of Financial Economics* 51 (1999), pp. 103–23.

Muscarella, Chris J., and Michael R. Vetsuypens. "Stock Splits: Signaling or Liquidity? The Case of ADR 'solo-splits'," *Journal of Financial Economics* 42 (1996), pp. 2–26.

Officer, Dennis T., and J. Ronald Hoffmeister. "ADRs: A Substitute for the Real Thing?" *Journal of Portfolio Management*, Winter (1987), pp. 61–65.

Park, Jinwoo. *The Impact of Information on ADR Returns and Variances: Some Implications,* unpublished Ph.D. dissertation from The University of Iowa, 1990.

Roll, Richard. "Industrial Structure and the Comparative Behavior of International Stock Market Indexes." *Journal of Finance* 47 (1992), pp. 3–42.

Rosenthal, Leonard. "An Empirical Test of the Efficiency of the ADR Market." *Journal of Banking and Finance* 7 (1983) pp. 17–29.

Rouwenhorst, K. Geert. "European Equity Markets and the EMU." *Financial Analysts Journal,* May/June (1999), pp. 57–64.

Schwartz, Robert A. *Equity Markets*. New York: Harper and Row, 1988.

Solnik, Bruno. "Capital Markets and International Monetary Variables." *Financial Analysts Journal* 40 (1984), pp. 69–73.

14 Interest Rate and Currency Swaps

本章考察的是利率
互换，包括单一货币及
交叉货币互换。利率互
换是规避长期利率风险
和外汇风险的工具。

CHAPTER 5 INTRODUCED forward contracts as a vehicle for hedging exchange rate risk; Chapter 7 introduced futures and options contracts on foreign exchange as alternative tools to hedge foreign exchange exposure. These types of instruments seldom have terms longer than a few years, however. Chapter 7 also discussed Eurodollar futures contracts for hedging short-term U.S.-dollar-denominated interest rate risk. In this chapter, we examine interest rate swaps, both single-currency and cross-currency, which are techniques for hedging long-term interest rate risk and foreign exchange risk.

The chapter begins with some useful definitions that define and distinguish between interest rate and currency swaps. Data on the size of the interest rate and currency swap markets are presented. The next section illustrates the usefulness of interest rate swaps. The following section illustrates the construction of currency swaps. The chapter also details the risks confronting a swap dealer in maintaining a portfolio of interest rate and currency swaps and shows how swaps are priced.

Types of Swaps

在进行利率互换方
式融资时，称为**对家**的
交易双方签订合约，定
期交换现金流。
    单一货币利率互换
    交叉货币利率互换

In interest rate swap financing, two parties, called **counterparties,** make a contractual agreement to exchange cash flows at periodic intervals. There are two types of interest rate swaps. One is a **single-currency interest rate swap.** The name of this type is typically shortened to *interest rate swap.* The other type can be called a **cross-currency interest rate swap.** This type is usually just called a *currency swap.*

In the basic ("plain vanilla") *fixed-for-floating rate* interest rate swap, one counterparty exchanges the interest payments of a floating-rate debt obligation for the fixed-rate interest payments of the other counterparty. Both debt obligations are denominated in the same currency. Some reasons for using an interest rate swap are to better match cash inflows and outflows and/or to obtain a cost savings. There are many variants of the basic interest rate swap, some of which are discussed below.

The World Bank's First Currency Swap

The World Bank frequently borrows in the national capital markets around the world and in the Eurobond market. It prefers to borrow currencies with low nominal interest rates, such as the deutsche mark and the Swiss franc. In 1981, the World Bank was near the official borrowing limits in these currencies but desired to borrow more. By coincidence, IBM had a large amount of deutsche mark and Swiss franc debt that it had incurred a few years earlier. The proceeds of these borrowings had been converted to dollars for corporate use. Salomon Brothers convinced the World Bank to issue Eurodollar debt with maturities matching the IBM debt in order to enter into a currency swap with IBM. IBM agreed to pay the debt service (interest and principal) on the World Bank's Eurodollar bonds, and in turn the World Bank agreed to pay the debt service on IBM's deutsche mark and Swiss franc debt. While the details of the swap were not made public, both counterparties benefited through a lower all-in cost (interest expense, transaction costs, and service charges) than they otherwise would have had. Additionally, the World Bank benefited by developing an indirect way to obtain desired currencies without going directly to the German and Swiss capital markets.

货币互换

使用货币互换的原
因有：节约筹资成本或
者为了规避长期外汇汇
率风险。

In a **currency swap,** one counterparty exchanges the debt service obligations of a bond denominated in one currency for the debt service obligations of the other counterparty denominated in another currency. The basic currency swap involves the exchange of *fixed-for-fixed rate* debt service. Some reasons for using currency swaps are to obtain debt financing in the swapped denomination at a cost savings and/or to hedge long-term foreign exchange rate risk. The International Finance in Practice box "The World Bank's First Currency Swap" discusses the first currency swap.

Size of the Swap Market

www.isda.org

This is the website of the International Swaps and Derivatives Association, Inc. This site describes the activities of the ISDA and provides educational information about interest rate and currency swaps, other OTC interest rate and currency derivatives, and risk management activities. Market survey data about the size of the swaps market are also provided at this site.

名义本金 (notional principal)

As the International Finance in Practice box suggests, the market for currency swaps developed first. Today, however, the interest rate swap market is larger. Exhibit 14.1 provides some statistics on the size and growth in the interest rate and currency swap markets. Size is measured by **notional principal,** a reference amount of principal for determining interest payments. The exhibit indicates that both markets have grown significantly since 1995, but that the growth in interest rate swaps has been by far more dramatic. The total amount of interest rate swaps outstanding increased from $12,811 billion at year-end 1995 to $127.6 trillion by mid-year 2004, an increase of nearly 900 percent. Total outstanding currency swaps increased 488 percent, from $1,197 billion at year-end 1995 to over $7 trillion by mid-year 2004.

While not shown in Exhibit 14.1, the five most common currencies used to denominate interest rate and currency swaps were the euro, U.S. dollar, Japanese yen, British pound sterling, and the Swiss franc.

The Swap Bank

互换银行（swap
bank）是指为交易双方
提供便利互换服务的金
融机构。

经纪人 (broker)
交易商 (dealer)

A **swap bank** is a generic term to describe a financial institution that facilitates swaps between counterparties. A swap bank can be an international commercial bank, an investment bank, a merchant bank, or an independent operator. The swap bank serves as either a **broker** or **dealer.** As a broker, the swap bank matches counterparties but does not assume any risk of the swap. The swap broker receives a commission for this service. Today, most swap banks serve as dealers or market makers. As a market maker, the swap bank stands willing to accept either side of a currency swap, and then later lay it off, or match it with a counterparty. In this capacity, the swap bank assumes a position

EXHIBIT 14.1

Size of Interest Rate and Currency Swap Markets: Total Notional Principal Outstanding Amounts in Billions of U.S. Dollars*

Year	Interest Rate Swaps	Currency Swaps
1995	12,811	1,197
1996	19,171	1,560
1997	22,291	1,824
1998	36,262	2,253
1999	43,936	2,444
2000	48,768	3,194
2001	58,897	3,942
2002	79,120	4,503
2003	111,209	6,371
2004 (mid-year)	127,570	7,033

*Notional principal is used only as a reference measure to which interest rates are applied for determining interest payments. In an interest rate swap, principal does not actually change hands. At the inception date of a swap, the market value of both sides of the swap are of equivalent value. As interest rates change, the value of the cash flows will change, and both sides may no longer be equal. This is interest rate risk. The deviation can amount to 2 to 4 percent of notional principal. Only this small fraction is subject to credit (or default) risk.

Sources: International Banking and Financial Market Developments, Bank for International Settlements, Table 18, p. 81, June 2000 and Table 19, p. A99, June 2002 and December 2004.

in the swap and therefore assumes certain risks. The dealer capacity is obviously more risky, and the swap bank would receive a portion of the cash flows passed through it to compensate it for bearing this risk.

Swap Market Quotations

www.bis.org
This is the website of the Bank for International Settlements. This site describes the activities and purpose of the BIS. Many online publications about foreign exchange and OTC derivatives are available at this site.

通常，互换银行按照同一货币的当地标准利率对利率互换中货币的利率进行报价，按照美元LIBOR对货币互换利率进行报价。

Swap banks will tailor the terms of interest rate and currency swaps to customers' needs. They also make a market in generic "plain vanilla" swaps and provide current market quotations applicable to counterparties with Aa or Aaa credit ratings. Consider a basic U.S. dollar fixed-for-floating interest rate swap indexed to dollar LIBOR. A swap bank will typically quote a fixed-rate bid-ask spread (either semiannual or annual) versus three-month or six-month dollar LIBOR flat, that is, no credit premium. Suppose the quote for a five-year swap with semiannual payments is 8.50−8.60 percent against six-month LIBOR flat. This means the swap bank will pay semiannual fixed-rate dollar payments of 8.50 percent against receiving six-month dollar LIBOR, or it will receive semiannual fixed-rate dollar payments at 8.60 percent against paying six-month dollar LIBOR.

It is convention for swap banks to quote interest rate swap rates for a currency against a local standard reference in the same currency and currency swap rates against dollar LIBOR. For example, for a five-year swap with semiannual payments in Swiss francs, suppose the bid-ask swap quotation is 6.60−6.70 percent against six-month LIBOR flat. This means the swap bank will pay semiannual fixed-rate SF payments at 6.60 percent against receiving six-month SF (dollar) LIBOR in an interest rate (a currency) swap, or it will receive semiannual fixed-rate SF payments at 6.70 percent against paying six-month SF (dollar) LIBOR in an interest rate (a currency) swap.

It follows that if the swap bank is quoting 8.50−8.60 percent in dollars and 6.60−6.70 percent in SF against six-month dollar LIBOR, it will enter into a currency swap in which it would pay semiannual fixed-rate dollar payments of 8.50 percent in return for receiving semiannual fixed-rate SF payments at 6.70 percent, or it will receive semiannual fixed-rate dollar payments at 8.60 percent against paying semiannual fixed-rate SF payments at 6.60 percent.

Exhibit 14.2 provides an illustration of interest rate swap quotations. Swap banks typically build swap yield curves such as this from the 90-day LIBOR rates implied in the Eurodollar interest rate futures contracts we discussed in Chapter 7.

EXHIBIT 14.2			Interest Rate Swap Quotations									
	Euro-€		£ Stlg		SwFr		US $		Yen			
Mar 03	Bid	Ask	Bid	Ask	Bid	Ask	Bid	Ask	Bid	Ask		
1 year	2.34	2.37	5.21	5.22	0.92	0.98	3.54	3.57	0.07	0.10		
2 year	2.62	2.65	5.14	5.18	1.23	1.31	3.90	3.94	0.20	0.23		
3 year	2.86	2.89	5.13	5.17	1.50	1.58	4.11	4.13	0.37	0.40		
4 year	3.06	3.09	5.12	5.17	1.73	1.81	4.25	4.28	0.55	0.58		
5 year	3.23	3.26	5.11	5.16	1.93	2.01	4.37	4.39	0.75	0.78		
6 year	3.38	3.41	5.11	5.16	2.10	2.18	4.46	4.50	0.94	0.97		
7 year	3.52	3.55	5.10	5.15	2.25	2.33	4.55	4.58	1.13	1.16		
8 year	3.63	3.66	5.10	5.15	2.37	2.45	4.62	4.66	1.29	1.32		
9 year	3.74	3.77	5.09	5.14	2.48	2.56	4.70	4.72	1.44	1.47		
10 year	3.82	3.85	5.08	5.13	2.56	2.64	4.75	4.79	1.56	1.59		
12 year	3.96	3.99	5.05	5.12	2.68	2.79	4.86	4.89	1.76	1.80		
15 year	4.10	4.13	5.01	4.10	2.83	2.93	4.98	5.01	1.99	2.02		
20 year	4.24	4.27	4.93	5.06	2.97	3.07	5.09	5.12	2.24	2.27		
25 year	4.31	4.34	4.87	5.00	3.07	3.17	5.13	5.17	2.38	2.41		
30 year	4.34	4.37	4.81	4.94	3.11	3.21	5.16	5.19	2.45	2.48		

Bid and ask rates as of close of London business. US $ is quoted annual money actual/360 basis against 3 months Libor, £ and Yen quoted on a semi-annual actual/365 basis against 6 months Libor, Euro/Swiss Franc quoted on annual bond 30/360 basis against 6 month Euribor/Libor with the exception of the 1 year rate which is quoted against 3 month Euribor/Libor.
Source: Financial Times, March 4, 2005, p. 25.

Interest Rate Swaps

Basic Interest Rate Swap

质量价差（QSD）

EXAMPLE 14.1

A Plain Vanilla Interest Rate Swap   As an example of a basic interest rate swap, consider the following example of a fixed-for-floating rate swap. Bank A is a AAA-rated international bank located in the United Kingdom. The bank needs $10,000,000 to finance floating-rate Eurodollar term loans to its clients. It is considering issuing five-year floating-rate notes indexed to LIBOR. Alternatively, the bank could issue five-year fixed-rate Eurodollar bonds at 10 percent. The FRNs make the most sense for Bank A, since it would be using a floating-rate liability to finance a floating-rate asset. In this manner, the bank avoids the interest rate risk associated with a fixed-rate issue. Bank A could end up paying a higher rate than it is receiving on its loans should LIBOR fall substantially.

Company B is a BBB-rated U.S. company. It needs $10,000,000 to finance a capital expenditure with a five-year economic life. It can issue five-year fixed-rate bonds at a rate of 11.25 percent in the U.S. bond market. Alternatively, it can issue five-year FRNs at LIBOR plus .50 percent. The fixed-rate debt makes the most sense for Company B because it locks in a financing cost. The FRN alternative could prove very unwise should LIBOR increase substantially over the life of the note, and could possibly result in the project being unprofitable.

A swap bank familiar with the financing needs of Bank A and Company B has the opportunity to set up a fixed-for-floating interest rate swap that will benefit each counterparty and the swap bank. Assume that the swap bank is quoting five-year U.S. dollar interest rate swaps at 10.375 – 10.50 percent against LIBOR flat. The key, or necessary condition, giving rise to the swap is that a **quality spread differential (QSD)** exists. A QSD is the difference between the default-risk premium differential

EXAMPLE 14.1(continued)

on the fixed-rate debt and the default-risk premium differential on the floating-rate debt. In general, the former is greater than the latter. The reason for this is that the yield curve for lower-quality debt tends to be steeper than the yield curve for higher-rated debt. Financial theorists have offered a variety of explanations for this phenomenon, none of which is completely satisfactory. Exhibit 14.3 shows the calculation of the QSD.

Given that a QSD exists, it is possible for each counterparty to issue the debt alternative that is least advantageous for it (given its financing needs), then swap interest payments, such that each counterparty ends up with the type of interest payment desired, but at a lower all-in cost than it could arrange on its own. Exhibit 14.4 diagrams a possible scenario the swap bank could arrange for the two counterparties. The interest rates used in Exhibit 14.4 refer to the percentage rate paid per annum on the notional principal of $10,000,000.

From Exhibit 14.4, we see that the swap bank has instructed Company B to issue FRNs at LIBOR plus .50 percent rather than the more suitable fixed-rate debt at 11.25 percent. Company B passes through to the swap bank 10.50 percent (on the notional principal of $10,000,000) and receives LIBOR in return. In total, Company B pays 10.50 percent (to the swap bank) plus LIBOR + .50 percent (to the floating-rate bondholders) and receives LIBOR percent (from the swap bank) for an **all-in cost** 总费用(all-in cost) (interest expense, transaction costs, and service charges) of 11 percent. Thus, through the swap, Company B has converted floating-rate debt into fixed-rate debt at an all-in cost .25 percent lower than the 11.25 percent fixed rate it could arrange on its own.

Similarly, Bank A was instructed to issue fixed-rate debt at 10 percent rather than the more suitable FRNs. Bank A passes through to the swap bank LIBOR percent and receives 10.375 percent in return. In total, Bank A pays 10 percent (to the fixed-rate Eurodollar bondholders) plus LIBOR percent (to the swap bank) and receives 10.375 percent (from the swap bank) for an all-in cost of LIBOR −.375 percent. Through the swap, Bank A has converted fixed-rate debt into floating-rate debt at an all-in cost .375 percent lower than the floating rate of LIBOR it could arrange on its own.

The swap bank also benefits because it pays out less than it receives from each counterparty to the other counterparty. Note from Exhibit 14.4 that it receives 10.50 percent (from Company B) plus LIBOR percent (from Bank A) and pays 10.375 percent (to Bank A) and LIBOR percent (to Company B). The net inflow to the swap bank is .125 percent per annum on the notional principal of $10,000,000. In sum, Bank A has saved .375 percent, Company B has saved .25 percent, and the swap bank has earned .125 percent. This totals .75 percent, which equals the QSD. Thus, if a QSD exists, it can be split in some fashion among the swap parties resulting in lower all-in costs for the counterparties.

In an interest rate swap, the principal sums the two counterparties raise are not exchanged, since both counterparties have borrowed in the same currency. The amount of interest payments that are exchanged are based on a notional sum, which may not equal the exact amount actually borrowed by each counterparty. Moreover, while Exhibit 14.4 portrays a gross exchange of interest payments based on the notional principal, in practice only the net difference is actually exchanged. For example, Company B would pay to the swap bank the net difference between 10.50 percent and LIBOR percent on the notional value of $10,000,000.

EXHIBIT 14.3

Calculation of Quality Spread Differential

	Company B	Bank A	Differential
Fixed-rate	11.25%	10.00%	1.25%
Floating-rate	LIBOR + .50%	LIBOR	.50%
			QSD = .75%

EXHIBIT 14.4

Fixed-For-Floating Interest Rate Swap*

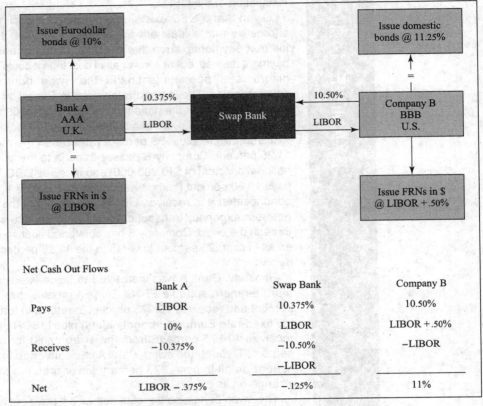

Net Cash Out Flows

	Bank A	Swap Bank	Company B
Pays	LIBOR	10.375%	10.50%
	10%	LIBOR	LIBOR + .50%
Receives	−10.375%	−10.50%	−LIBOR
		−LIBOR	
Net	LIBOR − .375%	−.125%	11%

*Debt service expressed as a percentage of $10,000,000 notional value.

In More Depth

EXAMPLE 14.2

Pricing the Basic Interest Rate Swap   After the inception of an interest rate swap, it may become desirable for one and/or the other counterparty to unwind or reverse the swap. The value of an interest rate swap to a counterparty should be the difference in the present values of the payment streams the counterparty will receive and pay on the notional principal. As an example, consider Company B from Example 14.1. Company B pays 10.50 percent to the swap bank and receives LIBOR percent from the swap bank on a notional value of $10,000,000. It has an all-in cost of 11 percent because it has issued FRNs at LIBOR + .50 percent.

Assume that one year later, the swap bank is quoting four-year dollar swaps at 9.00–9.125 percent versus LIBOR flat. This will also be a reset date for the FRNs. On any reset date, the present value of the future floating-rate payments paid or received at LIBOR on the notional value will always be $10,000,000. The present value of a

EXAMPLE 14.2 (continued)

hypothetical bond issue of $10,000,000 with four remaining 10.50 percent coupon payments at the new swap bid rate of 9 percent is $10,485,958 = $1,050,000 × $PVIFA_{9\%,4}$ + $10,000,000 × $PVIF_{9\%,4}$. The value of the swap is $10,000,000 − $10,485,958 = −$485,958. Thus, Company B should be willing to pay $485,958 to the swap bank to unwind or reverse the original swap. In essence, the market value of the swap is the present value of the difference between paying 10.50 percent and receiving 9 percent on the $10,000,000 notional value discounted at the new swap bid rate of 9 percent. That is: −$150,000 × $PVIFA_{9\%,4}$ = −$485,958.

Currency Swaps

Basic Currency Swap

EXAMPLE 14.3

A Basic Currency Swap   As an example of a basic currency swap, consider the following example. A U.S. MNC desires to finance a capital expenditure of its German subsidiary. The project has an economic life of five years. The cost of the project is €40,000,000. At the current exchange rate of $1.30/€1.00, the parent firm could raise $52,000,000 in the U.S. capital market by issuing five-year bonds at 8 percent. The parent would then convert the dollars to euros to pay the project cost. The German subsidiary would be expected to earn enough on the project to meet the annual dollar debt service and to repay the principal in five years. The only problem with this situation is that a long-term transaction exposure is created. If the dollar appreciates substantially against the euro over the loan period, it may be difficult for the German subsidiary to earn enough in euros to service the dollar loan.

An alternative is for the U.S. parent to raise €40,000,000 in the international bond market by issuing euro-denominated Eurobonds. (The U.S. parent might instead issue euro-denominated foreign bonds in the German capital market.) However, if the U.S. MNC is not well known, it will have difficulty borrowing at a favorable rate of interest. Suppose the U.S. parent can borrow €40,000,000 for a term of five years at a fixed rate of 7 percent. The current normal borrowing rate for a well-known firm of equivalent creditworthiness is 6 percent.

Assume a German MNC of equivalent creditworthiness has a mirror-image financing need. It has a U.S. subsidiary in need of $52,000,000 to finance a capital expenditure with an economic life of five years. The German parent could raise €40,000,000 in the German bond market at a fixed rate of 6 percent and convert the funds to dollars to finance the expenditure. Transaction exposure is created, however, if the euro appreciates substantially against the dollar. In this event, the U.S. subsidiary might have difficulty earning enough in dollars to meet the debt service. The German parent could issue Eurodollar bonds (or alternatively, Yankee bonds in the U.S. capital market), but since it is not well known its borrowing cost would be, say, a fixed rate of 9 percent.

A swap bank familiar with the financing needs of the two MNCs could arrange a currency swap that would solve the double problem of each MNC, that is, be confronted with long-term transaction exposure or borrow at a disadvantageous rate.

(continued)

比较优势（com-
parative advantage)

EXAMPLE 14.3 (continued)

(In order not to complicate this example any more than is necessary, it is assumed that the bid and ask swap rates charged by the swap bank are the same; that is, there is no bid-ask spread. This assumption is relaxed in Example 14.6.) The swap bank would instruct each parent firm to raise funds in its national capital market where it is well known and has a **comparative advantage** because of name or brand recognition. Then the principal sums would be exchanged through the swap bank. Annually, the German subsidiary would remit to its U.S. parent €2,400,000 in interest (6 percent of €40,000,000) to be passed through the swap bank to the German MNC to meet the euro debt service. The U.S. subsidiary of the German MNC would annually remit $4,160,000 in interest (8 percent of $52,000,000) to be passed through to the swap bank to the U.S. MNC to meet the dollar debt service. At the debt retirement date, the subsidiaries would remit the principal sums to their respective parents to be exchanged through the swap bank in order to pay off the bond issues in the national capital markets. The structure of this currency swap is diagrammed in Exhibit 14.5.

Exhibit 14.5 demonstrates that there is a cost savings for each counterparty because of their relative comparative advantage in their respective national capital markets. The U.S. MNC borrows euros at an all-in-cost (AIC) of 6 percent through the currency swap instead of the 7 percent it would have to pay in the Eurobond market. The German MNC borrows dollars at an AIC of 8 percent through the swap instead of the 9 percent rate it would have to pay in the Eurobond market. The currency swap also serves to contractually lock in a series of future foreign exchange rates for the debt service obligations of each counterparty. At inception, the principal sums are exchanged at the current exchange rate of $1.30/€1.00 = $52,000,000/€40,000,000. Each year prior to debt retirement, the swap agreement calls for the counterparties to exchange $4,160,000 of interest on the dollar debt for €2,400,000 of interest on the euro debt; this is a contractual rate of $1.7333/€1.00. At the maturity date, a final exchange, including the last interest payments and the reexchange of the principal sums, would take place: $56,160,000 for €42,400,000. The contractual exchange rate at year five is thus $1.3245/€1.00. Clearly, the swap locks in foreign exchange rates for each counterparty to meet its debt service obligations over the term of the swap.

EXHIBIT 14.5   **$/€ Currency Swap***

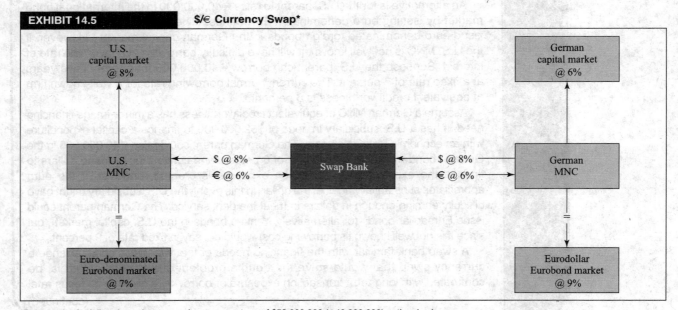

*Debt service in dollars (euros) expressed as a percentage of $52,000,000 (€40,000,000) notional value.

In More Depth

EXAMPLE 14.4

Equivalency of Currency Swap Debt Service Obligations   To continue with Example 14.3, it superficially appears that the German counterparty is not getting as good a deal from the currency swap as the U.S. counterparty. The reasoning is that the German counterparty is borrowing at a rate of 6 percent (€2,400,000 per year) but paying 8 percent ($4,160,000). The U.S. counterparty receives the $4,160,000 and pays €2,400,000. This reasoning is fraught with an ill appreciation for international parity relationships, as Exhibit 14.6 is designed to show. In short, the exhibit shows that borrowing euros at 6 percent is equivalent to borrowing dollars at 8 percent.

Line 1 of Exhibit 14.6 shows the cash flows of the euro debt in millions. Line 2 shows the cash flows of the dollar debt in millions. The all-in-cost (AIC) for each cash flow stream is also shown for each currency. Line 3 shows the contractual foreign exchange rates between the two counterparties that are locked in by the swap agreement. Line 4 shows the foreign exchange rate that each counterparty and the market should expect based on covered interest rate parity and the forward rate being an unbiased predictor of the expected spot rate, if we can assume that IRP holds between the 6 percent euro rate and the 8 percent dollar rate. This appears reasonable since these rates are, respectively, the best rates available for each counterparty who is well known in its national market. According to this parity relationship: $\overline{S}_t(\$/\euro) = S_0[1.08/1.06]^t$. For example, from the exhibit $1.350/€1.00 = $1.30[1.08/1.06]^2$.

Line 5 shows the equivalent cash flows in euros that have a present value of €40,000,000 at a rate of 6 percent. Without the currency swap, the German MNC would have to convert dollars into euros to meet the euro debt service. The expected rate at which the conversion would take place in each year is given by the implicit foreign exchange rates in Line 4. Line 5 can be viewed as a conversion of the cash flows of Line 2 via the implicit exchange rates of Line 4. That is, for year one, $4,160,000 has an expected value of €3,140,000 at the expected exchange rate of $1.325/€1.00. For year two, $4,160,000 has an expected value of €3,080,000 at an exchange rate of $1.350/€1.00. Note that the conversion at the implicit exchange rates converts 8 percent cash flows into 6 percent cash flows.

The lender of €40,000,000 should be indifferent between receiving the cash flows of Line 1 or the cash flows of Line 5 from the borrower. From the borrower's standpoint, however, the cash flows of Line 1 are free of foreign exchange risk because of the currency swap, whereas the cash flows of Line 5 are not. Thus, the borrower prefers the certainty of the swap, regardless of the equivalency.

Line 6 shows in dollar terms the cash flows based on the implicit foreign exchange rates of Line 4 that have a present value of $52,000,000. Line 6 can be viewed as a conversion of the 6 percent cash flows of Line 1 into the 8 percent cash flows of Line 6 via these expected exchange rates. A lender should be indifferent between these and the cash flow stream of Line 2. The borrower will prefer to pay the cash flows of Line 2, however, because they are free of foreign exchange risk.

EXHIBIT 14.6	Equivalency of Currency Swap Cash Flows						
	Time of Cash Flow						
	0	1	2	3	4	5	AIC
1. Euro debt cash flow	40	−2.40	−2.40	−2.40	−2.40	−42.40	6%
2. $ Debt cash flow	52	−4.16	−4.16	−4.16	−4.16	−56.16	8%
3. Contractual FX rate	1.300	1.7333	1.7333	1.7333	1.7333	1.3245	NA
4. Implicit FX rate	1.300	1.325	1.350	1.375	1.401	1.427	NA
5. Indifference euro cash flow	40	−3.14	−3.08	−3.03	−2.97	−39.35	6%
6. Indifference $ cash flow	52	−3.18	−3.24	−3.30	−3.36	−60.50	8%

Note: Lines 1 and 5 present alternative cash flows in euros that have present values of €40,000,000 at a 6 percent discount rate. The cash flows in Line 1 are free of exchange risk if the swap is undertaken, whereas the implicit cash flows of Line 5 are not if the swap is forgone. The certain cash flows are preferable. The uncertain euro cash flows of Line 5 are obtained by dividing the dollar cash flows of Line 2 by the corresponding implicit FX rate of Line 4. Analogously, Lines 2 and 6 present alternative cash flows in U.S. dollars that have present values of $52,000,000 at an 8 percent discount rate. The cash flows in Line 2 are free of exchange risk if the swap is undertaken, whereas the implicit cash flows of Line 6 are not if the swap is forgone. The certain cash flows are preferable. The uncertain dollar cash flows of Line 6 are obtained by multiplying the euro cash flows of Line 1 by the corresponding implicit FX rate of Line 4.

EXAMPLE 14.5

Pricing the Basic Currency Swap   Suppose that a year after the U.S. dollar–euro swap was arranged, interest rates have decreased in the United States from 8 percent to 6.75 percent and in the euro zone from 6 to 5 percent. Further assume that because the U.S. rate decreased proportionately more than the euro zone rate, the dollar appreciated versus the euro. Instead of being $1.325/€1.00 as expected, it is $1.310/€1.00. One or both counterparties might be induced to sell their position in the swap to a swap dealer in order to refinance at the new lower rate.

The market value of the U.S. dollar debt is $54,214,170; this is the present value of the four remaining coupon payments of $4,160,000 and the principal of $52,000,000 discounted at 6.75 percent. Similarly, the market value of the euro debt at the new rate of 5 percent is €41,418,380. The U.S. counterparty should be willing to buy its interest in the currency swap for $54,214,170 − €41,418,380 × 1.310 = −$43,908. That is, the U.S. counterparty should be willing to pay $43,908 to give up the stream of dollars it would receive under the swap agreement in return for not having to pay the euro stream. The U.S. MNC is then free to refinance the $52,000,000 8 percent debt at 6.75 percent, and perhaps enter into a new currency swap.

From the German counterparty's perspective, the swap has a value of €41,418,380 − $54,214,170/1.310 = €33,517. The German counterparty should be willing to accept €33,517 to sell the swap, that is, give up the stream of euros in return for not having to pay the dollar stream. The German MNC is then in a position to refinance the €40,000,000 6 percent debt at the new rate of 5 percent. The German firm might also enter into a new currency swap.

EXAMPLE 14.6

A Basic Currency Swap Reconsidered   As a more realistic example of a basic currency swap, it is necessary to recognize the bid-ask spread that the swap bank charges for making a market in currency swaps. To extend Example 14.3, assume

EXAMPLE 14.6 (continued)

that the swap bank is quoting five-year U.S. dollar (euro) currency swaps at 8.00–8.15 (6.00–6.10) percent against dollar LIBOR flat. Additionally, and more realistically, assume that the swap bank can deal with the U.S. MNC and the German MNC separately. Then the principal sums raised in the national capital markets by the U.S. MNC ($52,000,000) and the German MNC (€40,000,000) would be sold to the swap bank at the current spot rate of $1.30/€1.00 to obtain the desired currency, €40,000,000 for the U.S. MNC and $52,000,000 for the German MNC. The German subsidiary would annually remit €2,440,000 in interest (6.10 percent of €40,000,000) to its U.S. parent to be passed through to the swap bank. The swap bank, in turn, annually remits €2,400,000 (6 percent of €40,000,000) to the German MNC in order for it to meet the euro debt service. The U.S. subsidiary would annually remit $4,238,000 in interest (8.15 percent of $52,000,000) to its German parent to be passed through to the swap bank. The swap bank, in turn, annually remits $4,160,000 (8 percent of $52,000,000) to the U.S. MNC in order for it to meet the annual dollar debt service. At the debt retirement date, the subsidiaries would additionally remit the principal sums to their respective parents (dollars from the U.S. subsidiary of the German MNC and euros from the German subsidiary of the U.S. MNC) to be exchanged through the swap bank in order to pay off the bond issues in the national capital markets. The net result is that the U.S. MNC borrows euros at an AIC of 6.10 percent through the currency swap instead of the 7 percent rate it would have to pay in the Eurobond market. The German MNC borrows dollars at an AIC of 8.15 percent through the swap instead of the 9 percent rate it would have to pay in the Eurobond market. Exhibit 14.7 diagrams this swap.

EXHIBIT 14.7	$/€ Currency Swap with Bid-Ask Spreads*

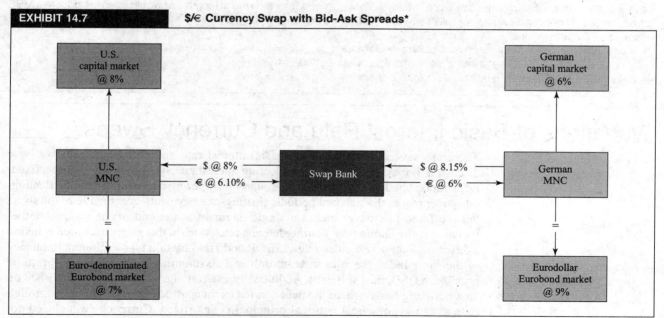

*Debt service in dollars (euros) expressed as a percentage of $52,000,000 (€40,000,000) notional value.

INTERNATIONAL FINANCE IN PRACTICE

AIG, Nomura, and IFC Link Up In Latin Swap Transaction

In what is being called a first for Brazilian future flows, American International Group (AIG) reportedly provided a cross-currency and interest rate swap to a yen transaction for Unibanco.

Underwritten by Nomura Securities, the 25 billion (US$229 million) bond was backed by dollar-denominated diversified payment rights (DPRs). While Moody's Investors Service, Standard & Poor's nor FitchRatings named the swap provider in their reports, all cited the AAA'-rated counterparty of the swap as key to the transaction's creditworthiness. The agencies rated the deal Baa1', BBB-', and BBB', respectively.

But AIG was not the only one in on the swap action. Sources said Nomura is acting as a backstop guarantor for the swap and that its exposure is, in turn, backed by the International Finance Corporation, a AAA' rated entity. "There are three parties here," said a source close to the deal.

According to the IFC, in the event of a default the multilateral would cover "up to 83% of the mark to market payment in case it's owed to Nomura." Officials from the organization added: "That payment is capped up to 30% of the notional amount [of the swap] of any particular time."

The swap agreement is a two-part invention. In addition to the trust switching U.S. dollar-denominated cash flows into Japanese yen to make the bond payments, the vehicle pays a floating interest rate under the swap, while AIG pays a fixed rate. The trust can partially or fully unwind the swap in specified circumstances.

Aside from the cascade of swap parties, the deal was a fairly conventional DPR. It is the fourth series off this trust, established in the Cayman Islands. Unibanco generates 6% of all the payment orders executed through the Brazilian banking system. Also underpinning the transaction is an initially steep overcollateralization. Set at $80 \times$ quarterly debt service, the OC shrinks to $12.5 \times$ with the onset of amortization. The bond has a coupon of 3.55%, according to a bank statement. It was unclear whether the deal priced at par. Nomura could not be reached for comment.

Issued as a private placement, the transaction closed November 14 and was bought by Japanese institutional investors, sources said.

Six correspondent banks have agreed to pledge their receivables for this transaction: American Express Bank, Bank of America, Citibank, Deutsche Bank Trust Company Americas, JPMorgan Chase Bank and The Bank of New York.

This Unibanco deal marks the first time a Brazilian future flows deal has been issued in a currency other than the greenback-denominated collateral, sources said. Currency mismatches cropped up in a number of Argentine deals when the country ditched its dollar peg and pesified the domestic economy. As there was no swap to fix the asymmetry between assets in devalued pesos and bond payments in dollars, it was only a matter of time for most of these transactions to crash. Swap talk is now swirling around Mexico's market, with players eager for the kind of length that would open the door to a MBS issuance in the U.S.

Source: Felipe Ossa, Private Placement Letter, December 1, 2003, p. 1.

Variations of Basic Interest Rate and Currency Swaps

另外，利率互换可以建立在分期付款的基础上，当名义本金随着时间推移逐步摊销时，互换的利息也逐期递减。

There are several variants of the basic interest rate and currency swaps we have discussed. For example, a fixed-for-floating interest rate swap does not require a fixed-rate coupon bond. A variant is a *zero-coupon-for-floating* rate swap where the floating-rate payer makes the standard periodic floating-rate payments over the life of the swap, but the fixed-rate payer makes a single payment at the end of the swap. Another variation is the *floating-for-floating* interest rate swap. In this swap, each side is tied to a different floating rate index (e.g., LIBOR and Treasury bills) for a different frequency of the same index (such as three-month and six-month LIBOR). For a swap to be possible, a QSD must still exist. Additionally, interest rate swaps can be established on an amortizing basis, where the debt service exchanges decrease periodically through time as the hypothetical notional principal is amortized. Currency swaps need not involve the swap of fixed-rate debt. *Fixed-for-floating* and *floating-for-floating* currency rate swaps are also frequently arranged. Additionally, *amortizing* currency swaps incorporate an amortization feature in which periodically the amortized portions of the notional principals are reexchanged. The International Finance in Practice box "AIG, Nomura, and IFC Link Up In Latin Swap Transaction" describes a fixed-for-floating, yen–dollar, currency swap entered into by the Brazilian private bank Unibanco to hedge the currency risk in a fixed-rate yen-denominated bond issue.

Risks of Interest Rate and Currency Swaps

利率风险指在互换银行还没来得及将互换转交给参与交易的另一方之前，利率就发生了不利的变化。

Some of the major risks that a swap dealer confronts are discussed here.

Interest-rate risk refers to the risk of interest rates changing unfavorably before the swap bank can lay off on an opposing counterparty the other side of an interest rate swap entered into with a counterparty. As an illustration, reconsider the interest rate swap example, Example 14.1. To recap, in that example, the swap bank earns a spread of .125 percent. Company B passes through to the swap bank 10.50 percent per annum (on the notional principal of $10,000,000) and receives LIBOR percent in return. Bank A passes through to the swap bank LIBOR percent and receives 10.375 percent in return. Suppose the swap bank entered into the position with Company B first. If fixed rates increase substantially, say, by .50 percent, Bank A will not be willing to enter into the opposite side of the swap unless it receives, say, 10.875 percent. This would make the swap unprofitable for the swap bank.

Basis risk refers to a situation in which the floating-rates of the two counterparties are not pegged to the same index. Any difference in the indexes is known as the basis. For example, one counterparty could have its FRNs pegged to LIBOR, while the other counterparty has its FRNs pegged to the U.S. Treasury bill rate. In this event, the indexes are not perfectly positively correlated and the swap may periodically be unprofitable for the swap bank. In our example, this would occur if the Treasury bill rate was substantially larger than LIBOR and the swap bank receives LIBOR from one counterparty and pays the Treasury bill rate to the other.

Exchange-rate risk refers to the risk the swap bank faces from fluctuating exchange rates during the time it takes for the bank to lay off a swap it undertakes with one counterparty with an opposing counterparty.

Credit risk is the major risk faced by a swap dealer. It refers to the probability that a counterparty will default. The swap bank that stands between the two counterparties is not obligated to the defaulting counterparty, only to the nondefaulting counterparty. There is a separate agreement between the swap bank and each counterparty.

Mismatch risk refers to the difficulty of finding an exact opposite match for a swap the bank has agreed to take. The mismatch may be with respect to the size of the principal sums the counterparties need, the maturity dates of the individual debt issues, or the debt service dates. Textbook illustrations typically ignore these real-life problems.

Sovereign risk refers to the probability that a country will impose exchange restrictions on a currency involved in a swap. This may make it very costly, or perhaps impossible, for a counterparty to fulfill its obligation to the dealer. In this event, provisions exist for terminating the swap, which results in a loss of revenue for the swap bank.

"标准化协议"减少了互换建立所需的时间，并提供了在何种情形下对方可提前终止互换协议的条款。

To facilitate the operation of the swap market, the International Swaps and Derivatives Association (ISDA) has standardized two swap agreements. One is the "Interest Rate and Currency Exchange Agreement" that covers currency swaps, and the other is the "Interest Rate Swap Agreement" that lays out standard terms for U.S.-dollar-denominated interest rate swaps. The standardized agreements have reduced the time necessary to establish swaps and also provided terms under which swaps can be terminated early by a counterparty.

Is the Swap Market Efficient?

The two primary reasons for a counterparty to use a currency swap are to obtain debt financing in the swapped currency at an interest cost reduction brought about through comparative advantages each counterparty has in its national capital market, and/or the benefit of hedging long-run exchange rate exposure. These reasons seem straightforward and difficult to argue with, especially to the extent that name recognition is truly important in raising funds in the international bond market.

进行利率互换的两
个主要原因是：更好地
使资产与负债的期限得
到匹配和／或通过获得
QSD来节约成本。

The two primary reasons for swapping interest rates are to better match maturities of assets and liabilities and/or to obtain a cost savings via the quality spread differential. In an efficient market without barriers to capital flows, the cost-savings argument through a QSD is difficult to accept. It implies that an arbitrage opportunity exists because of some mispricing of the default risk premiums on different types of debt instruments. If the QSD is one of the primary reasons for the existence of interest rate swaps, one would expect arbitrage to eliminate it over time and that the growth of the swap market would decrease. Quite the contrary has happened as Exhibit 14.1 shows; growth in interest rate swaps has been extremely large in recent years. Thus, the arbitrage argument does not seem to have much merit. Consequently, one must rely on an argument of **market completeness** for the existence and growth of interest rate swaps. That is, all types of debt instruments are not regularly available for all borrowers. Thus, the interest rate swap market assists in tailoring financing to the type desired by a particular borrower. Both counterparties can benefit (as well as the swap dealer) through financing that is more suitable for their asset maturity structures.

市场完备性

SUMMARY

本章对货币互换和利率互换进
行了说明，并详述了互换的应用问
题及与互换相关的风险。

1. 本章首先对利率互换和货币互
换进行了定义。基本的利率互换是固
定利率对浮动利率的互换，即互换交
易的一方将其固定利率债务的利息支
付与另一方浮动利率债务的利息支付
进行交换，而且两种债务均采用同一
种货币标价。在货币互换中，互换交
易的一方将其用某种货币表示的债券
的还本付息额与另一方用其他货币表
示的债券的还本付息额相交换。

2. 本章也讨论了互换银行的作
用。"互换银行"是用来描述为交易
双方提供互换服务的金融机构的通
称。互换银行起到经纪人或交易商
的作用。作为经纪人，互换银行为
互换双方的成交提供撮合服务，但
自身不承担任何互换风险。作为交
易商，互换银行乐意担当货币互换
交易任何一方的职能。

3. 本章给出了一个关于基本利
率互换的例子。不难发现，使互换
交易切实可行的一个必要条件是：
交易双方的固定和浮动利率的违约
风险利益间存在质量价差。此外，
因为互换双方的债务均采用相同的
货币标价，显然利率互换的双方并
不交换本金。利率互换是根据名义
本金来计算利息的。

4. 本章举例说明了利率互换开
始后的定价问题。显然，在互换开
始后，对交易的任何一方来说，利
率互换的价值等于按名义本金收取
以及支付的利息流现值之差。

5. 本章还列举了一个关于基本
货币互换的详例。该例子表明，货
币互换中交易双方的还本付息债务
成本实际上相等的。其名义差异可
用一系列国际平价关系来解释。

6. 本章举例说明了货币互换开
始后的定价问题。显然，在互换开
始后，对交易的任何一方来说，货
币互换的价值等于以某种货币标价
的收入现值与以另一种货币标价的

This chapter provides a presentation of currency and interest rate swaps. The discussion details how swaps might be used and the risks associated with each.

1. The chapter opened with definitions of an interest rate swap and a currency swap. The basic interest rate swap is a fixed-for-floating rate swap in which one counterparty exchanges the interest payments of a fixed-rate debt obligation for the floating-interest payments of the other counterparty. Both debt obligations are denominated in the same currency. In a currency swap, one counterparty exchanges the debt service obligations of a bond denominated in one currency for the debt service obligations of the other counterparty which are denominated in another currency.

2. The function of a swap bank was discussed. A swap bank is a generic term to describe a financial institution that facilitates the swap between counterparties. The swap bank serves as either a broker or a dealer. When serving as a broker, the swap bank matches counterparties, but does not assume any risk of the swap. When serving as a dealer, the swap bank stands willing to accept either side of a currency swap.

3. An example of a basic interest rate swap was presented. It was noted that a necessary condition for a swap to be feasible was the existence of a quality spread differential between the default-risk premiums on the fixed-rate and floating-rate interest rates of the two counterparties. Additionally, it was noted that there was not an exchange of principal sums between the counterparties of an interest rate swap because both debt issues were denominated in the same currency. Interest rate exchanges were based on a notional principal.

4. Pricing an interest rate swap after inception was illustrated. It was shown that after inception, the value of an interest rate swap to a counterparty should be the difference in the present values of the payment streams the counterparty will receive and pay on the notional principal.

5. A detailed example of a basic currency swap was presented. It was shown that the debt service obligations of the counterparties in a currency swap are effectively equivalent to one another in cost. Nominal differences can be explained by the set of international parity relationships.

6. Pricing a currency swap after inception was illustrated. It was shown that after inception, the value of a currency swap to a counterparty should be the difference in the present values of the payment stream the counterparty will receive in one currency and pay in the other currency, converted to one or the other currency denominations.

支出现值之差。计算现值时，这两种货币应换算为同一种货币单位。

7. 除了基本的"固定对浮动"的利率互换和"固定对固定"的货币互换外，还有许多其他的互换变体。其中的一种变体就是结合了名义本金分期付款的分期偿付互换。另一种变体是零息票对浮动利率的互换。其中，在整个互换期间，浮动利率支付者定期支付标准的浮动利率利息，但固定利率支付者仅在互换结束时进行一次性支付。还有一种变体是"浮动对浮动"的利率互换。在该互换中，交易双方采用不同的浮动利率指数或同一指数下的不同利息支付频次。

8. 本章对互换市场发展成长的原因进行了详尽的讨论。利率互换的存在和发展离不开完备的市场。换言之，因借款人通常无法获得所有的债务工具，所以利率互换市场有助于满足借款人所需的融资类型。

7. In addition to the basic fixed-for-floating interest rate swap and fixed-for-fixed currency swap, many other variants exist. One variant is the amortizing swap which incorporates an amortization of the notional principles. Another variant is a zero-coupon-for-floating rate swap in which the floating-rate payer makes the standard periodic floating-rate payments over the life of the swap, but the fixed-rate payer makes a single payment at the end of the swap. Another is the floating-for-floating rate swap. In this type of swap, each side is tied to a different floating rate index or a different frequency of the same index.

8. Reasons for the development and growth of the swap market were critically examined. It was argued that one must rely on an argument of market completeness for the existence and growth of interest rate swaps. That is, the interest rate swap market assists in tailoring financing to the type desired by a particular borrower when all types of debt instruments are not regularly available to all borrowers.

KEY WORDS

all-in cost, *341*	currency swap, *338*	single-currency interest
comparative	market	rate swap, *337*
advantage, *344*	completeness, *350*	swap bank, *338*
counterparty, *337*	notional principal, *338*	swap broker, *338*
cross-currency interest	quality spread	swap dealer, *338*
rate swap, *337*	differential (QSD), *340*	

QUESTIONS

1. Describe the difference between a swap broker and a swap dealer.

2. What is the necessary condition for a fixed-for-floating interest rate swap to be possible?

3. Discuss the basic motivations for a counterparty to enter into a currency swap.

4. How does the theory of comparative advantage relate to the currency swap market?

5. Discuss the risks confronting an interest rate and currency swap dealer.

6. Briefly discuss some variants of the basic interest rate and currency swaps diagrammed in the chapter.

7. If the cost advantage of interest rate swaps would likely be arbitraged away in competitive markets, what other explanations exist to explain the rapid development of the interest rate swap market?

8. Suppose Morgan Guaranty, Ltd. is quoting swap rates as follows: 7.75−8.10 percent annually against six-month dollar LIBOR for dollars and 11.25−11.65 percent annually against six-month dollar LIBOR for British pound sterling. At what rates will Morgan Guaranty enter into a \$/£ currency swap?

9. Assume a currency swap in which two counterparties of comparable credit risk each borrow at the best rate available, yet the nominal rate of one counterparty is higher than the other. After the initial principal exchange, is the counterparty that is required to make interest payments at the higher nominal rate at a financial disadvantage to the other in the swap agreement? Explain your thinking.

PROBLEMS

1. Alpha and Beta Companies can borrow for a five-year term at the following rates:

	Alpha	Beta
Moody's credit rating	Aa	Baa
Fixed-rate borrowing cost	10.5%	12.0%
Floating-rate borrowing cost	LIBOR	LIBOR + 1%

   a. Calculate the quality spread differential (QSD).

   b. Develop an interest rate swap in which both Alpha and Beta have an equal cost savings in their borrowing costs. Assume Alpha desires floating-rate debt and Beta desires fixed-rate debt. No swap bank is involved in this transaction.

2. Do problem 1 over again, this time assuming more realistically that a swap bank is involved as an intermediary. Assume the swap bank is quoting five-year dollar interest rate swaps at 10.7%–10.8% against LIBOR flat.

3. Company A is an AAA-rated firm desiring to issue five-year FRNs. It finds that it can issue FRNs at six-month LIBOR + .125 percent or at three-month LIBOR + .125 percent. Given its asset structure, three-month LIBOR is the preferred index. Company B is an A-rated firm that also desires to issue five-year FRNs. It finds it can issue at six-month LIBOR + 1.0 percent or at three-month LIBOR + .625 percent. Given its asset structure, six-month LIBOR is the preferred index. Assume a notional principal of $15,000,000. Determine the QSD and set up a floating-for-floating rate swap where the swap bank receives .125 percent and the two counterparties share the remaining savings equally.

4. A corporation enters into a five-year interest rate swap with a swap bank in which it agrees to pay the swap bank a fixed rate of 9.75 percent annually on a notional amount of €15,000,000 and receive LIBOR. As of the second reset date, determine the price of the swap from the corporation's viewpoint assuming that the fixed-rate side of the swap has increased to 10.25 percent.

5. Karla Ferris, a fixed income manager at Mangus Capital Management, expects the current positively sloped U.S. Treasury yield curve to shift parallel upward.

Ferris owns two $1,000,000 corporate bonds maturing on June 15, 1999, one with a variable rate based on 6-month U.S. dollar LIBOR and one with a fixed rate. Both yield 50 basis points over comparable U.S. Treasury market rates, have very similar credit quality, and pay interest semiannually.

Ferris wished to execute a swap to take advantage of her expectation of a yield curve shift and believes that any difference in credit spread between LIBOR and U.S. Treasury market rates will remain constant.

   a. Describe a six-month U.S. dollar LIBOR-based swap that would allow Ferris to take advantage of her expectation. Discuss, assuming Ferris's expectation is correct, the change in the swap's value and how that change would affect the value of her portfolio. [No calculations required to answer part a.]

   Instead of the swap described in part a, Ferris would use the following alternative derivative strategy to achieve the same result.

   b. Explain, assuming Ferris's expectation is correct, how the following *strategy* achieves the same result in response to the yield curve shift. [No calculations required to answer part b.]

Settlement Date	Nominal Eurodollar Futures Contract Value
12-15-97	$1,000,000
03-15-98	$1,000,000
06-15-98	$1,000,000
09-15-98	$1,000,000
12-15-98	$1,000,000
03-15-99	$1,000,000

   c. Discuss *one* reason why these two derivative strategies provide the same result.

6. Rone Company asks Paula Scott, a treasury analyst, to recommend a flexible way to manage the company's financial risks.

Two years ago, Rone issued a $25 million (U.S.$), five-year floating rate note (FRN). The FRN pays an annual coupon equal to one-year LIBOR plus 75 basis points. The FRN is noncallable and will be repaid at par at maturity.

Scott expects interest rates to increase and she recognizes that Rone could protect itself against the increase by using a pay-fixed swap. However, Rone's board of directors prohibits both short sales of securities and swap transactions. Scott decides to replicate a pay-fixed swap using a combination of capital market instruments.

a. Identify the instruments needed by Scott to replicate a pay-fixed swap and describe the required transactions.

b. Explain how the transactions in part a are equivalent to using a pay-fixed swap.

7. Dustin Financial owns a $10 million 30-year maturity, noncallable corporate bond with a 6.5 percent coupon paid annually. Dustin pays annual LIBOR minus 1 percent on its three-year term time deposits.

Vega Corporation owns an annual-pay LIBOR floater and wants to swap for three years. One-year LIBOR is now 5 percent.

a. Diagram the cash flows between Dustin, Vega, Dustin's depositors, and Dustin's corporate bond. Label the following items:

• Dustin, Vega, Dustin's depositors, and Dustin's corporate bond.

• Applicable interest rate at each line and specify whether it is floating or fixed.

• Direction of each of the cash flows.

Answer problem a in the template provided.

Template for problem a

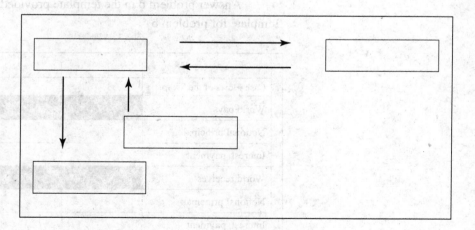

b. i. Calculate the first net swap payment between Dustin and Vega and indicate the direction of the net payment amount.

ii. Identify the net interest rate spread that Dustin expects to earn.

8. Ashton Bishop is the debt manager for World Telephone, which needs €3.33 billion Euro financing for its operations. Bishop is considering the choice between issuance of debt denominated in:

• Euros (€), or

• U.S. dollars, accompanied by a combined interest rate and currency swap.

a. Explain one risk World would assume by entering into the combined interest rate and currency swap.

Bishop believes that issuing the U.S.-dollar debt and entering into the swap can lower World's cost of debt by 45 basis points. Immediately after selling the debt issue, World would swap the U.S. dollar payments for Euro payments throughout the maturity of the debt. She assumes a constant currency exchange rate throughout the tenor of the swap.

Exhibit 1 gives details for the two alternative debt issues. Exhibit 2 provides current information about spot currency exchange rates and the 3-year tenor Euro/U.S. Dollar currency and interest rate swap.

EXHIBIT 1			
World Telephone Debt Details	Characteristic	Euro Currency Debt	U.S. Dollar Currency Debt
	Par value	€3.33 billion	$3 billion
	Term to maturity	3 years	3 years
	Fixed interest rate	6.25%	7.75%
	Interest payment	Annual	Annual

EXHIBIT 2		
Currency Exchange Rate and Swap Information	Spot currency exchange rate	$0.90 per Euro ($0.90/€1.00)
	3-year tenor Euro/U.S. Dollar fixed interest rates	5.80% Euro/7.30% U.S. Dollar

b. Show the notional principal and interest payment cash flows of the combined interest rate and currency swap.

Note: Your response should show both the correct currency ($ or €) and amount for *each* cash flow.

Answer problem b in the template provided.

Template for problem b

Cash Flows of the Swap				
World pays				
Notional principal				
Interest payment				
World receives				
Notional principal				
Interest payment				

c. State whether or not World would reduce its borrowing cost by issuing the debt denominated in U.S. dollars, accompanied by the combined interest rate and currency swap. Justify your response with *one* reason.

INTERNET EXERCISES

The website www.finpipe.com/intrateswaps.htm provides a brief description of interest rate swaps. Links at the bottom of the screen lead to other descriptions of derivative products, including currency swaps and other types of swaps that you will find interesting. It is a good idea to bookmark this site for future reference. Use it now to see how well you understand interest rate and currency swaps. If you cannot follow the discussions, go back and reread Chapter 14.

MINI CASE

The Centralia Corporation's Currency Swap

The Centralia Corporation is a U.S. manufacturer of small kitchen electrical appliances. It has decided to construct a wholly owned manufacturing facility in Zaragoza, Spain, to manufacture microwave ovens for sale in the European Union. The plant is expected to cost €5,500,000, and to take about one year to complete. The plant is to be financed over its economic life of eight years. The borrowing capacity created by this capital expenditure is $2,900,000; the remainder of the plant will be equity financed. Centralia is not well known in the Spanish or international bond market; consequently, it would have to pay 7 percent per annum to borrow euros, whereas the normal borrowing rate in the euro zone for well-known firms of equivalent risk is 6 percent. Alternatively, Centralia can borrow dollars in the United States at a rate of 8 percent.

Study Questions

1. Suppose a Spanish MNC has a mirror-image situation and needs $2,900,000 to finance a capital expenditure of one of its U.S. subsidiaries. It finds that it must pay a 9 percent fixed rate in the United States for dollars, whereas it can borrow euros at 6 percent. The exchange rate has been forecast to be $1.33/€1.00 in one year. Set up a currency swap that will benefit each counterparty.

2. Suppose that one year after the inception of the currency swap between Centralia and the Spanish MNC, the U.S. dollar fixed rate has fallen from 8 to 6 percent and the euro zone fixed rate for euros has fallen from 6 to 5.5 percent. In both dollars and euros, determine the market value of the swap if the exchange rate is $1.3343/€1.00.

15 International Portfolio Investment

近年来，私人和机构投资者在国际股票、债券及其他金融证券方面的证券组合投资呈显著上升的趋势，按美元来衡量已经超过了公司的对外直接投资。

IN RECENT YEARS, portfolio investments by individual and institutional investors in international stocks, bonds, and other financial securities have grown at a phenomenal pace, surpassing in dollar volume foreign direct investments by corporations. As Exhibit 15.1 shows, for instance, the dollar value invested in international equities (ADRs and local shares) by U.S. investors has steadily grown from a rather negligible level in the early 1980s to $200 billion in 1990 and $2,400 billion at the end of 2004. Exhibit 15.1 also shows that foreign equities as a proportion of U.S. investors' portfolio wealth rose from about 1 percent in the early 1980s to about 14 percent by 2004.[1] Considering that U.S. equities account for less than 50 percent of the world equity market capitalization, the volume of international investment may further increase.

近年来，国际证券组合投资的迅速增长反映了金融市场的全球化趋势。

The rapid growth in international portfolio investments in recent years reflects the globalization of financial markets. The impetus for globalized financial markets initially came from the governments of major countries that began to deregulate foreign exchange and capital markets in the late 1970s. For instance, the United Kingdom dismantled the investment dollar premium system in 1979, while Japan liberalized its foreign exchange market in 1980, allowing its residents, for the first time, to freely invest in foreign securities.[2] Even developing countries such as Brazil, India, Korea, and Mexico took measures to allow foreigners to invest in their capital markets by offering country funds or directly listing local stocks on international stock exchanges. In addition, recent advances in telecommunication and computer technologies have contributed to the globalization of investments by facilitating cross-border transactions and rapid dissemination of information across national borders.

---

[1]During the period 2000–2002, the dollar value of foreign equity holdings has declined somewhat, reflecting the worldwide market slump.

[2]Under the investment dollar premium system, U.K. residents had to pay a premium over the prevailing commercial exchange rate when they bought foreign currencies to invest in foreign securities. Since the premium increased the cost of cross-border portfolio investments, U.K. investors were discouraged from investing overseas.

EXHIBIT 15.1

U.S. Investment in Foreign Equities

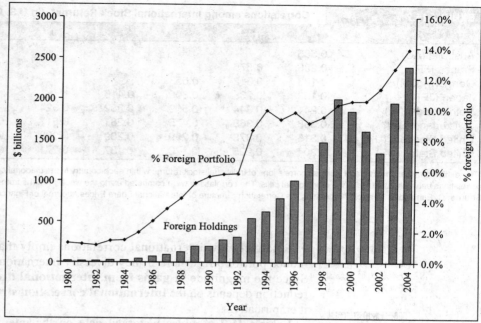

Source: The Federal Reserve Board, Flow of Funds Accounts of the United States, various issues.

In this chapter, we are going to focus on the following issues: (1) why investors diversify their portfolios internationally, (2) how much investors can gain from international diversification, (3) the effects of fluctuating exchange rates on international portfolio investments, (4) whether and how much investors can benefit from investing in U.S.-based international mutual funds and country funds, and (5) the possible reasons for "home bias" in actual portfolio holdings. This chapter provides a self-contained discussion of international portfolio investment; no prior knowledge of portfolio investment theory is assumed.

International Correlation Structure and Risk Diversification

It is clear even from casual observations that security prices in different countries don't move together very much. This suggests that investors may be able to achieve a given return on their investments at a reduced risk when they diversify their investments internationally rather than domestically. Investors diversify their portfolio holdings internationally for the same reason they may diversify domestically—to reduce risk as much as possible. As is suggested by the time-honored adage "Don't put all your eggs in one basket," most people are averse to risk and would like to diversify it away. Investors can reduce portfolio risk by holding securities that are less than perfectly correlated. In fact, the less correlated the securities in the portfolio, the lower the portfolio risk.

对国际组合投资风险分散化有专门的解释：即投资不同国家的有价证券回报的相关性要小于国内投资回报的相关性。

International diversification has a special dimension regarding **portfolio risk diversification:** Security returns are much less correlated across countries than within a country. Intuitively, this is so because economic, political, institutional, and even psychological factors affecting security returns tend to vary a great deal across countries, resulting in relatively low correlations among international securities. For instance, political turmoil in England may very well influence returns on most stocks in London, but it may have little or no impact on stock returns in, say, Finland. On the other hand, political upheaval in Russia may affect Finnish stock returns (due to the geographic proximity and the economic ties between the two countries), with little effect on China-Hong Kong SAR stock returns. In addition, business cycles are often asynchronous among countries, further contributing to low international correlations.

EXHIBIT 15.2		Correlations among International Stock Returns* (in U.S. Dollars)						
Stock Market	AU	FR	GM	JP	NL	SW	UK	US
Australia (AU)	0.586							
France (FR)	0.286	0.576						
Germany (GM)	0.183	0.312	0.653					
Japan (JP)	0.152	0.238	0.300	0.416				
Netherlands (NL)	0.241	0.344	0.509	0.282	0.624			
Switzerland (SW)	0.358	0.368	0.475	0.281	0.517	0.664		
United Kingdom (UK)	0.315	0.378	0.299	0.209	0.393	0.431	0.698	
United States (US)	0.304	0.225	0.170	0.137	0.271	0.272	0.279	0.439

*The exhibit provides the average pairwise correlations of individual stock returns within each country in the diagonal cells and the average pairwise correlations between countries in the off-diagonal cells. The correlations were computed using the weekly returns from the period 1973–1982.
Source: C. Eun and B. Resnick, "Estimating the Correlation Structure of International Share Prices," Journal of Finance, December 1984, p. 1314.

较低的国际相关性意味着投资者如果采取国际分散投资而不是国内投资，可以更有效地降低风险。

国际分散投资的利益

国际相关性结构

Relatively low international correlations imply that investors should be able to reduce portfolio risk more if they diversify internationally rather than domestically. Since the magnitude of **gains from international diversification** in terms of risk reduction depends on the **international correlation structure,** it is useful to examine it empirically.

Exhibit 15.2 provides historical data on the international correlation structure. Specifically, the table provides the average pairwise correlations of individual stock returns within each country in the diagonal entries, and the average pairwise correlations of stock returns between countries in the off-diagonal entries. The correlations are in terms of U.S. dollars and computed using the weekly return data from the period 1973–1982. As can be seen from the table, the average *intracountry* correlation is 0.653 for Germany, 0.416 for Japan, 0.698 for the United Kingdom, and 0.439 for the United States. In contrast, the average *intercountry* correlation of the United States is 0.170 with Germany, 0.137 with Japan, and 0.279 with the United Kingdom. The average correlation of the United Kingdom, on the other hand, is 0.299 with Germany and 0.209 with Japan. Clearly, stock returns tend to be much less correlated between countries than within a country.

如表15-2中的国际相关性结构所示，国际分散投资可以很有效地降低风险。

系统性（不可分散的）风险

The international correlation structure documented in Exhibit 15.2 strongly suggests that international diversification can sharply reduce risk. According to Solnik (1974), that is indeed the case. Exhibit 15.3, adopted from the Solnik study, first shows that as the portfolio holds more and more stocks, the risk of the portfolio steadily declines, and eventually converges to the **systematic** (or nondiversifiable) **risk.** Systematic risk refers to the risk that remains even after investors fully diversify their portfolio holdings. Exhibit 15.3 shows that while a fully diversified U.S. portfolio is about 27 percent as risky as a typical individual stock, a fully diversified international portfolio is only about 12 percent as risky as a typical individual stock. This implies that when fully diversified, an international portfolio can be less than half as risky as a purely U.S. portfolio.

Exhibit 15.3 also illustrates the situation from the Swiss perspective. The figure shows that a fully diversified Swiss portfolio is about 44 percent as risky as a typical individual stock. However, this Swiss portfolio is more than three times as risky as a well-diversified international portfolio. This implies that much of the Swiss systematic risk is, in fact, unsystematic (diversifiable) risk when looked at in terms of international investment. In addition, compared with U.S. investors, Swiss investors have a lot more to gain from international diversification. In sum, Exhibit 15.3 provides rather striking evidence supporting international, as opposed to purely domestic, diversification.[3]

---

[3]In Solnik's study, international portfolios were fully hedged against exchange risk and, as a result, both U.S. and Swiss investors faced the same risk in international portfolios, which was essentially determined by local stock market risks. The Solnik study also compared international diversification across countries versus across industries and found the former to be a superior strategy.

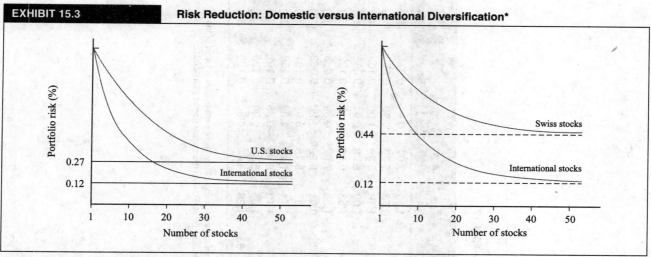

| EXHIBIT 15.3 | Risk Reduction: Domestic versus International Diversification* |

*Portfolio risk (%) represents the variance of portfolio returns divided by that of a typical individual stock.
Source: Reprinted with permission from Financial Analysts Journal, July/August 1974. © 1974, Financial Analysts Federation, Charlottesville, VA.
All rights reserved.

A cautionary note is in order here. A few studies, for example, Roll (1988) and Longin and Solnik (1995), found that international stock markets tend to move more closely together when the market volatility is higher. As was observed during the October 1987 market crash, most developed markets declined together. Considering that investors need risk diversification most precisely when markets are turbulent, this finding casts some doubt on the benefits of international diversification. However, one may say that unless investors liquidate their portfolio holdings during the turbulent period, they can still benefit from international risk diversification. Further, Solnik and Roulet (2000) found that the average correlation of 15 major stock markets with the world market increased by about 10 percent during the period 1971–1998. Although the correlation among international markets may have increased in recent years, securities are still less correlated across countries than within a country.

尽管国际市场间的
相关性近年来有了增加,
但不同国家间证券的相
关性仍然小于一个国家
内的证券的相关性。

Optimal International Portfolio Selection

理性投资者在选择
证券投资组合时会同时
考虑风险与收益。

**www.msci.com/equity/
index.html**

Provides an extensive coverage of world stock markets, including historical time series of major stock market indices around the world.

最优国际投资组合
(optimal international portfolios)

Rational investors would select portfolios by considering returns as well as risk. Investors may be willing to assume additional risk if they are sufficiently compensated by a higher expected return. So we now expand our analysis to cover both risk and return. We are going to first examine the risk-return characteristics of major world stock markets and then evaluate the potential gains from holding **optimal international portfolios**.

Exhibit 15.4 provides summary statistics of the monthly returns, in U.S. dollars, for 12 major stock markets during the period 1980–2001.[4] Let us first examine the correlation coefficients among these markets. The correlation of the U.S. stock market with a foreign market varies from 0.29 with Italy to 0.74 with Canada. Apart from Canada, the Dutch and U.K. markets have relatively high correlations, 0.62 and 0.58, respectively, with the U.S. market. The Dutch market, in fact, has relatively high correlations with many markets: for example, 0.70 with the U.K. and 0.71 with Germany. This is likely due to a high degree of internationalization of the Dutch economy. In contrast, the Italian and Japanese markets tend to have relatively low correlations with other markets. Generally speaking, neighboring countries, such as Canada and the United

[4]All the statistics in Exhibit 15.4 were computed using returns to the Morgan Stanley Capital International (MSCI) stock market indexes rather than individual stocks.

EXHIBIT 15.4

Summary Statistics of the Monthly Returns for 12 Major Stock Markets: 1980.1–2001.12
(All Statistics in U.S. Dollars)

Stock Market	Correlation Coefficients											Mean (%)	SD (%)	β^{a}	SHP[b]	(Rank)
	AU	CN	FR	GM	HK	IT	JP	NL	SD	SW	UK					
Australia (AU)												1.05	7.07	0.94	0.071	(10)
Canada (CN)	0.60											0.88	5.78	0.99	0.057	(11)
France (FR)	0.37	0.46										1.19	6.29	1.00	0.102	(6)
Germany (GM)	0.34	0.42	0.69									1.09	6.26	0.91	0.086	(9)
China-Hong Kong SAR (HK)	0.46	0.47	0.31	0.36								1.53	9.58	1.10	0.102	(6)
Italy (IT)	0.25	0.35	0.50	0.43	0.29							1.26	7.62	0.89	0.093	(8)
Japan (JP)	0.33	0.33	0.41	0.33	0.26	0.37						0.91	6.99	1.20	0.052	(12)
Netherlands (NL)	0.44	0.58	0.66	0.71	0.47	0.44	0.42					1.38	5.15	0.92	0.161	(1)
Sweden (SD)	0.44	0.49	0.49	0.54	0.39	0.44	0.39	0.54				1.71	7.28	1.08	0.159	(3)
Switzerland (SW)	0.38	0.46	0.61	0.67	0.34	0.35	0.41	0.70	0.49			1.13	5.40	0.85	0.107	(5)
United Kingdom (UK)	0.54	0.57	0.57	0.50	0.48	0.38	0.42	0.70	0.51	0.59		1.23	5.55	0.98	0.123	(4)
United States (US)	0.47	0.74	0.50	0.45	0.41	0.29	0.31	0.62	0.49	0.51	0.58	1.26	4.43	0.86	0.160	(2)

[a]β denotes the systematic risk (beta) of a country's stock market index measured against the world stock market index.

[b]SHP denotes the Sharpe performance measure, which is $(\bar{R}_i - R_f)/\sigma_i$, where $\bar{R}_i$ and σ_i are, respectively, the mean and standard deviation of returns to the ith market. Ranking of each market in terms of the Sharpe performance measure is provided in parentheses. The monthly risk-free interest rate, R_f, is 0.55%, which is the average monthly U.S. Treasury bill rate during the sample period 1980–2001.

Source: Returns on MSCI stock market indexes are from Datastream.

States, and Germany and Switzerland, tend to exhibit the highest pairwise correlations, most likely due to a high degree of economic interdependence.

全球β系数

Exhibit 15.4 also provides the mean and standard deviation (SD) of monthly returns and the world beta measure for each market. The **world beta** measures the sensitivity of a national market to world market movements.[5] National stock markets have highly individualized risk-return characteristics. The mean return per month ranges from 0.88 percent (10.56 percent per year) for Canada to 1.71 percent (20.52 percent per year) for Sweden, whereas the standard deviation ranges from 4.43 percent for the United States to 9.58 percent for China-Hong Kong SAR. Japan has the highest world beta measure, 1.20, while the United States has the lowest, 0.86. This means that the Japanese stock market is the most sensitive to world market movements and the U.S. market the least sensitive.

Lastly, Exhibit 15.4 presents the historical performance measures for national stock markets, that is,

$$\text{SHP} = (\bar{R}_i - R_f)/\sigma_i \qquad\qquad (15.1)$$

夏普绩效指标(SHP)
提供了一种调整风险的方法，反映的是单位标准偏离风险的超额回报。

where $\bar{R}_i$ and σ_i are, respectively, the mean and standard deviation of returns, and R_f is the risk-free interest rate. The above expression, known as the **Sharpe performance measure (SHP),** provides a "risk-adjusted" performance measure. It represents the excess return (above and beyond the risk-free interest rate) per standard deviation risk. In Exhibit 15.4, the Sharpe performance measure is computed by using the monthly U.S. Treasury bill rate as a proxy for the risk-free interest rate.

The Sharpe performance measure computed over our sample period, 1980–2001, ranges from 0.052 for Japan and 0.057 for Canada to 0.160 for the United States and 0.161 for the Netherlands. The Dutch market performed the best, closely followed by the U.S. and Swedish markets. The strong performance of the U.S. market is mainly due to its low risk. The lackluster performance of the Canadian market can be attributed to its low return. Similarly, Japan's poor performance is mainly due to its low mean return, which, in turn, reflects the long-term stagnation of the Japanese economy since the early 1990s. The German market also registered a lackluster performance, ranking ninth in terms of the Sharpe measure. In contrast, the U.K. market performed reasonably well, ranking fourth, owing to a respectable mean return combined with a relatively low risk. China-Hong Kong SAR has the second-highest mean return (1.53 percent per month) after Sweden but ranks sixth in terms of Sharpe performance measure, tying with France, due to its very high risk.

利用表15-4中的历史数据，从美元投资者的角度出发，我们可以求出最优国际投资组合。

Using the historical performance data represented in Exhibit 15.4, we can solve for the composition of the optimal international portfolio from the perspective of U.S. (or U.S. dollar-based) investors.[6] Exhibit 15.5 illustrates the choice of the optimal international portfolio (OIP). The result is presented in Exhibit 15.6. As can be seen from the next-to-last column of the table, U.S. investors' optimal international portfolio comprises:

Hong Kong market	=	1.61%
Italian market	=	1.14%
Dutch market	=	29.96%
Swedish market	=	26.45%
U.S. market	=	40.84%
Total	=	100.00%

---

[5]Formally, the world beta is defined as $\beta_i = \sigma_{iw}/\sigma_w^2$, where σ_{iw} is the covariance between returns to the ith market and the world market index, and σ_w^2 is the variance of the world market return. If, for example, the world beta of a market is 1.2, it means that as the world market moves up and down by 1 percent, the market goes up and down by 1.2%.

[6]The optimal international portfolio can be solved by maximizing the Sharpe ratio, i.e., $\text{SHP} = [E(R_p) - R_f]/\sigma_p$, with respect to the portfolio weights. Refer to the Appendix 15B for a detailed discussion.

EXHIBIT 15.5

Selection of the Optimal International Portfolio

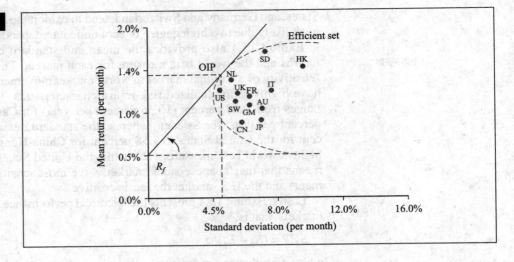

因为国际股票市场的收益－风险值随回报计量货币的汇率变化而变化，因此最优国际投资组合的构成因使用不同计量货币的各国投资者而异。

In their optimal international portfolio, U.S. investors allocate the largest share, 40.84 percent, of funds to their home market, followed by the Dutch and Swedish markets. The China-Hong Kong SAR and Italian markets receive relatively small weights. Seven markets-Australia, Canada, France, Germany, Japan, Switzerland, and U.K.—are not included in U.S. investors' optimal international portfolio.

Similarly, we can solve for the composition of the optimal international portfolio from the perspective of each of the national investors. Since the risk-return characteristics of international stock markets vary depending on the numeraire currency used to measure returns, the composition of the optimal international portfolio will also vary across national investors using different numeraire currencies. Exhibit 15.6 presents the composition of the optimal international portfolio from the currency perspective of each national investor.

For instance, the U.K. (or British pound–based) investors' optimal international portfolio comprises the Netherlands (43.49 percent), Sweden (33.18 percent), the United States (2.35 percent), and the United Kingdom (20.98 percent). Like U.S. investors, U.K. investors invest substantially in their domestic market partly because the domestic market is not subject to exchange rate fluctuations and thus has a low risk. It is clear from the table that the three best performing markets, the Netherlands, Sweden, and the United States, are most heavily represented in the optimal international portfolios. In fact, the Dutch, Swedish, and the U.S. markets are included in every national investor's optimal international portfolio and receive the largest weights. In contrast, the Canadian, French, and German markets are not included in any optimal portfolio, while the China-Hong Kong SAR and Italian markets are included in some portfolios with relatively small weights.

The last column of Exhibit 15.6 provides the composition of the optimal international portfolio in terms of the local currency (LC), constructed ignoring exchange rate changes. It is the optimal international portfolio that would have been obtained if exchange rates had not changed. As such, it can tell us the effect of currency movements on the compositions of international portfolios.

The LC optimal international portfolio comprises Australia (1.22 percent), China-Hong Kong SAR (3.62 percent), Italy (11.05 percent), the Netherlands (19.87 percent), Sweden (39.66 percent), the United Kingdom (8.57 percent), and the United States (16.01 percent). It is interesting to note that the U.K. is included in the LC optimal portfolio but not in the U.S. dollar-based investors' optimal portfolio. This implies that the weak performance of the British pound against the U.S. dollar should be responsible for the exclusion of the British market from the U.S. investors' optimal portfolio. In contrast, the Swiss market is not included in the LC optimal international portfolio but is included in some national investors' (such as the German and Dutch) optimal portfo-

EXHIBIT 15.6 Composition of the Optimal International Portfolio by Investors' Domicile (Holding Period: 1980–2001)

Stock Market	From the Perspective of Investors Domiciled in												
	AU	CN	FR	GM	HK	IT	JP	NL	SD	SW	UK	US	LC[a]
Australia	0.1178												0.0122
Canada													
France													
Germany													
China-Hong Kong SAR	0.0533	0.0331			0.0696		0.0447		0.0209			0.0161	0.0362
Italy		0.0262				0.0510			0.0380			0.0114	0.1105
Japan							0.0472						
Netherlands	0.2679	0.2853	0.6242	0.6193	0.3219	0.5541	0.4777	0.6081	0.4575	0.5508	0.4349	0.2996	0.1987
Sweden	0.3036	0.2392	0.3078	0.2541	0.3000	0.3546	0.3560	0.2571	0.2806	0.2618	0.3318	0.2645	0.3966
Switzerland			0.0195	0.0742				0.0776	0.0362	0.1813			
United Kingdom									0.0465		0.2098		0.0857
United States	0.2574	0.4162	0.0484	0.0523	0.3085	0.0403	0.0744	0.0573	0.1202	0.0061	0.0235	0.4084	0.1601
Total	1.0000	1.0000	1.0000	1.0000	1.0000	1.0000	1.0000	1.0000	1.0000	1.0000	1.0000	1.0000	1.0000
Risk-free rate (%)[b]	0.8145	0.6858	0.7447	0.4945	0.8005	0.9835	0.3486	0.5112	0.6902	0.3704	0.7651	0.5502	0.5502

[a] LC column provides the composition of optimal international portfolio without considering exchange rate changes.

[b] The risk-free rate denotes the average risk-free interest rate faced by investors domiciled in the corresponding country over the period 1980–2001. It is proxied by the one-month Treasury bill rate or eurocurrency interest rate.

EXHIBIT 15.7   Gains from International Diversification by Investor's Domicile (Monthly Returns: 1980–2001)

Investor's Domicile	Domestic Portfolio			Optimal International Portfolio			Gains from International Investment		
	Mean (%)	SD (%)	SHP	Mean (%)	SD (%)	SHP (%)	ΔSHP	(Δ%)[a]	ΔR(%)[b] (%p.a.)[c]
Australia	1.25	5.72	0.076	1.76	4.67	0.202	0.126	(166)	0.72 (8.64)
Canada	0.96	5.12	0.054	1.54	4.16	0.205	0.151	(280)	0.77 (9.24)
France	1.40	5.93	0.110	1.76	5.24	0.194	0.084	(76)	0.50 (6.00)
Germany	1.14	5.85	0.111	1.59	5.02	0.218	0.107	(96)	0.63 (7.56)
China-Hong Kong SAR	1.68	9.27	0.095	1.63	4.68	0.178	0.083	(87)	0.77 (9.24)
Italy	1.62	7.49	0.086	1.92	5.25	0.178	0.092	(107)	0.69 (8.28)
Japan	0.60	5.61	0.045	1.31	5.35	0.179	0.134	(298)	0.75 (9.00)
Netherlands	1.49	5.09	0.191	1.60	5.03	0.216	0.025	(13)	0.13 (1.56)
Sweden	2.06	7.26	0.188	1.85	4.82	0.241	0.053	(28)	0.38 (4.56)
Switzerland	1.12	4.89	0.154	1.51	5.20	0.219	0.065	(42)	0.32 (3.84)
United Kingdom	1.36	4.85	0.122	1.67	5.01	0.180	0.058	(48)	0.28 (3.36)
United States	1.26	4.43	0.161	1.42	4.51	0.193	0.032	(20)	0.14 (1.68)

[a] The number provided in parentheses represents the percentage increase in the Sharpe performance measure relative to that of the domestic portfolio, i.e., [ΔSHP/SHP(DP)] × 100, where ΔSHP denotes the difference in the Sharpe ratio between the optimal international portfolio and the domestic portfolio.

[b] This column provides the extra return accruing to the optimal international portfolio at the domestic-equivalent risk level.

[c] This column provides the annualized extra return accruing to the optimal international portfolio.

lios. This inclusion must be due to a strong performance of the Swiss franc rather than the Swiss stock market.

Having obtained optimal international portfolios, we can now evaluate the gains from holding these portfolios over purely domestic portfolios. We can measure the gains from holding international portfolios in two different ways: (1) the increase in the Sharpe performance measure, and (2) the increase in the portfolio return at the domestic-equivalent risk level. The increase in the Sharpe performance measure, DSHP, is given by the difference in the Sharpe ratio between the optimal international portfolio (OIP) and the domestic portfolio (DP), that is,

我们可用两种不同方法来衡量持有最优国际投资组合的收益性：夏普绩效指标的增量，投资国内相同风险水平的投资组合收益的增量。

$$\Delta SHP = SHP(OIP) - SHP(DP) \tag{15.2}$$

ΔSHP represents the extra return per standard deviation risk accruing from international investment. On the other hand, the increase in the portfolio return at the "domestic-equivalent" risk level is measured by the difference in return between the domestic portfolio (DP) and the international portfolio (IP) that has the same risk as the domestic portfolio. This extra return, $\Delta \overline{R}$ accruing from international investment at the domestic-equivalent risk level, can be computed by multiplying ΔSHP by the standard deviation of the domestic portfolio, that is,

$$\Delta \overline{R} = (\Delta SHP)(\sigma_{DP}) \tag{15.3}$$

Exhibit 15.7 presents both the measures of the gains from international investment from the perspective of each national investor. Let us first examine the results for U.S. investors. As can be seen from the last row of the table, the optimal international portfolio has a mean return of 1.42 percent per month and a standard deviation of 4.51 percent, whereas the U.S. domestic portfolio has a mean return of 1.26 percent and a standard deviation of 4.43 percent. The optimal international portfolio thus has a substantially higher return but a slightly higher risk than the domestic portfolio. As a result, the Sharpe performance measure increases from 0.161 to 0.193, a 20 percent increase. Alternately, U.S. investors can capture an extra return of 0.14 percent per month, or 1.68 percent per year, by holding an international portfolio at the domestic equivalent-risk, that is, at the standard deviation of 4.43 percent.

对有些国家的投资者来说，来自国际投资组合分散化（IPD）的收益要大得多。

The gains from international portfolio diversification (IPD) are much larger for some national investors, especially for Australian, Canadian, Italian, and Japanese investors. Each of these national investors can increase the Sharpe ratio by more than 100 percent. Japanese investors, for instance, can increase the Sharpe ratio by nearly 300 percent, or can capture an extra return of 9.0 percent per year at the Japan-equivalent risk level by holding their optimal international portfolio. Exhibit 15.7 indicates that the gains from IPD are relatively modest for investors from the Netherlands, Sweden, the United Kingdom, and the United States. Overall, the data presented in Exhibit 15.7 suggest that, regardless of domicile and numeraire currency, investors can potentially benefit from IPD to a varying degree.[7]

Effects of Changes in the Exchange Rate

美国居民投资于境外市场所获得的收益，不仅依赖于境外市场的获利情况，还和美元与当地货币的汇率有关系。

The realized dollar returns for a U.S. resident investing in a foreign market will depend not only on the return in the foreign market but also on the change in the exchange rate between the dollar and the local currency. Thus, the success of foreign investment rests on the performances of both the foreign security market and the foreign currency.

---

[7]In analyzing the gains from international investments, it was implicitly assumed that investors fully bear exchange risk. As will be discussed later, investors can hedge exchange risk using, say, forward contracts, therefore enhancing the gains. It is also pointed out that the preceding analyses are strictly "ex-post" in the sense that the risk-return characteristics of securities are assumed to be known to investors. In reality, of course, investors will have to estimate these characteristics, and estimation errors may lead to an inefficient allocation of funds.

| EXHIBIT 15.8 | Decomposition of the Variance of International Security Returns in U.S. Dollars[a] (Monthly Data: 1978.1–1989.12) |

		Components of Var $(R_{i\$})$[b]			
	Var$(R_{i\$})$	Var(R_i)	Var(e_i)	2Cov(R_i, e_i)	ΔVar
Bonds					
Canada	15.29	10.82 (70.76%)	1.72 (11.25%)	2.67 (17.46%)	0.08 (0.52%)
France	16.48	2.82 (17.11%)	12.74 (77.31%)	0.60 (3.64%)	0.32 (1.94%)
Germany	21.53	2.59 (12.03%)	13.84 (64.28%)	4.91 (22.81%)	0.19 (0.88%)
Japan	24.70	3.03 (12.27%)	15.13 (61.26%)	6.09 (24.66%)	0.45 (1.82%)
Switzerland	21.16	1.14 (5.39%)	17.64 (83.36%)	2.34 (11.06%)	0.04 (0.19%)
U.K.	27.67	8.88 (32.09%)	12.39 (44.78%)	6.08 (21.97%)	0.32 (1.16%)
U.S.	10.24	10.24 (100.00%)	0.00 (n.a.)	0.00 (n.a.)	0.00 (n.a.)
Stocks					
Canada	37.70	30.58 (81.11%)	1.72 (4.56%)	5.37 (14.24%)	0.03 (0.08%)
France	59.75	43.03 (72.02%)	12.74 (21.32%)	3.75 (6.28%)	0.23 (0.38%)
Germany	43.82	29.27 (66.80%)	13.84 (31.58%)	0.00 (0.00%)	0.71 (1.62%)
Japan	41.47	19.45 (47.24%)	15.13 (36.48%)	5.83 (14.06%)	1.06 (2.56%)
Switzerland	34.81	20.07 (57.66%)	17.64 (50.68%)	−3.76 (−10.80%)	0.86 (2.47%)
U.K.	40.96	29.27 (71.46%)	12.39 (30.25%)	−1.52 (−3.71%)	0.82 (2.00%)
U.S.	21.16	21.16 (100.00%)	0.00 (n.a.)	0.00 (n.a.)	0.00 (n.a.)

[a] The portfolio variances are computed using the monthly percentage returns.
[b] The relative contributions of individual components to the total portfolio risk appear in parentheses.
Source: Reprinted by permission, C. Eun and B. Resnick, "International Diversification of Investment Portfolios: U.S. and Japanese Perspectives," Management Science, Vol. 40, No. 1, January 1994. © 1994, The Institute of Management Sciences (currently INFORMS), 290 Westminster Street, Providence, RI 02903 USA.

Formally, the rate of return in dollar terms from investing in the ith foreign market, $R_{i\$}$, is given by

$$R_{i\$} = (1 + R_i)(1 + e_i) - 1$$
$$= R_i + e_i + R_i e_i \tag{15.4}$$

where R_i is the local currency rate of return from the ith foreign market and e_i is the rate of change in the exchange rate between the local currency and the dollar; e_i will be positive (negative) if the foreign currency appreciates (depreciates) against the dollar. Suppose that a U.S. resident just sold shares of British Petroleum (BP) she had purchased a year ago, and that the share price of BP rose 15 percent in terms of the British pound (i.e., $R = .15$), whereas the British pound depreciated 5 percent against the dollar over the one-year period (i.e., $e = -.05$). Then the rate of return, in dollar terms, from this investment will be calculated as: $R_{i\$} = (1 + .15)(1 - .05) - 1 = .0925$, or 9.25 percent.

The above expression suggests that exchange rate changes affect the risk of foreign investment as follows:

$$\text{Var}(R_{i\$}) = \text{Var}(R_i) + \text{Var}(e_i) + 2\text{Cov}(R_i, e_i) + \Delta\text{Var} \tag{15.5}$$

where the ΔVar term represents the contribution of the cross-product term, $R_i e_i$, to the risk of foreign investment. Should the exchange rate be certain, only one term, $\text{Var}(R_i)$, would remain in the right hand side of the equation. Equation 15.5 demonstrates that exchange rate fluctuations contribute to the risk of foreign investment through three possible channels:

式 (15-5) 表明, 汇率波动通过三种渠道影响对境外投资的风险: 汇率自身的波动性, Var(e_i), 与当地市场收益的协方差, Cov$(R_i e_i)$, 交叉积项的影响, ΔVar。

1. Its own volatility, $\text{Var}(e_i)$.
2. Its covariance with the local market returns, $\text{Cov}(R_i e_i)$.
3. The contribution of the cross-product term, ΔVar.

Exhibit 15.8 provides the breakdown of the variance of dollar returns into different components for both the bond and stock markets of six major foreign countries:

Canada, France, Germany, Japan, Switzerland, and the United Kingdom. Let us first examine the case of bond markets. The exhibit clearly indicates that a large portion of the risk associated with investing in foreign bonds arises from exchange rate uncertainty. Consider investing in a U.K. bond. As can be seen from the exhibit, the variance of U.K. bond returns is only 8.88 percent squared in terms of the British pound, but jumps to 27.67 percent squared when measured in dollar terms. This increase in volatility is due to the volatility of the exchange rate, $\text{Var}(e_i) = 12.39$, as well as its covariance with the local bond market returns, that is $2\text{Cov}(R_i, e_i) = 6.08$. As can be expected, the cross-product term contributes little. The Swiss market provides an extreme example; the local bond market returns account for only 5.39 percent of the volatility of returns in dollar terms. This means that investing in Swiss bonds largely amounts to investing in Swiss currency.

With the exception of Canada, exchange rate volatility is much greater than bond market volatility. And without exception, exchange rate changes are found to covary *positively* with local bond market returns. Empirical evidence regarding bond markets suggests that it is essential to control exchange risk to enhance the efficiency of international bond portfolios.

与债券市场相比，投资于国外股票市场的风险中，汇率波动的贡献作用相对较小。

Compared with bond markets, the risk of investing in foreign stock markets is, to a lesser degree, attributable to exchange rate uncertainty. Again, consider investing in the U.K. market. The variance of the U.K. stock market is 29.27 percent squared in terms of the British pound, but it increases to 40.96 percent squared when measured in terms of the U.S. dollar. The local market return volatility accounts for 71.46 percent of the volatility of U.K. stock market returns in dollar terms. In comparison, exchange rate volatility accounts for 30.25 percent of the dollar return variance, still a significant portion. Interestingly, the exchange rate covaries negatively with local stock market returns, partially offsetting the effect of exchange rate volatility. Exhibit 15.8 indicates that while exchange rates are somewhat less volatile than stock market returns, they will contribute substantially to the risk of foreign stock investments.

International Bond Investment

Although the world bond market is comparable in terms of capitalization value to the world stock market, so far it has not received as much attention in international investment literature. This may reflect, at least in part, the perception that exchange risk makes it difficult to realize significant gains from international bond diversification. It is worthwhile to explore this issue and determine if this perception has merit.

有必要研究国际债券投资问题并讨论国际债券投资意识是否有用。

Exhibit 15.9 provides summary statistics of monthly returns, in U.S. dollar terms, on long-term government bond indexes from seven major countries: Canada, France, Germany, Japan, Switzerland, the United Kingdom, and the United States. It also presents the composition of the optimal international portfolio for U.S. (dollar-based) investors. Note that European bond markets have very high correlations. For instance, the correlation of the German bond market is 0.89 with the French as well as Swiss bond markets, while the correlation between the French and Swiss bond markets is 0.81. These high correlations reflect the fact that as a group these European currencies float against the U.S. dollar.

In the optimal international portfolio, the U.S. bond receives the largest positive weight, followed by French and Japanese bonds. The Swiss bond, however, receives a negative weight, implying that U.S. investors should have borrowed in terms of the Swiss franc. The optimal portfolio has a monthly mean return of 1.06 percent and a standard deviation of 3.15 percent, resulting in a Sharpe performance measure of 0.337. Considering that the U.S. bond has a mean return of 0.86 percent, a standard deviation of 3.20 percent, and a Sharpe measure of 0.269, U.S. investors could have benefited modestly from holding the optimal international bond portfolio.

| EXHIBIT 15.9 | Summary Statistics of the Monthly Returns to Bonds and the Composition of the Optimal International Bond Portfolio (in U.S. Dollars: 1978.1–1989.12) | | | | | | | | | |

Bond Market	Correlation Coefficient						Mean (%)	SD (%)	SHP	Optimal International Portfolio[a] (Weight)
	CN	FR	GM	JP	SW	UK				
Canada (CN)							0.88	3.91	0.225	0.0218
France (FR)	0.36						0.83	4.06	0.204	0.4488
Germany (GM)	0.40	0.89					0.79	4.64	0.170	0.0204
Japan (JP)	0.27	0.68	0.64				1.07	4.97	0.215	0.2838
Switzerland (SW)	0.34	0.81	0.89	0.66			0.55	4.60	0.120	−0.4896
United Kingdom (UK)	0.40	0.52	0.56	0.51	0.54		0.94	5.26	0.179	0.0895
United States (US)	0.76	0.30	0.35	0.27	0.30	0.33	0.86	3.20	0.269	0.6254

[a] The optimal international bond portfolio is solved allowing for short sales and assuming a zero monthly risk-free interest rate. The optimal international portfolio has a mean return of 1.06% per month and standard deviation (SD) of 3.15%, with a Sharpe ratio (SHP) of 0.337.
Source: Reprinted by permission, C. Eun and B. Resnick, "International Diversification of Investment Portfolios: U.S. and Japanese Perspectives," Management Science, Vol. 40, No. 1, January 1994. © 1994, The Institute of Management Sciences (currently INFORMS), 290 Westminster Street, Providence, RI 02903 USA.

在国外债券投资中，汇率波动风险占主要地位。这意味着投资者可以通过恰当控制汇率风险来增加国际债券投资分散化的收益。

The preponderance of exchange risk in foreign bond investment suggests that investors may be able to increase their gains from international bond diversification if they can properly control the exchange risk. Recent studies indeed show that when investors control exchange risk by using currency forward contracts, they can substantially enhance the efficiency of international bond portfolios. Eun and Resnick (1994), for instance, show that when exchange risk is hedged, international bond portfolios tend to dominate international stock portfolios in terms of risk-return efficiency.[8]

The advent of the *euro,* the common European currency, is likely to alter the risk-return characteristics of the affected markets. Before the euro was introduced, for instance, the Italian and German bonds had quite different characteristics; the former was generally viewed as a high-risk and high-return investment, whereas the latter a low-risk and low-return investment, largely because the German mark was a hard currency while the Italian lira was a weak one. In the post-euro period, however, both German and Italian bonds (and all the other euro zone bonds) will be denominated and transacted in the common currency, rendering nationality of bonds a much less significant factor. Although euro zone bonds differ in terms of credit risk, their risk-return characteristics will converge to a large extent. This implies that non-euro currency bonds like British bonds would play an enhanced role in international diversification strategies as they would retain their unique risk-return characteristics.

International Mutual Funds: A Performance Evaluation

通过投资于国际共同基金，投资者可以：(1) 节约他们试图直接投资国外市场而必须承担的交易成本和信息成本，(2) 避免直接在国外市场进行证券组合投资所遇到的法律和制度壁垒，(3) 从职业基金经理的专业技术中获得潜在利益。

Currently, U.S. investors can achieve international diversification at home simply by investing in U.S.-based international mutual funds, which now number well over 300. By investing in international mutual funds, investors can (1) save any extra transaction and/or information costs they may have to incur when they attempt to invest directly in foreign markets, (2) circumvent many legal and institutional barriers to direct portfolio investments in foreign markets, and (3) potentially benefit from the expertise of professional fund managers.

[8]For further discussion of exchange risk hedging, readers are referred to Appendix 15A.

EXHIBIT 15.10

International Mutual Funds: A Performance Evaluation
(Monthly Returns: 1977.1–1986.12)

Fund	Mean (%)	SD (%)	β_{US}	R^2	SHP[a]
ASA	1.75	11.88	0.80	0.08	0.084
Canadian Fund	0.91	4.64	0.75	0.47	0.035
International Investors	2.34	10.09	0.72	0.09	0.157
Japan Fund	1.72	7.02	0.59	0.13	0.138
Keystone International	1.14	4.29	0.69	0.47	0.091
Merrill Lynch Pacific	1.82	5.45	0.32	0.06	0.196
New Perspective	1.47	3.99	0.80	0.73	0.179
Oppenheimer Global	1.94	6.35	1.02	0.47	0.186
Putnam International	1.64	5.91	0.62	0.20	0.150
Scudder International	1.46	4.23	0.50	0.26	0.168
Sogen International	1.48	3.36	0.70	0.78	0.217
Templeton Growth	1.48	4.13	0.84	0.74	0.176
United International Growth	1.41	3.86	0.71	0.61	0.172
Average	1.58	5.78	0.69	0.39	0.150
U.S. MNC Index	1.34	4.38	0.98	0.90	0.135
S&P 500	1.17	4.25	1.00	1.00	0.099
MSCI World Index	1.46	3.80	0.70	0.61	0.186

[a]The Sharpe measure is computed using the risk-free rate of 0.752%, which is the average monthly Treasury bill rate during the sample period.
Source: C. Eun, R. Kolodny, and B. Resnick, "U.S.-Based International Mutual Funds: A Performance Evaluation." This copyrighted material is reprinted with permission from the Journal of Portfolio Management, 488 Madison Avenue, New York, NY 10022.

国际共同基金的这些优势对私人小投资者特别有吸引力。这些私人小投资者愿意进行国际分散化投资，但他们缺乏必要的专业技术和对境外市场投资的直接途径。

These advantages of international mutual funds should be particularly appealing to small individual investors who would like to diversify internationally but have neither the necessary expertise nor the direct access to foreign markets. It is thus relevant to ask the following question: Can investors benefit from international diversification by investing in existing U.S.-based international mutual funds? To provide an answer to the above question, we are going to examine the historical performance of international mutual funds that invest a substantial portion of their assets in foreign markets.

Exhibit 15.10 provides the risk-return profiles of a sample of U.S.-based international mutual funds that have sufficient track records. Three funds—the ASA (which invests in South African gold-mining stocks), the Canadian Fund, and the Japan Fund—are single-country funds. Other funds invest more broadly. The table shows that all but one fund have a higher mean return than the U.S. stock market index, proxied by the Standard & Poor 500 Index, during the period of 1977.1–1986.12. The average mean return of the international mutual funds is 1.58 percent per month (18.96 percent per year). In comparison, the mean return on the S&P 500 is 1.17 percent per month (14.04 percent per year). The standard deviation of the international mutual funds ranges from 3.36 percent to 11.88 percent, with an average of 5.78 percent. In comparison, the S&P has a standard deviation of 4.25 percent.

这些结果表明样本基金给美国投资者带来了进行国际投资分散化的宝贵机遇。

Exhibit 15.10 also provides the U.S. beta measures of the international funds and the associated coefficient of determination (R^2) values.[9] Note that most funds have a U.S. beta value that is much less than unity. On average, U.S. stock market movements account for less than 40 percent of the fluctuations in the international fund returns. In contrast, U.S. stock market movements are known to account for about 90 percent of the fluctuations in U.S. domestic stock fund returns.[10] These results show that the sample

[9]The U.S. beta measures the sensitivity of the fund returns to the U.S. stock market returns. The coefficient of determination (R^2) measures the fraction of the variance of fund returns that can be explained by the U.S. market returns.
[10]See, for example, Sharpe (1966), pp. 127–28.

EXHIBIT 15.11

Performance of International Mutual Funds: 1977.1–1986.12

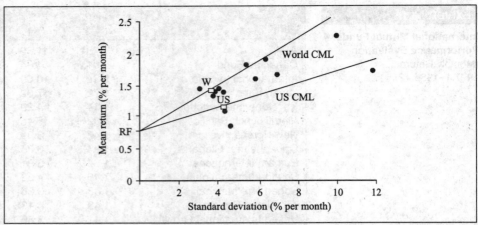

Note: Each international fund is denoted by a round dot (·). The risk-free rate (RF) is .752%, which is the average T-bill rate during the sample period. W and US, respectively, denote the MSCI World Index and the S & P 500.

funds provided U.S. investors with a valuable opportunity to diversify internationally. In contrast, the U.S. MNC Index, which comprises 60 U.S. multinational corporations with the highest proportions of international revenue, has a U.S. beta value of 0.98 and an R^2 value of 90 percent. This means that the share prices of MNCs behave much like those of domestic firms, without providing effective international diversification.[11]

Lastly, Exhibit 15.10 provides the Sharpe performance measures of international mutual funds. As the table shows, 10 out of 13 international funds outperformed the U.S. stock market index based on the Sharpe measure. The same point is illustrated in Exhibit 15.11, showing that only three international funds lie below the U.S. capital market line (CML).[12] This is in sharp contrast to the findings of previous studies showing that the majority of U.S. domestic mutual funds lie below the U.S. capital market line. Against the alternative benchmark of the World Index, however, the sample funds performed rather poorly. The average SHP value for the international funds, 0.15, is substantially less than the value for the World Index, 0.186. This seems to suggest that it is desirable to invest in a world index fund if available.[13]

这意味着，如果可以的话，投资于全球指数化证券投资基金也是非常有价值的。

In More Depth

除了国际共同基金，投资者还可通过以下途径在"家门口"实现国际分散化投资，而不必直接在外国证券市场投资：(1)国家基金；(2)美国存托凭证；(3)世界权益基准股份 (WEBS) 与 (4)对冲基金。

In addition to international mutual funds, investors may achieve international portfolio diversification "at home" by investing in (1) country funds, (2) American depository receipts (ADRs), (3) world equity benchmark shares (WEBS), or (4) hedge funds without having to invest directly in foreign stock markets. In the next section, we discuss each of these instruments.

[11]This result is consistent with Jacquillat and Solnik's study (1978), showing that multinational corporations of various countries have very low exposure (beta) to foreign stock market indexes.

[12]The capital market line (CML) is the straight line obtained by connecting the risk-free interest rate and the market portfolio.

[13]The capital asset pricing model (CAPM) suggests that if the world market portfolio is indeed mean-variance efficient, then the expected return on a portfolio will be determined by its world beta. This, in turn, implies that if investors hold parochial portfolios that are less than fully diversified globally, they are bearing some diversifiable risk for which there will be no compensation in terms of extra returns. Under this situation it would be optimal for investors to hold the world market portfolio, proxied by a world index fund, together with the risk-free asset, to achieve the desired combination of risk and return.

International Diversification through Country Funds

通过投资于国家基金，投资者可以：
1. 以最小的成本投资于单个国外市场；
2. 以国家基金为基础构建其个人的国际投资组合；
3. 进入以其他方式几乎无法进入的新兴市场。

就像其他封闭型基金一样，**封闭型国家基金（CECF）**也可以发行一定量的股份，像个股一样在东道国的股票交易所交易。

Recently, country funds have emerged as one of the most popular means of international investment in the United States as well as in other developed countries. As the name suggests, a country fund invests exclusively in stocks of a single country. Using country funds, investors can

1. Speculate in a single foreign market with minimum costs.
2. Construct their own *personal* international portfolios using country funds as building blocks.
3. Diversify into *emerging markets* that are otherwise practically inaccessible.

Many emerging markets, such as India, Brazil, China, Russia, and Turkey, still remain substantially segmented. As a result, country funds often provide international investors with the most practical, if not the only, way of diversifying into these largely inaccessible foreign markets.

The majority of country funds available, however, have a *closed-end* status. Like other closed-end funds, a **closed-end country fund (CECF)** issues a given number of shares that trade on the stock exchange of the host country as if the fund were an individual stock by itself. Unlike shares of open-end mutual funds, shares of a closed-end country fund cannot be redeemed at the underlying net asset value set at the home market of the fund. Currently, about 30 countries offer CECFs, a partial list of which is provided in Exhibit 15.12. In the United States, the majority of CECFs are listed on the New York Stock Exchange, with a few listed on the American Stock Exchange.

Since the share value of a fund is set on a U.S. stock exchange, it may very well diverge from the underlying net asset value (NAV) set in the fund's home market. The difference is known as a *premium* if the fund share value exceeds the NAV, or a *discount* in the opposite case. Exhibit 15.12 provides the magnitude of premiums/discounts for the sample CECFs. As indicated in the table, the average premium varies a great deal across funds, ranging from 63.17 percent (for the Korea Fund) to −24 percent (for the Brazil Fund). Like the Korea Fund, the Chian's Taiwan and Spain funds com-

EXHIBIT 15.12		U.S. and Home Market Betas of Closed-End Country Funds and Their Net Asset Values						
Region or Country	**Average Fund Premium (%)**	**Net Asset Value**			**Fund Share Value**			**Sample Period**
		β_{US}	β_{HM}	R_2	β_{US}	β_{HM}	R_2	
Australia	−14.77	0.62	0.48	0.13	0.25	0.81	0.60	1986.1–90.12
Brazil	−24.72	0.11	0.16	0.02	0.32	0.65	0.60	1988.4–90.12
Canada	−6.29	0.04	0.47	0.03	−0.19	0.29	0.11	1986.6–90.12
Germany	1.80	0.73	0.53	0.11	0.15	0.69	0.40	1986.7–90.12
India	−2.66	0.87	0.26	0.04	−0.27	0.66	0.40	1988.8–90.12
Italy	−12.49	0.89	0.68	0.21	0.13	0.57	0.28	1986.3–90.12
Korea	63.17	1.00	0.63	0.19	0.24	0.76	0.62	1985.1–90.12
Malaysia	−0.36	1.34	0.60	0.24	0.58	0.68	0.79	1987.6–90.12
Mexico	−21.14	0.99	0.53	0.13	0.33	0.75	0.62	1985.1–90.12
Spain	21.57	1.56	0.28	0.14	0.39	0.75	0.65	1988.7–90.12
South Africa	12.16	0.00	0.35	0.13	0.08	0.85	0.59	1985.1–90.12
Switzerland	−7.65	0.79	0.47	0.25	0.33	0.65	0.75	1987.8–90.12
China's Taiwan	37.89	1.46	0.39	0.26	0.19	0.40	0.13	1987.2–90.12
Thailand	−6.86	1.20	0.44	0.14	0.63	0.85	0.75	1988.2–90.12
U.K.	−16.55	1.04	0.62	0.36	0.55	0.73	0.37	1987.8–90.12
Average		0.84	0.46	0.16	0.25	0.67	0.51	

Source: E. Chang, C. Eun, and R. Kolodny, "International Diversification through Closed-End Country Funds," *Journal of Banking and Finance* (November 1995). Reprinted with permission of Elsevier Science.

manded large premiums, 37.89 percent and 21.57 percent, respectively. Like the Brazil Fund, the Mexico Fund traded at a steep discount, −21.14 percent on average. It was also observed that the fund premium/discount fluctuates widely over time. Most funds have traded at both a premium and a discount since their inception.[14] The behavior of the fund premium/discount implies that the risk-return characteristics of a CECF can be quite different from those of the underlying NAV.

Cash flows from CECFs are generated by the underlying assets held outside the United States. But CECFs are traded in the United States and their market values, determined in the United States, often diverge from the NAVs. This "hybrid" nature of CECFs suggests that they may behave partly like U.S. securities and partly like securities of the home market. To investigate this issue, consider the following "two-factor" market model:[15]

封闭型国家基金这种混合特性说明它们的行为部分地与美国证券相似，部分地与本国基金证券相似。

$$R_i = \alpha_i + \beta^{US}_i R_{US} + \beta^{HM}_i R_{HM} + e_i \qquad (15.6)$$

where:

R_i = the return on the ith country fund,

R_{US} = the return on the U.S. market index proxied by the Standard & Poor 500 Index,

R_{HM} = the return on the home market of the country fund,

β^{US}_i = the U.S. beta of the ith country fund, measuring the sensitivity of the fund returns to the U.S. market returns,

β^{HM}_i = the home market beta of the ith country fund, measuring the sensitivity of the fund returns to the home market returns, and

e_i = the residual error term.

Equation 15.6 is estimated for both the CECFs and their underlying net assets; that is, we run two regressions for each fund. In the first regression, the left-hand side (dependent) variable, R_i, is the return that U.S. investors receive on the CECF share itself. In the second regression, the left-hand side variable is the return on the NAV. The estimation results are provided in Exhibit 15.12.

Exhibit 15.12 shows that CECFs tend to have substantially higher U.S. beta values than their underlying NAVs. The average U.S. beta value is 0.84 for CECFs, but is only 0.25 for the NAVs. On the other hand, the average home market beta is 0.46 for CECFs, which is compared with 0.67 for the NAVs. In the case of Korea, for example, the fund (underlying net assets) has a U.S. beta of 1.00 (0.24) and a home market beta of 0.63 (0.76). In the case of Thailand, the fund (underlying net assets) has a U.S. beta of 1.20 (0.63) and a home market beta of 0.44 (0.85). In other words, CECF returns are substantially more sensitive to the U.S. market factor and less so to the home market factor than their corresponding NAVs. This implies that CECFs behave more like U.S. securities in comparison with the NAVs.[16] However, the majority of CECFs retain significant home market betas, allowing U.S. investors to achieve international diversification to a certain extent. Also noteworthy from the table is the fact that the

---

[14] A study by Bonser-Neal, Brauer, Neal, and Wheatley (1990) suggests that the country fund premium/discount reflects the barriers to direct portfolio investment in the home countries of the funds. They found that whenever these barriers were lowered, the fund premium declined.

[15] The returns to the home market, R_{HM}, employed in Equation 11.6 is, in fact, the "residual" obtained from regressing the home market returns on the U.S. market returns. U.S. investors who wish to diversify risk internationally will value exposure to the "pure" (or, orthogonal) foreign market risk, i.e., β_{HM}.

[16] This finding is consistent with the Bailey and Lim (1992) study showing that CECFs act more like U.S. securities than foreign stock market indexes.

EXHIBIT 15.13	**Summary Statistics of the Weekly Returns for Closed-End Country Funds and Their Net Asset Values and the Compositions of Optimal Portfolios (in U.S. Dollar Terms: 1989.1–1990.12)**							
	Country Fund Share			Net Asset Value			Optimal Portfolio	
Region or Country	**Mean (%)**	**SD (%)**	**Correlation with U.S.**	**Mean (%)**	**SD (%)**	**Correlation with U.S.**	**CECF (Weight)**	**NAV (Weight)**
Australia	0.46	5.64	0.12	0.01	1.78	0.25	0.0033	0.0000
Brazil	0.73	6.31	−0.01	0.29	7.55	−0.02	0.1271	0.0023
Canada	0.14	4.91	−0.31	−0.19	1.98	−0.19	0.0660	0.0000
Germany	0.78	9.70	0.22	0.38	4.67	−0.11	0.0253	0.0000
India	0.36	5.93	0.18	0.15	3.92	−0.21	0.0750	0.0882
Italy	0.44	7.00	0.22	0.39	2.20	0.25	0.0000	0.1044
Korea	−0.37	6.79	0.25	0.00	2.91	0.08	0.0000	0.0000
Malaysia	0.72	7.89	0.35	0.37	3.21	0.29	0.0000	0.0000
Mexico	1.11	6.07	0.50	0.77	2.63	0.24	0.2427	0.6026
Spain	0.39	8.76	0.40	0.03	3.08	0.29	0.0000	0.0000
South Africa	0.43	4.00	−0.13	0.36	5.06	−0.03	0.2993	0.0954
Switzerland	0.27	4.50	0.46	0.20	2.48	0.36	0.0000	0.0000
China's Taiwan	0.57	7.42	0.31	−0.06	7.95	0.05	0.0000	0.0000
Thailand	0.71	8.42	0.29	0.50	5.14	0.23	0.0000	0.0000
U.K.	0.35	4.01	0.44	0.27	4.08	0.23	0.0424	0.0616
U.S. Index	0.18	2.06	1.00	0.18	2.06	1.00	0.1189	0.0454
						Total = 1.0000		1.0000
						Mean = 0.58%		0.58%
						SD = 2.49%		1.81%
						SHP = 0.233		0.320

Source: E. Chang, C. Eun, and R. Kolodny, "International Diversification through Closed-End Country Funds," *Journal of Banking and Finance* (October 1995). Reprinted with permission of Elsevier Science.

coefficients of determination, R^2, tend to be quite low, 0.16 on average, for CECFs. This implies that CECFs are subject to significant *idiosyncratic* (or unique) risks that are related to neither the U.S. nor home market movements.

While CECFs behave more like U.S. securities, they provide U.S. investors with the opportunity to achieve international diversification at home without incurring excessive transaction costs. We now estimate the potential gains from international diversification using CECFs. Exhibit 15.13 provides the risk-return characteristics of 15 sample funds, as well as the U.S. stock market index, during the sample period 1989.1–1990.12. It also presents the composition of the optimal international portfolio comprising CECFs and, for comparison purposes, the composition of the corresponding optimal portfolio comprising the NAVs.

The optimal portfolio consisting of CECFs dominates the U.S. index in terms of risk-return efficiency; the Sharpe performance measure is 0.233 for the former and 0.087 for the latter. This point can be seen clearly from Exhibit 15.14, which traces out the efficient sets, separately, for CECFs and NAVs.

数据显示：相比于封闭型国家基金，资产净值型基金能提供更好的分散化投资机会。

The figure shows that the NAVs offer superior diversification opportunities compared to the CECFs. Consequently, those who can invest directly in foreign markets without incurring excessive costs are advised to do so. However, for the majority of investors without such opportunities, CECFs still offer a cost-effective way of diversifying internationally. Lastly, note that country funds from emerging markets receive significant weights in the optimal portfolio of CECFs. Specifically, the weight is 12.71 percent for the Brazil Fund, 7.50 percent for the India Fund, and 24.27 percent for the Mexico Fund. These emerging market funds as a whole receive about a 45 percent weight in the optimal CECF portfolio. This implies that CECFs from emerging markets can play an important role in expanding the investment opportunity set for internatitonal investors.

EXHIBIT 15.14

Efficient Sets: Country Funds versus Net Assets: 1989.1–1990.12

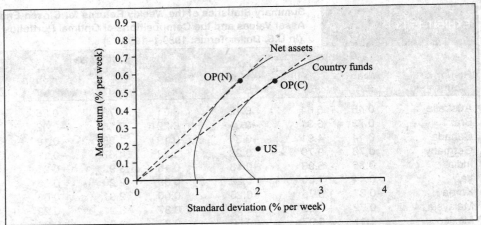

Note: OP(N) and OP(C) denote, respectively, the optimal portfolios comprising net assets and country funds. The efficient sets are illustrated by the dotted lines

International Diversification with ADRs

美国投资者使用美国存托凭证可以像使用国家基金一样，足不出户就能进行国际分散化投资。

U.S. investors can achieve international diversification at home using American depository receipts (ADRs), as well as country funds. As explained in Chapter 13, ADRs represent receipts for foreign shares held in the U.S. (depository) banks' foreign branches or custodians. Like closed-end country funds, ADRs are traded on U.S. exchanges like domestic American securities. Consequently, U.S. investors can save transaction costs and also benefit from speedy and dependable disclosures, settlements, and custody services. The International Finance in Practice box on page 376, "Live Here, Invest Abroad," describes the virtues of investing via ADRs. It is noted that like American investors, British and European investors may achieve international diversification at home using global depository receipts (GDRs), which represent ownership claims on those foreign shares that are listed on the London Stock Exchange.

A few studies examined the potential benefits of international diversification with ADRs. Officer and Hoffmeister (1987) found that adding ADRs to a domestic portfolio had substantial risk reduction benefits. Including as few as four ADRs in a representative U.S. stock portfolio reduced risk, measured by the standard deviation of returns, by as much as 25 percent without reducing the expected return. They also found that ADRs tend to have very low beta exposure to the U.S. stock market. During the sample period 1973–1983, ADRs were found to have an average U.S. beta of only 0.264.

Wahab and Khandwala (1993) found similar results. They reported that when investors hold an equally weighted portfolio of seven ADRs and the S&P 500, the annualized standard deviation of daily returns drops from 30.2 percent (for a purely domestic portfolio) to 17.5 percent. They also reported that most of the nonsystematic risk of the portfolio is eliminated by adding only seven ADRs to the S&P 500. Adding ADRs beyond seven did not reduce the portfolio risk materially, regardless of portfolio weights.

考虑到大部分的美国存托凭证来自发达国家，例如加拿大、日本、英国和美国等，因此投资者通过美国存托凭证进入新兴市场进行分散投资的机会是有限的。

Considering that the majority of ADRs are from such developed countries as Australia, Japan, and the United Kingdom, U.S. investors have a limited opportunity to diversify into emerging markets using ADRs. However, in a few emerging markets like Mexico, investors can choose from several ADRs. In this situation, investors should consider the relative advantages and disadvantages of ADRs and CECFs as a means of international diversification. Compared with ADRs, CECFs are likely to provide more complete diversification. As shown previously, however, the potential gains from investing in them tend to be reduced by premiums/discounts.

International Diversification with WEBS

全球权益基准股份
(WEBS)

www.ishares.com/

Provides extensive coverage of exchange-traded funds, including WEBS.

在本质上，世界权益基准股份是一种在交易所交易的开放式的国家基金，用来紧密跟踪国外股票市场指数的波动。

交 易 所 交 易 基 金
(ETF)

In April 1996, the American Stock Exchange (AMEX) introduced a class of securities called **World Equity Benchmark Shares (WEBS),** designed and managed by Barclays Global Investors. In essence, WEBS are exchange-traded open-end country funds that are designed to closely track foreign stock market indexes. Currently, there are 22 WEBS tracking the Morgan Stanley Capital International (MSCI) indexes for the following individual countries: Australia, Austria, Belgium, Brazil, Canada, China, France, Germany, Italy, Japan, Korea, Malaysia, Mexico, the Netherlands, Singapore, South Africa, Spain, Sweden, Switzerland, and the United Kingdom. The AMEX had previously introduced a similar security for the U.S. market, Standard & Poor's Depository Receipts (SPDRs) known as "spiders," that is designed to track the S&P 500 Index. Using **exchange traded funds (ETFs)** like WEBS and spiders, investors can trade a whole stock market index as if it were a single stock. Being open-end funds, WEBS trade at prices that are very close to their net asset values. In addition to single-country index funds, investors can achieve global diversification instantaneously just by holding shares of the S&P Global 100 Index Fund that is also trading on the AMEX with other WEBS.

A study by Khorana, Nelling, and Trester (1998) found that WEBS indeed track the underlying MSCI country indexes very closely. For example, the average correlation of daily returns between WEBS and the underlying country indexes is 0.97. They also found that the average correlation of WEBS with the S&P 500 Index is quite low, 0.22, which makes WEBS an excellent tool for international risk diversification. For those investors who desire international equity exposure, WEBS may well serve as a major alternative to such traditional tools as international mutual funds, ADRs, and closed-end country funds.

International Diversification with Hedge Funds

近年来，代表私人投资基金的对冲基金呈现显著上升的趋势。

Hedge funds which represent privately pooled investment funds have experienced a phenomenal growth in recent years. This growth of hedge funds has been mainly driven by the desire of institutional investors, such as pension plans, endowments, and private foundations, to achieve positive or absolute returns, regardless of whether markets are rising or falling. Unlike traditional mutual funds that generally depend on "buy and hold" investment strategies, hedge funds may adopt flexible, dynamic trading strategies, often aggressively using leverages, short positions, and derivative contracts, in order to achieve their investment objectives. These funds may invest in a wide spectrum of securities, such as currencies, domestic and foreign bonds and stocks, commodities, real estate, and so forth. Many hedge funds aim to realize positive returns, regardless of market conditions.

Legally, hedge funds are private investment partnerships. As such, these funds generally do not register as an investment company under the Investment Company Act and are not subject to any reporting or disclosure requirements. As a result, many hedge funds operate under rather opaque environments. Hedge fund advisors typically receive a management fee, often 1–2 percent of the fund asset value as compensation, plus performance fee that can be 20–25 percent of capital appreciation. Investors may not be allowed to liquidate their investments during a certain lock-up period. In the United States, only institutional investors and wealthy individuals are allowed to invest in hedge funds. In many European countries, however, retail investors are also allowed to invest in these funds.

Hedge funds tend to have relatively low correlations with various stock market benchmarks and thus allow investors to diversify their portfolio risk. In addition, hedge funds allow investors to access foreign markets that are not easily accessible. For example, J.P. Morgan provides access to the Jayhawk China Fund, a hedge fund

Live Here, Invest Abroad

Global consumers, global investors. Americans' appetite for products from abroad only begins with French champagne, Swiss chocolate and Japanese televisions. American investors are flocking to buy stock in the foreign corporations that make such goods—and not only through the already well-publicized route of mutual funds. They are purchasing shares of individual companies in the form of American depository receipts, or ADRs.

ADRs of about 1,300 foreign firms trade on U.S. stock markets, with one ADR certificate equaling a given number of shares of stock. In 1993, total ADR trading volume on the New York and American exchanges and Nasdaq topped $200 billion, up from $94 billion in 1991 and $41 billion in 1988. With an average of 15 new ADRs a month, the trend shows no signs of topping out.

It's easy to comprehend the enthusiasm. Last year, Merrill Lynch's ADR Composite Index, which tracks 184 ADRs and is the only index of its kind, chalked up a 29.9 percent gain. That was far ahead of the 10.1 percent gain in the Standard & Poor's 500-stock index and just slightly below the average 30.2 percent return for international stock funds. Some ADRs enjoyed triple-digit returns. From March 1, 1993, to Feb. 28, 1994, for example, the ADR price of the Signet Group, the U.K.'s largest retailer

Half a Dozen Winning ADRs

Of the 184 American depository receipts that trade on major U.S. exchanges, the six best performers over the year ended February 28 are listed below.

Company (Country)	Business	Recent Price	12-Month Price Change
Signet Group (Britain)	U.K./U.S. jewelry stores	$ 9.88	400.0%
Corimon (Venezuela)	Paints, chemicals, juices	15.50	189.4%
Fai Insurances (Australia)	Insurance	4.00	159.2%
Danka Business Sys. (Britain)	U.S./U.K. office equipment stores	43.13	143.6%
WPP Group (Britain)	Marketing/public relations	3.19	118.5%
Philips Electr. (Neth.)	Consumer electronics	27.75	108.4%

USN&WR—Basic data: Merrill Lynch International Quantitative Analysis.

虽然投资者能从对
冲基金中获益，但仍得
注意相关的风险。

investing in Chinese stocks not readily available in U.S. markets. Also, hedge funds may allow investors to benefit from certain global macroeconomic events. In fact, many hedge funds are classified as "global/macro" funds. Examples of global/macro funds include such well-known names as George Soros' Quantum Fund, Julian Robertson's Jaguar Fund, and Louis Bacon's Moore Global Fund. Some hedge funds were active during the British pound crisis of 1992 and Asian financial crisis of 1997. As is well known, George Soros correctly anticipated the withdrawal of the British pound from the European Monetary System (EMS) and bet on the pound depreciation upon the withdrawal. His funds reportedly took a $10 billion short position on the British pound and made about $1 billion dollar profit during September 1992. Soros funds also had short positions in the Thai baht and Malaysian ringgit during the Asian currency crisis of 1997. This touched off a series of acrimonious exchanges between the Malaysian Prime Minister Mahatir Mohamad and George Soros on whether hedge funds were responsible for the currency crisis.

While investors may benefit from hedge funds, they need to be aware of the associated risk as well. Hedge funds may make wrong bets based on the incorrect prediction of future events and wrong models. The failure of Long Term Capital Management (LTCM) provides an example of the risk associated with hedge fund investing. John Meriwether, a former fixed income trader at Salomon Brothers, founded LTCM in 1993. Teamed up with a group of veteran Wall Street traders and two Nobel laureates, Myron Scholes and Robert Merton, LTCM enjoyed a solid credibility and respectability among the investment community. Using its good name, LTCM pursued highly of fine jewelry, surged 400 percent to $9.38.

"U.S. stocks are increasingly pricey and precarious," explains Mark Coler, publisher of the Global Portfolio (800-582-9854; $195 for a one-year trial subscription), an ADR newsletter that compiles brokerage reports but doesn't make its own recommendations. "Many foreign shares still have some big gains ahead as a global economic recovery takes hold."

To buy ADRs, you don't have to dial overseas; all it takes is a quick call to a broker. ADRs are issued by the U.S. banks that hold the underlying foreign shares in custody and are sold in U.S. dollars through brokers, just like stocks.

Watch the News
ADRs open the door to a new world, but staying abreast of currency fluctuations and economic and political developments is a must. When Mexico's top presidential candidate was assassinated last week, for example, the ADR price of Teléfonos de México, the national telephone company, dropped by more than 6 percent overnight.

Many foreign firms, moreover, tell shareholders—including those back home—as little as possible. About 70 percent of foreign companies offering ADRs choose not to file financial statements with the Securities and Exchange Commission. Executive pay, lines of business and insider trading thus remain mysteries, and shareholders rarely get prospectuses or quarterly income reports. As a result, these companies' ADRs trade on the "pink sheets" segment of the over-the-counter market, a realm exempt from the rules of the bigger exchanges.

Big Feet
Prices can be hard to track in that thinly traded part of the market, but that doesn't mean the companies are fly-by-nights or start-ups. Most pink-sheeted ADRs are big-foot entities like Nestlé, Mitsubishi and Deutsche Bank that simply reject the arduous process of conforming to U.S. standards.

For investors who want to learn more, Chicago-based Morningstar Inc., a publisher of mutual fund reports, plans a late April start-up, Morningstar American Depository Receipts (800-876-5005; biweekly; $35 for a three-month trial subscription). The report will probe 700 ADRs, including about 300 pink sheeters and all of the others, with up to 10 years of data, business summaries and market snapshots, as well as a list of the five mutual funds owning the greatest number of a company's shares.

Investors hungry for foreign fare sans stomachache can dine at foreign stock mutual funds. "Overseas funds probably won't see quite as much action this year, but the good ones are still likely to outperform the U.S. market," says Michael Stolper, publisher of the Mutual Fund Monthly newsletter (800-426-6502; $49 annually). Two that Stolper recommends are GAM International, (800) 426-4685, and Janus Worldwide, (800) 525-3713. GAM, a nine-year-old fund, has had an average annual return of 25.6 percent. Janus Worldwide had a 1993 return of 28.4 percent—champagne and chocolate performance by any measure.

leveraged fixed income arbitrage strategies. Among other things, LTCM borrowed heavily and bet on international interest convergence between high- and low-quality debts. For example, LTCM bought Italian government bonds and sold German Bund futures. Initially, LTCM did well, realizing about 40 percent annual returns on equity in the first few years. But following the Asian and Russian currency crises, gradual convergence turned into a dramatic divergence. As a result, LTCM's debts increased and its capital base depleted, eventually leading to its downfall. Investors lost large sums of money.

Why Home Bias in Portfolio Holdings?

投资者实际所持有的投资组合与根据组合理论预测的投资组合有很大的不同。

As previously documented, investors can potentially benefit a great deal from international diversification. The actual portfolios that investors hold, however, are quite different from those predicted by the theory of international portfolio investment. Recently, various researchers, such as French and Porteba (1991), Cooper and Kaplanis (1994), Tesar and Werner (1993), Glassman and Riddick (1993), and Chan, Covrig, and Ng (2005), documented the extent to which portfolio investments are concentrated in domestic equities.

组合投资中的本国偏好

Exhibit 15.15, which is adopted from Cooper and Kaplanis (1994), shows the extent of **home bias in portfolio holdings.** U.S. investors, for instance, invested 98 percent of their funds in domestic equities as of 1987 when the U.S. stock market accounted

Stay-at-Home Shareholders

Pick up any investment newsletter these days and you will read about the joys of international investing. European investors, the story goes, should venture overseas before recession drags down continental bourses; Americans should flee before Wall Street's bubble bursts; all rich-country investors should rush into emerging markets, where shares are cheap after a dismal 1995. Many will no doubt be lured by these promises of easy pickings. But the case for diversifying has little to do with market fashion.

Despite the much-vaunted integration of the global economy, the things that can send a country's stockmarket reeling are still often unique to its own economy. By buying stakes in each other's economies, the world's investors should be able to pool their risks, thereby lowering them without sacrificing returns. One way to measure these potential gains is to compare two imaginary portfolios: a giant global mutual fund (unit trust) and one that invests solely in domestic securities. Using past stockmarket returns, and—crucially—adjusting for risk, one can gauge how much better off a global investor would be than a parochial one.

The chart shows such a comparison for a British investor. It compares the combinations of risks and returns that could have been attained using British assets in 1970–95 with those on investments in the Group of Seven countries as a whole. For any given level of risk, the punter could have earned more from an international portfolio.

Karen Lewis, an economist at the University of Pennsylvania's Wharton business school, has made similar calculations for America.* She reckons that, on various assumptions about how people feel about risk and about consuming today instead of tomorrow, an American who invested globally in 1969–93 would have

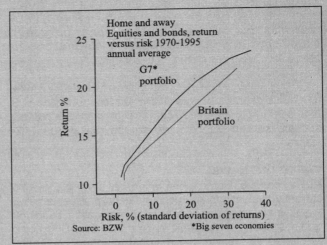

Home and away
Equities and bonds, return versus risk 1970-1995 annual average
G7* portfolio
Britain portfolio
Return %
Risk, % (standard deviation of returns)
Source: BZW   *Big seven economies

been between 10% and 50% better off than one who stayed at home. Her estimates, like the British example, are based only on the gains from investing in other G7 countries. A portfolio that also included emerging markets, which are far less correlated with rich ones than the rich ones are with each other, should offer even bigger rewards.

Economists have been aware of these opportunities for decades. Yet investors have been slow to cash in. Studies have found that, as recently as the early 1990s, Americans kept more than 90% of their assets at home, even though their securities markets accounted for less than half of the world's capitalization.

The bias towards domestic investment is even more striking when you consider human capital. Skills constitute a

---

EXHIBIT 15.15

The Home Bias in Equity Portfolios: December 1987

Country	Share in the World Market Value (%)	Proportion of Domestic Equities in the Portfolio (%)
France	2.6	64.4
Germany	3.2	75.4
Italy	1.9	91.0
Japan	43.7	86.7
Spain	1.1	94.2
Sweden	0.8	100.0
United Kingdom	10.3	78.5
United States	36.4	98.0
	Total = 100.0	

Source: Ian Cooper and Evi Kaplanis, "Home Bias in Equity Portfolios, Inflation Hedging, and International Capital Market Equilibrium," *Review of Financial Studies* 7 (1994) pp. 45–60. Reprinted by permission of Oxford University Press.

big share of most people's wealth, and their value is tied to the domestic economy's fortunes. A dedicated diversifier should therefore bet against his own country's equities, not invest in them.

Given these reasons to invest abroad, why are investors so fond of native shares? Economists have plenty of theories. For instance, investors may shun foreign shares because of cost: investing in many different markets can be expensive, especially after allowing for securities taxes and other capital controls.

But this explanation hardly solves the puzzle. Hurdles such as these have all been falling for years, yet the home-country bias has persisted. Between 1980 and 1990, for example, the share of rich countries' pension assets invested abroad barely budged. (Britain, however, has been an exception: the foreign share of its pension funds' investments went from about a tenth to a quarter during the decade.) Moreover, studies have found that, at least in rich countries, foreigners tend to turn over their shares even more often than domestic investors, casting doubt on the theory that they are deterred by excessive trading costs.

The Grass Is Greener

In a recent paper, Jun-Koo Kang and Rene Stultz, economists at the University of California-Riverside and Ohio State University, respectively, argue that investing overseas can be expensive even if explicit transaction costs are low.[†] Foreign investors may have less information than domestic ones about certain kinds of firms,— say, smaller ones. Knowing this, investors will shun shares in those companies. To test the idea, the economists looked at foreign equity investments in Japan between 1975 and 1991. They found that foreign investors were much more likely than domestic ones to prefer firms that, for example, were big and had little debt.

The study shows that, once foreigners decide to shun part of a country's market, they do best by also shying away from the country as a whole. Moreover, the best way to learn about foreign markets is probably to set up networks there to gather information and trade shares. This involves large fixed costs—which may explain why investors stay out of some countries altogether, but do a lot of trading in any they enter. Now that rich-country institutional investors have begun to incur these costs by putting down global roots, international equity investing should take off.

Besides these less tangible barriers, explicit barriers to foreign capital may still play a role in keeping investors out of some emerging markets. In another new paper, Ms. Lewis finds that the combined effect of capital controls and (for complicated reasons) non-tradable goods can go a long way towards explaining why investors shun some countries.[**]

It appears, therefore, that foreign investment has been hampered, at least until recently, by many of the factors that common sense would suggest: capital controls, opaque markets, and the high cost for fund managers of setting up overseas. In the past few years, these barriers have been falling—especially in emerging markets, where the gains from diversifying are biggest. So investors should soon start gobbling up foreign shares in record numbers. If they do not, economists may have to diversify into other theories.

[*]"Consumption, Stock Returns, and the Gains from International Risk-Sharing." NBER Working Paper No. 5410, January 1996.

[†]"Why Is There a Home Bias? An Analysis of Foreign Portfolio Equity Ownership in Japan." Unpublished, February 1996.

[**]"What Can Explain the Apparent Lack of International Consumption Risk Sharing?" Forthcoming in Journal of Political Economy, April 1996.

Source: The Economist, February 17, 1996, p. 75. © 1996 The Economist Newspaper Group, Inc.

下文将讨论出现组合投资的本国偏好的原因。

for only 36.4 percent of the world market capitalization value. Relatively speaking, French investors seem to invest more internationally—they put 35.6 percent of their funds in foreign equities and 64.4 percent in domestic equities. Considering, however, that the French share in the world market value is only 2.6 percent, French investors also display a striking degree of home bias in their portfolio holdings.

This home bias in actual portfolio holdings obviously runs counter to the strand of literature, including Grubel (1968), Levy and Sarnat (1970), Solnik (1974), Lessard (1976), and Eun and Resnick (1988), that collectively established a strong case for international diversification. This points to the following possibilities. First, domestic securities may provide investors with certain extra services, such as hedging against domestic inflation, that foreign securities do not. Second, there may be barriers, formal or informal, to investing in foreign securities that keep investors from realizing gains from international diversification. In what follows, we are going to examine possible reasons for the home bias in portfolio holdings.[17]

---

[17]For a survey of this issue, readers are referred to Uppal (1992).

首先，投资者可能面临与购买力平价相背而产生的特定国家的通货膨胀风险，而持有国内证券可对国内通货膨胀起到套期保值的作用。

其次，观察到的本国偏好可能反映的是限制对国外投资的制度与法律因素。

最后，额外的税金和交易/信息成本也限制了跨国投资者对国外有价证券的投资，致使引起了本国偏好。

First, consider the possibility that investors face country-specific inflation risk due to the violations of purchasing power parity and that domestic equities may provide a hedging service against domestic inflation risk. In this case, investors who would like to hedge domestic inflation risk may allocate a disproportionate share of their investment funds to domestic equities, resulting in home bias. This, however, is not a likely scenario. Those investors who are averse to inflation risk are likely to invest in domestic risk-free bonds rather than domestic equities, as the latter tends to be a poor hedge against inflation.[18] In addition, a study by Cooper and Kaplanis (1994) rules out inflation hedging as a primary cause for home bias.

Second, the observed home bias may reflect institutional and legal restrictions on foreign investments. For example, many countries used to restrict foreigners' ownership share of domestic firms. In Finland, foreigners could own at most 30 percent of the shares outstanding of any Finnish firm. In Korea, foreigners' ownership proportion was restricted to 20 percent of any Korean firm. As a result, foreigners had to pay premiums for local shares, which may reduce the gains from investing in those restricted markets. At the same time, some institutional investors may not invest more than a certain fraction of their funds overseas under the so-called *prudent man rule*. For example, Japanese insurance companies and Spanish pension funds may invest at most 30 percent of their funds in foreign securities. These inflow and outflow restrictions may contribute to the home bias in actual portfolio holdings.

Third, extra taxes and transaction/information costs for foreign securities can inhibit cross-border investments, giving rise to home bias. Investors often have to pay withholding taxes on dividends from foreign securities for which they may or may not receive tax credits in their home country. Transaction costs can be higher for foreign securities partly because many foreign markets are relatively thin and illiquid and partly because investment in foreign securities often involves transactions in foreign exchange markets. What's more, as argued by Merton (1987), investors tend not to hold securities with which they do not feel familiar. To the extent that investors feel familiar with domestic securities, but not with foreign securities, they are going to allocate funds to domestic, but not to foreign, securities. Consistent with the familiarity bias, Chan, Covrig, and Ng (2005) found that when a country is more remote from the rest of the world and has an uncommon language, domestic (foreign) investors tend to invest more (less) in the country's market. It is even possible that some investors may not be fully aware of the potential gains from international investments. Bailey, Kumar, and Ng (2004) found that the degree of home bias varies across investors. Using brokerage records of tens of thousands of U.S. individual investors, they examined ownership and trading of U.S.-listed foreign stocks and closed-end country funds. They found that wealthier, more experienced, and sophisticated investors are more likely to invest in foreign securities. The International Finance in Practice box on page 378, "Stay-at-Home Shareholders," further discusses the home-bias phenomenon.

The observed home bias in asset holdings is likely to reflect a combination of some of the factors mentioned above. Considering the ongoing integration of international financial markets, coupled with the active financial innovations introducing new financial products such as country funds and international mutual funds, home bias may be substantially mitigated in the near future.

---

[18]Fama and Schwert (1975) showed that common stocks are a perverse hedge against domestic inflation in that returns to common stocks are significantly negatively correlated with the inflation rate. In comparison, bond returns are positively correlated with the inflation rate.

SUMMARY

本章讨论了国际组合投资分散化的利益。国际组合投资分散化是20世纪80年代出现的一种主要的跨国投资形式，它与公司的对外直接投资形成了竞争。

1.近年来，国际组合投资（IPI）得到了迅速发展，其原因包括：（1）金融市场管制的解除，（2）国际共同基金、国家基金、全球跨国市场等投资工具的出现，从而使得投资者无需承担额外成本就可以进行国际分散化投资。

2.投资者为了减少风险而进行分散化投资，通过分散化投资使风险减少的程度取决于国家之间各种证券之间的协方差。由于国家之间证券收益的相关性小于国内证券之间的相关性，因此，投资者通过国际分散化投资比纯国内投资更能降低组合投资的风险。

3.通过充分的风险—收益分析，当各国国内投资的风险水平相等时，投资者可通过国际分散化投资来获得超额利益。实证表明，不管是用本币还是用标准币衡量收益，投资者均可以通过持有最优国际投资组合而获得超额收益。

4.通过其自身的波动性及其与当地市场收益的协方差，外汇汇率的不确定性风险会影响到国外投资的风险。总的来说，汇率的波动性本质上要大于债券市场收益的波动性，但会小于股票市场收益的波动性。这表明当投资者利用远期合约来控制汇率风险时，他们可以获得更多的分散化投资利益，尤其是在进行债券投资时。

5.投资者实际持有的美国国际共同基金的确为投资者提供了进行全球投资风险分散化的有效途径。此外，如果用夏普绩效指标进行衡量，绝大多数国际共同基金的业绩都好于美国股票市场指数。封闭型国家基金同样也为足不出国的美国投资者提供了一种获取国际分散化投资利益的机会。尽管如此，人们发现与其标的资产的净值相比，封闭型国家基金与美国有价证券非常类似。

6.虽然国际分散化投资的潜在收益巨大，许多投资者还是将其基金的很大部分用于投资国内有价证券，呈现一种所谓的本国偏好现象。本国偏好很可能反映了国际金融市场的不完备性：过高的交易成本及信息成本、对外国人的歧视性课税、国际投资中所存在的法律和制度性壁垒等。

This chapter discusses the gains from international portfolio diversification, which emerged as a major form of cross-border investment in the 1980s, rivaling foreign direct investment by firms.

1. International portfolio investment (IPI) has been growing rapidly in recent years due to (a) the deregulation of financial markets, and (b) the introduction of such investment vehicles as international mutual funds, country funds, and internationally cross-listed stocks, which allow investors to achieve international diversification without incurring excessive costs.

2. Investors diversify to reduce risk; the extent to which the risk is reduced by diversification depends on the covariances among individual securities making up the portfolio. Since security returns tend to covary much less across countries than within a country, investors can reduce portfolio risk more by diversifying internationally than purely domestically.

3. In a full-fledged risk-return analysis, investors can gain from international diversification in terms of "extra" returns at the "domestic-equivalent" risk level. Empirical evidence indicates that regardless of domicile and the numeraire currency used to measure returns, investors can capture extra returns when they hold their optimal international portfolios.

4. Foreign exchange rate uncertainty contributes to the risk of foreign investment through its own volatility as well as through its covariance with local market returns. Generally speaking, exchange rates are substantially more volatile than bond market returns but less so than stock market returns. This suggests that investors can enhance their gains from international diversification, especially in the case of bond investment, when they hedge exchange risk using, say, forward contracts.

5. U.S.-based international mutual funds that investors actually held did provide investors with an effective global risk diversification. In addition, the majority of them outperformed the U.S. stock market index in terms of the Sharpe performance measure. Closed-end country funds (CECFs) also provided U.S. investors with an opportunity to achieve international diversification at home. CECFs, however, were found to behave more like U.S. securities in comparison with their underlying net asset values (NAVs).

6. Despite sizable potential gains from international diversification, investors allocate a disproportionate share of their funds to domestic securities, displaying so-called home bias. Home bias is likely to reflect imperfections in the international financial markets such as excessive transaction/information costs, discriminatory taxes for foreigners, and legal/institutional barriers to international investments.

KEY WORDS

closed-end country fund (CECF), *371*
exchange traded funds (ETFs), *375*
gains from international diversification, *358*
home bias in portfolio holdings, *377*

international correlation structure, *358*
optimal international portfolios, *359*
portfolio risk diversification, *357*

Sharpe performance measure (SHP), *361*
systematic risk, *358*
world beta, *361*
World Equity Benchmark Shares (WEBS), *375*

QUESTIONS

1. What factors are responsible for the recent surge in international portfolio investment?

2. Security returns are found to be less correlated across countries than within a country. Why can this be?

3. Explain the concept of the world beta of a security.

4. Explain the concept of the Sharpe performance measure.

5. Explain how exchange rate fluctuations affect the return from a foreign market, measured in dollar terms. Discuss the empirical evidence on the effect of exchange rate uncertainty on the risk of foreign investment.

6. Would exchange rate changes always increase the risk of foreign investment? Discuss the condition under which exchange rate changes may actually reduce the risk of foreign investment.

7. Evaluate a home country's multinational corporations as a tool for international diversification.

8. Discuss the advantages and disadvantages of closed-end country funds (CECFs) relative to American depository receipts (ADRs) as a means of international diversification.

9. Why do you think closed-end country funds often trade at a premium or discount?

10. Why do investors invest the lion's share of their funds in domestic securities?

11. What are the advantages of investing via international mutual funds?

12. Discuss how the advent of the euro would affect international diversification strategies.

PROBLEMS

1. Suppose you are a euro-based investor who just sold Microsoft shares that you had bought six months ago. You had invested 10,000 euros to buy Microsoft shares for $120 per share; the exchange rate was $1.15 per euro. You sold the stock for $135 per share and converted the dollar proceeds into euro at the exchange rate of $1.06 per euro. First, determine the profit from this investment in euro terms. Second, compute the rate of return on your investment in euro terms. How much of the return is due to the exchange rate movement?

2. Mr. James K. Silber, an avid international investor, just sold a share of Nestlé, a Swiss firm, for SF5,080. The share was bought for SF4,600 a year ago. The exchange rate is SF1.60 per U.S. dollar now and was SF1.78 per dollar a year ago. Mr. Silber received SF120 as a cash dividend immediately before the share was sold. Compute the rate of return on this investment in terms of U.S. dollars.

3. In the above problem, suppose that Mr. Silber sold SF4,600, his principal investment amount, forward at the forward exchange rate of SF1.62 per dollar. How would this affect the dollar rate of return on this Swiss stock investment? In hindsight, should Mr. Silber have sold the Swiss franc amount forward or not? Why or why not?

4. Japan Life Insurance Company invested $10,000,000 in pure-discount U.S. bonds in May 1995 when the exchange rate was 80 yen per dollar. The company liquidated the investment one year later for $10,650,000. The exchange rate turned out to be 110 yen per dollar at the time of liquidation. What rate of return did Japan Life realize on this investment in yen terms?

5. At the start of 1996, the annual interest rate was 6 percent in the United States and 2.8 percent in Japan. The exchange rate was 95 yen per dollar at the time. Mr. Jorus, who is the manager of a Bermuda-based hedge fund, thought that the substantial interest advantage associated with investing in the United States relative to investing in Japan was not likely to be offset by the decline of the dollar against the yen. He thus concluded that it might be a good idea to borrow in Japan

and invest in the United States. At the start of 1996, in fact, he borrowed ¥1,000 million for one year and invested in the United States. At the end of 1996, the exchange rate became 105 yen per dollar. How much profit did Mr. Jorus make in dollar terms?

6. From Exhibit 15.4 we obtain the following data in dollar terms:

Stock Market	Return (Mean)	Risk (SD)
United States	1.26% per month	4.43%
United Kingdom	1.23% per month	5.55%

The correlation coefficient between the two markets is 0.58. Suppose that you invest equally, that is, 50 percent in each of the two markets. Determine the expected return and standard deviation risk of the resulting international portfolio.[19] This problem can be solved using the spreadsheet MPTSolver.xls.

7. Suppose you are interested in investing in the stock markets of seven countries— i.e., Canada, France, Germany, Japan, Switzerland, the United Kingdom, and the United States—the same seven countries that appear in Exhibit 15.9. Specifically, you would like to solve for the optimal (tangency) portfolio comprising the above seven stock markets. In solving the optimal portfolio, use the input data (i.e., correlation coefficients, means, and standard deviations) provided in Exhibit 15.4. The risk-free interest rate is assumed to be 0.5% per month and you can take a short position in any stock market. What are the optimal weights for each of the seven stock markets? This problem can be solved using the MPTSolver.xls spreadsheet.

8. The HFS Trustees have solicited input from three consultants concerning the risks and rewards of an allocation to international equities. Two of them strongly favor such action, while the third consultant commented as follows:

"The risk reduction benefits of international investing have been significantly overstated. Recent studies relating to the cross-country correlation structure of equity returns during different market phases cast serious doubt on the ability of international investing to reduce risk, especially in situations when risk reduction is needed the most."

a. Describe the behavior of cross-country equity return correlations to which the consultant is referring. Explain how that behavior may diminish the ability of international investing to reduce risk in the short run.

Assume the consultant's assertion is correct.

b. Explain why it might still be more efficient on a risk/reward basis to invest internationally rather than only domestically in the long run.

---

[19]The mean return on the portfolio is simply the weighted average of the returns on the individual securities that are included in the portfolio. The portfolio variance, on the other hand, can be computed using the following formula:

$$\text{Var}(R_p) = \sum_i \sum_j x_i x_j \sigma_{ij}$$

where x_i represents an investment weight for the ith security, and σ_{ij} denotes the variances and covariances among individual securities. In the case where the portfolio is comprised of two securities, its variance is computed as follows:

$$\text{Var}(R_p) = x_1^2 \sigma_1^2 + x_2^2 \sigma_2^2 + 2x_1 x_2 \sigma_{12}$$

The standard deviation, of course, is the square root of the variance. It is also noted that the covariance σ_{ij} is related to the correlation coefficient ρ_{ij} via $\sigma_{ij} = \rho_{ij} \sigma_i \sigma_j$, where σ_i is the standard deviation of returns on the ith security.

The HFS Trustees have decided to invest in non-U.S. equity markets and have hired Jacob Hind, a specialist manager, to implement this decision. He has recommended that an unhedged equities position be taken in Japan, providing the following comment and the table data to support his views:

"Appreciation of a foreign currency increases the returns to a U.S. dollar investor. Since appreciation of the Yen from 100¥/$U.S. to 98¥/$U.S. is expected, the Japanese stock position should not be hedged."

Market Rates and Hind's Expectations

	U.S.	Japan
Spot rate (yen per $U.S.)	n/a	100
Hind's 12-month currency forecast (yen per $U.S.)	n/a	98
1-year Eurocurrency rate (% per annum)	6.00	0.80
Hind's 1-year inflation forecast (% per annum)	3.00	0.50

Assume that the investment horizon is one year and that there are no costs associated with currency hedging.

c. State and justify whether Hind's recommendation (not to hedge) should be followed. Show any calculations.

9. Rebecca Taylor, an international equity portfolio manager, recognizes that an optimal country allocation strategy combined with an optimal currency strategy should produce optimal portfolio performance. To develop her strategies, Taylor produced the table below, which provides expected return data for the three countries and three currencies in which she may invest. The table contains the information she needs to make market strategy (country allocation) decisions and currency strategy (currency allocation) decisions.

Expected Returns for a U.S.-Based Investor

Country	Local Currency Equity Returns	Exchange Rate Returns	Local Currency Eurodeposit Returns
Japan	7.0%	1.0%	5.0%
United Kingdom	10.5	-3.0	11.0
United States	8.4	0.0	7.5

a. Prepare a ranking of the three countries in terms of expected equity-market return premiums. Show your calculations.

b. Prepare a ranking of the three countries in terms of expected currency return premiums from the perspective of a U.S. investor. Show your calculations.

c. Explain *one* advantage a portfolio manager obtains, in formulating a global investment strategy, by calculating both expected market premiums and expected currency premiums.

10. The Glover Scholastic Aid Foundation has received a €20 million global government bond portfolio from a Greek donor. This bond portfolio will be held in euros and managed separately from Glover's existing U.S. dollar-denominated assets. Although the bond portfolio is currently unhedged, the portfolio manager, Raine Sofia, is investigating various alternatives to hedge the currency risk of the portfolio. The bond portfolio's current allocation and the relevant country performance data are given in Exhibits 1 and 2. Historical correlations for the currencies being considered by Sofia are given in Exhibit 3. Sofia expects that future returns and correlations will be approximately equal to those given in Exhibits 2 and 3.

Exhibit 1. Glover Scholastic Aid Foundation Current Allocation Global Government Bond Portfolio

Country	Allocation (%)	Maturity (years)
Greece	25	5
A	40	5
B	10	10
C	10	5
D	15	10

Exhibit 2. Country Performance Data (in local currency)

Country	Cash Return (%)	5-year Excess Bond Return (%)	10-year Excess Bond Return (%)	Unhedged Currency Return (%)	Liquidity of 90-day Currency Forward Contracts
Greece	2.0	1.5	2.0	—	Good
A	1.0	2.0	3.0	−4.0	Good
B	4.0	0.5	1.0	2.0	Fair
C	3.0	1.0	2.0	−2.0	Fair
D	2.6	1.4	2.4	−3.0	Good

Exhibit 3. Historical Currency Correlation Table
(1998–2003, weekly observations)

Currency	€ (Greece)	A	B	C	D
€ (Greece)	1.00	−0.77	0.45	−0.57	0.77
A	—	1.00	−0.61	0.56	−0.70
B	—	—	1.00	−0.79	0.88
C	—	—	—	1.00	−0.59
D	—	—	—	—	1.00

a. Calculate the expected total annual return (euro-based) of the current bond portfolio if Sofia decides to leave the currency risk unhedged. Show your calculations.

b. Explain, with respect to currency exposure and forward rates, the circumstance in which Sofia should use a currency forward contact to hedge the current bond portfolio's exposure to a given currency.

c. Determine which *one* of the currencies being considered by Sofia should be the *best* proxy hedge for Country B bonds. Justify your response with *two* reasons.

Sofia has been disappointed with the low returns on the current bond portfolio relative to the benchmark—a diversified global bond index—and is exploring general strategies to generate excess returns on the portfolio. She has already researched two such strategies: duration management and investing in markets outside the benchmark index.

d. Identify *three* general strategies (other than duration management and investing in markets outside the benchmark index) that Sofia could use to generate excess returns on the current bond portfolio. Give, for *each* of the three strategies, a potential benefit specific to the current bond portfolio.

INTERNET EXERCISES

1. You would like to invest in the Mexican stock market and consider two alternative ways of investing in Mexico: (i) the Mexican closed-end country fund trading on the New York Stock Exchange and (ii) the WEBS for Mexico trading on the American Stock Exchange. Their websites are:

   www.themexicofund.com

   www.ishares.com/international/Americas/MSCI Mexico Index Fund

   Study all the relevant information from the websites and evaluate the relative merits and demerits of the two securities for your Mexican investment. Which one would you prefer?

2. You would like to evaluate the performance of the seven major stock markets of the world—Canada, France, Germany, Japan, the Netherlands, the United Kingdom, and the United States—for the last five years. In doing so, you want to use the Sharpe ratio, providing a risk-adjusted performance measure. Compute this Sharpe performance measure for each of the seven markets using the data from the following website: www.msci.com. Briefly discuss your findings.

MINI CASE

Solving for the Optimal International Portfolio

Suppose you are a financial adviser and your client, who is currently investing only in the U.S. stock market, is considering diversifying into the U.K. stock market. At the moment, there are neither particular barriers nor restrictions on investing in the U.K. stock market. Your client would like to know what kind of benefits can be expected from doing so. Using the data provided in problem 6, solve the following problems:

1. Graphically illustrate various combinations of portfolio risk and return that can be generated by investing in the U.S. and U.K. stock markets with different proportions. Two extreme proportions are (a) investing 100 percent in the United States with no position in the U.K. market, and (b) investing 100 percent in the U.K. market with no position in the U.S. market.

2. Solve for the optimal international portfolio comprising the U.S. and U.K. markets. Assume that the monthly risk-free interest rate is 0.5 percent and that investors can take a short (negative) position in either market. This problem can be solved using the spreadsheet MPTSolver.xls.

3. What is the extra return that U.S. investors can expect to capture at the U.S.-equivalent risk level? Also trace out the efficient set. Appendix 15.B provides an example.

REFERENCES & SUGGESTED READINGS

Adler, Michael, and Bernard Dumas. "International Portfolio Choice and Corporation Finance: A Synthesis." *Journal of Finance* 38 (1983), pp. 925–84.

Bailey, Warren, and J. Lim. "Evaluating the Diversification Benefits of the New Country Funds." *Journal of Portfolio Management* 18 (1992), pp. 74–80.

Bailey, Warren, Alok Kumar, and David Ng. "Venturing Abroad: Foreign Investments of U.S. Individual Investors." Working Paper (2004).

Bonser-Neal, C., G. Brauer, R. Neal, and S. Wheatley. "International Investment Restriction and Closed-End

Country Fund Prices." *Journal of Finance* 45 (1990), pp. 523–47.

Chan, Kalok, Vicentiu Covrig, and Lilian Ng. "What Determines the Domestic Bias and Foreign Bias? Evidence from Mutual Fund Equity Allocations Worldwide. *Journal of Finance* 60 (2005), pp. 1495–1534.

Chuppe, T., H. Haworth, and M. Watkins. "Global Finance: Causes, Consequences and Prospects for the Future." *Global Finance Journal* 1 (1989), pp. 1–20.

Cooper, Ian, and Evi Kaplanis. "Home Bias in Equity Portfolios, Inflation Hedging, and International Capital Market

Equilibrium," *Review of Financial Studies* 7 (1994), pp. 45–60.

Cumby, R., and J. Glen. "Evaluating the Performance of International Mutual Funds." *Journal of Finance* 45 (1990), pp. 497–521.

Errunza, Vihang, Ked Hogan, and Mao-Wei Hung. "Can the Gains from International Diversification Be Achieved without Trading Abroad?" *Journal of Finance* (1999), 2075–2107.

Eun, Cheol, and Bruce Resnick. "Exchange Rate Uncertainty, Forward Contracts and International Portfolio Selection." *Journal of Finance* 43 (1988), pp. 197–215.

Eun, Cheol, and Bruce Resnick. "International Diversification of Investment Portfolios: U.S. and Japanese Perspectives." *Management Science* 40 (1994), pp. 140–61.

Eun, Cheol, and Bruce Resnick. "International Equity Investments with Selective Hedging Strategies." *Journal of International Financial Markets,* Institutions and Money 7 (1997), pp. 21–42.

Eun, Cheol, Richard Kolodny, and Bruce Resnick. "Performance of U.S.-Based International Mutual Funds." *Journal of Portfolio Management* 17 (1991), pp. 88–94.

Fama, Eugene, and W. G. Schwert. "Asset Returns and Inflation." *Journal of Financial Economics* 5 (1975), pp. 115–46.

French, K., and J. Poterba. "Investor Diversification and International Equity Markets." *American Economic Review* 81 (1991), pp. 222–26.

Fung, William, and David Hsieh. "A Primer on Hedge Funds." *Journal of Empirical Finance* 6 (1999), pp. 309–31.

Glassman, Debra, and Leigh Riddick. "Why Empirical Portfolio Models Fail: Evidence That Model Misspecification Creates Home Asset Bias." Unpublished manuscript, 1993.

Grubel, H. G. "Internationally Diversified Portfolios." *American Economic Review* 58 (1968), pp. 1299–1314.

Jacquillat, B., and B. Solnik. "Multinationals Are Poor Tools for Diversification." *Journal of Portfolio Management* 4 (1978), pp. 8–12.

Jorion, Philippe. "Asset Allocation with Hedged and Unhedged Foreign Stocks and Bonds." *Journal of Portfolio Management* 15 (Summer 1989), pp. 49–54.

Khorana, A., E. Nelling, and J. Trester. "The Emergence of Country Index Funds." *Journal of Portfolio Management* (Summer 1998), pp. 78–84.

Larsen, Glen, Jr., and Bruce Resnick. "Universal Currency Hedging for International Equity Portfolios under Parameter Uncertainty." *International Journal of Business* 4 (1999), pp. 1–17.

Larsen, Glen, Jr., and Bruce Resnick. "The Optimal Construction of Internationally Diversified Equity Portfolios Hedged against Exchange Rate Uncertainty." *European Financial Management* 6 (2000), pp. 479–514.

Lessard, D. "World, Country and Industry Relationship in Equity Returns: Implications for Risk Reduction through International Diversification." *Financial Analyst Journal* 32 (1976), pp. 22–28.

Levy, H., and L. Sarnat. "International Diversification of Investment Portfolios." *American Economic Review* 60 (1970), pp. 668–675.

Longin, Francois, and Bruneo Solnik. "Is the Correlation in International Equity Returns Constant?: 1960–1990." *Journal of International Money and Finance* 14 (1995), pp. 3–26.

Merton, R. "A Simple Model of Capital Market Equilibrium with Incomplete Information." *Journal of Finance* 42 (1987), pp. 483–510.

Officer, Dennis, and Ronald Hoffmeister. "ADRs: A Substitute for the Real Thing?" *Journal of Portfolio Management* (Winter 1987), pp. 61–65.

Roll, Richard. "The International Crash of 1987." *Financial Analyst Journal* 44 (1988), pp. 19–35.

Sener, T. "Objectives of Hedging and Optimal Hedge Ratios: U.S. vs. Japanese Investors." *Journal of Multinational Financial Management* 8 (1998), pp. 137–53.

Sharpe, W. "Mutual Fund Performance." *Journal of Business,* A Supplement, No. 1, Part 2 (1966), pp. 119–38.

Solnik, Bruno. "Why Not Diversify Internationally?" *Financial Analyst Journal* 20 (1974), pp. 48–54.

Solnik, Bruno, and J. Roulet. "Dispersion as Cross-sectional, Correlation." *Financial Analyst Journal* 56 (2000), pp. 54–61.

Tesar, L., and I. Werner. "Home Bias and High Turnover." Unpublished manuscript, 1993.

Uppal, Raman. "The Economic Determinants of the Home Country Bias in Investors' Portfolios: A Survey." *Journal of International Financial Management and Accounting* 4 (1992), pp. 171–89.

Wahab, Mahmood, and Amit Khandwala. "Why Not Diversify Internationally with ADRs?" *Journal of Portfolio Management* (Winter 1993), pp. 75–82.

15A International Investment with Exchange Risk Hedging

In this appendix we show how hedging the exchange rate risk in an international portfolio can enhance the risk-return efficiency of an internationally diversified portfolio of financial assets. We begin by restating equations (15.4) and (15.5) from the text that state the return and variance of return to a U.S. dollar investor from investing in individual foreign security i:

$$R_{i\$} = (1 + R_i)(1 + e_i) - 1 \tag{15A.1a}$$

$$= R_i + e_i + R_i e_i \tag{15A.1b}$$

$$\approx R_i - e_i. \tag{15A.1c}$$

In equation (15A.1c), we ignore the cross-product term, $R_i e_i$, which is generally small, for discussion purpose. Consequently, the expected return to the U.S. dollar investor from investing in foreign security i can be approximated as:

$$\bar{R}_{i\$} \approx \bar{R}_i + \bar{e}_i \tag{15A.2}$$

Also, we can express the variance of dollar returns from the ith foreign security as follows:

$$\text{Var}(R_{i\$}) = \text{Var}(R_i) + \text{Var}(e_i) + 2\text{Cov}(R_i, e_i) \tag{15A.3}$$

Similarly, we can state the covariance between dollar returns from two different foreign securities as follows:

$$\text{Cov}(R_{i\$}, R_{j\$}) = \text{Cov}(R_i, R_j) + \text{Cov}(e_i, e_j) + \text{Cov}(R_i, e_j) + \text{Cov}(R_j, e_i) \tag{15A.4}$$

Now consider a simple exchange risk hedging strategy in which the U.S. dollar investor sells the expected foreign currency proceeds forward. In dollar terms, it amounts to exchanging the "uncertain" dollar return, $(1 + \bar{R}_i)(1 + e_i) - 1$, for the "certain" dollar return, $(1 + \bar{R}_i)(1 + f_i) - 1$, where $f_i = (F_i - S_i)/S_i$ is the forward exchange premium of the currency denominating security i. Although the expected foreign investment proceeds will be converted into U.S. dollars at the known forward exchange rate under this strategy, the unexpected foreign investment proceeds will have to be converted into U.S. dollars at the uncertain future spot exchange rate. The dollar rate of return under the hedging (H) strategy is thus given by

$$\bar{R}_{i\$H} = [1 + \bar{R}_i](1 + f_i) + [R_i - \bar{R}_i](1 + e_i) - 1 \tag{15A.5a}$$

$$= R_i + f_i + R_i e_i + \bar{R}_i(f_i - e_i) \tag{15A.5b}$$

Since the third and fourth terms of equation (15A.5b) are likely to be small in magnitude, the expected hedged return for the U.S. dollar investor can be approximated as follows:

$$\bar{R}_{i\$H} \approx \bar{R}_i + f_i \tag{15A.6}$$

Recall from the forward expectations parity discussion in Chapter 6 that f_i can be unbiased estimate of $\bar{e}_i$, i.e., $f_i = \bar{e}_i$. Comparison of equations (15A.1c) and (15A.6) thus indicates that the expected return to the U.S. dollar investor is approximately the same whether the investor hedges the exchange rate risk in the investment, or remains unhedged.

To the extent that the investor establishes an effective hedge to eliminate exchange rate uncertainty, the $\text{Var}(e_i)$ and $\text{Cov}(R_i, e_i)$ terms in equation (15A.3) will be close to zero. Similarly, the $\text{Cov}(e_i, e_j)$, $\text{Cov}(R_i, e_j)$, and $\text{Cov}(R_j, e_i)$ terms in equation (15A.4) will be close to zero. Consequently, given that f_i is a constant, it follows that

$$\text{Var}(R_{i\$H}) < \text{Var}(R_{i\$}), \text{ and}$$

$$\text{Cov}(R_{i\$H}, R_{j\$H}) < \text{Cov}(R_{i\$}, R_{j\$}).$$

The empirical results presented in Exhibit 15.8 generally support these relationships. It thus follows that the risk-return efficiency is likely to be superior if the investor hedges the exchange rate risk when investing internationally.

15B | Solving for the Optimal Portfolio

Here we explain how to solve for the optimal portfolio of risky securities when there exists a risk-free asset paying a certain risk-free interest rate, R_f. Once we assume that investors prefer more wealth to less and are averse to risk, we can solve for the "optimal" portfolio by maximizing the Sharpe ratio (SHPp) of the excess portfolio return to the standard deviation risk. In other words,

$$\text{Max SHPp} = [\bar{R}_p - R_f]/\sigma_p \tag{15B.1}$$

where $\bar{R}_p$ is the expected rate of return on the portfolio and σ_p is the standard deviation of the portfolio returns.

The expected portfolio return, $\bar{R}_p$, is just the weighted average of the expected returns to individual assets, $\bar{R}_i$, included in the portfolio, that is,

$$\bar{R}_p = \sum_i x_i \bar{R}_i \tag{15B.2}$$

where x_i denotes a fraction of wealth invested in the ith individual asset; the sum of fractions should add up to one, that is, $\sum_i x_i = 1$. The portfolio risk, σ_p, on the other hand, is related to the variances and covariances of individual asset returns as follows:

$$\sigma_p = [\sum_i \sum_j x_i x_j \sigma_{ij}]^{1/2} \tag{15B.3}$$

where σ_{ij} denotes the covariance of returns to the ith and jth assets. What's inside the bracket is the variance of portfolio return.

Now let us consider a simple case where the portfolio includes only two risky assets, A and B. In this case, the risk and return of the portfolio will be determined as follows:

$$\bar{R}_p = x_A \bar{R}_A + x_B \bar{R}_B \tag{15B.4}$$

$$\sigma_p = [x_A^2 \sigma_A^2 + x_B^2 \sigma_B^2 + 2 x_A x_B \sigma_{AB}]^{1/2} \tag{15B.5}$$

Suppose we now want to solve for the optimal portfolio using the two assets. We then first substitute Equations 15B.4 and 15B.5 in Equation 15B.1 and maximize SHPp with respect to the portfolio weights x's to obtain the following solution:

$$x_A = \frac{[\bar{R}_A - R_f]\sigma_B^2 - [\bar{R}_B - R_f]\sigma_{AB}}{[\bar{R}_A - R_f]\sigma_B^2 + [\bar{R}_B - R_F]\sigma_A^2 - [\bar{R}_A - R_f + \bar{R}_B - R_f]\sigma_{AB}}$$

$$x_B = 1 - x_A \tag{15B.6}$$

EXAMPLE Suppose we are trying to construct the optimal international portfolio using the U.S. (US) and Netherlands (NL) stock market indexes. From Exhibit 15.4 we obtain the following data (in percentage per month) for the two stock markets:

$$\bar{R}_{US} = 1.26; \quad \sigma_{US}^2 = 19.62$$

$$\bar{R}_{NL} = 1.38; \quad \sigma_{NL}^2 = 26.52$$

$$\sigma_{US,NL} = \sigma_{US}\sigma_{NL}\rho_{US,NL} = (4.43)(5.15)(0.62) = 14.14$$

Using the monthly risk-free rate of 0.55%, we can substitute the given data into Equation 15B.6 to obtain

$$x_{US} = \frac{(1.26-.55)(26.52)-(1.38-.55)(14.14)}{(1.26-.55)(26.52)+(1.38-.55)(19.62)-(1.26-.55+1.38-.55)(14.14)}$$

$$= .5319$$

$$x_{NL} = 1 - x_{US} = 1 - .5319 = .4681$$

The optimal international portfolio thus comprises 53.19 percent in the U.S. market and 46.81 percent in the Dutch market. The expected return and risk of the optimal portfolio can be computed as follows:

$$\bar{R}_{OP} = (.5319)(1.26\%) + (.4681)(1.38\%) = 1.32\%$$

$$\sigma_{OP} = [(.5319)^2 (19.62) + (.4681)^2 (26.52) + 2(.5319)(.4681)(14.14)]^{1/2}$$

$$= 4.29\%$$

The Sharpe performance measure of the optimal international portfolio is .180 [= (1.32 − .55)/4.29], which is compared with the Sharpe measure of .160 for the U.S. market. One can thus compute the extra return from holding the optimal international portfolio at the U.S. domestic-equivalent risk level as follows:

$$\Delta R_{US} = (\Delta SHP)(\sigma_{US}) = (.180 - .160)(4.43) = .089\%$$

or 1.07 percent per year.

PART FIVE

Financial Management of the Multinational Firm

PART FIVE covers topics on financial management practices for the MNC.

CHAPTER 16 discusses why MNCs make capital expenditures in productive capacity in foreign lands rather than just producing domestically and then exporting to overseas markets.

CHAPTER 17 deals with the international capital structure and the cost of capital of a MNC. An analytical argument is presented showing that the firm's cost of capital is lower when its shares trade internationally and if debt capital is sourced internationally.

CHAPTER 18 presents the adjusted present value (APV) framework of Donald Lessard that is useful for the parent firm in analyzing a capital expenditure in foreign operations.

CHAPTER 19 covers issues in cash management for the MNC. The chapter shows that if a MNC establishes a centralized cash depository and a multilateral system, the number of foreign cash flow transactions can be reduced, saving it money and giving it better control of its cash.

CHAPTER 20 provides a brief introduction to trade financing and countertrade. An example of a typical foreign trade transaction explains the three primary documents that are used in trade financing: letter of credit, time draft, and bill of lading.

CHAPTER 21 on the international tax environment opens with a discussion of the theory of taxation. Different methods of taxation are considered, and income tax rates in select countries are compared.

16 Foreign Direct Investment and Cross-Border Acquisitions

按照1981年的《自愿出口限制协议》，日本制造商不可增加对美国市场的汽车出口。

IN THE EARLY 1980s, Honda, a Japanese automobile company, built an assembly plant in Marysville, Ohio, and began to produce cars for the North American market. These cars were substitutes for imports from Japan. As the production capacity at the Ohio plant expanded, Honda began to export its U.S.-manufactured cars to other markets, including its home market, Japan. A few key factors seem to have motivated Honda to make investments in America. First, Honda wanted to circumvent trade barriers imposed on Japanese automobile manufacturers; under the 1981 *Voluntary Restraint Agreement*, Japanese manufacturers were not allowed to increase their automobile exports to the U.S. market. Second, direct investments in America might have been an integral part of Honda's overall corporate strategy designed to bolster its competitive position vis-à-vis its domestic rivals, such as Toyota and Nissan. Following Honda's lead, Toyota and Nissan themselves subsequently made direct investments in America.

It is noteworthy that the Japanese government had been urging the automobile companies to begin production in the United States. In the early 1980s, Japan exported about two million cars a year to the United States, compared to about 20,000 cars imported from the United States. The Japanese government wished to forestall the kind of protectionist sentiment that led to U.S. import quotas on Japanese-made TVs. When TV import quotas were introduced in 1977, virtually all Japanese TV makers were forced to build plants in the United States.

Honda's decision to build a plant in Ohio was welcomed by the United Auto Workers (UAW), an American labor union, which regarded the plant as a major job opportunity for its members. Honda also received several forms of assistance from the state of Ohio, including improved infrastructure around the plant site, access to the Transportation Research Center operated by Ohio State University, abatement of property taxes, and setting up a special foreign trade zone that allowed Honda to import automobile parts from Japan at a reduced tariff rate.

Firms become *multinational* when they undertake **foreign direct investments (FDI).** FDI often involves the establishment of new production facilities in foreign

www.unctad.org/statistics
Provides FDI data in an interactive format.
对外直接投资（FDI）

绿地投资
跨国并购

countries such as Honda's Ohio plant. FDI may also involve mergers with and acquisitions of existing foreign businesses. An example is provided by Ford, which recently acquired effective control of Mazda, a Japanese car manufacturer, as well as Jaguar, a British automobile company. Whether FDI involves a **greenfield investment** (that is, building brand-new production facilities) or **cross-border mergers and acquisitions,** it affords the multinational corporation (MNC) a measure of *control*. FDI thus represents an internal organizational expansion by MNCs.

事实上，跨国公司
的对外直接投资在加强
各国的经济联系以及决
定新兴全球经济的发展
方向上起着重要的作用。

According to a recent UN survey, the world FDI stock grew about twice as fast as worldwide exports of goods and services, which themselves grew faster than the world GDP by about 50 percent.[1] Indeed, FDI by MNCs now plays a vital role in linking national economies and defining the nature of the emerging global economy. By undertaking FDI on a global basis, such MNCs as Sony, Toyota, Royal Dutch Shell, IBM, GM, Coca-Cola, McDonald's, DaimlerChrysler, Bayer, and Nestlé have established their presence worldwide and become familiar household names. These MNCs deploy their formidable resources, tangible and intangible, irrespective of national boundaries, to pursue profits and bolster their competitive positions.

In this chapter, we discuss competing theories of FDI for the purpose of understanding the reasons firms undertake it. We also discuss in detail an increasingly popular mode of FDI, namely, cross-border mergers and acquisitions. In addition, we are going to discuss an extra dimension in FDI that would not particularly matter in domestic investments: how to measure and manage political risk associated with FDI. Our analysis of political risk is largely applicable to international portfolio investment as well. Once a MNC acquires a production facility in a foreign country, its operation will be subject to the "rules of the game" set by the host government. Political risk ranges from (unexpected) restrictions on the repatriation of foreign earnings to outright confiscation of foreign-owned assets. Needless to say, it is essential to the welfare of MNCs to effectively manage political risk. Before we discuss these issues, however, let us briefly review the global trends in FDI in recent years.

Global Trends in FDI

对外直接投资（FDI）
流量是现有FDI存量的增
量。

The recent trends in **FDI flows** are presented in Exhibit 16.1 and Exhibit 16.2. FDI flows represent new additions to the existing stock of FDI. As the exhibits show, during the five-year period 1999–2003, total annual worldwide FDI outflows amounted to about $840 billion on average. As can be expected, several developed countries are the dominant sources of FDI *outflows*. During the five-year period 1999–2003, the United States, on average, invested about $149 billion per year overseas, followed by the United Kingdom, which invested about $117 billion per year. France is the third most important source of FDI outflows, investing about $100 billion per year on average during the 5-year period. Germany and the Netherlands also invested heavily overseas, each exceeding $40 billion per year. After these "big five" come Spain ($36.9 billion), Japan ($30.7 billion), Canada ($29.2 billion), Switzerland ($22.9 billion), and Sweden ($19.4 billion). The developed countries mentioned above account for about 70 percent of the total worldwide FDI outflows during this five-year period. This implies that MNCs domiciled in these countries should have certain comparative advantages in undertaking overseas investment projects. It is interesting to note that China, a developing country, began to undertake FDI, albeit on a modest scale.

---

[1]Source: *World Investment Report 1998,* UNCTAD, United Nations.

EXHIBIT 16.1			Foreign Direct Investment—Outflows (Inflows) in Billions of Dollars			
Country	1999	2000	2001	2002	2003	Annual Average
Australia	−0.7	0.8	12.2	7.6	15.1	7.0
	(2.9)	(13.1)	(4.0)	(14.0)	(7.9)	(8.4)
Canada	17.2	44.7	36.1	26.4	21.5	29.2
	(24.7)	(66.8)	(27.5)	(21.0)	(6.6)	(29.3)
China	1.8	0.9	6.9	2.5	1.8	2.8
	(40.3)	(40.7)	(46.9)	(52.7)	(53.5)	(46.8)
France	126.9	177.4	86.8	49.4	57.3	99.6
	(46.5)	(43.3)	(50.5)	(48.9)	(47.0)	(47.2)
Germany	108.7	56.6	36.9	8.6	2.6	42.7
	(56.1)	(198.3)	(21.1)	(36.0)	(12.9)	(64.9)
Italy	6.7	12.3	21.5	17.1	9.1	13.4
	(6.9)	(13.4)	(14.9)	(14.5)	(16.4)	(13.2)
Japan	22.7	31.6	38.3	32.3	28.8	30.7
	(12.7)	(8.3)	(6.2)	(9.2)	(6.3)	(8.6)
Mexico	1.5	1.0	4.4	0.9	1.4	1.8
	(13.2)	(16.6)	(26.8)	(14.7)	(10.8)	(16.4)
Netherlands	57.6	75.6	48.0	34.6	36.1	50.4
	(41.2)	(63.9)	(51.9)	(25.6)	(19.7)	(40.4)
Spain	42.1	54.7	33.1	31.5	23.4	36.9
	(15.8)	(37.5)	(28.0)	(35.9)	(25.6)	(28.6)
Sweden	21.9	40.7	6.4	10.7	17.4	19.4
	(60.9)	(23.2)	(11.9)	(11.6)	(3.3)	(22.2)
Switzerland	33.3	44.7	18.2	7.6	10.9	22.9
	(11.7)	(19.3)	(8.9)	(5.6)	(12.2)	(11.5)
United Kingdom	201.5	233.4	58.9	35.2	55.1	116.8
	(88.0)	(118.8)	(52.6)	(27.8)	(14.5)	(60.3)
United States	209.4	142.6	124.9	115.3	151.9	148.8
	(283.4)	(214.0)	(159.5)	(62.9)	(29.8)	(149.9)
World	1,092.3	1,186.8	721.5	596.5	612.2	841.9
	(1,086.8)	(1,388.0)	(817.6)	(678.8)	(559.6)	(906.1)

Source: Adapted from World Investment Report 2004, UNCTAD.

Exhibits 16.1 and 16.2 also show FDI *inflows* by country. During the five-year period 1999–2003, the United States received the largest amount of FDI inflows, $150 billion per year on average, among all countries. The next most popular destinations of FDI flows were Germany ($64.9 billion), the United Kingdom ($60.3 billion), France ($47.2 billion), China ($46.8 billion), the Netherlands ($40.4 billion), Canada ($29.3 billion), Spain ($28.6 billion), and Sweden ($22.2 billion). These 9 countries account for about 54 percent of the total worldwide FDI inflows, suggesting these countries must have locational advantages for FDI over other countries. In contrast to its substantial role as an originating country of FDI outflows, Japan plays a relatively minor role as a host of FDI inflows; Japan received only $8.6 billion worth of FDI, on average, per year during the period 1999–2003, reflecting a variety of legal, economic, and cultural barriers to foreign investment in Japan. It is noted that FDI flows declined in 2001–2003, reflecting a slowdown of the world economy.

值得注意的是，近年来流入中国的FDI迅速增长。

It is noteworthy that FDI flows into China have dramatically increased in recent years. The amount of inflow increased from $3.5 billion in 1990 to $53.5 billion in 2003. By 2003, China had emerged as the second most important host country for FDI, trailing only the United States. MNCs might have been lured to invest in China not

EXHIBIT 16.2

Average Foreign Direct Investment per Year during 1999–2003 (Billions of Dollars)

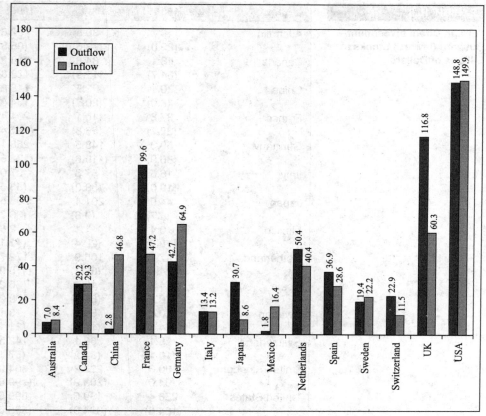

Source: Adapted from World Investment Report 2004, UNCTAD.

在发展中国家中，
墨西哥是另一个重要的
FDI流入国。

现在，我们再来看
看对**外直接投资**（FDI）
存量，即以往FDI流量的
累积数。

only by lower labor and material costs but also by the desire to preempt the entry of rivals into China's potentially huge market.

Among developing countries, Mexico is another country that experienced substantial FDI inflows, $16.4 billion on average per year. It is well known that MNCs are investing in Mexico, a low-cost country, to serve the North American as well as Mexican markets. It is also noteworthy that MNCs invested heavily, $28.6 billion per year, in Spain, where the costs of production are relatively low compared to other European countries such as France and Germany. Most likely, MNCs invested in Spain to gain a foothold in the huge single market created by the European Union, of which Spain is a member country.

Now, let us turn our attention to **FDI stocks,** which are the accumulation of previous FDI flows. The overall cross-border production activities of MNCs are best captured by FDI stocks. Exhibit 16.3 provides a summary of FDI stocks, both outward and inward, by country. As the exhibit shows, the total worldwide FDI stock, which was about $514 billion in 1980, rose to about $8,200 billion in 2003. In the case of the United States, FDI outward stock rose from $220 billion in 1980 to $2,069 billion in 2003. As of 2003, the United States, the U.K., France, Germany, the Netherlands, Japan, Switzerland, and Canada held the most outward FDI stocks. For FDI inward stock, on the other hand, the United States, the U.K., Germany, China, France, and the Netherlands are the most important hosts. Exhibit 16.4 shows the direction of FDI stocks among the three major economic centers, that is, the United States, the European Union, and Japan. Clearly, much of the FDI stocks are concentrated in these three major economic centers.

EXHIBIT 16.3					
Country	**1985**	**1990**	**1995**	**2000**	**2003**
Australia	6.7	30.5	52.8	98.8	117.1
	(25.0)	(73.6)	(95.8)	(108.7)	(174.2)
Canada	43.1	84.8	118.2	237.8	307.9
	(64.7)	(112.9)	(123.3)	(212.8)	(275.8)
China	0.1	2.5	15.8	25.8	37.0
	(6.0)	(20.7)	(134.9)	(348.3)	(501.5)
France	37.8	110.1	204.4	445.1	643.4
	(36.7)	(86.8)	(191.4)	(259.8)	(433.5)
Germany	59.9	148.5	258.1	483.9	622.5
	(36.9)	(119.6)	(192.9)	(470.9)	(544.6)
Italy	16.6	57.3	97.0	180.3	238.9
	(19.0)	(58.0)	(63.5)	(113.0)	(173.6)
Japan	44.0	201.4	238.5	278.4	335.5
	(4.7)	(9.8)	(36.7)	(50.3)	(89.7)
Mexico	0.4	1.1	2.6	7.5	13.8
	(18.8)	(22.4)	(41.1)	(97.2)	(165.9)
Netherlands	47.9	106.9	172.7	302.4	384.4
	(24.9)	(68.7)	(116.0)	(241.3)	(336.1)
Spain	4.5	15.7	36.2	159.9	207.5
	(8.9)	(65.9)	(109.2)	(144.9)	(230.3)
Sweden	10.8	50.7	73.1	123.2	189.3
	(4.3)	(12.6)	(31.1)	(94.0)	(143.2)
Switzerland	25.1	66.1	142.5	233.4	344.1
	(10.1)	(34.2)	(57.1)	(86.8)	(153.7)
United Kingdom	100.3	229.3	304.9	897.8	1,128.6
	(64.0)	(203.9)	(199.8)	(438.6)	(672.0)
United States	238.4	430.5	699.0	1,293.4	2,069.0
	(184.6)	(394.9)	(535.6)	(1,214.3)	(1,554.0)
World FDI Stock	738.8	1,758.2	2,897.6	5,983.3	8,196.9
	(972.2)	(1,950.3)	(2,992.1)	(6,089.9)	(8,245.1)

Foreign Direct Investment—Outward (Inward) Stocks in Billions of Dollars

Source: Adapted from World Investment Report 2004, UNCTAD.

Why Do Firms Invest Overseas?

为什么公司要选择在海外建厂生产，而不是直接从母公司出口或向东道国当地公司授权生产？

Why do firms locate production overseas rather than exporting from the home country or licensing production to a local firm in the host country? In other words, why do firms seek to extend corporate *control* overseas by forming multinational corporations? Unlike the theory of international trade or the theory of international portfolio investment, we do not have a well-developed, comprehensive theory of FDI. But several theories can shed light on certain aspects of the FDI phenomenon. Many of the existing theories, such as Kindleberger (1969) and Hymer (1976), emphasize various *market imperfections,* that is, imperfections in product, factor, and capital markets, as the key motivating forces driving FDI.

In what follows, we are going to discuss some of the key factors that are important in firms' decisions to invest overseas:

- Trade barriers
- Imperfect labor market
- Intangible assets
- Vertical integration
- Product life cycle
- Shareholder diversification services

EXHIBIT 16.4

FDI Stocks among the Triad and Economies In Which FDI from the Triad Dominates, 2001 (Billions of Dollars)

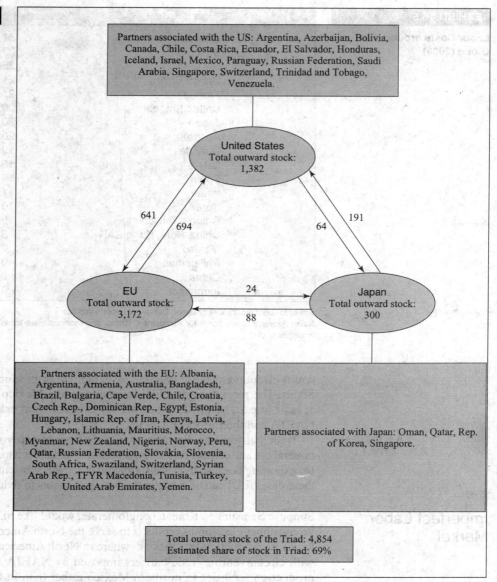

Partners associated with the US: Argentina, Azerbaijan, Bolivia, Canada, Chile, Costa Rica, Ecuador, El Salvador, Honduras, Iceland, Israel, Mexico, Paraguay, Russian Federation, Saudi Arabia, Singapore, Switzerland, Trinidad and Tobago, Venezuela.

United States
Total outward stock: 1,382

641   694   64   191

EU
Total outward stock: 3,172

24   88

Japan
Total outward stock: 300

Partners associated with the EU: Albania, Argentina, Armenia, Australia, Bangladesh, Brazil, Bulgaria, Cape Verde, Chile, Croatia, Czech Rep., Dominican Rep., Egypt, Estonia, Hungary, Islamic Rep. of Iran, Kenya, Latvia, Lebanon, Lithuania, Mauritius, Morocco, Myanmar, New Zealand, Nigeria, Norway, Peru, Qatar, Russian Federation, Slovakia, Slovenia, South Africa, Swaziland, Switzerland, Syrian Arab Rep., TFYR Macedonia, Tunisia, Turkey, United Arab Emirates, Yemen.

Partners associated with Japan: Oman, Qatar, Rep. of Korea, Singapore.

Total outward stock of the Triad: 4,854
Estimated share of stock in Triad: 69%

Source: UNCTAD, World Investment Report 2003; www.unctad.org/wir.
Note: Associate partners are the host economies in which the Triad member accounts for total FDI inward stocks or of total FDI inward flows within a 3-year average.

Trade Barriers

政府管制国际贸易往往是为了筹集税收、保护国内产业和实现其他经济政治目标。

面对出口贸易壁垒，公司可能决定将其生产转移到国外以规避贸易壁垒。

International markets for goods and services are often rendered imperfect by acts of governments. Governments may impose tariffs, quotas, and other restrictions on exports and imports of goods and services, hindering the free flow of these products across national boundaries. Sometimes, governments may even impose complete bans on the international trade of certain products. Governments regulate international trade to raise revenue, protect domestic industries, and pursue other economic policy objectives.

Facing barriers to exporting its products to foreign markets, a firm may decide to move production to foreign countries as a means of circumventing the trade barriers. A classic example for trade barrier–motivated FDI is Honda's investment in Ohio. Since the cars produced in Ohio would not be subject to U.S. tariffs and quotas, Honda

EXHIBIT 16.5

Labor Costs around the Globe (2003)

Region or Country	Average Hourly Cost ($)
Germany	31.25
Belgium	27.73
Sweden	25.18
United States	21.97
France	21.13
United Kingdom	20.37
Japan	20.09
Australia	20.05
Canada	19.28
Italy	18.35
Spain	14.96
Israel	11.73
Korea	10.28
China's Taiwan	5.84
China-Hong Kong SAR	5.54
Mexico	2.48
Philippines	0.66
China	0.60
Indonesia	0.22

Source: U.S. Department of Labor, Bureau of Labor Statistics.
Note: Average hourly costs for Philippines, China, and Indonesia are for 2001 and obtained from The Economist Intelligence Unit.

could circumvent these barriers by establishing production facilities in the United States. The recent surge in FDI in countries like Mexico and Spain can be explained, at least in part, by the desire of MNCs to circumvent external trade barriers set up by NAFTA and the European Union.

贸易壁垒也可能天生地来自运输成本。

Trade barriers can also arise *naturally* from transportation costs. Such products as mineral ore and cement that are bulky relative to their economic values may not be suitable for exporting because high transportation costs will substantially reduce profit margins. In these cases, FDI can be made in the foreign markets to reduce transportation costs.

Imperfect Labor Market

Suppose Samsung, a Korean conglomerate, would like to build production facilities for its consumer electronics products to serve the North American markets. Samsung could locate its production facilities anywhere in North America if the firm is concerned only with circumventing trade barriers imposed by NAFTA. Samsung chose to locate its production facilities in northern Mexico rather than in Canada or the United States, mainly because it wanted to take advantage of the lower costs of labor in Mexico.

在所有的要素市场中，劳动力市场是最不完善的。

Labor services in a country can be severely underpriced relative to its productivity because workers are not allowed to freely move across national boundaries to seek higher wages. Among all factor markets, the labor market is the most imperfect. Severe imperfections in the labor market lead to persistent wage differentials among countries. Exhibit 16.5 provides the hourly labor costs in the manufacturing sector for selected countries in 2003. Compared with Germany, hourly compensation for factory workers is about $16 less in Spain. The hourly compensation is only $2.48 in Mexico, compared with $21.97 in the U.S.

When workers are not mobile because of immigration barriers, firms themselves should move to the workers in order to benefit from the underpriced labor services. This is one of the main reasons MNCs are making FDIs in less developed countries such as Mexico, China, India, and Southeast Asian countries like Thailand, Malaysia, and Indonesia, where labor services are underpriced relative to their productivity. The recent surge in investment in China by companies from Japan, South Korea, and China's Taiwan can be attributable, in part, to the highly productive, low-cost workforces in China.

Intangible Assets

事实上，跨国公司
通常因其拥有无形资产
而享有比较优势。

内部化理论

Coca-Cola has invested in bottling plants all over the world rather than, say, licensing local firms to produce Coke. Coca-Cola chose FDI as a mode of entry into foreign markets for an obvious reason-it wanted to protect the formula for its famed soft drink. If Coca-Cola licenses a local firm to produce Coke, it has no guarantee that the secrets of the formula will be maintained. Once the formula is leaked to other local firms, they may come up with similar products, which will hurt Coca-Cola's sales. This possibility is known as the *boomerang* effect. In the 1960s, Coca-Cola, which had bottling plants in India, faced strong pressure from the Indian government to reveal the Coke formula as a condition for continued operations in India. Instead of revealing the formula, Coca-Cola chose to withdraw from India.[2]

MNCs may undertake overseas investment projects in a foreign country, despite the fact that local firms may enjoy inherent advantages. This implies that MNCs should have significant advantages over local firms. Indeed, MNCs often enjoy comparative advantages due to special **intangible assets** they possess. Examples include technological, managerial, and marketing know-how, superior R&D capabilities, and brand names. These intangible assets are often hard to package and sell to foreigners. In addition, the property rights in intangible assets are difficult to establish and protect, especially in foreign countries where legal recourse may not be readily available. As a result, firms may find it more profitable to establish foreign subsidiaries and capture returns directly by *internalizing* transactions in these assets. The internalization theory can help explain why MNCs, not local firms, undertake investment projects in foreign countries.

A strand of literature, including Caves (1982) and Magee (1977), places special emphasis on the role of market imperfections for intangible assets in motivating firms to undertake FDI. According to the **internalization theory** of FDI, firms that have intangible assets with a *public good* property tend to invest directly in foreign countries in order to use these assets on a larger scale and, at the same time, avoid the misappropriations of intangible assets that may occur while transacting in foreign markets through a market mechanism.[3]

Vertical Integration

一般而言，跨国公
司可能在那些原材料稳
定的国家进行对外直接
投资,以稳定原料的供应
和价格。

Suppose Royal Dutch Shell purchases a significant portion of crude oil for its refinery facilities from a Saudi oil company that owns the oil fields. In this situation, Royal Dutch Shell can experience a number of problems. For example, Royal Dutch Shell, the downstream firm, would like to hold the crude oil price down, whereas the Saudi oil company, an upstream firm, would like to push the price up. If the Saudi company has stronger bargaining power, Royal Dutch Shell may be forced to pay a higher price than it would like to, adversely affecting the firm's profits. In addition, as the world's demand for refined oil fluctuates, one of the two firms may have to bear excessive risk. The conflicts between the upstream and downstream firms can be resolved, however, if the two firms form a vertically integrated firm. Obviously, if Royal Dutch Shell controls the oil fields, the problems will disappear.

Generally speaking, MNCs may undertake FDI in countries where inputs are available in order to secure the supply of inputs at a stable price. Furthermore, if MNCs have monopolistic/oligopolistic control over the input market, this can serve as a barrier to entry to the industry. Many MNCs involved in extractive/natural resources industries tend to directly own oil fields, mine deposits, and forests for these reasons. Also, MNCs often find it profitable to locate manufacturing/processing facilities near the natural resources in order to save transportation costs. It would be costly to bring bulky bauxite ore to the home country and then extract the aluminum.

---

[2]Coca-Cola reentered the Indian market as India gradually liberalized its economy, improving the climate for foreign investments.

[3]Examples of public goods include public parks, lighthouses, and radio/TV broadcasting services. Once these goods are produced, it is difficult to preclude the public from using them, whether they are paying or not.

INTERNATIONAL FINANCE IN PRACTICE

Linear Sequence in Manufacturing: Singer & Company

Singer was one of the first United States–based companies that internationalized its operations. In August 1850, I.M. Singer invented a sewing machine and established I.M. Singer & Company in New York in 1851 to manufacture and sell the machines in the United States. To protect this innovative product, Singer had applied for and obtained domestic and some foreign patents by 1851. Until 1855, the company concentrated on fine-tuning its operations in the domestic market.

The first step towards internationalizing took place in 1855, when Singer & Co. sold its French patent for the single thread machine to a French merchant for a combination of lump-sum payment and royalties. This proved to be a bad experience for Singer as the French merchant was reluctant to pay royalties and handled competitors' products, leading to disputes and discouraging Singer from selling foreign patents to independent businesspersons. By 1856, Singer stopped granting territorial rights to independents in the domestic market due to bad experiences and began establishing its own sales outlets. Independent agents were not providing user instructions to buyers and failed to offer servicing. They were also reluctant to risk their capital by providing instalment payments as well as carrying large inventories.

Learning from its domestic problems, Singer used franchised agents as a mode of entry abroad; they sold and advertised the company's product in a given region. By 1858, Singer had independent businesspersons as foreign agents in Rio de Janeiro and elsewhere. Between September 1860 and May 1861, the company exported 127 machines to agents in Canada, Cuba, Curacao, Germany, Mexico, Peru, Puerto Rico, Uruguay, and Venezuela. Due to its domestic experience, Singer sped up the linear sequence, sometimes simultaneously using both franchised agents and its own sales outlets.

Singer also started extending its policy of establishing sales outlets to foreign markets. By 1861, it had salaried representatives in Glasgow and London. They established additional branches in England, to each of which the machines were sold on commission. By 1862, Singer was facing competition in England from imitators. Foreign sales of Singer machines increased steadily as the company was able to sell machines abroad at prices lower than in the United States because of the undervaluation of the dollar. In 1863, Singer opened a sales office in Hamburg, Germany, and later in Sweden. By 1866, the European demand for Singer machines surpassed supplies and competitors were taking advantage of Singer's inability to supply the machines. After the Civil War, the United States currency appreciated; at the same time, wages in the United States began to rise, increasing manufacturing costs and affecting firms' international competitiveness. As a result, some United States firms started establishing factories abroad.

In 1868, Singer established a small assembly factory in Glasgow, with parts imported from the United States. The venture proved to be successful and, by 1869, Singer decided to import tools from the United States to manufacture all parts in Glasgow. By 1874, partly due to the recession at home, Singer was selling more than half of its output abroad. Then, Singer started replacing locally financed independent agents with salaried-plus-commission agents. By 1879, its London regional headquarters had 26 offices in the United Kingdom and one each in Paris, Madrid, Brussels, Milan, Basel, Capetown, Bombay, and Auckland.

By the 1880s, the company had a strong foreign sales organization, with the London regional headquarters taking the responsibility for sales in Australia, Asia, Africa, the southern part of South America, the United Kingdom, and a large part of the European continent. The Hamburg office was in charge of northern and middle Europe, while the New York office looked after sales in the Caribbean, Mexico, the northern part of South America and Canada. By 1881, the capacity in Singer's three factories in Glasgow was insufficient to meet demand. Therefore, in 1882, Singer established a modern plant in Kilbowie near Glasgow with the latest United States machine tools and with a capacity equivalent to that of its largest factory in the United States. In 1883, Singer set up manufacturing plants in Canada and Australia. Through experience, Singer learned that it could manufacture more cost effectively in Scotland than in the United States for sales in Europe and other markets.

Source: World Investment Report 1996, UNCTAD, p. 77.

由于对外直接投资需要为跨国公司生产原材料的国外产业，所以纵向对外直接投资绝大多数都是后向的。但是，如果对外直接投资中包括销售跨国公司输出品的企业，那么对外直接投资就是前向的了。

Although the majority of vertical FDIs are *backward* in that FDI involves an industry abroad that produces inputs for MNCs, foreign investments can take the form of *forward* vertical FDI when they involve an industry abroad that sells a MNC's outputs. As is well known, U.S. car makers found it difficult to market their products in Japan. This is partly because most car dealers in Japan have a long and close business relationship with the Japanese car makers and are reluctant to carry foreign imports. To overcome this problem, U.S. car makers began to build their own network of dealerships in Japan to help sell their cars. This is an example of forward vertical FDI.

Product Life Cycle

产品生命周期理论

According to Raymond Vernon (1966), firms undertake FDI at a particular stage in the life cycle of the products that they initially introduced. Vernon observed that throughout the 20th century, the majority of new products, such as computers, televisions, and mass-produced cars, were developed by U.S. firms and first marketed in the United States. According to Vernon's **product life-cycle theory,** when U.S. firms first introduce new products, they choose to keep production facilities at home, close to customers. In the early stage of the product life cycle, the demand for the new product is relatively insensitive to the price and thus the pioneering firm can charge a relatively high price. At the same time, the firm can continuously improve the product based on feedback from its customers at home.

As demand for the new product develops in foreign countries, the pioneering U.S. firm begins to export to those countries. As the foreign demand for the product continues to grow, U.S. firms, as well as foreign firms, may be induced to start production in foreign countries to serve local markets. As the product becomes standardized and mature, it becomes important to cut the cost of production to stay competitive. A foreign producer operating in a low-cost country may start to export the product to the United States. At the same time, cost considerations may induce the U.S. firms to set up production facilities in a low-cost foreign country and export the product back to the United States. In other words, FDI takes place when the product reaches maturity and cost becomes an important consideration. FDI can thus be interpreted as a *defensive* move to maintain the firm's competitive position against its domestic and foreign rivals. The International Finance in Practice box "Linear Sequence in Manufacturing: Singer & Company" provides an interesting historical example supporting the product life-cycle view of FDI.

根据产品生命周期理论的预测，随着时间的推移，美国将从一个新产品的出口国变为进口国。

The product life-cycle theory predicts that over time the United States switches from an exporting country of new products to an importing country. The dynamic changes in the international trade pattern are illustrated in Exhibit 16.6. The prediction of the product life-cycle theory is consistent with the pattern of dynamic changes observed for many products. For instance, personal computers (PCs) were first developed by U.S. firms (such as IBM and Apple Computer) and exported to overseas markets. As PCs became a standardized commodity, however, the United States became a net importer of PCs from foreign producers based in such countries as Japan, Korea, and China's Taiwan, as well as foreign subsidiaries of U.S. firms.

It should be pointed out that Vernon's theory was developed in the 1960s when the United States was the unquestioned leader in R&D capabilities and product innovations. Increasingly, product innovations are taking place outside the United States as well, and new products are introduced simultaneously in many advanced countries. Production facilities may be located in multiple countries from the inception of a new product. The international system of production is becoming too complicated to be explained by a simple version of the product life-cycle theory.

Shareholder Diversification Services

资本市场的不完全性有可能促进公司的对外直接投资。

If investors cannot effectively diversify their portfolio holdings internationally because of barriers to cross-border capital flows, firms may be able to provide their shareholders with indirect diversification services by making direct investments in foreign countries. When a firm holds assets in many countries, the firm's cash flows are internationally diversified. Thus, shareholders of the firm can indirectly benefit from international diversification even if they are not directly holding foreign shares. Capital market imperfections thus may motivate firms to undertake FDI.

Although shareholders of MNCs may indirectly benefit from corporate international diversification, it is not clear that firms are motivated to undertake FDI for the purpose of providing shareholders with diversification services. Considering the fact that many barriers to international portfolio investments have been dismantled in recent years, enabling investors to diversify internationally by themselves, capital market imperfections as a motivating factor for FDI are likely to become less relevant.

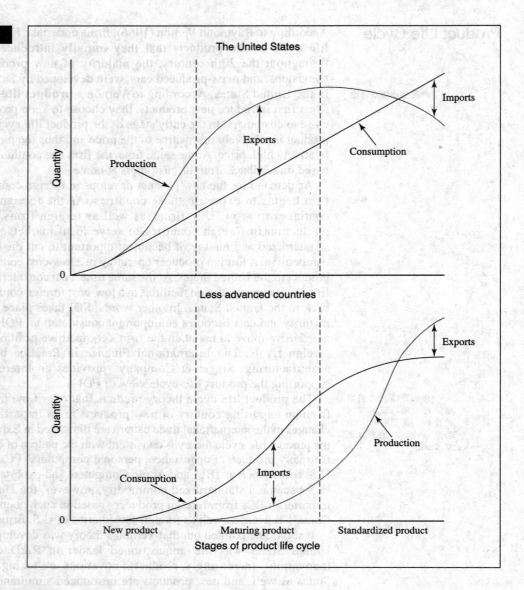

EXHIBIT 16.6

The Product Life Cycle

Cross-Border Mergers and Acquisitions

如前所述，对外直接投资既可以通过绿地投资，即在国外建立一家新的企业，也可以通过跨国并购，即合并或购买一家已经存在的外国企业来实现。

As previously mentioned, FDI can take place either through *greenfield investments,* which involve building new production facilities in a foreign country, or through *cross-border mergers and acquisitions,* which involve combining with or buying existing foreign businesses. In recent years, a growing portion of FDI has taken the form of cross-border mergers and acquisitions, accounting for more than 50 percent of FDI flows in terms of dollar amount. In 1998, for instance, British Petroleum purchased Amoco, a U.S. oil company, for $55 billion. Daimler-Benz of Germany acquired Chrysler, the third-largest U.S. car company, for $40.5 billion. And Hoechst, a major German pharmaceutical company, was acquired by Rhone-Poulenc SA (Life Sciences), a French company, for $21.2 billion. To top it all, Vodafone, a British telecommunication company, paid $203 billion to acquire Mannesmann, a major German company, in 2000. Exhibit 16.7 lists major cross-border mergers and acquisition (M&A) deals that were consummated during 1998–2003. The rapid increase in cross-border M&A deals can be attributed to the ongoing liberalization of capital markets and the integration of the world economy.

Firms may be motivated to engage in cross-border M&A deals to bolster their competitive positions in the world market by acquiring special assets from other firms or

EXHIBIT 16.7 **Top 40 Cross-Border M&A Deals Completed during 1998–2003**

No	Year	Deal Value ($ Billion)	Acquiring Company	Home Economy	Industry of the Acquiring Company	Acquired Company	Host Economy	Industry of the Acquired Company
1	2000	202.8	Vodafone AirTouch PLC	United Kingdom	Radiotelephone communications	Mannesmann AG	Germany	Radiotelephone communications
2	1999	60.3	Vodafone Group PLC	United Kingdom	Telecommunications	AirTouch Communications	United States	Telecommunications
3	1998	48.2	British Petroleum Co PLC (BP)	United Kingdom	Oil and gas; petroleum refining	Amoco Corp	United States	Oil and gas; petroleum refining
4	2000	46.0	France Telecom SA	France	Telephone communications, except radiotelephone	Orange PLC (Mannesmann AG)	United Kingdom	Telephone communications, except radiotelephone
5	1998	40.5	Daimler-Benz AG	Germany	Transportation equipment	Chrysler Corp	United States	Transportation equipment
6	2000	40.4	Vivendi SA	France	Water supply	Seagram Co Ltd	Canada	Motion picture and video tape production
7	1999	34.6	Zeneca Group PLC	United Kingdom	Drugs	Astra AB	Sweden	Drugs
8	1999	32.6	Mannesmann AG	Germany	Metal and metal products	Orange PLC	United Kingdom	Telecommunications
9	2001	29.4	Deutsche Telekom AG	Germany	Radiotelephone communications	VoiceStream Wireless Corp	United States	Radiotelephone communications
10	2000	27.2	BP Amoco PLC	United Kingdom	Petroleum refining	ARCO	United States	Petroleum refining
11	2000	25.1	Unilever PLC	United Kingdom	Creamery butter	Bestfoods	United States	Dried fruits, vegetables, and soup mixes
12	1999	21.9	Rhone-Poulenc SA	France	Chemicals and allied products	Hoechst AG	Germany	Chemicals and allied products
13	2000	19.4	Zurich Allied AG	Switzerland	Life insurance	Allied Zurich PLC	United Kingdom	Life insurance
14	1998	18.4	Zurich Versicherungs GmbH	Switzerland	Insurance	BAT Industries PLC-Financial	United Kingdom	Insurance
15	2000	16.5	UBS AG	Switzerland	Banks—non-US chartered	PaineWebber Group Inc	United States	Security brokers, dealers and flotation companies
16	2003	15.3	HSBC Holdings PLC (HSBC)	United Kingdom	Banks, non–US chartered	Household International Inc	United States	Personal credit institutions
17	2000	14.4	Vodafone AirTouch PLC	United Kingdom	Radiotelephone communications	Airtel SA	Spain	Radiotelephone communications
18	2001	13.8	British Telecommunications PLC	United Kingdom	Telephone communications, except radiotelephone	Viag Interkom GmbH & Co	Germany	Telephone communications, except radiotelephone
19	1999	13.6	Deutsche Telekom AG	Germany	Telecommunications	One 2 One	United Kingdom	Telecommunications
20	2000	13.5	Credit Suisse First Boston	United States	Security brokers, dealers and flotation companies	Donaldson Lufkin & Jenrette	United States	Commodity contracts brokers and dealers
21	1999	13.2	Repsol SA	Spain	Oil and gas; petroleum refining	YPF SA	Argentina	Oil and gas; petroleum refining
22	1999	12.6	Scottish Power PLC	United Kingdom	Electric, gas, and water distribution	Pacific Corp	United States	Electric, gas, and water distribution
23	2001	12.5	Citigroup Inc	United States	Commercial banks	Banacci	Mexico	Commercial banks
24	2001	12.5	Fortis(NL)NV	Netherlands	Life insurance	Fortis (B)	Belgium	Life insurance
25	2000	11.8	Cap Gemini SA	France	Business consulting services, nec	Ernst & Young-Consulting Bus.	United States	Business consulting services, nec
26	2001	11.5	Billiton PLC	United Kingdom	Miscellaneous metals ores	BHP Ltd	Australia	Steel works, blast furnaces, and rolling mills
27	2001	11.2	AXA Group (AXA-UAP)	France	Life insurance	AXA Financial Inc	United States	Life insurance
28	2001	11.1	DeBeers Consolidated Mines	South Africa	Miscellaneous nonmetallic minerals, except fuels	DB Investments	United Kingdom	Investors
29	2000	11.1	HSBC Holdings PLC	United Kingdom	Banks, non–US chartered	Credit Commercial deFrance	France	Banks, non–US chartered
30	2000	11.0	NTL Inc	United States	cable and other pay television services	CWC Consumer Co	United Kingdom	Telephone communications, except radiotelephone
31	1998	10.9	Texas Utilities Co	United States	Electric, gas, and water distribution	Energy Group PLC	United Kingdom	Electric, gas, and water distribution
32	1999	10.8	Wal-Mart Stores (UK) Ltd	United Kingdom	Investment and commodity firms, dealers, exchanges	ASDA Group PLC	United Kingdom	Retail trade-food stores
33	1999	10.8	Aegon NV	Netherlands	Insurance	Trans America Corp	United States	Insurance
34	2002	10.7	Vivendi Universal SA	France	Telephone communications, except radiotelephone	USA Networks Inc-Ent Asts	United States	Television broadcasting stations
35	2001	10.5	Nestlé SA	Switzerland	Food and beverages	Ralston Purina Co	United States	Dog, cat and pet food
36	2000	10.2	Telefonica SA	Spain	Telephone communications, except radiotelephone	Telecommunications de Sao Paulo	Brazil	Telephone communications, except radiotelephone
37	1998	10.2	Universal Studios Inc	United States	Motion picture production and distribution	PolyGram NV (Phillips Electrn)	Netherlands	Electronic and electrical equipment
38	1998	10.2	Roche Holding AG	Switzerland	Drugs	Corange Ltd	Bermuda	Drugs
39	1999	10.1	Global Crossing Ltd	Bermuda	Telecommunications	Frontier Corp	United States	Telecommunications
40	2001	9.8	NTT DoCoMo Inc	Japan	Telephone communications, except radiotelephone	AT&T Wireless Group	United States	Radiotelephone communications

Source: World Investment Report, various issues.

DaimlerChrysler: The First Global Car Colossus

By Bill Vlasic

The champagne was on ice at the Dorchester Hotel in London. Earlier in the day on May 6, the board of Chrysler Corp. and the management board of Daimler Benz approved a historic merger, creating a $130 billion automotive colossus known as DaimlerChrysler AG. The chief executives of two of the world's largest auto makers, Chrysler's Robert J. Eaton and Daimler's Jürgen Schrempp, strode across the room and sealed the largest merger in automotive history—and the third-largest deal ever—with a handshake. The mood was electric as the assembled executives prepared to pop the cork on a pact that would send shock waves around the world. "Both men were enormously energized," says a source close to the deal.

And why not? It looks like a marriage made in automotive heaven. In one bold stroke, the pending merger of Daimler and Chrysler dramatically changes the landscape of the global auto industry. By combining forces, Daimler, Germany's biggest industrial concern, and Chrysler, America's No. 3 carmaker, bring a range of hot-selling models and formidable financial muscle under one garage roof. Simply said, DaimlerChrysler is set to transform the way the auto industry operates worldwide.

The megadeal, which was set to be formally announced on May 7, unites two of the world's most profitable auto companies—with combined 1997 net earnings of $4.6 billion. And if ever a merger had the potential for that elusive quality —synergy—this could be the one. Mercedes-Benz passenger cars are synonymous with luxury and sterling engineering. Chrysler is renowned for its low-cost production of trucks, minivans, and sport-utility vehicles. Chrysler is almost wholly domestic, and Mercedes is increasing global sales—albeit within the confines of the luxury-car market. By spreading Chrysler's production expertise to Daimler operations and merging both product-development forces, the new company could cut costs by up to $3 billion annually—including $1.1 billion in purchasing costs, analysts say.

But DaimlerChrysler is about more than cutting costs and filling product and geographic gaps. It's about the emergence of a new category of global carmaker at a critical moment in the industry—when there is plant capacity to build at least 15 million more vehicles each year than will be sold. And overcapacity is expected to balloon to 18.2 million vehicles by 2002 as Asia continues to

decline, predicts Standard & Poor's DRI, a division of The McGraw-Hill Companies. Consolidation is inevitable; from about 40 auto companies now, to about 20 in the next century, says DRI analyst Sam Fiorani.

DaimlerChrysler, then, may be the first member of the 21st century 20. "The Mercedes-Chrysler deal sanctions the concept of auto mergers and is a major catalyst for more," says Joseph S. Phillippi, auto analyst for Lehman Brothers Inc. Eaton, in an Apr. 27 interview with BusinessWeek, predicted that Western auto makers with the wherewithal would snap up the troubled auto makers of South Korea and Southeast Asia. General Motors Corp., for example, is considering a big stake in Korea's beleaguered Daewoo. In Europe, auto makers such as Volvo, Fiat, PSA (Peugeot/Citröen), and Renault are ripe for takeover.

DaimlerChrysler will have the wherewithal. It will have $130 billion in annual sales and assets totaling $120 billion. It will have factories on four continents.

Indeed, both partners were giants in their own right. So why merge? Top executives at the two companies came to realize that if they continue to go it alone, their companies could survive as strong regional players—but might be forced onto the shoulder in a global industry. "There are world forces at work that are driving consolidation," Eaton said in the April interview. "Two factors are huge: the worldwide excess capacity in autos and the Asian economic crisis."

Eaton and Schrempp hatched their stunning plan in secret meetings over the past nine months in Germany and Detroit. Daimler was represented by Goldman, Sachs & Co. and Deutsche Bank, while CS First Boston represented Chrysler. The estimated $40 billion deal is being financed by a stock swap of two Chrysler shares for every one Daimler share. It will leave Chrysler shareholders with 43% of the combined entity, while Daimler stockholders control 57%, say sources familiar with the deal. That will make DaimlerChrysler a German company for tax and accounting benefits, these sources say.

But the company will have dual headquarters. A source close to Daimler says that Daimler and Chrysler headquarters will remain in Stuttgart and Auburn Hills, Mich., for

using their own assets on a larger scale. As a mode of FDI entry, cross-border M&As offer two key advantages over greenfield investments: speed and access to proprietary assets. A recent United Nations study aptly discusses why firms choose M&As as a mode of investment.[4]

Mergers and acquisitions are a popular mode of investment for firms wishing to protect, consolidate and advance their global competitive positions, by selling off divisions that fall

---

[4]Source: *World Investment Report 1996*, UNCTAD, p. 7.

some time to come. "Can you imagine Daimler leaving Stuttgart? Can you imagine Chrysler leaving Detroit?" It will also have CO-CEOS—to start. After three years, however, Eaton is expected to retire, allowing Schrempp to take full control, say sources familiar with the arrangement.

Investors immediately applauded—pushing Chrysler shares up 7³⁄₈ to 48¹³⁄₁₆ on May 6. "Chrysler has the trucks, vans, and SUVs, and Daimler has the luxury cars," says Seth M. Glickenhaus of Glickenhaus & Co., an investment firm that holds 8 million Chrysler shares. "There are enormous synergies in product."

One of the biggest opportunities is for the paired company to plunge into new markets that neither could assay alone. Neither has much of a presence in Latin America or Asia, although Daimler does sell heavy trucks there. Chrysler's inexpensive small cars will give Daimler a vehicle to drive into emerging markets. "With our [upscale] product portfolio, we will never be a mass marketer," says a source close to Daimler. "There are some markets where [Mercedes] will never be able to have an impact."

The first venture of the new merged company likely will be a barebones little car, smaller than Chrysler's subcompact Neon model, to sell in Asia and Latin America. "We would like a sub-Neon vehicle for the international market," says Eaton. "We started looking at projects four years ago, and it's something we're looking at harder now." Ironically, such a car may be powered by engines to be made in Brazil in a joint venture between Chrysler and BMW—Mercedes' archival in Germany. BMW declines to comment on the DaimlerChrysler union.

Indeed, most rivals are too stunned to react. Both Ford and GM declined to comment. On the other hand, many industry watchers immediately questioned whether the enormously divergent cultures of Auburn Hills and Stuttgart won't get in the way of all that synergy. "I can't imagine two more different cultures," says Furman Selz auto analyst Maryann N. Keller.

Chrysler's brushes with bankruptcy forged a culture dedicated to speedy product development, lean operations, and flashy design. Daimler remains a buttoned-down, engineering-driven bureaucracy known for conservatively styled products. "The reaction here is shock, excitement, enthusiasm, and concern," says one Chrysler exec.

Schrempp and Eaton are certainly an odd couple. Eaton, 58, is a Kansas-born engineer who worked his way up the ranks at GM before replacing Lee Iacocca as Chrysler chairman in 1993. His soft-spoken manner belies his reputation as a savvy manager. When he took the job at Chrysler, Motown observers expected that his rival, Robert A. Lutz, would bolt. Yet Eaton and Lutz came together to drive Chrysler to record sales and profits. Lutz, 66, now vice-chairman, is expected to retire soon.

Schrempp, who once trained as an auto mechanic, is also an engineer who climbed the corporate ladder to become CEO in 1995 after 28 years with Daimler. After he won the top post, he forced out his rival for the job, Helmut Werner, who had engineered a turnaround with hot products, like the M-class sport utility vehicles and SLK roadster, and youthful, irreverent marketing.

Can Chrysler and Mercedes live together? It could be tough because they will want to protect their vastly different brands. The Mercedes network "is not the kind of distribution system that Chrysler wants or needs, or even could use," says Keller. Nor is it likely that a Mercedes sedan will one day roll down a Chrysler line. "People buy Mercedes because they think they're made by guys in white coats," says Keller. "That image better not be contaminated by the idea that it's being built by a bunch of guys in Indiana."

So how will Chrysler and Mercedes help each other without losing their identities? Chrysler's slowly improving quality could take a quantum leap forward with help from Daimler engineers. And Daimler's diesel engines, for example, could help Chrysler in its efforts to sell subcompacts and minivans in Europe and elsewhere. Chrysler, for its part, has the industry's best supplier relations, while Daimler still relies on strong-arm techniques to get lower prices from its suppliers. Together, they can save on warehousing and logistics for cars and spare parts in both Europe and the U.S. They also can jointly make internal components like air-conditioning systems and door latches and pool their resources in developing basic technology.

Well before anyone knows if DaimlerChrysler is a success, however, its very existence could reshape the industry. Look for auto makers to scramble for partners to ensure survival as one of the 21st century 20. How that plays out is anybody's guess. "The odd man out here seems to be the Japanese," says Phillippi of Lehman Brothers. "Nissan and Honda in particular have only two legs to stand on: North America and Japan." That won't be enough in this race.

Source: BusinessWeek, May 18, 1998, pp. 40–43. Reprinted with permission.

outside the scope of their core competence and acquiring strategic assets that enhance their competitiveness. For those firms, "ownership" assets acquired from another firm, such as technical competence, established brand names, and existing supplier networks and distribution systems, can be put to immediate use towards better serving global customers, enhancing profits, expanding market share and increasing corporate competitiveness by employing international production networks more efficiently.

The International Finance in Practice box "DaimlerChrysler: The First Global Car Colossus" provides a real-world example involving the merger deal between Daimler, a German car company, and Chrysler, the third-largest U.S. car maker. As mentioned in the box, the combined company expects to cut costs by as much as $3 billion annually and fill product and geographic gaps. Anticipating the synergistic gains, stock prices of both companies rose upon the announcement of a $40.5 billion deal.

Cross-border acquisitions of businesses are a politically sensitive issue, as most countries prefer to retain local control of domestic firms. As a result, although countries may welcome greenfield investments, as they are viewed as representing new investment and employment opportunities, foreign firms' bids to acquire domestic firms are often resisted and sometimes even resented. Whether or not cross-border acquisitions produce **synergistic gains** and how such gains are divided between acquiring and target firms are thus important issues from the perspective of shareholder welfare and public policy. Synergistic gains are obtained when the value of the combined firm is greater than the stand-alone valuations of the individual (acquiring and target) firms.[5] If cross-border acquisitions generate synergistic gains and both the acquiring and target shareholders gain wealth at the same time, one can argue that cross-border acquisitions are mutually beneficial and thus should not be thwarted both from a national and global perspective.

Synergistic gains may or may not arise from cross-border acquisitions, depending on the motive of acquiring firms. In general, gains will result when the acquirer is motivated to take advantage of the market imperfections mentioned earlier. In other words, firms may decide to acquire foreign firms to take advantage of mispriced factors of production and to cope with trade barriers.

As previously mentioned, imperfections in the market for *intangible assets* can also play a major role in motivating firms to undertake cross-border acquisitions. According to the internalization theory, a firm with intangible assets that have a public good property such as technical and managerial know-how may acquire foreign firms as a platform for using its special assets on a larger scale and, at the same time, avoid the misappropriation that may occur while transacting in foreign markets through a market mechanism. Cross-border acquisitions may also be motivated by the acquirer's desire to acquire and internalize the target firm's intangible assets. In this *backward-internalization* case, the acquirer seeks to create wealth by appropriating the rent generated from the economy of scale obtained from using the target's intangible assets on a global basis. The internalization thus may proceed *forward* to internalize the acquirer's assets, or *backward* to internalize the target's assets.

Reflecting the increased importance of cross-border acquisitions as a mode of FDI, several researchers investigated the effects of cross-border acquisitions. Doukas and Travlos (1988) investigated the impact of international acquisitions on the stock prices of U.S. bidding firms. The study shows that shareholders of U.S. bidders experience significant positive abnormal returns when firms expand into new industries and geographic markets. When firms already have operations in the target firm's country, U.S. shareholders experience no significant abnormal returns. Harris and Ravenscraft (1991), on the other hand, studied shareholder wealth gains for U.S. firms acquired by foreign firms. They conclude that U.S. targets experience higher wealth gains when they are acquired by foreign firms than when acquired by U.S. firms.

Morck and Yeung (1992) also investigate the effect of international acquisitions on the stock prices of U.S. firms. They show that U.S. acquiring firms with information-based intangible assets experience a significantly positive stock price reaction upon foreign acquisition. This is consistent with the findings of their earlier work (1991) that the market value of the firm is positively related to its multinationality because of the firm's intangible assets, such as R&D capabilities, with public good nature. It is not the multinationality per se that contributes to the firm's value. Their empirical findings support the (forward-) internalization theory of FDI.

---

[5]Synergistic gains may arise if the combined companies can save on the costs of production, marketing, distribution, and R&D and redeploy the combined assets to the highest-value projects.

利润增值效应

换句话说，公司可能为了利用低价的生产要素或规避贸易壁垒而收购国外公司。

考虑到跨国收购在对外直接投资中占据着越来越重要的地位，一些研究人员开始研究跨国收购的效果。

EXHIBIT 16.8		Average Wealth Gains from Cross-Border Acquisitions: Foreign Acquisitions of U.S. Firms				
Country of Acquirer	Number of Cases	R&D/Sales (%)		Average Wealth Gains (in Million U.S.$)		
		Acquirer	Target	Acquirer	Target	Combined
Canada	10	0.21	0.65	14.93	85.59	100.53
Japan	15	5.08	4.81	227.83	170.66	398.49
U.K.	46	1.11	2.18	−122.91	94.55	−28.36
Other	32	1.63	2.80	−47.46	89.48	42.02
All	103	1.66	2.54	−35.01	103.19	68.18

Source: Reprinted from Journal of Banking and Finance 20, C. Eun, R. Kolodny, and C. Scheraga, "Cross-Border Acquisitions and Shareholder Wealth: Tests of the Synergy and Internalization Hypotheses," pp. 1559–82, ©1996 with kind permission from Elsevier Science-NL, Sara Burgerhartstreet 25, 1055 KV Amsterdam, The Netherlands.

Eun, Kolodny, and Scheraga (1996), on the other hand, directly measure the magnitude of shareholders' gains from cross-border acquisitions, using a sample of major foreign acquisitions of U.S. firms that took place during the period 1979–90. Their findings are summarized in Exhibit 16.8. First, the exhibit shows that U.S. target shareholders realized significant wealth gains, $103 million on average, regardless of the nationality of acquirers. Second, the wealth gains to foreign acquiring shareholders, however, varied greatly across acquiring countries. Shareholders of British acquirers experienced significant wealth reduction, −$123 million on average, whereas Japanese shareholders experienced major wealth increases, $228 million on average. Canadian acquisitions of U.S. firms produced modest wealth increases for their shareholders, $15 million on average.

Third, cross-border acquisitions are generally found to be synergy-generating corporate activities. Shareholders of the "paired" sample of U.S. targets and foreign acquirers experienced positive combined wealth gains, $68 million, on average. Synergistic gains, however, vary a great deal across acquiring countries. Japanese acquisitions generated large combined gains, $398 million, on average, which were shared by target shareholders (43 percent) and acquiring shareholders (57 percent).[6] In contrast, British acquisitions produced a somewhat negative combined wealth gain, −$28 million on average, and caused a wealth transfer from acquiring to target shareholders.

Eun、Kolodny和 Scheraga认为，日本收购者的巨大收益可以归功于对其目标公司的研发能力的成功内部化，其平均研发能力远高于其他国家的收购者。

Eun, Kolodny, and Scheraga argue that the significant gains for Japanese acquirers can be attributed to the successful internalization of the R&D capabilities of their targets, which have a much higher R&D intensity on average than the targets of acquirers from other countries. Thus, the desire to "backward" internalize the target's intangible assets appears to be an important driving force for Japanese acquisition programs in the United States. This supports the backward-internalization hypothesis.[7] In the case of British acquisitions, the average combined wealth gain was negative, and the acquiring shareholders lost substantial wealth. It thus appears that the managers of British firms often undertook negative NPV projects when they acquired U.S. firms. It is well known that corporate acquisitions can be driven by managers who pursue growth and diversification at the expense of shareholders' interests. As Jensen pointed out (1986), managers may benefit by expanding the firm beyond the size that maximizes shareholder wealth for various reasons.[8]

[6]This result is quite different from the findings of studies of domestic acquisitions showing that target shareholders capture the lion's share of synergistic gains.

[7]Japanese acquirers themselves are highly R&D intensive. This suggests that Japanese acquisitions of U.S. firms may generate technological synergies, and that Japanese firms may be capable of using U.S. target firms' technical know-how.

[8]For example, managers' payments are often positively related to the size of the assets they control, not just profits.

Stories Past and Present

An old story: Brazilian Tramways

The first electric trams in Brazil were built in 1891 by Thomson-Houston Company of Lynn, Massachusetts, which the following year became the General Electric Company. GE went on to build most of the early electric lines in Brazil and throughout Latin America, often retaining ownership. Other players soon entered the field, and, by 1907, a Canadian group had created South America's first great tramway empire, holding most of the lines in Rio de Janeiro and São Paulo as well as an assortment of telephone, gas, and water companies. The Canadians were bitterly and publicly opposed by a powerful Brazilian family, the Guinles, who also sought control of utilities in the major cities. The dispute profoundly affected the attitudes of Brazilians toward foreign-owned tramways. As a result of street riots and large-scale destruction of equipment in the city of Salvador, the Canadians curtailed their expansion efforts and in 1912 consolidated their assets into Brazilian Traction, Light & Power.

American & Foreign Power, the GE affiliate, eventually joined the fray and acquired 333 utilities in Brazil alone, with tramway systems in 13 Brazilian cities. By 1933, however, rising anti-Yankee sentiment led to freezing of tram fares at their 1909 level. A number of small companies shut down. Others switched to closed cars to increase fare collections. These cars were distinctly unpopular with riders because of the heat (and perhaps because of the better fare collection).

Still, on the eve of World War II, North American companies operated roughly two-thirds of Brazil's tramway systems. The lethal combination of parts shortages, increased hydroelectric power costs, and the effect of inflation on fixed fares led companies to cut back on service and, in some cases, to leave the business. In 1947, Brazilian Traction sold its São Paulo system to the municipal transport board, which then proceeded to raise fares by 250%. Rioting citizens pleaded for the foreigners and low rates. But, by 1950, a new president had vowed to rid Brazil of foreign corporations. AFP and most other foreign investors were quite willing by this point to sell their unprofitable tram systems to the Brazilians. By 1960, only Brazilian Traction's Rio system remained foreign owned; this last holdout went the way of the rest when it was acquired by the state in January 1965.

A recent story: Bangkok Toll Road

To help relieve Bangkok's horrible traffic congestion, a Japanese-led consortium was granted a 30-year concession to build a 12-mile toll road in the city. Just as part of the road was about to be opened in 1993, the Thai Expressway and Rapid Transit Authority (ETA) balked at the 30-baht toll that had been specified in the contract. Hesitating to absorb the proposed 10-baht toll reduction, the private consortium delayed opening the completed sections of road, and it halted further construction when its lenders suspended credit. Claiming to fear riots on the part of frustrated motorists who were angered at being unable to use the expressway, the ETA obtained a court order to force the road open and insisted on reopening negotiations to settle this and a number of other outstanding issues. Kumagai Gumi, the lead investor, reportedly with more than $100 million exposure, and its bankers, with still more at stake, cried foul, publicly accusing the Thai government of nationalizing the project. Eventually, Kumagai sold its 65% interest. And all this occurred in a country that is viewed as being very hospitable to foreign direct investment.

Source: Reprinted by permission of Harvard Business Review. From "Is Foreign Infrastructure Still Risky?" by Louis T. Wells and Eric S. Gleason, Sept./Oct. 1995. ©1995 by the President and Fellows of Harvard College; all rights reserved.

Political Risk and FDI

政治风险指因东道国的不利的政治走势而引起的对母公司的潜在损失。

In assessing investment opportunities in a foreign country, it is important for a parent firm to take into consideration the risk arising from the fact that investments are located in a foreign country. A sovereign country can take various actions that may adversely affect the interests of MNCs. In this section, we are going to discuss how to measure and manage **political risk,** which refers to the potential losses to the parent firm resulting from adverse political developments in the host country. Political risks range from the outright expropriation of foreign assets to unexpected changes in the tax laws that hurt the profitability of foreign projects.

Political risk that firms face can differ in terms of the incidence as well as the manner in which political events affect them. Depending on the incidence, political risk can be classified into two types:

1. *Macro risk,* where all foreign operations are affected by adverse political developments in the host country.
2. *Micro risk,* where only selected areas of foreign business operations or particular foreign firms are affected.

The predicament of Enron in Endia, Which we will discuss shortly, is an example of micro risk.

Depending on the manner in which firms are affected, political risk can be classified into three types:[9]

1. *Transfer risk,* which arises from uncertainty about cross-border flows of capital, payments, know-how, and the like.
2. *Operational risk,* which is associated with uncertainty about the host country's policies affecting the local operations of MNCs.
3. *Control risk,* which arises from uncertainty about the host country's policy regarding ownership and control of local operations.

Examples of transfer risk include the unexpected imposition of capital controls, inbound or outbound, and withholding taxes on dividend and interest payments. Examples for operational risk, on the other hand, include unexpected changes in environmental policies, sourcing/local content requirements, minimum wage law, and restriction on access to local credit facilities. Lastly, examples of control risk include restrictions imposed on the maximum ownership share by foreigners, mandatory transfer of ownership to local firms over a certain period of time (fade-out requirements), and the nationalization of local operations of MNCs.

近代史上发生过很多政治风险的例子。

Recent history is replete with examples of political risk. For example, when Gamal Nasser seized power in Egypt in the early 1950s, he nationalized the Suez Canal, which was controlled by British and French interests. Politically, this move was immensely popular throughout the Arab world. The International Finance in Practice box "Stories Past and Present" provides other historical examples showing how foreign investments can be decimated by nationalistic actions in a host country.

As Exhibit 16.9 shows, the frequency of expropriations of foreign-owned assets peaked in the 1970s, when as many as 30 countries were involved in expropriations each year. Since then, however, expropriations have dwindled to practically nothing. This change reflects the popularity of *privatization,* which, in turn, is attributable to widespread failures of state-run enterprises and mounting government debts around the world.

This, however, does not mean that political risk is a thing of the past. In 1992, the Enron Development Corporation, a subsidiary of the Houston-based energy company, signed a contract to build the largest-ever power plant in India, requiring a total investment of $2.8 billion. Severe power shortages have been one of the bottlenecks hindering India's economic growth. After Enron had spent nearly $300 million, the project was canceled by Hindu nationalist politicians in the Maharashtra state where the plant was to be built. Subsequently, Maharashtra invited Enron to renegotiate its contract. If Enron had agreed to renegotiate, it may have had to accept a lower profitability for the project. As can be seen from the Enron fiasco, the lack of an effective means of enforcing contracts in a foreign country is clearly a major source of political risk associated with FDI.

政治风险并不容易测量。

Political risk is not easy to measure. When Enron signed the contract to build a power plant in India, it perhaps could not have anticipated the victory of the Hindu

---

[9]Our discussion here draws on Kobrin (1979) and Root (1972).

Frequency of Expropriations of Foreign-Owned Assets

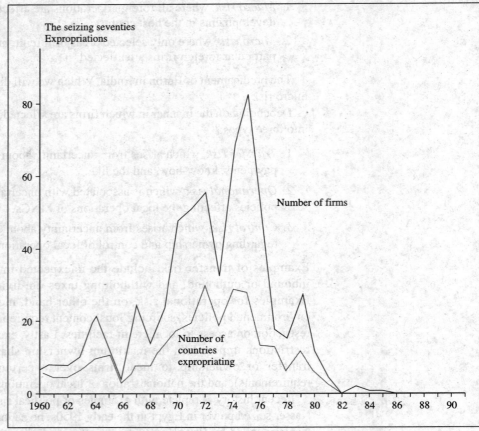

The seizing seventies
Expropriations

Number of firms

Number of countries expropriating

Source: The Economist, March 27, 1993, p. 19. ©1993 The Economist Newspaper Group, Inc. Reprinted with permission.

政治风险分析专家会对一些关键因素进行评估。

nationalist party. Difficult as it may be, MNCs still have to measure political risk for foreign projects under consideration. Experts of political risk analysis evaluate, often subjectively, a set of key factors such as:[10]

- *The host country's political and government system:* Whether the host country has a political and administrative infrastructure that allows for effective and streamlined policy decisions has important implications for political risk. If a country has too many political parties and frequent changes in government (like Italy, for example), government policies may become inconsistent and discontinuous, creating political risk.

- *Track records of political parties and their relative strength:* Examination of the ideological orientations and historical track records of political parties would reveal a great deal about how they would run the economy. If a party has a strong nationalistic ideology and/or socialist beliefs, it may implement policies that are detrimental to foreign interests. On the other hand, a party that subscribes to a liberal and market-oriented ideology is not very likely to take actions to damage the interests of foreign concerns. If the former party is more popular than the latter party and thus more likely to win the next general election, MNCs will bear more political risk.

---

[10]Our discussion here draws heavily on Morgan Stanley's system of evaluating political risk.

- *Integration into the world system:* If a country is politically and economically isolated and segmented from the rest of the world, it would be less willing to observe the rules of the game. North Korea, Iraq, Libya, and Cuba are examples. If a country is a member of major international organizations, such as the EU, OECD, and WTO, it is more likely to abide by the rules of the game, reducing political risk. In the same vein, as China joins the World Trade Organization (WTO), MNCs operating in China may face less political risk.

- *The host country's ethnic and religious stability:* As can be seen from the civil war in Bosnia, domestic peace can be shattered by ethnic and religious conflicts, causing political risk for foreign business. Additional examples are provided by Nigeria, Rwanda, Northern Ireland, Turkey, Israel, Sri Lanka, and Quebec.

- *Regional security:* Real and potential aggression from a neighboring country is obviously a major source of political risk. Kuwait is an example. Countries like South Korea and Taiwan may potentially face the same risk depending on the future course of political developments in East Asia. Israel and its Arab neighbors still face this risk as well.

- *Key economic indicators:* Often political events are triggered by economic situations. Political risk thus is not entirely independent of economic risk. For example, persistent trade deficits may induce a host country's government to delay or stop interest payments to foreign lenders, erect trade barriers, or suspend the convertibility of the local currency, causing major difficulties for MNCs. Severe inequality in income distribution (for example, in many Latin American countries) and deteriorating living standards (as in Russia after the collapse of the Soviet Union) can cause major political disturbances. Argentina's protracted economic recession and the eventual collapse of the peso–dollar parity led to the freezing of bank deposits, street riots, and three changes of the country's presidency in as many months in 2002.

跨国公司常常使用外部专家来对不同国家的政治风险进行专业评估。

MNCs may use in-house experts to do the analysis. But often, MNCs use outside experts who provide professional assessments of political risks in different countries. For example, Morgan Stanley offers an in-depth analysis of country/ political risks using a variety of data sources, including government and private sector publications, statistics provided by international organizations, newspaper articles, and on-site due diligence in countries with government officials and the private sector. Exhibits 16.10 and 16.11 provide such an analysis for two countries, South Korea and Hungary, both of which became full-fledged democracies in the last decade. The exhibits provide an example of how political risk analysis may be conducted.

www.euromoney.com/index.html

Provides data and articles from Euromoney.

国家风险是一个比政治风险更宽泛的指标，包括政治风险、信用风险和其他经济业绩。

Euromoney also provides such an assessment twice a year.[11] As Exhibit 16.12 shows, *Euromoney* provides country ratings by political risk, credit rating, economic performance, and other factors. It also provides the overall country risk ranking based on an opinion poll of economists and political analysts, plus market data and debt figures. **Country risk** is a broader measure of risk than political risk, as the former encompasses political risk, credit risk, and other economic performances. As of 2005, countries like Switzerland, Norway, and Luxembourg were considered practically free of political risk. In contrast, countries like Israel, India, Mexico, Russia, and Brazil were rated as having substantial political risk, while countries such as Argentina, Indonesia, and Zimbabwe were rated as among the most politically risky countries. Exhibit 16.12 shows that the ranking of countries by political risk closely coincides with that by overall country risk.

---

[11]Each year, *Euromoney* publishes its country risk ranking in the March and September issues.

EXHIBIT 16.10 | **Political Risk Analysis: South Korea**

Moody's: A1; S&P: A+, Outlook: Positive

Strengths	Weaknesses

Political
- Smooth transition to democracy (1987).
- Integrated into global and regional organizations.

Political
- Still a young democracy.
- More radical opposition party.
- Cost of potential unification with North Korea.
- Difficult labor relations.
- Anti-Western sentiment among students.

Economic
- Well-diversified economy.
- Strong manufacturing sector.
- Fast growth.
- Prudent fiscal management.
- Low unemployment.
- Well-diversified and competitive exports.
- Increasing foreign investment.
- Very favorable debt profile.

Economic
- Lacks natural resources and oil.
- Some foreign exchange controls.
- Financial sector needs reforms.
- Low foreign exchange reserves.
- Wage hikes eroding competitiveness.

Key Ratios (%)	1987	1988	1989	1990	1991
External Debt/Current Account Earnings	63	44	40	41	46
Debt Service/Current Account Earnings	17	10	9	11	10
Current Account Balance/GDP	7.5	8.1	2.4	−0.9	−3.1
Import Cover (Mos.)	1.1	3.1	3.2	2.7	2.2
Budget Balance (% of GDP)	1.5	2.1	0.3	0.4	−1.1

Source: IFS, World Bank Debt Tables, IIF, Monthly Statistical Bulletin of the Bank of Korea, Morgan Stanley Credit Research.

South Korea's economy is one of the most dynamic in the world. Economic fundamentals remain strong, and a well-developed industry geared toward exports has made South Korea's economy one of the fastest growing in the world during the past decade. Exports are diversified and competitive, and foreign portfolio investment has increased greatly following recent financial deregulation and easing of foreign exchange controls. Sound fiscal policy is evidenced by budget surpluses, unemployment is low and, by developing country standards, inflation is moderate. External debt at US$39 billion, or 46% of current account earnings, and the debt service ratio of 10% are very favorable. The country's few weaknesses include a lack of natural resources, dependence on imported oil and a financial system that needs to be deregulated, modernized and brought to world standards. The development of the financial sector is a requirement for the further development of the domestic economy and export sector and more effective macroeconomic management.

It is in the political area that the greatest risks lie. Despite great progress (a smooth transition to democracy through presidential elections in 1987), at times the political climate is uncertain as South Korea is still a young democracy and the main opposition party is radical. Anti-Western sentiment is prevalent among students and some labor demonstrators. Labor relations have been difficult, with major strikes occurring every spring. Although the military threat from North Korea has significantly diminished, the financial and social cost of a prospective reunification can be great. Finally, per capita income is still well below that of developed countries.

首先，当面对政治风险时，跨国公司可以对国外投资项目采用保守的方法。

Let us now turn to the issue of how to manage political risk. First, MNCs can take a conservative approach to foreign investment projects when faced with political risk. When a foreign project is exposed to political risk, the MNC can explicitly incorporate political risk into the capital budgeting process and adjust the project's NPV accordingly. The firm may do so either by reducing expected cash flows or by increasing the cost of capital. The MNC may undertake the foreign project only when the adjusted NPV is positive. It is important here to recognize that political risk may be diversifiable to some extent. Suppose that a MNC has assets in, say, 30 different countries. Since the political risks in different countries may not be positively correlated, the political risk associated with a single country may be diversifiable to some extent. To the extent that political risk is diversifiable, a major adjustment to the NPV may not be necessary. This consideration also suggests that MNCs can use geographic diversification of foreign investments as a means of reducing political risk. Put simply, don't put all your eggs in one basket.

EXHIBIT 16.11	Political Risk Analysis: Hungary

Moody's: Ba1; S&P: BB+, Outlook: Positive

Strengths	Weaknesses
Political	
• Smooth transition to multiparty system.	• Located in an unstable region.
• Pro-reform government and opposition.	• Uncertainty about relations with Slovakia.
• Associate member of the EEC.	
• Ethnically homogeneous.	
• Labor is accommodative of reform.	
Economic	
• Economic reform progressing rapidly.	• Reliance on imported oil.
• Much-eased foreign exchange controls.	• Major economic restructuring to be completed.
• Significantly liberalized trade system.	• Poor budgetary performance.
• Successful redirection of trade from East to West.	• High and growing unemployment.
• OECD accounts for 70% of trade.	
• Rapid accumulation of foreign exchange reserves.	
• Improved current account performance.	
• Rapid increase in foreign investment.	
• Rapidly improving debt profile.	

Key Ratios (%)	1987	1988	1989	1990	1991
External Debt/Current Account Earnings	327	299	266	218	177
Debt Service/Current Account Earnings	63	54	47	44	32
Current Account Balance/GDP	−3.4	−2.9	−5.0	0.8	0.8
Import Cover (Mos.)	3.9	3.5	2.5	2.1	5.2
Budget Balance (% of GDP)	−3.3	−0.2	−2.1	0.9	−4.1

Source: IFS, World Bank Debt Tables, IIF, National Bank of Hungary, Morgan Stanley Credit Research.

Hungary is unique as it is the only Eastern Bloc country to have made a smooth transition to a market economy without splitting or violence. The transition to a multiparty democracy was completed with the general elections in 1990. Hungary enjoys stability in a region torn by ethnic violence. Currently, the only threat to stability may come from the possible mistreatment of ethnic Hungarians in Slovakia after the Czechoslovak split. Hungary's willingness to pay has been very strong even during difficult times.

Hungary's economic transformation and resilience in the face of the collapse of Soviet trade are very impressive. During the past two years, the process of economic reform, started in 1968, has accelerated to develop a dynamic private sector, restructure the state sector and liberalize trade. The private sector now represents 30% of GDP, from only 10% in 1989. The trade system has been liberalized, with 90% of imports free of licensing, and tariffs have been lowered significantly. In light of the collapse of the Soviet Union and its economic difficulties, redirection of trade toward the West has been very successful with convertible currency exports increasing 45% in 1991 and 21% in the first seven months of 1992, and the OECD countries accounting for 70% of the trade. The current account continues to be in surplus, and the country has been able to attract more than half of all foreign investment in Eastern Europe. The debt profile has improved very quickly, with the debt ratio falling from 343% in 1986 to 177% in 1991. The debt service ratio has also improved from 85% in 1986 to 32% in 1991. On the negative side, the restructuring of the economy translates into a severe recession (GDP fell 10.2% in 1991 and is expected to fall another 5% this year) and high unemployment (currently about 11%).

其次，一旦跨国公司决定进行对外投资，可利用很多方法来降低所面临的政治风险。

Second, once a MNC decides to undertake a foreign project, it can take various measures to minimize its exposure to political risk. For example, a MNC can form a joint venture with a local company. The idea is that if the project is partially owned by a local company, the foreign government may be less inclined to expropriate it since the action will hurt the local company as well as the MNC. The MNC may also consider forming a consortium of international companies to undertake the foreign project. In this case, the MNC can reduce its exposure to political risk and, at the same time, make expropriation more costly to the host government. Understandably, the host government may not wish to take actions that will antagonize many countries at the same time. Alternatively, MNCs can use local debt to finance the foreign project. In this case, the MNC has an option to repudiate its debt if the host government takes actions to hurt its interests.

EXHIBIT 16.12

Country Risk Rankings

Rank	Country	Country Risk	Political Risk	Economic Performance	Credit Rating
	Weighting:	100.00	25.00	25.00	10.00
1	Norway	99.45	24.69	25.00	10.00
2	Switzerland	99.15	25.00	24.38	10.00
3	Luxembourg	99.10	24.90	24.43	10.00
4	United States	96.93	24.12	22.81	10.00
5	Denmark	95.63	24.69	21.18	10.00
6	Sweden	94.58	24.76	20.05	10.00
7	United Kingdom	93.55	24.52	19.26	10.00
8	Finland	93.52	24.77	18.99	10.00
9	Austria	93.43	24.59	19.07	10.00
10	Ireland	93.26	24.48	19.01	10.00
11	Netherlands	93.16	24.81	18.58	10.00
12	Canada	92.76	24.56	18.43	10.00
13	Japan	91.86	23.62	20.52	8.96
14	Belgium	91.74	23.84	18.75	9.38
15	Germany	91.17	24.19	17.21	10.00
16	France	90.78	24.08	16.93	10.00
17	Australia	90.58	24.13	17.00	9.79
18	Singapore	90.31	24.25	17.29	10.00
19	Iceland	89.75	22.93	19.02	8.54
20	Spain	87.82	23.24	14.82	10.00
21	New Zealand	87.45	23.56	14.66	9.58
22	Italy	86.50	22.61	15.58	8.54
23	Bermuda	83.75	20.62	17.72	8.96
25	Portugal	83.19	22.27	12.40	8.75
34	Bahamas	70.02	18.53	11.45	6.25
35	Czech Republic	69.38	19.31	10.53	6.67
37	South Korea	69.05	19.99	12.60	6.46
38	Hungary	68.82	17.58	10.36	6.67
41	Israel	66.28	15.62	11.29	6.46
42	Saudi Arabia	65.72	15.15	9.86	6.25
43	Chile	65.43	19.27	10.48	6.25
49	Mexico	62.68	16.99	9.50	5.00
56	Thailand	59.89	17.32	8.96	5.42
57	South Africa	58.21	15.29	7.95	5.21
60	India	56.34	15.33	8.77	3.96
61	Russia	53.51	13.53	8.63	4.38
66	Egypt	49.98	13.06	6.33	3.75
68	Brazil	49.04	12.44	7.91	2.29
73	Turkey	47.43	10.92	6.46	2.29
74	Iran	46.90	11.85	7.14	2.50
75	Vietnam	46.55	12.61	7.47	2.29
85	Indonesia	41.88	10.67	6.59	1.88
123	Bosnia-Herzegovina	33.67	6.01	4.18	0.63
141	Argentina	31.98	4.88	6.35	0.21
161	Sierra Leone	26.14	3.96	2.50	0.00
173	Zimbabwe	22.82	2.09	0.31	0.00
181	Cuba	14.07	2.81	8.43	0.00
185	Iraq	1.85	0.55	0.47	0.00

Source: Euromoney, March 2005.

第三，跨国公司可以购买保险来防止政治风险。

海外私人投资公司 (OPIC)

Third, MNCs may purchase insurance against the hazard of political risk. Such insurance policies, which are available in many advanced countries, are especially useful for small firms that are less well equipped to deal with political risk on their own. In the United States, the **Overseas Private Investment Corporation (OPIC),** a federally owned organization, offers insurance against (1) the inconvertibility of foreign currencies, (2) expropriation of U.S.-owned assets overseas, (3) destruction of U.S.-owned physical properties due to war, revolution, and other violent political events in foreign countries, and (4) loss of business income due to political violence. OPIC's primary goal is to encourage U.S. private investments in the economies of developing countries. Alternatively, MNCs may also purchase tailor-made insurance policies from private insurers such as Lloyd's of London.

When the political risk faced by a MNC can be fully covered by an insurance contract, the MNC can subtract the insurance premium from the expected cash flows from the project in computing its NPV. The MNC then can use the usual cost of capital, which would be used to evaluate domestic investment projects, in discounting the expected cash flows from foreign projects. Lastly, it is pointed out that many countries have concluded bilateral or multilateral investment protection agreements, effectively eliminating most political risk. As a result, if a MNC invests in a country that signed the investment protection agreement with the MNC's home country, it need not be overly concerned with political risk.

一种特定类型的政治风险就是跨国公司可能面临政府官员的腐败问题。

One particular type of political risk that MNCs and investors may face is corruption associated with the abuse of public offices for private benefits. Investors may often encounter demands for bribes from politicians and government officials for contracts and smooth bureaucratic processes. If companies refuse to make *grease payments,* they may lose business opportunities or face difficult bureaucratic red tape. If companies pay, on the other hand, they may risk violating laws or being embarrassed when the payments are discovered and reported in the media. Corruption can be found anywhere in the world. But it is a much more serious problem in many developing and transition economies where the state sector is large, democratic institutions are weak, and the press is often muzzled. U.S. companies are legally prohibited from bribing foreign officials by the Foreign Corrupt Practices Act (FCPA). In 1997, the OECD also adopted a treaty to criminalize the bribery of foreign officials by companies. Bribery thus is both morally and legally wrong for companies from most developed countries. Another particular risk that companies may face is extortion demands from Mafia-style criminal organizations. For example, the majority of companies in Russia are known to have paid extortion demands. To deal with this kind of situation, it is important for companies to hire people who are familiar with local operating environments, strengthen local support for the company, and enhance physical security measures.

SUMMARY

本章讨论了有关跨国公司对外直接投资的一些问题，而跨国公司对新兴全球经济的形成有着重要的影响。

1. 一旦公司开展对外直接投资，它就在进行跨国经营了。对外直接投资既可以是在国外建立全新的生产工厂，也可以是对现有的外国企业进行并购。

2. 在1999～2003年的五年里，全球对外直接投资总流出量平均每年约为8 400亿美元。美国既是对外直接投资的最大流入国，也是最大流出国。除了美国之外，法国、德国、荷

This chapter discusses various issues associated with foreign direct investments (FDI) by MNCs, which play a key role in shaping the nature of the emerging global economy.

1. Firms become *multinational* when they undertake FDI. FDI may involve either the establishment of new production facilities in foreign countries or acquisitions of existing foreign businesses.

2. During the recent five-year period 1999–2003, total annual worldwide FDI outflows amounted to about $840 billion on average. The United States is the largest recipient, as well as initiator, of FDI. Besides the United States, France, Germany, the Netherlands, and the United Kingdom are the leading sources of FDI outflows, whereas the United Kingdom, China, France, Germany, and the Netherlands are the major destinations for FDI in recent years.

兰和英国是对外直接投资的主要流
出国，而英国、中国、法国、德国
和荷兰是近年来对外直接投资的主
要流入国。

3. 现有的大多数对外直接投资理
论强调的是作为对外直接投资激励因
素的种种市场不完全性，即产品市场、
要素市场和资本市场方面的不完全性。

4. 按照对外直接投资的内部化
理论，那些拥有具有公共产品性质
的无形资产的公司为了在更大范围
内利用其资产，倾向于在国外进行
直接投资，同时，又能避免在国外
因市场交易而导致无形资产的滥用。

5. 根据雷蒙德·弗农的产品生
命周期理论，在新产品引入之初，
公司会选择在国内生产，从而比较
接近客户市场。一旦产品生产变得
标准化并趋向成熟，降低成本就成
了企业维持竞争力的主要因素。在
这一阶段，公司可选择在成本较低
的国家建立生产工厂。

6. 近年来，越来越多的对外直接
投资采取对现存企业进行并购的形式。
利润增值效应的产生可能起因于收购
者想要利用市场的诸多不完全性。

7. 无形资产市场的不完善性，
如研发能力，可能是促使跨国并购
的重要因素。前向并购可内部化收
购公司的无形资产，后向并购则可
内部化目标公司的无形资产。

8. 在评价政治风险时，专家们
通常都较为关注一些关键因素，如
东道国的政治和政府体制、政党的
历史及它们之间的相对实力、东道
国与世界政治经济体制的一体化程
度、东道国的种族和宗教稳定性、
地区的安全性和一些重要经济指标。

9. 在评价对外投资项目时，跨
国公司必须考虑政治风险的影响，
因为主权国家很可能改变游戏规则。
跨国公司可以提高资本成本或是降
低该项投资的预期现金流量，也可
以通过购买保单来应对政治风险。

3. Most existing theories of FDI put emphasis on various market imperfections, that is, imperfections in product, factor, and capital markets, as the key motivating forces driving FDI.

4. The *internalization* theory of FDI holds that firms that have intangible assets with a public good property tend to invest directly in foreign countries in order to use these assets on a larger scale and, at the same time, avoid the misappropriations that may occur while transacting in foreign markets through a market mechanism.

5. According to Raymond Vernon's product life-cycle theory, when firms first introduce new products, they choose to produce at home, close to their customers. Once the product becomes standardized and mature, it becomes important to cut production costs to stay competitive. At this stage, firms may set up production facilities in low-cost foreign countries.

6. In recent years, a growing portion of FDI has taken the form of cross-border acquisitions of existing businesses. *Synergistic* gains may arise if the acquirer is motivated to take advantage of various market imperfections.

7. Imperfections in the market for intangible assets, such as R&D capabilities, may play a key role in motivating cross-border acquisitions. The internalization may proceed *forward* to internalize the acquirer's intangible assets or *backward* to internalize the target's intangible assets.

8. In evaluating political risk, experts focus their attention on a set of key factors such as the host country's political/government system, historical records of political parties and their relative strengths, integration of the host country into the world political/economic system, the host country's ethnic and religious stability, regional security, and key economic indicators.

9. In evaluating a foreign investment project, it is important for the MNC to consider the effect of political risk, as a sovereign country can change the *rules of the game*. The MNC may adjust the cost of capital upward or lower the expected cash flows from the foreign project. Or, the MNC may purchase insurance policies against the hazard of political risks.

KEY WORDS

country risk, *413*
cross-border mergers and
  acquisitions, *395*
FDI flows, *395*
FDI stocks, *397*
foreign direct
  investments (FDI), *394*

greenfield
  investments, *395*
intangible assets, *401*
internalization
  theory, *401*
Overseas Private
Investment

Corporation
  (OPIC), *417*
political risk, *410*
product life-cycle
  theory, *403*
synergistic gains, *408*

QUESTIONS

1. Recently, many foreign firms from both developed and developing countries acquired high-tech U.S. firms. What might have motivated these firms to acquire U.S. firms?

2. Japanese MNCs, such as Toyota, Toshiba, and Matsushita, made extensive investments in Southeast Asian countries like Thailand, Malaysia, and Indonesia. In your opinion, what forces are driving Japanese investments in this region?

3. Since NAFTA was established, many Asian firms, especially those from Japan and Korea, have made extensive investments in Mexico. Why do you think these Asian firms decided to build production facilities in Mexico?

4. How would you explain the fact that China emerged as the second most important recipient of FDI after the United States in recent years?

5. Explain the internalization theory of FDI. What are the strengths and weaknesses of the theory?

6. Explain Vernon's product life-cycle theory of FDI. What are the strengths and weaknesses of the theory?

7. Why do you think the host country tends to resist cross-border acquisitions rather than greenfield investments?

8. How would you incorporate political risk into the capital budgeting process of foreign investment projects?

9. Explain and compare forward versus backward internalization.

10. What could be the reason for the negative synergistic gains for British acquisitions of U.S. firms?

11. Define *country risk*. How is it different from political risk?

12. What are the advantages and disadvantages of FDI as compared to a licensing agreement with a foreign partner?

13. What operational and financial measures can a MNC take to minimize the political risk associated with a foreign investment project?

14. Study the experience of Enron in India and discuss what we can learn from it for the management of political risk.

15. Discuss the different ways political events in a host country may affect local operations of a MNC.

16. What factors would you consider in evaluating the political risk associated with making FDI in a foreign country.

INTERNET EXERCISES

You are hired as a political consultant for General Motors Company, which is considering building automobile plants in three countries: Brazil and Poland. Choose a country and analyze the political risk of investing in that country. In doing so, utilize websites such as: www.odci.gov/publications/factbook, or any other relevant Internet resources. You may prepare a final report to GM using a similar format to Exhibit 16.10.

MINI CASE

Enron versus Bombay Politicians

On August 3, 1995, the Maharashtra state government of India, dominated by the nationalist, right-wing Bharatiya Janata Party (BJP), abruptly canceled Enron's $2.9 billion power project in Dabhol, located south of Bombay, the industrial heartland of India. This came as a huge blow to Rebecca P. Mark, the chairman and chief executive of Enron's international power unit, who spearheaded the Houston-based energy giant's international investment drive. Upon the news release, Enron's share price fell immediately by about 10 percent to $33½. Mark sprang to action to resuscitate the deal with the Maharashtra state, promising concessions. This effort, however, was met with scorn from BJP politicians. Enron's Dabhol debacle cast a serious doubt on the company's aggressive global expansion strategy, involving some $10 billion in projects in power plants and pipelines spanning across Asia, South America, and Middle East.

Enron became involved in the project in 1992 when the new reformist government of the Congress Party (I), led by Prime Minister Narasimha Rao, was keen on attracting foreign investment in infrastructure. After meeting with the Indian government officials visiting Houston in May, Enron dispatched executives to India to hammer out a "memorandum of understanding" in just 10 days to build a massive 2,015-megawatt Dabhol power complex. New Delhi placed the project on a fast track and awarded it to Enron without competitive bidding. Subsequently, the Maharashtra State Electricity Board (MSEB) agreed to buy 90 percent of the power Dabhol produces. Two other U.S. companies, General Electric (GE) and Bechtel Group, agreed to join Enron as partners for the Dabhol project.

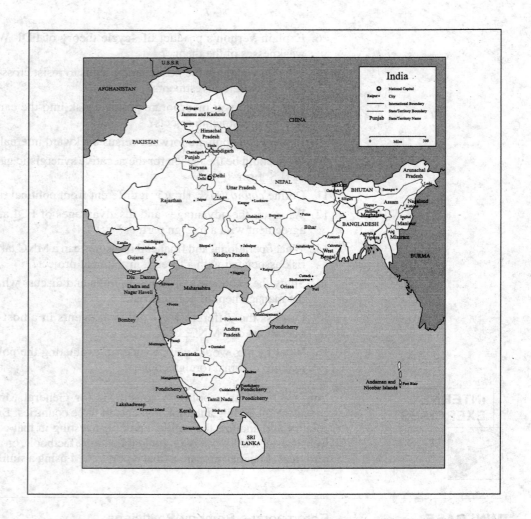

In the process of structuring the deal, Enron made a profound political miscalculation: It did not seriously take into consideration a rising backlash against foreign investments by an opposition coalition led by the BJP. During the state election campaign in early 1995, the BJP called for a reevaluation of the Enron project. Jay Dubashi, the BJP's economic advisor, said that the BJP would review all foreign investments already in India, and "If it turns out that we have to ask them to go, then we'll ask them to go." Instead of waiting for the election results, Enron rushed to close the deal and began construction, apparently believing that a new government would find it difficult to unwind the deal when construction was already under way. Enron was not very concerned with local political sentiments. Enron fought to keep the contract details confidential, but a successful lawsuit by a Bombay consumer group forced the company to reveal the details: Enron would receive 7.4 cents per kilowatt-hour from MSEB and Enron's rate of return would be 23 percent, far higher than 16 percent over the capital cost that the Indian government guaranteed to others. Critics cited the disclosure as proof that Enron had exaggerated project costs to begin with and that the deal might have involved corruption.

The BJP won the 1995 election in Maharashtra state and fulfilled its promise. Manohar Joshi, the newly elected chief minister of Maharashtra, who campaigned on a pledge to "drive Enron into the sea," promptly canceled the project, citing inflated project costs and too high electricity rates. This pledge played well with Indian voters with visceral distrust of foreign companies since the British colonial era. (It helps to recall that India was first colonized by a foreign company, the British East India Company.) By the time the project was canceled, Enron already had invested some $300 million. Officials of the Congress

Party who championed the Dabhol project in the first place did not come to the rescue of the project. The BJP criticized the Congress Party, rightly or wrongly, for being too corrupt to reform the economy and too cozy with business interests. In an effort to pressure Maharashtra to reverse its decision, Enron "pushed like hell" the U.S. Energy Department to make a statement in June 1995 to the effect that canceling the Enron deal could adversely affect other power projects. The statement only compounded the situation. The BJP politicians immediately criticized the statement as an attempt by Washington to bully India.

After months of nasty exchanges and lawsuits, Enron and Maharashtra negotiators agreed to revive the Dabhol project. The new deal requires that Enron cut the project's cost from $2.9 billion to $2.5 billion, lower the proposed electricity rates, and make a state-owned utility a new 30 percent partner of the project. A satisfied Joshi, the chief minister, stated: "Maharashtra has gained tremendously by this decision." Enron needed to make a major concession to demonstrate that its global power projects are still on track. The new deal led Enron to withdraw a lawsuit seeking $500 million in damages from Maharashtra for the cancellation of the Dabhol project.

Discussion Points

1. Discuss the chief mistakes that Enron made in India.
2. Discuss what Enron might have done differently to avoid its predicament in India.

REFERENCES & SUGGESTED READINGS

Aharoni, Yair. "The Foreign Investment Decision Process," *Harvard Business School,* 1966.

Caves, Richard. *Multinational Enterprise and Economic Analysis.* Cambridge, MA: Harvard University Press, 1982.

Doukas, John, and Nicholas Travlos. "The Effect of Corporate Multinationalism on Shareholders' Wealth: Evidence from International Acquisitions." *Journal of Finance* 43 (1988), pp. 1161–75.

Dunning, John. *Economic Analysis and the Multinational Enterprise.* New York: Praeger, 1975.

The Economist. "Multinationals, a Survey," March 27, 1993, pp. 4–20.

Eun, C., R. Kolody, and C. Scheraga. "Cross-Border Acquisitions and Shareholder Wealth: Tests of Synergy and Internalization Hypotheses." *Journal of Banking and Finance* 20 (1996), pp. 1559–82.

Harris, Robert, and David Ravenscraft. "The Role of Acquisitions in Foreign Direct Investment: Evidence from the U.S. Stock Market." *Journal of Finance* 46 (1991), pp. 825–44.

Hymer, Stephen. *The International Operations of National Firms: A Study of Direct Foreign Investment.* Cambridge, MA: MIT Press, 1976.

Jensen, Michael. "The Takeover Controversy: Analysis and Evidence." *Midland Corporate Finance Journal* 5 (1986), pp. 1–27.

Kang, Jun-Koo. "The International Market for Corporate Control: Mergers and Acquisitions of U.S. Firms by Japanese Firms." *Journal of Financial Economics* 35 (1993), pp. 345–71.

Kindleberger, Charles. *American Business Abroad.* New Haven, CT: Yale University Press, 1969.

Kobrin, Stephen. "Political Risk: A Review and Reconsideration." *Journal of International Business Studies* 10 (1979), pp. 67–80.

Mandel, Robert. "The Overseas Private Investment Corporation and International Investment." *Columbia Journal of World Business* 19 (1984), pp. 89–95.

Magee, Stephen. "Information and the Multinational Corporation: An Appropriability Theory of Direct Foreign Investment." In Jagdish N. Bhagwati (ed.), *The New International Economic Order.* Cambridge, MA: MIT Press, 1977.

Morck, Randall, and Bernard Yeung. "Why Investors Value Multinationality." *Journal of Business* 64 (1991), pp. 165–87.

—— . "Internalization: An Event Study Test." *Journal of International Economics* 33 (1992), pp. 41–56.

Ragazzione, Giorgio. "Theories of Determinants of Direct Foreign Investment." IMF Staff Papers 20 (1973), pp. 471–98.

Root, Franklin. "Analyzing Political Risks in International Business." In *The Multinational Enterprise in Transition,* ed. A. Kapoor and Philip Grub. Princeton: Darwin Press, 1972, pp. 354–65.

Rugman, Alan. "Internalization Is Still a General Theory of Foreign Direct Investment." Weltwirtschaftliche Archiv. 121 (1985), pp. 570–76.

Rummel, R. J., and David Heenan. "How Multinationals Analyze Political Risk." *Harvard Business Review* 56 (1978), pp. 67–76.

Vernon, Raymond. "International Investment and International Trade in the Product Cycle." *Quarterly Journal of Economics* 80 (1966), pp. 190–207.

—— . "The Product Cycle Hypothesis in a New International Environment." *Oxford Bulletin of Economics and Statistics* 41 (1979), pp. 255–67.

17 International Capital Structure and the Cost of Capital

近来，全球许多公司通过从国内外融资开始将其资本结构国际化。

资本结构

RECENTLY, MANY MAJOR firms throughout the world have begun to internationalize their capital structure by raising funds from foreign as well as domestic sources. As a result, these corporations are becoming *multinational* not only in the scope of their business activities but also in their **capital structure.** This trend reflects not only a conscious effort on the part of firms to lower the cost of capital by international sourcing of funds but also the ongoing liberalization and deregulation of international financial markets that make them accessible for many firms.

If international financial markets were completely integrated, it would not matter whether firms raised capital from domestic or foreign sources because the cost of capital would be equalized across countries. If, on the other hand, these markets are less than fully integrated, firms may be able to create value for their shareholders by issuing securities in foreign as well as domestic markets.

As discussed in Chapter 13, cross-listing of a firm's shares on foreign stock exchanges is one way a firm operating in a segmented capital market can lessen the negative effects of segmentation and also internationalize the firm's capital structure.[1] For example, IBM, Sony, and British Petroleum are simultaneously listed and traded on the New York, London, and Tokyo stock exchanges. By internationalizing its corporate ownership structure, a firm can generally increase its share price and lower its cost of capital. The International Finance in Practice box "The U.S. Welcomes the Alien Invasion," page 426, illustrates the rising popularity of raising capital internationally.

本章考察的是资本结构国际化对公司的资本成本和市场价值的作用。

In this chapter, we examine various implications of internationalizing the capital structure for the firm's cost of capital and market value. We also study existing

---

[1]Stapleton and Subrahmanyam (1977) pointed out that the firm may alternatively undertake foreign direct investment to mitigate the negative effects of segmented capital markets.

restrictions on foreign ownership of domestic firms and their effects on the firm's cost of capital. We are ultimately concerned with the MNC's ability to obtain capital at the lowest possible cost so that it can profitably take on the largest number of capital projects and maximize shareholders' wealth. We begin the chapter with a review of cost of capital concepts and basic asset pricing theory.

Cost of Capital

资本成本指一个投资项目为支付融资成本而必须实现的最小回报率。

The **cost of capital** is the minimum rate of return an investment project must generate in order to pay its financing costs. If the return on an investment project is equal to the cost of capital, undertaking the project will leave the firm's value unaffected. When a firm identifies and undertakes an investment project that generates a return exceeding its cost of capital, the firm's value will increase. It is thus important for a value-maximizing firm to try to lower its cost of capital.

加权平均资本成本 (WACC)

When a firm has both debt and equity in its capital structure, its financing cost can be represented by the **weighted average cost of capital.** It can be computed by weighting the after-tax borrowing cost of the firm and the cost of equity capital, using the capital structure ratio as the weight. Specifically,

$$K = (1 - \lambda)K_l + \lambda(1 - \tau)i \qquad (17.1)$$

where:

K = weighted average cost of capital,

K_l = cost of equity capital for a levered firm,

i = before-tax cost of debt capital (i.e., borrowing),

τ = marginal corporate income tax rate, and

λ = debt-to-total-market-value ratio.

In general, both K_l and i increase as the proportion of debt in the firm's capital structure increases.[2] At the optimal combination of debt and equity financing, however, the weighted average cost of capital (K) will be the lowest. Firms may have an incentive to use debt financing to take advantage of the tax-deductibility of interest payments. In most countries, interest payments are tax deductible, unlike dividend payments. The debt financing, however, should be balanced against possible bankruptcy costs associated with higher debt. A trade-off between the tax advantage of debt and potential bankruptcy costs is thus a major factor in determining the optimal capital structure.

最佳资本结构的选择很重要，因为一个追求股东财富最大化的企业会对新的资本支出进行融资，直到最后一单位新增投资的边际收益等于最后一单位新增融资的加权边际成本为止。

Choice of the optimal capital structure is important, since a firm that desires to maximize shareholder wealth will finance new capital expenditures up to the point where the marginal return on the last unit of new invested capital equals the weighted marginal cost of capital of the last unit of new financing to be raised. Consequently, for a firm confronted with a fixed schedule of possible new investments, any policy that lowers the firm's cost of capital will increase the profitable capital expenditures the firm takes on and increase the wealth of the firm's shareholders. Internationalizing the firm's cost of capital is one such policy.

Exhibit 17.1 illustrates this point. The value-maximizing firm would undertake an investment project as long as the internal rate of return (IRR) on the project exceeds the firm's cost of capital. When all the investment projects under consideration are ranked in descending order in terms of the IRR, the firm will face a negatively sloped IRR schedule, as depicted in the exhibit. The firm's optimal capital expenditure will then be determined at the point where the IRR schedule intersects the cost of capital.

---

[2]In Chapter 18, we distinguish between the cost of equity capital for a levered firm, K_l, and the cost of equity capital for an unlevered firm, K_u.

EXHIBIT 17.1

The Firm's Investment Decision
and the Cost of Capital

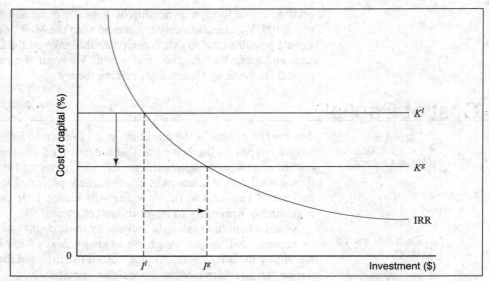

Note: K^l and K^g represent, respectively, the cost of capital under local and international capital structures; IRR represents the internal rate of return on investment projects; I^l and I^g represent the optimal investment outlays under the alternative capital structures.

然而必须注意到，
资本成本的下降不仅会
使新项目投资增加，也
会导致现有项目现金流
的重新估价，从而提高
企业的价值。

Now, suppose that the firm's cost of capital can be reduced from K^l under the local capital structure to K^g under an internationalized capital structure. As the exhibit illustrates, the firm can then increase its profitable investment outlay from I^l to I^g, contributing to the firm's value. It is important, however, to note that a reduced cost of capital increases the firm's value not only through increased investments in new projects but also through revaluation of the cash flows from existing projects.

Cost of Capital in Segmented versus Integrated Markets

The main difficulty in computing the financing cost (K) of a firm is related to the cost of equity capital (K_e). The cost of equity capital is the expected return on the firm's stock that investors require. This return is frequently estimated using the **Capital Asset Pricing Model (CAPM).** The CAPM states that the equilibrium expected rate of return on a stock (or more generally any security) is a linear function of the systematic risk inherent in the security. Specifically, the CAPM-determined expected rate of return for the ith security is:

通常用**资本资产定
价模型**(CAPM)来估计
企业股票的期望回报。

$$\overline{R}_i = R_f + (\overline{R}_M - R_f)\beta_i \tag{17.2}$$

where R_f is the risk-free rate of return and $\overline{R}_M$ is the expected return on the **market portfolio,** the market-value-weighted portfolio of all assets. **Beta,** β_i, is a measure of systematic risk inherent in security i. **Systematic risk** is the nondiversifiable market risk of an asset. The CAPM equation shows that the expected return of security i, $\overline{R}_i$, increases in β_i, the greater the market risk, the greater the expected return. Beta is calculated as $\mathrm{Cov}(R_i, R_M)/\mathrm{Var}(R_M)$, where $\mathrm{Cov}(R_i, R_M)$ is the covariance of future returns between security i and the market portfolio and $\mathrm{Var}(R_M)$ is the variance of returns of the market portfolio.

市场组合投资
β系数
系统风险

Now, suppose that international financial markets are segmented and, as a result, investors can only diversify domestically. In this case, the market portfolio (M) in the CAPM formula would represent the domestic market portfolio, which is often proxied by the S&P 500 Index in the United States. The relevant risk measure in pricing assets will be the beta measured against the domestic market portfolio. In segmented capital markets, the same future cash flows are likely to be priced differently across countries, as they would be viewed as having different systematic risks by investors from different countries.

On the other hand, suppose that international financial markets are fully integrated and, consequently, investors can diversify internationally. In this case, the market portfolio in the CAPM formula will be the "world" market portfolio comprising all assets in the world. The relevant risk measure then should be the beta measured against the world market portfolio. In integrated international financial markets, the same future cash flows will be priced in the same way everywhere. Investors would require, on average, lower expected returns on securities under integration than under segmentation because they can diversify risk better under integration.[3]

EXAMPLE 17.1

A Numerical Illustration   Suppose the domestic U.S. beta of IBM is 1.0, that is, $\beta_{IBM}^{U.B.} = 1.0$, which is the average beta risk level. In addition, let us assume that the expected return on the U.S. market portfolio is 12 percent, that is, $\overline{R}_{U.S} = 12\%$, and that the risk-free interest rate, which may be proxied by the U.S. Treasury bill rate, is 6 percent. If U.S. capital markets are segmented from the rest of the world, the expected return on IBM stock will be determined as follows:

$$\overline{R}_{IBM} = R_f + (\overline{R}_{U.S.} - R_f)\beta_{IBM}^{U.S.}$$
$$= 6 + (12 - 6)(1.0) = 12\%.$$

Considering the domestic beta risk of IBM, investors would require 12 percent return on their investment in IBM stock.

Suppose now that U.S. capital markets are integrated with the rest of the world and that the world beta measure of IBM stock is 0.8, that is, $\beta_{IBM}^{W} = 0.8$. If we assume that the risk-free rate is 6 percent and the expected return on the world market portfolio is 12 percent, that is, $R_f = 6\%$ and $\overline{R}_w = 12\%$, we can compute the expected return on IBM stock as follows:

$$\overline{R}_{IBM} = R_f + (\overline{R}_W - R_f)\beta_{IBM}^{W}$$
$$= 6 + (12 - 6)(0.8) = 10.8\%$$

In light of a relatively low world beta measure of 0.8, investors would require a lower return on IBM stock under integration than they would under segmentation.

很明显，国际金融市场的一体化或分割化对资本成本的决定有很大的影响。

Obviously, the integration or segmentation of international financial markets has major implications for determining the cost of capital. However, empirical evidence on the issue is less than clear-cut. Increasingly, researchers such as Harvey (1991) and Chan, Karolyi, and Stulz (1992) find it difficult to reject the international version of the CAPM, suggesting that international financial markets are integrated rather than segmented. Another group of researchers, including French and Poterba (1991), however, have documented that investors actually diversify internationally only to a limited extent, suggesting that international financial markets should be more segmented than integrated. In a study examining the integration of the Canadian and U.S. stock markets, on the other hand, Mittoo (1992) found that Canadian stocks cross-listed on U.S. exchanges are priced in an integrated market, and segmentation is predominant for those Canadian stocks that are not cross-listed.

---

[3]For a detailed discussion of the effect of integration/segmentation on the cost of capital, refer to Cohn and Pringle (1973) and Stulz (1995).

The U.S. Welcomes the Alien Invasion

Last year 7.5% of the $2.25 trillion worth of shares traded on the New York Stock Exchange (NYSE) came in the form of American depository receipts (ADRs). This percentage is likely to be even higher this year, helped by new issues from foreign companies, which are expected to surpass the record of 37 new listings set during 1993.

In addition to the NYSE's ADRs, a steady stream of depository receipts (DRs) trade over-the-counter, are listed on other exchanges such as Amex and Nasdaq, or are privately placed under Rule 144A and trade on the Portal system.

The depository receipts marketplace is becoming truly global. Until the late 1980s most DRs represented shares of European companies, but today investors in the United States can place orders domestically for dollar-denominated shares from countries as diverse as Chile, China, India and Mexico.

Investment bankers report the busiest schedule of offerings that they have ever seen in the depository receipts business, although volatility in many emerging markets has caused some concern among underwriters.

European DR issuance is being primarily driven by privatization programmes, notably those being implemented by France and Italy. In Asia, companies from China need capital to expand against a backdrop of runaway economic growth. And in Latin America the passage of the North American Free Trade Agreement (NAFTA) is expected to spur issuance from Mexico, while a dozen Chilean companies have plans to launch DRs this year. In addition, 1994 should witness the first DRs from countries including Sri Lanka, Pakistan, Peru and Uruguay.

The issuing companies are attracted by the growing demand for international equities in the form of ADRs from investors in the United States, accompanied by European and Asian demand for DRs that trade on exchanges outside the US—often referred to as global depository receipts.

Some companies urgently need to raise fresh capital in quantities unavailable at home. Others simply wish to broaden their investor base, and are being persuaded to set up an ADR programme without raising fresh capital.

But both groups have realized that in the global competition for capital those companies that broaden their investor base by actively courting the foreign investor stand a better chance of achieving a strong share price, and will be in a better position to raise capital as and when needed.

The message is clear. An ADR programme is becoming a necessity in order to gain full access to the US investor. And as the range of foreign shares available in depository receipt form grows many US investors may feel that there is even less of an incentive to hunt for stocks in overseas markets. This effect is magnified by the fact that issuance of depository receipts usually generates a great deal of research and broker interest, and pushes a company's story to the forefront of the many thousands seeking the attention of investors.

There are a range of options available to foreign companies wishing to access the depository receipt market. The simplest is the so-called level-one ADR, which entails setting up a programme under which existing domestic shares can be switched into DR form upon demand and trade over-the-counter. Similarly, level-two programmes may be set up under which existing shares can be transformed into DRs—but this time listed on an exchange.

这些研究表明国际金融市场已不再是分割的了，但还不是完全一体化的。

These studies suggest that international financial markets are certainly not segmented anymore, but still are not fully integrated. If international financial markets are less than fully integrated, which may be the case, there can be systematic differences in the cost of capital among countries.

Does the Cost of Capital Differ among Countries?

It has often been argued that U.S. firms "labored under the burden of heavier capital costs" relative to foreign rivals, especially in Japan and Germany. This argument, of course, implies that capital markets are less than fully integrated. It would be useful to directly compare the cost of capital across countries to see if the argument has any merit.

直接比较各国的资本成本就可看出这种评论是否具有合理性。

McCauley and Zimmer (1994) provide a direct comparison of the cost of capital among four major countries, Germany, Japan, the United Kingdom, and the United States. They first estimate the costs of debt and equity capital and then compute the cost of funds as the weighted average cost of capital using the capital structure in each country as the weight. They compute the cost of capital in real terms after adjusting for the inflation rate. In their study, the cost of debt is measured as the real, after-tax rate

Level-one and level-two programmes lack the benefits which come from the excitement created in the market by an offering of new stock. Nonetheless bankers do not feel that a company should ignore the market if it has no immediate capital-raising needs. "A level-one programme gives companies the chance to stand out," says Joseph Velli, an executive vice-president at Bank of New York, "and helps generate research product and broker interest."

UK companies such as Guinness and Tesco have built up a following by allowing existing shares to trade over-the-counter in the United States in the form of depository receipts. And more recently Telecommunicacoes Brasileiras (Telebras) has also successfully broadened its shareholder base with a level-one programme.

However, the majority of new depository receipt programmes do involve capital-raising. Until the 1980s this typically involved a European company selling ADRs to investors in the United States. But with Latin American and Asian companies doing more offerings, this is increasingly via a global depository receipt (GDR) offering which can tap simultaneously into investor demand from the US, Europe and Asia. Regardless of the terminology, both ADRs and GDRs represent the same basic structure of dollar-denominated securities.

Where capital is being raised, the major decisions a company has to make are whether to place stock privately under 144A or make a public offering; and, if the latter, where to list the depository receipts.

Currently there is a clear trend away from 144A issues toward full registration with the Securities and Exchange Commission.

"Even with a 144A placement, there is still a great deal of disclosure, the same roadshow, and a lot of work leading up to the offering," comments Bill Treut, who heads ADR sales for Latin American at Citibank.

Companies have realized that the accounting reconciliation problem is not as daunting a task as they previously thought. These factors have convinced many of them that it makes sense to take the extra steps needed to do a public offering.

"For particular reasons," Treut says, "some companies feel they have a limited window of opportunity" and can take advantage of the speed of the 144A process. "But without those special factors, the definite trend is toward full registration."

In 1991, $2.29 billion was raised via 144A placements; this rose to $3.83 billion in 1992, but fell back to $2.14 billion last year. Meanwhile, total capital raised via all DRs during 1993 was $9.54 billion, up from $5.26 billion in 1992, and $4.61 billion in 1991. That was preceded by three relatively quiet years in the wake of 1987, when $4.59 billion was raised.

One drawback with 144A placements is that they narrow the institutional investor base down to qualified institutional buyers (QIBs), and totally exclude the retail sector and smaller institutions. Second, liquidity is often not very good on the Portal secondary market trading system, so even the QIBs feel more comfortable buying public stock offerings.

The global trend toward harmonization of accounting standards is also having the effect of bringing more and more foreign companies closer to US accounting principles. This is putting foreign companies in a position where taking the step toward SEC filing for a public ADR issue is less of a challenge.

Source: Michael Marray, Euromoney, April 1994, pp. 61–63. Adapted with permission.

---

of interest faced by nonfinancial corporate borrowers. In estimating the cost of equity, McCauley and Zimmer first determine true, economic earnings, adjusting for various distortions like depreciation, inventory profits, and crossholdings of shares, and compare those internationally comparable earnings to the respective national market capitalizations.

The estimated debt and equity costs they compute are presented in Exhibits 17.2 and 17.3, respectively. As Exhibit 17.2 shows, prior to 1982, real debt costs were often negative and divergent among countries, reflecting the distortions of inflation. Since then, debt costs have become similar for U.S., Japanese, and British firms. German firms apparently enjoyed a lower cost of debt during the period 1982–88. Exhibit 17.3 shows that Japanese firms clearly enjoyed a lower cost of equity capital than the other three countries, especially during the period 1986–89. It is noteworthy, however, that the costs of equity of the four countries have converged in the 1990s.

Exhibit 17.4 shows the trend in the capital structure, as measured by the debt-to-equity value ratio, in each of the four countries. Clearly, Germany and Japan have higher debt ratios than the United States and the U.K. There are a few reasons for the higher debt ratios for German and Japanese firms. First, historically, the banking sector in both countries has played a much more important role in corporate financing than

值得注意的是，有4个国家的权益成本在20世纪90年代发生了聚合。

EXHIBIT 17.2

Effective Real After-Tax Cost of Debt

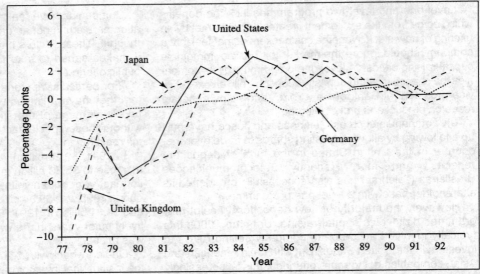

Source: Robert McCauley and Steven Zimmer, "Exchange Rates and International Differences in the Cost of Capital," in Y. Amihud and R. Levich (eds.), Exchange Rates and Corporate Performance (Burr Ridge, Ill.: Irwin, 1994).

stock markets. Second, both German and Japanese firms could carry high levels of debt without seriously exposing themselves to default risks since banks, which often belong to the same business concern or *keiretsu,* frequently hold bonds as well as stocks of these firms. This fact also tends to reduce the agency problems (or conflict of interest) between bondholders and stockholders.[4] The German and Japanese firms,

EXHIBIT 17.3

Cost of Equity

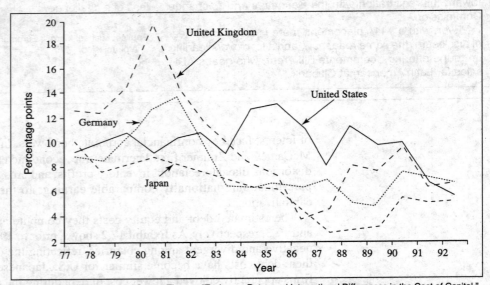

Source: Robert McCauley and Steven Zimmer, "Exchange Rates and International Differences in the Cost of Capital," in Y. Amihud and R. Levich (eds.), Exchange Rates and Corporate Performance (Burr Ridge, Ill.: Irwin, 1994).

---

[4]Recent evidence, summarized in Stulz (1996), also indicates that the agency costs of managerial discretion are lower in Japan than in the United States. This implies that Japanese managers are less likely to undertake unprofitable investment projects at the expense of existing shareholders. Unless closely monitored by shareholders, the management may pursue corporate empire building for its own interests. Stulz argues that if agency costs are indeed lower in Japan, then the cost of capital can be lower in Japan than the United States even if international financial markets are integrated.

EXHIBIT 17.4

Debt-to-Equity Value Ratios

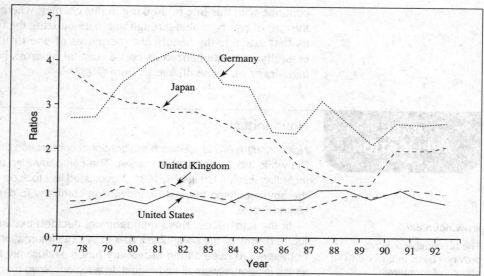

Source: Robert McCauley and Steven Zimmer, "Exchange Rates and International Differences in the Cost of Capital," in Y. Amihud and R. Levich (eds.), Exchange Rates and Corporate Performance (Burr Ridge, Ill.: Irwin, 1994).

however, "deleveraged" substantially in recent years, whereas the capital structure of American and British firms stayed relatively stable through time.

The cost of funds (that is, the weighted average cost of capital) advantages of Japanese and German firms are evident from Exhibit 17.5. The German firms' advantage stemmed mostly from low-cost, short-term debts, whereas the Japanese firms' advantage arose from both low debt and equity costs. Exhibit 17.5, however, also shows the differential cost of funds among countries diminishing in the 1990s.

然而当市场不完全时，国际融资能降低企业的资本成本。

In perfect markets, firms would be indifferent between raising funds abroad or at home. When markets are imperfect, however, international financing can lower the firm's cost of capital. In Chapter 12, for example, we saw that Eurobond financing was typically a less expensive form of debt financing than domestic bond financing. We

EXHIBIT 17.5

Real After-Tax Cost of Funds

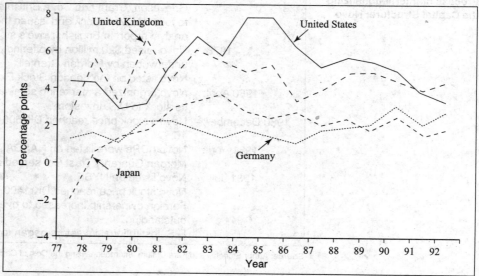

Source: Robert McCauley and Steven Zimmer, "Exchange Rates and International Differences in the Cost of Capital," in Y. Amihud and R. Levich (eds.), Exchange Rates and Corporate Performance (Burr Ridge, Ill.: Irwin, 1994).

continue with this line of thinking in this chapter, where we explore ways of lowering the cost of equity capital through internationalizing the firm's ownership structure. Let us first examine the historical experiences of one firm, Novo Industri, that has successfully internationalized its cost of capital by cross-border listings. Our discussion here draws on Stonehill and Dullum (1982).[5]

CASE APPLICATION

Novo Industri

Novo Industri A/S is a Danish multinational corporation that controls about 50 percent of the world industrial enzyme market. The company also produces health care products, including insulin. On July 8, 1981, Novo listed its stock on the New York Stock Exchange, thereby becoming the first Scandinavian company to directly raise equity capital in the United States.

In the late 1970s, Novo management decided that in order to finance the planned future growth of the company, it had to tap into international capital markets. Novo could not expect to raise all the necessary funds exclusively from the Danish stock market, which is relatively small and illiquid. In addition, Novo management felt that the company faced a higher cost of capital than its main competitors, such as Eli Lilly and Miles Lab, because of the segmented nature of the Danish stock market.

Novo thus decided to internationalize its cost of capital in order to gain access to additional sources of capital and, at the same time, lower its cost of capital. Initially, Novo increased the level of financial and technical disclosure, followed by Eurobond issue and the listing of its stock on the London Stock Exchange in 1978. In pursuing its goals further, Novo management decided to sponsor an American depository receipt (ADR) so that U.S. investors could invest in the company's stock using U.S. dollars rather than Danish kroners. Morgan Guarantee issued the ADR shares, which began trading in the over-the-counter (OTC) market in April 1981. On July 8, 1981, Novo sold 1.8 million ADR shares, raising Dkr. 450 million, and, at the same time, listed its ADR shares on the New York Stock Exchange. The chronology of these events is provided in Exhibit 17.6.

EXHIBIT 17.6

Process of Internationalizing the Capital Structure: Novo

1977:	Novo increased the level of its financial and technical disclosure in both Danish and English versions.
	Grieveson, Grant and Co, a British stock brokerage firm, started to follow Novo's stock and issued the first professional security analyst report in English. Novo's stock price: DKr200–225.
1978:	Novo raised $20 million by offering convertible Eurobond, underwritten by Morgan Grenfell.
	Novo listed on the London Stock Exchange.
1980 April:	Novo organized a marketing seminar in New York City promoting its stock to U.S. investors.
1980 December:	Novo's stock price reached DKr600 level; P/E ratio rose to around 16.
1981 April:	Novo ADRs were listed on NASDAQ (5 ADRs = one share)
	Morgan Guaranty Trust Co. served as the depository bank.
1981 July:	Novo listed on NYSE.
	Novo stock price reached DKr1400.
	Foreign ownership increased to over 50% of the shares outstanding.
	U.S. institutional investors began to hold Novo shares.

Source: Arthur Stonehill and Kare Dullum, Internationalizing the Cost of Capital (New York: John Wiley & Sons, 1982).

---

[5]Stonehill and Dullum (1982) provides a detailed analysis of the Novo case.

EXHIBIT 17.7

Novo B's Share Prices Compared to Stock Market Indices

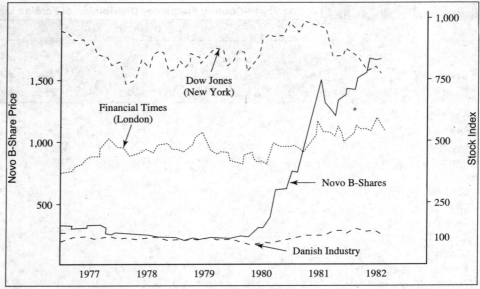

Source: Arthur I. Stonehill and Kare B. Dullum, Internationalizing the Cost of Capital: The Novo Experience and National Policy Implications (John Wiley & Sons, 1982), p. 73. Note that Novo A shares are nontradable shares held by the Novo Foundation. Reprinted with permission.

As can be seen from Exhibit 17.7, Novo's stock price reacted very positively to the U.S. listing.[6] Other Danish stocks, though, did not experience comparable price increases. The sharp increase in Novo's stock price indicates that the stock became fully priced internationally upon U.S. listing. This, in turn, implies that the Danish stock market was indeed segmented from the rest of the world. From the experiences of Novo, we can derive the following lesson: Firms operating in a small, segmented domestic capital market can gain access to new capital and lower the cost of capital by listing their stocks on large, liquid capital markets like the New York and London Stock Exchanges.

对于在小而分割的国内资本市场经营的公司，通过在纽约、伦敦等股票交易所等大型的、富有流动性的资本市场上市，就可以获得新的资本并降低资本成本。

Cross-Border Listings of Stocks

As we have seen from the case of Novo Industri, firms can potentially benefit from cross-border listings. As a result, cross-border listings of stocks have become quite popular among major corporations. Exhibit 17.8 presents the country-to-country frequency distribution of overseas listings that Sarkissian and Schill (2004) documented in their geographical analysis of cross-listings. As of 1998, their study period, there were 2,251 overseas listings. As can be seen from the bottom of Exhibit 17.8, U.S. and U.K. exchanges are, by far, the most popular hosts of overseas listings, probably reflecting the depth and credibility of these markets. Other important hosting markets include Belgium, France, Germany, Luxembourg, the Netherlands, and Switzerland, each hosting more than 100 foreign stocks. Examination of the exhibit suggests that to a certain extent, firms seem to prefer to list in neighboring markets. Out of the 266 Canadian overseas listings, 211 listings are on U.S. exchanges. New Zealand firms list heavily in Australia and vice versa. Similarly, Belgian firms list heavily in the Netherlands and vice versa. Sarkissian and Schill interpret this tendency as implying that the same

www.bankofny.com/adr
Provides general information about foreign firms that are cross-listed on U.S. stock markets.

---

[6]It is noted that Novo has dual-class shares: A-shares that are held by the Novo Foundation and nontradable and B-shares that are publicly tradable.

EXHIBIT 17.8   **Country-to-Country Frequency Distribution of Foreign Listings**

Home Country	Australia	Austria	Belgium	Brazil	Canada	Denmark	France	Germany	Ireland	Italy	Japan	Luxem.	Malaysia	Nether.	N. Zealand	Norway	Peru	Singapore	S. Africa	Spain	Sweden	Switz.	UK	USA
Argentina				1								3										2	1	12
Australia					4			2			4	1			45			3				2	10	26
Austria			1				2	8						1										
Belgium							7	3				4		7		1						4		1
Brazil												5											1	21
Canada	4		8				6	2			1			4				1	1			8	20	211
Chile																								22
Colombia												3												1
Czech R.																						5		
Denmark																1					1	1	3	3
Finland							1	2													3		2	4
France			11		1			7		1	2	2		7						1	3	5	6	23
Germany	17	7					13			2	9	6		12				1		2	1	26	11	11
Greece												1		1									4	2
Hungary	1											5											4	1
India												48											17	
Indonesia												1											2	4
Ireland																							58	14
Israel			2																				4	59
Italy			2				4	5						1						1				14
Japan	1		5	1			30	52				21		19				6				14	29	28
Korea												12											14	3
Luxem.			5				3	1						2						1	1		6	3
Malaysia											1							1					5	
Mexico																								30
Nether.		4	11				9	20	1	1		6						1			1	12	13	26
N. Zealand	17																							5
Norway					1		1	2						1							2	1	5	6
Peru																								3
Philippines												5						1						1
Poland												1											7	
Portugal								1															1	5
Singapore	2											2												1
S. Africa			9				15	5				4										4	40	11
Spain							4	4			4			1							2		4	5
Sweden		1	1		5		3	3			2					2		2				4	12	12
Switz.		1	1		1		5	10			4			1									1	5
Thailand												2						1						
Turkey												1											6	
UK	6		8		4	1	13	1013		8		1	3	12		2		7	1			4		77
USA	8		31		27		32	42			23	1		71		3	2				5	67	104	
Venezuela												1												3
Total	40	25	106	1	37	8	148	1179	13	4	60	150	3	140	45	10		234	2	4	17	157	406	659

Source: Sergei Sarkissian and Michael Schill. "The Overseas Listing Decision: New Evidence of Proximity Preference." Review of Financial Studies 17(2004).

EXHIBIT 17.9	Foreign Firms Listed on the New York Stock Exchange (Selected)
Country	**Firms**
Australia	Broken Hill Prop., Cole Myers, FAI, News Corporation, Western Mining, Westpac
Brazil	Aracruz Celulose, Gerdau, Telebras, Unibanco
Canada	Alcan Aluminum, Avalon, Canadian Pacific, Domtar, Mitel, Northern Telecom, Seagram
China	China Eastern Airlines, Hauneng Power International, Shanghai Petrochemical
Finland	Metso Corp., Nokia Corp., UPM-Kymmene
France	Elf Acquitaine, France Telecom, Rhone Poulenc, Thomson Multimedia, TOTALFina
Germany	Celanese, Deutsche Telecom, DaimlerChrysler, Hoechst, SAP, VEBA
Italy	Benetton, Fiat, Luxottica, Montedison, Telecom Italia
Japan	Canon, Fuji Photo Film, Japan Air Lines, Kirin Brewery, Kubota, Mitsui Co., NEC, Nissan Motor, Sanyo Electric, Sony, Toyota Motor
Korea	Korea Electric Power, Korea Telecom, Pohang Iron & Steel, SK Telecom
Mexico	Cemex, Impresas ICA, Grupo Televisa, Telefonos de Mexico, Vitro
Netherlands	Aegon, KLM, Philips, Polygram, Royal Dutch Petrol., Unilever, ABN AMRO Holdings
Russia	Tatnet, Rostelecom, Vimpel-Communications
South Africa	ASA Limited
Spain	Banco Bilbao, Banco Central, Banco Santan., Emprosa National, Repsol, Telefon. Nac.
United Kingdom	Attwoods, Barclays, Bass Public, Beazer, BET, British Airways, British Gas, British Petrol., British Steel, British Telecom., Cable & Wireless, Glaxo, Grand Met

Source: NYSE Factbook, 2003.

proximity preference that is believed to be responsible for "home bias" in portfolio holdings may also influence firms' choice of overseas listing venues. Exhibit 17.9 provides a partial list of overseas stocks that are listed on the NYSE.

一般来讲，公司可通过股票的境外上市来获益。

Generally speaking, a company can benefit from cross-border listings of its shares in the following ways:

1. The company can expand its potential investor base, which will lead to a higher stock price and a lower cost of capital.

2. Cross-listing creates a secondary market for the company's shares, which facilitates raising new capital in foreign markets.[7]

3. Cross-listing can enhance the liquidity of the company's stock.

4. Cross-listing enhances the visibility of the company's name and its products in foreign marketplaces.

5. Cross-listed shares may be used as the "acquisition currency" for taking over foreign companies.

6. Cross-listing may improve the company's corporate governance and transparency.

The last point deserves detailed discussion here. Consider a company domiciled in a country where shareholders' rights are not well protected and controlling shareholders (e.g., founding families and large shareholders) derive substantial private benefits, such as perks, inflated salaries, bonuses, and even thefts, from controlling the company. Once the company cross-lists its shares on the New York Stock Exchange (NYSE), London Stock Exchange (LSE), or other foreign exchanges that impose stringent disclosure and listing requirements, controlling shareholders may not be able to continue to divert company resources to their private benefit. As argued by Doidge, Karolyi, and Stulz (2001), in spite of the "inconveniences" associated with a greater public scrutiny

---

[7]Chaplinsky and Ramchand (1995) report that, compared with exclusively domestic offerings, global equity offerings enable firms to raise capital at advantageous terms. In addition, they report that the negative stock price reaction that equity issue often elicits is reduced if firms have a foreign tranche in their offer.

and enhanced transparency, controlling shareholders may choose to cross-list the company shares overseas, as it can be ultimately in their best interest to bond themselves to "good behavior" and to be able to raise funds to undertake profitable investment projects (thereby increasing share prices). This implies that if a foreign company does not need to raise capital, it may not choose to pursue U.S. listings, so that controlling shareholders can continue to extract private benefits from the company. The aforementioned study shows that other things being equal, those foreign companies that are listed on U.S. exchanges are valued nearly 17 percent higher, on average, than those that are not, reflecting investors' recognition of the enhanced corporate governance associated with U.S. listings. Since the London Stock Exchange also imposes stringent disclosure and listing requirements, foreign firms cross-listed on the exchange may also experience positive revaluation due to the effect of enhanced corporate governance.[8]

A study by Lang, Lins, and Miller (2003) shows that cross-listing can enhance firm value through improving the firm's overall information environments. Specifically, they show that foreign firms that cross-list in U.S. exchanges enjoy greater analyst coverage and increased forecast accuracy for firms' future earnings relative to those firms that are not cross-listed. They further show that firms that have greater analyst coverage and higher forecasting accuracy have a higher valuation, other things equal. These findings are consistent with the findings of other studies that cross-listed firms generally enjoy a lower cost of capital and better corporate governance.

尽管存在着潜在利益，但由于成本的缘故，并不是所有的公司都寻求海外上市。

Despite these potential benefits, not every company seeks overseas listings because of the costs.

1. It can be costly to meet the disclosure and listing requirements imposed by the foreign exchange and regulatory authorities.

2. Once a company's stock is traded in overseas markets, there can be volatility spillover from those markets.

3. Once a company's stock is made available to foreigners, they might acquire a controlling interest and challenge the domestic control of the company.

根据各种调查，披露方面的要求是影响海外上市的最大障碍。

According to various surveys, disclosure requirements appear to be the most significant barrier to overseas listings. For example, adaptation to U.S. accounting rules, which is required by the U.S. Security and Exchange Commission (SEC), is found to be the most onerous barrier facing foreign companies that consider NYSE listings. According to a German survey conducted by Glaum and Mandler (1996), one-third of the German sample firms are, in principle, interested in U.S. listings but view the required adaptation of financial statements to the U.S. Generally Accepted Accounting Rules (US-GAAP) as a major obstacle. Daimler-Benz, a German firm listed on the NYSE, employs US-GAAP as well as German accounting law and publishes two versions of consolidated financial statements with different reported earnings.[9] As can be seen from Exhibit 17.10, the company's net earnings were positive by German accounting rules but negative by American rules in 1993 and 1994. In light of the costs and benefits of overseas listings, a foreign listing should be viewed as an investment project to be undertaken if it is judged to have a positive net present value (NPV) and thus adds to the firm's value.

---

[8]As Dahya, McConnell, and Travlos (2002) point out, the standard of corporate governance has been raised significantly in the United Kingdom since the "Cadbury Committee" issued the *Code of Best Practice* in 1992, recommending that corporate boards include at least three outside directors and that the positions of chairman and CEO be held by different individuals.

[9]Unlike U.S. accounting rules, German accounting rules are driven by tax considerations and creditor protection. For this reason, prudence, not a true and fair view, is the dominant accounting principle. German managers are granted broad discretion in accounting policy, and they try to achieve income smoothing.

EXHIBIT 17.10

Daimler-Benz's Net Profit/Loss (DM bn): German vs. American Accounting Rules

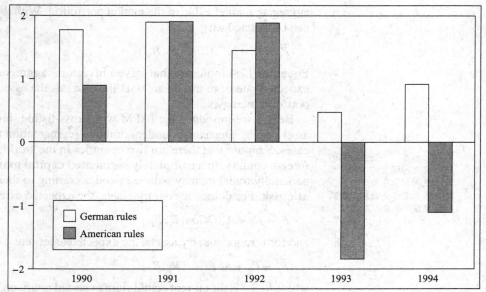

Source: The Economist, May 20, 1995.

In an extensive survey of the academic literature on the corporate decision to cross-list shares, Karolyi (1996) reports, among other things, that: (1) the share price reacts favorably to cross-border listings; (2) the total postlisting trading volume increases on average, and, for many issues, home-market trading volume also increases; (3) liquidity of trading in shares improves overall; (4) the stock's exposure to domestic market risk is significantly reduced and is associated with only a small increase in global market risk; (5) cross-border listings resulted in a net reduction in the cost of equity capital of 114 basis points on average; and (6) stringent disclosure requirements are the greatest impediment to cross-border listings. A detailed study by Miller (1999) also confirms that dual listing can mitigate barriers to international capital flows, resulting in a higher stock price and a lower cost of capital. Considering these findings, cross-border listings of stocks seem to have been, on average, positive NPV projects.

In More Depth

Capital Asset Pricing under Cross-Listings[10]

这里我们要讨论仅有部分资产可进行国际交易背景下的国际资产定价模型。

国际资产定价模型 (IAPM)

可在国际间交易的资产

不可在国际间交易的资产

风险厌恶水平

To fully understand the effects of international cross-listings, it is necessary to understand how assets will be priced under the alternative capital market regimes. In this section, we discuss an **International Asset Pricing Model (IAPM)** in a world in which some assets are internationally tradable while others are not. For ease of discussion, we will assume that cross-listed assets are **internationally tradable assets** while all other assets are **internationally nontradable assets**.

It is useful for our purpose to recalibrate the CAPM formula. Noting the definition of beta, the CAPM Equation 17.2 can be restated as:

$$\overline{R}_i = R_f + [(\overline{R}_M - R_f)/Var(R_M)]Cov(R_i, R_M) \tag{17.3}$$

For our purposes in this chapter, it is best to define $[(\overline{R}_M - R_f)/Var(\overline{R}_M)]$ as equal to $A^M M$, where A^M is a **measure of aggregate risk aversion** of all investors and M is the

[10]Readers may skip the theoretical discussion presented in this section and proceed to the numerical example without losing continuity.

aggregate market value of the market portfolio.[11] With these definitions, Equation 17.3 can be restated as:

$$\overline{R}_i = R_f + A^M M Cov(R_i, R_M) \tag{17.4}$$

Equation 17.4 indicates that, given investors' aggregate risk-aversion measure, the expected rate of return on an asset increases as the asset's covariance with the market portfolio increases.

Before we introduce the IAPM with cross-listing, however, let us first discuss the asset pricing mechanism under complete segmentation and integration as benchmark cases. Suppose that there are two countries in the world, the domestic country and the foreign country. In a **completely segmented capital market** where no assets are internationally tradable, they will be priced according to their respective **country systematic risk.** For domestic country assets, the expected asset return is calculated as

在一个完全分割的资本市场上，不存在可进行国际交易的资产，所以资产分别按照国家系统风险进行定价。

$$\overline{R}_i = R_f + A^D D Con(R_i, R_D) \tag{17.5}$$

and for foreign country assets, the expected asset return is calculated as

$$\overline{R}_g = R_f + A^F F Cov(R_g, R_F) \tag{17.6}$$

where $\overline{R}(\overline{R}_g)$ is the current equilibrium expected return on the ith (gth) domestic (foreign) asset, R_f is the risk-free rate of return that is assumed to be common to both domestic and foreign countries, $A^D(A^F)$ denotes the risk-aversion measure of domestic (foreign) investors, $D(F)$ denotes the aggregate market value of all domestic (foreign) securities, and $Cov(R_i, R_D)[Cov(R_g, R_F)]$ denotes the covariance between the future returns on the ith (gth) asset and returns on the **domestic (foreign) country market portfolio.**

本（外）国市场投资组合
完全一体化的世界资本市场
全球系统风险

By comparison, in **fully integrated world capital markets** where all assets are internationally tradable, each asset will be priced according to the **world systematic risk.** For both domestic and foreign country assets

$$\overline{R}_i = R_f + A^W W Cov(R_i, R_W) \tag{17.7}$$

世界市场组合投资

where A^W is the aggregate risk-aversion measure of world investors, W is the aggregate market value of the **world market portfolio** that comprises both the domestic and foreign portfolios, and $Cov(R_i, R_W)$ denotes the covariance between the future returns of the ith security and the world market portfolio.

我们马上会看到，在有些资产可进行国际交易而有些资产不可以进行国际交易的部分一体化的世界金融市场上，资产定价关系变得更加复杂。

As we will see shortly, the asset pricing relationship becomes more complicated in **partially integrated world financial markets** where some assets are internationally tradable (that is, those that are cross-listed) while others are nontradable.

To tell the conclusion first, internationally tradable assets will be priced *as if* world financial markets were completely integrated. Regardless of the nationality, a tradable asset will be priced solely according to its world systematic risk as described in Equation 17.7. Nontradable assets, on the other hand, will be priced according to a world systematic risk, reflecting the spillover effect generated by the traded assets, as well as a country-specific systematic risk. Due to the **pricing spillover effect,** nontradable assets will *not* be priced as if world financial markets were completely segmented.

定价溢出效应

For nontradable assets of the domestic country, the pricing relationship is given by

$$\overline{R}_i = R_f + A^W W Cov^*(R_i, R_w) + A^D D[Cor(R_i, R_D) - Cov^*(R_i, R_D)] \tag{17.8}$$

where $Cov^*(R_i, R_D)$ is the *indirect* covariance between the future returns on the ith nontradable asset and the domestic country's market portfolio that is induced by tradable assets. Formally,

$$Cov^*(R_i, R_D) = \sigma_i \sigma_D \rho_{iT} \rho_{TD} \tag{17.9}$$

---

[11]Here we assume, in fact, that investors' risk-aversion measure is constant.

Where σ_i and σ_D are, respectively, the standard deviations of future returns of the ith asset and the domestic country's market portfolio; ρi_T is the correlation coefficient between the ith nontradable asset and portfolio T of tradable assets, and ρ_{TD} is the correlation coefficient between the returns of portfolio T and the domestic country's market portfolio. Similarly, $Cov^*(R_i, R_W)$ is the *indirect* covariance between the ith nontradable asset and the world market portfolio. Nontradable assets of the foreign country will be priced in an analogous manner; thus, it is necessary to concentrate only on the pricing of nontradable assets in the domestic country.

间接的全球系统风险

Equation 17.8 indicates that nontradable assets are priced according to: (1) the **indirect world systematic risk,** $Cov^*(R_i, R_W)$, and, (2) the *pure* domestic systematic risk, $Cov(R_i, R_D) - Cov^*(R_i, R_D)$, which is the domestic systematic risk, net of the part induced by tradable assets. Despite the fact that nontradable assets are traded only within the domestic country, they are priced according to an indirect world systematic risk as well as a country-specific systematic risk. This partial international pricing of nontradable assets is due to the pricing spillover effect generated by tradable assets. (The asset pricing spillover effect was first expounded in Alexander, Eun, and Janakiramanan, 1987.)

尽管不可交易资产
只被本国投资者所持有，
但它们部分地得到国际
化定价，这反映了可交
易资产的溢出效应。

Although nontradable assets are exclusively held by domestic (local) investors, they are priced partially internationally, reflecting the spillover effect generated by tradable assets. As can be inferred from Equation 17.8, nontradable assets will not be subject to the spillover effect and thus be priced solely domestically only if they are not correlated at all to tradable assets. This, of course, is not a very likely scenario. The pricing model also implies that if the domestic and foreign market portfolios can be exactly replicated using tradable assets, all nontradable, as well as tradable, assets will be priced fully internationally as if world financial markets were completely integrated.

搭便车

The IAPM has a few interesting implications. First, international listing (trading) of assets in otherwise segmented markets directly integrates international capital markets by making these assets tradable. Second, firms with nontradable assets essentially get a **free ride** from firms with tradable assets in the sense that the former indirectly benefit from international integration in terms of a lower cost of capital and higher asset prices, without incurring any associated costs. Appendix 17A makes this point clear using numerical simulations.

The asset pricing model with nontraded assets demonstrates that the benefits from partial integration of capital markets can be transmitted to the entire economy through the pricing spillover effect. The pricing spillover effect has an important policy implication: *To maximize the benefits from partial integration of capital markets, a country should choose to internationally cross-list those assets that are most highly correlated with the domestic market portfolio.*

Consistent with the theoretical analyses presented above, many firms have indeed experienced a reduction in the cost of capital when their stocks were listed on foreign markets. In their study of foreign stocks listed on U.S. stock exchanges, Alexander, Eun, and Janakiramanan (1988) found that foreign firms from such countries as Australia and Japan experienced a substantial reduction in the cost of capital. Canadian firms, in contrast, experienced a rather modest reduction in the cost of capital upon U.S. listings, probably because Canadian markets were more integrated with U.S. markets than other markets when U.S. listings took place.

The Effect of Foreign Equity Ownership Restrictions

结果，发达国家与
发展中国家的政府经常
对外国人所能持有的本
地企业所有权的最大百
分比施加限制。

While companies have incentives to internationalize their ownership structure to lower the cost of capital and increase their market values, they may be concerned, at the same time, with possible loss of corporate control to foreigners. Consequently, governments in both developed and developing countries often impose restrictions on the maximum

EXHIBIT 17.11	Restrictions on Equity Ownership by Foreigners: Historical Examples
Country	Restrictions on Foreigners
Australia	10% in banks, 20% in broadcasting, and 50% in new mining ventures.
Canada	20% in broadcasting, and 25% in bank/insurance companies.
China	Foreigners are restricted to B shares; locals are eligible for A shares.
France	Limited to 20%.
India	Limited to 49%.
Indonesia	Limited to 49%.
Mexico	Limited to 49%.
Japan	Maximum of 25–50% for several major firms; acquisition of over 10% of a single firm subject to approval of the Ministry of Finance.
Korea	Limited to 20%.
Malaysia	20% in banks and 30% in natural resources.
Norway	0% in pulp, paper, and mining, 10% in banks, 20% in industrial and oil shares, and 50% in shipping companies.
Spain	0% in defense industries and mass media. Limited to 50% for other firms.
Sweden	20% of voting shares and 40% of total equity capital.
Switzerland	Foreigners can be restricted to bearer shares.
U.K.	Government retains the veto power over any foreign takeover of British firms.

Source: Various publications of Price Waterhouse.

percentage ownership of local firms by foreigners. In countries like India, Mexico, and Thailand, foreigners are allowed to purchase no more than 49 percent of the outstanding shares of local firms. These countries want to make sure that foreigners do not acquire majority stakes in local companies. France and Sweden once imposed an even tighter restriction of 20 percent. In Korea, foreigners were allowed to own only 20 percent of the shares of any local firm until recently.

In Switzerland, a local firm can issue two different classes of equity shares, bearer shares and registered shares. Foreigners are often allowed to purchase only bearer shares. In a similar vein, Chinese firms issue A shares and B shares, and foreigners are allowed to hold only B shares. Exhibit 17.11 lists examples of historical restrictions on foreign ownership of local firms for various countries. Obviously, these restrictions are imposed as a means of ensuring domestic control of local firms, especially those that are considered strategically important to national interests.[12]

Pricing-to-Market Phenomenon

换句话说，由于对外国投资者实施了法律限制，所以股价可能呈现出**市场双重定价现象**(PTM)。

Suppose that foreigners, if allowed, would like to buy 30 percent of a Korean firm, but they are constrained to purchase at most 20 percent due to ownership constraints imposed on foreigners. Because the constraint is effective in limiting desired foreign ownership, foreign and domestic investors may face different market share prices. In other words, shares can exhibit a dual pricing or **pricing-to-market (PTM) phenomenon** due to legal restrictions imposed on foreigners.

CASE APPLICATION	Nestlé[13]

The majority of publicly traded Swiss corporations have up to three classes of common stock: (1) registered stock, (2) voting bearer stock, and (3) nonvoting bearer stock. Until

[12]Stulz and Wasserfallen (1995) suggest a theoretical possibility that firms may impose restrictions on foreigners' equity ownership to maximize their market values. They argue that when domestic and foreign investors have differential demand functions for a firm's stocks, the firm can maximize its market value by discriminating between domestic and foreign investors.

[13]The Nestlé case was briefly mentioned in Chapter 1. We offer an in-depth analysis of the case here.

EXHIBIT 17.12

Price Spread between Bearer and Registered Shares of Nestlé

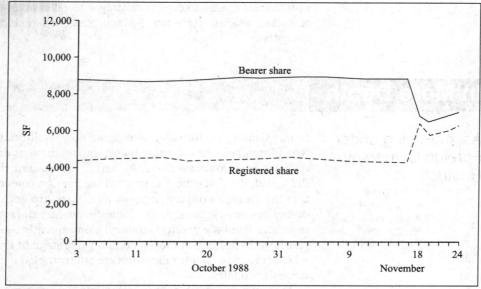

Source: Financial Times, November 26, 1988, p. 1. Adapted with permission.

recently, foreigners were not allowed to buy registered stocks; they were only allowed to buy bearer stocks. Registered stocks were made available only to Swiss nationals.

In the case of Nestlé, a well-known Swiss multinational corporation that derives more than 95 percent of its revenue from overseas markets, registered shares accounted for about 68 percent of the votes outstanding. This implies that it was practically impossible for foreigners to gain control of the firm. On November 17, 1988, however, Nestlé announced that the firm would lift the ban on foreigners buying registered shares. The announcement was made after the Zurich Stock Exchange closed.

Nestlé's board of directors mentioned two reasons for lifting the ban on foreigners. First, despite the highly multinational nature of its business activities, Nestlé maintained a highly nationalistic ownership structure. At the same time, Nestlé made high-profile cross-border acquisitions, such as Rowntree (U.K.) and Carnation (U.S.). Nestlé's practices thus were criticized as unfair and incompatible with free-market principles. The firm needed to remedy this situation. Second, Nestlé realized that the ban against foreigners holding registered shares had the effect of increasing its cost of capital, negatively affecting its competitive position in the world market.

As Exhibit 17.12 illustrates, prior to the lifting of the ban on foreigners, (voting) bearer shares traded at about twice the price of registered shares. The higher price for bearer shares suggests that foreigners desired to hold more than they were allowed to in the absence of ownership restrictions imposed on them. When the ban was lifted, however, prices of the two types of shares immediately converged; the price of bearer shares declined by about 25 percent, whereas that of registered shares increased by about 35 percent. Because registered shares represented about two-thirds of the total number of voting shares, the total market value of Nestlé increased substantially when it fully internationalized its ownership structure. This, of course, means that Nestlé's cost of equity capital declined substantially.

Hietala (1989) documented the PTM phenomenon in the Finnish stock market. Finnish firms used to issue restricted and unrestricted shares, with foreigners allowed to purchase only unrestricted shares. Unrestricted shares accounted for at most 20 percent of the total number of shares of any Finnish firm. Because of this legal restriction, if foreigners desired to hold more than 20 percent of a Finnish firm, dual pricing could result. Indeed, Hietala found that most Finnish firms exhibited the PTM phenomenon, with unrestricted shares trading at roughly a 15 percent to 40 percent premium relative to restricted shares. Recently, Finland abolished restrictions imposed on foreigners altogether.

In More Depth

Asset Pricing under Foreign Ownership Restrictions[14]

在本小节中，我们正式探讨一下当外国人遭遇所能持有的本国企业所有权份额的上限时，均衡资产价格是如何定价的。

In this section, we formally investigate how equilibrium asset prices are determined when foreigners are subject to ownership restrictions on the maximum proportionate ownership of domestic firms. As before, we assume that there are two countries in the world, the domestic country and the foreign country. For simplicity, we assume that the foreign country imposes an ownership constraint on investors from the domestic country, but that the domestic country does not impose any constraints on investors from the foreign country. Consequently, domestic country investors are restricted to holding at most a certain percentage of the shares of any foreign firms, whereas foreign country investors are not restricted in any way from investing in the domestic country.

Since we assume that there are no investment restrictions on domestic shares, both domestic and foreign country investors face the same price for the same domestic asset, which equals the perfect capital market price. As far as domestic assets are concerned, the law of one price prevails. For foreign shares, however, the PTM phenomenon applies.

Specifically, domestic country assets will be priced according to Equation 17.7, the fully integrated world capital market's IAPM. Foreign shares will be priced differently, depending upon whether the investor is from the foreign or domestic country. Investors from the domestic country will pay a premium above and beyond the *perfect market price* that would prevail in the absence of restrictions, whereas investors from the foreign country will receive a discount from the perfect market price. This implies that the domestic country investors would require a lower return on foreign country shares than the foreign country investors.

Eun and Janakiramanan (1986) offer the following solutions for the equilibrium rates of return for foreign asset i from the domestic and the foreign country investors' perspectives, respectively:

$$\overline{R}_i^d = R_f + A^W W Cov(R_i, R_W) - (A^W W - \delta A^D D)[Cov(R_i, R_F) - Cov(R_i, R_S)] \quad \textbf{(17.10)}$$

$$\overline{R}_i^f = R_f + A^W W Cov(R_i, R_W) + [(1-\delta)A^D D - A^W W]$$
$$[Cov(R_i, R_F) - Cov(R_i, R_s)] \quad \textbf{(17.11)}$$

投资组合替代

净外国市场风险

where δ represents the fraction of the *i*th foreign firm that domestic country investors as a whole are allowed to own. In the above equations, portfolio S refers to the **substitution portfolio,** which is the portfolio of domestic country assets that is most highly correlated with the foreign market portfolio F. Portfolio S can thus be regarded as the domestic country investors' best *home-made* substitute for the foreign market portfolio F.

According to the above model, the equilibrium rates of return depend critically on (1) the severity of the ownership constraint (δ) and, (2) the ability of domestic country investors to replicate the foreign market portfolio using their domestic assets, which is measured by the **pure foreign market risk,** $Cov(R_i, R_F) - Cov(R_i, R_S)$. In the special case where portfolio S is a perfect substitute for the foreign market portfolio F, we have $Cov(R_i, R_F) = Cov(R_i, R_S)$. In this event, the foreign asset will be priced as if world capital markets are fully integrated from both the domestic and foreign investors' perspectives, even though an ownership constraint is in force. In general, however, domestic country

[14]Readers may proceed to the numerical example without losing continuity.

investors will pay premiums for foreign assets (that is, accept a lower rate of return than the perfect capital market rate) to the extent that they cannot precisely replicate the foreign market portfolio using domestic assets. Foreign country investors, on the other hand, will get a discount (that is, receive a higher rate than the perfect capital market rate).

EXAMPLE 17.2

A Numerical Illustration To illustrate the effect of foreign ownership restrictions on the firm's cost of equity capital, we conduct a numerical simulation using the model economy described in Exhibit 17.13.

Exhibit 17.13 provides the standard deviations and correlation matrix of our model economy. Firms D1 to D4 belong to the domestic country and firms F1 to F4 belong to the foreign country. For simplicity, the correlation matrix reflects the stylized fact that asset returns are typically less correlated between countries than within a country; the pairwise correlation is uniformly assumed to be 0.50 within a country and 0.15 between countries. Both domestic and foreign investors are assumed to have the same aggregate risk-aversion measure, and the risk-free rate is assumed to be 9 percent.

Exhibit 17.14 considers the case in which the foreign country imposes a 20 percent ownership constraint ($\delta_F = 20$ percent), whereas the domestic country does not impose any constraint on foreign investors. In this case, domestic country assets are priced as if the capital markets were completely integrated. Foreign country assets, however, are priced to market.

In general, the exhibit shows that the firm's cost of capital tends to be higher under the 20 percent ownership constraint than under complete integration. This implies that restricting foreign equity ownership in a firm will have a negative effect on the firm's cost of equity capital. For comparison purposes, we again provide the results obtained under complete segmentation and integration. Specifically, consider foreign firm F1. The exhibit shows that with the 20 percent ownership constraint, the firm's cost of capital is 22.40 percent, which is computed as a weighted average of the required returns by the domestic and foreign country investors in F1. Note that in the absence of the restriction, the firm's cost of capital would have been substantially lower, 19.03 percent. It is also noteworthy that when the PTM phenomenon prevails, the firm's cost of capital depends on which investors, domestic or foreign, supply capital. The exhibit also provides the case where both the domestic and foreign countries impose restrictions at the 20 percent level, that is, $\delta_D = 20\%$ and $\delta_F = 20\%$. Interpretation of this case is left to readers.

EXHIBIT 17.13		Description of the Model Economy							
	Expected Future	**Standard Deviation of Share**	**Correlation Matrix**						
Firm	Share Price ($)	Price ($)	D2	D3	D4	F1	F2	F3	F4
D1	100	16	.50	.50	.50	.15	.15	.15	.15
D2	100	20		.50	.50	.15	.15	.15	.15
D3	100	24			.50	.15	.15	.15	.15
D4	100	28				.15	.15	.15	.15
F1	100	18					.50	.50	.50
F2	100	22						.50	.50
F3	100	26							.50
F4	100	30							

Note: Firms D1 to D4 are from the domestic country, whereas firms F1 to F4 are from the foreign country. The risk-free interest rate is assumed to be 9%. The domestic and foreign country investors are assumed to have the same aggregate (absolute) risk-aversion measure.

Asset	Complete Segmentation	σ-constraint		Complete Integration
		$\delta_D = 20\%$ $\delta_F = 20\%$	$\delta_F = 20\%$	
A. Equilibrium Asset Prices ($)[a]				
D1	81.57	83.04/87.45	85.25	85.25
D2	78.53	80.45/86.22	83.34	83.34
D3	75.30	77.75/85.07	81.41	81.41
D4	71.88	74.86/83.82	79.34	79.34
F1	79.19	86.91/81.12	87.86/80.16	84.01
F2	75.87	85.66/78.31	86.87/77.11	81.99
F3	72.34	84.50/75.38	85.92/73.96	79.94
F4	68.62	83.24/72.28	84.90/70.62	77.76
B. Cost of Equity Capital (%)				
D1	22.59	19.15	17.30	17.30
D2	27.34	22.54	19.99	19.99
D3	32.80	26.24	22.84	22.84
D4	39.12	30.46	26.04	26.04
F1	26.28	21.54	22.40	19.03
F2	31.80	25.34	26.48	21.97
F3	38.24	39.96	32.82	25.09
F4	45.73	47.95	38.85	28.60

[a]The two figures indicate the asset prices for domestic/foreign country investors, respectively.

The Financial Structure of Subsidiaries

One of the problems faced by financial managers of multinational corporations is how to determine the financial structure of foreign subsidiaries. According to Lessard and Shapiro (1984), there are three different approaches to determining the subsidiary's financial structure:

1. Conform to the parent company's norm.

2. Conform to the local norm of the country where the subsidiary operates.

3. Vary judiciously to capitalize on opportunities to lower taxes, reduce financing costs and risks, and take advantage of various market imperfections.

Which approach to take depends largely on whether and to what extent the parent company is responsible for the subsidiary's financial obligations. When the parent is fully responsible for the subsidiary's obligations, the independent financial structure of the subsidiary is irrelevant; it is the parent's overall financial structure that becomes relevant. When the parent is legally and morally responsible for the subsidiary's debts, potential creditors will examine the parent's overall financial conditions, not the subsidiary's.

When, however, the parent company is willing to let its subsidiary default, or the parent's guarantee of its subsidiary's financial obligations becomes difficult to enforce across national borders, the subsidiary's financial structure becomes relevant. In this case, potential creditors will examine the subsidiary's financial conditions closely to assess default risk. As a result, the subsidiary should choose its own financial structure to reduce default risk and thus financing costs.

In reality, the parent company cannot let its subsidiary default on its debts without expecting its worldwide operations to be hampered in one way or another. Default by a subsidiary can deplete the parent's reputational capital, possibly increase its own cost of capital, and certainly make it difficult to undertake future projects in the country where default occurred. Various surveys, including one by Robert Stobaugh, strongly

采取哪种方式很大程度上取决于母公司是否对子公司债务承担完全责任或承担责任的程度。

在现实中，如果母公司认为其全球经营并未受到某种形式的妨碍，公司是不会让它的子公司因债务而破产的。

suggest that parent firms of MNCs indeed will not allow their subsidiaries to default, regardless of circumstances.

An immediate implication of the parent's legal and moral obligation to honor its subsidiary's debts is that the parent should monitor its subsidiary's financial conditions closely and make sure that the firm's overall financial conditions are not adversely affected by the subsidiary's financial structure. What really matters is the marginal impact that the subsidiary's financial structure may have on the parent's worldwide financial structure. The subsidiary's financial structure should be chosen so that the parent's overall cost of capital can be minimized.

根据上面的讨论，前两种决定子公司财务结构的方式都不能被认为是合适的。

In light of the above discussion, neither the first nor the second approach to determining the subsidiary's financial structure can be deemed appropriate. The first approach, which calls for replicating the parent's financial structure, is not necessarily consistent with minimizing the parent's overall cost of capital. Suppose the subsidiary can locally borrow at a subsidized interest rate because the host government is eager to attract foreign investments. In this situation, the subsidiary should borrow locally and exploit the lower interest rate, even if this means that the subsidiary's debt ratio will exceed the parent's norm. If deemed necessary, the parent can simply lower its own debt ratio. In other words, the distribution of debt between the parent and the subsidiary can be adjusted to take advantage of the subsidized loans. Also, in a special case where the subsidiary is operating in a country that regulates its financial structure, it would be difficult to replicate the parent's norm even if that were desirable.

The second approach, proposed by Stonehill and Stitzel (1969), calls for adopting the local financing norm. In essence, the approach is based on "When in Rome, do as the Romans do." By following the local norm, the firm can reduce the chance of being singled out for criticism. This approach makes sense only when the parent is not responsible for the subsidiary's obligations, and the subsidiary has to depend on local financing due to, say, segmentation of financial markets. Otherwise, it does not make much sense. Suppose each foreign subsidiary conforms to the local financing norm, which reflects the host country's cultural, economic, and institutional environments. Then, the parent firm's worldwide financial structure will be determined strictly in a "residual" manner. The overall financial structure so determined is not likely to be the optimal one that minimizes the parent's overall cost of capital. When the host country's norm reflects, for example, the immature nature of local financial markets, a subsidiary of the MNC with ready access to global financial markets should not slavishly follow the local norm. Doing so means that the MNC gives up its advantage in terms of a lower cost of capital.

This brings us to the third approach, which appears to be the most reasonable and consistent with the goal of minimizing the firm's overall cost of capital. The subsidiary should take advantage of subsidized loans as much as possible whenever available. It should also take advantage of tax deductions of interest payments by borrowing more heavily than is implied by the parent's norm when the corporate income tax rate is higher in the host country than in the home country, unless foreign tax credits are useful.

Apart from the tax factor, political risk is another factor that should be considered in choosing the method of financing the subsidiary. Political risk generally favors local financing over the parent's direct financing. The parent company can renounce the subsidiary's local debt in the event that the subsidiary's assets are expropriated. When the subsidiary is financed by local creditors and shareholders, the chance of expropriation itself can be lowered. When a subsidiary is operating in a developing country, financing from such international development agencies as the World Bank and International Finance Corporation will lower political risk. When the choice is between external debt and equity financing, political risk tends to favor the former. This is the case because the host government tolerates repatriation of funds in the form of interest much better than dividends.

总之，既然母公司在法律和（或）道德上对子公司的财务债务承担责任，它在决定子公司财务结构时就要考虑后者对母公司整体财务结构的影响。

To summarize, since the parent company is responsible, legally and/or morally, for its subsidiary's financial obligations, it has to decide the subsidiary's financial structure considering the latter's effect on the parent's overall financial structure. The subsidiary, however, should be allowed to take advantage of any favorable financing opportunities available in the host country, because that is consistent with the goal of minimizing the overall cost of capital of the parent. If necessary, the parent can adjust its own financial structure to bring about the optimal overall financial structure.

SUMMARY

本章讨论了跨国公司的资本成本问题。随着金融市场的不断自由化和管制的日益放松，全球的大型公司通过允许外国人持有公司的股票和债券来实现公司资本结构的国际化。

1. 资金成本的国际比较表明，虽然近些年主要国家的资金成本趋于一致，但国际金融市场尚未实现完全一体化。这表明企业可通过在海外审慎筹资来提高公司的市场价值。

2. 如果企业在分割的资本市场上经营，可通过在境外股票市场的境外上市来降低市场分割所产生的负面影响，进而实现股票的国际交易。

3. 企业可通过境外上市来获益，主要利益有二：（1）更低的资本成本，更高的股价；（2）新的资本来源渠道。

4. 如果企业的股票在处于非分割资本市场的外国交易所境外上市，那么股票就会按照全球系统风险来定价，将国际资本市场看成实现了完全一体化。不可在国际间交易的资产应按照国别系统风险和间接的全球系统风险进行定价，以反映可在国际间交易的资产所产生的定价溢出效应。

5. 尽管世界金融市场呈现出更为自由化的趋向，但许多国家仍然对国外投资进行限制，尤其是对外国投资者所能持有的当地企业的最大股权比例实施限制。在对所有权存在限制的情况下，外国和本国的投资者可能面临不同的股价，结果产生了市场双重定价现象。市场双重定价现象通常会导致企业整体资本成本的上升。

6. 为了实现整体资本成本的最小化，母公司应决定其子公司的融资方式。就母公司对子公司的债务承担责任而言，子公司自身的财务结构是不相关的。

In this chapter, we have discussed the cost of capital for a multinational firm. Reflecting the trend toward more liberalized and deregulated financial markets, major corporations of the world are internationalizing their capital structure by allowing foreigners to hold their shares and debts.

1. International comparison of the cost of funds indicates that while the costs of funds are converging among major countries in recent years, international financial markets are less than fully integrated. This suggests that firms can increase their market values by judiciously raising capital overseas.

2. When a firm is operating in a segmented capital market, it can reduce the negative effects by cross-listing its stock on foreign stock markets, thereby making the stock internationally tradable.

3. A firm can benefit from international cross-listings in terms of (a) a lower cost of capital and a higher stock price, and (b) access to new sources of capital.

4. When a firm's stock is cross-listed on foreign exchanges in an otherwise segmented capital market, the stock will be priced according to the world systematic risk as if international capital markets were fully integrated. Internationally nontradable assets will be priced according to a country-specific systematic risk and an indirect world systematic risk, reflecting the pricing spillover effect generated by internationally tradable assets.

5. Although the trend is toward more liberal world financial markets, many countries still maintain restrictions on investment by foreigners, especially the maximum percentage ownership of a local firm by foreigners. Under an ownership constraint, foreign and domestic country investors may face different share prices, resulting in the pricing-to-market phenomenon (PTM). PTM generally raises the firm's overall cost of capital.

6. The parent company should decide the financing method for its own subsidiary with a view to minimizing the parent's overall cost of capital. To the extent that the parent is responsible for its subsidiary's financial obligations, the subsidiary's own financial structure is irrelevant.

KEY WORDS

beta, *424*
Capital Asset
   Pricing Model
   (CAPM), *424*
capital structure, *422*
completely segmented
   capital market, *436*
cost of capital, *423*

country systematic
   risk, *436*
domestic (foreign)
   country market
   portfolio, *436*
free ride, *437*
fully integrated world
   capital markets, *436*

indirect world systematic
   risk, *437*
International Asset
   Pricing Model
   (IAPM), *435*
internationally
   nontradable asset, *435*

QUESTIONS

1. Suppose that your firm is operating in a segmented capital market. What actions would you recommend to mitigate the negative effects?

2. Explain why and how a firm's cost of capital may decrease when the firm's stock is cross-listed on foreign stock exchanges.

3. Explain the pricing *spillover effect*.

4. In what sense do firms with nontradable assets get a *free ride* from firms whose securities are internationally tradable?

5. Define and discuss *indirect world systematic risk*.

6. Discuss how the cost of capital is determined in segmented versus integrated capital markets.

7. Suppose there exists a nontradable asset with a perfect positive correlation with a portfolio *T* of tradable assets. How will the nontradable asset be priced?

8. Discuss what factors motivated Novo Industri to seek U.S. listing of its stock. What lessons can be derived from Novo's experiences?

9. Discuss foreign equity ownership restrictions. Why do you think countries impose these restrictions?

10. Explain the *pricing-to-market phenomenon*.

11. Explain how the premium and discount are determined when assets are priced to market. When would the law of one price prevail in international capital markets even if foreign equity ownership restrictions are imposed?

12. Under what conditions will the foreign subsidiary's financial structure become relevant?

13. Under what conditions would you recommend that the foreign subsidiary conform to the local norm of financial structure?

PROBLEMS

Answer problems 1–3 based on the stock market data given by the following table.

	Correlation Coefficients				
	Telmex	**Mexico**	**World**	**SD (%)**	**R̄ (%)**
Telmex	1.00	.90	0.60	18	?
Mexico		1.00	0.75	15	14
World			1.00	10	12

The above table provides the correlations among Telmex, a telephone/communication company located in Mexico, the Mexico stock market index, and the world market index, together with the standard deviations (SD) of returns and the expected returns (R̄). The risk-free rate is 5%.

1. Compute the domestic country beta of Telmex as well as its world beta. What do these betas measure?

2. Suppose the Mexican stock market is segmented from the rest of the world. Using the CAPM paradigm, estimate the equity cost of capital of Telmex.

3. Suppose now that Telmex has made its shares tradable internationally via cross-listing on NYSE. Again using the CAPM paradigm, estimate Telmex's equity cost of capital. Discuss the possible effects of international pricing of Telmex shares on the share prices and the firm's investment decisions.

INTERNET EXERCISES

You are the controlling shareholder of Dragon Semicon based in China's Taiwan, a company with a strong growth potential. In order to fund future growth, you are considering listing the company stock either on the New York or the London stock exchange. Visit the websites of the two exchanges and find out and compare their listing and disclosure requirements for foreign companies.

REFERENCES & SUGGESTED READINGS

Adler, Michael. "The Cost of Capital and Valuation of a Two-Country Firm." *Journal of Finance* 29 (1974), pp. 119–32.

Alexander, Gordon, Cheol Eun, and S. Janakiramanan. "Asset Pricing and Dual Listing on Foreign Capital Markets: A Note." *Journal of Finance* 42 (1987), pp. 151–58.

——. "International Listings and Stock Returns: Some Empirical Evidence." *Journal of Financial and Quantitative Analysis* 23 (1988), pp. 135–51.

Bailey, Warren, and Julapa Jagtiani. "Foreign Ownership Restrictions and Stock Prices in the Thai Market." *Journal of Financial Economics* 36 (1994), pp. 57–87.

Black, Fisher. "International Capital Market Equilibrium with Investment Barriers." *Journal of Financial Economics* 1 (1974), pp. 337–52.

Bodie, Zvi, Alex Kane, and Alan J. Marcus. *Investments,* 2nd ed. Burr Ridge, Ill.: Irwin, 1993.

Chan, K. C., Andrew Karolyi, and Rene Stulz. "Global Financial Markets and the Risk Premium on U.S. Equity." *Journal of Financial Economics* 32 (1992), pp. 137–67.

Chaplinsky, Susan, and Latha Ramchand. "The Rationale for Global Equity Offerings." University of Virginia Working Paper, 1995.

Cohn, Richard, and John Pringle. "Imperfections in International Financial Markets: Implications for Risk Premia and the Cost of Capital to Firms." *Journal of Finance* 28 (1973), pp. 59–66.

Dahya, J., J. McConnell, and N. Travlos. "The Cadbury Committee, Corporate Performance, and Top Management Turnover." *Journal of Finance* 57 (2002), pp. 461–483.

Doidge, Craig, Andrew Karolyi, and Rene Stulz. "Why Are Foreign Firms Listed in the U.S. Worth More?" Ohio State University Working Paper (2001).

Errunza, Vihang, and Etienne Losq. "International Asset Pricing under Mild Segmentation: Theory and Test." *Journal of Finance* 40 (1985), pp. 105–24.

Eun, Cheol, and S. Janakiramanan. "A Model of International Asset Pricing with a Constraint on the Foreign Equity Ownership." *Journal of Finance* 41 (1986), pp. 897–914.

French, K., and J. Poterba. "Investor Diversification and International Equity Markets." *American Economic Review* 81 (1991), pp. 222–26.

Glaum, Martin, and Udo Mandler. "Global Accounting Harmonization from a German Perspective: Bridging the GAAP." Europa-Universitaet Viadrina Working Paper, 1996.

Harvey, Campbell. "The World Price of Covariance Risk." *Journal of Finance* 46 (1991), pp. 111–57.

Hietala, Pekka. "Asset Pricing in Partially Segmented Markets: Evidence from the Finnish Markets." *Journal of Finance* 44 (1989), pp. 697–718.

Jayaraman, N., K. Shastri, and K. Tandon. "The Impact of International Cross Listings on Risk and Return: The Evidence from American Depository Receipts." *Journal of Banking and Finance* 17 (1993), pp. 91–103.

Karolyi, G. Andrew. "What Happens to Stocks That List Shares Abroad? A Survey of the Evidence and its Managerial Implications." University of Western Ontario Working Paper, 1996.

Lang, Mark, Karl Lins, and Darius Miller. "ADRs, Analysts, and Accuracy: Does Cross Listing in the United States Improve a Firm's Information Environment and Increase Market Value?" *Journal of Accounting Research* 41 (2003), pp. 317–45.

Lee, Kwang Chul, and Chuck C. Y. Kwok. "Multinational Corporations vs. Domestic Corporations: International Environmental Factors and Determinants of Capital Structure." *Journal of International Business Studies* 19 (1988), pp. 195–217.

Lessard, D., and A. Shapiro. "Guidelines for Global Financing Choices." *Midland Corporate Finance Journal* 3 (1984), pp. 68–80.

Loderer, Claudio, and Andreas Jacobs. "The Nestlé Crash." *Journal of Financial Economics* 37 (1995), pp. 315–39.

McCauley, Robert, and Steven Zimmer. "Exchange Rates and International Differences in the Cost of Capital." In Y. Amihud and R. Levich (eds.), *Exchange Rates and Corporate Performance*. Burr Ridge, IL: Irwin, 1994, pp. 119–48.

Miller, Darius. "The Market Reaction to International Cross-listing: Evidence from Depository Receipts." *Journal of Financial Economics* 51 (1999), pp. 103–23.

Mittoo, Usha. "Additional Evidence on Integration in the Canadian Stock Market." *Journal of Finance* 47 (1992), pp. 2035–54.

Ross, Stephen A., Randolph W. Westerfield, and Jeffrey F. Jaffee. *Corporate Finance,* 3rd ed. Burr Ridge, Ill.: Irwin, 1987.

Sarkissian, Sergei, and Michael Schill. "The Overseas Listing Decision: New Evidence of Proximity Preference." *Review of Financial Studies* 17 (2004), pp. 769–809.

Stapleton, Richard, and Marti Subrahmanyan. "Market Imperfections, Capital Market Equilibrium and Corporation Finance." *Journal of Finance* 32 (1977), pp. 307–21.

——. *Capital Market Equilibrium and Corporate Financial Decisions.* Greenwich, Conn.: JAI Press, 1980.

Stobaugh, Robert. "Financing Foreign Subsidiaries of U.S.-Controlled Multinational Enterprises." *Journal of International Business Studies* (1970), pp. 43–64.

Stonehill, Arthur, and Kare Dullum. *Internationalizing the Cost of Capital.* New York: John Wiley and Sons, 1982.

Stonehill, Arthur, and Thomas Stitzel. "Financial Structure and Multinational Corporations." *California Management Review* (1969), pp. 91–96.

Stulz, Rene. "On the Effect of Barriers to International Investment." *Journal of Finance* 36 (1981), pp. 923–34.

——. "Pricing Capital Assets in an International Setting: An Introduction." *Journal of International Business Studies* 16 (1985), pp. 55–74.

——. "The Cost of Capital in Internationally Integrated Markets: The Case of Nestlé." *European Financial Management* 1 (1995), pp. 11–22.

——. "Does the Cost of Capital Differ across Countries? An Agency Perspective." *European Financial Management* 2 (1996), pp. 11–22.

Stulz, Rene, and Walter Wasserfallen. "Foreign Equity Investment Restrictions, Capital Flight, and Shareholder Wealth Maximization: Theory and Evidence." *Review of Financial Studies* 8 (1995), pp. 1019–57.

Subrahmanyam, Marti. "On the Optimality of International Capital Market Integration." *Journal of Financial Economics* 2 (1975), pp. 3–28.

17A Pricing of Nontradable Assets: Numerical Simulations

To further explain the theoretical results presented in the preceding section, we provide a numerical illustration in which we assume a two-country and eight-firm world as described by Exhibit 17.13 to arrive at the equilibrium stock prices and expected rates of return, or costs of equity capital, under the alternative structures of international capital markets.

Exhibit 17A.1 presents the equilibrium asset prices and the costs of equity capital for each of the eight firms as computed according to the asset pricing models presented earlier. As the exhibit shows, cross-listing of domestic asset D1 on the foreign exchange in an otherwise segmented market decreases the equilibrium cost of equity capital from 22.59 percent (under segmentation) to 17.30 percent upon cross-listing. Clearly, international trading of the asset leads to a decrease in the cost of capital.

Once asset D1 is cross-listed, it will be priced (at $85.25) to yield the same expected rate of return that it would obtain under complete integration. Moreover, when the domestic asset is cross-listed, other domestic assets, which remain internationally nontradable, also experience a decrease in their costs of equity capital. Take asset D2 for example; the cost of capital falls from 27.34 percent under segmentation to 23.72 percent after cross-listing asset D1. This reflects the spillover effect generated by asset D1 when it becomes internationally tradable. Additionally, Exhibit 17A.1 shows that when foreign asset F1 is cross-listed in the domestic country, it will lower its own cost of equity capital as well as that of the other foreign firms. The exhibit shows that when F1 is cross-listed, its cost of equity capital falls from 26.28 percent to 19.03 percent, the same as if capital markets were completely integrated. Moreover, other foreign assets that remain internationally nontradable also experience a decrease in their costs of capital as a result of the spillover effect from the cross-listing of F1.

EXHIBIT 17A.1

International Capital Market Equilibria: The Effect of Cross-Listings

Asset	Complete Segmentation	Cross-Listing Asset D1	Cross-Listing Assets D1 and F1	Complete Integration
A. Equilibrium Asset Prices ($)				
D1	81.57	85.25	85.25	85.25
D2	78.53	80.83	80.37	83.34
D3	75.30	78.06	77.51	81.41
D4	71.88	75.10	74.45	79.34
F1	79.19	78.57	84.01	84.01
F2	75.87	75.11	78.36	81.99
F3	72.34	71.45	75.29	79.94
F4	68.62	67.59	72.02	77.76
B. Cost of Equity Capital (%)				
D1	22.59	17.30	17.30	17.30
D2	27.34	23.72	24.42	19.99
D3	32.80	28.11	29.02	22.84
D4	39.12	33.16	34.32	26.04
F1	26.28	27.28	19.03	19.03
F2	31.80	33.14	27.62	21.97
F3	38.24	39.96	30.97	25.09
F4	45.73	47.95	36.10	28.60

18 International Capital Budgeting

净现值（NPV）

IN THIS BOOK, we have taken the view that the fundamental goal of the financial manager is shareholder wealth maximization. Shareholder wealth is created when the firm makes an investment that will return more in a present value sense than the investment costs. Perhaps the most important decisions that confront the financial manager are which capital projects to select. By their very nature, capital projects denote investment in capital assets that make up the productive capacity of the firm. These investments, which are typically expensive relative to the firm's overall value, will determine how efficiently the firm will produce the product it intends to sell, and thus will also determine how profitable the firm will be. In total, these decisions determine the competitive position of the firm in the product marketplace and the firm's long-run survival. Consequently, a valid framework for analysis is important. The generally accepted methodology in modern finance is to use the **net present value (NPV)** discounted cash flow model.

本章旨在详细阐述一种分析跨国公司进行海外资本项目投资的方法。

In Chapter 16, we explored why a MNC would make foreign direct investment in another country. In Chapter 17, we discussed the cost of capital for a multinational firm. We saw that a firm that could source funds internationally rather than just domestically could feasibly have a lower cost of capital than a domestic firm because of its greater opportunities to raise funds. A lower cost of capital means that more capital projects will have a positive net present value to the multinational firm. Our objective in this chapter is to detail a methodology for a multinational firm to analyze the investment in a capital project in a foreign land. The methodology we present is based on an analytical framework formalized by Donald Lessard (1985). The adjusted present value (APV) methodology is an extension of the NPV technique suggested for use in analyzing domestic capital expenditures. As will be seen, the APV methodology facilitates the analysis of special cash flows that are unique to international capital expenditures.

Most readers will already be familiar with NPV analysis and its superiority in comparison to other capital expenditure evaluation techniques as a tool for assisting the financial manager in maximizing shareholder wealth. Therefore, the chapter begins with only a brief review of the basic NPV capital budgeting framework. Next, the basic NPV framework is extended into an APV model by way of analogy to the Modigliani-Miller equation for the value of a levered firm. Following this, the APV model is extended to make it suitable for use by a MNC analyzing a foreign capital investment. The chapter includes a case application showing how to implement the APV decision framework.

Review of Domestic Capital Budgeting

The basic net present value (NPV) capital budgeting equation can be stated as:

$$NPV = \sum_{t=1}^{T} \frac{CF_t}{(1+K)^t} + \frac{TV_T}{(1+K)^T} - C_0 \tag{18.1}$$

where:

CF_t = expected after-tax cash flow for year t,
TV_T = expected after-tax terminal value, including recapture of working capital,
C_0 = initial investment at inception,
K = weighted-average cost of capital,
T = economic life of the capital project in years.

资本项目的NPV等于全部现金流入量现值（包括项目结束时的现金流入量）与所有现金流出量现值的差额。

The NPV of a capital project is the present value of all cash inflows, including those at the end of the project's life, minus the present value of all cash outflows. The *NPV rule* is to accept a project if NPV ≥ 0 and to reject it if NPV < 0.

The internal rate of return (IRR) payback method, and the profitability index are three additional methods for analyzing a capital expenditure. The IRR method solves for the discount rate, that is, the project's IRR, that causes the NPV to equal zero. In many situations a project will have only a single IRR, and the IRR decision rule is to select the project if the IRR ≥ K. However, under certain circumstances a project will have multiple IRRs, thus causing difficulty in interpreting the simple decision rule if one or more IRRs are less than K. The payback method determines the period of time required for the cumulative cash inflows to "pay back" the initial cash outlay; the shorter the payback period the more acceptable is the project. However, the payback method ignores the time value of money. The profitability index is computed by dividing the present value of cash inflows by the initial outlay; the larger the ratio, the more acceptable is the project. However, when dealing with mutually exclusive projects, a conflict may arise between the profitability index and the NPV criterion due to the scale of the investments. If the firm is not under a capital rationing constraint, it is generally agreed that conflicts should be settled in favor of the NPV criterion. Overall, the NPV decision rule is considered the superior framework for analyzing a capital budgeting expenditure.

总体而言，NPV决策原则是分析资本预算支出的最优框架。

For our purposes, it is necessary to expand the NPV equation. First, however, it is beneficial if we discuss annual cash flows. In capital budgeting, our concern is only with the change in the firm's total cash flows that are attributable to the capital expenditure. CF_t represents the **incremental** change in total firm cash flow for year t resulting from the capital project. Algebraically CF_t can be defined as:

增量

$$CF_t = (R_t - OC_t - D_t - I_t)(1 - \tau) + D_t + I_t(1 - \tau) \tag{18.2a}$$

$$= NI_t + D_t + I_t(1 - \tau) \tag{18.2b}$$

Equation 18.2a presents a very detailed expression for incremental cash flow that is worth learning so that we can easily apply the model. The equation shows that CF_t is the sum of three flows, or that the cash flow from a capital project goes to three different groups. The first term, as Equation 18.2b shows, is expected income, NI_t, which belongs to the equity holders of the firm. Incremental NI_t is calculated as the after-tax $(1 - \tau)$ value of the change in the firm's sales revenue, R_t, generated from the project, minus the corresponding operating costs, OC_t, minus project depreciation, D_t, minus interest expense, I_t. (As we discuss later in the chapter, we are only concerned with the interest expense that is consistent with the firm's optimal capital structure and the borrowing capacity created by the project.) The second term represents the fact that depreciation is a *noncash* expense, that is, D_t is subtracted in the calculation of NI_t only for tax purposes. It is added back because this cash did not actually flow out of the firm in year t. D_t can be viewed as the recapture in year t of a portion of the original investment, C_0, in the project. The last term represents the firm's after-tax payment of interest to debtholders.

$$CF_t = (R_t - OC_t - D_t)(1 - \tau) + D_t \qquad (18.2c)$$

$$= NOI_t(1 - \tau) + D_t \qquad (18.2d)$$

Equation 18.2c provides a computationally simpler formula for calculating CF_t. Since $I_t(1 - \tau)$ is subtracted in determining NI_t in Equation 18.2a and then added back, the two cancel out. The first term in Equation 18.2c represents after-tax net operating income, $NOI_t(1 - \tau)$, as stated in Equation 18.2d.

$$CF_t = (R_t - OC_t)(1 - \tau) + \tau D_t \qquad (18.2e)$$

$$= OCF_t(1 - \tau) + \tau D_t \qquad (18.2f)$$

$$= \text{nominal after-tax incremental cash flow for year } t$$

Equation 18.2e provides yet an even simpler formula for calculating CF_t. It shows the result from Equation 18.2c of combining the after-tax value of the depreciation expense, $(1 - \tau)D_t$, with the before-tax value of D_t. The result of this combination is the amount τD_t in Equation 18.2e, which represents the tax saving due to D_t being a tax-deductible item. As summarized in Equation 18.2f, the first term in Equation 18.2e represents after-tax operating cash flow, $OCF_t(1 - \tau)$, and the second term denotes the tax savings from the depreciation expense.[1]

The Adjusted Present Value Model

为继续我们的讨论,
需对NPV模型进行扩充。

To continue on with our discussion, we need to expand the NPV model. To do this, we substitute Equation 18.2f for CF_t in Equation 18.1, allowing us to restate the NPV formula as:

$$\text{NPV} = \sum_{t=1}^{T} \frac{OCF_t(1-\tau)}{(1+K)^t} + \sum_{t=1}^{T} \frac{\tau D_t}{(1+K^t)} + \frac{TV_T}{(1+K)^T} - C_0 \qquad (18.3)$$

In a famous article, Franco Modigliani and Merton Miller (1963) derived a theoretical statement for the market value of a levered firm (V_l) versus the market value of an equivalent unlevered firm (V_u). They showed that

$$V_l = V_u + \tau \text{Debt} \qquad (18.4a)$$

Assuming the firms are ongoing concerns and the debt the levered firm issued to finance a portion of its productive capacity is perpetual, Equation 18.4a can be expanded as:

$$\frac{NOI(1-\tau)}{K} = \frac{NOI(1-\tau)}{K_u} + \frac{\tau I}{i} \qquad (18.4b)$$

资本的全部权益成本   where i is the levered firm's borrowing rate, $I = i$Debt, and K_u is the cost of equity for an **all-equity** financed firm.

---

[1] Annual cash flows might also include incremental working capital funds. These are ignored here to simplify the presentation.

Recall from Chapter 17 that the weighted average cost of capital can be stated as:

$$K = (1 - \lambda)K_l + \lambda i(1 - \tau) \tag{18.5a}$$

where K_l is the cost of equity for a levered firm, and λ is the optimal debt ratio. In their article, Modigliani-Miller showed that K can be stated as:[2]

$$K = K_u(1 - \tau\lambda) \tag{18.5b}$$

Recall that Equation 18.2a can be simplified to Equation 18.2d. What this implies is that regardless of how the firm (or a capital expenditure) is financed, it will earn the same NOI. From Equation 18.5b, if $\lambda = 0$ (that is, an all-equity financed firm), then $K = K_u$ and $I = 0$; thus in Equation 18.4a $V_l = V_u$. However, if $\lambda > 0$ (that is, a levered firm), then $K_u > K$ and $I > 0$, thus $V_l > V_u$. For Equation 18.4b to hold as an equality, it is necessary to add the present value of the tax savings the levered firm receives. The main result of Modigliani and Miller's theory is that the value of a levered firm is greater than an equivalent unlevered firm earning the same NOI because the levered firm also has tax savings from the tax deductibility of interest payments to bondholders that do not go to the government. The following example clarifies the tax savings to the firm from making interest payments on debt.

EXAMPLE 18.1

Tax Savings from Interest Payments Exhibit 18.1 provides an example of the tax savings arising from the tax deductibility of interest payments. The exhibit shows a levered and an unlevered firm, each with sales revenue and operating expenses of $100 and $50, respectively. The levered firm has interest expense of $10 and earnings before taxes of $40, while the unlevered firm enjoys $50 of before-tax earnings since it does not have any interest expense. The levered firm pays only $16 in taxes as opposed to $20 for the unlevered firm. This leaves $24 for the levered firm's shareholders and $30 for the unlevered firm's shareholders. Nevertheless, the levered firm has a total of $34 (= $24 + $10) of funds available for investors, while the unlevered firm has only $30. The extra $4 comes from the tax savings on the $10 before-tax interest payment.

调整后的现值(APV)

APV模型是关于资本
预算的价值可加性模型。

价值可加性

By direct analogy to the Modigliani-Miller equation for an unlevered firm, we can convert the NPV Equation 18.3 into the **adjusted present value (APV)** model:

$$APV = \sum_{t=1}^{T} \frac{OCF_t(1-\tau)}{(1+K_u)^t} + \sum_{t=1}^{T} \frac{\tau D_t}{(1+i)^t} + \sum_{t=1}^{T} \frac{\tau I_t}{(1+i)^t} + \frac{TV_T}{(1+K_u)^T} - C_0 \tag{18.6}$$

The APV model is a **value-additivity** approach to capital budgeting. That is, each cash flow that is a source of value is considered individually. Note that in the APV model, each cash flow is discounted at a rate of discount consistent with the risk inherent in that cash flow. The OCF_t and TV_T are discounted at K_u. The firm would receive these cash flows from a capital project regardless of whether the firm was levered or unlevered. The tax savings due to interest, τI_t, are discounted at the before-tax borrowing rate, i, as in Equation 18.4b. It is suggested that the tax savings due to depreciation,

---

[2]To derive Equation 18.5b from Equation 18.5a, it is necessary to know that $K_l = K_u + (1-\tau)(K_u - i)$ (Debt/Equity).

EXHIBIT 18.1

Comparison of Cash Flows Available to Investors

	Levered	Unlevered
Revenue	$100	$100
Operating costs	−50	−50
Net operating income	50	50
Interest expense	−10	−0
Earnings before taxes	40	50
Taxes @.40	−16	−20
Net income	24	30
Cash flow available to investors	$24 + 10 = $34	$ 30

APV模型对国内公司分析国内资本项目十分有用。

τD_t, also be discounted at i because these cash flows are relatively less risky than operating cash flows if tax laws are not likely to change radically over the economic life of the project.[3]

The APV model is useful for a domestic firm analyzing a domestic capital expenditure. If APV ≥ 0, the project should be accepted. If APV < 0, the project should be rejected. Thus, the model is useful for a MNC for analyzing one of its domestic capital expenditures or for a foreign subsidiary of the MNC analyzing a proposed capital expenditure from the subsidiary's viewpoint.

Capital Budgeting from the Parent Firm's Perspective

事实上，一个在子公司看来APV为正的项目，在母公司看来APV可能为负。

The APV model as stated in Equation 18.6 is not useful for the MNC in analyzing a foreign capital expenditure of one of its subsidiaries from the MNC's, or parent's, perspective. In fact, it is possible that a project may have a positive APV from the subsidiary's perspective and a negative APV from the parent's perspective. This could happen, for example, if certain cash flows are blocked by the host country from being legally remitted to the parent or if extra taxes are imposed by the host country on foreign exchange remittances. A higher marginal tax rate in the home country may also cause a project to be unprofitable from the parent's perspective. If we assume the MNC owns the foreign subsidiary, but domestic shareholders own the MNC parent, it is the currency of the parent firm that is important because it is that currency into which the cash flows must be converted to benefit the shareholders whose wealth the MNC is attempting to maximize.

Donald Lessard (1985) developed an APV model that is suitable for a MNC to use in analyzing a foreign capital expenditure. The model recognizes that the cash flows will be denominated in a foreign currency and will have to be converted into the currency of the parent. Additionally, Lessard's model incorporates special cash flows that are frequently encountered in foreign project analysis. Using the basic structure of the APV model developed in the previous section, Lessard's model can be stated as:

$$\text{APV} = \sum_{t=1}^{T} \frac{\overline{S}_t OCF_t (1-\tau)}{(1+K_{ud})^t} + \sum_{t=1}^{T} \frac{\overline{S}_t \tau D_t}{(1+i_d)^t} + \sum_{t=1}^{T} \frac{\overline{S}_t \tau I_t}{(1+i_d)^t} + \frac{\overline{S}_T TV_t}{(1+K_{ud})^T} -$$

$$S_0 C_0 + S_0 RF_0 + S_0 CL_0 - \sum_{t=1}^{T} \frac{\overline{S}_t LP_t}{(1+i_d)^t} \tag{18.7}$$

Several points are noteworthy about Equation 18.7. First, the cash flows are assumed to be denominated in the foreign currency and converted to the currency of the parent at the expected spot exchange rates, $\overline{S}_t$, applicable for year t. The marginal

---

[3]Booth (1982) shows under what circumstances the NPV and APV methods will be precisely equivalent.

corporate tax rate, τ, is the larger of the parent's or the foreign subsidiary's because the model assumes that the tax authority in the parent firm's home country will give a foreign tax credit for foreign taxes paid *up to* the amount of the tax liability in the home country. Thus, if the parent's tax rate is the larger of the two, additional taxes are due in the home country, which equals the difference between the domestic tax liability and the foreign tax credit: On the other hand, if the foreign tax rate is larger, the foreign tax credit more than offsets the domestic tax liability, so no additional taxes are due. (Foreign tax credits are covered in detail in Chapter 21.) It is also noted that each of the discount rates has the subscript d, indicating that once the foreign cash flows are converted into the parent's home currency, the appropriate discount rates are those of the domestic country.

In Equation 18.7, the OCF_t represents only the portion of operating cash flows available for remittance that can be legally remitted to the parent firm. Cash flows earned in the foreign country that are blocked by the host government from being repatriated do not provide any benefit to the stockholders of the parent firm and are not relevant to the analysis. Additionally, cash flows that are repatriated through circumventing restrictions are not included here.

As with domestic project analysis, it is important to include only incremental revenues and operating costs in calculating the OCF_t. An example will help illustrate the concept. A MNC may presently have a sales affiliate in a foreign country that is supplied by merchandise produced by the parent or a manufacturing facility in a third country. If a manufacturing facility is put into operation in the foreign country to satisfy local demand, sales may be larger overall than with just a sales affiliate if the foreign subsidiary is better able to assess market demand with its local presence.

However, the former manufacturing unit will experience **lost sales** as a result of the new foreign manufacturing facility; that is, the new project has *cannibalized* part of an existing project. Thus, incremental revenue is not the total sales revenue of the new manufacturing facility but rather that amount minus the lost sales revenue. However, if the sales would be lost regardless, say because a competitor who is better able to satisfy local demand is gearing up, then the entire sales revenue of the new foreign manufacturing facility is incremental sales revenue.

Equation 18.7 includes additional terms representing cash flows frequently encountered in foreign projects. The term $S_0 RF_0$ represents the value of accumulated **restricted funds** (of amount RF_0) in the foreign land from existing operations that are freed up by the proposed project. These funds become available only *because* of the proposed project and are therefore available to offset a portion of the initial capital outlay. Examples are funds "whose use is restricted by exchange controls"[4] or funds on which additional taxes would be due in the parent country if they are remitted. RF_0 equals the difference between the face value of these funds and their present value used in the next best alternative. The extended illustration at the end of this chapter will help clarify the meaning of this term.

The term $S_0 CL_0 - \sum_{t=1}^{T} \dfrac{\bar{S}_t LP_t}{(1+i_d)^t}$ denotes the present value in the currency of the parent firm of the benefit of below-market-rate borrowing in foreign currency. In certain cases, a **concessionary loan** (of amount CL_0) at a below-market rate of interest may be available to the parent firm if the proposed capital expenditure is made in the foreign land. The host country offers this financing in its foreign currency as a means of attracting economic development and investment that will create employment for its citizens. The benefit to the MNC is the difference between the face value of the concessionary loan converted into the home currency and the present value of the similarly converted concessionary loan payments (LP_t) discounted at the MNC's normal

---

[4]Lessard (1985, p. 577).

domestic borrowing rate (i_d). The loan payments will yield a present value less than the face amount of the concessionary loan when they are discounted at the higher normal rate. This difference represents a subsidy the host country is willing to extend to the MNC if the investment is made. It should be clear that the present value of the loan payments discounted at the normal borrowing rate represents the size of the loan available from borrowing at the normal borrowing rate with a debt service schedule equivalent to that of the concessionary loan.

Recall that to calculate the firm's weighted-average cost of capital, it is necessary to know the firm's optimal debt ratio. When considering a capital budgeting project, it is never appropriate to think of the project as being financed separately from the way the firm is financed, for the project represents a portion of the firm. When the asset base increases because a capital project is undertaken, the firm can handle more debt in its capital structure. That is, the borrowing capacity of the firm has increased because of the project. Nevertheless, the investment and financing decisions are separate. There is an optimal capital structure for the firm; once this is determined, the cost of financing is known and can be used to determine if a project is acceptable. We do not mean to imply that *each* and every capital project is financed with the optimal portions of debt and equity. Rather, some projects may be financed with all debt or all equity or a suboptimal combination. What is important is that in the long run the firm does not stray too far from its optimal capital structure so that overall the firm's assets are financed at the lowest cost. Thus, the interest tax shield term $S_t \tau I_t$ in the APV model recognizes the tax shields of the **borrowing capacity** created by the project *regardless* of how the project is financed. Handling the tax shields in any other way would bias the APV favorably or unfavorably, respectively, if the project was financed by a larger or smaller portion of debt. This is an especially important point in international capital budgeting analysis because of the frequency of large concessionary loans. The benefit of concessionary loans, which are dependent on the parent firm making the investment, is recognized in a separate term.[5]

Generality of the APV Model

Lessard's APV model includes many terms for cash flows frequently encountered in analyzing foreign capital expenditures. However, *all* possible terms are not included in the version presented as Equation 18.7. Nevertheless, the reader should now have the knowledge to incorporate into the basic APV model terms of a more unique nature for specific cash flows encountered in a particular analysis.

For example, there may be tax savings or deferrals that come about because of multinational operations. That is, the MNC may be able to shift revenues or expenses among its affiliates in a way that lowers taxes, or be able to combine profits or affiliates from both low and high tax environments in a manner that results in lower overall taxes. Tax deferrals are possible by reinvesting profits in new capital projects in low-tax countries.

Additionally, through interaffiliate transfer pricing strategies, licensing arrangements, royalty agreements, or other means, the parent firm might be able to repatriate some funds that are meant to be blocked, or restricted, by the host country.[6] These cash flows are the counterpart to the unrestricted funds available for remittance as part of operating cash flows. As with the cash flows arising from tax savings or deferrals, it may be difficult for the firm to accurately estimate the size of these cash flows or their duration. Since these cash flows will exist regardless of how the firm is financed, they should be discounted at the all-equity rate.

One of the major benefits of the APV framework is the ease with which difficult cash flow terms, such as tax savings or deferrals and the repatriation of restricted funds, can be handled. The analyst can first analyze the capital expenditure as if they

借款能力

国际资本预算分析必须考虑到经常存在大量的优惠性贷款这一点。

APV框架的一个主要优点是便于处理税收补偿或税收递延、受限资金回笼等涉及现金流期限的问题。

---

[5]Booth (1982) shows that tax shields calculated using the concessionary loan rates are also theoretically correct.
[6]Chapter 19 covers interaffiliate transfer pricing strategies, licensing arrangements, and royalty agreements as methods the parent firm might use to repatriate funds restricted by the host country.

did not exist. Additional cash flow terms do not need to be explicitly considered unless the APV is negative. If the APV is negative, the analyst can calculate how large the cash flows from other sources need to be to make the APV positive, and then estimate whether these other cash inflows will likely be that large.

Estimating the Future Expected Exchange Rate

The financial manager must estimate the future expected exchange rates, $\overline{S}_t$, in order to implement the APV framework. Chapter 6 provided a wide variety of methods for estimating exchange rates. One quick and simple way to do this is to rely on PPP and estimate the future expected spot rate for year t as:

$$\overline{S}_t = S_0(1 + \overline{\pi}_d)^t / (1 + \overline{\pi}_f)^t \qquad (18.8)$$

where $\overline{\pi}_d$ is the expected long-run annual rate of inflation in the (home) domestic country of the MNC and $\overline{\pi}_f$ is the rate in the foreign land.

As noted in Chapter 6, PPP is not likely to hold precisely in reality. Nevertheless, unless the financial manager suspects that there is some systematic long-run bias in using PPP to estimate $\overline{S}_t$ that would result in a systematic over- or underestimate of the series of expected exchange rates, then PPP should prove to be an acceptable tool. Alternatively, the analyst may choose to use long-dated forward prices to estimate the future expected spot exchange rates, or use an IRP forecast.

CASE APPLICATION

The Centralia Corporation

The Centralia Corporation is a midwestern manufacturer of small kitchen electrical appliances. The market segment it caters to is the midprice range. It specializes in small and medium-size microwave ovens suitable for small homes, apartment dwellers, or office coffee lounges. In recent years it has been exporting microwave ovens to Spain, where they are sold through a sales affiliate in Madrid. Because of different electrical requirements in Western Europe, the ovens Centralia manufactured for the Spanish market could not be used elsewhere in Europe without an electrical converter. Thus, the sales affiliate concentrated its marketing effort just in Spain. Sales are currently 9,600 units a year and have been increasing at a rate of 5 percent.

Centralia's marketing manager has been keeping abreast of integration activities in the European Union. All obstacles to the free movement of goods, services, people, and capital among the member states of the EU have been removed. Additionally, further integration promises a commonality among member states of rail track size, telephone and electrical equipment, and a host of other items. These developments have led the marketing manager to believe that a substantial number of microwave oven units could be sold throughout the EU and that the idea of a manufacturing facility should be explored.

The marketing and production managers have jointly drawn up plans for a wholly owned manufacturing facility in Zaragoza, which is located about 325 kilometers northeast of Madrid. Zaragoza is located just a couple hundred kilometers from the French border, thus facilitating shipment out of Spain into other EU countries. Additionally, Zaragoza is located close enough to the major population centers in Spain so that internal shipments should not pose a problem. A major attraction of locating the manufacturing facility in Zaragoza, however, is that the Spanish government has promised to arrange for a large portion of the construction cost of the production facility to be financed at a very attractive interest rate if the plant is built there. Any type of industry that will improve the employment situation would be a benefit, as the current unemployment rate in Spain exceeds 19 percent. Centralia's executive committee has instructed the financial manager to determine if the plan has financial merit. If the manufacturing facility is built, Centralia will no longer export units for sale in Europe. The necessary information follows.

On its current exports, Centralia receives $180 per unit, of which $35 represents contribution margin. The sales forecast predicts that 25,000 units will be sold within the EU during the first year of operation and that this volume will increase at the rate of 12 percent per year. All sales will be invoiced in euros. When the plant begins operation, units will be priced at €200 each. It is estimated that the current production cost will be €160 per unit. The sales price and production costs are expected to keep pace with inflation, which is forecast to be 2.1 percent per annum for the foreseeable future. By comparison, long-run U.S. inflation is forecast at 3 percent per annum. The current exchange rate is $1.32/€1.00.

The cost of constructing the manufacturing plant is estimated at €5,500,000. The borrowing capacity created by a capital expenditure of this amount is $2,904,000. The Madrid sales affiliate has accumulated a net amount of €750,000 from its operations, which can be used to partially finance the construction cost. The marginal corporate tax rate in Spain and the United States is 35 percent. The accumulated funds were earned under special tax concessions offered during the initial years of the sales operation, and taxed at a marginal rate of 20 percent. If they were repatriated, additional tax at the 35 percent marginal rate would be due, but with a foreign tax credit given for the Spanish taxes already paid.

The Spanish government will allow the plant to be depreciated over an eight-year period. Little, if any, additional investment will be required over that time. At the end of this period, the market value of the facility is difficult to estimate, but Centralia believes that the plant should still be in good condition for its age and that it should therefore have reasonable market value.

One of the most attractive features of the proposal is the special financing the Spanish government is willing to arrange. If the plant is built in Zaragoza, Centralia will be eligible to borrow €4,000,000 at a concessionary loan rate of 5 percent per annum. The normal borrowing rate for Centralia is 8 percent in dollars and 7 percent in euros. The loan schedule calls for the principal to be repaid in eight equal installments. In dollar terms, Centralia uses 12 percent as its all-equity cost of capital.

Here is a summary of the key points:

The current exchange rate in American terms is $S_0 = \$1.32/€1.00$.

$\bar{\pi}_f = 2.1\%$

$\bar{\pi}_d = 3\%$

The initial cost of the project in U.S. dollars is

$S_0 C_0 = \$1.32 \times €5,500,000 = \$7,260,000.$

For simplicity, we will assume that PPP holds and use it to estimate future expected spot exchange rates in American terms as:

$\bar{S}_t = 1.32(1.03)^t/(1.021)^t.$

The before-tax incremental operating cash flow per unit at $t = 1$ is €200 − 160 = €40.

The nominal contribution margin in year t equals €40(1.021)$^{t-1}$.

Incremental lost sales in units for year t equals 9,600(1.05)^t.

Contribution margin per unit of lost sales in year t equals $35(1.03)^t.

The marginal tax rate, τ, equals the Spanish (or U.S.) rate of 35 percent.

Terminal value will initially be assumed to equal zero.

Straight-line depreciation is assumed; $D_t = €687,500 = €5,500,000/8$ years.

$K_{ud} = 12\%.$

$i_c = 5\%.$

$i_d = 8\%.$

EXHIBIT 18.2			Calculation of the Present Value of the After-Tax Operating Cash Flows				
Year (t)	$\bar{S}_t$	Quantity	$\bar{S}_t \times$ Quantity $\times €40$ $\times (1.021^{t-1})$ (a) $	Quantity Lost Sales	Quantity Lost Sales $\times \$35.00$ $\times (1.03)^t$ (b) $	$\bar{S}_t OCF_t$ (a + b) $	$\dfrac{\bar{S}_t OCF_t (1-\tau)}{(1+K_{ud})^t}$ $
1	1.3316	25,000	1,331,636	(10,080)	(363,384)	968,252	561,932
2	1.3432	28,000	1,536,175	(10,584)	(393,000)	1,143,175	592,366
3	1.3552	31,360	1,772,131	(11,113)	(425,029)	1,347,102	623,246
4	1.3672	35,123	2,044,331	(11,669)	(459,669)	1,584,662	654,603
5	1.3792	39,338	2,358,340	(12,252)	(497,132)	1,861,208	686,465
6	1.3914	44,059	2,720,581	(12,865)	(537,648)	2,182,932	718,862
7	1.4036	49,346	3,138,462	(13,508)	(581,467)	2,556,995	751,826
8	1.4160	55,267	3,620,530	(14,184)	(628,856)	2,991,674	785,386
							5,374,685

In Exhibit 18.2 the present value of the expected after-tax operating cash flows from Centralia establishing the manufacturing facility in Spain is calculated. Column (a) presents the annual revenue in dollars from operating the new manufacturing facility. These are calculated each year by multiplying the expected quantity of microwave ovens to be sold times the year one incremental operating cash flow of €40 per unit. This product is in turn multiplied by the Euro zone price inflation factor of 2.1 percent. For example, for year $t = 2$ the factor is $(1.021)^{t-1} = (1.021)$. The euro sales estimates are then converted to dollars at the expected spot exchange rates. Column (b) presents the annual lost sales revenues in dollars that are expected to result if the manufacturing facility is built and the parent firm no longer sells part of its production through the Spanish sales affiliate. These are calculated by multiplying the estimated quantity of lost sales in units by the current contribution margin of $35 per unit, which is in turn multiplied by a 3 percent U.S. price inflation factor. The incremental dollar operating cash flows are the sum of columns (a) and (b), which are converted to their after-tax value and discounted at K_{ud}. The sum of their present values is $5,374,685.

The present value of the depreciation tax shields τD_t is calculated in Exhibit 18.3. The tax savings on the annual straight-line depreciation of €687,500 is converted to dollars at the expected future spot exchange rates and discounted to the present at the domestic borrowing rate of 8 percent. The present value of these tax shields is $1,892,502.

The present value of the benefit of the concessionary loan is calculated in Exhibits 18.4 and 18.5. Exhibit 18.4 finds the present value of the concessionary loan payments in dollars. Since the annual principal payment on the €4,000,000 concessionary loan is the same each

EXHIBIT 18.3	Year (t)	$\bar{S}_t$	D_t €	$\dfrac{\bar{S}_t \tau D_t}{(1+i_d)^t}$ $
Calculation of the Present Value of the Depreciation Tax Shields	1	1.3316	687,500	296,690
	2	1.3434	687,500	277,134
	3	1.3552	687,500	258,868
	4	1.3672	687,500	241,805
	5	1.3792	687,500	225,867
	6	1.3914	687,500	210,980
	7	1.4036	687,500	197,074
	8	1.4160	687,500	184,084
				1,892,502

Year (t)	$\bar{S}_t$ (a) €	Principal Payment (b) €	I_t (c) €	$\bar{S}_t LP_t$ (a) × (b + c) $	$\dfrac{\bar{S}_t LP_t}{(1 + i_d)^t}$ $
1	1.3316	500,000	200,000	932,145	863,097
2	1.3434	500,000	175,000	906,777	777,415
3	1.3552	500,000	150,000	880,890	699,279
4	1.3672	500,000	125,000	854,476	628,065
5	1.3792	500,000	100,000	827,528	563,202
6	1.3914	500,000	75,000	800,038	504,160
7	1.4036	500,000	50,000	771,999	450,454
8	1.4160	500,000	25,000	743,404	401,638
		4,000,000			4,887,311

EXHIBIT 18.4

Calculation of the Present Value of the Concessionary Loan Payments

year, the interest payments decline as the loan balance declines. For example, during the first year, interest of €200,000 (= .05 × €4,000,000) is paid on the full amount borrowed. During the second year interest of €175,000 (= .05 × (€4,000,000 − 500,000)) is paid on the outstanding balance over year two. The annual loan payment equals the sum of the annual principal payment and the annual interest charge. The sum of their present values in dollars, converted at the expected spot exchange rates, discounted at the domestic borrowing rate of 8 percent, is $4,887,311. This sum represents the size of the equivalent loan available (in dollars) from borrowing at the normal borrowing rate with a debt service schedule equivalent to that of the concessionary loan.

Exhibit 18.5 concludes the analysis of the concessionary loan. It shows the difference between the dollar value of the concessionary loan and the equivalent dollar loan value calculated in Exhibit 18.4. The difference of $392,689 represents the present value of the benefit of the below market rate financing of the concessionary loan.

The present value of the interest tax shields is calculated in Exhibit 18.6. The interest payments in column (b) of Exhibit 18.6 are drawn from column (c) of Exhibit 18.4. That is, we follow a conservative approach and base the interest tax shields on using the concessionary loan interest rate of 5 percent. The concessionary loan of €4,000,000 represents 72.73 percent of the project cost of €5,500,000. By comparison, the borrowing capacity created by the project is $2,904,000, which implies an optimal debt ratio λ for the parent firm of 40.0% = $2,904,000/$7,260,000 of the dollar cost of the project. Thus, only 55.0 percent (= 40.0%/72.73%) of the interest payments on the concessionary loan should be used to calculate the interest tax shields. At the domestic borrowing rate of 8 percent, the present value of the interest tax shields is $183,807.

To calculate the amount of the freed-up restricted remittances it is first necessary to gross up the after-tax value of the net accumulation of €750,000, on which the Madrid sales affiliate has previously paid taxes at the rate of 20 percent. This amount is €937,500 = €750,000/(1 − .20). The dollar value of this sum at the current spot exchange rate S_0 is $1,237,500 = $1.32 (€937,500). If Centralia decided not to establish a manufacturing facility in Spain, the €750,000 should be repatriated to the parent firm. It would be required to pay additional taxes in the U.S. in the amount of $185,625 = (.35 − .20) $1,237,500. If the manufacturing facility is built, the

EXHIBIT 18.5

Calculation of the Present Value of the Benefit from the Concessionary Loan

$$S_0 CL_0 - \sum_{t=1}^{T} \frac{\bar{S}_t LP_t}{(1 + i_d)^t} = \$1.32 \times €4{,}000{,}000 - 4{,}887{,}311 = \$392{,}689$$

EXHIBIT 18.6

Calculation of the Present Value of the Interest Tax Shields

Year (t)	$\bar{S}_t$ (a)	I_t (b) €	λ/Project Debt Ratio (c)	$\bar{S}_t \tau(.55)I_t$ (a × b × c × τ) $	$\dfrac{\bar{S}_t \tau(.55)I_t}{(1+i_d)^t}$ $
1	1.3316	200,000	0.55	51,268	47,470
2	1.3434	175,000	0.55	45,255	38,799
3	1.3552	150,000	0.55	39,132	31,064
4	1.3672	125,000	0.55	32,897	24,181
5	1.3792	100,000	0.55	26,550	18,069
6	1.3914	75,000	0.55	20,088	12,659
7	1.4036	50,000	0.55	13,510	7,883
8	1.4160	25,000	0.55	6,815	3,682
					183,807

€750,000 should not be remitted to the parent firm. Thus, freed-up funds of $185,625 result from the tax savings, which can be applied to cover a portion of the equity investment in the capital expenditure.

The APV = $5,374,685 + 1,892,502 + 392,689 + 183,807 + 185,625

    − 7,260,000

    = $769,308.

There appears little doubt that the proposed manufacturing facility will be a profitable venture for Centralia. Had the APV been negative or closer to zero, we would want to consider the present value of the after-tax terminal cash flow. We are quite uncertain as to what this amount might be, and, fortunately, in this case we do not have to base a decision on this cash flow, which is difficult at best to forecast.

Risk Adjustment in the Capital Budgeting Analysis

风险调整贴现率法
是处理这种情况的标准
方法。

调整APV模型中风
险的第二种方法就是
"确定等值法"。

The APV model we presented and demonstrated is suitable for use in analyzing a capital expenditure that is of average riskiness in comparison to the firm as a whole. Some projects may be more or less risky than average, however. The *risk-adjusted discount method* is the standard way to handle this situation. This approach requires adjusting the discount rate upward or downward for increases or decreases, respectively, in the systematic risk of the project relative to the firm as a whole. In the APV model presented in Equation 18.7, only the cash flows discounted at K_{ud} incorporate systematic risk; thus, only K_{ud} needs to be adjusted when project risk differs from that of the firm as a whole.[7]

A second way to adjust for risk in the APV framework is the *certainty equivalent method*. This approach extracts the risk premium from the expected cash flows to convert them into equivalent riskless cash flows, which are then discounted at the risk-free rate of interest. This is accomplished by multiplying the risky cash flows by a certainty-equivalent factor that is unity or less. The more risky the cash flow, the smaller is the certainty-equivalent factor. In general, cash flows tend to be more risky the further into the future they are expected to be received. We favor the risk-adjusted discount rate method over the certainty-equivalent approach because we find that it is easier to adjust the discount rate than it is to estimate the appropriate certainty-equivalent factors.[8]

---

[7]See Ross, Westerfield, and Jaffe (2002, Chapter 12) for a treatment of capital budgeting using discount rates adjusted for project systematic risk.

[8]See Brealey and Myers (2003, Chapter 9) for a more detailed discussion of the certainty equivalent method of risk adjustment.

Sensitivity Analysis

The way we have approached the analysis of Centralia's expansion into Spain is to obtain a point estimate of the APV through using expected values of the relevant cash flows. The expected values of these inputs are what the financial manager expects to obtain given the information he had at his disposal at the time the analysis was performed. However, each cash flow does have its own probability distribution. Hence, the realized value that may result for a particular cash flow may be different than expected. To examine these possibilities, the financial manager typically performs a sensitivity analysis. In a *sensitivity analysis,* different scenarios are examined by using different exchange rate estimates, inflation rate estimates, and cost and pricing estimates in the calculation of the APV. In essence, the sensitivity analysis allows the financial manager a means to analyze the business risk, economic exposure, exchange rate uncertainty, and political risk inherent in the investment. Sensitivity analysis puts financial managers in a position to more thoroughly understand the implications of planned capital expenditures. It also forces them to consider in advance actions that can be taken should an investment not develop as anticipated.

在敏感性分析中，用不同的汇率估计值、通货膨胀估计值及成本与价格的估计值来计算不同情形下的APV。

Purchasing Power Parity Assumption

The APV methodology we developed assumes that PPP holds and that future expected exchange rates can be forecasted accordingly. As noted, relying on the PPP assumption is a common and conceptually satisfying way to forecast future exchange rates. Assuming no differential in marginal tax rates, when PPP holds and all foreign cash flows can be legally repatriated to the parent firm, it does not make any difference if the capital budgeting analysis is done from the perspective of the parent firm or from the perspective of the foreign subsidiary. To see this, consider the following simple example.

EXAMPLE 18.2

The PPP Assumption in Foreign Capital Expenditure Analysis. A capital expenditure of FC30 by a foreign subsidiary of a U.S. MNC with a one year economic life is expected to earn a cash flow in local currency terms of FC80. Assume inflation in the foreign host country is forecast at 4 percent per annum and at 2 percent in the United States. If the U.S. MNC's cost of capital is 7.88 percent, the Fisher equation determines that the appropriate cost of capital for the foreign subsidiary is 10 percent: $1.10 = (1.0788)(1.04)/(1.02)$. Consequently, the project NPV in foreign currency terms is $NPV_{FC} = FC80/(1.10) - FC30 = FC42.73$. If the current spot exchange rate is FC2.00/\$1.00, $\bar{S}_1$ (FC/\$) = 2.00 (1.04)/(1.02) = 2.0392 by PPP. In U.S. dollar terms, $NPV_\$ = (FC80/2.0392)/(1.0788) - FC30/2.00 = \$21.37$. Note that according to the law of one price, NPV_{FC}/S_0 (FC/\$) = $NPV_\$ = FC42.73/2.00 = \$21.37$. This is the expected result because both the exchange rate forecast and the discount rate conversion incorporate the same differential in expected inflation rates. Suppose, however, that $\bar{S}_1$ (FC/\$) actually turns out to be FC5.00/\$1.00, that is, the foreign currency depreciates in real terms versus the dollar, then $NPV_\$ = -\$0.17$ and the project is unprofitable from the parent's perspective.

Real Options

Throughout this chapter, we have recommended the APV framework for evaluating capital expenditures in real assets. The APV was determined by making certain assumptions about revenues, operating costs, exchange rates, and the like. This approach treats risk through the discount rate. When evaluated at the appropriate discount rate, a positive

通过对收入、运营成本、利率等进行某些假设，就可确定APV值。

APV implies that a project should be accepted and a negative APV implies that it should be rejected. A project is accepted under the assumption that all future operating decisions will be optimal. Unfortunately, the firm's management does not know at the inception date of a project what future decisions it will be confronted with because all information concerning the project has not yet been learned. Consequently, the firm's management has alternative paths, or options, that it can take as new information is discovered. Options pricing theory is useful for evaluating investment opportunities in real assets as well as financial assets, such as foreign exchange that we considered in Chapter 7. The application of options pricing theory to the evaluation of investment options in real projects is known as **real options.**

The firm is confronted with many possible real options over the life of a capital asset. For example, the firm may have a *timing option* about when to make the investment; it may have a *growth option* to increase the scale of the investment; it may have a *suspension option* to temporarily cease production; and, it may have an *abandonment option* to quit the investment early. All of these situations can be evaluated as real options.

In international capital expenditures, the MNC is faced with the political uncertainties of doing business in a foreign host country.[9] For example, a stable political environment for foreign investment may turn unfavorable if a different political party wins power by election—or worse, by political coup. Moreover, an unexpected change in a host country's monetary policy may cause a depreciation in its exchange rate versus the parent firm's home currency, thus adversely affecting the return to the shareholders of the parent firm. These and other political uncertainties make real options analysis ideal for use in evaluating international capital expenditures. Real options analysis, however, should be thought of as an extension of discounted cash flow analysis, not as a replacement of it, as the following example makes clear.

实物期权

在资本资产运营期内，公司会遇到很多可能发生的真实期权。

在国际资本支出方面，跨国公司在东道国经商时会面临政治风险的影响。

EXAMPLE 18.3

Centralia's Timing Option   Suppose that the sales forecast for the first year for Centralia in the case application had been for only 22,000 units instead of 25,000. At the lower figure, the APV would have been −$55,358. It is doubtful that Centralia would have entered into the construction of a manufacturing facility in Spain in this event. Suppose further that it is well known that the European Central Bank has been contemplating either tightening or loosening the economy of the European Union through a change in monetary policy that would cause the euro to either appreciate to $1.45/€1.00 or depreciate to $1.20/€1.00 from its current level of $1.32/€1.00. Under a restrictive monetary policy, the APV would be $86,674, and Centralia would begin operations. On the other hand, an expansionary policy would cause the APV to become an even more negative −$186,464.

Centralia believes that the effect from any change in monetary policy will be known in a year's time. Thus it decides to put its plans on hold until it learns what the ECB decides to do. In the meantime, Centralia can obtain a purchase option for a year on the parcel of land in Zaragoza on which it would build the manufacturing facility by paying the current landowner a fee of €5,000, or $6,600.

The situation described is a classic example in which real options analysis is useful in evaluating a capital expenditure. In this situation, the purchase option of €5,000 represents the option premium of the real option and the initial investment of €5,500,000 represents the exercise price of the option. Centralia will only exercise its real option if the ECB decides to follow a restrictive policy that would cause the APV

[9]It may be helpful to review the discussion on political risk in Chapter 16.

下述案例运用二项
式期权定价模型更直观地
展示了时间期权的价值。

to be a positive $86,674. The €5,000 seems like a small amount to allow Centralia the flexibility to postpone making a costly capital expenditure until more information is learned. The following example explicitly values the timing option using the binomial options pricing model.

EXAMPLE 18.4

Valuing Centralia's Timing Option   In this example, we value the timing option described in the above example using the binomial options pricing model developed in Chapter 7. We use Centralia's 8 percent borrowing cost in dollars and 7 percent borrowing cost in euros as our estimates of the domestic and foreign risk-free rates of interest. Depending upon the action of the ECB, the euro will either appreciate 10 percent to $1.45/€1.00 or depreciate 9 percent to $1.20/€1.00 from its current level of $1.32/$1.00. Thus, u = 1.10 and d = 1/1.10. = .91. This implies that the risk-neutral probability of an appreciation is q = [(1 + i_d)/(1 + i_f) − d]/(u − d) = [(1.08)/(1.07) − .91]/(1.10 − .91) = .52 and the probability of a depreciation is 1 − q = .48. Since the timing option will only be exercised if the APV is positive, the value of the timing option is C = .52($86,674)/(1.08) = $41,732. Since this amount is in excess of the $6,600 cost of the purchase option on the land, Centralia should definitely take advantage of the timing option it is confronted with to wait and see what monetary policy the ECB decides to pursue.

SUMMARY

本章对资本预算的NPV模型进行了回顾，并将该模型扩展为APV模型以适用于跨国公司的境外资本支出分析。

1. 回顾了适用于国内资本预算的NPV模型。NPV是现金流入现值与现金流出现值间的差额。如果某一资本项目的NPV≥0，那么应接受该项目。

2. 对税后现金流公式进行了完整的界定并介绍了它的各种变体，而这对于将NPV模型扩展为APV模型非常必要。

3. 为了计算进行债务融资公司的价值，通过类比莫迪里亚尼－米勒（MM）模型，本章建立了APV资本预算模型。APV模型将经营现金流量从融资现金流量间分离了出来。此外，对各类现金流量按与个别现金流量内在风险相当的贴现率进行了贴现。

4. 本章还对APV模型做了进一步的扩展，以适应跨国公司母公司的国外资本项目分析。其中，现金流量转为用母公司所在国货币衡量，并对APV模型增加附加条件以便处理国际资本预算中经常发生的现金流量。

5. 通过案例应用来说明APV模型的应用。

This chapter presents a review of the NPV capital budgeting framework and expands the methodology into the APV model that is suitable for analyzing capital expenditures of a MNC in a foreign land.

1. The NPV capital budgeting framework in a domestic context is reviewed. The NPV is the difference between the present value of the cash inflows and outflows. If NPV ≥ 0 for a capital project, it should be accepted.

2. The annual after-tax cash flow formula was thoroughly defined and presented in a number of variations. This was necessary to expand the NPV model into the APV model.

3. The APV model of capital budgeting was developed by analogy to the Modigliani-Miller formula for the value of a levered firm. The APV model separates the operating cash flows from the cash flows due to financing. Additionally, each cash flow is discounted at a rate of discount commensurate with the inherent risk of the individual cash flow.

4. The APV model was further expanded to make it amenable for use by a MNC parent analyzing a foreign capital project. The cash flows were converted into the parent firm's home currency, and additional terms were added to the model to handle cash flows that are frequently encountered in international capital projects.

5. A case application showing how to apply the APV model was presented and solved.

KEY WORDS

adjusted present value (APV), 452	concessionary loan, 454	net present value (NPV), 449
all-equity cost of capital, 451	incremental cash flow, 450	real option, 462
borrowing capacity, 455	lost sales, 454	restricted funds, 454
		value-additivity, 452

QUESTIONS

1. Why is capital budgeting analysis so important to the firm?
2. What is the intuition behind the NPV capital budgeting framework?
3. Discuss what is meant by the *incremental* cash flows of a capital project.
4. Discuss the nature of the equation sequence, Equations 18.2a to 18.2f.
5. What makes the APV capital budgeting framework useful for analyzing foreign capital expenditures?
6. Relate the concept of *lost sales* to the definition of incremental cash flows.
7. What problems can enter into the capital budgeting analysis if project debt is evaluated instead of the *borrowing capacity* created by the project?
8. What is the nature of a *concessionary* loan and how is it handled in the APV model?
9. What is the intuition of discounting the various cash flows in the APV model at specific discount rates?
10. In the Modigliani-Miller equation, why is the market value of the levered firm greater than the market value of an equivalent unlevered firm?
11. Discuss the difference between performing the capital budgeting analysis from the parent firm's perspective as opposed to the project perspective.
12. Define the concept of a real option. Discuss some of the various real options a firm can be confronted with when investing in real projects.
13. Discuss the conditions under which the capital expenditure of a foreign subsidiary might have a positive NPV in total currency terms but be unprofitable from the parent firm's perspective.

PROBLEMS

1. The Alpha Company plans to establish a subsidiary in Hungary to manufacture and sell fashion wristwatches. Alpha has total assets of $70 million, of which $45 million is equity financed. The remainder is financed with debt. Alpha considered its current capital structure optimal. The construction cost of the Hungarian facility in forints is estimated at HUF2,400,000,000, of which HUF1,800,000,000 is to be financed at a below-market borrowing rate arranged by the Hungarian government. Alpha wonders what amount of debt it should use in calculating the tax shields on interest payments in its capital budgeting analysis. Can you offer assistance?

2. The current spot exchange rate is HUF250/$1.00. Long-run inflation in Hungary is estimated at 10 percent annually and 3 percent in the United States. If PPP is expected to hold between the two countries, what spot exchange rate should one forecast five years into the future?

3. The Beta Corporation has an optimal debt ratio of 40 percent. Its cost of equity capital is 12 percent and its before-tax borrowing rate is 8 percent. Given a marginal tax rate of 35 percent, calculate (a) the weighted-average cost of capital, and (b) the cost of equity for an equivalent all-equity financed firm.

4. Zeda, Inc., a U.S. MNC, is considering making a fixed direct investment in Denmark. The Danish government has offered Zeda a concessionary loan of DKK 15,000,000 at a rate of 4 percent per annum. The normal borrowing rate for the Zeda is 6 percent in dollars and 5.5 percent in Danish krone. The load schedule calls for the principal to be repaid in three equal annual installments. What is the present value of the benefit of the concessionary loan? The current spot rate is DKK5.60/$1.00 and the expected inflation rate is 3 percent in the U.S. and 2.5 percent in Denmark.

5. Suppose that in the case application in the chapter the APV for Centralia had been −$60,000. How large would the after-tax terminal value of the project need to be before the APV would be positive and Centralia would accept the project?

6. With regard to the Centralia case application in the chapter, how would the APV change if:

   a. The forecast of $\bar{\pi}_d$ and/or $\bar{\pi}_f$ are incorrect?

   b. Depreciation cash flows are discounted at K_{ud} instead of i_d?

   c. The host country did not provide the concessionary loan?

INTERNET EXERCISES

Concessionary financing is very important as a source of funds to encourage private sector investment in developing countries. As an example of this, see the Ceylon *Daily News* article at http://origin.dailynews.lk/2002/04/12/bus11.html calling for concessionary financing from the DFCC Bank to support private sector investments in power generation in Sri Lanka. Many such articles can be found on the Internet by searching under the key words *concessionary financing*.

MINI CASE 1   Dorchester, Ltd.

Dorchester, Ltd. is an old-line confectioner specializing in high-quality chocolates. Through its facilities in the United Kingdom, Dorchester manufactures candies that it sells throughout Western Europe and North America (United States and Canada). With its current manufacturing facilities, Dorchester has been unable to supply the U.S. market with more than 225,000 pounds of candy per year. This supply has allowed its sales affiliate, located in Boston, to be able to penetrate the U.S. market no farther west than St. Louis and only as far south as Atlanta. Dorchester believes that a separate manufacturing facility located in the United States would allow it to supply the entire U.S. market and Canada (which presently accounts for 65,000 pounds per year). Dorchester currently estimates initial demand in the North American market at 390,000 pounds, with growth at a 5 percent annual rate. A separate manufacturing facility would, obviously, free up the amount currently shipped to the United States and Canada. But Dorchester believes that this is only a short-run problem. They believe the economic development taking place in Eastern Europe will allow it to sell there the full amount presently shipped to North America within a period of five years.

Dorchester presently realizes £3.00 per pound on its North American exports. Once the U.S. manufacturing facility is operating, Dorchester expects that it will be able to initially price its product at $7.70 per pound. This price would represent an operating profit of $4.40 per pound. Both sales price and operating costs are expected to keep track with the U.S. price level; U.S. inflation is forecast at a rate of 3 percent for the next several years. In the U.K., long-run inflation is expected to be in the 4 to 5 percent range, depending on which economic service one follows. The current spot exchange rate is $1.50/£1.00. Dorchester explicitly believes in PPP as the best means to forecast future exchange rates.

The manufacturing facility is expected to cost $7,000,000. Dorchester plans to finance this amount by a combination of equity capital and debt. The plant will increase Dorchester's borrowing capacity by £2,000,000, and it plans to borrow only that amount. The local community in which Dorchester has decided to build will provide $1,500,000 of debt financing for a period of seven years at 7.75 percent. The principal is to be repaid in equal installments over the life of the loan. At this point, Dorchester is uncertain whether to raise the remaining debt it desires through a domestic bond issue or a Eurodollar bond issue. It believes it can borrow pounds sterling at 10.75 percent per annum and dollars at 9.5 percent. Dorchester estimates its all-equity cost of capital to be 15 percent.

The U.S. Internal Revenue Service will allow Dorchester to depreciate the new facility over a seven-year period. After that time the confectionery equipment, which accounts for the bulk of the investment, is expected to have substantial market value.

Dorchester does not expect to receive any special tax concessions. Further, because the corporate tax rates in the two countries are the same—35 percent in the U.K. and in the United States—transfer pricing strategies are ruled out.

Should Dorchester build the new manufacturing plant in the United States?

MINI CASE 2   **Strik-it-Rich Gold Mining Company**

The Strik-it-Rich Gold Mining Company is contemplating expanding its operations. To do so it will need to purchase land that its geologists believe is rich in gold. Strik-it-Rich's management believes that the expansion will allow it to mine and sell an additional 2,000 troy ounces of gold per year. The expansion, including the cost of the land, will cost $500,000. The current price of gold bullion is $425 per ounce and one-year gold futures are trading at $450.50 = $425 (1.06). Extraction costs are $375 per ounce. The firm's cost of capital is 10 percent. At the current price of gold, the expansion appears profitable: NPV = ($425 − 375) × 2,000/.10 − $500,000 = $500,000. Strik-it-Rich's management is, however, concerned with the possibility that large sales of gold reserves by Russia and the United Kingdom will drive the price of gold down to $390 for the foreseeable future. On the other hand, management believes there is some possibility that the world will soon return to a gold reserve international monetary system. In the latter event, the price of gold would increase to at least $460 per ounce. The course of the future price of gold bullion should become clear within a year. Strik-it-Rich can postpone the expansion for a year by buying a purchase option on the land for $25,000. What should Strik-it-Rich's management do?

REFERENCES & SUGGESTED READINGS

Ang, James S., and Tsong-Yue Lai. "A Simple Rule for Multinational Capital Budgeting." *The Global Finance Journal* 1 (1989), pp. 71–75.

Booth, Lawrence D. "Capital Budgeting Frameworks for the Multinational Corporation." *Journal of International Business Studies* (Fall 1982), pp. 113–23.

Brealey, Richard A., and Stewart C. Myers. *Principles of Corporate Finance,* 7th ed. New York: McGraw-Hill/Irwin, 2003.

Endleson, Michael E. "Real Options: Valuing Managerial Flexibility (A)." *Harvard Business School Note* (March 31, 1994).

Holland, John. "Capital Budgeting for International Business: A Framework for Analysis." *Managerial Finance* 16 (1990), pp. 1–6.

Lessard, Donald R. "Evaluating International Projects: An Adjusted Present Value Approach." In Donald R. Lessard (ed.), *International Financial Management: Theory and Application,* 2nd ed. New York: Wiley, 1985, pp. 570–84.

Luenberger, David G. "Evaluating Real Investment Opportunities." *Investment Science.* New York: Oxford University Press, 1998, pp. 337–43.

Luehrman, Timothy A. "Capital Projects as Real Options: An Introduction." *Harvard Business School Note* (March 22, 1995).

Luehrman, Timothy A. "Investment Opportunities as Real Options: Getting Started on the Numbers." *Harvard Business Review* (July–August 1998) pp. 51–67.

Modigliani, Franco, and Merton H. Miller. "Corporate Income Taxes and the Cost of Capital: A Correction." *American Economic Review* 53 (1963), pp. 433–43.

Ross, Stephen A., Randolph W. Westerfield, and Jeffrey F. Jaffe. *Corporate Finance,* 6th ed. New York: McGraw-Hill/Irwin, 2002.

Shapiro, Alan C. "Capital Budgeting for the Multinational Corporation." *Financial Management* (spring 1978), pp. 7–16.

19 Multinational Cash Management

我们关注的是现金收支的规模、标价货币以及这些现金收支发生在跨国公司的哪些子公司。

OUR PRIMARY CONCERN in this chapter is with the efficient management of cash within a MNC. We are concerned with the size of cash balances, their currency denominations, and where these cash balances are located among the MNC's affiliates. Efficient cash management techniques can reduce the investment in cash balances and foreign exchange transaction expenses, and it can provide for maximum return from the investment of excess cash. Additionally, efficient cash management techniques result in borrowing at the lowest rate when a temporary cash shortage exists.

The chapter begins with a case application that develops a centralized cash management system for a MNC. The system we develop includes interaffiliate netting and a centralized cash depository. The benefits of a centralized system are clearly detailed. A second case application is used to illustrate transfer pricing strategies and the unbundling of services as two means for a MNC to reposition cash between affiliates and, under certain circumstances, reduce its overall income tax liability. The chapter concludes with a discussion on moving blocked funds from a host country that has imposed foreign exchange restrictions.

The Management of International Cash Balances

现金管理是指在现金预算期间，公司在交易收支方面用于支付预期现金流出的**交易余额**投资，以及作为**风险预备金**而占用的资金。

预防性现金余额（Precautionary cash balances）

不论公司只从事国

Cash management refers to the investment the firm has in **transaction balances** to cover scheduled outflows of funds during a cash budgeting period and the funds the firm has tied up in precautionary cash balances. **Precautionary cash balances** are necessary in case the firm has underestimated the amount needed to cover transactions. Good cash management also encompasses investing excess funds at the most favorable rate and borrowing at the lowest rate when there is a temporary cash shortage.

Many of the skills necessary for effective cash management are the same regardless of whether the firm has only domestic operations or if it operates internationally.

内业务，还是从事国际
化业务，都必须掌握众多
有效的现金管理方法。

For example, the cash manager of a domestic firm should source funds internationally to obtain the lowest borrowing cost and to place excess funds wherever the greatest return can be earned. Firms with multinational operations, however, regularly deal in more than one currency, and hence the cost of foreign exchange transactions is an important factor in efficient cash management. Moreover, multinational operations require the firm to decide on whether the cash management function should be centralized at corporate headquarters (or elsewhere) or decentralized and handled locally by each affiliate. In this chapter, we make a strong case for centralized cash management.

CASE APPLICATION

Teltrex's Cash Management System

We use a case problem for a company named Teltrex International to illustrate how a centralized cash management system works. Teltrex is a U.S. multinational firm with headquarters in California's Silicon Valley. It manufactures low-priced quartz watches which it markets throughout North America and Europe. In addition to its manufacturing facilities in California, Teltrex has three sales affiliates in Canada, Germany, and the United Kingdom.

现金预算是关于现
金收付的时间和规模的
具体计划。

The foundation of any cash management system is its cash budget. The **cash budget** is a plan detailing the time and the size of expected cash receipts and disbursements. Teltrex prepares a cash budget in advance for the fiscal year (updating it periodically as the year progresses), using a weekly time interval as the planning frequency. Exhibit 19.1 presents a payments matrix for one week during the cash budget planning horizon; it summarizes all interaffiliate cash receipts and disbursements of Teltrex and the receipts from and disbursements to external parties with which Teltrex does business. Exhibit 19.1 is denominated in U.S. dollars, the reporting currency of the parent firm. However, the functional currency of each foreign affiliate is the local currency.

Exhibit 19.1 shows, for example, that the U.S. parent expects to receive the equivalent of $30,000 in Canadian dollars from its Canadian affiliate, the equivalent of $35,000 in euros from its German affiliate, and the equivalent of $60,000 in British pounds sterling from its affiliate in the United Kingdom. In total, it expects to receive $125,000 from interaffiliate transactions. Additionally, the U.S. parent expects to receive $140,000 from external parties, say, from sales in the United States. In total, the parent expects to receive $265,000 in cash during the week. On the disbursements side, the U.S. parent expects to make payments in dollars in the amounts of $20,000 to its Canadian affiliate,

---

EXHIBIT 19.1		Cash Receipts and Disbursements Matrix for Teltrex ($000)					
		Disbursements					
Receipts	U.S.	Canada	Germany	U.K.	External	Total Internal	Total Receipts
U.S.	—	30	35	60	140	125	265
Canada	20	—	10	40	135	70	205
Germany	10	25	—	30	125	65	190
U.K.	40	30	20	—	130	90	220
External	120	165	50	155	—	—	490[a]
Total Internal	70	85	65	130	—	350	—
Total Disbursements	190	250	115	285	530[b]	—	1,370[c]

[a]Total cash disbursed by the U.S. parent firm and its affiliates to external parties.
[b]Total cash received by the U.S. parent firm and its affiliates from external parties.
[c]Balancing check figure.
Note: $350,000 is shifted among the various affiliates; $530,000 − $490,000 = $40,000 = increase in cash balances for Teltrex during the week.

EXHIBIT 19.2		Teltrex's Interaffiliate Cash Receipts and Disbursements Matrix ($000)				
		Disbursements				
Receipts	U.S.	Canada	Germany	U.K.	Total Receipts	Net[a]
U.S.	—	30	35	60	125	55
Canada	20	—	10	40	70	(15)
Germany	10	25	—	30	65	0
U.K.	40	30	20	—	90	(40)
Total Disbursements	70	85	65	130	350	0

[a]Net denotes the difference between total receipts and total disbursements for each affiliate.

$10,000 to its German affiliate, and $40,000 to its British affiliate. It also expects to make external disbursements of $120,000 to, say, suppliers for component parts and to cover other operating costs. Analogous cash flows exist for the three affiliates.

Exhibit 19.1 shows that the equivalent of $350,000 in interaffiliate cash flows are expected to flow among the parent and its three affiliates. Note that no increase in cash in the MNC occurs as a result of interaffiliate transactions. Interaffiliate transactions effectively represent taking money out of one pocket of the MNC and putting it into another. However, Teltrex expects to receive the equivalent of $530,000 from external parties and make payments of $490,000 to other external parties. From these external transactions, a net increase of $40,000 in cash among the affiliates is expected during the week.

Netting Systems

Let's first consider the interaffiliate transactions that make up part of Exhibit 19.1. Later we will examine the transactions Teltrex expects to have with external parties. Exhibit 19.2 presents only the portion of Teltrex's receipts and disbursements matrix from Exhibit 19.1 that concerns interaffiliate cash flows.

Exhibit 19.2 shows the amount that each affiliate is to pay and receive from the other. Without a netting policy, 12 foreign exchange transactions will take place among the four affiliates. In general, if there are N affiliates, there will be a maximum of $N(N-1)$ transactions; in our case $4(4-1) = 12$. Exhibit 19.3 diagrams these 12 transactions.

Exhibit 19.3 indicates that the equivalent of $350,000 in funds flows among the four affiliates in 12 foreign exchange transactions. This represents a needless use of administrative time in arranging the transactions and a waste of corporate funds in making the

EXHIBIT 19.3

Teltrex's Interaffiliate Foreign Exchange Transactions without Netting ($000)

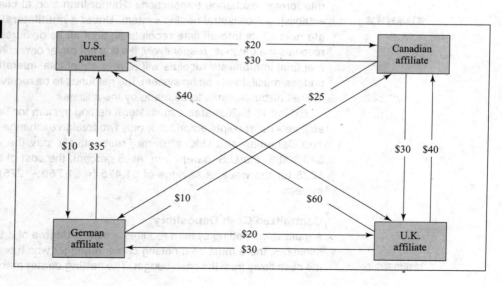

EXHIBIT 19.4

Bilateral Netting of Teltrex's Interaffiliate Foreign Exchange Transactions ($000)

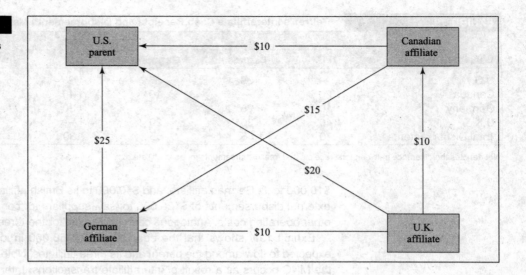

transactions. The cost of transferring funds is in the range of .25 percent to 1.5 percent of the transaction; this includes transaction expenses and the opportunity cost of funds tied up in interaffiliate float. If we assume a cost of .5 percent, the cost for transferring $350,000 is $1,750 for the week.

The 12 transactions can be reduced at least by half through bilateral netting. Under a **bilateral netting** system, each pair of affiliates determines the net amount due between them, and only the net amount is transferred. For example, the U.S. parent and the Canadian affiliate would net the $30,000 and the $20,000 to be received from one another. The result is that only one payment is made; the Canadian affiliate pays the U.S. parent an amount equivalent to $10,000. Exhibit 19.4 shows the results of bilateral netting among Teltrex's four affiliates.

在双边净额结算制度下，关联公司的各方确定相互间到期的净额并对此做转账处理。

From Exhibit 19.4, it can be seen that a total of $90,000 flows among the four affiliates of Teltrex in six transactions. Bilateral netting can reduce the number of foreign exchange transactions among the affiliates to N (N − 1)/2, or less. The equivalent of $260,000 in foreign exchange transactions is eliminated through bilateral netting. At .5 percent, the cost of netting interaffiliate foreign exchange transactions is $450, a savings of $1,300 (= $1,750 − 450) over a non-netting system.

Exhibit 19.2 implies a way to limit interaffiliate transfers to no more than (N − 1) separate foreign exchange transactions. Rather than stop at bilateral netting, the MNC can establish a multilateral netting system. Under a **multilateral netting** system, each affiliate nets all its interaffiliate receipts against all its disbursements. It then transfers or receives the balance, respectively, if it is a net payer or receiver. Recall from Exhibit 19.1 that total interaffiliate receipts will always equal total interaffiliate disbursements. Thus, under a multilateral netting system, the net funds to be received by the affiliates will equal the net disbursements to be made by the affiliates.

多边净额结算

Exhibit 19.5 illustrates a multilateral netting system for Teltrex. Because the German affiliate's net receipts equal zero, only two foreign exchange transactions are necessary. The Canadian and U.K. affiliates, respectively, pay the equivalent of $15,000 and $40,000 to the U.S. parent firm. At .5 percent, the cost of transferring $55,000 is only $275 for the week, a savings of $1,475 (= $1,750 − 275) with a multilateral netting system.

Centralized Cash Depository

净额结算中心

A multilateral netting system requires a certain degree of administrative structure. At the minimum, there must be a netting center manager who has an overview of the interaffiliate cash flows from the cash budget. The **netting center** manager determines the amount

EXHIBIT 19.5

Multilateral Netting of Teltrex's Interaffiliate Foreign Exchange Transactions ($000)

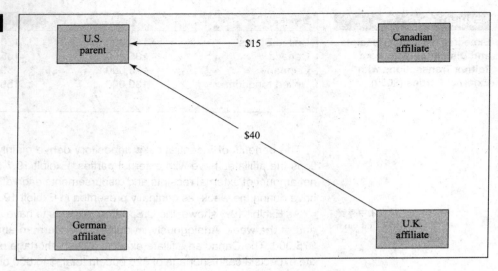

中央现金库

of the net payments and which affiliates are to make or receive them. A netting center does not imply that the MNC has a central cash manager, however. Indeed, the multilateral netting system presented in Exhibit 19.5 suggests that each affiliate has a local cash manager who is responsible for investing excess cash and borrowing when there is a temporary cash shortage.

Exhibit 19.6 presents a modified diagram of multilateral netting for Teltrex with the addition of a centralized depository. Under a centralized cash management system, unless otherwise instructed, all interaffiliate payments will flow through the central cash depository.

As Exhibit 19.6 shows, the Canadian affiliate remits the equivalent of $15,000 to the central depository and the U.K. affiliate remits the equivalent of $40,000. In turn, the central depository remits $55,000 to the U.S. parent. One might question the wisdom of this system. It appears as if the foreign exchange transactions have doubled from $55,000 in Exhibit 19.5 to $110,000 in Exhibit 19.6. But that is not the case. The Canadian and U.K. affiliates might be instructed to remit to the central depository in U.S. dollars. Alternatively, the central depository could receive the remittances in Canadian dollars and British pounds sterling and exchange them for dollars before transferring the funds to the U.S. parent. (There is the expense of an additional wire transfer, however.)

EXHIBIT 19.6

Multilateral Netting of Teltrex's Interaffiliate Foreign Exchange Transactions with a Centralized Depository ($000)

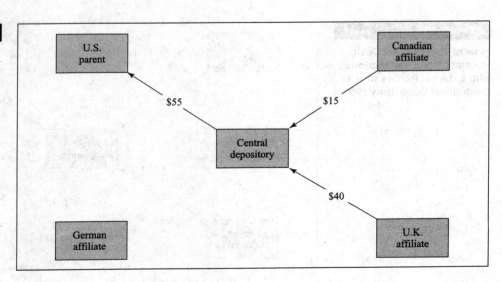

Affiliate	Receipts	Disbursements	Net
United States	$140,000	$120,000	$20,000
Canada	135,000	165,000	(30,000)
Germany	125,000	50,000	75,000
United Kingdom	130,000	155,000	(25,000)
			$40,000

按照现金集中存管制（centralized cash depository），各关联公司自己持有交易收支头寸和风险预备金。

www.treasury-management.com

This is the website of the online magazine Treasury Management International. TMI articles are written by corporate treasurers. Many articles on international cash management can be found at this site.

闲散资金(mislocated funds)

资金移动（funds mobilization）

The benefits of a central cash depository derive mainly from the business transactions the affiliates have with external parties. Exhibit 19.7 presents a table showing the net amount of external receipts and disbursements each affiliate of Teltrex is expected to have during the week, as originally presented in Exhibit 19.1.

As Exhibit 19.7 shows, the U.S. parent expects to have net receipts of $20,000 by the end of the week. Analogously, in dollars, the German affiliate expects net receipts of $75,000. The Canadian affiliate expects a cash shortage of $30,000, and the U.K. affiliate expects a cash shortage of $25,000. In total, $40,000 of net receipts are expected for the MNC as a whole.

With a **centralized cash depository,** excess cash is remitted to the central cash pool. Analogously, the central cash manager arranges to cover shortages of cash. The central cash manager has a global view of the MNC's overall cash position and needs. Consequently, there is less of a chance for mislocated funds; that is, there is less of a chance for funds being denominated in the wrong currency. Moreover, because of his global perspective, the central cash manager will know the best borrowing and investing rates. A centralized system facilitates funds mobilization, where systemwide cash excesses are invested at the most advantageous rates and cash shortages are covered by borrowing at the most favorable rates. Without a centralized cash depository, one affiliate might end up borrowing locally at an unfavorable rate, while another is investing temporary surplus funds locally at a disadvantageous rate. Exhibit 19.8 diagrams the cash payments for Teltrex depicted in Exhibit 19.7, showing the flows to and from the central cash pool.

Exhibit 19.8 shows that the U.S. parent will remit $20,000 of excess cash from transactions with external parties to the central cash pool, and similarly, the German affiliate will remit the $75,000 it has obtained. Both the Canadian and U.K. affiliates will have their cash shortages of $30,000 and $25,000, respectively, covered by the central

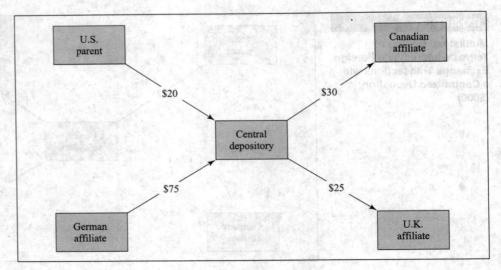

pool. In total, a net increase of $40,000 is expected at the central cash depository at the end of the week. The diagram shows that a total of $150,000 of cash is expected to flow to ($95,000) and from ($55,000) the cash depository.

In More Depth

Bilateral Netting of Internal and External Net Cash Flows

Up to this point, we have handled the multilateral netting of interaffiliate cash flows (Exhibit 19.6) *and* the net receipts of the affiliates from the transactions with external parties (Exhibit 19.8) as two separate sets of cash flows through the central cash depository. While it was easier to develop the concepts in that manner, it is not necessary, practical, or efficient to do it that way in practice. Instead, the two sets of net cash flows can be bilaterally netted, with the resulting net sums going through the central depository. This will further reduce the number, size, and expense of foreign exchange transactions for the MNC. Exhibit 19.9 calculates the net amount of funds from Teltrex affiliates to flow through the central depository.

Exhibit 19.9 shows the result of netting the cash receipts that would flow through the central cash depository via multilateral netting with the net cash flows that would flow through the central depository as a result of external transactions. As the exhibit shows, the U.S. parent will receive a single payment from the cash pool of $35,000 and the Canadian affiliate will receive $15,000. The German affiliate will remit to the central depository $75,000 and the U.K. affiliate will remit $15,000. In total, the central depository receives $90,000 and disburses $50,000, for an expected net increase in cash of $40,000 for the week. Instead of two separate sets of cash flows totaling $55,000 from the multilateral netting and $150,000 from transactions with external parties, there is only one set of cash flows after the netting totaling $140,000. Thus, there is a savings on foreign exchange transactions of $65,000 for the week. Exhibit 19.10 diagrams the resulting $140,000 of cash flows for Teltrex that are calculated in Exhibit 19.9.

EXHIBIT 19.9			
Net Cash Flows of Teltrex Affiliates through the Central Cash Depository ($000)	**Affiliate**	**Net Receipts from Multilateral Netting[a]**	**Net Excess Cash from Transactions with External Parties[b]**	**Net Flow[c]**
	United States	$55,000	$20,000	$35,000
	Canada	($15,000)	($30,000)	$15,000
	Germany	0	$75,000	($75,000)
	United Kingdom	($40,000)	($25,000)	($15,000)
				($40,000)

[a]Net receipt from (payment to) the central depository resulting from multilateral netting, as shown in Exhibit 19.2.
[b]Net excess (shortage) of cash to be remitted to (covered by) the central depository, as shown in Exhibit 19.7.
[c]A positive amount in this column denotes a payment to an affiliate from the central cash depository; a negative amount denotes a payment from the affiliate.

Reduction in Precautionary Cash Balances

An additional benefit of a centralized cash depository is that the MNC's investment in precautionary cash balances can be substantially reduced without a reduction in its ability to cover unforeseen expenses. To see how this is accomplished, consider the receipts and disbursements each affiliate of Teltrex expected to make with external parties during the week. Assume, for simplicity, that each affiliate will have to make

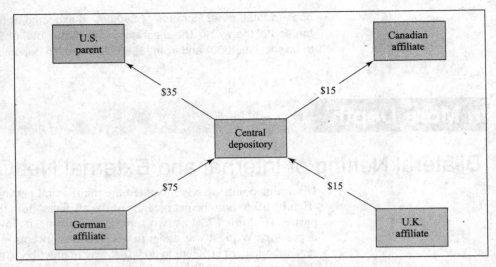

all its planned payments to external parties before it receives any cash from other external sources. For example, from Exhibit 19.7, the Canadian affiliate expects to have to pay to external parties the equivalent of $165,000 before it receives any of the expected $135,000 in receipts. Thus, the Canadian affiliate will need a transactions balance of $165,000 to cover expected transactions.

As previously mentioned, a firm keeps a precautionary cash balance to cover unexpected transactions during the budget period. The size of this balance depends on how safe the firm desires to be in its ability to meet unexpected transactions. The larger the precautionary cash balance, the greater is the firm's ability to meet unexpected expenses, and the less is the risk of financial embarrassment and loss of credit standing. Assume that cash needs are normally distributed and that the cash needs of one affiliate are independent from the others. If Teltrex follows a conservative policy, it might keep three standard deviations of cash for precautionary purposes, in addition to the cash needed to cover expected transactions for the planning period. Thus, the probability that Teltrex would experience a cash shortage is only .13 of 1 percent; it will have sufficient cash to cover transactions 99.87 percent of the time.

按照现金分散存管制，各关联公司自己持有交易收支尺寸和风险预备金。

Under a decentralized cash management system, each affiliate would hold its own transaction balance and precautionary cash. Exhibit 19.11 shows the total cash held for transactions and precautionary purposes by each affiliate and by Teltrex as a whole.

As can be seen from Exhibit 19.11, Teltrex needs the equivalent of $490,000 in cash to cover expected transactions and an additional $615,000 in precautionary balances to cover unexpected expenses, for a total of $1,105,000. A centralized cash management system will greatly reduce the investment in precautionary cash balances. Under a centralized system, the amount of cash held by the MNC is viewed as a portfolio. Each affiliate will continue to hold cash sufficient to cover its expected cash transactions, but the precautionary cash balances are held by the central cash manager at the central

Affiliate	Expected Transactions (a)	Standard Deviation (b)	Expected Needs plus Precautionary (a + 3b)
United States	$120,000	$50,000	$ 270,000
Canada	165,000	70,000	375,000
Germany	50,000	20,000	110,000
United Kingdom	155,000	65,000	350,000
Total	$490,000		$1,105,000

cash depository. In the event one of the affiliates experiences a cash shortage, funds would be wired from precautionary cash held in the central cash pool.

From portfolio theory, the standard deviation of the portfolio of cash held by the centralized depository for N affiliates is calculated as:[1]

$$\text{Portfolio Std. Dev.} = \sqrt{(\text{Std.Dev.Affiliate } 1)^2 + \ldots + (\text{Std.Dev.Affiliate } N)^2}$$

For our example,

$$\text{Portfolio Std. Dev.} = \sqrt{(\$50,000)^2 + (\$70,000)^2 + (\$20,000)^2 + (\$65,000)^2}$$

$$= \$109,659.$$

Thus under a centralized system, only $328,977 (= 3 × $109,659) needs to be held for precautionary purposes by Teltrex's central cash manager. A total of $818,977 (= $490,000 + $328,977) is held by Teltrex. The reduction in precautionary cash balances under the centralized system is $286,023 (= $1,105,000 − $818,977), a sum that most likely can be used more profitably elsewhere, rather than standing by as a potential safety net.

Cash Management Systems in Practice

按照现金分散存管制，各关联公司自己持有交易收支尺寸和风险预备金。

Multilateral netting is an efficient and cost-effective mechanism for handling interaffiliate foreign exchange transactions. Not all countries allow MNCs the freedom to net payments, however. Some countries allow interaffiliate transactions to be settled only on a gross basis. That is, all receipts for a settlement period must be grouped into a single large receipt and all disbursements must be grouped into a single large payment. The reason for requiring gross settlement is precisely the opposite of the reason that MNCs desire to net. By limiting netting, more needless foreign exchange transactions flow through the local banking system, thus generating income for the local banks that handle them.

A study by Collins and Frankle (1985) surveyed the cash management practices of the *Fortune* 1000 firms. The researchers received a 22 percent response rate from their questionnaire. Of the responding firms, 163 were involved in international operations. Thirty-five percent of the international respondents reported using some type of intracorporate netting and 23 percent had centralized funds concentration.

In another study, Bokos and Clinkard (1983) found that the most frequently cited benefits of a multilateral netting system were:

1. The decrease in the expense associated with funds transfer, which in some cases can be over $1,000 for a large international transfer of foreign exchange.

2. The reduction in the number of foreign exchange transactions and the associated cost of making fewer but larger transactions.

3. The reduction in intracompany float, which is frequently as high as five days even for wire transfers.

4. The savings in administrative time.

5. The benefits that accrue from the establishment of a formal information system, which serves as the foundation for centrally managing transaction exposure and the investment of excess funds.

Bokos and Clinkard note that several international banks offer multilateral netting software packages that calculate the net currency positions of each affiliate. Some packages integrate the netting function with foreign exchange exposure management. In an

---

[1]The standard deviation formula assumes that interaffiliate cash flows are uncorrelated with one another.

article, Srinivasin and Kim (1986) develop a sophisticated network optimization approach for netting interaffiliate cash payments that is computationally efficient and visually appealing.

Transfer Pricing and Related Issues

转移价格

显然，转移价格越高，转出部门的毛利润越高，转入部门的毛利润就越低。

Within a large business firm with multiple divisions, goods and services are frequently transferred from one division to another. The process brings into question the **transfer price** that should be assigned, for bookkeeping purposes, to the goods or services as they are transferred between divisions. Obviously, the higher the transfer price, the larger will be the gross profits of the transferring division relative to the receiving division. Even within a domestic firm, it is difficult to decide on the transfer price. Within a MNC, the decision is further compounded by exchange restrictions on the part of the host country where the receiving affiliate is located, a difference in income tax rates between the two countries, and import duties and quotas imposed by the host country.

CASE APPLICATION

Mintel Products Transfer Pricing Strategy

Low versus High Markup Policy

Mintel Products, Inc., manufactures goods for sale in the United States and overseas. Finished goods are transferred from the parent firm to its wholly owned sales affiliate for overseas retail sale. Mintel's financial manager, Hilary Van Kirk, has decided that the firm's transfer pricing strategy should be reevaluated as part of a routine review of the operations of the sales affiliate. Van Kirk has decided to explore both a low and a high markup policy. The analysis is to be done in U.S. dollars. She notes that both the parent firm and the sales affiliate have a 40 percent income tax rate, that the variable production cost of one unit is $1,500, and that the unit retail sales price charged by the sales affiliate to the final customer is $3,000. As a first step in her analysis, Van Kirk prepares Exhibit 19.12. The upper portion of the exhibit presents the analysis of a low markup policy,

---

EXHIBIT 19.12

Low versus High Transfer Pricing Strategy between Mintel Affiliates with the Same Income Tax Rate

	Manufacturing Affiliate	Sales Affiliate	Consolidated Company
Low Markup Policy			
Sales revenue	$2,000	$3,000	$3,000
Cost of goods sold	1,500	2,000	1,500
Gross profit	500	1,000	1,500
Operating expenses	200	200	400
Taxable income	300	800	1,100
Income taxes (40%)	120	320	440
Net income	180	480	660
High Markup Policy			
Sales revenue	$2,400	$3,000	$3,000
Cost of goods sold	1,500	2,400	1,500
Gross profit	900	600	1,500
Operating expenses	200	200	400
Taxable income	700	400	1,100
Income taxes (40%)	280	160	440
Net income	420	240	660

where the transfer price is set at $2,000. The lower portion of the exhibit analyzes the effect of a high markup policy, where the transfer price is $2,400 per unit.

Van Kirk notices from Exhibit 19.12 that the low markup policy results in larger pretax income, income taxes, and net income per unit in the selling country. On the other hand, the high markup policy has the opposite effect, that is, higher taxable income, income taxes, and net profit per unit in the manufacturing country. She also notes that because the income tax rates are the same in both countries, the consolidated results are identical regardless of whether the MNC follows a low or high transfer pricing scheme.

Exchange Restrictions

Van Kirk wonders if Mintel should be indifferent between the low and high markup policies, since the consolidated results are the same. She reasons, however, that if the distribution country imposes exchange restrictions limiting or blocking the amount of profits that can be repatriated to the manufacturing parent, Mintel would no longer be indifferent between the two markup policies. It obviously would prefer the high markup policy. According to Exhibit 19.12, the higher markup allows $240 per unit to be repatriated to the parent that otherwise may have been blocked. This amount represents the $400 higher markup minus the $160 additional taxes paid in the parent country.

Van Kirk notes that the low markup policy is disadvantageous from the host country's perspective. If the transferring affiliate attempts to reposition funds by changing from the low to the high markup policy, the exchange controls have been partially bypassed and there is a loss of tax revenue in the host country. Thus, the host country may take measures to enforce a certain transfer price. She decides she needs to brush up on how this might be accomplished and also to consider the effect of a difference in income tax rates between the two affiliates.

Differential Income Tax Rates

As a second step, Van Kirk prepares Exhibit 19.13, which examines the low versus high markup policies when the tax rate in the transferring country is assumed to be 25 percent, or 15 percent less than the marginal tax rate of 40 percent in the receiving country.

EXHIBIT 19.13	Manufacturing Affiliate	Sales Affiliate	Consolidated Company
Low versus High Transfer Pricing Strategy between Mintel Affiliates with Differential Income Tax Rates			
Low Markup Policy			
Sales revenue	$2,000	$3,000	$3,000
Cost of goods sold	1,500	2,000	1,500
Gross profit	500	1,000	1,500
Operating expenses	200	200	400
Taxable income	300	800	1,100
Income taxes (25%/40%)	75	320	395
Net income	225	480	705
High Markup Policy			
Sales revenue	$2,400	$3,000	$3,000
Cost of goods sold	1,500	2,400	1,500
Gross profit	900	600	1,500
Operating expenses	200	200	400
Taxable income	700	400	1,100
Income taxes (25%/40%)	175	160	335
Net income	525	240	765

Van Kirk notes from Exhibit 19.13 that the consolidated taxable income is $1,100 under both markup policies. However, Mintel would no longer be indifferent when there is a differential in the income tax rates. In the absence of governmental restrictions on the transfer price, the MNC would prefer a high markup policy when the tax rate in the parent country is lower than the tax rate in the receiving country. Consolidated net income for Mintel would be $60 [= ($2,000 − 2,400) × (.25 − .40)] per unit greater under the high versus the low markup policy. The high markup policy results in $400 per unit of taxable income being shifted from the receiving country to the transferring country, where it is taxed at a 15 percent lower rate. Consequently, the consolidated income taxes paid by Mintel drop from $395 to $335 per unit.

If the tax rate in the receiving country is lower than in the parent country, it is not clear that a low markup policy should be pursued. Van Kirk recalls that U.S. MNCs are taxed on their worldwide income. Hence, income repatriated to the U.S. parent from a receiving country with a low tax rate would be "grossed up" to its pretax amount so that U.S. taxes could be figured. A credit for the taxes paid in the receiving country would be given against taxes owed in the United States. Thus, pursuing a low markup policy would not result in a dollar tax savings if net income was to be repatriated. However, if the net income of the foreign subsidiary was to be reinvested in the host country, the low markup policy would result in a tax savings and allow more funds for reinvestment. Nevertheless, this would only be temporary, Van Kirk reasons. At some point, profitable investment opportunities would be exhausted, and the parent firm and its stockholders would desire some return on the investment made—and this means repatriation.

Regulations Affecting Transfer Prices

Van Kirk believes that governmental authorities within a host country would be quite aware of the motives of MNCs to use transfer pricing schemes to move blocked funds or evade tax liabilities. After doing some research, she learns that most countries have regulations controlling transfer prices. In the United States, Section 482: Allocation of Income and Deductions Among Taxpayers of the U.S. Internal Revenue Code stipulates that the transfer price must reflect an arm's-length price, that is, a price the selling affiliate would charge an unrelated customer for the good or service. The Internal Revenue Service (IRS) . . . "may distribute, apportion, or allocate gross income, deductions, credits, or allowances between or among such organizations . . . [if it is] necessary in order to prevent evasion of taxes or clearly to reflect the income of any such organizations . . ." Moreover, in the event of conflict, the burden of proof lies with the taxpayer to show that the IRS has unreasonably established the transfer price and determined taxable income.

She learns that there are three basic methods prescribed by the IRS, and recognized internationally, for establishing arm's-length prices of tangible goods. The method considered the best is to use a comparable uncontrolled price between unrelated firms. While this method seems reasonable and theoretically sound, it is difficult to use in practice because many factors enter into the pricing of goods and services between two business enterprises. The Code allows for some adjustments because differences in the terms of sale, the quantity sold, quality differences, and the date of sale are all factors that can realistically affect the sale price among various customers. Thus, what is a reasonable price for one customer may not be reasonable for another. The next best method is the resale price approach, which can be used if, among other things, there is no comparable uncontrolled sales price. Under this method, the price at which the good is resold by the distribution affiliate is reduced by an amount sufficient to cover overhead costs and a reasonable profit. However, it may be difficult to determine the value added by the distribution affiliate. The third method is the cost-plus approach, where an appropriate profit is added to the cost of the manufacturing affiliate. This method assumes that the manufacturing cost is readily accountable. Additionally, a group of

EXHIBIT 19.14

Low versus High Transfer Pricing Strategy between Mintel Affiliates with Differential Income Tax Rates and a 5 Percent Import Duty

	Manufacturing Affiliate	Sales Affiliate	Consolidated Company
Low Markup Policy			
Sales revenue	$2,000	$3,000	$3,000
Cost of goods sold	1,500	2,000	1,500
Import duty (5%)	—	100	100
Gross profit	500	900	1,400
Operating expenses	200	200	400
Taxable income	300	700	1,000
Income taxes (25%/40%)	75	280	355
Net income	225	420	645
High Markup Policy			
Sales revenue	$2,400	$3,000	$3,000
Cost of goods sold	1,500	2,400	1,500
Import duty (5%)	—	120	120
Gross profit	900	480	1,380
Operating expenses	200	200	400
Taxable income	700	280	980
Income taxes (25%/40%)	175	112	287
Net income	525	168	693

methods collectively referred to as fourth methods can be applied to approximate arm's-length prices when the three basic methods are not applicable. The fourth methods include those based on financial and economic models and econometric techniques. The comparable uncontrolled price method and fourth methods are used for determining an arm's-length transfer price for intangible goods, whereas cost methods are used for pricing services.

The Organization for Economic Cooperation and Development Model Tax Convention sets out the same methods as the IRS Code for use by member countries. Van Kirk concludes that all methods present operational difficulties of some type and are also difficult for the taxing authority to evaluate. Thus, transfer pricing manipulation cannot be completely controlled and the potential exists for maneuverability by the MNC to reposition funds or reduce its tax liability.

The International Finance in Practice box "Transfer Pricing Is the Most Important International Tax Issue" discusses a recent survey by the international accounting firm Ernst & Young.

Import Duties

After some reflection, Van Kirk concludes that import duties are another factor that need to be considered. When a host country imposes an ad valorem import duty on goods shipped across its borders from another country, the import tax raises the cost of doing business within the country. An ad valorem duty is a percentage tax levied at customs on the assessed value of the imported goods. She reasons that an import tax will affect the transfer pricing strategy a MNC uses, but that, in general, the income tax will have the greatest after-tax effect on consolidated net income. To analyze the effect of an import duty on Mintel, she prepares Exhibit 19.14, which shows the low versus high transfer price alternatives presented in Exhibit 19.13 with the imposition of a 5 percent import duty by the receiving country.

Transfer Pricing Is the Most Important International Tax Issue

Transfer pricing is the most important international tax issue that multinational enterprises (MNEs) now face, according to a new survey by Ernst & Young.

Eighty-six percent of MNE parent company respondents and 93 percent of subsidiary respondents to the Ernst & Young Transfer Pricing 2003 Global Survey identified transfer pricing as the most important international tax matter they are currently dealing with, and indicated that audits by tax authorities are becoming a rule, rater than an exception.

Transfer pricing involves the price at which transactions between units of multinational companies take place, including the inter-company transfer of goods, property, services, loans and leases.

The Ernst & Young Survey revealed that 59 percent of all MNEs with revenues of US$5 billion or more, and 71 percent of all US-based MNEs regardless of revenues, had been subject to a transfer pricing audit somewhere in their organization since 1999. Seventy-six percent of all company respondents total Ernst & Young that they "believe that a transfer pricing examination will occur within their group during the next two years."

According to Ernst & Young, MNEs believe that the chance of being subjected to a transfer pricing audit is increasing because more and more countries are adopting transfer pricing legislation; those that already have legislation are stepping up their enforcement efforts. Moreover, audits will become more challenging because, according to survey participants, revenue authorities are more sophisticated. Tax authority feedback reinforced this observation, as many countries indicate they are investing more in training and encouraging their examiners to use all the examination tools available, reports Ernst & Young.

The survey indicated that if an MNE is subject to an adjustment as the result of a transfer pricing examination, there is almost a one-in-three chance that it will be threatened with a penalty, and a one-in-seven chance that one will actually be imposed. Ernst & Young expects these rates to increase as countries, including the United States, step up compliance and penalty enforcement.

In addition, the Survey revealed that 40 percent of the reported transfer pricing adjustments result in double taxation.

"This figure is alarmingly high, but perhaps lower than might be expected, given that only 19 percent of reported cases with adjustments were appealed," said Robert D. M.

Comparison of Exhibits 19.13 and 19.14 shows Van Kirk that under the low markup policy, Mintel would receive $60 less (= $645 − 705) per unit if a 5 percent import duty was imposed by the host country. The $60 represents the after-tax cost of the $100 import duty on the $2,000 per unit transfer price cost of the good. Mintel would still prefer the high markup policy as before, however, as it results in an increase in net income from $645 to $693 per unit. The difference in the net incomes between the two markup policies is only $48, in comparison to $60 without the 5 percent import tax. The loss of $12 represents the after-tax cost of an additional $20 of import duty per unit when the transfer price is $2,400 instead of $2,000 per unit.

Unbundling Fund Transfers

As Van Kirk knows, host countries are well aware of transfer pricing schemes used by MNCs to evade taxes within its borders or to avoid exchange restrictions. She wonders if there are ways to avoid suspicion from host country governmental authorities, and the administrative hassle likely to arise from such an inquiry, when the firm is merely trying to repatriate a sufficient amount of funds from a foreign affiliate to make the investment worthwhile. To learn more about transfer pricing strategies and related issues, she decides to attend a one-day seminar on the topic she saw advertised by a professional organization to which she belongs. She hopes it is beneficial, as the registration fee is $1,500 for the day!

As it turns out, the money was well spent. In addition to making the acquaintance of financial managers from other companies, one thing Van Kirk learned at the conference was that a MNC is likely to fare better if, instead of lumping all costs into a single

Turner, Global CEO of Ernst & Young's Transfer Pricing Services. "Of the appeals actually made by parent MNEs, 51 percent involved the competent authority process, 26 percent went to court and seven percent sought arbitration," said Mr. Turner.

The Ernst & Young survey found that MNE experiences with the competent authority process, which is a tax treaty process under which two governments agree to resolve the issue, vary. In many cases, although the competent authority process may take a year or two to reach resolution, the authorities eliminate or reduce the double taxation. Those MNEs who have used the competent authority process generally appear to have had a favorable experience, as most would go to competent authority again or even consider an Advance Pricing Agreement.

The survey also revealed that many multinationals fail to re-examine their transfer pricing policies in the wake of mergers or acquisitions.

"Because of the increasing scrutiny of transfer pricing policies, it is essential for an MNE to review the impact of any business change on its risk profile. In many cases, this will highlight the multinational's need to re-design core elements of its transfer pricing policies," according to Mr. Turner.

Mr. Turner also pointed out that while nearly half (46%) of the survey's Parents respondents had been through a merger or acquisition in the last two years, "only 18 percent of these MNEs either recognized the need or used the oppor-tunity to reexamine their overall transfer pricing policies. In fact, almost half of the survey respondents who went through a business combination simply used the transfer pricing policies of the dominant player in the transaction, thereby potentially missing legitimate planning opportunities. Moreover, a failure to adjust transfer pricing following major business changes may leave an MNE exposed when the years in question come up for review."

According to the Survey report, the sale of tangible goods remains the most commonly audited transaction among MNEs. The percentage of audits of tangible goods transactions is deceasing, however, while the percentage of audits relating to service and intangible property transactions is increasing.

Mr. Turner observed that "intercompany services are becoming a much larger part of the 'services economy' and we are seeing services transactions with larger monetary value. Despite this, MNEs tend to shy away from documenting these types of transactions, as they consider administrative or managerial services and financing transactions to be de minimis. With no or minimal documentation, these transactions appear to be the weakest link in an MNE's transfer pricing armor, giving revenue investigators more room to propose an adjustment."

Source: Ernst & Young, November 5, 2003. Reprinted with permission of LexisNexis.

transfer price, the parent firm unbundled the package to recognize the cost of the physical good and each service separately that it provides the affiliate. A detailing of the charges makes it easier, if ever necessary, to present and support to the taxing authority of a host country that each charge is legitimate and can be well substantiated. For instance, in addition to charging for the cost of the physical good, the parent firm could charge a fee for technical training of the affiliate's staff, a share of the cost of worldwide advertising or other corporate overhead, or a royalty or licensing fee as payment for use of well-recognized brand names, technology, or patents. The royalty or licensing fee represents remuneration for expense previously incurred by the parent for development or having made the product one that is desirable to own.

As a final step in her analysis, Van Kirk prepares Exhibit 19.15, which reproduces the low versus high markup policy analysis for Mintel with differential income tax rates presented in Exhibit 19.13. In addition, Exhibit 19.15 shows that a $2,000 transfer price and $400 per unit charge for royalties and fees results in the same consolidated net income of $765 as does the high markup policy with a $2,400 transfer price. By comparison, the low markup policy only provides $705 per unit consolidated net income. This is the case, regardless of whether a portion of the $480 net income of the sales affiliate is repatriated to the manufacturing affiliate as a dividend, because the tax rate in the distribution country is higher. As Van Kirk learned at the conference, the strategy of recognizing specific services may be acceptable to the host government, whereas the high markup policy may not, if $2,400 appears to be more than an arm's-length price for the transferred good.

	Manufacturing Affiliate	Sales Affiliate	Consolidated Company
Low Markup Policy			
Sales revenue	$2,000	$3,000	$3,000
Cost of goods sold	1,500	2,000	1,500
Gross profit	500	1,000	1,500
Operating expenses	200	200	400
Taxable income	300	800	1,100
Income taxes (25%/40%)	75	320	395
Net income	225	480	705
High Markup Policy			
Sales revenue	$2,400	$3,000	$3,000
Cost of goods sold	1,500	2,400	1,500
Gross profit	900	600	1,500
Operating expenses	200	200	400
Taxable income	700	400	1,100
Income taxes (25%/40%)	175	160	335
Net income	525	240	765
Low Markup Policy and Royalty			
Sales revenue	$2,000	$3,000	$3,000
Royalty and fee income	400	—	—
Cost of goods sold	1,500	2,400	1,500
Gross profit	900	600	1,500
Operating expenses	200	200	400
Taxable income	700	400	1,100
Income taxes (25%/40%)	175	160	335
Net income	525	240	765

Miscellaneous Factors

转移价格还会影响东道国居民对跨国公司子公司的感觉。

Transfer pricing strategies may be beneficial when the host country restricts the amount of foreign exchange that can be used for importing specific goods. In this event, a lower transfer price allows a greater quantity of the good to be imported under a quota restriction. This may be a more important consideration than income tax savings, if the imported item is a necessary component needed by an assembly or manufacturing affiliate to continue or expand production.

Transfer prices also have an effect on how divisions of a MNC are perceived locally. A high markup policy leaves little net income to show on the affiliate's books. If the parent firm expects the affiliate to be able to borrow short-term funds locally in the event of a cash shortage, the affiliate may have difficulty doing so with unimpressive financial statements. On the other hand, a low markup policy makes it appear, at least superficially, as if affiliates, rather than the parent firm, are contributing a larger portion to consolidated earnings. To the extent that financial markets are inefficient, or securities analysts do not understand the transfer pricing strategy being used, the market value of the MNC may be lower than is justified.

很显然，转移定价策略会影响国际资本支出的分析。

Obviously, transfer pricing strategies have an effect on international capital expenditure analysis. A very low (high) markup policy makes the APV of a subsidiary's capital expenditure appear more (less) attractive. Consequently, in order to obtain a meaningful analysis, arm's-length pricing should be used in the APV analysis to determine after-tax operating income, regardless of the actual transfer price employed. A separate term in the APV analysis can be used to recognize tax-savings from transfer pricing strategies. This was the recommended approach detailed in Chapter 18.

Blocked Funds

For a variety of reasons, a country may find itself short of foreign currency reserves, and thus impose exchange restrictions on its own currency, limiting its conversion into other currencies so as not to further reduce scarce foreign currency reserves. When a country enforces exchange controls, the remittance of profits from a subsidiary firm to its foreign parent is blocked. The blockage may be only temporary, or it may be for a considerable period of time. A lengthy blockage is detrimental to a MNC. Without the ability to repatriate profits from a foreign subsidiary, the MNC might as well not even have the investment as returns are not being paid to the stockholders of the MNC.

Prior to making a capital investment in a foreign subsidiary, the parent firm should investigate the potential of future funds blockage. This is part of the capital expenditure analysis outlined in Chapter 18. The APV framework developed in that chapter only considers the expected operating cash flows that are available for repatriation.

因此，跨国公司应
该非常熟悉转移冻结资
金的方法，以便有利于
股东。

Unexpected funds blockage after an investment has been made, however, is a political risk with which the MNC must contend. Thus, the MNC should be familiar with methods for moving blocked funds so as to benefit its stockholders. Several methods for moving blocked funds have already been discussed in this chapter and others. For example, transfer pricing strategies and unbundling services are methods the MNC might be able to use to move otherwise blocked funds. These methods were covered earlier in this chapter. Moreover, in Chapter 8, leading and lagging of payments were discussed primarily as a means of controlling transaction exposure. However, leading and lagging payments may be used as a strategy for repositioning funds within a MNC. Additional strategies that may be useful for moving blocked funds are *export creation* and *direct negotiation*.

出口创造就是用子
公司被冻结的资金来支
付有利于母公司和其他
子公司的出口。

Export creation involves using the blocked funds of a subsidiary in the country in which they are blocked to pay for exports that can be used to benefit the parent firm or other affiliates. Thus, instead of using repatriated funds to pay for goods or services that will benefit the MNC, blocked funds are used. Examples include: using consulting firms located in the host country where funds are blocked, instead of a firm in the parent country, to provide necessary consulting work that benefits the MNC; transferring personnel from corporate headquarters to the subsidiary offices where they will be paid in the blocked local currency; using the national airlines of the host country when possible for the international travel of all MNC executives, where the reservations and fare payments are made by the subsidiary; and holding business conferences in the host country, instead of elsewhere, where the expenses are paid by the local subsidiary. All of these possibilities not only benefit the MNC, since these goods and services are needed, but they also benefit various industries within the host country.

东道国希望能吸引
有利于本国经济发展、
有利于提高本国劳动力
技能的外国产业。

Host countries desire to attract foreign industries that will most benefit their economic development and the technical skills of its citizens. Thus, foreign investment in the host country in industries that produce export goods, such as automobiles or electronic equipment, or in industries that will attract tourists, such as resort hotels, is desirable. This type of investment provides good employment and training for the country's citizens and is also a source, rather than a use, of foreign exchange. The host country should not expect a MNC to make beneficial investment within its borders if it is not likely to receive an appropriate return. Consequently, MNCs in desirable industries may be able to convince the host country government through direct negotiation that funds blockage is detrimental to all.

SUMMARY

本章讨论了跨国经营企业的现金管理，并重点分析了多边净额结算制度和转移定价策略问题。此外，借助于案例来说明现金集中存管制的优点和转移定价策略的应用。

1. 多边净额结算制度有利于降低关联公司间的外汇交易次数和相应支出。

2. 中央现金库有助于消除资金错置问题，也有利于资金的流动。中央现金管理部门应从全球角度寻求最佳的借款利率和最优的投资收益率。

3. 现金集中存管制和现金库可降低跨国公司在现金余额准备方面的投资，从而节省公司的资金支出。

4. 转移定价策略是实现资金在跨国公司内部重新配置的方法，也是降低税负以及从实施外汇管制的东道国转移冻结资金的可行办法。

5. 分类资金转移、出口创造和直接谈判也是从实施外汇管制的东道国转移冻结资金的可行办法。

This chapter discussed cash management in the multinational firm. Special attention was given to the topics of multilateral netting and transfer pricing policy. Case applications were used to show the benefits of centralized cash management and to examine transfer pricing strategies.

1. A multilateral netting system is beneficial in reducing the number of and the expense associated with interaffiliate foreign exchange transactions.

2. A centralized cash pool assists in reducing the problem of mislocated funds and in funds mobilization. A central cash manager has a global view of the most favorable borrowing rates and most advantageous investment rates.

3. A centralized cash management system with a cash pool can reduce the investment the MNC has in precautionary cash balances, saving the firm money.

4. Transfer pricing strategies are a means to reposition funds within a MNC and a possible technique for reducing tax liabilities and removing blocked funds from a host country that has imposed foreign exchange restrictions.

5. Unbundling fund transfers, export creation, and direct negotiation are other means for removing blocked funds from a host country that is enforcing foreign exchange restrictions.

KEY WORDS

bilateral netting, *470*
cash budget, *468*
cash management, *467*
centralized cash depository, *472*

multilateral netting, *470*
netting center, *470*
precautionary cash balances, *467*

transaction balances, *467*
transfer price, *476*

QUESTIONS

1. Describe the key factors contributing to effective cash management within a firm. Why is the cash management process more difficult in a MNC?

2. Discuss the pros and cons of a MNC having a centralized cash manager handle all investment and borrowing for all affiliates of the MNC versus each affiliate having a local manager who performs the cash management activities of the affiliate.

3. How might a MNC use transfer pricing strategies? How do import duties affect transfer pricing policies?

4. What are the various means the taxing authority of a country might use to determine if a transfer price is *reasonable*?

5. Discuss how a MNC might attempt to repatriate blocked funds from a host country.

PROBLEMS

1. Affiliate A sells 5,000 units to Affiliate B per year. The marginal income tax rate for Affiliate A is 25 percent and the marginal income tax rate for Affiliate B is 40 percent. The transfer price per unit is currently $2,000, but it can be set at any level between $2,000 and $2,400. Derive a formula to determine how much annual after-tax profits can be increased by selecting the optimal transfer price.

2. Affiliate A sells 5,000 units to Affiliate B per year. The marginal income tax rate for Affiliate A is 25 percent and the marginal income tax rate for Affiliate B is 40 percent. Additionally, Affiliate B pays a tax-deductible tariff of 5 percent on imported merchandise. The transfer price per unit is currently $2,000, but it can be set at any level between $2,000 and $2,400. Derive (a) a formula to determine the effective marginal tax rate for Affiliate B, and (b) a formula to determine how much annual after-tax profits can be increased by selecting the optimal transfer price.

The Transfer Pricing Management Benchmarking Association conducts benchmarking studies to identify the best transfer pricing processes that will improve the overall operations of its members. Its website is **www.tpmba.com.** Go to this website to learn about the objectives of the association and the events it sponsors. You may be interested in receiving its free newsletter.

MINI CASE 1

Efficient Funds Flow at Eastern Trading Company

The Eastern Trading Company of Singapore purchases spices in bulk from around the world, packages them into consumer-size quantities, and sells them through sales affiliates in China-Hong Kong SAR, the United Kingdom, and the United States. For a recent month, the following payments matrix of interaffiliate cash flows, stated in Singapore dollars, was forecasted. Show how Eastern Trading can use multilateral netting to minimize the foreign exchange transactions necessary to settle interaffiliate payments. If foreign exchange transactions cost the company .5 percent, what savings result from netting?

Eastern Trading Company Payments Matrix (S$000)

	Disbursements				
Receipts	Singapore	China-Hong Kong SAR	U.K.	U.S.	Total Receipts
Singapore	—	40	75	55	170
China-Hong Kong SAR	8	—	—	22	30
U.K.	15	—	—	17	32
U.S.	11	25	9	—	45
Total disbursements	34	65	84	94	277

MINI CASE 2

Eastern Trading Company's Optimal Transfer Pricing Strategy

The Eastern Trading Company of Singapore ships prepackaged spices to China-Hong Kong SAR, the United Kingdom, and the United States, where they are resold by sales affiliates. Eastern Trading is concerned with what might happen in China-Hong Kong now that control has been turned over to China. Eastern Trading has decided that it should reexamine its transfer pricing policy with its China-Hong Kong affiliate as a means of repositioning funds from China-Hong Kong SAR to Singapore. The following table shows the present transfer pricing scheme, based on a carton of assorted, prepackaged spices, which is the typical shipment to the China-Hong Kong sales affiliate. What do you recommend that Eastern Trading should do?

Eastern Trading Company Current Transfer Pricing Policy with China-Hong Kong SAR Sales Affiliate

	Singapore Parent	China-Hong Kong SAR Affiliate	Consolidated Company
Sales revenue	S$300	S$500	S$500
Cost of goods sold	200	300	200
Gross profit	100	200	300
Operating expenses	50	50	100
Taxable income	50	150	200
Income taxes (20%/17.5%)	10	26	36
Net income	40	124	164

MINI CASE 3

Eastern Trading Company's New MBA

The Eastern Trading Company of Singapore presently follows a decentralized system of cash management where it and its affiliates each maintain their own transaction and precautionary cash balances. Eastern Trading believes that it and its affiliates' cash needs are normally distributed and independent from one another. It is corporate policy to maintain two and one-half standard deviations of cash as precautionary holdings. At this level of safety there is a 99.37 percent chance that each affiliate will have enough cash holdings to cover transactions.

A new MBA hired by the company claims that the investment in precautionary cash balances is needlessly large and can be reduced substantially if the firm converts to a centralized cash management system. Use the projected information for the current month, which is presented below, to determine the amount of cash Eastern Trading needs to hold in precautionary balances under its current decentralized system and the level of precautionary cash it would need to hold under a centralized system. Was the new MBA a good hire?

Affiliate	Expected Transactions	One Standard Deviation
Singapore	S$125,000	S$40,000
China-Hong Kong SAR	60,000	25,000
United Kingdom	95,000	40,000
United States	70,000	35,000

REFERENCES & SUGGESTED READINGS

Bokos, W. J., and Anne P. Clinkard. "Multilateral Netting." *Journal of Cash Management* 3 (1983), pp. 24–34.

Collins, J. Markham, and Alan W. Frankle. "International Cash Management Practices of Large U.S. Firms." *Journal of Cash Management* 5 (1985), pp. 42–48.

Srinivasin, Venkat, and Yong H. Kim. "Payments Netting in International Cash Management: A Network Optimization Approach." *Journal of International Business Studies* 17 (1986), pp. 1–20.

U.S. Internal Revenue Code. Chicago: Commerce Clearing House, 1993.

20 International Trade Finance

IN MODERN TIMES, it is virtually impossible for a country to produce domestically everything its citizens need or demand. Even if it could, it is unlikely that it could produce all items more efficiently than producers in other countries. Without international trade, scarce resources are not put to their best uses.

与国内贸易相比，国际贸易困难更多，风险也更大。

International trade is more difficult and risky, however, than domestic trade. In foreign trade, the exporter may not be familiar with the buyer, and thus not know if the importer is a good credit risk. If merchandise is exported abroad and the buyer does not pay, it may prove difficult, if not impossible, for the exporter to have any legal recourse. Additionally, political instability makes it risky to ship merchandise abroad to certain parts of the world. From the importer's perspective, it is risky to make advance payment for goods that may never be shipped by the exporter.

The present chapter deals with these issues and others. The chapter begins with an example of a simple yet typical foreign trade transaction. The mechanics of the trade are discussed, delineating the institutional arrangements that have been developed over time to facilitate international trade in light of the risks we have identified. The three basic documents needed in a foreign trade transaction—a letter of credit, a time draft, and a bill of lading—are discussed in detail. It is shown how a time draft becomes a banker's acceptance, a negotiable money market instrument.

The second part of the chapter discusses the role of the Export-Import Bank, an independent government agency founded to offer competitive assistance to U.S. exporters through loans, financial guarantees, and credit insurance. The chapter concludes with a discussion of various types of countertrade transactions. Countertrade transactions can collectively be defined as foreign trade transactions in which the seller provides the buyer with goods or services in return for a reciprocal promise from the seller to purchase goods or services from the buyer.

A Typical Foreign Trade Transaction

To understand the mechanics of a typical foreign trade transaction, it is best to use an illustration. Consider a U.S. importer, who is an automobile dealer, and who desires to purchase automobiles from a Japanese exporter, the manufacturer. The two do not know one another and are obviously separated by a great distance. If the Japanese manufacturer could have his way, he would have the U.S. importer pay *cash in advance* for the shipment, since he is unfamiliar with the creditworthiness of the auto dealer.

If the auto dealer could have his way, he ideally would prefer to receive the cars on consignment from the auto manufacturer. In a *consignment* sale, the exporter retains title to the merchandise that is shipped. The importer only pays the exporter once he sells the merchandise. If the importer cannot sell the merchandise, he returns it to the exporter. Obviously, the exporter bears all the risk in a consignment sale. Second best for the auto dealer would be to receive the car shipment on credit and then to make payment, thus not paying in advance for an order that might not ever be received.

怎样才能找到一种令进出口双方都满意的折衷的外贸交易形式呢?

How can the situation be reconciled so that the foreign trade transaction is satisfactory for both the exporter and the importer? Fortunately for the auto dealer and the auto manufacturer, they are not the first two parties who have faced such a dilemma. Over the years, an elaborate process has evolved for handling just this type of foreign commerce transaction. Exhibit 20.1 presents a schematic of the process that is typically followed in foreign trade. Working our way through Exhibit 20.1 in a narrative fashion will allow us to understand the mechanics of a trade and also the three major documents involved.

Exhibit 20.1 begins with (1) the U.S. importer placing an order with the Japanese exporter, asking if he will ship automobiles under a letter of credit. If the auto manufacturer agrees to this, he will inform the U.S. importer of the price and the other terms of sale, including the credit terms. For discussion purposes, we will assume the length of the credit period is 60 days. The U.S. importer will (2) apply to his bank for a letter of credit for the merchandise he desires to purchase, providing his bank with the terms of the sale.

信用证 (L/C) 是进口商开户行开出的一种保证书。在出口商按信用证条款的规定提交信用证上所明确列出的各项有关证件后,进口商开户行将代表进口商向出口商支付货款。

A **letter of credit (L/C)** is a guarantee from the importer's bank that it will act on behalf of the importer and pay the exporter for the merchandise if all relevant documents specified in the L/C are presented according to the terms of the L/C. In essence, the importer's bank is substituting its creditworthiness for that of the unknown U.S. importer.

The L/C is (3) sent via the importer's bank to the exporter's bank. Once the L/C is received, the exporter's bank will (4) notify the exporter. The Japanese exporter will (5) then ship the cars.

远期汇票

提单 (B/L)

银行承兑汇票 (B/A)

After shipping the automobiles, the Japanese exporter will (6) present to his bank a (60-day) time draft, drawn according to the instructions in the L/C, the bill of lading, and any other shipping documents that are required, such as the invoice and a packing list. A **time draft** is a written order instructing the importer or his agent, the importer's bank, to pay the amount specified on its face on a certain date (that is, the end of the credit period in a foreign trade transaction). A **bill of lading (B/L)** is a document issued by the common carrier specifying that it has received the goods for shipment; it can serve as title to the goods. The exporter's bank (7) presents the shipping documents and the time draft to the importer's bank. After taking title to the goods via the bill of lading, the importer's bank accepts the time draft, creating at this point a **banker's acceptance (B/A),** a negotiable money market instrument for which a secondary market exists. The importer's bank charges an acceptance commission, which is deducted at the time of final settlement. The acceptance commission is based on the term-to-maturity of the time draft and the creditworthiness of the importer.

One of several things can happen with the B/A. It can be returned to the Japanese exporter, who will hold it for 60 days and then present it for payment to the importer's

EXHIBIT 20.1 Process of Typical Foreign Trade Transaction

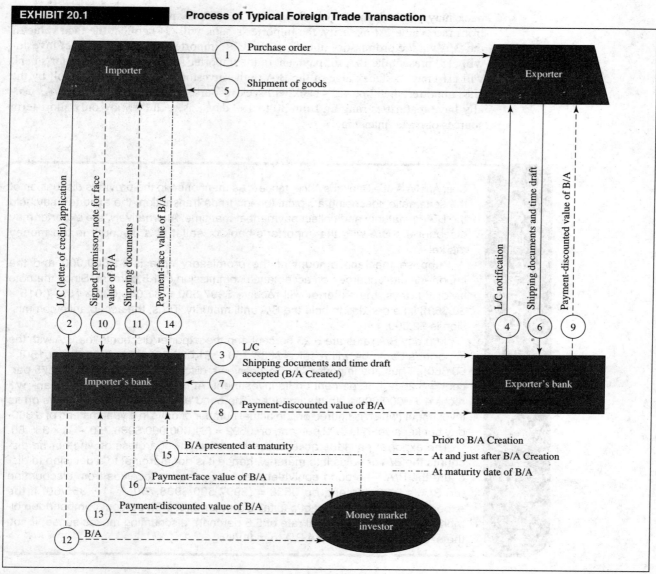

Source: Adapted from Instruments of the Money Market, Federal Reserve Bank of Richmond, 1986. Used by permission.

bank at maturity. Should the exporter suddenly find he needs funds prior to the maturity date, the B/A can be sold at a discount in the money market. Since their risks are similar, banker's acceptances trade at rates similar to rates for negotiable bank certificates of deposit. Alternatively, as in Exhibit 20.1, the Japanese exporter could instruct its bank to have the B/A (8) discounted by the importer's bank and (9) pay that amount to it. Analogously, the exporter's bank may decide to hold the B/A to maturity as an investment, and pay the Japanese exporter the discounted equivalent.

The U.S. importer (10) signs a (60-day) promissory note with his bank for the face value of the banker's acceptance, due on the maturity date of the B/A. In return, the exporter's bank (11) provides the auto dealer with the shipping documents needed to take possession of the automobiles from the common carrier.

If the B/A is not held by the Japanese exporter or the exporter's bank, the importer's bank may hold it for 60 days until maturity when it will collect the face value from the U.S. importer via the promissory note. Alternatively, as in Exhibit 20.1, the importer's bank may (12) sell the B/A in the money market to an investor at a (13) discount from face value. At maturity, the importer's bank will (14) collect the face value of the B/A via the promissory note from the U.S. importer, the money market investor will (15) present the B/A for payment to the importer's bank, and the importer's bank will (16) pay the face value of the B/A to the investor. In the event of default by the U.S. importer, the importer's bank will seek recourse against the importer. B/As usually have maturities ranging from 30 to 180 days; as such they are only short-term sources of trade financing.

EXAMPLE 20.1

Cost Analysis of a Banker's Acceptance   As mentioned in the previous discussion of the schematic describing a typical foreign trade transaction, the exporter may hold the B/A to maturity and collect payment at that time. Alternatively, the exporter may discount the B/A with the importer's bank or sell it at a discount in the money market.

Suppose the face amount of the promissory note is $1,000,000 and the importer's bank charges an acceptance commission of 1.5 percent. Since the note is for 60 days, the exporter will receive $997,500 = $1,000,000 × [1 − (.015 × 60/360)] if he decides to hold the B/A until maturity. Thus, the acceptance commission is $2,500.

If 60-day B/A rates are 5.25 percent and the exporter discounts the B/A with the importer's bank, he will receive $988,750 = $1,000,000 × [1 − ([.0525 + .0150] × 60/360)]. Thus, the importer's bank receives a discount rate of interest of 6.75 percent = 5.25 + 1.50 percent on its investment. At maturity the importer's bank will receive $1,000,000 from the importer. The bond equivalent yield it receives on its investment (which is figured on the actual number of days in a year instead of a 360-day banker's year) is 6.92 percent, or .0692 = ($1,000,000/$988,750 − 1) × 365/60.

The exporter pays the acceptance commission regardless of whether he discounts the B/A or holds it to maturity, hence it is not marginal to a decision to discount the B/A. The bond equivalent rate the exporter receives from discounting the B/A is 5.38 percent, or .0538 = ($997,500/$988,750 − 1) × 365/60. If the exporter's opportunity cost of capital is greater than 5.38 percent compounded bimonthly (an effective annual rate of 5.5 percent), discounting makes sense; if not, the exporter should hold the B/A to maturity.

Forfaiting

www.afia-forfaiting.org

The website of the Association of Forfaiters in the Americas, Inc. It provides information on forfaiting for exporters, importers, and financial institutions.

福费庭是一种典型的为资本货物销售进行中期融资的方法。

Forfaiting is a type of medium-term trade financing used to finance the sale of capital goods. Forfaiting involves the sale of promissory notes signed by the importer in favor of the exporter. The *forfait,* usually a bank, buys the notes at a discount from face value from the exporter. In this way, the exporter receives payment for the export and does not have to carry the financing. The forfait does not have recourse against the exporter in the event of default by the importer. The promissory notes are typically structured to extend out in a series over a period of from three to seven years, with a note in the series maturing every six months. Since forfaiting transactions are typically used to finance capital goods, they usually are for amounts of $500,000 or more. Forfaiting began in Switzerland and Germany, but it has now spread throughout most of Western Europe and into the United States. Forfait transactions are typically denominated in Swiss francs, euros, and U.S. dollars.

The International Finance in Practice box "First Islamic Forfaiting Fund Set Up" discusses how forfaiting meets Islamic finance practices.

First Islamic Forfaiting Fund Set Up

While selling debt at a reduced value, strictly forbidden under the terms of Islamic finance, is inherent in forfaiting as this involves the sale of a discounted letter of credit (LC), Norton Rose and WestLB have recently managed to structure a forfaiting fund aimed at institutional investors requiring Islamically compliant investment opportunities.

The WestLB-Tricon Forfaiting Fund is a Bermuda-registered entity allowing investors to participate in a Shari'ah compliant investment strategy involving commodity and trade finance, including forfaiting asset receivables. Islamic finance is a relatively new field that has only existed for around two decades and financing solutions to accommodate it continue to be rolled out.

Mohammed Paracha, an associate and London-based member of Norton Rose's Islamic finance group, tells Trade Finance: "Financial institutions have for some time recognized that the requirements of Middle Eastern investors are not being met. With so much wealth in the region, people are looking at innovative ways to tap into Islamic money and it was decided that there was a need to get Islamic money into a product that could be combined with forfaiting assets and

we have been able to develop an investment fund which has been structured to adhere to Shari'ah principles whilst at the same time making use of forfaiting assets."

It is understood that the fund is now up and running, and that its investment strategy includes investing in LCs (or similar trade paper) across all sectors, though screening is required to ensure that the products underlying the LCs do not run counter to Shari'ah principles. According to Paracha, the structure is a complex one. He says: "It was quite a difficult exercise, and there had to be a sign-off by Islamic scholars to verify that Shari'ah strictures had been met with. There was also the issue of working across UK and Bermudan jurisdictions."

Paracha continues: "We also had to be careful in ensuring that the pool of non-Islamic forfaiting assets was not used to directly satisfy the Islamically compliant obligations under the commodity and trade financing arrangements."

Source: Trade Finance, November 2003, p. 1.

Government Assistance in Exporting

www.export.gov

A U.S. government website with information on export counseling, programs and services, and financing and insurance.

鉴于出口创造的利益，大部分发达国家的政府通常对国内出口商提供信贷补助形式的竞争性援助，这种补助可扩展至进口商。

The Export-Import Bank and Affiliated Organizations

美国进出口银行

www.exim.gov

Website of the Export-Import Bank of the United States (Eximbank). The site provides details of the Eximbank and its services.

美国进出口银行最重要的目标有：营运资金保证、对国外借款人直接贷款、贷款担保和信用保险。

Success in international trade is fundamentally important for a country. Success in exporting implies that there is demand for a country's products, that its labor force is benefiting from employment, and that some resources are used for technological advancement. To be successful in international trade requires a country's export-oriented firms to be good marketers, that is, to be competitive in terms of product offerings, promotion, price, delivery capability, and service provided to importers. Equally important, however, is for firms to be competitive in terms of extending credit to importers.

Because of the benefits that accrue from exporting, the governments of most developed countries offer competitive assistance to domestic exporters in the form of subsidized credit that can be extended to importers. Also, credit insurance programs that guarantee financing extended by private financial institutions are common. In this section, we discuss the main features of programs available to U.S. exporters.

In 1934, the **Export-Import Bank (Eximbank) of the United States** was founded, and subsequently chartered in 1945, as an independent government agency to facilitate and finance U.S. export trade. Eximbank's purpose is to provide financing in situations where private financial institutions are unable or unwilling to because: (1) the loan maturity is too long; (2) the amount of the loan is too large; (3) the loan risk is too great; or (4) the importing firm has difficulty obtaining hard currency for payment.

To meet its objectives, Eximbank provides service through several types of programs. Some of the most important of these are working capital guarantees, direct loans to foreign borrowers, loan guarantees, and credit insurance.[1]

---

[1]Much of the discussion in this section is drawn from the Export-Import Bank website, www.exim.gov/.

Through its *Working Capital Guarantee Program,* Eximbank facilitates the expansion of U.S. exports by encouraging commercial lenders to make working capital loans to U.S. exporters. The Eximbank loan guarantee covers 90 percent of the loan principal and accrued interest, and it is backed by the full faith and credit of the U.S. government.

Through its *Medium and Long-Term Loan Program,* Eximbank will facilitate direct credit to foreign buyers of U.S. exports. Disbursements go to the U.S. exporter, and the export products go to the foreign importer. The *Long-Term Program* covers repayment terms in excess of seven years and a loan amount greater than $10 million. The *Medium-Term Program* covers repayment terms of seven years or less and loan amounts of $10 million or less. Both programs cover financing up to 85 percent of the export contract value. The *Private Export Funding Corporation (PEFCO),* established in 1970 by a group of commercial banks and industrial corporations, frequently cooperates in loans with the Eximbank under these programs by providing liquidity via the purchase of notes issued by Eximbank to finance the loans.

Through its *Medium and Long-Term Guarantee Program,* Eximbank guarantees the loans made by private financial institutions to foreign importers. Interest charged on these loans is usually at a floating rate. The guarantees, which commit the full faith and credit of the U.S. government, cover financing up to 85 percent of the export contract value. The guarantees cover 100 percent of the loan principal and accrued interest against loss due to commercial and political risks. Guarantees covering only political risks are available.

Through its *Export Credit Insurance Program,* Eximbank helps U.S. exporters develop and expand their overseas sales by protecting them against loss should a foreign buyer or other foreign debtor default for political or commercial reasons. Insurance policies may cover both comprehensive commercial and political credit risks, or only specific political risks.

In the United Kingdom, the *Exports Credits Guarantee Department (ECGD)* performs functions similar to those of the Eximbank and FCIA. Formed in 1919, the ECGD provides assistance to exporters through direct insurance coverage against non-payment by the importer due to commercial and political risks and by guaranteeing bank loans to foreign borrowers. The exporter, who is considered to be the true beneficiary, pays to ECGD the guaranteed bank loan insurance premium.

www.ecgd.gov.uk

The official website of the Exports Credits Guarantee Department.

www.eximbankindia.com

Website of the Export-Import Bank of India. The EXIM India was set up in 1982 to finance, facilitate, and promote India's international trade. It is the counterpart of the Eximbank of the United States. There are several websites providing information about various countries' export-import banks.

Countertrade

www.countertrade.org/

Official site of the Global Offset and Countertrade Association (GOCA). The GOCA provides a forum for companies involved in countertrade and a resource for companies exploring the possibilities held by countertrade.

Countertrade is an umbrella term used to describe many different types of transactions, each "in which the seller provides a buyer with goods or services and promises in return to purchase goods or services from the buyer."[2] Countertrades may or may not involve the use of money. If money is not exchanged, the trade is a type of barter. Regardless, countertrade usually results in a two-way flow of commodities.

Countertrade arrangements can be traced back to prehistoric times and they have been used throughout history whenever money was scarce. While it is difficult to determine the exact volume of countertrade, the practice is nevertheless widespread. According to Hammond (1990), some estimates put countertrade at only 5 percent of total world trade, whereas other estimates are as high as 40 percent. Moreover, countertrade transactions are not accounted for in official trade statistics. In the new millennium, the IMF, the World Bank, and the U.S. Department of Commerce estimate that as much as half of all international trade transactions will be conducted as countertrade.[3] Most recently, a surge of countertrade activity occurred in the 1980s, when the Third World debt crisis left the debtor countries without sufficient foreign exchange reserves or bank lines of credit to carry on normal commerce.[4]

---

[2]Definition from Hennart (1989).
[3]See Anyane-Ntow and Harvey (1995, p. 47) for this estimate.
[4]See Chapter 11 for a discussion of the extent and severity of the Third World debt crisis.

Forms of Countertrade

Hennart (1989) identifies six forms of countertrade: barter, clearing arrangement, switch trading, buy-back, counterpurchase, and offset. The first three do not involve the use of money, whereas the latter three do.

Barter is the direct exchange of goods between two parties. While money does not exchange hands in a barter transaction, it is common to value the goods each party exchanges in an agreed-upon currency. It is often necessary to place a monetary value on the goods for accounting, taxation, and insurance purposes.

Hammond (1990) describes barter as "a rather primitive way to do business. It fosters bilateral trade which, in turn, under mercantilist economies and imperialistic policies, fostered a tight system of colonial dependency with protected markets and captive sources of raw materials." He notes that barter flourished until after World War II when the Bretton Woods fixed exchange rate system was established that provided for currency convertibility and fostered free trade.

Today, barter transactions are typically one-time exchanges of merchandise that take place when circumstances warrant. Schaffer (1989) describes a modern example of barter that took place between General Electric (GE) and Rumania. GE had agreed to sell Rumania a turbine generator for cash. The Rumanian loan financing subsequently fell through, and in order to complete the deal, GE agreed to accept Rumanian products, which it in turn sold for cash through its trading company.

A *clearing arrangement* (also called a bilateral clearing agreement) is a form of barter in which the counterparties (governments) contract to purchase a certain amount of goods and services from one another. Both parties set up accounts with each other that are debited whenever one country imports from the other. At the end of an agreed-upon period of time, any account imbalances are settled for hard currency, or by the transfer of goods. The clearing arrangement introduces the concept of credit to barter transactions, and means bilateral trade can take place that does not have to be immediately settled. Account balances are periodically determined and any trade imbalances are settled in an agreed-upon currency. Anyane-Ntow and Harvey (1995) note that bilateral clearing agreements have usually taken place between Third World and Eastern European countries. They cite the 1994 agreement between China and Saudi Arabia with a $1 billion target as an example.

A *switch trade* is the purchase by a third party of one country's clearing agreement imbalance for hard currency, which is in turn resold. The second buyer uses the account balance to purchase goods and services from the original clearing agreement counterparty who had the account imbalance. Anyane-Ntow and Harvey (1995) give the example of a switch trade when the United States exported fertilizers to Pakistan through a Rumanian-Pakistani clearing agreement.

A *buy-back transaction* involves a technology transfer via the sale of a manufacturing plant. As part of the transaction, the seller agrees to purchase a certain portion of the plant output once it is constructed. As Hennart (1989) notes, money enters into the agreement in two ways. First, the plant buyer borrows hard currency in the capital market to pay the seller for the plant. Second, the plant seller agrees to purchase enough of the plant output over a period of time to enable the buyer to pay back the borrowed funds. A buy-back transaction can be viewed as a form of direct investment in the purchasing country. Examples of buy-back transactions include Japan's agreements with China's Taiwan, Singapore, and Korea to exchange computer chip production equipment for a certain percentage of the output.[5]

A *counterpurchase* is similar to a buy-back transaction, but with some notable differences. The two counterparties are usually an Eastern importer and a Western exporter of technology. The major difference between a buy-back and a counterpurchase transaction is that in the latter, the merchandise the Western seller agrees

Hennart (1989)定义了六种反购贸易形式：易货贸易、结算协定、转手贸易、回购贸易、互购和补偿贸易。

结算协定（又称双边结算协定）是一种易货贸易形式，贸易双方签订合约向对方购买一定量的商品或劳务。

---

[5]See Anyane-Ntow and Harvey (1995, p. 48).

Armed Forces Tops In Countertrade List

The Armed Forces of the Philippines (AFP) leads all government agencies in countertrade transactions, accounting for a total of $143.4 million worth from 1989 to August 2004 based on figures provided by the Philippine International Trading Corporation (PITC). Countertrade refers to reciprocal and compensatory agreements involving the purchase of goods or services by the seller from he buyer of this product or arrangements where the seller assists the buyer in reducing the net cost of the purchase through some form of compensatory financing.

The AFP yesterday announced that the Philippines recently benefited from two countertrade transactions by the military. In February last year, the Philippine Army procured $2.1 million worth of Squad Automatic Weapons from FN Herstal of Belgium, with a countertrade commitment of $1.8 million or 85% of the contract price.

The program has paved the way for the development of Philippine semi-processed rubber exports worldwide through a financing scheme packaged by Raifeissen Centrobank of Austria, the designated trading partner of FN Herstal under the Countertrade Program of the Philippines.

The assistance has opened doors to new exports markets including Czech Republic, Australia, Italy, Germany, and New Zealand, officials added. The AFP also purchased $7.6 million worth of HF/SSB Transceivers and Manpack Communications equipment from Harris Corp. in December 2003 and February 2004. As a direct beneficiary of the coun-tertrade program, the military received some $6.1 million worth of offset activities.

Under the arrangement Harris Corporation is obligated to an 80% offset of some $6.2 million and a 20% counterpurchase or $1.5 million. Some of he offset benefits included software upgrades for 324 Manpack Communication units, donation of additional Manpack batteries, donation of one automated test set and spare modules, officials said.

The government countertrade program was established under Executive Order 120, which provides that all government procurements equivalent of $1 million and above have to have a countertrade component of at least 50% of the value of the supply contract. In response, the Department of National Defense issued Dept. Circular 4 dated July 20 2001 requiring countertrade to be part of the AFP's acquisition program for all projects costing more than $1 million.

The AFP is closely followed by the National Food Authority with a total of $136.6 million worth of countertrade transactions. More than $300 million worth of Philippine products have been exported under the Countertrade Program of the Government through its foreign procurement.

Source: Karl Lester M. Yap, BusinessWorld, August 17, 2004, p. 1.

to purchase is unrelated and has not been produced on the exported equipment. The seller agrees to purchase goods from a list drawn up by the importer at prices set by the importer. Goods on the list are frequently items for which the buyer does not have a ready market. As an example of a counterpurchase, Anyane-Ntow and Harvey (1995) cite the agreement to exchange Italian industrial equipment for Indonesian rubber.

An *offset transaction* can be viewed as a counterpurchase trade agreement involving the aerospace/defense industry. Offset transactions are reciprocal trade agreements between an industrialized country and a country that has defense and/or aerospace industries. Hammond (1990) cites the example of the sale of F-16 jet fighters manufactured by General Dynamics to Turkey and Greece in exchange for olives, hydroelectric power projects, the promotion of tourism, and aircraft coproduction.

The International Finance in Practice box "Armed Forces Tops In Countertrade List" discusses how the Armed Forces of the Philippines uses offset transactions and counterpurchases to obtain military equipment.

Some Generalizations about Countertrade

Hammond (1990)发现，关于反购贸易，人们既有支持的，也有反对的。

Countertrade transactions became very prominent in international trade in the 1980s and 1990s. Arguments both for and against countertrade transactions can be made. Hammond (1990) notes that there are both negative and positive incentives for a country to be in favor of countertrade. Negative incentives are those that are forced upon a country or corporation whether or not it desires to engage in countertrade. They include the conservation of cash and hard currency, the improvement of trade imbalances, and the maintenance of export prices. Positive reasons from both the country and corporate perspectives include enhanced economic development, increased employment, technology transfer, market expansion, increased profitability, less costly sourcing of supply, reduction of surplus goods from inventory, and the development of marketing expertise.

Those against countertrade transactions claim that such transactions tamper with the fundamental operation of free markets, and, therefore, resources are used inefficiently. Opponents claim that transaction costs are increased, that multilateral trade is restricted through fostering bilateral trade agreements, and that, in general, transactions that do not make use of money represent a step backwards in economic development.

Hennart (1989) empirically studied all 1,277 countertrade contracts between June 1983 and December 31, 1986, that were reported in *Countertrade Outlook*. Of these transactions, 694 were clearing arrangements, 171 were classified as barters, 298 as counterpurchases, 71 as buy-backs, and 43 as offsets. The countries involved were classified into the World Bank categories of: Developed, Organization of Petroleum Exporting Countries (OPEC) Members, Centrally Planned Economies (CPE), Middle-Income, and Low-Income.

Hennart发现每一国家群体都有参与特定类型反购贸易的倾向。

Hennart found that each country grouping had a propensity to engage in certain types of countertrade transactions. OPEC, middle-income, and low-income countries used more counterpurchases; CPEs more buy-backs; and developed and middle-income countries engaged in more offsets. Barter was most common between two middle-income countries, between developed and middle-income countries, and between middle-income countries and CPEs.

Hennart claims the high frequency of buy-backs among CPEs is consistent with their use as a substitute for foreign direct investment. The reasons that CPEs and low-income countries do not actively engage in offset transactions are twofold: CPEs are not allowed to purchase Western weapons, and low-income developing countries cannot afford sophisticated weapons systems typically sold via offset transactions. Barter between two middle-income countries (the most frequent) is consistent with the two countries desiring to avoid the repayment of external debt. The absence of barter between OPEC countries and between developed countries is consistent with the use of barter to bypass cartels and commodity arrangements. The analysis of Marin and Schnitzer (1995) is consistent with Hennart's conclusions.

无论反购贸易对全球经济是好是坏，随着世界贸易的增加，反购贸易也必将增加。

Whether countertrade transactions are good or bad for the global economy, it appears certain that they will increase in the near future as world trade increases.

SUMMARY

进出口贸易和贸易融资是本章所讨论的主要内容。

1. 与国内贸易相比，国际贸易往往更为困难，因为国际贸易涉及到国内贸易中无需考虑的商业风险和政治风险因素。为使本国居民能够得到他们所需要的商品和劳务，具有强大的国际贸易竞争力对一国而言是非常重要的。

2. 外贸交易一般需要三种基本单证：信用证、远期汇票和提单。远期汇票可以成为可流通的货币市场工具，即所谓的银行承兑汇票。

3. 福费庭是进行中期贸易融资的一种形式，银行以折价形式从进口商那里购买一系列以出口商为受益人的本票。

4. 进出口银行通过对国外进口商提供直接贷款、进行贷款担保和

Export and import transactions and trade financing are the main topics discussed in this chapter.

1. Conducting international trade transactions is difficult in comparison to domestic trades. Commercial and political risks enter into the equation, which are not factors in domestic trade. Yet it is important for a country to be competitively strong in international trade in order for its citizens to have the goods and services they need and demand.

2. A typical foreign trade transaction requires three basic documents: letter of credit, time draft, and bill of lading. A time draft can become a negotiable money market instrument called a banker's acceptance.

3. Forfaiting, in which a bank purchases at a discount from an importer a series of promissory notes in favor of an exporter, is a medium-term form of trade financing.

4. The Export-Import Bank provides competitive assistance to U.S. exporters through direct loans to foreign importers, loan guarantees, and credit insurance to U.S. exporters.

对美国出口商提供信用保险来帮助美国出口商增强竞争力。

　5. 反购贸易作为国际贸易的形式之一已变得越来越重要。反购贸易有很多种形式，但仅有一小部分涉及到货币的使用。在反购贸易中，卖方向买方提供商品和劳务，同时向买方承诺购买商品和劳务。

5. Countertrade transactions are gaining renewed prominence as a means of conducting international trade transactions. There are several types of countertrade transactions, only some of which involve the use of money. In each type, the seller provides the buyer with goods or services in return for a reciprocal promise from the seller to purchase goods or services from the buyer.

KEY WORDS

banker's acceptance (B/A), 488	Export-Import Bank (Eximbank) of the United States, 491	letter of credit (L/C), 488
bill of lading (B/L), 488		time draft, 488
countertrade, 492	forfaiting, 490	

QUESTIONS

1. Discuss some of the reasons why international trade is more difficult and risky from the exporter's perspective than is domestic trade.

2. What three basic documents are necessary to conduct a typical foreign commerce trade? Briefly discuss the purpose of each.

3. How does a time draft become a banker's acceptance?

4. Discuss the various ways the exporter can receive payment in a foreign trade transaction after the importer's bank accepts the exporter's time draft and it becomes a banker's acceptance.

5. What is a forfaiting transaction?

6. What is the purpose of the Export-Import Bank?

7. Do you think that a country's government should assist private business in the conduct of international trade through direct loans, loan guarantees, and/or credit insurance?

8. Briefly discuss the various types of countertrade.

9. Discuss some of the pros and cons of countertrade from the country's perspective and the firm's perspective.

10. What is the difference between a buy-back transaction and a counterpurchase?

PROBLEMS

1. Assume the time from acceptance to maturity on a $2,000,000 banker's acceptance is 90 days. Further assume that the importing bank's acceptance commission is 1.25 percent and that the market rate for 90-day B/As is 7 percent. Determine the amount the exporter will receive if he holds the B/A until maturity and also the amount the exporter will receive if he discounts the B/A with the importer's bank.

2. The time from acceptance to maturity on a $1,000,000 banker's acceptance is 120 days. The importer's bank's acceptance commission is 1.75 percent and the market rate for 120-day B/As is 5.75 percent. What amount will the exporter receive if he holds the B/A until maturity? If he discounts the B/A with the importer's bank? Also determine the bond equivalent yield the importer's bank will earn from discounting the B/A with the exporter. If the exporter's opportunity cost of capital is 11 percent, should he discount the B/A or hold it to maturity?

INTERNET EXERCISES

The chapter indicated that banker's acceptances were negotiable money market instruments. You might be interested in including B/As in your portfolio. Fiscal Agents Financial Services Group is an investment advisory service specializing in helping investors structure portfolios to meet their needs. Search the **www.fiscalagents.com** website to learn what Fiscal Agents has to say about B/As as an investment.

MINI CASE

American Machine Tools, Inc.

American Machine Tools is a midwestern manufacturer of tool-and-die-making equipment. The company has had an inquiry from a representative of the Estonian government about the terms of sale for a $5,000,000 order of machinery. The sales manager spoke with the Estonian representative, but he is doubtful that the Estonian government will be able to obtain enough hard currency to make the purchase. While the U.S. economy has been growing, American Machine Tools has not had a very good year. An additional $5,000,000 in sales would definitely help. If something cannot be arranged, the firm will likely be forced to lay off some of its skilled workforce.

Is there a way that you can think of that American Machine Tools might be able to make the machinery sale to Estonia?

REFERENCES & SUGGESTED READINGS

Anyane-Ntow, Kwabena, and Santhi C. Harvey. "A Countertrade Primer." *Management Accounting* (April 1995), pp. 47–50.

Hammond, Grant T. *Countertrade, Offsets and Barter in International Political Economy.* New York: St. Martin's Press, 1990.

Hennart, Jean-Francois. "Some Empirical Dimensions of Countertrade." *Journal of International Business Studies* (Second Quarter, 1989), pp. 243–70.

Marin, Dalia, and Monika Schnitzer. "Tying Trade Flows: A Theory of Countertrade with Evidence." *The American Economic Review* 85 (1995), pp. 1047–64.

Neumeir, Shelley. "Why Countertrade Is Getting Hot," *Fortune,* June 29, 1992, p. 25.

Schaffer, Matt. *Winning the Countertrade War.* New York: John Wiley and Sons, 1989.

21 International Tax Environment

本章介绍的国际税收环境对跨国公司的税收计划制定和国际金融资产投资都很重要。

THE PURPOSE OF THIS CHAPTER is to provide a brief introduction to the international tax environment that will be useful to multinational firms in their tax planning and also informative to investors in international financial assets. Tax regulation is a complex topic at the domestic level. It is obviously a much more complex topic at the international level. Hence, this chapter is designed to serve only as an introduction.

The chapter begins with a discussion of the two main objectives of taxation: tax neutrality and tax equity. After this theoretical foundation has been established, the main types of taxation are discussed. Next follows discussions of how taxes are typically levied throughout the world, the purpose of foreign tax credits, and tax treaties between nations. The chapter concludes by examining various types of organizational structures that exist for reducing tax liabilities. Since it is not possible to thoroughly address taxation from the viewpoint of all national taxpayers, by necessity the perspective is from the U.S. taxpayer's viewpoint when the discussion needs to be country specific.

Some taxation issues have been introduced earlier in other chapters because a thorough presentation of the topic under discussion required it. For example, Chapter 18 on international capital budgeting required some elementary knowledge of the concepts of worldwide taxation of active foreign-source income and foreign tax credits applied against a MNC's domestic tax liability. This topic will be revisited in this chapter to provide a more detailed and structured understanding of these issues. Additionally, Chapter 19 on multinational cash management investigated the viability of transfer pricing strategies for reducing a MNC's tax liability. Because this topic was covered sufficiently in Chapter 19, it is given only minor treatment in this chapter.

The Objectives of Taxation

要了解国际税收环境，有必要了解征税的两个基本目标：税收中性和税负平等。

Two basic objectives of taxation have to be discussed to help frame our thinking about the international tax environment: tax neutrality and tax equity.

Tax Neutrality

Tax neutrality has its foundations in the principles of economic efficiency and equity. Tax neutrality is determined by three criteria. **Capital-export neutrality** is the criterion that an ideal tax should be effective in raising revenue for the government and not have any negative effects on the economic decision-making process of the taxpayer. That is, a good tax is one that is efficient in raising tax revenue for the government and does not prevent economic resources from being allocated to their most appropriate use no matter where in the world the highest rate of return can be earned. Obviously, capital-export neutrality is based on worldwide economic efficiency.

A second neutrality criterion is **national neutrality.** That is, taxable income is taxed in the same manner by the taxpayer's national tax authority regardless of where in the world it is earned. In theory, national tax neutrality is a commendable objective, as it is based on the principle of equality. In practice, it is a difficult concept to apply. In the United States, for example, foreign-source income is taxed at the same rate as U.S.-earned income and a foreign tax credit is given against taxes paid to a foreign government. However, the foreign tax credit is limited to the amount of tax that would be due on that income if it were earned in the United States. Thus, if the tax rate paid on foreign-source income is greater than the U.S. tax rate, part of the credit may go unused. Obviously, if the U.S. tax authority did not limit the foreign tax credit to the equivalent amount of U.S. tax, U.S. taxpayers would end up subsidizing part of the tax liabilities of U.S. MNCs' foreign earned income.

The third neutrality criterion is **capital-import neutrality.** To illustrate, this criterion implies that the tax burden a host country imposes on the foreign subsidiary of a MNC should be the same regardless of the country in which the MNC is incorporated and the same as that placed on domestic firms. Implementing capital-import neutrality means that if the U.S. tax rate were greater than the tax rate of a foreign country in which a U.S. MNC earned foreign income, additional tax on that income above the amount paid to the foreign tax authority would *not* be due in the United States. The concept of capital-import neutrality, like national neutrality, is based on the principle of equality, and its implementation provides a level competitive playing field for all participants in a single marketplace, at least with respect to taxation. Nevertheless, implementing capital-import neutrality means that a sovereign government follows the taxation policies of foreign tax authorities on the foreign-source income of its resident MNCs and that domestic taxpayers end up paying a larger portion of the total tax burden. Obviously, the three criteria of tax neutrality are not always consistent with one another.

Tax Equity

The underlying principle of **tax equity** is that all similarly situated taxpayers should participate in the cost of operating the government according to the same rules. Operationally, this means that regardless of the country in which an affiliate of a MNC earns taxable income, the same tax rate and tax due date apply. A dollar earned by a foreign affiliate is taxed under the same rules as a dollar earned by a domestic affiliate of the MNC. The principle of tax equity is difficult to apply; as we will see in a later section, the organizational form of a MNC can affect the timing of a tax liability.

Types of Taxation

This section discusses the three basic types of taxation that national governments throughout the world use in generating revenue: income tax, withholding tax, and value-added tax.

Income Tax

Many countries in the world obtain a significant portion of their tax revenue from imposing an **income tax** on personal and corporate income. An income tax is a **direct tax,** that is, one that is paid directly by the taxpayer on whom it is levied. The tax is levied on **active income,** that is, income that results from production by the firm or individual or from services that have been provided.

One of the best guides detailing corporate income tax regulations in most countries is the PriceWaterhouseCoopers annual *Corporate Taxes: Worldwide Summaries*. Exhibit 21.1 is derived from the PriceWaterhouseCoopers summaries. It lists the normal,

EXHIBIT 21.1 Corporate Percentage Income Tax Rates from Certain Countries[a]

Country	Tax Rate	Region or Country	Tax Rate	Region or Country	Tax Rate	Region or Country	Tax Rate
Antigua & Barbuda	35	Croatia	20	Kazakhstan	30	Russian Federation	24
Argentina	35	Cyprus	15	Kenya	30	St. Lucia	33
Australia	30	Czech Republic	28	Korea	29.7	Saudi Arabia	30
Austria	34	Denmark	30	Latvia	15	Singapore	20
Azerbaijan	24	Dominican Republic	25	Liechtenstein	20	Slovak Republic	25
Bahamas	0	Ecuador	25	Lithuania	15	Slovenia	25
Bahrain	0	Estonia	26	Luxembourg	22.88	Solomon Islands	30
Barbados	36	Faroe Islands	20	China-Hong Kong SAR	15.75	South Africa	30
Belgium	33.99	Fiji	31	Malaysia	28	Spain	35
Bermuda	0	Finland	29	Malta	35	Sri Lanka	39.25
Bolivia	25	France	35.46	Mauritius	25	Swaziland	30
Botswana	25	Germany	26.38	Mexico	33	Sweden	28
Brazil	33.76	Ghana	32.5	Mozambique	32	Switzerland	30
British Virgin Islands[b]	15/0	Greece	35	Namibia	35	Tahiti	40
Brunei Darussalam	30	Guatemala	31	Netherlands	34.5	China's Taiwan	25
Bulgaria	19.5	Guyana	35	Netherlands Antilles	34.5	Tanzania	30
Cambodia	20	Honduras	30	New Caledonia	30	Thailand	30
Canada	33.1	China-Hong Kong SAR	17.5	New Zealand	33	Trinidad & Tobago	30
Cayman Islands	0	Hungary	16	Norway	28	Turkey	33
Channel Islands, Guernsey	20	India	35.875	Oman	30	Uganda	30
Channel Islands, Jersey	20	Indonesia	30	Pakistan	41	Ukraine	25
Chile	17	Iran	25	Panama	30	United Kingdom	30
China	33	Ireland	12.5	Paraguay	30	United States	35
Colombia	36.7	Isle of Man	18	Peru	30	Uruguay	35
Congo	40	Israel	36	Philippines	32	Uzbekistan	18
Costa Rica	30	Italy	33	Poland	19	Venezuela	34
		Ivory Coast	35	Portugal	33	Vietnam	28
		Jamaica	33.33	Puerto Rico	39	Zambia	35
		Japan	46.2	Romania	27.5	Zimbabwe	30.9

[a]The table lists normal, standard, or representative upper-end marginal tax rates for nonfinancial corporations.

[b]In the British Virgin Islands, a nonresident company incorporated as an international business company is tax exempt.

Source: Derived from PriceWaterhouseCoopers, Corporate Taxes: Worldwide Summaries, 2004.

standard, or representative upper-end marginal income tax rates for domestic nonfinancial corporations for 113 countries. As the exhibit shows, national tax rates vary from a low of zero percent in such tax haven countries as Bahrain, Bermuda, the British Virgin Islands, and the Cayman Islands to well over 40 percent in some countries. The current U.S. marginal tax rate of 35 percent is positioned toward the upper end of the rates assessed by the majority of countries.

Withholding Tax

预提税是间接税，即一项由并未直接产生税源收入的纳税人所承担的税。

非主营收入 (Passive income)

间接税 (indirect tax)

www.taxsites.com/ international.html

www.taxup.com

These websites provide tax and accounting information by country.

税收协定 (tax treaties)

增值税 (VAT) 是一项对商品（或劳务）在不同生产环节转移时的价值增加部分课征的间接税。

A **withholding tax** is a tax levied on passive income earned by an individual or corporation of one country within the tax jurisdiction of another country. **Passive income** includes dividends and interest income, and income from royalties, patents, or copyrights paid to the taxpayer. A withholding tax is an **indirect tax,** that is, a tax that is borne by a taxpayer who did not directly generate the income that serves as the source of the passive income. The tax is withheld from payments the corporation makes to the taxpayer and turned over to the local tax authority. The withholding tax assures the local tax authority that it will receive the tax due on the passive income earned within its tax jurisdiction.

Many countries have **tax treaties** with one another specifying the withholding tax rate applied to various types of passive income. Exhibit 21.2 lists the *basic* withholding tax rates the U.S. imposes on other countries through its tax treaties with them. For specific types of passive income, the tax rates may be different from those presented in the exhibit.[1] Withholding tax rates imposed through tax treaties are bilateral; that is, through negotiation two countries agree as to what tax rates apply to various categories of passive income.

Note from Exhibit 21.2 that withholding tax rates vary by category of passive income from zero to 30 percent. It is also noteworthy that withholding tax rates vary significantly among countries within an income category. For example, the United States withholds 0 percent on interest income from taxpayers residing in most Western European countries, but 30 percent from taxpayers residing in Pakistan. The exhibit also shows that the United States withholds 30 percent of passive income from taxpayers that reside in countries with which it does not have withholding tax treaties. Exhibit 21.2 also indicates that according to the withholding tax treaty with a country, the *general* tax rate on dividends paid to foreign payees from portfolio investment in a U.S. firm is frequently higher than the *direct* dividend rate applied to investors with a substantial ownership share.

Value-Added Tax

www.eurunion.org/ legislat/VATweb.htm

This website discusses practical aspects of value-added taxation in the European Union.

A **value-added tax (VAT)** is an indirect national tax levied on the value added in the production of a good (or service) as it moves through the various stages of production. There are several ways to implement a VAT. The "subtraction method" is frequently followed in practice.

EXAMPLE 21.1

Value-Added Tax Calculation As an example of the subtraction method of calculating VAT, consider a VAT of 15 percent charged on a consumption good that goes through three stages of production. Suppose that Stage 1 is the sale of raw materials to the manufacturer at a cost of €100 per unit of production. Stage 2 results in a finished good shipped to retailers at a price of €300. Stage 3 is the retail sale to the final consumer at a price of €380. €100 of value has been added in Stage 1, resulting in a VAT of €15. In Stage 2 the VAT is 15 percent of €300, or €45, with a credit of €15 given against the value added in Stage 1. In Stage 3, an additional VAT of €12 is due on the €80 of value added by the retailer. Since the final consumer pays a price of €380, he effectively pays the total VAT of €57 (= €15 + €30 + €12), which is 15 percent of €380. Obviously, a VAT is the equivalent of imposing a national sales tax. Exhibit 21.3 summarizes the VAT calculation.

---

[1]See the 2004 PriceWaterhouseCoopers *Corporate Taxes: Worldwide Summaries* for exceptions to the basic withholding tax rates.

EXHIBIT 21.2

U.S. Tax Treaty Percentage Withholding Tax Rates with Selected Countries[a]

Country	Interest Paid by U.S. Obligors—General	Dividends[b]		Royalties[c]
		Paid by U.S. Corporations—General	Qualifying for Direct Dividend Rate	
Nontreaty countries	30	30	30	30
Australia	10	15	5	0
Austria	0	15	5	0
Barbados	5	15	5	5
Belgium	15	15	5	0
Canada	10	15	5	0
China, People's Republic of	10	10	10	10
Commonwealth of Independent States	0	30	30	0
Cyprus	10	15	5	0
Czech Republic	0	15	5	10
Denmark	0	15	5	0
Egypt	15	15	5	0
Estonia	10	15	5	5
Finland	0	15	5	5
France	0	15	5	5
Germany	0	15	5	0
Greece	0	30	30	0
Hungary	0	15	5	0
Iceland	0	15	5	0
India	15	25	15	10
Indonesia	10	15	10	10
Ireland, Republic of	0	15	5	0
Israel	17.5	25	12.5	15
Italy	15	15	5	10
Jamaica	12.5	15	10	10
Japan	10	10	5	0
Kazakhstan	10	15	5	10
Korea, Republic of	12	15	10	15
Latvia	10	15	5	5
Lithuania	10	15	5	5
Luxembourg	0	15	5	0
Mexico	15	10	5	10
Morocco	15	15	10	10
Netherlands	0	15	5	0
New Zealand	10	15	15	10
Norway	0	15	15	0
Pakistan	30	30	15	0
Philippines	15	25	20	15
Poland	0	15	5	10
Portugal	10	15	5	10
Romania	10	10	10	15
Russia	0	10	5	0
Slovak Republic	0	15	5	10
Slovenia	5	15	5	5
South Africa	0	15	5	0
Spain	10	15	10	8
Sweden	0	15	5	0
Switzerland	0	15	5	0
Thailand	15	15	10	8
Trinidad and Tobago	30	30	30	15
Tunisia	15	20	14	10
Turkey	15	20	15	5
Ukraine	0	15	5	10
United Kingdom	0	15	5	0
Venezuela	10	15	5	5

[a]The exhibit shows the basic treaty withholding tax rates; see the original source for exceptions and rates that apply to special situations.
[b]No U.S. tax is imposed on a dividend paid by a U.S. corporation that received at least 80 percent of its gross income from an active foreign business for the three-year period before the dividend is declared.
[c]Royalties: The rate is different if the royalties are industrial/motion pictures and television/other.
Source: PriceWaterhouseCoopers, Corporate Taxes: Worldwide Summaries, 2004, pp. 899–903. Used by permission.

	Production Stage	Selling Price	Value Added	Incremental VAT
EXHIBIT 21.3	1	€100	€100	€15
Value-Added Tax Calculation	2	€300	€200	€30
	3	€380	€80	€12
				Total VAT €57

In many European countries (especially the EU) and also Latin American countries, VAT has become a major source of taxation on private citizens. Many economists prefer a VAT in place of a personal income tax because the latter is a disincentive to work, whereas a VAT discourages unnecessary consumption. A VAT fosters national saving, whereas an income tax is a disincentive to save because the returns from savings are taxed. Moreover, national tax authorities find that a VAT is easier to collect than an income tax because tax evasion is more difficult. Under a VAT, each stage in the production process has an incentive to obtain documentation from the previous stage that the VAT was paid in order to get the greatest tax credit possible. Of course, some argue that the cost of record keeping under a VAT system imposes an economic hardship on small businesses.

特别是在欧盟，增值税的一个难题就是各国课征增值税的税率并不都相同。

A problem with a VAT, especially in the EU, is that not all countries impose the same VAT tax rate. For example, in Denmark the VAT rate is 25 percent, but in Germany it is only 16 percent. Consequently, consumers who reside in a high-VAT country can purchase goods less expensively by simply shopping across the border in a lower-VAT country. Indeed, *The Wall Street Journal* reports that Danish customers frequently *demand* the lower German VAT rate on their purchases in Denmark![2] This problem should eventually be resolved, or at least mitigated, in the EU countries as it is expected that a harmonization in VAT rates among member states will occur. The International Finance in Practice box "The TAXING Devil You Know" presents an interesting discussion of implementing VAT in the United States as one means of tax reform.

National Tax Environments

有两种基本的税收管辖权：全球所得课税和区域所得课税。

The international tax environment confronting a MNC or an international investor is a function of the tax jurisdictions established by the individual countries in which the MNC does business or in which the investor owns financial assets. There are two fundamental types of tax jurisdiction: the *worldwide* and the *territorial*. Unless some mechanism were established to prevent it, double taxation would result if all nations were to follow both methods simultaneously.

Worldwide Taxation

全球课税或居住地课税体制

The **worldwide** or **residential** method of declaring a national tax jurisdiction is to tax national residents of the country on their worldwide income no matter in which country it is earned. The national tax authority, according to this method, is declaring its tax jurisdiction over people and businesses. A MNC firm with many foreign affiliates would be taxed in its home country on its income earned at home and abroad. Obviously, if the host countries of the foreign affiliates of a MNC also tax the income earned within their territorial borders, the possibility of double taxation exists, unless a mechanism is established to prevent it.

Territorial Taxation

本土课税体制或来源地课税体制

The **territorial** or **source** method of declaring a tax jurisdiction is to tax all income earned within the country by any taxpayer, domestic or foreign. Hence, regardless of

[2]See Horwitz (1993).

The TAXING Devil You Know

If you could create a national tax system from scratch, it likely wouldn't bear much resemblance to America's system today. It would enable people and businesses to figure their tax quickly and easily, without an accountant, attorney, or computer software. If would generate about as much revenue as the present system, to avoid a wrenching reduction of government spending all at once—or at all, depending on your preference. But it would save Americans and their government the billions of dollars spent each year on tax planning, preparation of complex returns, audits, and prosecution.

What's Fair?

You would strive for fairness in your simplified new system, but you would quickly discover that the perception of fairness is entirely subjective. Some folks think that progressive taxation—higher tax rates on higher amounts of income—is the essence of fairness. But others believe fairness means taxing every dollar at the same rate. Maybe you believe that income from different sources should be taxed at the same rate. But others believe that investment income should be taxed at a higher—or lower—rate than income earned in wages and salaries.

To some people, a fair tax code is full of incentives for behavior that they believe to be socially desirable: getting married, having children, owning a home, giving to charity, investing, saving for retirement. Ditto for businesses: incentives to buy new equipment, hire more employees, drill for oil, pay for health insurance. Whatever. But other folks believe that a fair tax code lets people and firms spend their money as they please. Therefore all tax deductions, however well-intentioned, should be abolished.

Some ambitious reformers think the income tax should be replaced by (or reduced and supplemented by) a national retail-sales tax collected by merchants. This would stimulate saving by taxing only consumption. The burden on the poor and middle class could be eased by rebating some of the sales tax or by exempting food, clothing, and medicine. Others prefer a European-style value-added tax (VAT), which would be levied on goods and services at every stage of production and folded into final prices. In a growing economy, the VAT would raise prodigious amounts of money in a way almost invisible to tax-paying voters—appealing to some members of Congress but appalling to others.

An American flat tax of 16 percent or 17 percent could be coupled with a high standard deduction that would exempt low-income folks, and millions of lower-middle-income households, from paying any federal tax. But Congress waffled on abolishing all itemized deductions—including the wildly popular breaks for mortgage interest and charitable giving—so that flat rate would probably have to be in the mid-20 percent range to generate today's level of revenue. Ironically, conservatives diminish the chances of their preferred reform, the flat tax, each time they persuade Congress to cut taxes within our present code. Example: the new 15 percent rate on dividends.

You've probably figured out by now why most Americans see sweeping tax reform as a fine idea in principle, but don't agree on which reform to embrace.

Scary Implications

In assessing the prospects of sweeping tax reform, remember that just 25 years ago, top marginal rates of 70 percent and higher were common throughout the Western democracies. Those rates have been cut in half—a remarkable political feat. But the next big tax-reform ideas—the flat tax, national sales tax, and VAT—are vastly bolder, and scarier in their economic implications, than the rate cuts of the 1980s. So, merits aside, the odds of enactment are very slim. Most Americans seem to prefer the devil they know to the devil they can only imagine.

Source: Knight Kiplinger, Kiplinger's Personal Finance, November 2004, Vol. 58 Issue 11, p. 58.

---

the nationality of a taxpayer, if the income is earned within the territorial boundary of a country, it is taxed by that country. The national tax authority, according to this method, is declaring its tax jurisdiction over transactions conducted within its borders. Consequently, local firms and affiliates of foreign MNCs are taxed on the income earned in the *source* country. Obviously, if the parent country of the foreign affiliate also levies a tax on worldwide income, the possibility of double taxation exists, unless a mechanism is established to prevent it.

避免双重征税的通常方式是一国不对其国内居民的外国来源所得征税。

Foreign Tax Credits

外国税收抵扣

The typical approach to avoiding double taxation is for a nation not to tax foreign-source income of its national residents. An alternative method, and the one the United States follows, is to grant to the parent firm **foreign tax credits** against U.S. taxes for taxes paid to foreign tax authorities on foreign-source income.[3] In general, foreign tax credits are categorized as direct or indirect. A *direct* foreign tax credit is computed for direct taxes paid on active foreign-source income of a foreign branch of a U.S. MNC or on the indirect withholding taxes withheld from passive income distributed by the foreign subsidiary to the U.S. parent. For foreign subsidiaries of U.S. MNCs, an *indirect* foreign tax credit is computed for income taxes *deemed paid* by the subsidiary. The deemed-paid tax credit corresponds to the portion of the distribution of earnings available for distribution that were actually distributed. For example, if a wholly owned foreign subsidiary pays out dividends equal to 50 percent of the earnings available for distribution, the deemed-paid tax credit is 50 percent of the foreign income taxes paid by the foreign subsidiary.

在给定的税收年度
里，外国税收抵扣适用
一个总的限额，即对外
国来源的应税所得额有
一个最大的总的税收抵
扣限制。

In a given tax year, an *overall limitation* applies to foreign tax credits; that is, the maximum total tax credit is limited to the amount of tax that would be due on the foreign-source income if it had been earned in the United States. The maximum tax credit is figured on worldwide foreign-source income; losses in one country can be used to offset profits in another. Excess tax credits for a tax year can be carried back two years and forward five years. Examples of calculating foreign tax credits for U.S. foreign branch and subsidiary operations are provided in the next section. Value-added taxes paid may not be included in determining the amount of the foreign tax credit, but they are nevertheless indirectly expensed as part of the cost of a good or service.

Individual U.S. investors may take a tax credit for the withholding taxes deducted from the dividend and interest income they received from the foreign financial assets in their portfolios.

Organizational Structures for Reducing Tax Liabilities

因此，为减少税收
负担，管理部门有必要
熟悉在跨国公司生命周
期各阶段所适用的各种
组织形式。

Countries differ in how they tax foreign-source income of their domestic MNCs. Additionally, regardless of the twin objectives of tax neutrality and tax equity, different forms of structuring a multinational organization within a country can result in different tax liabilities for the firm. Thus, it behooves management to be familiar with the different organizational structures that can be useful at various stages in the life cycle of the MNC for reducing tax liabilities. The following discussion on MNC organizational structure relates to U.S. tax regulations.

Branch and Subsidiary Income

国外分公司

国外子公司

An overseas affiliate of a U.S. MNC can be organized as a branch or a subsidiary. A **foreign branch** is not an independently incorporated firm separate from the parent; it is an extension of the parent. Consequently, active or passive foreign-source income earned by the branch is consolidated with the domestic-source income of the parent for determining the U.S. tax liability, regardless of whether or not the foreign-source income has been repatriated to the parent. A **foreign subsidiary** is an affiliate organization of the MNC that is independently incorporated in the foreign country, and one in which the U.S. MNC owns at least 10 percent of the voting equity stock. A foreign subsidiary in which the U.S. MNC owns more than 10 but less than 50 percent of the voting equity is a *minority foreign subsidiary* or an *uncontrolled foreign corporation*. Active and passive foreign-source income derived from a minority foreign subsidiary is taxed in the United States only when remitted to the U.S. parent firm via a dividend. A foreign subsidiary in which the U.S. MNC owns more than 50 percent of the voting equity is a *controlled foreign corporation*. Active foreign-source income from a controlled foreign corporation is taxed in the United States only as remitted to the U.S. parent, but passive income is taxed in the

---

[3]In general, as Kuntz and Peroni (1994) note, the United States claims only a "limited taxing jurisdiction over nonresident alien individuals and foreign corporations. Foreign persons pay U.S. taxes only on income that has a sufficient nexus with the U.S."

United States as earned, even if it has not been repatriated to the parent. A more detailed discussion on controlled foreign corporations is reserved for later in this section.

EXAMPLE 21.2

Foreign Tax Credit Calculations   Exhibit 21.4 presents examples of calculating the foreign tax credits for both a foreign branch and a wholly owned foreign subsidiary of a U.S. MNC in the host countries of Finland and Pakistan. The examples use the actual domestic marginal income tax rates presented in Exhibit 21.1 and the withholding tax treaty rates with respect to the United States. Both Finland and Pakistan tax foreign branch income at the same rate as domestic taxable income. The examples show the total tax liability for $100 of foreign taxable income when any excess foreign tax credits can be used and when they cannot. As a rule, excess tax credits can be carried back two years and forward five years. The examples assume that all after-tax foreign-source income available for remittance is immediately remitted to the U.S. parent.

Exhibit 21.4 indicates that when the U.S. MNC can use the full excess tax credits, the total tax liability is $35 per $100 of foreign taxable income, or 35 percent, the same amount due on $100 of taxable income earned in the United States. This is true: (1) regardless in which country the foreign affiliate is located; (2) whether the foreign affiliate is established as a branch or a subsidiary; and (3) regardless of the size of the income tax and withholding tax rates. A MNC that consistently generates excess foreign tax credits will never be able to use them in the allowable time. Thus, the more typical situation is that excess foreign tax credits go unused.

When excess tax credits go unused, the foreign tax liability for a branch is greater than the corresponding U.S. tax liability when the foreign income tax rate is greater than the U.S. rate of 35 percent. For a foreign subsidiary, the foreign tax liability is greater than the corresponding U.S. tax liability when: [foreign income tax rate + withholding tax rate − (foreign income tax rate × withholding tax rate)] is greater than the U.S. income tax rate of 35 percent. To illustrate, a foreign subsidiary in Pakistan for which excess foreign tax credits cannot be used has a total tax liability of: $.41 + .0375 − (.41 × .0375) = .4321$, or 43.21 percent versus 35 percent in the United States.

EXHIBIT 21.4

Examples of Calculating U.S. Foreign Tax Credits for Branch and Subsidiary Operations

	Finland		Pakistan	
	Branch	Subsidiary	Branch	Subsidiary
Foreign income tax rate	29%	29%	41%	41%
Withholding tax rate	N/A	5%	N/A	3.75%
Taxable income	100	100	100	100
Foreign income tax	−29	−29	−41	−41
Net available for remittance	71	71	59	59
Withholding tax[a]	0	−4	0	−2
Net cash to U.S. parent	71	67	59	57
Gross-up: Income tax	29	29	41	41
Gross-up: Withholding tax	0	4	0	2
U.S. taxable income	100	100	100	100
U.S. income tax at 35%	35	35	35	35
Less foreign tax credit:				
Income tax	−29	−29	−41	−41
Withholding tax	0	−4	0	−2
Net U.S. tax (excess credit)	6	2	(6)	(8)
Total tax: Excess credit used	35	35	35	35
Total tax: Excess credit not used	35	35	41	43

[a]100 percent of the funds available for remittance are assumed to be declared as dividends.

This example suggests that the management of a MNC should be aware of the current tax rates levied by various host countries when deciding where to locate foreign affiliate operations. Moreover, the exhibit indicates that there can be a difference in the tax liability due on foreign-source income depending upon the organizational structure selected for the foreign affiliate. Thus, the management of a MNC must be aware of any differences in the taxation of income by a particular host country when deciding whether to organize a foreign operation as a branch or subsidiary. For example, new foreign affiliates frequently experience operating losses in the early years of operation. If this situation is expected, it may be beneficial for a U.S. MNC to originally establish overseas operations as a foreign branch of the parent because branch operating losses are consolidated with the parent firm's earnings for tax purposes. Alternatively, when foreign-source income is to be reinvested abroad to expand foreign operations, it may be preferable to organize as a minority foreign subsidiary if the foreign income tax rate is less than the U.S. income tax rate because the tax liability in the United States can be deferred until the subsidiary remits a dividend to the U.S. parent.

Payments to and from Foreign Affiliates

In Chapter 19, we discussed transfer pricing strategies that may help a U.S. MNC to minimize its global tax liability. Since the discussion there was sufficient, we will only recap the major points in this chapter. Recall that a *transfer price* was the accounting value assigned to a good or service as it was transferred from one affiliate to another. We learned that the higher the transfer price, the larger will be the gross profits of the transferring division relative to the receiving division. Consequently, it is beneficial to follow a high markup policy on transferred goods and services from the parent to a foreign affiliate when the income tax rate in the host country is greater than the tax rate in the parent country because there will be less taxable income remaining in the high-tax host country. However, when the parent country has the higher tax rate, it is not instantly clear that a low markup policy should be pursued. Since U.S. MNCs are taxed on their worldwide income, earnings repatriated to the United States from a low-tax host country would be grossed up to figure the additional tax due in the United States. However, if foreign-source retained earnings were needed for reinvestment in the host country, a low markup policy would result in a tax savings (assuming, of course, that undistributed profits are not highly taxed by the host country).

We also learned from Chapter 19 that governmental authorities are quite aware of transfer pricing schemes used by MNCs to reduce their worldwide tax liability, and most countries have regulations controlling transfer prices. These regulations typically state that the transfer price must reflect an *arm's-length price,* that is, a price the selling affiliate would charge an unrelated customer for the good or service. However, an arm's-length price is frequently difficult to establish and evaluate; thus, there exists a window of opportunity for some maneuverability by a MNC to use transfer pricing strategies to reduce its worldwide tax liability.

但是，合理的价格常常难以确立和核定，所以，跨国公司尚有在一定限度内使用转移定价策略减少其整体税负的机会。

Tax Havens

税收天堂国家是指这些国家对被动收入征收较低的公司所得税和预提税。

A **tax haven** country is one that has a low corporate income tax rate and low withholding tax rates on passive income. Some major tax haven countries, which are suggested by the income tax rates presented in Exhibit 21.1, are the Bahamas, Bahrain, Bermuda, British Virgin Islands, Cayman Islands, Channel Islands (Guernsey and Jersey), and the Isle of Man. Additionally, in Panama, foreign-source income is exempt from taxation.

In Ireland and the Netherlands Antilles, special tax incentives or tax holidays are granted for businesses that will earn hard currency or develop export markets. In Puerto Rico, certain businesses are granted a reduced flat income tax rate of 7 percent applicable to industrial development income, which in some cases may be further reduced to 0 percent. In Liechtenstein and in many instances in Switzerland, holding companies are exempt from certain income taxes.

As Dot-Coms Go Bust In U.S., Bermuda Hosts an Odd Little Boomlet

HAMILTON, Bermuda—Operating out of a hurricane-proof command center in a former U.S. military base, Paven Bratch is a tax examiner's nightmare.

Although his Internet company, music and video merchant Playcentric.com, has just 10 employees, didn't go live until September and has yet to turn a profit, it has the structure of a major multinational. Its computer servers are located here, its operating unit is in Barbados, and it has a distribution deal with a big record-store chain in Toronto. The 36-year-old Mr. Bratch figures this setup will save him so much on corporate income taxes and other expenses that he'll be able to undercut Amazon.com Inc.'s prices by more than 45% and still make a bundle.

"One thing that always amazes me is, why would anyone who's planning on generating a profit locate themselves in a full-tax jurisdiction?" he says.

'First Generation'

Plenty of dot-coms are asking themselves the same question these days. Undaunted by their industry's growing ranks of flameouts and hoping to emerge as one of the profitable few, dozens of them are popping up in tax havens around the world.

In Bermuda, they range from tiny publisher ISI Publications Ltd., which sells hard-to-find business books under the domain name Booksonbiz.com, to E*Trade Group Inc., the big online stockbroker, which is locating its international trading operations here. Further south, on the Caribbean island of Antigua, an American trader has set up Indextrade.com to allow small investors to bet on swings in market indexes, while in Cyprus, a former British jazz singer is doing a brisk business by listing vessels such as a Soviet-era submarine on Ships-for-sale.com.

"These merchants are the first generation who can really domicile anywhere," says Andrea Wilson, chief executive of Bermuda-based First Atlantic Commerce Ltd., which provides credit-card payment systems for e-businesses. "They can be a virtual corporation if they choose."

The trend started with Internet gambling companies, which fled to the Caribbean to avoid the long arm of U.S. law. But now, thanks to an explosion of new telecommunications links to places such as Bermuda and Britain's Channel Islands—and an ambitious push by promoters in such countries as Panama to set up facilities capable of hosting hundreds or thousands of Web sites each—more-legitimate Internet companies are starting to make the leap offshore.

A Wealth of Ambiguity

There are serious questions about whether some of the structures would pass muster with the Internal Revenue Service and its foreign counterparts. But many accountants figure there's enough ambiguity in the industrial world's offshore tax codes that e-commerce companies could, at least theoretically, rack up tax-free profits for years before the authorities sort things out.

The issues are often murkier than for a standard offshore tax shelter, because they involve technological innovations that the U.S. Treasury couldn't have anticipated when it began laying the ground rules for offshore taxation in the 1960s. For instance, nobody's entirely sure how to tax the earnings of a programmer who sells his software by allowing buyers to download it from a Web site hosted on a computer server in a zero-tax jurisdiction.

Some tax attorneys take the position that the sale takes place where the server is located, and that the business owes no corporate or sales tax in the buyer's home country. "It would be no different than you or I getting on a plane, flying to the Bahamas, and buying a T-shirt in the hotel," says Lazaro Mur, a Miami tax attorney.

New telecommunications options have brought Bermuda and much of the Caribbean even closer than a plane ride away. Cable & Wireless PLC's phone monopoly among former British colonies in the region is breaking up, and C&W's new competitors are starting to lace the seabed with modern fiber-optic lines, breaking down old technological barriers to working offshore.

At the same time, so-called server farms—warehouses built to accommodate row upon row of computer servers—are sprouting up to accommodate high-tech newcomers. At Fort Clayton, a former U.S. military base in Panama, local entrepreneurs plan to open a 50,000-square-foot "high-tech hotel" later this month they say will be capable of hosting as many as 1.2 million Web sites.

HavenCo, a self-proclaimed "data haven," announced plans last year to host Web sites from an antiaircraft platform abandoned by the British after World War II. The North Sea platform has a colorful history: In 1966, a retired British army major seized control of it and has operated it for years as the sovereign "Principality of Sealand."

Ryan Lackey, HavenCo's chief technical officer, says the company, which spent the summer upgrading electrical power and air conditioning on Sealand, has more than 30 servers up and running, connected to the mainland by satellite and wireless service, and hopes to expand to as many as 5,000.

He says the company has fielded "several thousand" sales inquiries. "The big thing people really want is e-mail servers, because in the past people have been getting their e-mail servers subpoenaed," he says. He adds that HavenCo would only comply with subpoenas issued by the Court of Sealand. "But there's no Court of Sealand, so it's very unlikely."

Tax savings are the big selling point for many of the installations. "Offshore + Ecommerce = Tax Free Heaven," screams a banner ad for Bahamas.net, which offers server facilities in the Bahamas for as low as $2,200 a month.

Bermuda, which has a rich history of helping foreigners shave taxes, also is doing its best to encourage the migration offshore. Its two biggest banks, Bank of Bermuda Ltd. and Bank of N.T. Butterfield & Son Ltd., have launched major e-commerce initiatives, establishing systems to allow online merchants to bill customers in several major currencies. A common refrain among business leaders on this tiny fishhook-shaped island is that Bill Gates would be a much-richer man today if he had originally established Microsoft here.

The pitch helped reel in Robert Edwards, an editorial cartoonist who lives in Canterbury, England. Not long ago he went looking for help in setting up a Web site to sell works by him and about 30 other artists from around the world. Tipped off to Bermuda by a visiting delegation of businesspeople, he registered his company online through Appleby, Spurling & Kempe, a local law firm here, and was quickly directed to Web designers, a hosting site and a credit-card intermediary, First Atlantic.

Late last year, at a total cost of less than $200,000, his Drawnandquartered.com went live, offering 4,000 artworks, which can be downloaded online with a credit card, for $200 and up. His company doesn't pay any income or sales taxes, and he only has to pay personal-income tax on the salary he draws. "I'm a perfect example of how it can be done," he says.

Playcentric's Mr. Bratch, a former Procter & Gamble Co. manager, says he relied on advice from an international tax attorney in structuring the online retailer, which will market its compact disks, videos and DVDs partly through packaged-goods makers who want to reward loyal customers. Mr. Bratch, a Canadian citizen, put his operating unit in Barbados, which, unlike Bermuda, has a tax treaty with Canada, in order to take advantage of the Caribbean nation's corporate income-tax rate of just 2%.

He says he located his computer operations in Bermuda because of its extensive banking and telecommunications infrastructure. Its attractions include a state-of-the-art server facility built in an old U.S. naval base by 360networks Inc.'s

TeleBermuda International unit, which laid an undersea fiber-optic cable to the U.S. in 1997.

Tax considerations also helped lure Todd Middagh, chief executive of Originals Online Ltd., to Bermuda. His brainchild: a site that will allow importers, exporters and shipping companies to swap legally binding trade documents online, instead of wasting days with couriers. "It's a digital product, global in nature, 24-hours-a-day world-wide," says Mr. Middagh, who has already attracted the interest of several major grain companies, including Archer Daniels Midland Co.

"We're going to be in almost every jurisdiction over time," he says. Meanwhile, Mr. Middagh, a native of Canada, will be presiding over the company from his house here, which overlooks the Atlantic Ocean.

Scott Rubman, a Long Island, N.M., real-estate attorney whose family has long been in the fur trade, is putting together Furs.com, a Bermuda-based site that plans to match mink farmers in, say, Norway, with fur-coat manufacturers in North America and China. As an American, Mr. Rubman may face a bigger hurdle in shielding any offshore profits from taxation. Unlike many other countries, the U.S. taxes its citizens on their income world-wide.

"If you move offshore strictly to evade taxes, that's something the U.S. will always look at," says Mr. Rubman, who is getting plenty of advice from U.S. tax experts. "When you have a legitimate business purpose to transact business offshore, I'd think the U.S. would be supportive of that."

And if the U.S. isn't supportive? Cryptographer Vince Cate thinks he has that covered. In 1998, the onetime Carnegie-Mellon University Ph.D. candidate walked into the U.S. Embassy in Barbados and renounced his American citizenship, declaring that he was henceforth a citizen of Mozambique, thanks to a document he purchased for $5,000 over the Internet.

Then, he went back to the Caribbean island of Anguilla, where he had developed a reputation as a computer-encryption visionary. Among his many ventures, he has taken over the operations of an online marketer of driver's-license information that had run afoul of a new privacy law in Texas. Mr. Cate plans to build the business without paying a cent of taxes.

"Because I'm not a U.S. citizen, I'm not in the United States, and Anguilla has no taxes, I don't believe I have any problem," he says.

Source: Michael Allen, The Wall Street Journal, January 8, 2001, pp. A1, A8. Reprinted by permission of The Wall Street Journal, © 2001 Dow Jones & Company, Inc. All Rights Reserved Worldwide.

税收天堂一度被跨国公司用作建立全资所有的"账面"公司的地点，该公司反过来拥有跨国公司经营的所有外国附属机构。

Tax havens were once useful as locations for a MNC to establish a wholly owned "paper" foreign subsidiary that in turn would own the operating foreign subsidiaries of the MNC. Hence, when the tax rates in the host countries of the operating affiliates were lower than the tax rate in the parent country, dividends could be routed through the tax haven affiliate for use by the MNC, but the taxes due on them in the parent country could continue to be deferred until a dividend was declared by the tax haven subsidiary. These days the benefit of a tax haven subsidiary for U.S. MNCs has been greatly reduced by two factors: One is that the present corporate income tax rate in the United States is not especially high in comparison to most non-tax-haven countries, thus eliminating the need for deferral; the second factor is that the rules governing controlled foreign corporations (the topic to be discussed next) have effectively eliminated the ability to defer passive income in a tax haven foreign subsidiary. As the International Finance in Practice box "As Dot-Coms Go Bust in U.S., Bermuda Hosts an Odd Little Boomlet" suggests, however, certain tax advantages may obtain for dot.com companies domiciled in tax haven countries that engage in e-commerce.

Controlled Foreign Corporation

控 股 外 国 公 司 (CFC) 是指美国股东拥有50%以上有表决权股份的外国子公司。

The Tax Reform Act of 1986 created a new type of foreign subsidiary called a controlled foreign corporation. The purpose of the reform was to prevent the tax deferral of certain income in tax haven countries and to raise taxes by reducing the benefit gained by U.S. MNCs from foreign tax credits. **A controlled foreign corporation (CFC)** is a foreign subsidiary that has more than 50 percent of its voting equity owned by U.S. shareholders. A U.S. shareholder is any U.S. citizen, resident, partnership, corporation, trust, or estate that owns (or indirectly controls) 10 percent or more of the voting equity of the CFC. Thus, six nonaffiliated U.S. shareholders each owning exactly 10 percent of the voting equity would be required for a foreign corporation to be designated a CFC. Alternatively, a wholly owned subsidiary of a U.S. MNC would be a CFC.

附则F所得

The undistributed income of a minority foreign subsidiary of a U.S. MNC is tax deferred until it is remitted via a dividend. This rule is modified for Subpart F income of CFCs, which is subject to immediate taxation. **Subpart F income** includes income of a type that is relatively easy to transfer between countries and that is subject to a low foreign tax levy. Special rules apply for calculating foreign tax credits for CFCs. Much Subpart F income can be classified into four distinct categories or "baskets" of income: passive income, high withholding tax interest, financial services income, and shipping income. The allowable foreign tax credit limit is figured separately for each basket. Operating income of the CFC goes into the overall basket. The result is that high taxes paid in one country on income classified into one basket cannot be used to offset low taxes paid in another country on income classified into a different basket. This procedure results in more excess foreign tax credits, which are unlikely to be completely used.

SUMMARY

本章对跨国公司和国际金融资产投资者所面临的国际税收环境做了简单的介绍。

1. 税收的两个主要目标是税收中性和税收公平。经济效率和平等原理是税收中性的理论基础。税收公平原则是指所有情况相似的纳税人应该依据相同的规则分担政府运作的成本。

2. 税收的三种基本类型分别是所得税、预提税和增值税。本章给出了许多国家的公司所得税并做了相应的比较。类似地，本章还给出并比

This chapter provided a brief introduction to the international tax environment that confronts MNCs and investors in international financial assets.

1. The twin objectives of taxation are tax neutrality and tax equity. Tax neutrality has its foundations in the principles of economic efficiency and equity. Tax equity is the principle that all similarly situated taxpayers should participate in the cost of operating the government according to the same rules.

2. The three basic types of taxation are income tax, withholding tax, and value-added tax. Corporate income tax rates from many countries were listed and compared. Similarly, the withholding tax rates for certain countries for various types of foreign-source income for which the U.S. has bilateral tax treaties were listed and compared.

较了与美国签订有双边协定的一些国家对各种外国来源所得征收的预提税。

3.各国通常对居民纳税人的全球所得和外国纳税人在其境内的经营所得课税。如果各国同时采用两种方式，那么就会发生双重课税问题，除非能建立起一套防止双重课税的机制。作为减少双重课税的一种手段，本章引入了外国税收抵扣概念。本章从美国跨国公司的角度，举例说明了在三个采用不同公司所得税率的国家里分公司和子公司的外国税收抵扣的计算。

4.不同的组织结构形式会影响跨国公司的税负。当分公司和子公司的经营面临不同的税收时，情况更是如此。此外，本章还对转移定价策略、在税收天堂国家或地区开展经营的子公司、本国居民控股的国外公司和外国销售公司进行了界定和讨论。

3. Nations often tax the worldwide income of resident taxpayers and also the income of foreign taxpayers doing business within their territorial boundaries. If countries simultaneously apply both methods, double taxation will result unless a mechanism is established to prevent it. The concept of the foreign tax credit as a means to eliminate double taxation was developed. Examples were presented from the perspective of a U.S. MNC showing the calculation of the foreign tax credits for branch and subsidiary operations in three countries with different corporate income tax rates.

4. Different forms of organizational structure can affect the tax liability of a MNC. Specifically, there are differences in taxation between branch and subsidiary operations. Transfer pricing strategies, subsidiary operations in tax haven countries, foreign-controlled corporations, and foreign sales corporations were also defined and discussed.

KEY WORDS

active income, *499*

capital-export neutrality, *499*

capital-import neutrality, *499*

controlled foreign corporation (CFC), *510*

direct tax, *499*

foreign branch, *505*

foreign subsidiary, *505*

foreign tax credits, *504*

income tax, *499*

indirect tax, *501*

national neutrality, *499*

passive income, *501*

residential taxation, *503*

source taxation, *503*

Subpart F income, *510*

tax equity, *499*

tax haven, *507*

tax neutrality, *499*

tax treaty, *501*

territorial taxation, *503*

value-added tax (VAT), *501*

withholding tax, *501*

worldwide taxation, *503*

QUESTIONS

1. Discuss the twin objectives of taxation. Be sure to define the key words.

2. Compare and contrast the three basic types of taxation that governments levy within their tax jurisdiction.

3. Show how double taxation on a taxpayer may result if all countries were to tax the worldwide income of their residents and the income earned within their territorial boundaries.

4. What methods do taxing authorities use to eliminate or mitigate the evil of double taxation?

5. There is a difference in the tax liability levied on foreign-source income depending upon whether a foreign branch or subsidiary form of organizational structure is selected for a foreign affiliate. Please elaborate on this statement.

PROBLEMS

1. There are three production stages required before a pair of skis produced by Fjord Fabrication can be sold at retail for NOK2,300. Fill in the following table to show the value added at each stage in the production process and the incremental and total VAT. The Norwegian VAT rate is 24 percent.

Production Stage	Selling Price	Value Added	Incremental VAT
1	NOK 450		
2	NOK1,900		
3	NOK2,300		
			Total VAT

2. The Docket Company of Asheville, NC, USA, is considering establishing an affiliate operation in the city of Wellington, on the south island of New Zealand. It is undecided whether to establish the affiliate as a branch operation or a wholly

owned subsidiary. New Zealand taxes income of both resident corporations and branch operations at a flat rate of 33 percent. It also withholds taxes at a rate of 15 percent on dividends paid by resident corporations to recipients in the United States. The United States has an income tax rate of 35 percent on income earned worldwide, but gives a tax credit for taxes paid to another country. Based on this information, is a branch or subsidiary the recommended form for the affiliate?

INTERNET EXERCISES

The website www.taxsites.com/international.html is a comprehensive site that provides links to many other websites categorized into the following topics: country-specific sites, IRS Resources, European Union and VAT, Students and Scholars, Tax Associations, Other Resources, Tax Treaties, and Governments. For example, go to the Worldwide-Tax section under Other Resources and learn about the history of taxation.

MINI CASE

Sigma Corp.'s Location Decision

Sigma Corporation of Boston is contemplating establishing an affiliate operation in the Mediterranean. Two countries under consideration are Spain and Cyprus. Sigma intends to repatriate all after-tax foreign-source income to the United States. At this point, Sigma is not certain whether it would be best to establish the affiliate operation as a branch operation or a wholly owned subsidiary of the parent firm.

In Cyprus, the marginal corporate tax rate is 15 percent. Foreign branch profits are taxed at the same rate. In Spain, corporate income is taxed at 35 percent, the same rate as in the United States. Additionally, foreign branch with the U.S. income in Spain is also taxed at 35 percent. The withholding tax treaty rates with the U.S. on dividend income paid from Cyprus is 0 percent and 10 percent paid from Spain.

The financial manager of Sigma has asked you to help him determine where to locate the new affiliate and which organizational structure to establish. The location decision will be largely based on whether the total tax liability would be smallest for a foreign branch or a wholly owned subsidiary in Cyprus or Spain.

REFERENCES & SUGGESTED READINGS

Bischel, Jon E., and Robert Feinscheiber. *Fundamentals of International Taxation*, 2nd ed. New York: Practicing Law Institute, 1985.

Horwitz, Tony. "Continental Shift: Europe's Borders Fade and People and Goods Can Move Freely." *The Wall Street Journal*, May 18, 1993.

Isenberg, Joseph. *International Taxation: U.S. Taxation of Foreign Taxpayers and Foreign Income*, Vols. I and II. Boston: Little, Brown, 1990.

Kaplan, Richard L. *Federal Taxation of International Transactions: Principles, Planning and Policy*. St. Paul, Minn.: West, 1988.

Kopits, George, ed. *Tax Harmonization in the European Community: Policy Issues and Analysis*. International Monetary Fund Occasional Paper, No. 94, Washington, D.C., June 1992.

Kuntz, Joel D., and Robert J. Peroni. *U.S. International Taxation*, Vols. I and II. Boston: Warren, Gorham and Lamont, 1994.

Metcalf, Gilbert E. "Value-Added Taxation: A Tax Whose Time Has Come?" *Journal of Economic Perspectives* 9 (1995), pp. 121–40.

PriceWaterhouseCoopers. *Corporate Taxes: Worldwide Summaries*. New York: John Wiley and Sons, Inc., 2004.

U.S. Internal Revenue Code, Part III. Income From Sources Without the United States. Chicago: Commerce Clearing House, 1993.

Glossary

Active Income Income which results from production or services provided by an individual or corporation.

Adjusted Present Value (APV) A present value technique which discounts a firm's cash flows at different rates depending on the risk of the cash flows.

Agency Market A market in which the broker takes the client's order through the agent, who matches it with another public order.

Agency Problem Managers who are hired as the agents working for shareholders may actually pursue their own interests at the expense of shareholders, causing conflicts of interest. Agency problems are especially acute for firms with diffused share ownership.

All-Equity Cost of Capital The required return on a company's stock in the absence of debts.

All-in-Cost All costs of a swap, which are interest expense, transaction cost, and service charges.

American Depository Receipt (ADR) A certificate of ownership issued by a U.S. bank representing a multiple of foreign shares that are deposited in a U.S. bank. ADRs can be traded on the organized exchanges in the U.S. or in the OTC market.

American Option An option which can be exercised at any time during the option contract.

Appreciate In the context of a domestic currency, a decrease (an increase) in a foreign exchange rate relative to another currency when stated in terms of the domestic (foreign) currency.

Arbitrage The act of simultaneously buying and selling the same or equivalent assets or commodities for the purpose of making certain, guaranteed profits.

Ask Price *See* Offer Price.

B

Balance of Payments A country's record of international transactions presented in a double-entry bookkeeping form.

Balance Sheet Hedge Intended to reduce translation exposure of a MNC by eliminating the mismatch of exposed net assets and exposed net liabilities denominated in the same currency.

Bank Capital Adequacy The amount of equity capital and other securities a bank holds as reserves against risky assets to reduce the probability of a bank failure.

Banker's Acceptance (B/A) A negotiable money market instrument for which a secondary market exists and is issued by the Importer's Bank once the bill of lading and time draft are accepted. It is essentially a promise that the bank will pay the draft when it matures.

Basle Accord Established in 1988 by the Bank for International Settlements, this act established a framework to measure bank capital adequacy for banks in the Group of Ten and Luxembourg.

Bearer Bond A bond in which ownership is demonstrated through possession of the bond.

Bid Price The price at which dealers will buy a financial asset.

Bilateral Netting A system in which a pair of affiliates determines the net amount due between them and only this amount is transferred.

Bill of Lading (B/L) In exporting, a document issued by a common carrier specifying that it has received goods for shipment and which can also serve as title to the goods.

Bimetallism A double standard maintaining free coinage for both gold and silver.

Brady Bonds Loans converted into collateralized bonds with a reduced interest rate devised to resolve the international debt crisis in the late 1980s. Named after the U.S. Treasury Secretary Nicholas Brady.

Bretton Woods System An international monetary system created in 1944 to promote postwar exchange rate stability and coordinate international monetary policies. Otherwise known as the gold-exchange system.

C

Cadbury Code The Cadbury Committee appointed by the British government issued the *Code of Best Practice* in corporate governance for British companies, recommending, among other things, appointing at least three outside board directors and having the positions of CEO and board chairman held by two different individuals.

Call Market A market in which market and limit orders are accumulated and executed at specific intervals during the day.

Call Option An option to "buy" an underlying asset at a specified price.

Capital Account Balance-of-payment entry capturing all sales and purchases of financial assets, real estate, and businesses.

Capital-Export Neutrality The idea that an ideal tax is one which is effective in raising revenue for the government and, at the same time, does not prevent economic resources from being deployed most efficiently no matter where in the world the highest return can be earned.

Capital-Import Neutrality The idea that an ideal tax burden imposed by a host country on a foreign subsidiary of a MNC should be the same regardless of which country the MNC is incorporated in and should be the same burden as placed on domestic firms.

Cash Budget In cash management, a plan which details the time and size of expected receipts and disbursements.

Cash Management The handling of cash within a firm such as the investment a firm has in transaction balances, funds tied up in precautionary cash balances, investment of excess funds at the most favorable rate, and borrowing at the lowest rate when there is a temporary cash shortage.

Central Cash Depository In a MNC, it is a central cash pool in which excess cash from affiliates is collected and invested or used to cover system-wide shortages of cash.

Closed-End Country Fund (CECF) A country fund (fund invested exclusively in the securities of one country) which issues a given number of shares that are traded on the host country exchange as if it were an individual stock. These shares are not redeemable at the underlying net asset value set in the home market.

Comparative Advantage   David Ricardo used the notion of comparative advantage to justify international trade. Specifically, if countries specialize production in those industries where they can produce goods and services more efficiently (in relative terms) than other countries, and engage in trade, all countries will be better off.

Competitive Effect   Refers to the effect of exchange rate changes on the firm's competitive position, which, in turn, affects the firm's operating cash flows.

Complete Contract   Refers to the contract that specifies exactly what each party will do under all possible future contingencies.

Concessionary Loan   A loan below the market interest rate offered by the host country to a parent MNC to encourage capital expenditures in the host country.

Contingent Claim Security   *See* Derivative Security.

Contingent Exposure   The risk due to uncertain situations in which a firm does not know if it will face exchange risk exposure in the future.

Continuous Market   A market in which market and limit orders can be executed any time during business hours.

Controlled Foreign Corporation (CFC)   A foreign subsidiary in which U.S. shareholders own more than 50 percent of the voting equity stock.

Conversion Effect   Refers to the fact that the dollar amount converted from a given cash flow from foreign operation will be affected by exchange rate changes.

Convertible Bond   A bond which can be exchanged for a pre-determined number of equity shares of the issuer.

Corporate Governance   The economic, legal, and institutional framework in which corporate control and cash flow rights are distributed among shareholders, managers, and other stakeholders of the company.

Counterparty   One of the two parties involved in financial contracts who agrees to exchange cash flows on particular terms.

Countertrade   Transactions in which parties exchange goods or services. If these transactions do not involve an exchange of money, they are a type of barter.

Country Risk   In banking and investment, it is the probability that unexpected events in a country will influence its ability to repay loans and repatriate dividends. It includes political and credit risks.

Covered Interest Arbitrage   A situation which occurs when IRP does not hold, thereby allowing certain arbitrage profits to be made without the arbitrageur investing any money out of pocket or bearing any risk.

Cross Exchange Rate   An exchange rate between a currency pair where neither currency is the U.S. dollar.

Cross-Currency Interest Rate Swap   Typically called a "currency swap." One counterparty exchanges the debt service obligations of a bond denominated in one currency for the debt service obligations of the other counterparty that are denominated in another currency.

Cross-hedging   Involves hedging a position in one asset by taking a position in another asset.

Cross-Listing   The act of directly listing securities on foreign financial exchanges. Cross-listing will require meeting the listing and disclosure standards of foreign exchanges.

Cumulative Translation Adjustment (CTA)   Used in the current rate method of translating foreign currency financial statements, this equity account allows balancing of the balance sheet by accounting for translation gains and losses.

Currency Board   An extreme form of the fixed exchange rate regime under which local currency is fully backed by the U.S. dollar or another chosen standard currency.

Currency Futures   A standardized foreign exchange contract with a future delivery date that is traded on organized exchanges.

Currency Swap   One counter party exchanges the debt service obligations of a bond denominated in one currency for the debt service obligations of the other counter party denominated in another currency.

Current Account   Balance-of-payment entry representing the exports and imports of goods and services, and unilateral transfer.

Current/Noncurrent Method   In dealing with foreign currency translation, the idea that current assets and liabilities are converted at the current exchange rate while noncurrent assets and liabilities are translated at the historical exchange rates.

Current Rate Method   In dealing with foreign currency translation, the idea that all balance sheet accounts are translated at the current exchange rate except stockholder's equity, which is translated at the exchange rate on the date of issuance.

D

Dealer Market   A market in which the broker takes the trade through the dealer, who participates in trades as a principal.

Debt-for-Equity Swap   The sale of sovereign debt for U.S. dollars to investors desiring to make equity investment in the indebted nation.

Depreciate   In the context of a domestic currency, an increase (a decrease) in a foreign exchange rate relative to another currency when stated in terms of the domestic (foreign) currency.

Derivative Security   A security whose value is contingent upon the value of the underlying security. Examples are futures, forward, and options contracts.

Direct Tax   A tax paid directly by the taxpayer on whom the tax is levied.

Diversification of the Market   A strategy for managing operating exposure in which a firm diversifies the market for its product. Thus, exchange rate changes in one country may be offset by opposite exchange rate changes in another.

Draft   A written order instructing the importer or his agent to pay the amount specified on its face at a certain date.

Dual Currency Bond   A straight fixed-rate bond which pays coupon interest in the issue currency, but at maturity pays the principal in a currency other than the issue currency.

E

Economic Exposure   The possibility that cash flows and the value of the firm may be affected by unanticipated changes in the exchange rates.

Edge Act Bank   Federally chartered subsidiaries of U.S. banks which may engage in the full range of international banking operations. These banks are located in the United States.

Efficient Market Hypothesis   Hypothesis stating that financial markets are informationally efficient in that the current asset prices reflect all the relevant and available information.

Elasticity of Demand   A measure of the sensitivity of demand for a product with respect to its price.

EURIBOR   The rate at which interbank deposits of the euro are offered by one prime bank to another in countries that make up the EMU as well as prime banks in non-EMU EU countries and major prime banks in non-EU countries.

Euro   The common European currency introduced in 1999 of the 11 countries of the EU that make up the EMU.

Eurobond   A bond issue denominated in a particular currency but sold to investors in national capital markets other than the issuing country.

Eurocurrency   A time deposit of money in an international bank located in a country other than the country which issues the currency.

European Central Bank (ECB)   The central bank of the 11 countries that make up the EMU, responsible for maintaining price stability via monetary policy.

European Currency Unit (ECU)   A basket currency made up of a weighted average of the currencies of the 12 members of the European Union. The precursor of the euro.

European Monetary System (EMS)   Replaced the snake in 1979. A system to establish monetary stability in Europe and promote European economic and political unification.

European Monetary Union (EMU)   The monetary union of 11 countries of the EU that irrevocably fixed their exchange rates and use the common euro currency.

European Option   An option which can be exercised only at the maturity date of the contract.

European Union (EU)   A regional economic integration in Western Europe, currently with 15 member states, in which all barriers to the free flow of goods, capital, and people have been removed. EU plans to complete economic unification including a single currency.

Exchange Rate Mechanism (ERM)   The procedure, prior to the introduction of the euro, by which EMS member countries collectively manage their exchange rates based on a parity grid system, a system of par values between ERM countries.

Exchange Rate Pass-through   The relationship between exchange rate changes and the price adjustments of internationally traded goods.

Exercise Price   The prespecified price paid or received when an option is exercised.

Export-Import Bank (Eximbank) of the United States   Chartered in 1945, it is an independent government agency which facilitates and finances U.S. export trade by financing exports in situations where private financial institutions are unable or unwilling to provide financing.

Exposure Coefficient   The coefficient obtained from regressing the home currency value of assets on the foreign exchange rate under consideration. This provides a measure of the firm's economic exposure to currency risk.

Exposure Netting   Hedging only the net exposure by firms which have both payables and receivables in foreign currencies.

F

Financial Hedges   Refers to hedging exchange risk exposure using financial contracts such as currency forward and options contracts.

Fisher Effect   Theory stating that the nominal interest rate is the sum of the real interest rate and the expected inflation rate.

Flexible Sourcing Policy   A strategy for managing operating exposure that involves sourcing from areas where input costs are low.

Floating Rate Note   Medium-term bonds which have their coupon payments indexed to a reference rate such as the three-month U.S. dollar LIBOR.

Foreign Bond   Refers to a bond offered by a foreign borrower to the investors in a national capital market and denominated in that nation's currency. Example: An American company selling yen-denominated bonds in Japan to local investors.

Foreign Branch   An overseas affiliate of a MNC which is not an independently incorporated firm but is rather an extension of the parent.

Foreign Direct Investment (FDI)   Investment in a foreign country that gives the MNC a measure of control.

Foreign Exchange Markets   Encompass the conversion of purchasing power from one currency into another, bank deposits of foreign currencies, and trading in foreign currency spot, forward, futures, swap, and options contracts.

Foreign Exchange Risk   The risk of facing uncertain future exchange rates.

Foreign Subsidiary   An affiliate organization of a MNC which is independently incorporated in a foreign country.

Foreign Tax Credit   Used to avoid double taxation on a parent firm with foreign subsidiaries. It is the credit given to the parent firm against taxes due in the host country based on the taxes paid to foreign tax authorities on foreign-source income.

Forfaiting   A form of medium-term trade financing used to finance exports in which the exporter sells promissory notes to a bank at a discount, thereby freeing the exporter from carrying the financing.

Forward Expectations Parity   Theory stating that the forward premium or discount is equal to the expected change in the exchange rate between two currencies.

Forward Market   A market for trading foreign exchange contracts initiated today but to be settled at a future date.

Forward Market Hedge   A method of hedging exchange risk exposure in which a foreign currency contract is sold or bought forward.

Forward Premium/Discount   The amount over (under) the spot exchange rate for a forward rate that is often expressed as an annualized percent deviation from the spot rate.

Forward Rate Agreement   An interbank contract that is used to hedge the interest rate risk in mismatched deposits and credits.

Free Cash Flow   It represents a firm's internally generated fund in excess of the amount needed to finance all investment projects with positive net present values.

Functional Currency   For a foreign subsidiary of a MNC, it is the currency of the primary economic environment in which the entity operates. This is typically the local currency of the country in which the entity conducts most of its business.

G

General Agreement on Tariffs and Trade (GATT) A multilateral agreement between member countries to promote international trade. The GATT played a key role in reducing international trade barriers.

Gold Exchange Standard A monetary system in which countries hold most of their reserves in the form of a currency of a particular country. That country is on the gold standard.

Gold Standard A monetary system in which currencies are defined in terms of their gold content. The exchange rate between a pair of currencies is determined by their relative gold contents.

Gresham's Law Under the bimetallic standard, the abundant metal was used as money while the scarce metal was driven out of circulation, based on the fact that the ratio of the two metals was officially fixed.

H

Hedger One who attempts to eliminate the risk of an unfavorable price change in an asset by taking an offsetting position in another asset, usually a derivatives contract.

Hedging via the Invoice Currency A method of hedging exchange risk exposure by invoicing in terms of the home currency of the firm.

Home Bias In portfolio holdings, the tendency of an investor to hold a larger portion of the home country securities than is optimum for diversification of risk.

I

Income Tax A direct tax levied on the active income of an individual or corporation.

Indirect Tax A tax levied on a taxpayer's income which was not directly generated by the taxpayer and serves as passive income for the taxpayer.

Initial Performance Bond An initial collateral deposit needed to establish an asset position.

Interest Rate Parity (IRP) An arbitrage equilibrium condition holding that the interest rate differential between two countries should be equal to the forward exchange premium or discount. Violation of IRP gives rise to profitable arbitrage opportunities.

International Banking Facility (IBF) Banking operation within domestic U.S. banks that act as foreign banks in the U.S. and, as such, are not bound by domestic reserve requirements or FDIC insurance requirements. They seek deposits from non-U.S. citizens and can make loans only to foreigners.

International Fisher Effect A theory stating that the expected change in the spot exchange rate between two countries is the difference in the interest rates between the two countries.

International Monetary System The institutional framework within which international payments are made, movements of capital are accommodated, and exchange rates among currencies are determined.

Intrinsic Value The immediate exercise value of an American option.

J

Jamaica Agreement International monetary agreement in January 1976 by which flexible exchange rates were accepted and gold was abandoned as an international reserve asset.

J-curve Effect Refers to the initial deterioration and eventual improvement of the trade balance following a depreciation of a country's currency.

L

Law of One Price The requirement that similar commodities or securities should be trading at the same or similar prices.

Lead/Lag Strategy Reducing transaction exposure by paying or collecting foreign financial obligations early (lead) or late (lag) depending on whether the currency is hard or soft.

Letter of Credit (L/C) A guarantee from the Importer's Bank that it will act on behalf of the importer and pay the exporter for merchandise if all documentation is in order.

Limit Order An order away from the market price which is held until it can be executed at the desired price.

Liquidity The ability of securities to be bought and sold quickly at close to the current quoted price.

London Interbank Offered Rate (LIBOR) The interbank interest rate at which a bank will offer Eurocurrency deposits to another bank in London. LIBOR is often used as the basis for setting Eurocurrency loan rates. The loan rate is determined by adding a risk premium to LIBOR.

Louvre Accord An agreement in 1987, prompted by the dollar's decline, in which the G-Seven countries (i) cooperate to achieve greater exchange rate stability and (ii) consult and coordinate their macroeconomic policies.

M

Maastricht Treaty Treaty signed in December 1991 states that the European Union will irrevocably fix exchange rates among member countries by January 1999 and introduce a common European currency which will replace individual national currencies.

Maintenance Performance Bond Collateral needed to maintain an asset position.

Managed Float System Established by the Louvre Accord in 1987, it allows the G-7 countries to jointly intervene in the exchange market to correct over- or undervaluation of currencies.

Market Completeness A market is complete if each state of the economy is matched by security payoff.

Market Imperfections Various frictions, such as transaction costs and legal restrictions, that prevent the markets from functioning perfectly.

Market Order An order executed at the best price available (market price) when the order is received in the market.

Marking-to-Market The process of establishing daily price gains and losses in the futures market by the change in the settlement price of the futures contract.

Merchant Bank Banks which perform traditional commercial banking as well as investment banking activities.

Monetary/Nonmonetary Method In dealing with foreign currency translation, the idea that monetary balance sheet accounts such as accounts receivable are translated at the current exchange rate while nonmonetary balance sheet accounts such as stockholder's equity are converted at the historical exchange rate.

Money Market Hedge A method of hedging transaction exposure by borrowing and lending in the domestic and foreign money markets.

Multilateral Netting A system in which all affiliates each net their individual interaffiliate receipts against all their disbursements and transfer or receive the balance, respectively, if it is a net payer or receiver.

Multinational Corporation (MNC) Refers to a firm that has business activities and interests in multiple countries.

N

National Neutrality The idea that an ideal tax on taxable income would tax all income in the same manner by the taxpayer's national tax authority regardless of where in the world it is earned.

Negotiable Certificate of Deposit (NCD) A negotiable bank time deposit.

Net Present Value (NPV) A capital budgeting method in which the present value of cash outflows is subtracted from the present value of expected future cash inflows to determine the net present value of an investment project.

Netting Center In multilateral netting, it determines the amount of net payments and which affiliates are to make or pay them.

North American Free Trade Agreement (NAFTA) Created in 1994, it includes the U.S., Canada, and Mexico as members in a free trade area. NAFTA aims to eliminate tariffs and import quotas over a 15-year period.

Notional Principal A reference amount of principal used for determining payments under various derivative contracts.

O

Offer Price The price at which a dealer will sell a financial asset.

Offshore Banking Center A country in which the banking system is organized to allow external accounts beyond the normal economic activity of the country. Their primary function is to seek deposits and grant loans in currencies other than the host country currency.

Open Interest The total number of short or long contracts outstanding for a particular delivery month in the derivative markets.

Operating Exposure The extent to which the firm's operating cash flows will be affected by random changes in the exchange rates.

Operational Hedges Long-term, operational approaches to hedging exchange exposure that include diversification of the market and flexible sourcing.

Optimum Currency Area A geographical area that is suitable for sharing a common currency by virtue of a high degree of factor mobility within the area.

Option A contract giving the owner the right, but not the obligation, to buy or sell a given quantity of an asset at a specified price at some date in the future.

Options Market Hedge Use of put and call options to limit the downside risk of transaction exposure while preserving the upside potential. The price of such flexibility is the option premium.

Over-the-Counter (OTC) Market Trading market in which there is no central marketplace; instead, buyers and sellers are linked via a network of telephones, telex machines, computers, and automated dealing systems.

P

Par Value The nominal or face value of stocks or bonds.

Passive Income Income not directly generated by an individual or corporation, such as interest income, royalty income, and copyright income.

Plaza Accord G-5 agreement in 1985 that depreciation of the dollar is desirable to correct the U.S. trade deficits.

Political Risk Potential losses to the parent firm resulting from adverse political developments in the host country.

Portfolio Risk Diversification Portfolio risk is minimized by investing in multiple securities which do not have strong correlations between one another.

Precautionary Cash Balance Emergency funds a firm maintains in case it has underestimated its transaction cash balance.

Price-Specie-Flow Mechanism Under the gold standard, it is the automatic correction of payment imbalances between countries. This is based on the fact that, under the gold standard, the domestic money stock rises or falls as the country experiences inflows or outflows of gold.

Primary Market The market in which new security issues are sold to investors. In selling the new securities, investment bankers can play a role either as a broker or a dealer.

Privatization Act of a country divesting itself of ownership and operation of business ventures by turning them over to the free market system.

Product Differentiation Creating a perception among consumers that a firm's product(s) are different from those offered by competitors, thereby reducing price sensitivity of demand.

Purchasing Power Parity (PPP) A theory stating that the exchange rate between currencies of two countries should be equal to the ratio of the countries' price levels of a commodity basket.

Put An option to sell an underlying asset at a prespecified price.

Q

Quality Spread Differential (QSD) The difference between the fixed interest rate spread differential and the floating interest rate spread differential of the debt of two counterparties of different creditworthiness. A positive QSD is a necessary condition for an interest swap to occur that ensures that the swap will be beneficial to both parties.

Quantity Theory of Money An identity stating that for each country, the general price level times the aggregate output should be equal to the money supply times the velocity of money.

R

Random Walk Hypothesis A hypothesis stating that in an efficient market, asset prices change randomly (i.e., independently of historical trends), or follow a "random walk."

Thus, the expected future exchange rate is equivalent to the current exchange rate.

Real Exchange Rate Measures the degree of deviation from PPP over a period of time, assuming PPP held at the beginning of the period.

Real Option The application of options pricing theory to the evaluation of investment options in real projects.

Registered Bond A bond whose ownership is demonstrated by associating the buyer's name with the bond in the issuer's records.

Reinvoice Center A central financial subsidiary of a multinational corporation where intrafirm transaction exposure is netted, and the residual exposure is managed.

Reporting Currency The currency in which a MNC prepares its consolidated financial statements. Typically this is the currency in which the parent firm keeps its books.

Residential Taxation *See* Worldwide Taxation.

Residual Control Rights Refers to the right to make discretionary decisions under those contingencies that are not specifically covered by the contract.

Reversing Trade A trade in either the futures or forward market that will neutralize a position.

S

Sarbanes-Oxley Act The U.S. Congress passed this law in 2002 to strengthen corporate governance. The act requires the creation of a public accounting oversight board. It also requires that the CEO and the CFO sign off the company's financial statements.

Secondary Market A market in which investors buy and sell securities to other investors; the original issuer is not involved in these trades. This market provides marketability and valuation of the securities.

Shareholder Wealth Maximization This represents the most important objective of corporate management that managers of companies should keep in mind when they make important corporate decisions. Managers can maximize shareholder wealth by maximizing the market value of the firm.

Sharpe Performance Measure (SHP) A risk-adjusted performance measure for a portfolio which gives the excess return (above the risk-free interest rate) per standard deviation risk.

Shelf Registration Allows bond issuer to pre-register a securities issue which will occur at a later date.

Single-Currency Interest Rate Swap Typically called an "interest rate swap." There are many variants; however, all involve swapping interest payments on debt obligations that are denominated in the same currency.

Smithsonian Agreement In December 1971, the G-10 countries agreed to devalue the U.S. dollar against gold and most major currencies in an attempt to save the Bretton Woods system.

Snake European version of fixed exchange rate system which appeared as the Bretton Woods system declined.

Source Taxation *See* Territorial Taxation.

Special Drawing Rights (SDR) An artificial international reserve created by the International Monetary Fund (IMF) which is a currency basket currently comprised of five major currencies.

Specialist On exchange markets in the U.S., each stock is represented by a specialist who makes a market by holding an inventory of the security.

Speculator One who attempts to profit from a favorable, but uncertain, price change in an asset by acquiring a position in it.

Spot (Exchange) Rate Price at which foreign exchange can be sold or purchased for immediate (within two business days) delivery.

Straight Fixed-Rate Bond Bonds with a specified maturity date that have fixed coupon payments.

Striking Price *See* Exercise Price.

Stripped Bond A synthetic zero coupon bond created by an investment bank via selling the rights to a specific coupon payment or the bond principal of a coupon bond, typically a U.S. Treasury bond.

Subpart F Income Income of controlled foreign corporations which is subject to immediate U.S. taxation and includes income that is relatively easy to transfer between countries and is subject to a low foreign tax levy.

Swap Bank A generic term to describe a financial institution which facilitates currency and interest rate swaps between counterparties.

Swap Broker Function of a swap bank in which it matches counterparties but does not assume any risk of the swap; however, it does receive a commission for this service.

Swap Dealer Function of a swap bank in which it makes a market in one or the other side of a currency or interest rate swap.

Swap Transaction The simultaneous spot sale (purchase) of an asset against a forward purchase (sale) of an approximately equal amount of the asset.

Syndicate A group of Eurobanks banding together to share the risk of lending Eurocredits.

T

Tax Equity The idea that all similarly situated taxpayers should participate in the cost of operating the government according to the same rules.

Tax Haven A country that has a low corporate income tax rate and low withholding tax rates on passive income.

Tax Neutrality A principle in taxation, holding that taxation should not have a negative effect on the decision-making process of taxpayers.

Technical Analysis A method of predicting the future behavior of asset prices based on their historical patterns.

Temporal Method In dealing with foreign currency translation, the idea that current and noncurrent monetary accounts as well as accounts which are carried on the books at current value are converted at the current exchange rate. Accounts carried on the books at historical cost are translated at the historical exchange rate.

Territorial Taxation A method of declaring tax jurisdiction in which all income earned within a country by any taxpayer, domestic or foreign, is taxed.

Theory of Comparative Advantage An argument which supports the existence of international trade. This theory states that it is mutually beneficial for countries to specialize in production of goods for which they can produce most efficiently and then engage in trade.

Time Draft   A written order instructing the importer or the importer's bank to pay a specific sum of money on a certain date. Used in import-export trade financing.

Tobin Tax   A tax on the international flow of hot money proposed by Professor Tobin for the purpose of discouraging cross-border financial speculation.

Transaction Cash Balance   Funds a firm has marked to cover scheduled outflows during a cash budgeting period.

Transaction Exposure   The potential change in the value of financial positions due to changes in the exchange rate between the inception of a contract and the settlement of the contract.

Transfer Price   The price assigned, for bookkeeping purposes, to the receiving division within a business for the cost of transferring goods and services from another division.

Translation Exposure   The effect of an unanticipated change in the exchange rates on the consolidated financial reports of a MNC.

Triangular Arbitrage   The process of trading U.S. dollars for a second currency and subsequently trading this for a third currency. This third currency is then traded for U.S. dollars. The purpose of such trading is to earn arbitrage profit via trading from the second currency to the third.

Triffin Paradox   Under the gold exchange standard, the reserve-currency country should run a balance of payments deficit, but this can decrease confidence in the reserve currency and lead to the downfall of the system.

U

Uncovered Interest Rate Parity   This parity condition holds that the difference in interest rates between two countries is equal to the expected change in exchange rate between the countries' currencies.

Universal Bank   International banks that provide such services as consulting in foreign exchange hedging strategies, interest rate and currency swap financing, and international cash management.

V

Value-Added Tax (VAT)   An indirect national tax which is levied on the value added in the production of a good or service as it moves through the various stages of production.

W

Withholding Tax   An indirect tax levied on passive income earned by an individual or corporation of one country within the tax jurisdiction of another country.

World Beta   A measure of the sensitivity of an asset or portfolio to the world market movements. This is a measure of the world systematic risk.

World Equity Benchmark Shares (WEBS)   WEBS are exchange-traded, open-end country funds designed to closely track national stock market indices. WEBS are traded on the American Stock Exchange (AMEX).

World Trade Organization (WTO)   Permanent international organization created by the Uruguay Round to replace GATT. The WTO will have power to enforce international trade rules.

Worldwide Taxation   A method of declaring national tax jurisdiction in which national residents of the country are taxed on their worldwide income regardless of which country it is earned in.

Y

Yankee Bond (Stock)   Bond (stock) directly sold to U.S. investors by foreign companies.

Z

Zero Coupon Bond   A bond that pays no coupon interest and simply returns the face value at maturity.

华章系列教材·会计与财务管理

会计与财务管理教材译丛

书号	书名	作者	定价
7-111-14615-8	会计学：教程与案例（财务会计分册，原书第 11 版）	罗伯特 N. 安东尼	58.00
7-111-14615-8	会计学：教程与案例（管理会计分册，原书第 11 版）	罗伯特 N. 安东尼	54.00
	本书第 12 版即将由机械工业出版社出版		
7-111-17405-4	会计学：企业决策的基础（财务会计分册，第 13 版）	罗伯特 R. 迈格斯	52.00
7-111-17405A	会计学：企业决策的基础（管理会计分册，第 13 版）	罗伯特 R. 迈格斯	59.00
	本书第 14 版即将由机械工业出版社出版		
7-111-12625-4	公司理财（原书第 6 版）	斯蒂芬·罗斯	78.00
	本书第 8 版即将由机械工业出版社出版		
7-111-14657-3	公司理财（精要版）	斯蒂芬·罗斯	60.00
7-111-14317-5	用 Excel 和 Acess 学习会计学（附光盘）	格伦·欧文	33.00
7-111-12268-2	审计与其他保证服务（原书第 13 版）	O. 雷·惠延顿	85.00
7-111-12202-X	管理会计学：在动态商业环境中创造价值（原书第 5 版）	罗纳德 W. 希尔顿	75.00
7-111-19865-4	审计学：基于国际审计准则的视角（原书第 2 版）	里克·海斯	49.00
7-111-13233-5	管理控制系统（原书第 11 版）	罗伯特 N. 安东尼	98.00
7-111-13635-7	财务会计：概念、方法与应用（原书第 10 版）	克莱德 P. 斯蒂克尼	59.00
7-111-13670-5	财务会计：概念、方法与应用习题集（原书第 10 版）	克莱德 P. 斯蒂克尼	43.00
7-111-14069-9	财务与会计研究方法与方法论	鲍勃·赖安	30.00
7-111-17322	财务会计理论(原书第 3 版)	威廉 R. 斯科特	41.00
7-111-07248-0	成本会计：为管理创造价值（原书第 5 版）	米切尔·马赫	68.00
7-111-11523-6	政府与非赢利组织会计导论（原书第 4 版）	约瑟夫 R. 拉扎克	65.00
7-111-22995-7	公司财务原理（原书第 8 版）	理查德 A. 布雷利	108.00
7-111-15900-4	公司财务报告（原书第 4 版）	E. 理查德·布朗利二世	69.00
7-111-14993-9	财务报告与分析（原书第 2 版）	劳伦斯·莱佛辛	62.00
7-111-14831-2	兼并收购与公司重组	帕特里克 A. 高根	56.00
7-111-14240-3	会计学原理学习指南与习题集 I（原书第 5 版）	乔尔·勒纳	38.00
7-111-14355-8	会计学原理学习指南与习题集 II（原书第 4 版）	乔尔·勒纳	31.00
7-111-12142-2	财务管理精要（原书第 12 版）	尤金 F. 布里格姆	49.00
7-111-14438-4	财务管理实务（原书第 3 版）	威廉 R. 拉舍	59.00
7-111-13010-3	财务管理基础（原书第 3 版）	彼得·阿特勒尔	46.00
7-111-21679-7	国际财务管理（原书第 4 版）	凯奥尔 S. 尤恩	69.00
7-111-22258-3	国际会计与跨国企业（原书第 6 版）	李 H. 拉德鲍	60.00
7-111-17107-1	跨国财务（原书第 3 版）	科特 C. 巴特勒	54.00

21 世纪经典原版经济管理教材文库

7-111-15966-7	会计学：企业决策的基础（财务会计分册，原书第 13 版）	罗伯特 R. 迈格斯	58.00
7-111-15966-7	会计学：企业决策的基础（财务会计分册，原书第 13 版）	罗伯特 R. 迈格斯	45.00
	本书第 14 版即将由机械工业出版社出版		

7-111-12494-4	会计学：财务会计分册（第20版）	卡尔 S. 沃伦	58.00
7-111-12494-4	会计学：管理会计分册（第20版）	卡尔 S. 沃伦	58.00
7-111-21552-3	会计学：教程与案例（财务会计分册）第12版	罗伯特 N. 安东尼	65.00
7-111-21558-5	会计学：教程与案例（管理会计分册）第12版	罗伯特 N. 安东尼	66.00
7-111-20280-5	公司财务原理(原书第8版)	理查德 A. 布雷利	98.00
7-111-13732-9	财务管理精要（原书第12版）	尤金 F. 布里格姆	90.00
7-111-10796-9	管理会计学：在动态商业环境中创造价值（原书第5版）	罗纳德 W. 希尔顿	78.00
7-111-20600-2	国际财务管理（原书第4版）	凯奥尔 S. 尤恩	58.00
7-111-06553-0	财务管理分析（原书第5版）	罗伯特 C. 希金斯	43.00
7-111-15819-9	公司理财（原书第7版）(英文版)	斯蒂芬 A. 罗斯	210.00
7-111-12556-8	高级经理财务管理：创造价值的过程(原书第2版)	克劳德·维埃里	65.00
7-111-06552-2	财务管理精要（原书第11版）	弗雷德·韦斯顿	89.00
7-111-06400-3	财务管理：理论与实务（原书第8版）	尤金·布里格姆	128.00
7-111-06414-3	财务会计（原书第9版）	罗伯特·迈格斯	86.00
7-111-21202-7	经济环境下的财务会计（原书第6版）	杰米 J. 帕拉特	88.00
7-111-06423-2	成本会计（原书第5版）	迈克尔·马赫	86.00
7-111-20455-7	国际会计与跨国企业（原书第6版）	李 H. 拉德鲍	58.00
7-111-21201-0	中级会计（原书第12版）	唐纳德 E. 基索	146.00
7-111-21203-4	财务会计（原书第5版）	杰里 J. 韦安特	98.00
高等院校财务管理专业核心课程教材			
7-111-16973	财务会计（修订版）	赵书和	36
7-111-17900	会计学原理（修订版）	韩星	28
7-111-17048	财务分析	鲁爱民	26
7-111-16968	计算机财务管理（附光盘）	边泓	29
7-111-18323	审计学	刘建军	38
7-111-18358	成本与管理会计	赵书和 高方露	36
7-111-17620	财务法规	肖沂娃	35
7-111-17972	财务管理	李冠众	28
7-111-21193	国际财务管理	余娟	30
会计学专业新企业会计准则系列教材			
7-111-22730	基础会计学	徐泓	32
7-111-23453	成本会计学：有效管理的工具	赵桂娟	38
	中级财务会计	马建威	即将出版
	高级财务会计	王竹泉	即将出版
	税务会计与税收筹划	王素荣	即将出版
	管理会计学	陈良华	即将出版
	审计学	陈郡	即将出版
其他相关教材			
7-111-22171	会计信息系统	韩庆兰	34
7-111-22612	会计审计专业英语	罗殿英	25
7-111-21427	财务管理专业英语	刘媛媛	25

机械工业出版社 华章公司
Huazhang Graphics & Information Co., Ltd

教师服务登记表

尊敬的老师：

您好！感谢您购买我们出版的 _____ 教材。

机械工业出版社华章公司本着为服务高等教育的出版原则，为进一步加强与高校教师的联系与沟通，更好地为高校教师服务，特制此表，请您填妥后发回给我们，我们将定期向您寄送华章公司最新的图书出版信息。为您的教材、论著或译著的出版提供可能的帮助。欢迎您对我们的教材和服务提出宝贵的意见，感谢您的大力支持与帮助！

个人资料（请用正楷完整填写）

教师姓名		□先生 □女士	出生年月		职务		职称： □教授 □副教授 □讲师 □助教 □其他

学校			学院			系别	

联系电话	办公： 宅电： 移动：		联系地址及邮编	
			E—mail	

学历		毕业院校		国外进修及讲学经历	

研究领域	

主讲课程	现用教材名	作者及出版社	共同授课教师	教材满意度
课程： □专 □本 □研 □MBA 人数： 学期：□春□秋				□满意 □一般 □不满意 □希望更换
课程： □专 □本 □研 □MBA 人数： 学期：□春□秋				□满意 □一般 □不满意 □希望更换
课程： □专 □本 □研 □MBA 人数： 学期：□春□秋				□满意 □一般 □不满意 □希望更换

备注	已出版著作		译著	
	著书计划	方向一		
		方向二		
	是否愿意从事翻译工作 □是 □否	翻译方向		
	意见和建议			

填妥后请选择以下任何一种方式将此表返回：（如方便请赐名片）
地　址：北京市西城区百万庄南街1号　华章公司营销中心　　邮编：100037
电　话：(010) 68353079　88378995　传真：(010) 68995260
E-mail: hzedu@hzbook.com　markerting@hzbook.com　图书详情可登录http://www.hzbook.com网站查询